THE POLITICS OF THE ADMINISTRATIVE PROCESS

Fourth Edition

Donald F. Kettl
University of Pennsylvania

James W. Fesler (late)
Yale University

CQ PRESS

A Division of SAGE
Washington, D.C.

CQ Press
2300 N Street, NW, Suite 800
Washington, DC 20037

Phone: 202-729-1900; toll-free, 1-866-4CQ-PRESS (1-866-427-7737)

Web: www.cqpress.com

Cover design by designfarm, Takoma Park, Maryland
Typesetting by Auburn Associates, Inc., Baltimore, Maryland

⊗ The paper used in this publication exceeds the requirements of the American National Standard for Information Sciences—Permanence of Paper for Printed Library Materials, ANSI Z39.48-1992.

Printed and bound in the United States of America

12   11   10   09   08   1   2   3   4   5

Library of Congress Cataloging-in-Publication Data

Kettl, Donald F.
    The politics of the administrative process / Donald F. Kettl, James W. Fesler.—
4th ed.
        p. cm.
    Includes bibliographical references and index.
    ISBN 978-0-87289-599-7 (pbk. : alk. paper)   1. Public administration—United
States—Textbooks. I. Fesler, James W. (James William), 1911–2005. II. Title.

    JK421.K4817 2009
    351.73—dc22
                                                                                2008040942

For our students

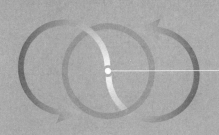

Contents

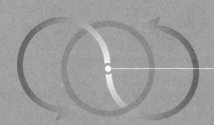

Figures, Tables, and Boxes

Figures

Tables

Boxes

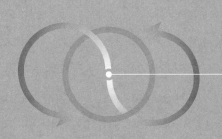
Any road map of how government does what it does has to start with public administration. Policymakers might make policy, but their ideas, big and small, rarely have any meaning apart from their execution. Whether the issue is climate change or homeland security, police protection or highway maintenance, administration lies at the core of public action. The administrative process is thus inevitably political, since it involves translating political decisions into practical steps. Each step brings in critical decisions about public values, which means that politics infuses public administration. Public administration thus raises critical questions about efficacy—does the process really produce a government that works?—and accountability—does the process produce action that is responsive to the will of public officials and to the citizens who elect them?

It so often is easy for politicians and citizens to ignore the central importance of public administration. They view—wrongly, as this book shows—administrative issues as less important or less interesting than the sensational battles fought over public policy. In fact, however, public administration provides the real life and true meaning to U.S. government and public policy. Without appropriate follow-through, even the biggest and best policy ideas will disappoint and possibly even enrage citizen taxpayers.

Public administration can be stunningly intricate. No one can listen in on air traffic controllers working the flight patterns around Chicago's O'Hare International Airport without coming away with a profound sense of awe for these employees of the Federal Aviation Administration. They have their own language and an uncanny ability to scan radar screens while barking out orders that keep aircraft safe distances apart. At any given moment, the lives of tens of thousands of people literally hang in the balance. Air traffic controllers must cope with crowded skies and unpredictable weather, and they have zero room for error. They guide planes as carefully as the best choreographers direct their dancers. They sit in small rooms, invisible to passengers settled in their seats, but without them modern aviation would be impossible.

Public administration can also be remarkably diverse. Public administrators teach in public schools and colleges, manage student loan programs, safeguard U.S. borders, rescue boaters in trouble, process Social Security checks, and run job-training programs. They also pick up garbage, manage the money supply, build bridges and highways, ensure that grocery-store scales are accurate, and provide care for disabled veterans. The demands to which administrators must respond are equally numerous and varied and sometimes even contradictory. Citizens want government programs to be efficient and effective, responsive and accountable; they want government to work, but they don't want to pay too much for it. They want new ideas quickly put into practice and problems fixed immediately. They expect the government to treat all citizens equally and government administrators to ensure that all citizens are protected from discrimination. Indeed, public administration encompasses such an enormous array of roles and responsibilities that it is nearly impossible to describe them all in detail. It is, however, possible to outline the common themes in organization and management, as well as the shared goals of institutions designed to serve the interests of democracy and the public.

Good public administration is essential to good democracy because it brings policy ideas to life. Even more fundamentally, public administration helps define what policy ideas really mean. The nation's founders realized that the rich diversity of the United States, even in the late 1700s, would make it hard to arrive at clear decisions on important issues. They demonstrated genius not so much in figuring out how to resolve the public's inevitable disagreements but in devising institutions that could help resolve them, over time, in peaceful ways. The unique system of U.S. government creates opportunities to debate—and even revisit—big policy issues. This multilevel, multibranch system has helped citizens work through their policy differences, even as it has made it harder to get things done. The system tends to prefer ambiguity over clarity in its processes and structures. After all, the founders built it to accomplish political, not administrative, ends, and the most important of these is accommodating the vast range of interests that from time to time might threaten to tear the nation apart. As a result, the founders sacrificed some measure of efficiency for the sake of political stability.

This long and rich political tradition frames a central question for U.S. government. In many ways, administration is an afterthought to policy and politics, but without effective administration, neither policy nor politics have much meaning. Indeed, without effective administration, the public would become restless, and politicians would have a hard time remaining in office. How does bureaucracy *really* work in a democracy where bureaucratic responsibility, a cornerstone of the democratic process, sometimes stands at odds with important governmental efficiencies?

In a sense, public administration tells the story of how the system moves ambitious policy ideas into practice, through the basic mechanisms of bureaucracy as well as the intricate channels of politics. Public administration is about getting results (the administration part), but doing so in a way that is responsive and accountable to the political process and the nation's ideals (the public part). It shares some approaches and techniques with business administration, although the public sector often employs complex strategies and tactics that business executives who enter government find surprising. Public administration differs distinctly from business administration in that its job is to bring life to the public will. Indeed, the politics of the administrative process make it different and fascinating. That is the puzzle this book explores.

As many readers know, this book has enjoyed a long life. James W. Fesler wrote the original volume, *Public Administration: Theory and Practice,* published by Prentice-Hall (1980). Later, the distinguished publisher Ed Artinian brought it to his press, Chatham House. He encouraged Fesler, and me as Fesler's new coauthor, to write a new version, *The Politics of the Administrative Process* (1991). With Artinian's nurturing and enthusiasm, a second edition appeared (1996). Several years after Artinian's untimely death, CQ Press acquired Chatham House. The book is now in its fourth edition, with thanks to the strong support of CQ Press and SAGE Publications. The book has continued since Jim Fesler's death in 2005 at the age of 94, building steadily on the foundation he established throughout his career as one of America's most distinguished scholars of public administration. This fourth edition contains significant changes from the previous editions, including a fresh and extensive examination of the role of administrative accountability and political power in chapter 1, which continues throughout the book.

Organization of the Book

Following this careful look at politics and administration in chapter 1, *The Politics of the Administrative Process* explores the issues in five parts. Part 1 considers what government does and how it does it. Chapter 2 examines the basic issues of administrative responsibility and the meaning of the "administrative state." Chapter 3 lays out government's strategies and tactics, as well as the growth of government's reliance on nongovernmental partners to do its work.

Part 2 moves on to probe the theories underlying organizations and their structure. Chapter 4 charts the basics of organizational theory, and chapter 5 examines the enduring instinct of policymakers and administrators alike to reform organizational structure. Chapters 6 and 7 analyze the structure of the executive branch and the problems that periodically hamper good organizational performance.

Part 3 addresses the role of people inside these organizational structures. Civil service systems have long defined the basic rules and procedures for hiring and firing government workers, and that constitutes the focus of chapter 8. Chapter 9 asks how government can make the most of the intellectual capital its employees bring to the job.

Part 4 carefully examines how administrative agencies accomplish their missions. Administration is about making decisions, and chapter 10 analyzes the theories about this process. Chapter 11 applies these theories to budgeting, which is the most important administrative decision and which drives much of administrative action. Chapter 12 explores how implementers transform decisions into practice.

Part 5 takes on the theme of government accountability, with chapter 13 probing the strategies of regulation and the courts. Chapter 14 concludes the book by returning to the central themes of executive power and accountability and examines, in particular, the control of administration by legislatures.

Key Features

This fourth edition of *The Politics of the Administrative Process* benefits greatly from the many suggestions and recommendations of students and instructors over the years. It maintains many of the features of the previous editions, including the early chapters' focus on what government does. It contains substantial new material on accountability, and it examines the debate about the increase of executive power that accompanied the administration of George W. Bush.

To enhance the new material, the tables and figures have been completely updated. Many are brand new. Readers will also find key concepts bolded within the text and listed at the end of each chapter for ease of review, and a comprehensive glossary at the back of the book defines all the key concepts. Each chapter concludes with a list of suggested readings and a discussion of websites to aid further study. Photos illustrate key conceptual points made in the text and help bring life to the material.

Perhaps most important, *The Politics of the Administrative Process* features case studies for each chapter. In the third edition, these cases appeared in a special appendix. In this fourth edition, they are integrated into the text, with new cases to illustrate many of the book's major themes and with updating of some of the third edition's cases. These original "ripped from the headlines" cases provide for each chapter fertile material for applying the book's theories to cutting-edge problems of practice. They feature all the functional areas of public bureaucracy and cover a wide variety of fundamental federal, state, and local issues, including the following:

- waterboarding detainees held by the U.S. government in Guantanamo Bay
- the bailout of the financial markets in the 2008 economic tsunami
- the grounding of thousands of flights because of aircraft wiring problems
- new strategies for rethinking the government's civil service system
- the battle over financing Philadelphia's public transit system
- the use of Tasers by local police to subdue suspects
- 100 words government bureaucrats should not use

Ancillaries

Written by Lia Howard of the University of Pennsylvania, a website for students and new instructor ancillaries, available to adopters for download at www.cqpress.com/college, support this fourth edition:

- An instructor's manual—with helpful chapter summaries, lecture outlines, talking points for further discussion, and sample syllabi—assists with course preparation.
- A complete test bank of more than 350 multiple-choice, true-or-false, and essay questions has been crafted specifically for the book and is available with *Respondus* test-generation software.
- Tables and figures from the book are provided in PDF and PowerPoint formats for easy use in lectures.

The new companion website at http://college.cqpress.com/adminprocess offers students a great way to review and self-test. The website includes chapter summaries, discussion questions, flashcards, and annotated links to helpful resources and organizations, including some that provide further research materials on the cases, and most important, quizzes with immediate grading that help focus and direct students' reading and study.

Acknowledgments

I was fortunate to have had the chance to cut my teeth on public administration in Jim Fesler's seminar. He later became my dissertation adviser—and I was his last student. He was a giant in the field, a keen thinker who forged new paths between political realities and administrative pragmatism. His stamp on the field was unmistakable, and I benefitted immeasurably from the chance to work with him. The carrying on of his work through this book is the memorial he wanted most, and it is an honor for me to be entrusted with it.

I am grateful to my colleagues, who have enriched my understanding of public administration. I have also learned a great deal from practitioners in the field. I have spent decades working closely with real-world policy problems, and the lessons I have learned—which theories work, which fall short—powerfully enliven this volume. I thank these practitioners, who have been some of my best teachers. Most of all, I am grateful to my students. They are our future leaders and, in many cases, future public servants. The quality of government depends critically on them, and it is to them that this edition is dedicated.

I would like also to thank the reviewers for this edition who made many fine and useful recommendations: James Carruth, University of Memphis; Jeremy Duff,

Michigan State University; Christopher Leu, California State University, Northridge; and Lori Riverstone-Newell, Illinois State University.

At CQ Press, I would like to thank Charisse Kiino, Elise Frasier, Allie McKay, Gwenda Larsen, and Steve Pazdan. Elaine Dunn, the copy editor, did a fabulous job clarifying the prose. I am grateful indeed to all of them for their invaluable help in bringing the fourth edition of this book to life.

AEC	Atomic Energy Commission
AFGE	American Federation of Government Employees
AFSCME	American Federation of State, County, and Municipal Employees
AIDS	Acquired Immune Deficiency Syndrome
APA	Administrative Procedure Act of 1946
BIA	Bureau of Indian Affairs
BOB	Bureau of the Budget
CBO	Congressional Budget Office
CDC	Centers for Disease Control and Prevention
CEQ	Council on Environmental Quality
CFR	Code of Federal Regulations
CIA	Central Intelligence Agency
CPSC	Consumer Product Safety Commission
DHS	Department of Homeland Security
DIA	Defense Intelligence Agency
DOD	Department of Defense
EDA	Economic Development Administration
EOP	Executive Office of the President
EPA	Environmental Protection Agency
FAA	Federal Aviation Administration
FBI	Federal Bureau of Investigation
FCC	Federal Communications Commission
FDA	Food and Drug Administration
FDIC	Federal Deposit Insurance Corporation
Fed	Federal Reserve Board
FEMA	Federal Emergency Management Agency
FHA	Federal Highway Administration
FLRA	Federal Labor Relations Authority
FTC	Federal Trade Commission
GAO	Government Accountability Office (formerly General Accounting Office)
GDP	Gross domestic product
GIS	Geographic information system
GPP	Government Performance Project

GPRA	Government Performance and Results Act
GS	General Schedule of Classification and Pay
GSA	General Services Administration
HEW	Department of Health, Education, and Welfare
HHS	Department of Health and Human Services
HR	Human resources
HUD	Department of Housing and Urban Development
ICC	Interstate Commerce Commission
INS	Immigration and Naturalization Service
IRS	Internal Revenue Service
JCS	Joint Chiefs of Staff
LGA	Local Government Association (U.K.)
MBO	Management by objectives
MIL-SPECS	Military specifications
MSPB	Merit Systems Protection Board
NAPA	National Academy of Public Administration
NASA	National Aeronautics and Space Administration
NHTSA	National Highway Traffic Safety Administration
NIH	National Institutes of Health
NIMBY	"Not in my backyard"
NMA	National Motorists Association
NPR	National Performance Review
NSC	National Security Council
NYPD	New York Police Department
OECD	Organization for Economic Cooperation and Development
OGE	Office of Government Ethics
OMB	Office of Management and Budget
OPA	Office of Price Administration
OPM	Office of Personnel Management
OSD	Office of the Secretary of Defense
OSHA	Occupational Safety and Health Administration
PART	Program Assessment Rating Tool
PPBS	Planning-Programming-Budgeting System
RIF	Reductions in force
SEC	Securities and Exchange Commission
SEPTA	Southeastern Pennsylvania Transportation Authority
SES	Senior Executive Service
SSA	Social Security Administration
TABOR	Taxpayer Bill of Rights

Taser	Thomas A. Swift Electric Rifle
TQM	Total quality management
TSA	Transportation Security Administration
TVA	Tennessee Valley Authority
USDA	U.S. Department of Agriculture
ZBB	Zero-base budgeting

Politics and Administration

In the spring of 2008, analysts at Iowa State University conducted a survey of scientists at the federal Environmental Protection Agency (EPA). Nearly 1,600 scientists responded, and 60 percent of them said that they personally had felt political interference in their work over the previous five years. Hundreds complained about the "selective or incomplete use of data to justify a specific regulatory outcome" and that they had been told to "inappropriately exclude or alter technical information" in EPA documents.[1]

The survey came on the heels of a decision late in 2007 by EPA Administrator Stephen L. Johnson to deny a request by the state of California to impose tough greenhouse gas standards on vehicle emissions. The state wanted a waiver so it could force automobile manufacturers to meet stricter standards than required by federal law. Johnson told Gov. Arnold Schwarzenegger that California's pollution problem was not exclusive to the state. The nation would be better off, he said, with "an aggressive standard" for all fifty states instead of the lower standard California sought for cars sold within its borders.[2]

EPA's experts, however, had argued in favor of granting California's request. They quietly complained later that they had been overruled, but they made their complaints anonymously because they feared retribution if their names became public. Inside sources said that Johnson stopped communicating with technical staffers once the internal opposition surfaced and made the decision without having them write a formal justification. That, one source said, was "very highly unusual." Some EPA officials suspected that Johnson made his decision after meeting with Vice President Dick Cheney and after a Chrysler executive had made the case against the California standards.[3] California Sen. Barbara Boxer (D) savaged the Bush administration, calling its top officials "environmental outlaws." She concluded, "Every time the EPA deviates from what their scientists recommend, we know one thing for sure: People will get sick, and some will die."[4]

Following EPA's decision to deny California's request to impose tough greenhouse gas emission standards on vehicles, Gov. Arnold Schwarzenegger (center) announced on November 8, 2007, that the state was filing suit against the federal government to force a decision on whether the state's policy would prevail.

The battles over EPA policy were epic. Environmentalists charged that the Bush administration was steered more by politics than by good policy. Some internal EPA scientists argued the case for California's tougher standards. Automobile manufacturers quietly made the case that higher mileage standards and tougher greenhouse gas rules would make cars more expensive and cost American jobs. Chrysler made its case with a position paper submitted to the Office of Management and Budget, the regulatory oversight arm for the executive branch. The stakes were huge: the state of California was trying to circumvent federal policy by creating stricter state rules. Because the state is such a huge market, car makers would have had little choice but to comply. California's standards would in practice have set the national standard, since car makers would have found it very complicated—and very expensive—to engineer one car for California and a different one for other states. The car makers were worried about the cost of meeting California's higher standards and about the challenge of meeting different standards in different states. They wanted one policy, set in Washington, at a lower level. It was a tough political battle about matters of science that had enormous stakes.

The discovery that politics lies at the core of public administration reaches back to a famous scene in the movie *Casablanca*, often voted by critics as the best movie of all time. Police Captain Renault tells everyone in a nightclub, "I'm shocked, shocked to find that gambling is going on in here!"—just before a dealer hands him his own winnings. Many of the players in the administrative process say they are shocked by the political pressures that others try to impose. They raise fundamental questions of ethics in the decisions that some of the players make.

At the core of the administrative process is an impossible dilemma. Everyone expects fair and impartial provision of our public services. We expect efficiency and effectiveness. Americans have never much liked politics, and they have long been suspicious about the exercise of political power (the inescapable fallout, no doubt, of having fought a revolution against a king to establish the country). We expect government to be responsive to our views and responsible to professional norms.

Much as we dislike politics, we cannot escape the fact that politics lies at the core of the administrative process. EPA Administrator Johnson's decision might have been wise (on the grounds that it makes no sense to allow each state to set its own air pollution policy) or dangerous (on the argument advanced by the state of California that, if the federal government was not going to move aggressively against global warming, it would do so). The decision was administrative, but it was also inevitably political. Johnson struggled to balance conflicting political values.

The administrative process is political for several important reasons. The decisions of elected officials typically have little meaning until they are implemented. Their implementation, in turn, requires the choice among competing values— whether, for example, Johnson should lean more heavily toward uniform national standards for vehicle emissions or encourage state-level experimentation and variation. Different political interests, from automobile manufacturers to environmentalists, had very different ideas about how best to set that balance. Political forces press hard on administration. Administrative decisions have political consequences. New York Mayor John Lindsay is famous for the way his administration botched snow removal following a February 1969 blizzard and for how the administrative failure haunted his failed reelection campaign. Administration, inevitably, is the translation of politics into the reality that citizens see every day.

Americans don't much like politics. We have high expectations about administration. But our distaste for politics spills over into administration, to the point that "bureaucracy" has become a dirty word. "That's so bureaucratic" is a catchphrase for rules that get in the way of action, for routines that seem mindless, for processes that create inefficiency, and for a public-be-damned approach that prevents responsive service. In fact, "bureaucracy" is not a purely public form of action. Rather, it is a generic strategy for marshaling large organizations to do complex jobs. After all, Microsoft, Apple, Toyota, and Whole Foods are bureaucracies. Neither is it an inherently inefficient and unresponsive strategy. It is remarkable that the Social Security Administration gets checks to 50 million Americans every month and that air traffic controllers handle safely 87,000 flights a day. The key to the politics of the administrative process is to ensure that it is efficient, effective, responsive, and ethical. Those are the challenges that frame the big questions in this book.

Historical Roots

These tensions have deep roots in American history. Not only do we not much like politics—we like bureaucracy even less. The United States is a country born of revolution, not only against the king of England but also against his administrators stationed in the colonies. The Boston tea party was a public act of rebellion against the king's tax collectors. The Declaration of Independence condemns King George III, saying, "He has erected a multitude of New Offices, and sent hither swarms of Officers to harass our people and eat out their substance." Americans revolted not so much against England as against the way that royal administrators exercised power on behalf of George III and Parliament. What drove the revolutionaries meeting in Philadelphia to a declaration of independence from the crown was a long list of grievances based in England's exercise of administrative power, which led them to declare "That these united Colonies are, and of Right ought to be Free and Independent States."

Signing the document required tremendous bravery, but declaring independence was the easy part. Winning the war against Britain and then making independence stick proved far more difficult. Few gave the colonists much of a chance against the most powerful army in the world, yet the colonists won (with a large measure of help from France). The victory would have had little meaning if the new country could not find a way to govern itself. The difficulty of the fledgling government in putting down a rebellion led by Daniel Shays in western Massachusetts in 1786 and 1787 led the nation's founders to conclude that they needed a more powerful government, and that in turn helped lead to the constitutional convention in Philadelphia.

Determining what role administrators ought to play in the new constitution, however, proved difficult. No one wanted to create the foundation for renewed tyranny. Neither did they want to have a government so weak that they risked invasion. The founders delicately balanced the legislative, judicial, and executive powers, but they said very little about how the government would exercise those powers, especially through the executive branch. Article II of the Constitution vests "the executive power" in the president, but there is little to define what this executive power is. The founders dealt with the problem by putting limits on the presidency, through the power of the other two branches, and by leaving the rest vague. In part, they had great respect for the ability of the nation to work these tough problems out. But in larger part, they knew that going any further down the road of defining executive power risked fracturing the fragile coalition that brought the Constitution together. What wasn't there couldn't draw political fire, so they left the big administrative questions for later leaders to work out.

There is, of course, profound irony in this decision. The American revolution grew from charges of abuse of administrative power. The founders were determined to prevent a recurrence of such abuse. But when given the chance to prescribe how this should happen, they sidestepped the question, because they knew that a more detailed answer would court more political conflict. From its first moments, American public administration was grounded in politics—the political battle against the king, followed by the delicate political balance to get the Constitution ratified. The political issues about public administration flowed through Washington's two presidential terms, as John Adams and other Federalists battled with Thomas Jefferson and his colleagues about just how far the government's power should go. Defining the nature of executive power produced the first big split in the new nation and soon led to the creation of political parties with very different views on how that power ought to be exercised.

The Progressives and Public Power

By the end of the nineteenth century, the puzzle of executive power became even more complex and important. Large private trusts monopolized some industries, including oil and transportation. Upton Sinclair's *The Jungle* (1906) focused a strong spotlight on conditions in the meatpacking industry, including unsafe working conditions and low wages. Reformers, who came to be known as the **Progressives,** campaigned for stronger government regulation to protect citizens from private power and more public programs to improve the lives of ordinary Americans. The Progressives' campaign, however, had to solve two tough problems. One was the pervasive corruption of many governments, especially in the nation's largest cities. Lincoln Steffens and other muckrakers exposed graft and poor management in cities ranging from St. Louis to New York. How could governments be trusted with more power if corruption channeled more public money into a handful of well-connected interests? The other problem was Americans' long-standing distrust of public power. How could governments be trusted with more power if, in the American revolutionary tradition, government power was the foundation of tyranny?

The reformers argued they could produce a stronger government while holding it more accountable. Woodrow Wilson, a prominent political scientist and Progressive reformer before becoming president, believed that government could learn how to effectively use the tools of power without producing corruption or tyranny. The answer, he argued, was subjecting bureaucratic power to political accountability. Public administrators can use the best tools, regardless of who invented them, without running the risk of kinglike tyranny:

> If I see a murderous fellow sharpening a knife cleverly, I can borrow his way of sharpening the knife without borrowing his probable intention to commit murder with it; and so, if I see a monarchist dyed in the wool managing a public bureau well, I can learn his business methods without changing one of my republican spots.[5]

For Wilson, the "republican spots" meant the techniques of democratic accountability: the exercise of administrative power under the control and supervision of elected officials. Elected officials, answerable to citizens, made policy; administrators, accountable to elected officials, carried it out. Protection against tyranny came through separating political decision making from administrative policy implementation.

This **policy-administration dichotomy,** as it became known, formed the basis of a generations-long intellectual battle over the place of politics in administration and the role of administration in politics. We will return to the puzzle later in the book, but for now, the critical point is the centrality of the question. Politics permeates public administration. Elected officials might make policy, but most policy has no meaning until administrators carry it out. Government is about politics, about the choice of values to guide public action. Public administration carries out that action. Politics is inevitably about administration, and administration inevitably involves politics.

The Search for Responsible Government

The challenge is how to ensure the best possible administration—the implementation of public programs efficiently and effectively—and grant administrators enough power to get the job done without allowing them to exercise that power in ways that threaten liberty and democratic government. In the country's first years, the founders battled over whether to allow the creation of a national bank, which would increase governmental power over private finance to enhance trade and commerce. The nation returned to the debate in 1913 to establish a permanent national bank, the Federal Reserve, as part of a reform period that saw the creation of new federal agencies to regulate commerce, protect the food supply, and break the backs of industrialists who had established monopolies in several industries. Franklin D. Roosevelt followed with his New Deal, which vastly expanded the scale and scope of governmental activity. During the 1960s, Lyndon B. Johnson's War on Poverty pushed government's role up another notch. In the early twenty-first century, the George W. Bush administration sought additional power to investigate the lives of ordinary citizens in an effort to root out terrorism. The nature of the struggle changes with the times, but the basic issues are as old as the United States: creating a responsible administration strong enough to do the public's work without becoming so strong as to raise the specter of tyranny that the nation's founders shed their blood to rid out.

Nothing is more basic in a constitutional, democratic system than a responsible public service. As citizens, we expect our administrators to deliver public services efficiently and effectively—and we expect that they will do so in a way that is responsive to the public and accountable to its elected officials. We expect a process that is fair and administrators who are professional. But how should we define these complex—

and often competing—conceptions of responsibility? Most important, how can we best achieve the obvious goal of responsible public service?

If the questions are simple, the answers are complex. "Bureaucrat bashing" only increases officials' resentment, demoralization, and reluctance to take initiatives. Empowerment of employees risks having their actions fall out of sync with the expectations of policymakers. Citizens and elected officials often expect the impossible. They expect administrators to "do more with less" as a matter of routine.

Bureaucratic responsibility has two elements. One is accountability: faithful obedience to the law, to higher officials' directions, and to standards of efficiency and economy. The other is ethical behavior: adherence to moral standards and avoidance even of the appearance of unethical actions. The two elements overlap and are generally compatible, but not always. Administrators may sometimes feel that acting morally requires them to disobey their superiors or to blow the whistle on colleagues and alert the media. Administrators must balance their own professional judgment with the sometimes conflicting standards set by their multiple overseers. One ultimately expects that public administrators will act in the public interest, but discovering what that means and how best to achieve it is often anything but clear.

This problem is central to American public administration, and it dates from the earliest days of the Republic. Alexander Hamilton chose for his second in command at the Treasury Department a notorious speculator who appropriated $200,000 for his private use and never repaid the government.[6] Americans have struggled ever since to balance freedom and flexibility for administrators with the need to hold them accountable to elected officials. But the idea of accountability is deceptively complex.

The Constitution and the law are the central elements of bureaucratic accountability. We expect bureaucrats to follow them both, as set down on paper, shaped by legislators, interpreted by the courts, and defined by their executive branch superiors. Indeed, that is the meaning of the often-repeated phrase "a government of laws, not of men." We expect that administrators will be subordinate to the sources of political legitimacy.

These propositions are indisputable. They lie at the very core of democratic government and the American political tradition. However, it is difficult to specify them in theory or to achieve them in practice. The central challenge is how best to define the role of bureaucratic power in the democratic system and how best to hold bureaucrats accountable.

Theoretical Approaches

The problem of how to balance bureaucratic power and accountability is enduring, and over the years many different answers have emerged. One is based in the law, because bureaucrats' authority is delegated authority. Citizens elect policymakers, in legislatures and in the executive. Through the peculiarly American separation-of-powers system, these elected officials make policy and delegate responsibility for executing that policy to administrators. Top administrators delegate authority for carrying out these programs to lower-level administrators, through the chain of command. In this approach, John P. Burke explains, "the emphasis falls on the strict obedience of the individual bureaucrat to hierarchy, the orders of superiors, and the explicit laws, regulations, and procedures that these superiors and other legitimate political authorities establish."[7] This formula is only a broad sketch, and it requires considerable elaboration to fit the real world. As we will see in later chapters, organization theory has developed intriguing variations in this traditional approach. Nevertheless, it is the fundamental idea connecting public administration to constitutional democracy. It is the key strategy that explains how to make bureaucrats powerful enough to do their job without making them so powerful that they threaten democratic rule.

A second approach views political power and administrative efficiency as inherently incompatible.[8] The advocates of this approach contend that democracy by its very nature fosters inefficiency. They say that the policymaking process creates fuzzy goals and conflicting mandates. It surely establishes multiple opportunities for discussion and debate, but this political participation gets in the way of defining a clear policy and providing administrators with the resources to carry it out. If democracy is inefficient, according to these theorists, it nevertheless provides the only way for the people to rule. It builds on government by the majority with protection of the rights of the minority. In a democracy, policy decisions emerge from an untidy process of interest group pressures, shifting legislative coalitions, responsiveness to legislators' desire to accommodate their constituencies, and executives' attentiveness to the groups electing them; advocacy and compromise triumph. Administration, in contrast, aspires to efficiency. The merit system of staffing, the rise of professions with expert knowledge, and the complexity of government functions all reinforce the need and capability for efficiency. Indeed, the people tend to demand efficiency, and when administrators foul up, they face complaints from citizens about wasting tax dollars and failing to achieve programs' goals. Faced with the fundamentally contrasting values of responsiveness and efficiency, along with the very different skills required to accomplish them both amid the public's conflicting expectations, administrators often struggle to seek the best practice of one or the other—and often fall short on both.

A third approach tries to reconcile the conflicts in the first two approaches by viewing administration in a democracy as a process of exchange, in which each side trades resources that others want.[9] For example, as we will see in chapter 10, bureaucrats are experts and often have far more information about policies than policy-makers. Policymakers can provide budget dollars, but they need bureaucrats' information to determine where best to apply the money and how best to serve their own political needs. Bureaucrats can be induced to share information because they gain something thereby: well-informed controllers will be less likely to make disruptive and misguided interventions.[10] In sum, the approach suggests, a marketlike relationship exists between administrators and their controllers.

The problem, at its core, is how to make bureaucrats powerful enough to do their jobs—to determine the best way to pick up garbage, run a state university, plow snow, distribute social security payments, or inspect airliners—but not so powerful that elected officials cannot hold them accountable. This is the central and eternal problem in the politics of the administrative process. It is central because it focuses sharply on the central puzzle of bureaucracy. Citizens pay taxes with the expectation government will solve their problems. They do not expect they will need to surrender their liberty to make government work. It is eternal because no democracy has ever found an answer that has remained stable for long. Citizens and their elected officials expect to be able to hold public administrators accountable for their actions, both in what they do and in how they do it.

Accountability Systems

We use the word *accountability* a great deal, but we rarely stop to ask ourselves what it means, how it works, what we seek to control, or who controls whom. Let us examine these issues in turn.

What Is Accountability?

Accountability is a relationship between people (who is accountable to whom?) about things (what are they accountable for?). It is the foundation of bureaucracy in a democracy, because accountability is the ability of policymakers to *control* administrators' actions. Control, in turn, can be either positive (requiring an agency to do something it ought to do) or negative (seeking to prevent an agency from doing something it should not do). Sins of omission as well as sins of commission are subject to investigation, criticism, instructions, and sanctions. The principal focus of control is on discovering bureaucratic errors and requiring their correction—a largely negative approach that tends to become dominant for several reasons. First, it is easier to see—and to criticize—sins of commission, for they tend to be the stories that attract media attention; the more intense the news coverage, the stronger the policymakers' reaction is likely to be. In 2004 the abuse of Iraqi prisoners by a small group of American soldiers drew media coverage for months, while the effective military service—and considerable suffering—of other American troops in Iraq got little attention in comparison. Second, an external control body (such as Congress or a state legislature) can more easily identify specific problems to be solved than it can devise a broader strategy to be followed. Oversight hearings promptly focused on the behavior of that handful of troops, but Congress struggled to sort out the far more complex issues underlying American policy in the region. Our discussion focuses on efforts of policymakers to shape administrative behavior. It therefore focuses primarily on the negative aspects of external control: correcting bureaucratic behavior that policymakers believe is not in the public interest. But we must explore that issue also in the context of the often confusing dynamics of the underlying policy.

It would be easier to solve the problem of accountability if we assumed that policymakers actually *wanted* to control administrators. In fact, many of them really do not. Policymakers are often reluctant to specify policy goals too carefully, because that would in turn make them responsible for the results. Policymakers often like to keep some distance between the decisions they make and the consequences that flow from them. When problems occur—from accidents in the space program to slow response time of fire trucks—reporters and top officials usually look for someone to blame. If control were an unbroken chain from policymakers to administrators, the links of accountability would lead directly to the top and blame would land in the laps of elected officials. These officials certainly do not want to encourage problems but when, inevitably, problems do occur, there is political value in a loose chain of command that points the finger of responsibility elsewhere. When the independent commission investigating the 9/11 Al Qaeda attacks set out to identify those responsible for preventing the attacks, its members discovered that the patterns of responsibility were so unclear that it was impossible to fix the blame. Despite heavy pressure to hold someone accountable for failures in intelligence and security, no one was fired. When Hurricane Katrina in 2005 produced the worst administrative failure in American history, only the administrator of the Federal Emergency Management Agency, Michael Brown, lost his job, despite manifest problems throughout the federal, state, and local policy system.

Even if elected officials actually wanted a clear chain of accountability, it would create a "gotcha" effect: if administrators knew they would have to answer for every problem, they would have to work in a demoralizing climate of distrust. In many cases, good administration requires the exercise of professional judgment. How likely is it that some drugs will cause deformities in humans, or that landing an airplane in a thunderstorm is likely to be unsafe? How can a dangerous chemical dump best be cleaned? When a storm wobbles between snow, ice, and rain, when is it best to plow the roads, and how many chemicals should be applied to keep them clear (and what damage to the environment and to the roadway might the chemicals cause)? If we create a climate that punishes risk-taking, we are likely to get too-safe decisions that interfere with getting government's job done. Excessive controls increase red tape and delay action. So much energy can be spent attempting to control administrative activities—and filing the paperwork to document that the control standards have been met—that there may be little money or time left to do the job. Controls that are too tight, therefore, may reduce administration's responsiveness to its public. Indeed, as British scholar Peter Self put it, "The tensions between the requirements of responsibility or 'accountability' and those of effective executive action can reasonably be described as *the* classic dilemma of public administration."[11]

Discretion is inevitable—and desirable—in administrative action. The process of filling in the gap between broad policy at the top and specific actions on the front line requires the constant exercise of judgment. Legislators can never specify all the factors that administrators must weigh in making decisions; even if they could, the necessity of reaching legislative compromise typically produces vague, sometimes even conflicting, guidance. Not all circumstances are the same, and good administration requires adapting general policies to special needs. Hence, effective administration always entails discretion. We want to give administrators enough room to make the right decisions yet we want to hold them accountable. Administrators must follow the law and meet the goals of public policy.

Who ultimately is accountable for what? That, in fact, is a question that stretches back centuries. The Roman satirist Juvenal asked two millennia ago: *"Quis custodiet ipsos custodes?"*—"Who is to watch the watchers?"[12] Who will control the controllers, to ensure that they get the balance right? We all want accountability, but there is no absolute standard for accountability, and a large number of hands tussle over what it ought to look like. Accountability thus is not only a relationship. It is also an uneasy one, with the balance among competing forces constantly in flux.[13]

What Should We Seek to Control?

When we look at performance, we focus on three elements of accountability: fiscal, process, and programmatic.[14] **Fiscal accountability** is the most traditional and widespread. We seek to ensure that agency officials spend money on the programs they are charged with managing—and only on those programs. This issue cuts both ways. On the one hand, we want to make sure that, in fact, the money is spent. A recurring complaint in the early 2000s was that the Department of Homeland Security failed to distribute quickly enough to state and local governments the funds that Congress had appropriated to support their security efforts. On the other hand, we want to make sure that the money is spent according to the law and is not wasted. The Defense Department inspector general launched a major investigation in 2004 when it was revealed that contractors in Iraq appeared to be paying exorbitant prices for gasoline. In 2008, investigators found that handheld computers purchased to support the 2010 census would not work, and they scrambled to put together a paper-based backup system. "Following the money" is a time-honored technique for ensuring financial accountability.

Process accountability is concerned with *how* agencies perform their tasks. While we often argue about the meaning of procedural fairness, government agencies regularly find themselves charged with unfair treatment. Massive problems in the 2000 presidential election focused national attention on the voting machines that Americans used and whether problems with those machines had prevented some votes from being counted. Those complaints about process led to a massive investment in new machinery for future elections, but new problems continued to ripple through the electoral system.

Program accountability is the newest and most difficult objective of control systems. Is a public program achieving its purpose, as defined in law? The U.S. Government Accountability Office, the investigative arm of Congress, has increasingly conducted program analyses to measure how well federal agencies answer this question. At the local, state, and federal level, governments have developed sophisticated performance-measurement systems to gauge how well programs met their goals. These new systems increasingly try to put hard numbers on the tough question of whether programs actually work.

Everyone agrees that citizens deserve accountability for their hard-earned tax dollars. But we tend to measure accountability in these three different ways—sometimes relying more on one standard than another and rarely trying to reconcile all three into an overall picture of an agency's performance.

Solutions?

The twin problems of making administration work efficiently and ensuring it is democratically accountable are deep and lasting. Administrators can follow the basic doctrine of accountability, through the hierarchical system of delegated authority. When that path leaves gaps, they can use their best judgment to discover the intent of the policy, rely on their professional judgment to determine how best to achieve that intent, and consult with the controllers to resolve uncertainties.[15]

But this formula brings no magic. Administrators face multiple controllers, and these controllers may not always agree on an agency's priorities. A congressional statute may suggest a set of priorities that conflicts with the president's, leaving agency heads, appointed by the president, to choose which to obey; appointees who choose the legislature's course could find themselves replaced by appointees more willing to follow the president's wishes. Moreover, when an agency head seeks clarification of Congress's priorities, there is no "Congress" to talk to—only a congressional committee or its chair, whose interpretation may not conform to the view of Congress as a whole. Of course, if Congress had spoken clearly to begin with, such conflicts would not have arisen. For officials at the state and local level, who might have to answer for how they spend federal money, the problem compounds itself.

These real-world conflicts leave administrators responsible for resolving many uncertainties, for which they must rely heavily on their own internal compasses—their personal character, professional training, devotion to the public service, and respect for faithful execution of the law. When controllers give conflicting directions or confusing signals, administrators face a conflict of loyalties. They can choose an option called **voice**: remaining in their positions and fighting for what they think is right, even if that risks dismissal. Or, they can choose **exit**: resigning, possibly with a public attack on the controller whose mandate they condemn.[16] But they know that the exit option may put the policies they care about at even greater risk, for they can be replaced by people who will bend more easily to the very pressures they have battled against. In fact, the idea of a conscience-driven exit from government is more popular in the press than in reality, because civil servants often have families to support, college tuition to pay, and relatively few job options at hand. In contrast, most high political appointees, cushioned by established reputations and extensive contacts outside government, can often exit to private-sector jobs at higher salaries. Furthermore, an attack by a resigning official is usually only a one-day media event, so anyone deciding to resign in protest must weigh the short-term political effect against the long-term personal impact.

In the end, the solution to the problem of accountability hinges on the balance between forces that come from outside administrators, including efforts by outside controllers, and forces that emerge from administrators themselves, including their character, background, and training. Theorists for generations have debated which forces are—and should be—more important. Should we assume that external controllers can never know enough about an administrator's actions and that setting the administrator's internal compass is most important? Or should we assume that we need to insist on extensive external controls to compensate for the tendency of administrators sometimes to stray off course? Two great figures in American public administration, Carl J. Friedrich and Herman Finer, staged an historic debate in the 1940s, deliberating over how much to rely on formal prescriptions and control mechanisms and how much must depend on what we have called the inner compasses of persons entrusted with public responsibilities.[17] They were not able to resolve this debate, and neither scholars nor practitioners since have done any better. Accountability, in the final analysis, is a fine balance between external and internal controls. This balance, in turn, depends critically on ethical behavior by administrators.

Governmental Power and Administrative Ethics

Citizens and elected officials alike demand a higher standard of ethics than typically prevails in the private sector. Indeed, that ethical upgrade often comes as a shock for political appointees who come to government from the private sector.[18] As Calvin Mackenzie writes,

> At one time or another in their work lives, most business leaders have found jobs in their own companies for family members or friends, have entered into contracts with firms in which they had a financial interest, or have accepted substantial gifts from people with whom they regularly do business. . . . When public officials engage in similar activities, however, they break the law.[19]

The pursuit of high ethical behavior in government raises a different tradeoff. On the one hand, we want skilled employees who can ensure that government's work is done well. In particular, we don't want to make the process of screening and hiring officials to be so burdensome, in the pursuit of high ethical standards, that we drive away good people. On the other hand, the public expects that those who exercise the public's trust will meet high standards and that, in particular, they will not use their power to line their own pockets, advantage their friends, or trade in the future on the relationships they developed in public service.

The issue is one that crosses all governmental boundaries. Philadelphia Mayor Michael A. Nutter emphatically made the point in his January 2008 inaugural address. "There is nothing government does that cannot be done ethically and transparently," he said. His goal, he told Philadelphians, was "a government that serves all of us, not a few."[20] Nutter's speech underlined the recurring central themes of public administration: creating government power to serve citizens; holding that power accountable to elected officials and, ultimately, to voters; doing so ethically, according to high standards of public service; and ensuring accountability through transparency.

The Public Service

In the end, the quality of government's work depends on the quality of the individuals recruited and retained in the public service, on their respect for bureaucratic accountability and ethical behavior, and especially on their commitment to the constitutional, democratic system. Instilling such values is a societal task; it depends on communication by family, schools, and peers. It also depends on creating a system that is accountable within our political system—especially since, in so many ways, the politics of the administrative process shapes the performance of American government.

Those capabilities encompass much more than they did in the past. Public administration is no longer primarily the direct execution of governmental programs. Much of it now is administration by proxy, the delegation to and supervision of activities by third parties—state and local governments, profit-oriented corporations, and nonprofit organizations. This new mission calls for a degree of sophistication and a continuing awareness that government is different, with obligations that eclipse those of the nongovernmental agents whose energies it enlists. The added complexity creates a greater challenge, but it also conveys a far greater reward.

The government needs to provide incentives and opportunities that invite the ablest citizens to join in and to delight in public service. Few of them will then fail to welcome the challenge of helping "to form a more perfect union, establish justice, insure domestic tranquility, provide for the common defense, and secure the blessings of liberty to ourselves and our posterity."[21] Encouraged by such possibilities, they will recognize that the public service, as President George H. W. Bush said, is "the highest and noblest calling."[22] Few vocations offer greater promise for improving the lives of so many of the world's citizens.

Case 1

From the Front Lines of Government Power: Waterboarding, the CIA, and Government Contractors

At the February 7, 2008, hearing before the House Permanent Select Committee on Intelligence, CIA Director Michael V. Hayden (right) conferred with Director of National Intelligence Mike McConnell. House members grilled Hayden on waterboarding and other techniques used to extract information from suspected terrorists.

On February 7, 2008, the House Permanent Select Committee on Intelligence held its annual hearing to assess the threats that the nation faced around the world. In the middle of the hearing, Rep. Jan Schakowsky (D-Ill.), questioned Central Intelligence Agency (CIA) Director Michael V. Hayden about the use of waterboarding on individuals suspected of plotting terrorism against the United States.

The technique, in which interrogators pour water over the hooded heads of suspects in a way that simulates drowning, came under harsh attack in the years after the September 11 attacks. Critics argued that the technique amounted to torture and should not be used by the United States, regardless of the danger. Proponents argued that it was not torture and that it constituted a reasonable approach to questioning individuals who might have knowledge about pending terrorist attacks on Americans.

In the midst of the questioning came a huge surprise. Not only did Hayden publicly reveal that the CIA had used waterboarding, but he also said that contractors—nongovernmental employees hired to work for the government—had been involved in the government's interrogation programs. Moreover, he thought that the contractors had participated in the waterboarding, but he was not sure.

Here is the transcript of their conversation:[1]

REP. SCHAKOWSKY: So are you saying, you know, you had harsh interrogation techniques that are often justified by this ticking-time-bomb scenario that, you know attacks are imminent? But why has the CIA employed harsh interrogation techniques, even once those immediate, imminent threats have passed?

GEN. HAYDEN: Well, all the techniques that we've used have been deemed to be lawful. We used waterboarding on three individuals under what were fairly unique historic circumstances: number one, a belief across the community that further catastrophic attacks were imminent; number two, an admittedly weak understanding of the workings of al Qaeda. No, those two situations do not pertain at the current time. The third leg of the stool, on which we stood at that point in time, was the inherent lawfulness of the activity. Now, all three of those things have changed. We have far more knowledge of al Qaeda. And although the threat continues, the imminence of the attack is not apparent to us.

REP. SCHAKOWSKY: Okay, my time is ticking away. . . . Are contractors involved in CIA detention interrogation programs?

GEN. HAYDEN: Absolutely.

REP. SCHAKOWSKY: Were contractors involved in the waterboarding of al Qaeda detainees?

GEN. HAYDEN: I'm not sure of the specifics. I'll give you a tentative answer: I believe so. And I can give you a more detailed answer—

REP. SCHAKOWSKY: And are they bound by the same rules enforced for other government personnel?

GEN. HAYDEN: They are bound by the same rules enforced for the Office of the Central Intelligence Agency.

REP. SCHAKOWSKY: Thank you.

Questions to Consider

1. Do you believe that the government should allow harsh interrogation techniques such as waterboarding? Note that Congress has delegated substantial power to the CIA, but it has neither approved nor denied the CIA's power to use this technique.

2. How can—and should—CIA employees be held accountable for the use of such power?

3. Do you think it matters, in answering question 2, whether the individual performing the waterboarding is a CIA employee or a private contractor?

4. Do you think it matters that the CIA director was not sure whether or not contractors were the ones performing the waterboarding?

Notes

1. House Permanent Select Committee on Intelligence, Annual Worldwide Threat Assessment (February 7, 2008), http://www.fas.org/irp/congress/2008_hr/020708transcript.pdf.

Key Concepts

exit **13**

fiscal accountability **11**

policy-administration dichotomy **6**

process accountability **12**

program accountability **12**

Progressives **5**

voice **13**

For Further Reading

Burke, John P. *Bureaucratic Responsibility.* Baltimore: Johns Hopkins University Press, 1986.

Finer, Herman. "Administrative Responsibility in Democratic Government." *Public Administration Review* 1 (Summer 1941): 335–350.

Friedrich, Carl J. "Public Policy and the Nature of Administrative Responsibility." In *Public Policy,* edited by Carl J. Friedrich and E. S. Mason, 3–24. Cambridge, Mass.: Harvard University Press, 1940.

Gruber, Judith E. *Controlling Bureaucracies: Dilemmas in Democratic Governance.* Berkeley: University of California Press, 1987.

Hirschman, Albert O. *Exit, Voice, and Loyalty: Responses to Decline in Firms, Organizations, and States.* Cambridge, Mass.: Harvard University Press, 1970.

Landau, Martin. "Redundancy, Rationality, and the Problem of Duplication and Overlap." *Public Administration Review* 29 (July–August 1969): 346–358.

Rohr, John A. *Ethics for Bureaucrats: An Essay on Law and Values.* 2nd ed. New York: Marcel Dekker, 1989.

Suggested Websites

Extensive discussion on federal ethics laws and policies can be found on the website of the U.S. Office of Government Ethics, **http://www.usoge.gov.**

More broadly, the Council on Governmental Ethics Laws, **http://www.cogel.org,** tracks policies on ethics. In addition, many state and local governments have their own sites—which search engines can readily locate—detailing laws and regulations on ethics.

PART I

The Nature of Government

The subject of our book, public administration, does not exist in the abstract. Rather, its meaning comes from the job it has to do. Political decisions typically have meaning only in the ways that public administrators bring them to life, and the pursuit of that mission is what shapes the nature of public administration and the jobs that public administrators do.

But not all administration is the same. Administrative strategies and tactics vary tremendously within each level of government and between levels of government. Understanding administration thus depends on understanding the tasks that administrators must accomplish. Even more fundamentally, it requires understanding the sources of bureaucratic power and how elected officials, in a world of growing complexity, can hold administrators accountable for *how* they do the work they do.

2

Administrative Responsibility

Not long ago, one of this book's authors, Don Kettl, struggled out of bed for an early-morning trip to Washington, D.C. From his apartment, he rode an elevator down and, outside his building, caught a trolley to Philadelphia's 30th Street train station. He came out of the underground tunnel at the station just as the sun was coming up, and just in time to scoot across the street as the "don't walk" sign was flashing. As he waited for the train, the barking of a bomb-sniffing dog echoed throughout the concourse. The dog had not spotted a suspicious package—he was a pup in training and was just learning how to focus on the job at hand instead of all the people milling around the platforms. The train, fortunately, was on time, and it was a pretty ride, across the estuaries of the Chesapeake Bay before rolling into Union Station at the foot of Capitol Hill. A quick trip on Washington's Metro got him to a meeting in a nearby federal office building.

This tale, of course, is more than just about the trip of a sometime road warrior and textbook author. It is also a map of government—and government administration—in action. The elevator had an inspection sticker certifying that the Pennsylvania Department of Labor and Industry had found the elevator safe, for which the author was grateful (since it would have been a long fall down an empty shaft to the basement). The inspection might have been performed by a private company licensed by the state, but the state government stood behind the certificate pasted on the elevator's wall. The Southeastern Pennsylvania Transportation Authority (SEPTA), a regional government whose services traveled into three states, ran the trolley. The city of Philadelphia's Traffic Engineering Division managed the walk/don't walk sign, and the excited puppy was an employee of Amtrak's own police department. Amtrak is really the National Railroad Passenger Corporation, a quasi-governmental corporation that operates like a private company but is controlled by government officials and subsidized by public money. The Chesapeake Bay is more scenic because of the efforts of Pennsylvania and Maryland, in concert with the U.S. Environmental Protection Agency, to ensure the waterway is clean. Like SEPTA,

Washington's Metro is a regional transportation authority. Its stations contain hidden security devices to detect terrorist threats, with security provided by a complicated network of federal, state, regional, and local law enforcement agencies.

This is only the beginning. None of us can even get our days started without encountering government bureaucracy. The water we drink, the cars we drive, the bicycles we pedal, the streets we walk—all are the product of government bureaucracy in action. Often without noticing, we are surrounded by **public administration.** Without it, public policy would have little real meaning and virtually no practical effect. Indeed, over the years, public administration's role in society has become so pervasive that many observers have pointed to the rise of the **administrative state.**[1] Dwight Waldo wrote a doctoral dissertation by this title and published it in 1948. Since then, some observers have condemned the spread of government and its power. Others have seen the trend as an inevitable—even desirable—reaction to the growing complexity of social problems and Americans' adamant demands for solutions to them. Some fear that the growth of government has empowered nameless, faceless bureaucrats with greater control over our lives. Some plead for more businesslike practices in the hope of making government more efficient. Others counter that government and business are so fundamentally different that there is surprisingly little that corporate practice can teach **public bureaucracy.** Americans have widespread debates about the role of public administration and often criticize it for reaching too deeply into our lives. We have found, however, that we cannot do without it.

These debates have produced a wide array of approaches to the study of public administration, but one issue dominates: **administrative responsibility.** Americans expect, indeed insist, that the nation's bureaucracy be held accountable to elected officials and, through them, to the people. Since the earliest days of the nation's history, that has been the central concern about public administration, and it remains so today. Critics sometimes complain that government bureaucracy has no bottom line. In fact, government does have a bottom line: administrative responsibility, not only for administering programs efficiently but also for ensuring that both the process and its results are accountable to elected officials and, ultimately, to the people. Americans care deeply about what government does—whether its agencies pick up the trash effectively or prevent dangerous food products from being sold in stores—and about how it does it—including making sure that people are treated fairly and that government officials do not abuse their power. How it works is the cornerstone of the politics of the administrative process.

An Administrative State?

Especially since the end of World War II, citizens have demanded far more of government. These demands have led to the creation of more administrative agencies, a larger number of civil servants, and higher government spending. This expansion has brought us to what Waldo characterized as the era of the administrative state and has inspired generations of debate about the implications of a bigger bureaucracy for a strong, vibrant democracy.[2]

Emphasizing government's growing size, Waldo's phrase *administrative state* points to the enormous discretion that government administrators exercise, and it also suggests the possibility that such discretion could disrupt traditional constitutional arrangements. However, in global perspective, America's "big government" does not appear so big. As Figure 2.1 reveals, the combined spending of all American governments—national, state, and local—amount to little more than a third of the nation's gross domestic product, the measure of the total amount of goods and services produced by the economy. Among twenty-eight major industrial countries, the United States ranks eighth from the bottom. By contrast, Sweden and France spend 52 percent of their economic output on government, and Denmark is right behind

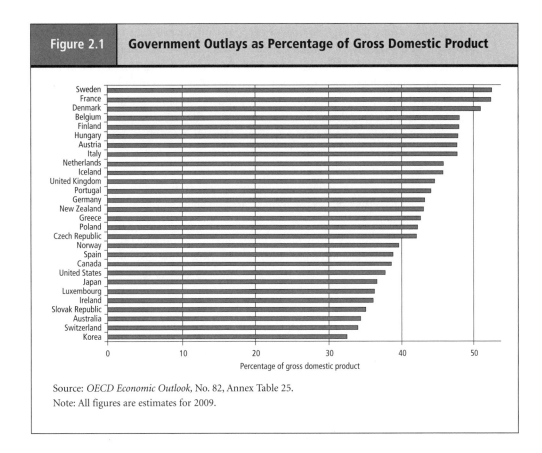

| Figure 2.1 | **Government Outlays as Percentage of Gross Domestic Product** |

Source: *OECD Economic Outlook*, No. 82, Annex Table 25.

Note: All figures are estimates for 2009.

at 51 percent. Thus, we begin with a profound paradox. Americans look at their bureaucracy and see big government. In fact, their government is smaller than in most other countries in the industrialized world.

Where does this distorted perception of American bureaucracy's size and power come from? As we see in chapter 3, government's power flows from more than just the money it spends. Government increasingly enlists citizens and private companies as proxies in managing government programs, including contracts and regulation. That means government's fingers are in more pies than ever before. But it is also clear that some of this perception results from a sense that government administrators too often have too much power, and exercise too much discretion, in excess of what the government is constitutionally empowered to do. It is surely true that administrators exercise discretion far more than in the past. Yet, as we will see later in the book, a vast assortment of legal and political forces—legislative bodies, courts, chief executives, political appointees, and interest groups—now exercise so much control over administrators' discretion that a countercomplaint frequently arises: too often, public administrators find their hands tied as they struggle to manage programs effectively.

Citizens may not agree. Their principal contacts with government are with administrative agencies and their employees, and they often find the administrative system so complex that they do not know where to turn with their problems. They complain about budgetary, regulatory, and spending policies and programs. They frequently vent their unhappiness about political decisions on the administrators charged with carrying them out.

We all complain of red tape, a term attributed to the ribbon used to tie up English documents presented to the king. Later, after the American Civil War, veterans had to show proof of their service to receive their pensions, and the war records were bound in red ribbon. In both cases, administrators had to "cut the red tape" to get to the papers. The term stuck as the term of art for slicing through paperwork to solve the real problems.

Yet despite people's often loud complaints about bureaucracy, they count on firefighters to extinguish fires, police officers to arrest criminals, snowplow operators to clear the roads, Social Security clerks to process checks for senior citizens, and guards to maintain order in prisons. At all levels of American government, elected officials shape very ambitious policies, and then they rely on these unelected bureaucrats, working in administrative agencies, to transform those ambitions into reality. Without effective work by these bureaucrats, much of what citizens seek as a society could never be achieved.

Public administration thus is about deep, profound issues: how citizens' aspirations become translated into policy; how government tries to make these services as effective, efficient, and fair as possible; and how the work of government can ultimately be held accountable to citizens. The connections between democracy and bureaucracy are intimate—indeed, they lie at the core of the politics of the administrative process and the rise of the administrative state.

The Bureaucracy Problem

Public administration is the study of government bureaucracy. The term *bureaucracy* itself comes from the French word *bureau,* with its roots in the fourteenth century. At the French Chamber of Accounts, field administrators placed their financial records on a brown woolen cloth, *la bure,* which covered the table where they faced the king's auditors. The room thus came to be called "the bureau," and the way these officials did their work became known as "bureaucracy." The term has long held its pejorative connotation. In an 1836 novel Balzac characterized the bureaucracy as "a gigantic power manipulated by dwarfs," and as "that heavy curtain hung between the good to be done and him who commands it."[3] Such disparagement was scarcely surprising or new. In the New Testament, Jesus faced widespread criticism for naming a government tax collector as one of his apostles.

Even in its derogatory sense, bureaucracy embodies a deep contradiction.[4] On the one hand, it refers to a red-tape-bound set of civil servants, who are viewed as inefficient, unresponsive, negative, bored, impolite, and unhelpful to citizens seeking services. On the other hand, the word conjures up visions of a body of all-too-efficient officials who have amassed tremendous power and who arbitrarily decide matters without due process. Bureaucracy is at once too inefficient to accomplish much of anything and so powerful that its force is impossible to resist.

In the study of public administration, the term has a neutral meaning. Indeed, bureaucracy has long been used to define the organization and structure of complex organizations, in both the public and private sectors. Large private companies, from power utilities to auto manufacturers, are bureaucracies. Many charitable organizations, such as the American Red Cross and the American Cancer Society, are bureaucracies. Indeed, the oldest continuously functioning bureaucracy in the world is a religious one, the Roman Catholic Church. (The New Testament, in fact, records that after the ascension of Jesus, one of the first acts of the new church was to create a formal organization to carry on the work of its charismatic founder.) In this book, we use the word *bureaucracy* to refer to public organizations: the formal, rational system of relations among persons vested with administrative authority to carry out public programs. In chapter 4 we examine this interpretation of bureaucracy—and some of its alternatives—more fully.

Despite this neutral cast, the pejorative meanings of the term are never far from our minds. The often contradictory images of bureaucracy point to very real problems of large-scale administration. They also shape the politics of public administration.

As presidential candidates, both Jimmy Carter and Ronald Reagan campaigned on "bureaucracy bashing" themes; Bill Clinton dealt with calls to shrink the bureaucracy; both Presidents Bush campaigned on a conservative agenda to reduce government (even though they both increased it); and John McCain and Barack Obama sparred on who could best promote change.

Other countries have struggled with the same conflicts. A foreign prime minister once complained, "Creating the appearance of work, taking cover behind hollow rhetoric, bureaucracy may hold back the improvement of the economic mechanism, dampen independence and initiative, and erect barriers to innovation." A second said, "Bureaucratism remains a serious problem in the political life of our party and state. The overstaffing, overlapping and unwieldiness of Government organs, confusion of their responsibilities and buck-passing are . . . major causes of bureaucratism. We must therefore reform these organs from top to bottom." The first speaker was prime minister of the former Soviet Union, the second acting prime minister of the People's Republic of China.[5] The impulse to reform the bureaucracy has driven government officials around the world.[6]

If political leaders, both at home and abroad, perceive bureaucracy and red tape as such fundamental evils, one wonders why powerful government officials do not simply abolish them. The answer is that complexity and red tape are inherent in large organizations, especially in government, where public policy embraces a broad array of complex goals.[7] Indeed, it would be impossible to pursue the vast array of ambitious programs that citizens expect without a bureaucracy—and its accompanying red tape. Any real effort to shred the tape would require a fundamental redefinition of the role of government in society. Politicians have tried to do so—including efforts by the Reagan administration in the 1980s and House Speaker Newt Gingrich in the 1990s—but the fundamental patterns have endured. Those who have sought to shrink the size of government quickly found that most Americans like most of the government they are getting. Citizens in the United States, like those everywhere, just do not much like to pay taxes for what they receive. Americans regularly complain about the size of bureaucracy and want it cut—except for *their* bureaucracy and the programs that serve them.

Bureaucracy and Size

The scope of governmental activities is broad, and public administration operates on a grand scale. Consider the comparison of the public and private sectors. In 2007, the federal government spent $2.5 trillion, about the same as the total combined sales of the world's fifteen largest corporations. Federal spending was more than seven times larger than the sales of the world's largest company, Wal-Mart. State and local governments spent another $1.8 billion. Indeed, as Table 2.1 shows, each of the federal

Table 2.1	Size of Largest Public and Private Organizations		
Rank	**Organization**	**Category**	**Sales or outlays** (in $ billions)
1	**Health and Human Services**	**Federal department**	**699.24**
2	**Social Security Administration***	**Federal department**	**567.18**
3	**Defense**	**Federal department**	**548.92**
4	**Treasury**	**Federal department**	**524.99**
5	Wal-Mart Stores	Retailing	348.65
6	ExxonMobil	Oil and gas operations	335.09
7	Royal Dutch/Shell Group	Oil and gas operations	318.85
8	BP	Oil and gas operations	265.91
9	General Motors	Consumer durables	207.35
10	**California**	**State government**	**203.64**
11	DaimlerChrysler	Consumer durables	199.99
12	Chevron	Oil and gas operations	195.34
13	Toyota Motor	Consumer durables	179.02
14	Total	Oil and gas operations	175.05
15	ConocoPhillips	Oil and gas operations	167.58
16	General Electric	Conglomerates	163.39
17	Ford Motor	Consumer durables	160.12
18	ING Group	Insurance	153.54
19	CitiGroup	Banking	146.56
20	Allianz	Insurance	125.33
21	HSBC Holdings	Banking	121.51
22	**New York**	**State government**	**120.68**

Source: "Forbes 2000," *Forbes* (March 29, 2007), http://www.forbes.com/lists/2007/18/biz_07forbes2000_The-Global-2000_Sales. html; U.S. Office of Management and Budget, *Budget of the United States Government: Historical Tables, Fiscal Year 2008*, Estimate; and statistics from the California and New York state governments.

Note: New York figures are for 2007–2008 Enacted Budget. California figures are for 2007–2008. Otherwise statistics are for 2007.

* Social Security Administration (on budget only)

government's four largest departments spends more than Wal-Mart sells. California's state budget ranks between General Motors and DaimlerChrysler, while that of New York is just below a multinational bank.

The federal government's customers are 300 million Americans (not including, as one might, the people in other countries who benefit from foreign-aid programs). No private company can claim such a large customer base. The U.S. Postal Service moves 700 million pieces of mail each day, or 212 billion pieces per year. The Internal Revenue Service receives 224 million tax returns in a year, and more than 50 million Americans receive benefits from the Social Security Administration.

The different interests of these customers, however, often push the government in very different directions. The U.S. Department of Agriculture subsidizes tobacco growers and promotes foreign sales of tobacco, but the Office of the Surgeon General requires health warnings on tobacco packages and advertisements. The Federal Aviation Administration is charged both with promoting and with regulating air traffic. Citizens count on government not only to do ambitious, different, and sometimes contradictory things and to do them all equally well.

Of course, public administration can sometimes be small in scale: thousands of tiny towns throughout the nation are clearly engaged in small-scale administration, and within a large bureaucracy it is possible to study a single subunit of a bureau and even a face-to-face working group within that subunit. Nevertheless, the large scale and complex form of government bureaucracies shape the key issues of government's behavior and performance.

The Meaning of Public Administration

Analysts and scholars have never agreed on a common definition of public administration.[8] Examples of public administration abound, from the prosaic delivery of mail, collection of trash, and licensing of motor vehicles to overseeing the dramatic landing of cameras and spacecraft on Mars, the dispatching of Peace Corps volunteers to scores of countries, helping citizens recover from hurricanes, and the pinpoint mapping of dangerous storms through satellite images. But examples do not add up to a definition. To define a subject is to fix its boundaries or, if the boundaries turn out to be fuzzy, to identify its essence, its core character. For public administration this has proved so intractable a problem that its scholarly study has long been said to be suffering a "crisis of identity."

A two-step approach, defining first "administration" and then "public" might seem promising, but it fails. Dictionary editors and scholars have stumbled over the first step, sometimes using other words that themselves need definition, as in "administration is executing." Other writers characterize administration as cooperative human action that has a high degree of rationality, which means that the cooperative action is intended to maximize the realization of certain goals.[9] But this formulation seems to embrace even a child's persuading two friends to share instant messages on a cell phone. Still other writers, operating at a less abstract level, say that

106 also

administration is concerned with "how, not what," with "means, not ends," with "process, not substance," with efficiency, not other values—a set of dichotomies that provoke debate rather than providing definition.

A better starting point for understanding the meaning of public administration is to clarify its distinctness from private administration. We begin by evaluating the argument that administration is administration wherever it exists, whether in the public or the private sector. Next we examine policy execution versus **policymaking.** This separates the administrative processes, in which government administration shares similarities with private administration, from the distinctly public nature of government decisions. Finally, we emphasize the ways that administrative responsibility in public administration differs in both form and content from its analog in private enterprises. Of central importance to public bureaucracies, administrative responsibility defines the very essence of our puzzle—and of this book.

Public versus Private Administration

Public administration is *public*: it is the administration of specifically governmental affairs. Yet it is also administration, a kind of activity found in all large organizations. For years a debate has brewed about how to treat public administration: Are its basic features the same as administration of all sorts? Is it therefore simply a subset of more generic management issues? Or does it have special elements that make it distinctly public and thus require separate attention? A number of schools of thought seek to answer these questions.

Leading the movement toward a generic approach to administration are sociologists who specialize in **organizational theory** and many business school students of management. At the broadest level, some organizational theorists contend that administration is administration, whatever its setting, and that the problems of organizing people, leading them, and supplying them with resources to do their jobs are the same regardless of setting.[10] More practically oriented thinkers have argued that politics is about conflict and that "political conflict is at the center of management life"; management is fundamentally about managing that conflict, regardless of its organizational setting.[11] Most broadly, Barry Bozeman has argued that "all organizations are public because public authority affects some of the behavior or processes of all organizations." Thus, organizations are neither purely public nor purely private, but all organizations, he contends, share public and private features independent of their legal or formal status.[12] In fact, a leading British political scientist, William A. Robson, has noted that "modern American theory is heavily committed to the view that one can discuss every kind of administration in a generalized manner." This effort, he explains, is like "an effort to produce a treatise on ball games, as distinct from studies of golf, or tennis, or football, or polo, or baseball."[13]

Indeed, the distinction between the public and private sectors has gradually become more blurred. As Dwight Waldo pointed out in 1980, "in the United States—and I believe much more widely—there is a movement away from a sharp distinction between *public* and *private*, and *toward* a blurring and mingling of the two."[14] As government becomes more involved in business, and as more business organizations are incorporated into the provision of public services, such blurring is unmistakable. But our central question remains: Is there something distinctly *public* about public administration?

The response of private-sector managers who move into top public-sector positions is a solid yes. They have universally underlined crucial differences between the two.[15] Scholars have emphasized other differences as well.[16] One can distinguish public agencies in two ways: First, and most crucially, public organizations do the public's business—they administer law. Second, there are important differences of character—public organizations have fundamentally different processes from those of private organizations and work in a different environment.

The Critical Role of Public Authority

The most fundamental distinction between public and private organizations is the rule of law. Public organizations exist to *administer the law,* and every element of their being—their structure, staffing, budget, and purpose—is the product of legal authority. Every action taken by a public administrator ultimately "must be traceable to a legal grant of authority; those of private firms need not be," as Harold F. Gortner, Julianne Mahler, and Jeanne Bell Nicholson argue.

> Managers of private firms can generally take any action, establish any policy, or use any means of operation not specifically prohibited. Public managers, in contrast, may not do so in the absence of specific grants of authority. Private organizations can act unless proscribed or forbidden; public ones may act *only* if the authority is granted. As a veteran public manager remarked. . . . "For the private organization, it is a matter of 'go until I say stop'; but to the public manager the message is 'don't go unless I tell you to.' "[17]

Indeed, the law not only requires government officials to administer the law; the federal **Antideficiency Act** explicitly forbids them from spending anything on any purpose not explicitly authorized by law.[18] In the private sector, by contrast, officials are allowed to do anything not explicitly forbidden by law.[19]

Public administration thus exists to implement law. In the American system, authority flows from the people to those they elect to govern them. When a legislature passes a law and an executive signs it, the law does not implement itself. That is the task the legislature delegates to the administrator, and it is this chain of authority, flowing from the people through elected institutions to the public administrator,

Six weeks after Hurricane Katrina hit the Gulf Coast in 2005, 2,616 trailers sat in a staging area in Selma, Alabama, awaiting inspections and clearance before being moved to the devastated area. Investigators later discovered that many of the trailers leaked toxic levels of formaldehyde.

that makes public administration distinctively public. Faithful execution of these laws is the highest calling of public administrators. It is the core of administrative responsibility. Public and private administration thus differ most sharply and fundamentally on the foundation of every administrative action.

Public management scholar Steven Kelman points to a fundamental difference between public and private management. All organizations, he says, must balance goals and constraints. Goals are the good things they try to do—the value they produce, the objectives they seek to accomplish. Constraints are the negative forces they must jump and the rules they must abide by in pursuing their goals. Ideally, they would find the right balance that ensures good results and strong accountability. For private organizations, the balance leans toward the goals. With fewer constraints, they sometimes encounter the Enron problem, christened after the energy management company whose free-wheeling tactics caused it to collapse in 2001, leaving shareholders and employees broke. For public organizations, the balance leans toward the constraints. With more constraints, government sometimes struggles to accomplish the objectives that policymakers set for it. This, he says, is the Katrina problem—red tape that restrains the ability of government to do its job. Public and private organizations share the need to balance goals and constraints, but the forces underlying their operations tend to push them in different directions. That, in turn, frames very different problems for their leaders and for the people they serve.[20]

Characteristic Public Processes

In addition to this fundamental legal distinction, there typically are important differences between public and private organizational processes. Although they are not fixed in law—and although some private-sector organizations share these public-sector characteristics—there tend to be regular differences in the way public-sector organizations do business.[21] The following are some examples of these private- versus public-sector differences:

- *Career service.* Whereas private-sector organizations tend to be led by individuals who devote their careers to the organization, American public bureaucracies tend to be headed by relative amateurs whose tenure is of short duration. Assistant secretaries in federal departments, for example, typically serve only eighteen months and spend much of their time in office simply learning their jobs.
- *Measures of performance.* The private sector has the market in which to test its **performance.** Few public-sector organizations, by contrast, have any "direct way of evaluating their outputs in relation to the cost of the inputs used to make them," as Anthony Downs puts it.[22] For public administrators, compliance with the law is the ultimate measure of performance, but laws often are vague and give little guidance.
- *Competing standards.* Whereas efficiency is the ultimate private standard, public administrators are expected to manage both efficiently and equitably. These two standards often compete: what is fair often is not the most efficient, and vice versa. As economist Arthur Okun notes, the balance between equality and efficiency is "the big tradeoff."[23]
- *Public scrutiny.* To a far greater degree than in the private sector, public administrators work under public scrutiny. Public administrators labor under laws whose very titles, such as "Government in the Sunshine," underline the role of public **oversight,** covering both internal and external operations. This "goldfish-bowl effect" is in stark contrast with the much more limited public scrutiny that private organizations receive. Dealing with the media has long been a feature of public administrative activity.[24]
- *Persuasion.* In the private sector, managers tend to manage by authority. They give orders and expect them to be obeyed. In the public sector, by contrast, administration depends far more on persuasion and the balancing of conflicting political demands.
- *Oversight.* Public administrators must answer not only to their superiors but also to legislators and the courts. Administrators must appear before legislative committees to explain their activities and must answer complaints raised in court. If the private sector has one bottom line—the financial statement—the public sector has several: accountability to higher-level administrative officials, to the chief executive, to legislators, to the courts, and ultimately to the public.

We tend sometimes to separate public and private activities by the profit motive. To be sure, this is an important difference, but it does not clearly distinguish the two sectors. Private organizations sometimes submerge profit making to other goals. Some **nongovernmental organizations** are nonprofit; they exist to advance social agendas. Furthermore, some public organizations, such as the U.S. Postal Service, simulate the market by imposing fees and charges. Such strategies are on the rise as reformers attempt to make public organizations more efficient.

Most fundamentally, however, public organizations are public because they administer the law and because their very being springs from the law. Moreover, public organizations typically operate in a different environment from that of private organizations. Wallace Sayre once wryly suggested that "business and public administration are alike only in all unimportant respects."[25] It is the challenge of public service that distinguishes public from private administration.

Policy Execution versus Policy Formation

Public administration shares with private administration many basic features of policy execution. From managing computer systems to processing forms, the basic work often is similar. But public-sector execution differs fundamentally in the goals to be served and the standards by which it is judged. Indeed, part of what makes public administration public is its execution of the will of the people as defined by governmental institutions. Because public administration contributes to both the shaping and the execution of policies, it is often very different indeed from private administration. We look first at the more familiar function—that of execution.

Policy Execution

Consider what it means when we say that the government has "adopted" a policy. In our system, this normally means that the elected policymakers have enacted a law forbidding, directing, or permitting members of the society to behave in specified ways. Then what happens? The law is merely printed paper. The task of public administration is to translate the print of statute books into changed behavior by members of society—individuals, groups, organizations, and businesses—to convert words into action, form into substance.

This is a complex task. It means expanding some individuals' opportunities by extending governmental services and protections to them. It means regulating some individuals' freedom by drawing taxes from them, discovering and prosecuting those who engage in forbidden behaviors, granting or denying permission to engage in certain activities (for example, licensing radio and television stations and selling prescription drugs), and manipulating the environment of subsidies and interest rates. The government administers some enterprises itself, either as monopolies or as competitors of private enterprises: local libraries and the Social Security Administration function largely as monopolies; the U.S. Postal Service and the Tennessee Valley Authority compete with private companies. Reformers have increasingly sought to bring private competition into local schools, and public schools increasingly have to compete with private schools and parents schooling their children at home. The government also administers the defense establishment and foreign affairs, including hundreds of outposts over the world. The range is immense, and the pattern is a mixture of old and new concerns.

Authorizing these governmental activities, giving policy direction, and providing the resources needed to accomplish them are among the central tasks of the elective legislature and chief executive. But all this initiative merely permits something to happen; it does not *make* it happen. Administration is what translates these paper declarations of intent into reality. It seeks to shape the behavior of citizens to match policy goals and seeks to deliver the benefits promised in legislation.

Administration as execution cannot be taken for granted. If it is weak or unresponsive, it will enfeeble the political system itself. For example, in many developing countries the critical problem is not so much the government's political instability as it is the government's incapacity to carry out its decisions. Public policies, no matter how bold or innovative, are worthless if government cannot put them into effect. When Hurricane Katrina put most of New Orleans under water in 2005, official government policy was to provide help quickly. The government staggered in doing so, not because its officials did not want to but because executing the policy proved tremendously complex. Making policy does not ensure results happen.

Policy Formation

Administration's second role is played out at two stages of the policy-formation process: (1) before the constitutionally empowered legislature and chief executive have made their policy decisions, and (2) after they have enacted statutes or issued executive orders, and then passed on to administrators the job of making sense of them. In the first stage, proposals for statutes and for amendments of statutes flow from many sources, of which administrative agencies are among the most important. An agency in a given program field is likely to possess much factual information about needs and trends in that field; to have an expert staff for the analysis of such data; to have discovered the defects in existing statutes through the experience of trying to apply them; and to have a strong devotion to the program's objectives and so to their fuller realization. Often, though not always, the agency is trusted as a less biased source of information than other available sources, such as organized interest groups.

In our time, two developments have enhanced the role that administrative agencies play at this initiating and preparatory stage of policymaking. One is the increased technicality of public policy, paralleled by a growth in the specialized competence of administrative agency staffs. Economic stabilization policies, for example, must be guided by sophisticated information, analysis, and advice from professional economists, as well as by the value preferences and political sense of the elected president and members of Congress. Expert knowledge and advice are essential to policy development for national defense weaponry, space exploration, public health, research and development, education, poverty, urban renewal, energy, air and water pollution, and a host of other program areas. Most of the government's experts are in the administrative agencies.

The second development is the marked expansion of the chief executive's role as a major agenda setter for government policymaking. The chief executive—president, governor, mayor, county executive—initiates many of the proposals that legislatures review. Typically the executive shapes this program through consultation with the agency-based experts of the executive branch. Although they are not the only sources of the executive's ideas, they are strategically situated to initiate and counsel on policy proposals that may win the executive's influential sponsorship. And, to complete the circle, the executive's need for expert help has grown as public policy problems have become increasingly technical.

The second stage of the policy-formation process occurs after statutes are on the books. Often, and particularly in important and complex fields, the statutes are not clear enough that what happens afterward can be regarded as execution in the narrow sense. Legislative behavior follows no consistent pattern, sometimes yielding highly detailed statutory measures and other times resulting in only the fuzzy identification of a problem that administrators are directed to wrestle with. In effect, then, the administrator must make policy by trying to decide what the legislators meant.

There are several reasons for such delegation, whether deliberate or inadvertent, of policymaking power. In a new policy field in which there is little experience to build on, the legislature sometimes wants something done but can make only a vague gesture in the direction that action should take. In a field in which technology or other features are expected to change rapidly, the statute must permit flexible action by the agency, rather than requiring frequent returns to the legislature for enactment of new language. Some subjects, such as licensing of liquor stores and the operation of taxis, simply do not lend themselves to specification of criteria that would confine administrative discretion. Statutes often do specify some conditions—for example, requirements that liquor store owners must not have criminal records and that liquor stores not be located near schools—but they offer few guidelines about how to choose among the numerous applicants who meet these simple criteria. In addition, the ingenuity of businesspeople can often generate clever ways of evading any highly specific prohibitions in a statute. Hence, Congress broadly forbids "unfair methods of competition . . . and unfair or deceptive acts in commerce," leaving the administrative agency and the courts to give content to those vague terms "unfair" and "deceptive."

At times, the legislative process itself is so stormy and full of crosscurrents that the resulting statutes incorporate contradictory policy guidelines, leaving agency managers to use their own judgment in making sense out of the mishmash. Sometimes, too, the necessity of reaching a compromise solution leads to legislative language that papers over disagreement—but whose deliberate ambiguity leaves the agency wide scope for administrative interpretation. Most agencies, furthermore, administer many statutes, passed by different legislatures with differing preferences, so that the need to reconcile the accumulated set of legislative instructions forces some exercise of agency discretion. Finally, the legislature may not appropriate sufficient funds to allow an agency to carry out a program as enacted. Unless the legislature itself gives specific direction, the agency must then decide whether to spread the money thinly or, more commonly, to choose which of its objectives it will pursue with vigor and which it will slight.

In essence, then, public administration includes the shaping of policy on the way up, the execution of policy after it has been made, and discretion about policy matters on the way down.

The Policy-Administration Dichotomy

As scholars studied public administration early in the twentieth century, they prominently developed the theme of separating policy—that is, the political work of making policy—from administration. As we saw in chapter 1, this dichotomy resulted both from the need to identify a distinctive field of study and, probably more so, from the efforts to reform city government and then state and national governments in the late nineteenth and early twentieth centuries. Reformers worked to root out political corruption, the mother's milk of machine-style politics. Establishing a neutral realm for administration, protected by civil service laws and governed by a drive for businesslike efficiency, would both dry up the patronage resources of political machines and leave policymaking organs of government as the proper realm for democratic politics.

Today the dual goals of assuring a nonpartisan body of civil servants remain unchanged: loyal service to a long succession of officials from different political parties and the achievement of efficient administration. The obvious fact that administrative staffs share in the policy-formation function—as well as the inevitably fuzzy line between policy and administration—has led many students to reject the policy-administration dichotomy. Analysts have tried to reestablish the distinction by forbidding administrators from participating in political activities, but that line may waver. Civil servants need to be respectful of the policy goals of elected officials and sensitive to the political implications of their policy suggestions. But civil servants have other obligations as well—to long-range policy goals, continuity and consistency, effective administration, and resistance to corruption. Furthermore, they must balance an administration's preferences against legislative and judicial mandates.

In sum, civil servants have a kind of responsibility that is distinguishable from that of politically elected officials. Policy and administration are certainly intertwined, but the motivations and behaviors of policymakers and public administrators are very different. Separating them is one of the core issues of public administration.

Administrative Responsibility

Every well-developed organization has some system for holding subordinates accountable to their superiors. Nowhere is the system so complex and confining as in government.[26] Statutes and regulations specify elaborate procedures that seriously limit administrators' discretionary authority. Legislative committees call administrators to testify, often on the same matter before a variety of such bodies and often to answer criticisms of actions and proposed actions. Members of legislative staffs closely monitor administrative actions in agencies of interest to their superiors. Budget offices typically review proposed regulations and information-gathering proposals in addition to reviewing financial requests and setting personnel ceilings.

From the career administrators' perspective, this is a formidable control system. Yet, as we have earlier suggested, administrative responsibility goes beyond these external controls on behavior. There are internalized guides to conduct—internalized, that is, by administrators themselves. They know, to begin with, that they serve in government and that therefore they must be sensitive to the legitimate roles of other elements of the government, roles that include control of administrative behavior. Second, they have a loyalty to their agencies and the programs entrusted to them. Third, in a civil service now markedly populated by professional experts, they are loyal to their professions' standards and motivated to win the regard of members of the profession who are outside the government. All these commitments build administrative responsibility, even though at times they may not all point in the same direction.[27]

A major problem is how to maximize what we have called internalized controls so as to allow reduction of the burdensome red tape resulting from elaborate external controls. Solution of that problem requires an enhanced degree of trust between the political and the civil service strata of government.

The Study of Public Administration

How, then, should we think about public administration?[28] Dwight Waldo has suggested that we face a difficult task, that of reconciling the political ideas of the small Greek city-state (the *polis*) with the large-scale administrative example of the Roman Empire, both of which the American system inherited.[29] One way of addressing this task, as we have seen, is to claim that administration and policy (or politics) are separate spheres. This was substantially the view of Woodrow Wilson and Frank J. Goodnow, writing in the late nineteenth and early twentieth centuries.[30] Nicholas Henry identifies 1900–1926 as the period when the politics-administration dichotomy reigned. He then traces later periods: 1927–1937, when students affirmed the existence of clear principles of public administration; 1938–1950, marked by rejection of the politics-administration dichotomy and loss of confidence in principles, along with reactions leading to the next period; 1950–1970, years of reorientation to public administration as political science; and, overlapping and contradicting that, a 1956–1970 emphasis on management, often borrowing from business management, together with the rise of public policy studies (focused on effective achievement of policy objectives); and, finally, the post-1970 reversion to a specific focus on public administration, with work often lodged in distinct schools of public administration that are hospitable to management methods but also sensitive to the public-interest commitment of administrators of governmental affairs.[31]

In our study, we need to confront three questions. First, is public administration something that we can generalize about regardless of historical context? Second, is it generalizable regardless of place, circumstance, and level of government? Third, if we are to make a start toward even limited generalizations, how shall we proceed? To such fundamental questions, we must offer perplexing answers:

1. Public administration is timeless but is time-bound.[32]
2. It is universal but is also culture-bound and varies with situations.
3. It is complex but is intelligible only by a simplified model or a step-by-step combining of such models.

We consider the first two puzzling answers together, because time and space are related variables.

Time and Space: Critical or Noncritical Variables?

Public administration has a longer history and a wider geographic range than almost any other aspect of government. It has been the instrument of ancient empires, of monarchies, of both democracies and dictatorships, of both developed and developing countries. Carl J. Friedrich has cogently argued that the achievement of representative government in Western Europe depended on the prior development of effective bureaucracies by undemocratic regimes.[33] Indeed, revolutions that seek to transform the structure of political authority are at the same time struggles for control of the bureaucracy.

In the United States, public administration received scant discussion from the nation's founders or for decades after the writing of the Constitution. In 1835 Alexis de Tocqueville was amazed at the neglect of the subject in the United States, compared with experience in his native France:

> The public administration is, so to speak, oral and traditional. But little is committed to writing and that little is soon wafted away forever, like the leaves of the Sibyl, by the smallest breeze. . . . The instability of administration has penetrated into the habits of the people . . . and no one cares for what occurred before his time: no methodical system is pursued, no archives are formed, and no documents are brought together when it would be very easy to do so. . . . Nevertheless, the art of administration is undoubtedly a science, and no science can be improved if the discoveries and observations of successive generations are not connected together in the order in which they occur. . . . But the persons who conduct the administration in America can seldom afford any instruction to one another. . . . Democracy, pushed to its furthest limits, is therefore prejudicial to the art of government; and for this reason it is better adapted to a people already versed in the conduct of administration than to a nation that is uninitiated in public affairs.[34]

Woodrow Wilson and the Science of Administration

In 1887, early in his scholarly career and before he turned to presidential politics, Woodrow Wilson wrote, "the poisonous atmosphere of city government, the crooked secrets of state administration, the confusion, sinecurism, and corruption ever and again discovered in the bureau at Washington forbid us to believe that any clear conceptions of what constitutes good administration are as yet very widely current in the United States."[35] Noting that "the functions of government are every day becoming more complex and difficult" and "are also vastly multiplying in number," Wilson pleaded for "a science of administration which shall seek to straighten the paths of government, to make its business less unbusinesslike, to strengthen and purify its organization, and to crown its duties with dutifulness." Such a science, he noted, existed on the European continent and was to be found reflected in, for example, Prussian and French practice. He anticipated that comparative study would yield "one rule of good administration for all governments alike. So far as administrative functions are concerned, all governments have a strong structural likeness; more than that, if they are to be uniformly useful and efficient, they *must* have a strong structural likeness."

A Princeton professor before he was president, Woodrow Wilson wrote an article entitled "The Study of Administration." Long after Wilson's death, it became a classic.

From one point of view, then, public administration has universal elements, independent of time, place, and political system. The many individuals who serve in any public bureaucracy must be selected, compensated, given specific assignments, controlled, disciplined when necessary, and so on. To pay them and to support other governmental activities (minimally, provision for military forces and construction of roads), a revenue system must be devised, the receipts allocated by some kind of budgetary system, and accounting and other recordkeeping methods worked out.

To say that there are such universal elements implies that governments' accumulated experience in dealing with these elements constitutes a rich fund of knowledge requiring only skillful analysis to save wasteful repetition of errors. As Wilson stated, "the object of administrative study is to rescue executive methods from the confusion and costliness of empirical experiment and set them upon foundations laid deep in stable principle."

Despite expectations that more than a century of study of public administration should by now have yielded stable principles, that has not yet happened. Wilson based his analysis on a perception of administration as a neutral instrument, distinct from policy, politics, and particular regime. Such a perception seemed essential to define a distinct field of study, separate from the study of policy and politics. It may also have sprung from the **neutrality doctrine** of civil service reformers, who had succeeded in getting the Pendleton Civil Service Act passed just four years before Wilson's essay appeared in the *Political Science Quarterly*. But it was an especially critical assumption for Wilson's thesis that "nowhere else in the whole field of politics, it would seem, can we make use of the historical, comparative method more safely than in this province of administration." That is, we can learn administration from the Prussian and French (Napoleonic) autocracies without being infected by their political principles.

Over against this line of argument were two contradictory themes. One was that administration must be fitted to the particular nation's political ideas and constitutional system. The science of administration, Wilson wrote,

> is not of our making; it is a foreign science, speaking very little of the language of English or American principles. . . . It has been developed by French and German professors, and is consequently in all parts adapted to the needs of a compact state, and made to fit highly centralized forms of government. . . . If we would employ it, we must Americanize it, and that not formally, in language merely, but radically, in thought, principle, and aim as well. It must learn our constitutions by heart; must get the bureaucratic fever out of its veins; must inhale much free American air.

Wilson advanced a second theme that blurs the distinction he made elsewhere between policy and administration. He contended that the "lines of demarcation, setting apart administrative from nonadministrative functions . . . run up hill and down dale, over dizzy heights of distinction and through dense jungles of statutory enactment, hither and thither around 'ifs' and 'buts,' 'whens,' and 'however,' until they become altogether lost to the common eye." It is true Wilson suggested "some roughly definite criteria": "public administration is detailed and systematic execution of public law," "every particular application of general law," "the detailed execution" of "the broad plans of governmental action," the "special means" as distinguished from the "general plans." Yet he went on to plead for the vesting of "large powers and unhampered discretion" as the indispensable conditions of administrative responsibility.

Here, then, are Wilson's basic contradictions: He contends that public administration needs to be interpreted in the light of a particular country's political ideas and kind of government, but at the same time he sees it as a neutral instrument. He seeks a goal of "one rule of good administration for all governments alike," but he notes that different settings can produce different problems. He explains that administrators have large powers and great discretion, but he says that the administrative cannot readily be distinguished from the nonadministrative aspects of government.

Much of the literature on administration since Wilson's time has been troubled by the same contradictions that he inadvertently set forth. The reason is that each of the positions he embraced has its contribution to make to the whole truth. A number of problems are common to all or most public bureaucracies. It is possible to consider many of these in terms of a simple criterion, which Wilson put in language closely paralleled in the administrative literature of our own time: how government can do things "with the utmost possible efficiency and at the least possible cost either of money or of energy." Yet there are also problems, some of them among the most critical for administration, that require different criteria and different answers in dissimilar social and political systems, at the several stages of national development, and even in the individual agencies of a single government.

The experiences of Western experts asked to advise developing countries have demonstrated how difficult these dilemmas are. Western models have not proved very suitable for understanding the role of the bureaucracy in non-Western political systems. And, insofar as developing countries have looked to the West for models, they have struggled to choose which ones to follow. A substantial comparative administration movement appeared in the 1960s, but the movement virtually evaporated until the global public management revolution that began in the late 1980s helped to rejuvenate it. Time and space are interlinked in the recent and growing literature on the history of governmental administration.[36] Moreover, as Christopher Pollitt argues, the deep traditions of behavior and culture have a powerful influence over administrative action. The pace of social change has accelerated around the world, and "this makes considerations of time and of the past even *more* important, not less so."[37] We need to understand where administration comes from to understand how the long shadow of the past shapes the way we think about the present and future.

Complexity and Simplicity

Any real organizational system is extremely complex, and it is therefore impossible to describe any such system fully. It might appear to be a reasonable assumption that the main features of the system can be described—for example, by a single model that simplifies *total* reality in order to clarify *essential* reality. Even this assumption is wrong, however, for three reasons.

First, the complexity of any large-scale organization seems not to be one of the kinds of puzzles that a single key will unlock. Instead, there are so many ways of looking at an organization that no single model can be expected to embrace them all, as can be seen from the following list of complicating factors:[38]

- An organization (as we have seen) is both a policy-program-decision-making set of processes and a policy-program-decision-executing set of processes, and they intertwine.
- It is both a way of dividing up work and a way of coordinating work.
- It is both a formal, prescribed structure of relations among offices and organization units and an arena for the dynamic conflict of ambitious persons and units intent on expanding or at least maintaining their status and power.

- It both persists over time despite changes in its personnel (*complete* change in the case of long-lived organizations) and at any single point in time is a particular group of individuals, each with his or her special set of psychological needs and frustrations.
- It is both a top-down system of authority, conformity, and compliance and a down-up system for the flow to the top of innovative ideas, proposed solutions to problems, claims on resources, and reports of trouble signs in program execution and content.
- It is an information storage and retrieval system and a communication network, subject to overloads of information, misreading of signals, and supplementations and wire crossing by informal grapevines.
- It usually includes both a headquarters staff and a far-flung field service, the former organized by functions and the latter by geographical areas— a feature that hinders their effective linkage.
- Its decision-making process must embrace the broad choices in which the personal value preferences and educated guesses of officials play a large part; it must provide for other major choices for which quantified data and other scientific evidence can clarify the options and reduce the role of mere hunches; and it must program the narrow choices capable of routine handling by clerks and automatic data-processing machines.
- It looks both inward and outward, having to maintain internal effectiveness and to adapt to the external environment in which it encounters the pressures of other organizations, the sea changes and temporary crises of the society and the economy, and the often poorly articulated needs of the customers of its service.
- It can be likened to a physical system such as a machine, or it can be likened to the system of a biological organism such as an animal or a living plant.
- It can be judged successful if it simply survives, or instead it can be so judged only if it achieves the purpose that justifies its existence.

Second, it is hard to produce a single model because most writers on organizations have sought to describe organization in the abstract. Realities are often far more complex, and theorizing has often become disconnected from concrete experience.[39]

Third, organization theorists do not agree on a single theory or model. Theories and models of organization abound, each usually intended as the way of seeing what an organization essentially is but, in fact, each selecting only one or a very few of the characteristic features of organizations (usually from those identified above). The complexity of an organization can be accurately portrayed only by a combination of the partial truths that most models have expressed. We can imagine each model's bit of truth being mapped on a transparent sheet of paper; when one is placed on top of another, the series of overlays comes closer to the real organization than any single sheet does.[40]

In chapter 3, we move from this foundation—the nature of public administration—to explore what it does and how it does it.

Case 2

From the Front Lines of the Administrative State: Enforcement of Speeding Laws and Police Discretion

On an overpass along Interstate 10 in Mobile, Alabama, State Trooper Corporal Chip Burgerson clocked a car going 92 mph. Troopers eventually stopped and ticketed the driver. The website speedtrap.org warns drivers that troopers often work this road in teams of ten to twenty.

Attention motorists! Driving up the East Coast soon? You might want to check out a website sponsored by the National Motorists Association (NMA), called Speed Trap Exchange, at http://www.speedtrap.org. Here's what their writers have to say about a particularly notorious stretch of Interstate 83 near York, Pennsylvania:

> The Interstate goes from 65 to 55 mph but with absolutely no change in
> the highway construction, condition, or population densities as it's out in

the country. It just so happens that just off the Loganville exit is a state police barracks which makes it awful convenient for them to work this stretch of road.[1]

A reader posts a comment below that entry, chiming in with her two cents' worth, "My mother lives in PA, and I have seen troopers measuring speed in that area—especially where that little cut-out is on the southbound hill of I-83. Troopers in PA have to use stationary radar, so they have learned to be quite creative with their hiding places." Even if we'd like to spare this person a ticket on her way to her mother's house, doesn't it seem a little, well, *dishonest* to share this kind of information? Isn't the speed limit the speed limit after all?

Ethically challenged? Maybe. But in fact, the idea that the speed limit is whatever the officially posted limit says it is misses the point. The posted limit may be the official maximum, but everyone knows that these posted limits often have little meaning in reality, a fact that the NMA apparently both recognizes and embraces.

Sometimes, traffic moves along at barely a crawl. Congestion, poor road engineering, and the unpredictable behavior of drivers can limit speeds. On clogged roads, the posted limit can seem a distant dream instead of a realistic limit. On wide-open roads, in contrast, many drivers have discovered that, if they drive at the posted limit, most other traffic goes flying past them.

So what is the real speed limit? It's the speed at which one can safely drive without being pulled over by the police or state trooper and issued a citation. On an interstate highway, the conventional wisdom is that a driver can drive at 5, or perhaps 7, miles per hour over the posted limit with little fear of being stopped and ticketed.

Does that mean that if the posted speed is 65 mph, the speed limit is *really* about 72 mph? Not quite. If a driver is clocked going 71 in a 65-mph zone, the fact that the speed is under the conventional-wisdom limit would be no defense. Police officers can—and do—issue citations for driving at that speed. But if the police stopped everyone going just a bit over the posted limit, they would spend all their days and nights stopping just about everyone. Aggressive speeders might then get a free pass, because the police would be so busy stopping people driving just a few miles over the limit that they might not catch the superspeeders, drunk drivers, and others who are reckless on the road. As a result, the highway death toll might shoot up. In short, the real speed limit is determined less by what the posted limit is than by how the police choose to enforce it.

It is one thing for elected officials to pass a law, create a policy—such as a speed limit—and post it for all to see. It is quite another to translate that policy into action. When it comes to the speed limit, how that process works depends on the discretion that police officers and state troopers exercise as they drive up and down the nation's highways. The police invest a great deal of time in deciding how best to exercise that discretion: where most effectively to concentrate their energy, according to their best judgment about how to save the most lives, improve traffic flow, and (sometimes) increase the flow of cash to the local government.

Government policy on control of speeding depends not only on how the police translate the official limits into their operating plans but also on how individual police officers, often operating alone in cars with no supervision, decide to exercise their own discretion. Should a police officer ticket a husband driving fast to get his wife to the hospital because she is in labor? Should the officer just issue a warning to someone who says, "Gee, officer, this is my first ticket"? Should the officer concentrate on easy pickings—drivers with out-of-state licenses who will most likely want to settle quickly so they can get back on their way? And should the officers' commanders—and the elected officials who set policy—worry if different officers make these decisions in different ways, so that the real speed limit depends ultimately on the subjective discretion of the officer operating the radar in the police car?

The work of government bureaucrats (for that is what police officers are) extends far beyond enforcement, reaching into policy planning, development, and research. Some of the world's leading experts on traffic safety work for the U.S. Department of Transportation's Federal Highway Administration (FHA). A fascinating study conducted by the FHA in 1992 found that changes in the speed limit—lowering it by as much as 20 mph or raising it by as much as 15 mph—had little actual effect on drivers' speed. Moreover, the FHA found, *most* drivers regularly exceed the speed limit. Lowering the speed limit below the 50th percentile (that is, to a speed lower than that at which half the drivers drive) did not reduce accidents—but it did increase the number of violations.

Where should state and local governments set the speed limit? The FHA determined that it should be set at the 85th percentile (the speed on any given road at which 85 percent of the drivers drive slower and 15 percent drive faster). Because most accidents are caused by people who drive *very* fast, setting the limit at the 85th percentile would allow most drivers to drive as fast as is reasonable and safe, and it would allow the police to focus their attention on those drivers who are most likely to cause accidents.[2]

Having that data in hand isn't the end of the story, however. Policymakers often resist such seemingly sound advice on setting the speed limit as different constituents weigh in on the ramifications of raising or lowering the limit. Higher speeds burn more gasoline, so environmentalists often favor lower limits. In many western states, drivers chafe at even high limits and press for limits as high as possible and enforcement as loose as possible. A string of accidents on a road can create enormous pressure on policymakers and police officers for a crackdown. Citizens demand that their governments respond to their preferences. When it comes to speed limits, policymakers need—and want—administrators to be accountable because, if lax enforcement of speeding laws causes accidents, the political costs for politicians can be very high. But when it comes to setting and enforcing speed limits, that's a tough trade-off. In the end, one thing is clear: the posted speed limit is one thing, but the government's actual policy against speeding may be quite another.

Questions to Consider

1. The announced policy on speeding usually does not match the policy as the police actually enforce it. Why? What forces are at work?
2. Should citizens worry that there seems to be such a gap between policy and administration?
3. Where the speed limit policy posted on traffic signs and the actual enforcement behavior of the police differ, what issues are potentially the most difficult to resolve?
4. Police are bureaucrats—but so are the technical experts who have conducted published studies on the speed limits. What impact can—and should—government's bureaucratic experts have on its policy?
5. Who is responsible for what in this surprisingly complex system: framing policy options, setting overall policy, setting patrol strategies, and enforcing the policy on the roads? What does this tell us about the politics of the administrative process?

Notes

1. See Speed Trap Exchange, http://www.speedtrap.org/speedtraps/comments.asp?state=PA&city=York&st=18369 (accessed November 9, 2004).
2. Federal Highway Administration, U.S. Department of Transportation, *Effects of Raising and Lowering Speed Limits,* Report FHWA-RD-92-084 (October 1992). See also Elizabeth Alicandri and Davey L. Warren, "Managing Speed," *Public Roads* (January–February 2003), http://www.tfhrc.gov/pubrds/03jan/10.htm.

Key Concepts

administrative responsibility **22**	oversight **32**
administrative state **22**	performance measures **32**
Antideficiency Act **30**	policymaking, or policy formation **29**
neutrality doctrine **40**	public administration **22**
nongovernmental organizations **33**	public bureaucracy **22**
organizational theory **29**	

For Further Reading

Fry, Brian R. *Mastering Public Administration: From Max Weber to Dwight Waldo.* New York: Chatham House, 1998.

Goodsell, Charles T. *The Case for Bureaucracy: A Public Administration Polemic.* 4th ed. Washington, D.C.: CQ Press, 2004.

Okun, Arthur. *Equality and Efficiency: The Big Tradeoff.* Washington, D.C.: Brookings Institution, 1975.

Waldo, Dwight. *The Administrative State: A Study of the Political Theory of American Public Administration.* New York: Ronald Press, 1948.

Wilson, Woodrow. "The Study of Administration." *Political Science Quarterly* 2 (June 1887). Reprinted in *Political Science Quarterly* 56 (December 1941): 481–506.

Suggested Websites

The Internet contains a vast reservoir of information about public administration and public organizations. A good place to start an exploration of the subject is with the associations that focus most on the field: the American Society for Public Administration (**www.aspanet.org**) and the National Academy of Public Administration (**www.napawash.org**).

Moreover, the federal government has an excellent search engine that provides easy access to the huge amount of data, reports, and programs produced by the government: **www.firstgov.gov.** In addition, **http://www.searchgov.org** is another valuable source for information about the federal government's activities. Most state and local governments have their own websites as well. This link—**http://www.statelocalgov .net/index.cfm**—provides an easy index to the state and local government websites.

3

What Government Does—
And How It Does It

In the last chapter, we saw that Americans are ambivalent about government policy, politics, and administration. They also tend to be cynical about how well government works. Most Americans believe that "people in government waste a lot of tax money." When asked about this in public opinion polls, the number has gone from 43 percent in 1958 to a high of 78 percent in 1980 to 61 percent in 2004 (see Figure 3.1). But despite this cynicism about waste, public expectations about government services have risen steadily. We expect government to keep the environment clean and to provide the elderly with adequate health care. We expect it to find cures for diseases and to ensure the national defense. We expect it to stop terrorism and keep our tomatoes safe to eat. In fact, when major problems and disasters arise, from plane crashes to oil spills, our first reaction often is, "Why didn't the government keep the problem from occurring?" And our second reaction? "How can the government prevent it from happening again?" When an outbreak of salmonella swept the country and sickened hundreds of people in the summer of 2008, the cause lay somewhere in the food chain, created and managed by private sector companies. But citizens looked to government to identify the source—tainted tomatoes, or something else—and to make sure the problem did not recur.

Americans regularly complain about their government, but they continue to believe that their political system offers the best possible means of governance. They treasure basic principles such as the separation of powers and access to government officials. They value the system of checks and balances. In fact, some candidates for federal office have deliberately played to divided party control. Keeping Congress and the White House under the control of different parties, they contend, is better for everyone. But Americans also harbor grave suspicions about whether people in government really pay attention to what ordinary people think and about whether government runs public programs efficiently. A measure by pollsters assessing political efficacy—whether people believe they have a say in what government does and whether public officials care about what people think—has hovered around 50 percent

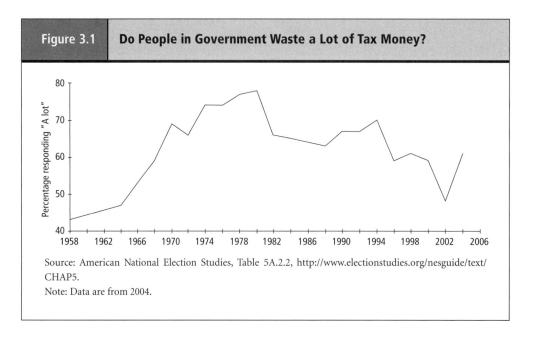

| Figure 3.1 | Do People in Government Waste a Lot of Tax Money? |

Source: American National Election Studies, Table 5A.2.2, http://www.electionstudies.org/nesguide/text/CHAP5.

Note: Data are from 2004.

since the 1980s (see Figure 3.2). Trust in government fell during the Vietnam War and the Watergate scandal and has hovered between 30 and 40 percent for most of the years since (see Figure 3.3).

Americans fret over tales of military contracting abuse and overpriced gasoline for troops in Iraq. Headlines trumpet stories about waste in federal housing grants and health programs as well as reports of muddled performance throughout government. Sometimes these problems are the direct result of our endless search for responsiveness in government—because we create checks and cross-checks that make it difficult to manage government efficiently. Sometimes these problems are the product of mismanagement. And very often it is hard to tell the difference. Since the 1960s, Americans have tended to think that "the system is good, but it is not performing well because the people in charge are inept and untrustworthy." Indeed, "the public suspects that unchecked power will be abused by self-interested power-holders."[1]

Public administrators have always been at the center of these swirling suspicions. For political candidates, running against government and its bureaucrats has become a can't-miss campaign strategy—an easy way to build public support. Once elected, however, these candidates have to work with the very institutions they have campaigned against; then they are likely to find that it is one thing to run against government to get elected, and quite another to make government work once in office. Repeated constantly, this campaign ploy only feeds the endless cycle of citizens' cynicism.

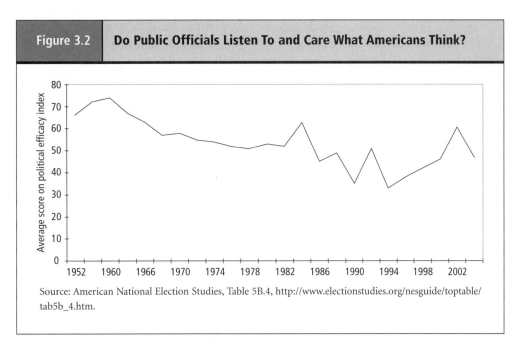

Figure 3.2 | **Do Public Officials Listen To and Care What Americans Think?**

Source: American National Election Studies, Table 5B.4, http://www.electionstudies.org/nesguide/toptable/tab5b_4.htm.

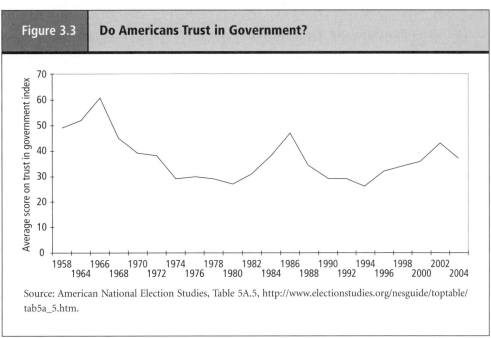

Figure 3.3 | **Do Americans Trust in Government?**

Source: American National Election Studies, Table 5A.5, http://www.electionstudies.org/nesguide/toptable/tab5a_5.htm.

All these harsh perceptions have deep implications for our study of public administration. The self-interested power of faceless bureaucrats is one of the strongest, most negative images in American political culture. Furthermore, in the public's mind, "bigness" and "badness" are inextricably linked. There is a strong sense that government is getting bigger and that, as its size grows, it gets badder, with growing problems of performance. Since the Revolution, Americans have feared concentrated governmental power, and politicians have regularly campaigned to shrink the size of government (even though the promise to make government smaller rarely comes with a list of programs to cut).[2] At the same time, Americans want bureaucracy to be open and responsive, even if administration takes longer and effectiveness suffers.

Many of these images and fears are based on profound misunderstandings about the nature of governmental activity. Quoting from the Gospel according to St. John, two students of American public administration have warned: "Judge not according to the appearance."[3] In examining American public administration, this is good advice, for how things actually work is not always the way they appear. Our search for understanding about the responsiveness and effectiveness of American public administration depends, first and most fundamentally, on understanding the answers to two important questions: (1) What does government do? and (2) How does government do it?

The Functions of Government

Consider the following scenarios:

- The Social Security Administration distributes more than 50 million monthly payments, totaling $614 billion in benefits in 2008. The benefits amount to 40 percent of the income of the elderly. Indeed, the program has been a major force in dramatically reducing the poverty of older Americans.[4]
- In 1989 the Federal Deposit Insurance Corporation (FDIC), best known for its bank-window stickers promising $100,000 insurance for each account, took over the management of two hundred financially troubled savings and loan institutions. As part of this process, the FDIC found itself the temporary owner of 12 percent of the Dallas Cowboys football team.[5]
- Inspectors for the Food and Drug Administration, alerted in March 1989 to the possibility that terrorists might attempt to poison imported fruit, managed to find two grapes—in a shipment of 364,000 *crates* of grapes—that had been injected with cyanide.[6]

- The Federal Aviation Administration quietly manages the nation's air traffic. Its air traffic controllers handle 87,000 flights a day and 64 million takeoffs and landings a year. At any given time, 5,000 planes are in the air.[7]
- In 2008, the City of New York Fire Department responded to tens of thousands of structural fires, with an average response time of just 4 minutes 23 seconds. Ambulances arrived at the scene of life-threatening emergencies in an average of 6 minutes 23 seconds—even in the city's famously snarled traffic.[8]
- The Port of Los Angeles is the nation's busiest. A department of the City of Los Angeles, its facilities service more than 8.5 million containers of cargo per year.[9]

The scope of the American government's activities is nothing short of remarkable. From controlling drug safety to researching AIDS, from protecting the food supply to protecting the nation's finances, from arresting criminals to protecting waterfalls, government agencies oversee an amazing variety of services. Public administration is central to all these operations.

Any discussion of what government does, and how public administrators help do it, must begin with a look at how government has changed over the past century. No matter how measured, its growth has been dramatic. The federal, state, and local governments combined, which spent $1.6 billion in 1902, saw that amount rise to $70.3 billion in 1950, and to $4.5 trillion in 2007. But if government is huge, what it does varies dramatically by level of government.

The traditional way of viewing the American federal system was as a **layer cake** of compartmentalized functions. Other analysts argued that the division of functions was not cleanly separated but was intricately mixed, like a **marble cake.**[10] American government, however, is really neither a layer cake nor a marble cake—or any kind of cake at all. Instead, different levels of government concentrate on different kinds of services. The levels of American government do not share these functions equally but specialize in performing different functions, as Table 3.1 shows. The federal government, for example, has primary responsibility for national defense (although the states run the national guard). It runs the postal service and space exploration, and it spends more than the other two levels of government put together on veterans' services, protection of natural resources, and trust programs (such as Social Security). State governments have primary responsibility for higher education, welfare, highways, correction (including jails), and public safety inspections. In some states, liquor stores are government-owned monopolies. In Pennsylvania, for example, a former liquor control board commissioner was also a wine

Table 3.1	**Concentration of Government Spending**

Level of government with primary responsibility

Federal	State	Local	Mixed responsibility
Defense	Higher education	Elementary education	Health
Postal service	Welfare	Libraries	Hospitals
Space	Highways	Police	
Veterans' services	Corrections	Fire	
Natural resources and environment	Inspections	Parks	
Social Security	Liquor stores	Housing and community development	
		Sanitation	
		Utilities	

Note: "Primary responsibility" means accounting for more than 50 percent of direct government spending for the function.

aficionado, and his state liquor stores featured his "chairman's selections" (that is, a government official was also serving as the state's quasi-official wine steward). Finally, local governments carry primary responsibility for basic services such as fire protection, police, and elementary and secondary education. On a few services, including health and hospitals, governmental responsibilities are balanced among the levels of government.

In almost no area does any level of government have exclusive responsibility for any major function. Federal and state governments provide aid to local schools. Local governments pass resolutions on foreign policy issues. America's intergovernmental system is a world of blended functions. This is the product of the nation's vibrant politics. On important issues, everyone wants a voice on policy, and there are few barriers to governments getting involved in each other's business. If the blended system is a logical product of America's politics, it also creates many of its administrative cross-pressures. The fact that political pressures lead to shared policymaking also means that no single level of government has full responsibility for anything. That fundamentally muddies accountability and increases the system's complexity. The diversity of public administration not surprisingly matches the diversity of the American republic.

What the Federal Government Does

Over the years, more federal spending has become concentrated in just a few categories. In just over forty years, from 1963 to 2007, spending for entitlements grew from 32 percent to 60 percent of total government outlays. (**Entitlements** are programs such as Social Security and Medicare, to which individuals are "entitled" by law; legislation defines who is eligible for the programs and prescribes how much they receive.) Defense is the second-largest piece of the federal spending pie, though it has gone in the opposite direction from entitlements, declining from 48 percent of all federal spending in 1963 to just 20 percent in 2007. Interest on the national debt amounts to another 9 percent of the total. These three categories combined account for 89 percent of all federal spending. Everything else—from federal grants to highway building to foreign aid, federal prisons, and AIDS research—accounts for the rest. Indeed, as Figure 3.4 shows, the recent history of federal spending is a story of

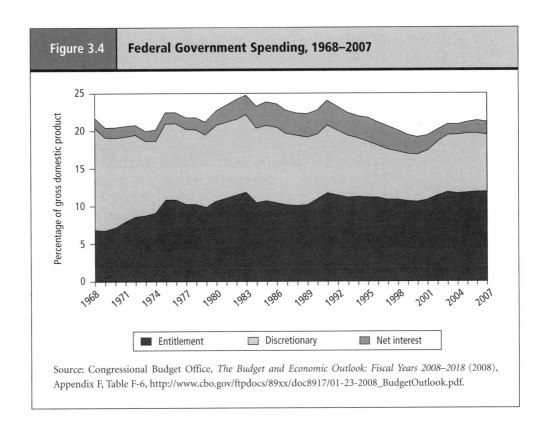

| Figure 3.4 | **Federal Government Spending, 1968–2007** |

Source: Congressional Budget Office, *The Budget and Economic Outlook: Fiscal Years 2008–2018* (2008), Appendix F, Table F-6, http://www.cbo.gov/ftpdocs/89xx/doc8917/01-23-2008_BudgetOutlook.pdf.

much more money concentrated in far fewer categories, led by the huge increase in entitlement spending.

Such figures surprise most Americans. In fact, a public opinion poll conducted on election night in 1994 revealed that 30 percent of citizens responding thought that defense was the largest category of spending, 27 percent said foreign aid, and 15 percent said Social Security (which is actually the single largest program).[11] In another poll in 2001, respondents thought that America spent too much on foreign aid. How much was the appropriate amount? The poll results suggested about 10 percent—ten times more than the actual total.[12] Americans believe that their government is very large, when in fact (as we saw in chapter 2) it ranks among the world's smallest. There is often a vast gulf between what citizens think about what government does and what is true.

At the bottom of all these numbers are two stubborn facts. First, a large part of the federal budget—two-thirds of the total—goes simply to writing checks, for entitlement programs and for interest on the national debt (most of which comes back to American citizens). Second, a very small share of federal employees manage these programs. Almost all federal employees work to administer the remaining one-third of the budget: they are the prison guards, civilian Defense Department employees supporting the armed forces, FBI agents, passport officers, virus researchers, national park managers, and the millions of other workers who make federal programs work. As a result, a very small percentage of the federal budget actually goes to pay the salaries of bureaucrats. The total personnel cost (including both wages and fringe benefits) budgeted for the civilian workers in the federal executive branch was just 7 percent in 2005. Adding those who work for the postal service, in the federal government's other branches, and in the armed services brought the total to only 13.8 percent.[13] (Budget-cutters often argue for reducing the number of federal employees to help balance the budget, but there simply is not much money there: cutting the number of federal bureaucrats by 10 percent would trim federal spending by only 0.7 percent, or less than two months' worth of the expense of fighting the 2003 war in Iraq.)

The federal budget describes what the government does but not how it does it. It certainly does not describe at all well what most federal employees do.

What State Governments Do

State governments differ significantly from the federal government in three ways. First, state governments concentrate their services on welfare, higher education, highways, and prisons. They run retirement programs (through insurance trusts), but this accounts for a far smaller share of state than federal spending (see Figure 3.5). Second, state governments play a major banking role in American federalism. They receive federal grants and administer them, for projects ranging from highway

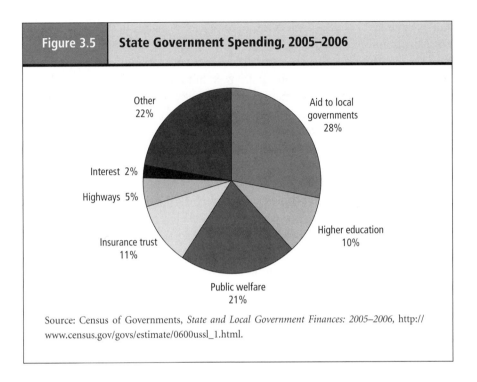

Figure 3.5 | **State Government Spending, 2005–2006**

Other 22%

Aid to local governments 28%

Interest 2%

Highways 5%

Insurance trust 11%

Higher education 10%

Public welfare 21%

Source: Census of Governments, *State and Local Government Finances: 2005–2006*, http:// www.census.gov/govs/estimate/0600ussl_1.html.

construction and social services to Medicaid and welfare. Almost 30 percent of their spending, on average, goes to local governments. As the middle layer of the system, state governments play an intermediary role in the system's finances: they levy taxes to support state programs, but they devote most of their fiscal energy to managing federal programs and distributing aid to local governments.

Third, state spending patterns, especially when compared with federal spending, have stayed relatively constant over time. As the interstate highway system was built during the 1950s and 1960s, spending on road construction rose; then, as highway spending shrank in the late 1970s, welfare spending grew to replace it. Since World War II, however, the patterns of state spending have been much more stable than those of the federal government. And while state governments make some payments to individuals—principally for welfare—they generally play a much smaller redistributive role than does the federal government.

What Local Governments Do

The first thing any observer of local administrative patterns notices is their incredible variety. Most states are divided into counties, and the counties are subdivided in turn into cities, towns, and townships. However, Connecticut has no county governments, and in Virginia the counties and cities are completely separate. In some states, counties are enormously powerful; in others, they are principally field offices for the state government. Moreover, there is an amazing variety of special-district governments. School districts dominate in scope and power, but numerous other special-district governments are charged with managing everything from water and sewage to airports and bridges.

If it is hard to characterize local governments, it is at least possible to count them. In 2002 there were 87,525 local governments, more than half of them comprised of school districts and special districts. The number of local governments is down substantially since before World War II, largely because of a huge drop in the number of school districts. However, the number of other special districts has quickly grown in number, almost tripling from 1952 to 2002 (see Table 3.2).

Despite their remarkable number and variety, local governments share a common purpose: compared with other levels of government in the United States, they are singularly devoted to providing goods and services (see Figure 3.6). Of the $1.4 trillion that local governments spent in 2006, education—mostly for elementary and secondary schools—accounted for 36 percent. Local governments also concentrated on building roads; protecting citizens with police and fire services; providing health programs, hospitals, and welfare; and supplying utilities, from water and public transportation to gas and electric power in some jurisdictions.

Table 3.2	Number of Governments					
Type of government	**1952**	**1962**	**1972**	**1982**	**1992**	**2002**
Federal	1	1	1	1	1	1
State	50	50	50	50	50	50
Local	116,756	91,186	78,218	81,780	84,955	87,525
Total units	116,807	91,237	78,269	81,831	85,006	87,576
Type of local government						
County	3,052	3,043	3,044	3,041	3,043	3,034
Municipal	16,807	18,000	18,517	19,076	19,279	19,429
Township and town	17,202	17,142	16,991	16,734	16,656	16,504
School district	67,355	34,678	15,781	14,851	14,422	13,506
Special district	12,340	18,323	23,885	28,078	31,555	35,052

Source: U.S. Census Bureau, *2002 Census of Governments,* vol. 1, no. 1, Government Organization, Series GC02(1)-1.

| Figure 3.6 | **Local Government Spending, 2005–2006** |

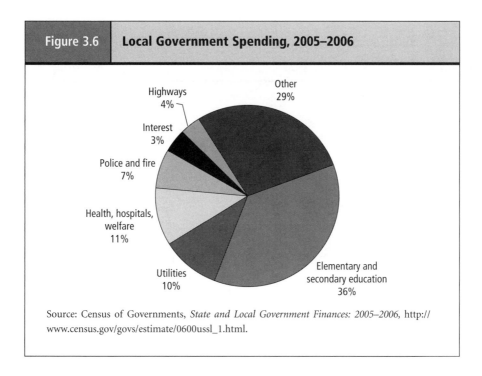

Highways
4%

Other
29%

Interest
3%

Police and fire
7%

Health, hospitals,
welfare
11%

Utilities
10%

Elementary and
secondary education
36%

Source: Census of Governments, *State and Local Government Finances: 2005–2006,* http://www.census.gov/govs/estimate/0600ussl_1.html.

The pattern of local government spending varies tremendously. In some states, the state government accounts for most of the spending. In Vermont, for example, the state government accounts for 89 percent of all spending by state and local governments, while in Delaware (83 percent), Hawaii (82 percent), and Arkansas (81 percent), the balance of state-local spending also tilts heavily to the state level. In other states, however, local governments account for more spending. In Nevada and Colorado, for example, local government spending is 45 percent of the total, and Florida, Texas, Illinois, and New York are not far behind (see Table 3.3). This relatively high proportion of spending at the local level often results from the fact that, unlike states in which the state government funds most local schools, in these and some other states, the local governments themselves raise most of the revenue for school spending. Thus it is very hard to describe the "typical" state or local government, because of the wide differences among them.

The one thing we can say about local governments, in general, is that they concentrate far more on **direct delivery of services** than do governments at other levels. Working on the front lines of government programs, they spend most of their time and resources on the services that citizens encounter every day: police and fire, schools and hospitals, roads and sanitation. However, even this common characteristic masks remarkable diversity in how the service delivery function is carried out

Table 3.3	State versus Local Spending as a Percentage of Total State Spending: A Ranking

More state dominance			Less state dominance		
Rank		Percentage	Rank		Percentage
1	Vermont	89	41	Ohio	63
2	Delaware	83	42	Tennessee	63
3	Hawaii	82	43	Georgia	61
4	Arkansas	81	44	New Jersey	60
5	New Mexico	79	45	New York	57
6	Alaska	77	46	Illinois	57
7	Kentucky	75	47	Texas	57
8	West Virginia	75	48	Florida	56
9	Montana	74	49	Colorado	55
10	Utah	72	50	Nevada	55

Source: U.S. Census Bureau, *State and Local Government Finances* series, http://www.census.gov/govs/www/estimate.html.

Note: Data are for 2000.

and what role the states play in financing it. All these variations are part of the rich texture of federalism and of American political tradition.

The Growth of Government

The one thing that everyone thinks they know about American government is that it has grown substantially over the past generation. But, although there is little agreement about how to measure its size, the most common methods of assessment offer a surprising conclusion: government has grown fastest at the state and local levels. One way of gauging government's size is by spending, and as Figure 3.7 shows, government spending per capita more than tripled in recent decades. In 1980 the federal government spent a third more than state and local governments. By 2000, however, state and local spending had grown so quickly that spending was about even.

If one chooses instead to measure the size of government in terms of the number of government employees, the growth of state and local governments is even more dramatic. Whereas federal employment has increased only slightly since the late 1960s, the number of state and local government employees has grown rapidly, tripling over the same period (see Figure 3.8). State and local government activity has

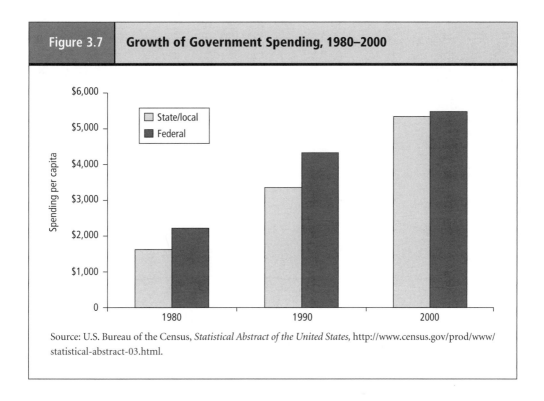

| Figure 3.7 | **Growth of Government Spending, 1980–2000** |

Source: U.S. Bureau of the Census, *Statistical Abstract of the United States,* http://www.census.gov/prod/www/statistical-abstract-03.html.

increased in many functions, from direct provision of services to planning and support. Overall, however, the big story is not that government has grown, but that the growth has been fastest at the state and local levels.

The Tools of Government

One helpful way of understanding the work of government is to see public administration not just as a collection of departments, bureaus, and agencies but as a collection of basic tools. As Christopher C. Hood puts it:

> We can imagine government as a set of administrative tools—such as tools for carpentry or gardening, or anything else you like. Government administration is about social control, not carpentry or gardening. But there is a toolkit for that, just like anything else. What government does to us—its subjects or citizens—is to try to shape our lives by applying a set of administrative tools, in many different combinations and contexts, to suit a variety of purposes.[14]

Government operates through a wide array of tools. Some are **direct tools**— including the provision of goods and services, such as police and fire protection; income support, such as Social Security; and the cost of doing business, such as basic

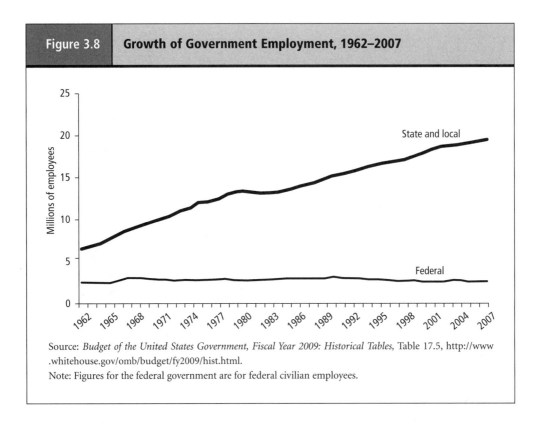

| Figure 3.8 | **Growth of Government Employment, 1962–2007** |

Source: *Budget of the United States Government, Fiscal Year 2009: Historical Tables,* Table 17.5, http://www
.whitehouse.gov/omb/budget/fy2009/hist.html.
Note: Figures for the federal government are for federal civilian employees.

organizational management and the payment of interest on the national debt. But government has also undergone a quiet "revolution that no one noticed," a rising share of government programs operated through **indirect tools** of action.[15] Such indirect tools include the contracting out of government programs to nongovernmental partners; grants, to encourage other levels of government to do things they might not otherwise have done; vouchers, to allow citizens to purchase services from private organizations; and loan programs, to enhance the ability of individuals and private organizations to borrow private money to pursue public goals.

Good numbers on the government's tools are deceptively difficult to come by. The government simply does not keep its books in a way that makes it simple to chart who does its work. But a perceptive analysis by Lester M. Salamon shows just how important this variety of tools is: direct government expenditures, he estimates, total just 28 percent of the federal government's financial operations; indirect tools account for the rest. Moreover, more than half of the federal government's financial activity, Salamon estimates, lies outside the regular budgetary process, so it is not subject to regular review or formal accounting.[16]

Assessing the usage rates of these indirect tools at the state and local level is impossible, since those governments do not track the trends in a comparable way. Even a casual look at the expansion of state and local contracting, regulations, special tax preferences, and similar tools, however, shows that the shift toward indirect tools is a lively trend throughout American government. Social service programs have come to rely far more on contracting than they used to, and the state and local governments have been equally creative in constructing tax incentives for corporations and regulatory strategies to encourage business development.

Examination of the tools of government reveals a double paradox. First, while most people think of government bureaucrats when they think of government services, much of the federal government's activity is implemented through indirect tools in which the government is only one partner in a series of complex relationships. Second, although we tend to focus most of our attention on the budget as a way of understanding and controlling government's actions, much of the government's activity, at all levels, escapes the budgetary process. Any careful look at what government does must therefore include both its direct and indirect tools.

Direct Administration

Direct administration is what most people think of when they think of public administration. From police and fire protection to air-traffic control and inspection of food safety, administrators provide a remarkable range of government services. As we have seen, however, such services represent only a part—at the federal level, a small part—of governmental activity. There is a large and often hidden paradox here. Most of the

An investigator from FDA's San Francisco field office (left) worked with an investigator from the California Department of Health Services to collect soil samples. They were tracking the source of a 2006 E. coli outbreak in spinach, which originated in California farms and sickened people throughout the United States and Canada.

federal employees shown in Figure 3.8 are involved in managing the government's direct programs, but most of the federal government's financial activity occurs through indirect tools. At the state and local levels, far more government employees are involved in direct administration.

Grants

Much governmental activity occurs *between* levels of government. Sometimes one level of government wishes to provide financial assistance to another level—often to encourage those other governments to do what they could not otherwise afford or might not otherwise choose to do. Many state governments, as we have seen, provide a large share of the support for local schools, to help improve the quality of education and to level out the financial disparities among local governments. Sometimes one level of government wants to induce another level to perform a certain service in a particular way. For example, the federal government created the interstate highway system to encourage state governments to build modern high-speed roads; it provided 90 cents of every construction dollar, and the states naturally found the funds irresistible. In fact, the use of this tool dates from the Ordinance of 1787—before the drafting of the Constitution—which provided land grants to the states for education. Since then, **federal grants** have been used for everything from supporting land-grant colleges to helping states provide medical care for the poor. As Donald Haider argues, "federal grants are the oldest, most widely used, and probably the best-understood tool that the federal government has available to carry out public policy."[17]

We return to the role of grants in implementing public programs in chapter 12. In the meantime, we can note that the administration of grants differs significantly from direct administration. Administrators at one level must supervise administrators at another, whose behavior they cannot directly control but must attempt to influence through the grant system. This indirect process requires substantially different administrative skills from those employed in supervising the work of employees in one's own agency.

Contracts

While governments have always relied on **contracts**—to feed and supply armies, for example—their use has increased markedly since World War II. As we see in chapter 12, the growing complexity of government has led to greater reliance on private-sector experts and outside organizations. In a contract, government administrators sign a formal agreement with private parties, and the agreement embodies a quid pro quo: the government agrees to pay a certain amount of money in exchange for a good or a service.

Contract administration thus requires the government to employ officials to set the standards for contracts, to negotiate effective programs at low prices, and to oversee the results that contractors produce. While newspaper stories about Pentagon contracting scandals remind us about both the scope of federal contracting and how difficult it can be to administer contracts well, they disguise the degree to which government at all levels is reliant on contracting. From the management of cafeterias in federal office buildings to the construction of roads by local governments, contractors play an important role in many government activities. The effective management of contracts poses a growing challenge for public administrators.

Regulations

Budgetary spending measures only one part of governmental activity, because regulatory programs can significantly expand government's power while expending relatively little money. A mere handful of government regulators can promulgate extensive and costly rules that apply to entire industries or large segments of the population. Even the volume of **regulations**—there are more than two hundred volumes in the *Code of Federal Regulations,* the federal government's compendium of rules—does not provide a really good gauge of their size or scope. The rules are wide ranging: there are twenty volumes of rules on agriculture, eighteen covering the Internal Revenue Service's tax regulations, and one on the Panama Canal.

Even a casual look around us shows the breadth and importance of regulation by all levels of government. Federal food experts found the tainted grapes. State regulators check the management of many banks and insurance companies. Local inspectors ensure the accuracy of the scales grocery stores use to measure and charge for our food. Everything from the cars we drive, the bicycles we peddle, the clothes we wear, the banks we use, the air we breathe, and the food we eat to the airplanes in which we fly is covered by regulations—and by public administrators who write and enforce them. We return to a discussion of regulatory agencies in chapter 12.

Tax Expenditures

Governments at all levels include a wide variety of features in their tax codes to give individuals and taxpayers special advantages in paying their taxes. These features do more than ease taxpayers' burdens. They also serve as incentives to promote many different social and economic policies, to encourage taxpayers to do some things and avoid doing others. Such tax advantages are called by a variety of names—tax breaks, tax loopholes, and **tax expenditures** (which is the term we use, to emphasize their relationship to regular spending). Tax expenditures reduce the cost of homeownership and thus encourage taxpayers to buy rather than rent their homes, for example. The federal tax deduction for mortgage interest and local property taxes, which makes family homes much cheaper to own, will cost the federal government $166 billion by 2013.[18] Other tax expenditures exempt from income taxes the interest taxpayers earn on state and local government bonds and thereby reduce the cost of state and local governments' borrowing. The special tax breaks for oil and gas exploration encourage more exploration for these resources.

Most state income taxes use federal tax law to structure their systems, so federal tax expenditures spill over into the state level as well. Moreover, many local governments have devised their own special tax preferences, especially those designed to promote economic development. Many local economic growth programs, including enterprise zones and tax increment financing zones, create special tax abatements to encourage investment in economically depressed areas.

Proponents of tax expenditures often promote them as "free" programs. The government does not have to budget or spend any money on these programs, which hides their cost. In fact, of course, they are scarcely free: tax expenditures cost the government money, by taking away from revenues instead of adding to spending. But even if the cost factor is the same, the administrative consequences are very different. Tax expenditures require tax administrators to write and enforce rules, which can be a much more complex task than direct administration.[19]

Loan Programs

The federal government has become the largest lender in the country. From guaranteeing student loans to extending credit to farmers, the federal government provides financial assistance through a broad range of **loan programs.** (Other levels of government have their own programs as well, but the federal government plays by far the most important role in this area.) Federal lending began during the Great Depression, but it grew dramatically during the late 1970s and early 1980s. As budget deficits swelled, members of Congress seeking new ways of funding federal programs found that loans provided an easy answer. As Rep. Willis D. Gradison Jr. (R-Ohio) put it, federal loans are "a technique used during a period of budget stringency to do good things where the cost doesn't show up until later."

Although the federal government dominates government credit policy, lending programs are administered in a highly decentralized fashion. Loans for college students and home mortgages, for example, are administered by local banks under the supervision of state and federal agencies. Government loan programs thus are part of the subtle and complex public-private mixture of administrative strategies that have grown in the American system, especially since 1945.

Implications for Public Administration

The many threads in this discussion of what government does and how it does it suggest three broad implications.

1. *The job of government varies by level.* Local governments tend to concentrate on direct provision of goods and services. State governments

provide many goods and services directly as well, but they also play a crucial intermediary role in the American federal system by transferring money to local governments (especially for public schools) and administering grants from the federal government (especially for welfare and Medicaid). The federal government, by contrast, devotes most of its administrative energy to national defense and the transfer function.

2. *The job of government varies by function.* The growth of transfer functions emphasizes that different kinds of governmental programs require different administrative approaches. Providing goods and services, from education to national defense, requires sharp technical skills. Administrators work to develop the best techniques: the best way to train teachers, the right kind of audiovisual aids, textbooks that do not promote stereotypes or advance the "wrong" values, tests that most appropriately measure students' achievements. In direct provision of goods and services, most administrative action is internal to the government's bureaucracy.

   By contrast, administering transfer programs involves extensive action external to the government bureaucracy. Instead of mailing checks for welfare and Social Security, government could directly provide such services as government-run shelters for those who could not afford their own homes, government-run kitchens for those who could not afford food, and so on. Transfer payments serve both to make the government's administrative task easier and to preserve dignity and free choice for the recipients. They also fundamentally change the administrative task: instead of providing the necessary services, the government seeks to determine the size of the check to which the law entitles a recipient. That is a very different kind of government-citizen interaction than would be involved in direct services, and it requires a different collection of administrative skills.

3. *The job of government varies by who finally provides the goods and services.* Even services that formerly were offered directly by government are now being provided instead through contracts, intergovernmental grants, tax expenditures, and loan programs. Just as in transfer programs, much of the administrative work is external to the governmental bureaucracy. When contractors manufacture weapons for defense or collect local garbage, governmental officials are "in the uncomfortable position of being held responsible for programs they do not really control."[20]

   There is, in short, a difference between who *provides* a service, by creating a program and paying for it, and who *produces* it by actually administering the service.[21] As government has grown bigger, more and more of its growth has come about through providing more services but relying on nongovernmental agents and organizations—or sometimes governments at other levels—to produce them.

Such **government by proxy**—the use of third-party agents to deliver programs that the government funds—is thus different from transfer programs because the responsibility of government officials extends far beyond simply ensuring that checks are mailed out correctly, and different from directly administered programs because government officials do not control those who finally provide the service. Each kind of program requires a different approach to administration, tailored to the special problems and needs that the program presents. We explore this problem in more depth in chapter 12.

Conclusion

If there truly is a crisis of confidence in American government, its roots are not necessarily in big government. While government unquestionably has gotten bigger, it has not become more concentrated. Instead, the problems that lie at the heart of the so-called crisis stem from government's growing complexity. More and more, government programs rely on intricate relationships among levels of government or between government and private contractors or other agents. There has, moreover, been a growing disconnection between the raising and spending of governmental money. Those responsible for the performance of governmental programs are not always within the same level of government, and often they are not within government itself.

That complicates the task of accountability. Traditional approaches to accountability, as we see in the next chapter, depend on a direct link between government policymakers and the administrators executing government decisions. When the chain of implementation stretches beyond a government agency to another level of government—or even to nongovernmental partners—traditional approaches to government are strained. This certainly does not mean that the growth of government's reliance on indirect tools makes accountability impossible. Nor does it necessarily make it more difficult, although holding government's partners accountable often requires different and more complex approaches. But it does mean that accountability is often different from what government has been used to in the past, and that raises new challenges for government accountability.

Indeed, from filling out income tax forms to borrowing money through student loans to working as government contractors, all citizens have come to be more involved in the performance of government programs. Public functions are more intricately interwoven with the private sector, and this interweaving brings new complexities into the administration of government. If government depends both on public and private values, whose values are to prevail in the inevitable conflicts, and who will work out solutions to these conflicts?

These fundamental issues, which underline the crucial problems of accountability and performance in public administration, will follow us through the book as we explore the value of traditional theories of management, both public and private, and as we examine the challenges of the new approaches, both to existing notions of public administration and to lasting values of American democracy.

Case 3

From the Front Lines of What Government Does: Getting the Flu Shot

The 2004 flu vaccine shortage swept the country from coast to coast. At a San Francisco Safeway store, hundreds of people were turned away while others pushed and shoved their way in line to get one of the 400 doses of vaccine that were available.

In late fall 2004, 72-year-old Bill Wolfson raced to get to Runnemede Senior Center in Camden County, New Jersey, in such a rush to get there that he ran a stop sign. Wolfson had heard that Runnemede was holding a flu-shot clinic, and he wanted to be there when the clinic opened. Wolfson had suffered seven heart attacks, he had three sisters to care for, and he wanted to make sure he was healthy enough to get to the casinos during the winter.[1] His health problems and those of his sisters, he argued, made him a high-risk candidate for the vaccine. New Jersey health officials weren't so sure.

In most years, of course, that medical history would have been more than enough to qualify anyone for a flu shot. In the 2004 flu season, however, things were very different. An American company, Chiron, had discovered that 4.5 million doses of the flu vaccine being manufactured in its Liverpool, England, plant were contaminated with bacteria. The company was unsure about how far the contamination had spread, so it took off the market all 46 million doses it was manufacturing for the season, dramatically reducing the amount of the vaccine that would be available in the U.S. market. Flu annually kills 36,000 people in the United States, and public health officials understandably worried that a vaccine shortage would drive that number even higher in 2004–2005.

As was soon widely reported, the nation was dependent on just two companies for the vaccine—Chiron, which manufactured its U.S.-bound vaccine in England, and Aventis Pasteur, a French company that manufactured its vaccine for American customers in American plants, using eggs from Pennsylvania farms. Learning that Chiron's problems had eliminated almost half the nation's supply, doctors and public health officials scrambled to determine how best to make up the difference for Bill Wolfson and millions of others like him around the country.

In years past, flu vaccinations had been given free at many public health clinics. Medicare patients—Americans over the age of 55—could have the government pay for their flu shots at their family doctors' offices, and Americans with health insurance usually found that they were covered as well. Anyone could pay $15 or $20 for the vaccine at walk-in clinics in pharmacies and other locations.

Even with the wide availability of the vaccines, many Americans historically had chosen to avoid taking the needle. For the most part, that hadn't presented a major problem. Relatively low demand coupled with spotty administration in some states—the public health systems in some were slow to distribute the vaccines or set up few public vaccination clinics—typically hadn't built to a crisis situation during flu season. But the flu struck early in the winter of 2003 in a particularly nasty form, causing the deaths of at least five Colorado children. Adams County chief deputy coroner Mark Chavez said, "We have never had a string of deaths like this."[2] Local public health officials who previously had not been able to get people to line up for immunizations were soon swamped by the quick and sometimes fatal spread of the illness. That led to a surge in demand for the vaccine as the winter wore on, and many people were determined to get their shots early in the 2004 flu season.

This combination—memories of the previous year's problems and the sudden disappearance of half the nation's vaccine supply—led to near panic in some communities. A flu vaccine black market, with doses fetching up to $800, sprang up. Doctors reported that burglars were breaking into their offices late at night and looting vaccines from their refrigerators. Seniors with walkers and canes came to public health clinics at 5:00 a.m. and stood in line for hours, only to discover that the handful of doses on hand disappeared within minutes of the clinics' opening.

John Kerry made the vaccine debacle a big issue in his 2004 presidential campaign, and the flu vaccine problem quickly became entangled in everything from the George W. Bush administration's plans for Social Security reform to Kerry's charges that Bush had mismanaged health policy. But the one issue that the election furor missed was the central one: the chronically poor condition of the nation's public health system.

The American company's Liverpool plant had been shut down by British government regulators, whose decision surprised the Food and Drug Administration (FDA), the lead U.S. regulatory agency. As officials at the FDA and the Centers for Disease Control and Prevention, the chief federal agency tracking health problems, struggled to devise a policy to help alleviate the shortage, state officials complained that they were getting little useful information or guidance from the federal government. Meanwhile, local public health agencies, which ran public clinics and worked with local doctors, had to cope with the long lines and worried citizens.

Those public health officers were forced to ask some tough questions—most important, how had the nation become totally dependent on just two companies for its entire flu vaccine supply? Part of the explanation was that demand was hard to forecast: in some years, when relatively few patients sought the vaccine, manufacturers were left with unsold supplies that could not be used the next year; in other years, demand surged and unhappy patients could not get the shots they wanted. Company officials added that government regulations made it hard for them to make much money in the business, and fewer companies were interested in competing.

Further complicating the issue was the process for manufacturing the vaccines, which are grown in hens' eggs over a six-month period. Because mutations in the flu virus make each year's flu strain different from that of the year before, manufacturers have to guess long in advance of the flu season which strains are most likely to occur so they can prepare the most effective vaccine. The extended timetable of the manufacturing process means that neither policymakers nor manufacturers can second-guess either the formula decided on or the appropriate quantity to be produced.

The combination of uncertain markets and costly government regulations, the vaccine manufacturers said, had led many of them to abandon the field. That reasoning, in turn, led some analysts to propose that the government intervene in the market to help make it more profitable, perhaps by guaranteeing in advance the purchase of a sufficient number of doses to make the business more profitable.

But all the sudden attention paid to these high-level issues proved of little reassurance to the 72-year-old man and his friends, many of whom did not receive a flu shot and who ended up hoping to get through the winter without contracting a serious illness.

Questions to Consider

1. What role does—and should—government play in vaccinating the nation's citizens against the flu?
2. Consider the roles of the federal, state, and local governments in flu vaccine policy. What does this say about how responsibility and accountability are distributed in the administrative process?
3. How have international forces come to shape the impact of government policy at even the lowest levels of American government?
4. Should the United States change its policy regarding flu vaccines? If so, how?

Notes

1. Monica Yant Kinney, "Flu-Shot Scarcity Stinging Seniors," *Philadelphia Inquirer,* October 17, 2004, B1.
2. Quoted in Kieran Nicholson and Karen Augé, "Flu Claims 5th Colorado Child," *Denver Post.com,* http://www.denverpost.com/Stories/0%2C1413%2C36%257E24769%257E 1805090%2C00.html (accessed December 3, 2003).

Key Concepts

contracts **64**	indirect tools **62**
direct delivery of services **59**	layer cake organization **53**
direct tools **61**	loan programs **66**
entitlements **55**	marble cake organization **53**
federal grants **64**	regulations **65**
government by proxy **68**	tax expenditures **65**

For Further Reading

Hood, Christopher C. *The Tools of Government.* Chatham, N.J.: Chatham House, 1983.

Kerwin, Cornelius. *Rulemaking: How Government Agencies Make Law and Write Policy.* Washington, D.C.: CQ Press, 2003.

Kettl, Donald F. *Government by Proxy: (Mis?) Managing Federal Programs.* Washington, D.C.: CQ Press, 1988.

Kettl, Donald F. *The Next Government of the United States: Why Our Institutions Fail Us and How to Fix Them.* New York: Norton, 2008.

Salamon, Lester M., ed. *The Tools of Government: A Guide to the New Governance.* New York: Oxford University Press, 2002.

Suggested Websites

For research on how the federal government spends its money, the basic source is the federal budget, published by the Office of Management and Budget (**http://www .whitehouse.gov/omb/**). OMB annually publishes two useful reports: *Analytical Perspectives,* which provides background information on issues such as federal taxing, spending, and lending programs; and *Historical Tables,* which provides long-term data on federal budget trends. Many of the key budget tables are available for download in Excel format.

In addition, the Congressional Budget Office (**http://www.cbo.gov**) assembles federal budget data and is especially useful for tracking trends in entitlement and discretionary spending and in federal government revenue.

The best source of information about trends in state and local government finances is the U.S. Census Bureau (**http://www.census.gov/govs/www/index.html**). For international comparisons, the "statistics" portal at the Organization for Economic Cooperation and Development (**http://www.oecd.org/home**) is valuable. OECD is an international organization that tracks the policy and financial issues facing nations around the world.

PART II

Organizational Theory and the Role of Government's Structure

The organization is the basic building block of public adminis-tration. Done badly, the work of complex organizations can cre-ate all the pathologies that make bureaucracies "bureaucratic." Done well, bureaucratic structure makes it possible to accom-plish the complex tasks that society wishes to pursue. There is a long intellectual history of thinking about how best to structure organizations—and, given the problems, there is also an equally long history of efforts to reform bureaucracy.

Every choice about how to build bureaucracy or how to fix it is inevitably political: it represents an emphasis of some values over others. And because it is political, no choice has proven very stable for very long. The values of individuals shift, and as they change, so do the ways they arrange organizational structure. In the chapters that follow, we examine the basic foundations of organizational theory, the strategies to reform it, how organiza-tional structure affects the behavior of political executives, and how efforts to reorganize bureaucracy can improve the way it functions.

4

Foundations of Organizational Theory

The basic building block of large-scale administration is *structure*—a formal arrangement of the relationships among the persons and groups engaged in the administrative enterprise. The traditional model of organizational theory begins with officials at the top, connected to individuals at the bottom through **hierarchy,** the top-down delegation of authority from higher officials to lower ones. The top official sets policy for the organization and then delegates responsibility for pieces of that policy to subordinates, who answer to the top official through channels of authority. The pattern then cascades throughout the organization, as subordinates become superiors to the workers on the next lower level. The chain of authority ensures accountability from top to bottom. The result is the familiar organization chart that dominates both the abstract model and the operating reality of complex organizations (see Figure 4.1). In the traditional approach to organizations, hierarchy defines the basic shape, and authority shapes the fundamental relationships.

This hierarchical model is the dominant approach, but four major theories challenge some of its basic premises: The **humanist approach,** rooted in the dynamics of human relations, condemns the impersonality of bureaucratic hierarchies and so pleads for the humanizing of organizations. The **pluralist approach,** emphasizing the realities of political life, posits a less orderly model of organizational interactions. The **government-by-proxy approach** notes that government delegates authority to other governments, to private organizations, and to mixed public-private enterprises as well as within its own **organizational structure,** and so develops a mixed model. The **formal approach** returns to a structural perspective but adds a very different theoretical twist.

There is a variety of approaches describing how organizations work, but there is little agreement on which theoretical approach works best or which best fits the public sector. In this chapter, we will examine the competing theories and explore their implications.[1]

Figure 4.1	**Hierarchical Bureaucracy**

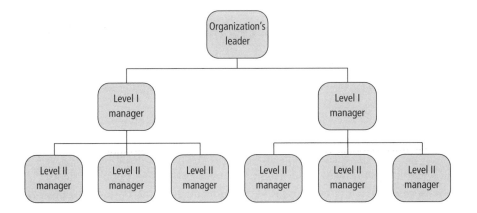

The Structural Approach to Large Organizations

Students of organizations have long begun their work by looking at structure, the basic building block of large administrative enterprises. Reformers often work by rearranging boxes to improve the organization's function. Critics often condemn restructuring as "just moving boxes around on the organization chart." Either way, structure is the fundamental element of organizational theory.

We need to make a clear distinction between *positions* and the *persons* who occupy them. The structural approach certainly considers the personal relations among the chief executive, the department heads, the bureau chiefs, the division directors, and the section chiefs. But anyone who has carefully studied bureaucratic behavior knows that patterns of behavior persist regardless of who holds a position. Although no one in the U.S. government puts a personal stamp on a position as much as does the person who is the president, we do not hesitate to speak of "the presidency" or "the president" as an office with certain powers and a reasonably determinate scope of expected behavior, independent of the incumbent. Hence, we tend to focus on bureaucratic positions—and the patterns of behavior in them—more than on the people who hold the jobs, especially when we seek a long-term perspective on how organizations work.

The concept of an administrative position abstracted from its current human occupant has a close kinship with the concept of *role* as it is used in sociology and psychology. Although these scholarly disciplines expect a person's role to be defined by the expectations of adjacent fellow workers (including peers, superiors, and subordinates), those expectations in turn derive substantially from the person's formal position in the organization. The relation of role to organizational position is captured by the social psychologists Daniel Katz and Robert L. Kahn, who write:

> In any organization we can locate each individual in the total set of ongoing relationships and behaviors that make up the organization. The key concept for this is *office* [i.e., position], by which is meant a particular point in organizational space; space in turn is defined in terms of a structure of interrelated offices and the patterns of activities associated with them. . . . Associated with each office is a set of *activities* or expected behaviors. These activities constitute the *role* to be performed, at least approximately, by any person who occupies that office. . . .
>
> To a considerable extent the role expectations . . . are determined by the broader organizational context. The technology of the organization, the structure of its subsystems, its formal policies, and its rewards and penalties dictate in large degree the content of a given office. . . . The structural properties of organization are sufficiently stable so that they can be treated as independent of the particular persons in the role-set.[2]

Formal organization, then, shapes the fundamental behavioral pattern of people in administration. The roles in which people work create expectations (formal and informal), and the expectations powerfully shape their behavior. In governments, the structural arrangements have always had a special importance, because these arrangements flow from the political society's basic ideas. We need to appreciate these arrangements if we are to be able to make the leap from democratic ideals, founded on voting by the people and representative government by elected officials, to the complex job of carrying out government policy through a large, powerful, unelected bureaucracy. To those following the structural approach, that is no great leap, and we see why in the following section. To those who object to the structural approach, the problem can be significant. We explore that issue later in this chapter and in the next.

Authority and Hierarchy

The central problem of political societies is the distribution and structure of power. In constitutional systems, the government is accorded power that, within the stated limits, is legitimate—that is, power conferred through the constitution, rather than naked power seized from the people. Wrapped in this cloak of constitutional legitimacy, the government expects citizens to comply with its decisions and most citizens do so voluntarily, regardless of their personal agreement or disagreement with the specific content of those decisions and regardless of the severity of punishment for noncompliance. In sum, a government possessed of legitimacy is said to have **authority** —that is, rightful power to make decisions within constitutionally defined limits, with the expectation of widespread compliance.[3]

[handwritten margin note: authority exercised in pub admin comes from the people]

A government's authority is exercised through institutions and the people who occupy institutional positions. Elements of authority are vested in designated major bodies and offices (e.g., legislature, courts, chief executive, government agencies). The constitution that distributes authority among these major bodies also limits the kind and scope of authority allotted to each one; the keystone of the legitimacy of their decisions is compliance with the conditions prescribed in the constitution. And because, in democratic theory, the constitution flows from the people's support, the authority exercised by public institutions ultimately flows from a grant of power from the people.

This is the short-form explanation for the legitimacy of governmental power. Administrative authority is a further extension of this concept. Administrators have legitimacy because their power is authorized by higher-level officials, especially elected officials; administrative authority is delegated authority. Note, though, that the idea of delegated authority has two applications. First, an administrative agency can expect most citizens to comply with its decisions because, within its field of activity, the government agency is vested with the government's legitimacy. Second, the legislature, the courts, and the chief executive expect administrators to comply with *their* decisions because they bear a higher legitimacy, through the popular vote of the people and the nature of constitutional government. Now, put these two applications together: citizens owe obedience to an administrative agency, but their obligation extends only as long as the agency's demands comply with the relevant constitutional, legislative, judicial, and executive limitations and instructions.

Thus, the structuring of authority in administration, with its emphasis on linking power and legitimacy, has theoretical and historical roots in such great political questions as the nature of "the State," the legitimacy of governments themselves, the limits to their powers, and the rights of revolution and civil disobedience. The answers reached provide premises for elaborate bodies of doctrine about the delegation of power, the legal liability of government executives and their agencies for wrongs done private citizens, and the right of public servants individually to expose wrongdoing and collectively to strike. Public administration, being government in action, cannot be understood without an appreciation of its relation to these great political, doctrinal, and moral issues.

Administrative Implications

Six basic propositions flow from the view of public administration as a structuring of authority:

1. *Principals and agents.* In a democracy, the **principals** are the elected officials who make policy and delegate responsibility to public administrators. Their **agents** are the administrators charged with carrying out

the law, which leads to the concept of **agencies** as the organizations established to do the work.

2. *Narrow, defined specialization.* Such an agency is assigned by law a particular field of activity and a set of responsibilities (e.g., execution of particular statutes).

3. *Internal specialized structure.* The agency has an internal structure that divides responsibilities among bureaus (or whatever its principal units are called) and, further down, among individual positions.

4. *Rules of the game.* The agency has a set of procedures that identify which units and position holders do what in what sequence during the flow of business through the agency.

5. *Staff of experts.* The agency has a staff of officials and employees who are expected to contribute to performance of the kind of activity and the specific responsibilities assigned to the agency. Although the staff is constantly losing and gaining members, this by itself does not alter the stable expectations about the nature of the members' contributions.

6. *Outside definition of roles and responsibilities.* Other parts of the government—such as the legislature, chief executive, and judiciary—have authority to abolish the agency; to continue, add to, or contract the scope of its field of activity and its responsibilities; to fix the amount of funds it can use; to appoint some staff members and specify how others shall be chosen; and to impose structural and procedural requirements on its organization and operation.

The government agency does not spontaneously spring into being but is formally created by a constitutionally legitimate body or official. The agency cannot choose its own objectives. Rather, citizens and constitutional officials expect it to operate in a limited range of subject matter and to fulfill responsibilities assigned to it by an outside authority. The agency is not simply a social pattern developed out of who likes whom or who can seize and hold power. Rather, it has a formal organizational structure intended to specify who is meant to do what and who is meant to have authority over whom. Its officials and employees are not supposed to serve private groups' interests that are incompatible with their official responsibilities, to mobilize colleagues to subvert the agency's objectives, or to use their power for personal gain. Instead, they are judged by their service to the agency and its objectives. The agency is not set up and left to proceed on its own as an autonomous "closed organization" or to wrestle with a vague set of forces called "the environment." Rather, it remains part of a very specific environment—the government—whose major legitimate power holders have authority to appraise its performance, determine the input of resources to it, and alter its mission and activities.

These propositions, based on the structure of authority, do not guarantee that the work of public administrators will be free of problems. The lawmaking body may establish an agency that is not needed. The assignment of responsibilities may be vague, and they may overlap those of other agencies. The internal structure of an agency may be poorly designed. And any feature of the legitimate power model may be subverted by developments not taken into account by the model itself. Aggressive individuals or groups in an agency may seize or gradually accumulate power and, in the process, undermine the formal structure of authority. An agency may generate such internal dynamics and so powerful a set of allies that superior holders of authority will hesitate to challenge its independent actions. Or a superior holder of authority may induce an agency to make decisions that serve private economic, political, or personal interests that are incompatible with the larger public purpose. Although these and other practical possibilities require our attention, they do not destroy the usefulness of our starting with theories based on the structuring of authority. Indeed, they help to emphasize the fundamental role that hierarchical authority plays in structuring the legitimacy of bureaucratic power—and they point to the ways in which that power can be misused or redirected.

Two Models: Classical and Bureaucratic

The premise that legitimate power is the starting point for developing the structure of public administration is also the premise of two schools of administrative thought that developed in the first half of the twentieth century. They assume a higher source of authority for the agency's existence and powers. They see the fundamental organizational problem as one of setting up internal units and subunits, each charged with a specified portion of the agency's activities. This is a top-down approach. Critics have often labeled it authoritarian because it assumes a subordination of lower units to higher units—often called a *chain of command.*

Both the classical and the bureaucratic schools of thought rely on values in addition to legitimacy. Among these added values, rationality is the most important, partly because both schools view organizations simply as neutral instruments for achieving whatever policy objectives (that is, political values) the state's rulers may choose. The models are therefore meant to be politically neutral; they are designed to be rational, which is equated with efficiency.

The Classical Model

The classical theory of organization reached its peak in the 1930s, when Luther Gulick published its most persuasive exposition.[4] It still has wide currency, both as a theory in itself and as the foundation for other approaches. The theory begins at the top of the organization, with clear, bounded jurisdictions of authority and responsi-

"... Clear *boundaries* + *jurisdictions of authority* + *responsibility*"

bility. It moves on to further subdivision of these jurisdictions among the positions immediately under the top positions, and it continues through all administrative levels. Its prime value is efficiency, whose twin elements are differentiation (sometimes labeled specialization) of functions and coordination of responsibilities. What Gulick views as objective principles of organization provide guides on how to organize.

efficiency

The classical school builds on six specific doctrines:

1. *Bases of organization.* Organizations can be structured according to four different strategies:
   a. Purpose (e.g., defense, education, crime control)
   b. Process (e.g., accounting, engineering, typing, purchasing)
   c. Clientele (e.g., Indians, children, veterans, the elderly)
   d. Place (e.g., the Tennessee Valley, New England, Mississippi, Latin America)

6 points

base

2. *Mutually exclusive alternatives.* When policymakers design an organization, they must recognize that the four bases of organization are mutually exclusive and that one must be given precedence over the others. In other words, it is impossible to give equal weight, for example, to organization by both purpose and place. However, that does not mean that one base of organization must be used throughout the organization. As Gulick pointed out, if an organization is erected on one base, "it becomes immediately necessary to recognize the other[s] in constructing the secondary and tertiary divisions of work."[5]

1 main base

3. *Focus on purpose at the top.* Although organization designers have four alternatives, in general the executive branch of a government should be organized at its top level by major purposes (not by any of the other three bases or by a mixture). Each department should include all activities that contribute to its purpose.

focus on singular purpose at top

4. *Span of control.* Any executive can effectively oversee only a limited number of immediate subordinates. Therefore, the number of departments under the chief executive, the number of bureaus under a department head, and so on, should not exceed the executive's span of control—the number of subordinates he or she can effectively supervise.

limited # of subordinates

5. *Single head for agencies.* Administrative authority and responsibility should be vested in single administrators, not in plural-membership ("collegial") bodies such as boards and commissions, because under such arrangements, the fixing of individual responsibility for mistakes is difficult, and clear-cut decisions are less likely than fuzzy compromises among the members.

single head

6. *Separate line and staff.* Line activities and staff activities should be sharply distinguished. Line activities are those operations *directly* related to the major purpose of the agency—that is, the achievement of a public objective through service to or regulation of the whole public or particular segments of it. Staff activities, in contrast, are *assisting* functions to facilitate the work of the line officials—for example, research, policy and program analysis, planning, budgeting, personnel administration, and procurement of supplies. Essentially, line executives exercise powers of decision and command, whereas staff officials are—or should be—restricted to advising and providing raw materials.

The classical model has been closely associated with the pursuit of efficiency, as well as closely related ideas such as a commitment to a civil service of qualified persons selected by merit and a single-budget system for the whole executive branch. The classical model also anticipates a rational decision-making process, through which higher officials draw on the specialized knowledge at lower levels and decision makers at lower levels are furnished criteria and subjected to controls that assure conformity with higher policy. It has attracted a large collection of critics over the years, but in public administration its principles remain important in creating the basic building blocks of the field.

The Bureaucratic Model

Max Weber, a German sociologist, is the intellectual father of the **bureaucratic model,** and sociologists are its contemporary exponents and refiners. Bureaucratic theory is similar to classical theory, although it arose through a different path of study. Moreover, it gained prominence in the United States only after World War II; Weber originally wrote in German, and his views did not become widely accessible to American readers until the English translation appeared in 1946, long after his death in 1920.[6]

Weber focused an important part of his work on why people feel an obligation to obey commands without asking whether they agree with each one. He suggested that a stable system of authority cannot depend purely on appeals to subordinates' sense of self-interest, nor on their liking or admiration of their superior, nor on their sense of the ideal. Instead, a stable pattern of obedience must rest on a belief by subordinates in the legitimacy of the system of authority, which leads them to defer to superiors and, ultimately, to the source of command in that system.

Weber found it useful to think in terms of three "pure" models of legitimate authority: traditional, charismatic, and legal-rational. **Traditional authority** rests on belief in the sacredness of immemorial traditions ("what actually, allegedly, or pre-

3 types of authority

traditional

sumably has always existed"); it thus depends on the loyalty of individuals to some- _Charismatic_
one who has become "chief" in a traditional way. **Charismatic authority** rests on
personal devotion to an individual because of the exceptional sanctity, heroism, or
exemplary character of this person. Both of these types of authority may be exercised
in an arbitrary way or through revelations and inspirations. The bureaucratic model
holds, therefore, that both types of authority lack rationality.

By contrast, **rational-legal authority** (Weber used both terms interchangeably _rational-legal_
in characterizing this model) rests in "the legally established impersonal order." He
found it useful to describe this as an "ideal type" of bureaucracy, by which he meant
not "something to be desired" but rather the "basic characteristics" of a bureaucratic
system. Obedience is due "the persons exercising the authority of office under it only
by virtue of the formal legality of their commands and only within the scope of
authority of the office."[7] "The official duty . . . is fixed by _rationally established_ norms,
by enactments, decrees, and regulations, in such a manner that the legitimacy of the
authority becomes the legality of the general rule, which is purposely thought out,
enacted, and announced with formal correctness."[8] Persons in a corporate body, "in
so far as they obey a person in authority, do not owe this obedience to him as an individual, but to the impersonal order."[9] This approach establishes the basic structure
for accountability, because it describes the flow of power and responsibility from top
officials to those at the bottom of the organization.

To Weber, such a bureaucratic structure leads to efficiency. He wrote:

> Experience tends universally to show that the purely bureaucratic type of
> administrative organization . . . is . . . from a purely technical point of view,
> capable of attaining the highest degree of efficiency and is in this sense for-
> mally the most rational known means of carrying out imperative control
> over human beings. It is superior to any other form in precision, in stability,
> in the stringency of its discipline, and in its reliability. It thus makes possible
> a particularly high degree of calculability of results for the heads of the
> organization and for those acting in relation to it.[10]

To achieve such rational efficiency, Weber explains, the organization requires
two conditions (which are similar to those in the classical approach). First, laws and
administrative regulations establish "fixed and official jurisdictional areas" as part of _Conditions_
a systematic division of labor, each area being assigned "regular activities . . . as offi- _for_
cial duties" and "the authority to give the commands required for the discharge of _rational-legal_
these duties" (subject to rules delimiting the use of coercive means for obtaining _authority to_
compliance). Members of the bureaucracy can be efficient only if the scope of their _exist_
responsibilities is sharply defined. Second, "the principles of office hierarchy and of
levels of graded authority mean a firmly ordered system of super- and subordination
in which there is supervision of the lower offices by the higher ones." Efficiency also

depends on clear patterns of hierarchy and authority, from the top to the bottom of the organization.[11]

Weber, like the classical theorists, complements the organizational requisites with other characteristics of a full-fledged rational bureaucracy. He specifies particularly that officials should be full-time, salaried, and selected on the basis of technical qualifications. But, again as with the classical theory, the human beings who constitute "the bureaucratic machine" seem stripped of their human differences: "The individual cannot squirm out of the apparatus in which he is harnessed . . . the professional bureaucrat is chained to his activity by his entire material and ideal existence. In the great majority of cases he is only a single cog in an ever-moving mechanism which prescribes to him an essentially fixed route of march."[12] Weber's image of the individual as a cog in a machine has long been one of the principal criticisms of bureaucracy and the object of parody—from Charlie Chaplin's famous silent movie, *Modern Times,* to the satire on the Korean War, *M.A.S.H.,* which led to a long-running television comedy.

It is an oddity of the history of administrative study that, despite the similarities of the two theories, classical organizational theory has been scathingly attacked by many modern students of administration, whereas bureaucratic organizational theory continues to command their profound respect. Classical theory has, to some theorists, seemed impersonal and autocratic, as well as too unrefined; Weber's bureaucratic theory, on the other hand, seemed to paint a richer canvas. To be sure, Weber has attracted much criticism. For example, critics have pointed out that he both emphasizes the importance of hierarchical authority and recognizes that bureaucracy builds on specialized, professional knowledge and technical competence among subordinates, which expertise gives them a kind of authority that can conflict with the top-down patterns of organizational authority.[13] Despite these criticisms, however, Weber's concepts remain central to modern sociological analyses of bureaucratic organization.

Systems Theory

Systems theory has arisen as a major alternative to the hierarchical approach. It is the most ambitious effort to generalize about *all* organizations, public and private, large and small. Indeed, the theory has an enormous scope. A system can be any set of related parts—from the universe to a molecule. Its application to organizations, therefore, draws on analogies to both physical and biological phenomena.[14]

A system can be either closed or open. **Closed-system theorists** analogize an organization to a physical system, such as a machine, whose own operation is substantially unaffected by its environment. A common example is the heating system of a house: the thermostat is set for a given room temperature; when the temperature falls below the set point, the thermostat triggers the furnace, and when the temperature rises again to the level set on the thermostat, the thermostat turns off the furnace. (Room temperature is an environmental factor affecting the timing of the thermostatic system's activity, but the system's operation is self-contained—once set, it reads the temperature changes and performs its function, without the need for anyone to intervene.)

Open-system theorists see an organization as something akin to a biological organism, such as an animal or a plant living in the environment. A common example is the human body's normal temperature of 98.6 degrees Fahrenheit: when an individual contracts a disease from outside the system (that is, from outside the body), the body's temperature rises in response and the body's own system—sometimes with help from a physician—tries to kill the disease and restore the temperature to normal. Systems theorists have tended to be fascinated with nature's processes for restoring normalcy. Their tendency to look at both the nature of the system and that of the forces that pull it back to equilibrium has often led them to produce static, rather than dynamic, models of organizations.

open
(like an organism)

Most systems approaches to organizational theory treat an organization as an open system—that is, one that interacts with its environment. The essential elements are these: an organization is a system that receives **inputs** of resources (equipment, supplies, the energies of employees), which it **throughputs** and transforms to yield **outputs** (products or services). (Some of the input resources, however, go for use in maintaining the organization itself as a system—that is, for overhead costs.) Such a system also operates a **feedback loop**: Some feedback can be negative, in flagging problems that must be corrected. Some feedback can be positive, in identifying things that work well. In either case, this information can adjust the inputs and the system so that it produces better outputs at a lower cost. The usual graphic representation is shown in Figure 4.2.

| Figure 4.2 | **Systems Theory** |

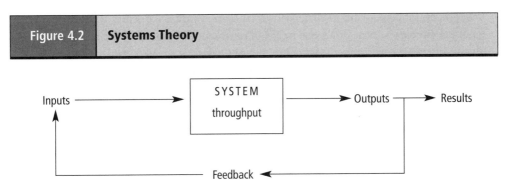

Even though open-systems models dominate, the closed system remains important. Many large organizations have tried to reduce their dependence on an uncertain environment by bringing much of that environment within their own systems—sometimes by manufacturing their own component parts instead of relying on outside suppliers, sometimes by attempting to buy out their competitors. In recent years, however, some corporations have moved in precisely the opposite direction, by relying on "just in time" delivery of supplies and equipment from outside suppliers. This practice, they believe, makes their own systems more lean and efficient, and it gives them greater flexibility in getting the material they need. Government agencies seek autonomy in selecting employees, purchasing supplies, and evaluating their own program outputs. In sum, open systems often try to reduce risks by evolving toward closed systems. Sometimes they are willing to take extra risks in exchange for greater flexibility.

Two important elements in the classical and bureaucratic theories of organizational structure come into sharp focus in systems theory: agency jurisdictions, which define **system boundaries**; and agency missions, which define **system purpose.**

System Boundaries

For both classical and bureaucratic theories, boundaries are essential, so that the authority and responsibility of each department and each bureau will be clear. A system, too, must have boundaries, so that one can tell what is within the system and what is outside it. This inside-outside distinction is vital for two reasons. First, systems theorists need to identify inputs to the system from the environment (the outside) and the system's outputs to the environment. These transactions occur at the system's boundaries. Second, the theory distinguishes two requisites for the survival of a system: its capacity to manipulate or adapt to its external environment, and its capacity to suppress or moderate internal threats.

It is often difficult to see a business corporation as a neatly bounded organizational system, and the problems are even greater in the public sector. One can formally assert, of course, that the Department of Agriculture is a distinct system with precise boundaries, everything else in the government and outside it being merely the department's environment. More broadly, one can treat the department, its pressure groups, and Congress's agricultural committees as a "system." Nevertheless, legal, political, and organizational realities allow the department far less autonomy and clarity of boundaries than the corporate analogy would require. The Department of Agriculture is a part of the executive branch, so many of its important decisions require the concurrence of other departments, the president, and central agencies (such as the Office of Management and Budget). Indeed, decisions directly affecting agriculture may actually lie with other agencies or with the president. These active sharers of decision-making authority cannot realistically be analogized to a business corporation's competitors, suppliers, and customers. To be sure, the Department of Agriculture does have a distinctive identity within the executive branch, but its identity rests in its core of concerns, not in the sharpness of its boundaries.

System Purpose

Classical theory, you will recall, proposes that the executive branch should be organized at the top by major purpose. Systems theory goes much further. It asserts that every organizational system has a purpose, goal, or objective—its translation of inputs into outputs.

Systems theory also borrows heavily from the idea of a biological system. Living organisms, of course, are systems. They take in inputs (nutrients) from the environment, process them, and turn them into outputs (activities or behaviors that characterize the organism's way of living). Of course, the first imperative of all organisms is simply to survive.[15] Systems theorists conclude that the same is true for organizations as well. Business corporations must take in more money than they spend or they cannot long stay in business; according to systems theory, a corporation's long life is, therefore, a sign of the success of its system.

Systems theorists then extend the basic argument to sociologists' views about human beings. Unlike most organisms, humans are moral beings, and they seek a purpose beyond themselves. When they join in complex organizations, these organizations likewise seek to serve broader purposes. As Lord Ashby explained long ago in writing about universities as organizations:

> Among living organisms it is assumed that the prime function is to survive.
> . . . Among social institutions one cannot make so simple an assumption.
> The biological analogy breaks down. It is not enough to say that the function
> of a university is to survive. It has functions over and above survival: in other
> words, it has purpose. . . . Unlike the biologist, the university administrator
> cannot eschew teleology; he must squarely face the fact that universities do
> not exist simply for their own sakes, as daffodils and sparrows and mice do;
> they have a purpose.[16]

Thus, systems theory focuses on an organization's purpose and how best to achieve it—how best to translate inputs into outputs. Systems theorists conclude that organizations need to be understood in terms of their purposes and that purposes define the nature of organizations. However, this is often difficult in practice, because—especially in the case of government agencies—organizational purposes often multiply and sometimes conflict.

Is it the purpose of the Department of Agriculture to advocate the American farmer's interests? Or is it to assure that the agricultural sector contributes to stability and growth of the national economy, serves consumer needs, adjusts to world trade conditions and American foreign policy, and forgoes products and practices that endanger public health? Is its purpose to serve the interests of large-scale, commercial farm corporations? Or is it to reduce the poverty of small-scale farmers and migratory farm workers? Is it both, and, if so, in what proportions? Congress does not provide the answers, for Congress has assigned the department multiple and conflicting purposes without conveying a sense of which is more important. The president, as chief executive, does not provide the answers either. President Nixon said in 1971 that he wanted his secretary of agriculture "to speak for the farmers to the president" rather than "for the president to the farmers,"[17] and, contrarily, that "when any department or agency begins to represent a parochial interest, then its advice and support inevitably become less useful to the man who must serve *all* of the people as their president."[18] Nothing has changed in the generation since.

Nor can a department's own definition of its mission help to solve this problem. The 1973 official statement of purpose and functions (since revised) was ridiculously vague: "The Department of Agriculture (USDA) is directed by law to acquire and diffuse useful information on agricultural subjects in the most general and comprehensive sense. *To accomplish this purpose,* the Department functions in the areas of research, education, conservation, marketing, regulatory work, agricultural adjustment, surplus disposal, and rural development."[19] Rather than a useful declaration of goals, such rhetorical flourishes are instead a part of the department's performance—they are carefully designed to enlist external and internal support. Systems theory needs a clear statement of an organization's objectives so that the organization's performance can be measured against the stated objectives; circular reasoning will not help.

The 1993 Government Performance and Results Act required federal departments to define their purpose and measure their results. The George W. Bush administration amplified these requirements and then tied the departments' success in achieving their goals to budget decisions. (We examine these innovations more in chapter 11 while exploring the budgetary process.) This process put hard numbers on some elements of the department's performance, but its overall mission remained fuzzily defined. In its 2003 annual report, the USDA defined its mission: "to provide leadership on food, agriculture, natural resources and related issues based on sound public policy, the best-available science and efficient management."[20] That hazy affirmation provided little advance on the department's statement of thirty years earlier.

Government agencies certainly do not fade away because their goals are vague. Indeed, the fuzzy nature of their boundaries provides extra flexibility in coping with the complex policy and political environments in which they operate. (That is, in a systems sense, they have more flexibility in responding to external stimuli.) What we know is that an agency operates in a field of activity, such as agriculture, national defense, transportation, or public health. The agency may not monopolize the field, and the field's boundaries may be imprecise. The objectives pursued by the agency, and the priorities among them, may shift with changes in political control of the executive and legislative branches (to name only the most obvious of many factors). These features of the real world help explain how government agencies actually operate. But they require relaxation of system theory's demand that every organizational system have precisely described boundaries and purposes.

Challenges to the Dominant Theories

The models and theories described so far have much in common. Each offers a rather formal, abstract view of an organization with clear goals and sharply defined boundaries. Systems theory views an organization as a "black box" that translates inputs into outputs. The classical model looks inside the black box and sees organizational units and subunits as clearly bounded and arranged to provide a hierarchical structuring of authority that is often pictured as a pyramid.[21]

These approaches focus on the organization's basic structure and on the relationship among its elements. Over time, they have drawn fire from three directions. Humanists charge that the various structural approaches are authoritarian—that their focus on boundaries stifles the creativity of the human beings who are the organization's life blood. Pluralists charge that the classical and bureaucratic models ignore the political system, give an unreal portrayal of the executive branch, and conflict with democratic values. Other critics from the government-by-proxy perspective contend that government agencies rely increasingly on other levels of government and on private and nonprofit organizations to administer public functions. To the degree that governments in fact do depend on such indirect administration, traditional patterns of hierarchy and authority are uprooted and displaced. All three approaches, therefore, raise fundamental challenges to the structuralist perspectives embodied by Weber, Gulick, and systems theory. We discuss each of these approaches in detail below.

The Humanist Challenge

The humanist challenge to the structural models looks inside the bureaucracy, focusing on the life of individual workers within the organization. Most of this challenge arises from research in industry and large corporations.

Jobs, Productivity, and Happiness

Industrial managers have long recognized that the business organization's performance depends on the productivity of individual workers. Among the major factors in a worker's productivity are the design of the job and the procedures that all workers follow. The **scientific management movement,** which developed the profession of industrial engineering, dates back to the early 1900s, when Frederick W. Taylor began to study how long it took workers to accomplish specified tasks. The movement used time-and-motion studies to find the most efficient way of completing these tasks, which led, in turn, to patterns for specialization and standardization of jobs and designed procedures to guide the flow of work from job to job.[22] This single-minded pursuit of efficiency was, even then, perceived as dehumanizing. Taylor unfortunately wrote that because of "the grinding monotony" of the work, "one of the first requirements for a man who is fit to handle pig iron as a regular occupation is that he shall be so stupid and so phlegmatic that he more nearly resembles in his mental make-up the ox than any other type."[23]

Such views reinforced the concern that bureaucratic work was dehumanizing. Organizational reformers sought to make the work more rewarding and the organizations perform better. The humanist challenge built on basic questions of motivation: why an individual joins a particular organization, stays with it, performs well, leaves.[24] Money helps, but it does not adequately explain variations among companies or among a single company's work groups. Important research in the late 1920s and 1930s at the Hawthorne Works of the Western Electric Company showed how variations in working conditions could affect the motivation and productivity of workers.[25] Researchers concluded they had found a "Hawthorne effect"—paying attention to workers as individuals increased their productivity. This research helped establish that human behavior matters to organization. That left questions about how, how much, and how it connected with authority and hierarchy.

The **human relations movement,** which peaked in the 1950s and again in the antiestablishment mood of the late 1960s, sought to answer these questions and to establish a link to the managerial approach. Both were concerned with workers' productivity and such related matters as absenteeism and turnover. The humanists argued that happy workers were more productive, and their early research studies confirmed this. Happiness, or satisfaction, as it was usually called, was not a matter of monetary and promotional rewards but of the interpersonal relations in the small face-to-face group of fellow workers and their immediate supervisor. According to the humanists, an atmosphere that generates satisfaction, and presumably productivity, does not flow from bureaucratic structure but from a commitment to participation by the workers in reaching decisions for the group. In such a system, the supervisor is not autocratic and directive, but informal, consultative, trusting, and concerned for the team members' welfare.

Although such arguments seemed promising, researchers found that (1) these conditions make some workers happy and some unhappy—some workers like to participate in decision making but others resist having to share the risk and responsibility for big decisions; and (2) happy workers are not necessarily more productive workers.[26] Though many research studies consistently showed that "job satisfaction is related to absences and turnover; they have been equally consistent in showing negligible relationships between satisfaction and level of performance or productivity."[27] This determination broke the link to the managerial approach, the shared concern for ways to improve productivity.

Ideology

After these findings, what remained was a normative commitment to the individual's opportunity for "self-actualization" (creativity, self-direction, the realization of one's full potential as a human being) and to the equality of persons (and thus minimal subordination to a leader's direction and maximal participation in decision making). Members of the human relations movement insisted that large, formal organizations, with their hierarchical authority structure, are repressive. Chris Argyris wrote that organization planners

> assume that efficiency is increased by a fixed hierarchy of authority. The man at the top is given formal power to hire and fire, reward and penalize, so that employees will work for the organization's objectives.
>
> The impact of this design-feature on human personality is clearly to make the individuals dependent on, passive and subordinate to the leader. The results are obviously to lessen their self-control and shorten their time-perspective . . . pushing individuals back from active toward passive, from being aware of long time-perspectives toward having only a short time-perspective. In all these four ways, the result is to move employees back from adulthood toward immaturity.[28]

The human relations school has been severely attacked, through four lines of argument.[29] First, most of the early research presenting empirical proof of the doctrines was conducted by "true believers," and other scholars found it seriously flawed. Those who rejected the traditional hierarchical approach embraced the human relations school; those devoted to the traditional approach tended to reject the human relations movement out of hand.

Second, the sweeping contrast of the bad hierarchical organization with the ideal humanist organization was overdrawn, resting on assertion rather than scientific study of organizations. Many writers simply adopted Douglas McGregor's distinction between two different approaches to organization and management: Theory X, which relied on hierarchical authority; and Theory Y, which relied on motivation; McGregor advocated Theory Y.[30] (See Box 4.1 for a summary of McGregor's theory.) The simplicity of his argument made it persuasive to those seeking to capture the

[handwritten margin notes: Commitment to an individual's self-actualization became a norm as did equality]

[handwritten margin notes: Attack on human relations movement 1) little empirical evidence 2) not as drastic of a difference b/w hierarchical structure and HR +]

Box 4.1	**McGregor's Theory X and Theory Y**

<table>
<tr><th>Theory X</th><th>Theory Y</th></tr>
<tr>
<td>

1. The average human being has an inherent dislike for work and will avoid it if he can.
2. Because of this human characteristic of dislike of work, most people must be coerced, controlled, directed, threatened with punishment to get them to put forth adequate effort toward the achievement of organizational objectives.
3. The average human being prefers to be directed, wishes to avoid responsibility, has relatively little ambition, wants security above all.

</td>
<td>

1. The expenditure of physical and mental effort in work is as natural as play or rest.
2. External control and the threat of punishment are not the only means for bringing about effort toward organizational objectives.
3. Commitment to objectives is a function of the rewards associated with their achievement.
4. The average human being learns, under proper conditions, not only to seek but to accept responsibility.
5. The capacity to exercise a relatively high degree of imagination, ingenuity, and creativity in the solution of organizational problems is widely, not narrowly, distributed in the population.
6. Under the conditions of modern industrial life, the intellectual potentialities of the average human being are only partially utilized.

</td>
</tr>
</table>

Source: Douglas McGregor, *The Human Side of Enterprise* (New York: McGraw-Hill, 1960), 33–49.

human relations approach, but it provided scant guidance to those trying to think more carefully and systematically about organizational management. Recent studies have rejected this simple contrast. Instead, the theory leads to prescriptions for tailoring leadership and participatory styles to the particular circumstances.[31] However, this call to adapt strategies to specific situations thwarts the search for general propositions, which is the essence of theory.

Third, although the human relations school was committed to development of "the whole person," the job was treated as if it were the worker's whole life. Critics made the obvious point that in societies with limited workdays and workweeks, most people obtain important satisfactions off the job. A high overall level of happiness often comes despite only moderate satisfaction with the job's sociopsychological attributes.

Fourth, the school's normative commitments blocked out awareness that a qualified leader needs to lead. Curiously, it was Abraham Maslow, a psychologist much admired by humanists, who made the point most sharply:

The writers on the new style of management have a tendency to indulge in certain pieties and dogmas of democratic management that are sometimes in striking contrast to the realities of the situation.

With dogma occupying this front-rank position, it is not surprising that human relations theory has evaded the problem of the very superior boss. The participative kind of management, where subordinates work toward a good solution to a problem, is often an inappropriate setting for the superior boss. He is apt to get restless and irritated. . . . The less intelligent subordinates are also affected adversely. Why should they sweat for three days to work toward the solution of a particular problem when they know all the time that the superior can see the solution in three minutes. . . .

The relationship of the boss to the people whom he might have to order around or fire or punish is, if we are realistic about it, not a friendly relation among equals. . . . This hard reality ought to have some impact on the theories of participative, democratic management.[32]

in reality, a tough boss making difficult decisions may be needed?

Sensitivity Training and Organization Development

Many members of the human relations school concluded that large organizations would work better only if their top officials changed their behavior. If higher executives were more "authentic" in their own interpersonal relations—deemphasizing their competitive, hierarchical positions and developing instead their own identities as human beings interacting with other human beings—the psychological atmosphere of the whole organization would be transformed. To achieve this behavioral modification, the executives needed to be trained in new attitudes, the leaders of the human relations school contended. Business corporations embraced the approach, and selected executives were sent off to participate in "team building" or **sensitivity training** activities. The movement began in the 1960s and has continued into the twenty-first century. Newer approaches have brought managers together for exercises that focus on interpersonal skills and the development of effective teams. Some approaches have even used nature-based challenges, such as developing a team to build a bridge across a river or relying on teammates to catch blindfolded employees as they fell backward.

if top dogs became more sensitive to others, the whole org would improve

Objective assessments of the human relations approach do not report much reliable evidence to support its claims.[33] Although many participants value the experience and alter their behavior back on the job, the new behavior may either improve or lessen their effectiveness in their organizations. The effects of the experience usually fade after a few months; the organizations often are left unchanged, and underlying organizational problems sometimes continue to fester.

not much evidence for this

Despite its uneven impact on organizational performance, the antibureaucratic school has had a profound effect on the study of organizations. It has become a rallying point for those seeking to move the study and practice of organizations past the

Establishments like Outward Bound offer skills-based exercises, such as wall climbing, to encourage teamwork among members of an organization.

structural approaches to new ones founded on interpersonal relationships. Improving those relationships, human relations theorists have long argued, has been the foundation for improving organizational performance.

The Pluralist Challenge

The pluralist challenge to the formal, structural model is externally oriented and emphasizes the responsiveness of a government organization to society's politically active interest groups. It focuses on the ability of these outside groups to shape a bureaucracy's behavior.

The pluralist model assumes a society characterized by the political interplay of groups, each seeking to have it interests prevail. It regards administration as a set of battlegrounds to which the interest groups carry their struggles from the electoral and legislative arenas.[34] It perceives a fragmented administrative structure linked with a fragmented Congress. Overhead direction is weak: the president is so occupied with policy and political leadership, international affairs, and other demands on his energies that he can give only partial and periodic attention to administrative responsibilities, and the department heads he appoints, birds of passage as they are, only rarely achieve effective control of the bureaus in their charge. Far from being a symmetrical pyramid, the executive branch is a jumble of structures, each pushed around by political crosscurrents. The task of administration, at least at its highest levels, is the same as the task of politics—to facilitate the peaceful resolution of conflicts, according to the distribution of power among groups in our society, and to use the interplay of these groups to seek the public interest.

Administrative organizations, according to the pluralistic model, are the products of this conflict and accommodation of interests.[35] Their survival as individual agencies depends on their command of sufficient outside support to withstand assault by disadvantaged interests. Their top officials can retain their power only as they adjust their use of power to the preferences of the supporting groups—or if they succeed in winning sufficient support from other groups to break free from the original supporters. The president appears in this model as the spokesperson not for the nation in the sense of "all the people" but for the specific combination of forces that enables him to attain power and that makes it possible for him to retain and exercise power. He is, in a sense, just another player—more a man with influence than a man with effective authority. To survive, administrative agencies must be responsive to Congress, and especially to congressional committees and their leaders, for both substantive power and appropriations derive from Congress. This has a sobering influence on administrators inclined to look to the president for their sole guidance.

Organization Culture

A variant of the pluralistic approach emphasizes the variety of **organization cultures**.[36] Agencies differ in many ways, which makes suspect any generalizations about the structure of authority. Some have such strong interest group support that they enjoy substantial autonomy within the executive branch; some enjoy such support without creating and mobilizing it; others foster the birth of sympathetic organizations. Some have such records of devotion to the public interest or to professional standards that they can resist interest group pressure and politically motivated efforts to intervene; others are orphans in the storm, the easy victims of unsympathetic interest groups, politicians, and sister agencies. An agency physically consolidated in one building differs from one whose headquarters units and staff members are scattered among many buildings or among capital suburbs and distant cities.[37]

The concept of organization culture stresses these and many other differences among agencies. One can enter a state liquor-control agency or an athletics-regulating agency and sense a different atmosphere from that in, say, a banking or insurance department or a labor department. In Washington, "one has only to walk into the ancient Treasury Department building . . . to sense the atmosphere of a conservative financial institution."[38] Even more is this the case with the independent Federal Reserve, which additionally illustrates the possibility of a culture in which one "subordinate" (the New York Federal Reserve Bank) at various times dominates the system.[39] The Forest Service and the National Park Service, located in different departments, will probably never be merged because they cannot forget a bitter controversy early in this century. The Forest Service, too, has a professional esprit de corps, a decentralization practice, and a systematic socialization of its rangers to the agency's norms that substitutes for centralization.[40] Other agencies often have difficulty maintaining morale and effective control of their field-office employees.

Critics have sometimes dismissed the organization culture approach as being too fuzzy to guide either theory or practice. However, after the space shuttle *Columbia* disintegrated on reentry from orbit on February 1, 2003, killing all seven astronauts on board, the National Aeronautics and Space Administration (NASA) went through a deep soul-searching investigation about how the accident had happened. Subsequent investigation revealed that the accident had been caused by hot gases pouring through a hole in the leading edge of the right wing and eating away at the internal support, until the wing gave way and the *Columbia* broke up; the hole, in turn, had been caused by the impact of a piece of insulation at launch. NASA's cameras had caught the impact, but meetings held while the shuttle was in orbit had concluded that it posed little risk.

Investigators later determined that NASA had developed a culture that was unreceptive to airing and resolving problems. In fact, an extensive survey of NASA employees a year after the disaster found that "there appear to be pockets [within NASA] where the management chain has (possibly unintentionally) sent signals that the raising of issues is not welcome. This is inconsistent with an organization that truly values integrity." How should NASA solve the problem? NASA's report concluded, "There is an opportunity and need to become an organization whose espoused values are fully integrated into its culture—an organization that 'lives the values' by fostering cultural integrity."[41]

Hal Gehman, who headed the NASA-convened board that investigated the February 1, 2003, *Columbia* space shuttle accident, asked a question during a public hearing six weeks after the disaster. The board found that NASA had slipped back into many of the same problems that had contributed to the *Challenger* disaster years before.

Critics may wonder whether the idea of organization culture has any real bite, but NASA's top officials concluded that it lay at the center of the factors that had caused the *Columbia* disaster. NASA administrator Sean O'Keefe said bluntly, "We need to create a climate where open communications is not only permissible, but is encouraged."[42] Together with outside experts brought in to help prevent future disasters, NASA's leader concluded that organizational culture was real, that NASA's culture had contributed to the accident, and that with hard work it could be changed.

Assessment

The hierarchical and pluralistic models perform different functions. The pluralistic model yields a more realistic description and explanation of what goes on in administration and politics, but the fragmentation it describes and even celebrates as part of the genius of the American political system affords little or no guidance as to what direction we should move in if we have the opportunity to express a preference or to exert influence. This model slides across the line dividing description from prescription—what *is* from what *ought to be*—but it does not tell reformers how to change organizations. The organization culture variation of pluralist theory even suggests that change may be fleeting, because cultures are deep-seated, rooted in particular functions and histories that alter only slowly and incrementally.

The hierarchical model, in contrast, draws strength from the wide support it has long enjoyed. It is the pattern advocated by every reorganization commission that surveys the whole sweep of federal administration. After the September 11 attacks, reformers argued for the need to "connect the dots" among related government agencies that failed to coordinate their information and operations. Congress created a new Department of Homeland Security designed to bring related agencies together under the same bureaucratic umbrella. It was, in short, a classic case of pursuing the hierarchic model and its prescriptions for clarifying missions and responsibilities.

Much of what are widely regarded as advances in national administration in the past several decades can best be understood as attempts to apply to a pluralistic government the arrangements implied by the hierarchic administrative model. Nevertheless, such proposals must be acted on by political people. The power group forces and the organization cultures identified by the pluralistic model often block reforms designed to strengthen hierarchical administration.

The tension between the two models is by no means simply that between reality and unsubstantiated belief. The very multiplicity of social forces and interest groups, along with the intensity of their competition for governmental favor, makes anarchy unacceptable. We need administrative institutions and processes that contribute rationality and order rather than happenstance and confusion; that are designed to seek the general interest rather than merely to reflect particular private, often selfish, interests; and that take the long view of policy goals rather than the short view of tactical maneuvers. The role of government in a democracy has always been to combine energies for widely shared objectives, whether for national security against foreign enemies, for maintenance of the legal system, or for the affirmative promotion of economic and social welfare. We should therefore not be surprised that efforts to improve government and its administration often emphasize the coordination, rationality, and legitimacy found in the hierarchic model—and that such efforts need to be accommodated to the variety of interest groups, congressional committees, and government agencies whose competing interests are the central fact of the pluralistic model.

The Challenge of Government by Proxy

All of these theories assume that a government's programs are carried out by the government's own employees through the government's own bureaucracies. What if that is not substantially true? Suppose that much of the government's work is farmed out to other governments and to private organizations, or to entities whose mix of public and private control puts them outside the administrative hierarchy. The supposition is true. As we saw in chapter 3, government has come to rely substantially on a wide variety of tools—and it manages many of these tools through strategies and tactics that are not based on traditional hierarchical governmental bureaucracies.[43]

This development calls for reconsideration of organizational theory. The more government administration relies on third-party tools—government by proxy—the less it fits the classical and bureaucratic models. Hiring, firing, and direct management of work are hierarchical powers that work poorly, if at all, when dealing with grants and contracts. To manage the programs effectively, government must seek other forms of leverage, especially through contract law and performance measurement. But the government cannot readily monitor all these outside agents, nor can it cancel large grants and contracts for violation of the prescribed conditions without damaging its programs and the public served.

Some scholars have suggested that an approach built on organizational networks might help to explain these problems better.[44] Such networks, Eugene Bardach explains, consist of "a set of working relationships among actors such that any relationship has the potential both to elicit action and to communicate information in an efficient manner."[45] Pragmatic in its exploration of how organizations share common ground—missions, clients, and goals—and coordinate their work, this approach has been developed by administrative scholars who sought to explain the management of public programs but found existing theories lacking. For example, they have discovered that most social service programs work through complex networks: a chain of federal grant money, frequently supplemented by state grant funds, that is passed on to local governments and administered through government organizations as well as for-profit and nonprofit contractors. These programs, in turn, connect with local schools, police departments, antidrug programs, programs managed through churches, and volunteer organizations, among others. The growth of this movement has given rise to extensive research into "collaborative governance," including a 2007 special issue of *Public Administration Review* that examined the rise of networked strategies for government action.[46]

Network analysis is distinguished from other approaches by two characteristics. Scholars debate whether networks constitute an approach, a theory, a method, or a prescription, but there is rising recognition of the power of collaborative approaches to public administration. On one level, the network approach is important for what it is not: it is based neither on traditional hierarchical control of organizations nor on market-based transactions among them. Organizations help one another because they discover that collaboration advances their own goals as well. On another level, such interdependence has come to define more governmental programs. Whereas traditional administration begins by assuming that the legislature delegates to government agencies the job of managing programs, network analysis begins with the discovery that the management of programs depends on the interconnections among those who actually implement programs, and that links of the implementation process often lie outside the bureaucratic chain of command. Some networks connect different agencies within a single department; the performance of a state's human services department typically depends on the network connecting its child welfare, health, and social service agencies. Some networks, especially those for federal grant programs, connect different departments at different levels of government. The performance of government programs depends on how well these networks function.

Compared with traditional hierarchical authority, network analysis is in its relative infancy. Its proponents disagree about whether it is a broad-based theory or simply a useful approach. But in moving past the traditional theories of hierarchy and in exploring the pragmatic tactics that managers develop to tackle the problems of government by proxy, network analysis offers fresh insights for government's emerging issues.

Formal Models of Bureaucracy

By the 1980s, many theorists were unhappy with the development of the various theories of public bureaucracy. They liked the fundamental simplicity of the hierarchical model, but they found that it did not yield enough clear propositions about just how to organize bureaucracy. They did not believe that the systems model produced enough insight, and they found the human relations approach too imprecise. As the government-by-proxy model emerged, they believed that it moved too far from the hierarchical approach, which in their view still provided the best foundation for bureaucratic theory. So they adapted economic propositions to produce new, formal models of bureaucracy.[47]

The formal approach to organizational theory fundamentally transformed public administration. Theorists began with elemental questions. Identifying individuals as the basic building blocks of economic systems, they asked: What motivates them? How do these motivations shape their behavior? How does their behavior shift as they come together in formal organizations? Traditional public administration assumed that authority relationships between superiors and subordinates shaped the basic relationships within an organization: individuals did what they did because superiors asked them to do it. The formal approach, by contrast, began with the proposition, borrowed from microeconomics, that individuals seek their self-interest: workers agree to work because the work provides them valued rewards, such as pay and fulfillment; employers agree to pay workers to get the job done, and the market determines how much employers must pay and what employees will agree to accept.

These basic assumptions have led to approaches that view bureaucracies as networks of contracts, built around systems of hierarchies and authority.[48] Each of these networks consists of relationships between superiors and subordinates, and each relationship has a variety of **transaction costs**—especially the cost to the supervisor of supervising the subordinate. As originally developed by Nobel laureate Ronald Coase in 1937, this theory has made several advances.[49] Beginning with the motivations of individuals, it explains how they fit into organizations. It charts the problems that such motivations can cause within organizations and identifies the problems that supervisors have in overseeing subordinates. By building on the concept of a contract between individuals and the organization, the theory links organizational theory to economics and its related ideas.

Principals and Agents

From this foundation, theorists developed **principal-agent theory,** an approach that details the contracts between superiors and subordinates. A top-down alternative to hierarchical authority, this approach stipulates that higher-level officials (principals) initiate the contracts and then hire subordinates (agents) to implement them. It also provides an alternative theory of accountability: workers (agents) are responsible to top-level officials (principals) not because they have been ordered to do so but because they have negotiated contracts in which they agreed to pursue specific actions in exchange for specific rewards. Principal-agent theory thus offers an elegant and theoretically powerful solution to the problems with which traditional public administration struggled for nearly a century. The task of devising the most efficient organizational structure and the best operating processes becomes a matter of constructing the best contracts. In both cases, the measure of "best" is the same: the ability of the organization to produce the most efficient and responsive goods and services possible.

Because principals and agents operate through contracts, results will be only as good as the contracts. Theorists contend that predictable problems grow out of any contractual relationship. To write a good contract requires good information. But principals can never know enough about their agents to make sure they have selected the best ones, and that lack of insight can produce adverse selection problems, in which ill-chosen agents cannot or choose not to do what their principals want. Moreover, principals can never observe their agents' behavior closely enough to be sure that their performance matches the terms of the contract—a lack of knowledge that can produce moral hazard problems, in which agents perform differently than the principals had in mind.

Principal-agent theory thus focuses on information and the incentives for using that information as the critical problems of public administration. Principals need to learn the right things about their agents before hiring them, and they need to improve their monitoring of agents' behavior to learn what results they produce. They can use this improved knowledge to adjust agents' incentives and to redesign organizations to reduce the risks from adverse selection and moral hazard. And because conventional wisdom and formal theory alike predict that bureaucrats resist change, principals can use this analysis to improve performance and oversight.

For public administration, this approach produces a straightforward theory: Institutions headed by elected officials, such as the presidency and Congress, create bureaucracies; that is, bureaucracies can be viewed as agents for the principals'—elected officials'—wishes. The principals design bureaucracies' incentives and sanctions to enhance their control, and when the principals detect bureaucratic behavior that does not match their policy preferences, they use these incentives and sanctions to change that behavior. Among the important sanctions are the president's appointment power and the budgetary leverage that the branches share.[50]

Principal-agent theory thus has introduced a simple, precise solution to the enduring puzzle of how principals should manage their relationships with their agents. Since these are market-based relationships, with costs and benefits on both sides, it makes sense to structure the relationship through a basic tool of the market, a contract, which specifies what the principal wants and what the principal will pay. When both the principal and the agent sign it, they thereby resolve the uncertainties that otherwise would surround their relationship—and potentially undermine their work. Moreover, principal-agent analysis has provided an inductive approach to theory-building. Starting with a simple assumption—that individuals seek their self-interest—the theorists have built propositions about why individuals join organizations, how organizations structure their work, and what problems can emerge from such relationships. Those propositions, in turn, have produced hypotheses—for example, that rational bureaucrats seek to maximize their budgets—that seem to explain much commonly observed administrative behavior. Principal-agent theory not only has helped to develop an alternative explanation of bureaucratic behavior but has also identified the pathologies that, especially by the late 1970s, seemed so often to afflict bureaucratic behavior.

Its very popularity, however, has stirred heavy criticism, especially from theorists who contend that the search for rationality robs the study of organizations of their very life. Economic theories of organization, Charles Perrow argues, represent "a challenge that resembles the theme of the novel and movie *The Invasion of the Body-Snatchers,* in which human forms are retained but all that we value about human influence, and resentment of domination—has disappeared."[51] Even one of formal theory's strongest voices, Terry M. Moe, agrees, commenting that the inner workings of bureaucracies tend to evaporate from most of these models. Instead, they appear "as black boxes that mysteriously mediate between interests and outcomes. The implicit claim is that institutions do not matter much."[52] Theorists from the structural approaches often add that the same goes for the people inside these institutions.

This debate leads to several important conclusions about the formal approaches to bureaucracy. First, although they are intriguing, they are not theoretically mature. Their proponents frankly acknowledge that large holes remain in their arguments and that far more work needs to be done. In particular, even though the approaches build from models of individual behavior, many of the models are peculiarly people-free. Public administration, at the least, has demonstrated that bureaucratic behavior matters, and if they are to be successful, the formal approaches will need to become more sophisticated about modeling that behavior. Second, the approaches lead in different, even contradictory, directions. The theorists have engaged in lively, even heated, arguments among themselves about which formal approach is most useful, and the battles are nowhere close to resolution. Third, the theoretical propositions are far more elegant than their empirical tests. The behaviors they seek to model are extremely complex and not easily reducible to equations and statistics. To conduct empirical tests, the formalists must impose large constraints and look only at pieces of the puzzle. That, they contend, is a natural part of theory building.

Traditional public administrationists have found the assumptions and models of the formal approach arbitrary and unrealistic; practically inclined researchers and practitioners have found them unpersuasive. Nevertheless, the formal models do provide theoretical elegance and a clear, logical set of propositions that many scholars find extremely powerful in a discipline that has long been searching for an intellectual anchor.

Conclusion

How can theorists look at the phenomenon of public organizations and reach such different interpretations?[53] Despite the multiple and contradictory approaches, three broader propositions surface. First, each approach embodies a significant truth about government organizations. Each has enjoyed a long life because it has captured at least an important nugget of reality, for a large number of analysts.

Second, as a mere matter of common sense, the error of these approaches lies in overgeneralization: not all organizations are the same; not all small groups are the same; not all jobs are the same. Therefore, we need to take situational variables into account. That recognition suggests an agenda for research, but pursuing the variation risks losing the capacity for broader generalization, which of course is the essence of building a theory.

Third, a step away from grand-scale theorizing leads to two more modest points. One is the direct study of reality—understanding how the context of public agencies can affect their behavior. The other is the formulation of middle-range theories—that is, theories that attempt to explain only a limited range of phenomena. For example, which organizational arrangements appear most likely to save a regulatory agency from being dominated by those it is meant to regulate? Is coordination of the elements of a complex program more likely under a hierarchical authority arrangement or under an interagency committee? What are the major frustrations of government executives, of civil servants, and of clients? Can they be significantly reduced, and how? Does an effective use of networks promise greater effectiveness in public administration?

If, as we have suggested, each of the approaches reviewed in this chapter contributes something that is true, then together they may be viewed as painting a rich portrait of a complex reality, including the following:

- The formal models of bureaucracy provide great intellectual power in explaining what bureaucracies are and how they work. They also furnish a bridge between twenty-first-century concerns and the fundamental issues that helped shape public administration at the beginning of the twentieth century. However, critics have pointed out that they provide little practical guidance to public administrators, and in the minds of many theorists they have not produced a firm foundation in research.

- The growth of government by proxy is a fact, one that forces a shift from sole reliance on hierarchical authority to honing of bargaining and negotiation skills. Yet, because the execution of farmed-out work by contractors and grant-receiving organizations is susceptible to corruption and other abuses, governmental officials need to devise incentives for faithful performance, to monitor behavior, and to apply sanctions.
- The pluralist approach soundly emphasizes the societal and political environment in which powerful interest groups intervene in administration to achieve their objectives. How such groups' often narrow interests can receive due attention without sacrifice of the larger public interest is an issue that tends to redirect attention to the role of hierarchical responsibility.
- The humanist approach, though flawed in several ways, usefully reminds us that individual workers' incentives and teamwork matter in gauging the effectiveness of administration.
- A systems approach, however simple to portray, is in fact complex in application. As with pluralism, its contribution lies in its emphasis on the interplay between an administrative system and its environment. In addition, its attention to feedback reminds us that organizations learn from experience over time.
- The structural approach, with which we started, goes back to first principles about government, viewing authority—legitimate power—as the heart of the matter. Executive branch departments are agents that hold authority that is delegated and restricted by other elements of the constitutional system—Congress, the president, and the courts. In turn, each such agency organizes a hierarchy for further delegating and restricting authority and for holding subordinates accountable for their use of such authority. Despite more than a century of criticism and complaint about this approach, it remains the foundation for both the theories and practice of public administration.

These first principles, linked to the concept of authority, are the building blocks for understanding organizational structure, staffing, the making and implementing of decisions, budgeting, and the enforcement of bureaucratic responsibility. The other approaches are complementary to this structural orientation, variously reinforcing or modifying its thrusts.

We need to tolerate the ambiguities of organizational theory. Physical scientists have long lived with both the wave theory of light and the particle theory of light, despite their contradiction. Our problem seems less troublesome in comparison.

Case 4

From the Front Lines of Organizational Theory: Is the FBI from Mars and the CIA from Venus?

Is this Venus and Mars meeting in conjunction? CIA director George Tenet (right) talks with FBI director Robert Mueller before they appeared at a Senate hearing in February 2003 on world-wide threats to U.S. security.

A uthor John Gray has made a global reputation with his best-seller, *Men Are from Mars, Women Are from Venus.* His argument: that men expect women to think and talk like men, that women expect men to think and talk like women, and that "our relationships are filled with unnecessary friction and conflict."[1]

He must be on to something. His Mars/Venus books have sold more than 30 million copies in forty languages. In fact, thanks to appearances on *Oprah* and *Live with Regis,* his first book was the best-selling book of the 1990s.

Some people think Gray's guide to male-female relationships helps explain the tensions between governments as well. Journalist Siobhan Gorman thinks so. She writes that the key agencies responsible for protecting the United States from terrorist attacks, the Central Intelligence Agency (CIA) and the Federal Bureau of investigation (FBI), "have such different approaches to life that they remain worlds apart"—and even White House–ordered relationship counseling might not be enough to bring them together.[2]

Prior to the September 11 attacks, government intelligence agencies spread across the nation and around the world had collected fragments of information, hints and warnings about the potential attacks from numerous disparate sources. But the information never came together to paint a picture of the disaster about to occur. Even in retrospect, it isn't certain that the picture would ever have been clear enough for the government to stop the attacks. However, we didn't have a chance to find out because high bureaucratic barriers prevented the flow of information.

In the months after the attacks, critics and reformers universally called on government to "connect the dots"—to do a much better job of weaving together the information collected by the various intelligence agencies. That process, they all concluded, would make America safer by helping top officials identify the greatest threats. Everyone agreed that the intelligence system needed better coordination, and a quiet consensus began to build that bureaucratic battles between the intelligence agencies were undermining the nation's security.

The national commission investigating the September 11 attacks confirmed that deep divisions between the nation's intelligence agencies had frustrated the government's ability to uncover valuable clues and, perhaps, take steps to prevent the attacks. Commission chairman Thomas Kean declared that the government had not been able to protect its citizens from attack because of "a failure of policy, management, capability and, above all, a failure of imagination." Who or what was to blame? Kean's commission answered, "There's no single individual who is responsible for our failures." The commission's recommendation? Create a new cabinet-level national intelligence director to oversee the nation's network of fifteen different intelligence agencies.[3] A single head of intelligence, the commission argued, would improve coordination and break down the barriers that had prevented the sharing of intelligence before the attacks. This national intelligence director needed to be able to steer the agencies' investigations, coordinate the information they collected, and provide clear advice to the president. That complex assignment, the commission concluded, required a new position at the highest level of the federal government—with the power to hire and fire employees and to control the intelligence budget.

At the center of the organizational battle was a decades-old struggle between the CIA and the FBI. "It's not that [FBI agents and CIA officers] don't like each other, but they're really different people," explained Jim Simon, who had worked as an analyst in the CIA. "They have a hard time communicating."[4]

For years, the two agencies had made an uneasy peace: the CIA focused on digging out information abroad on threats to the United States, while the FBI concentrated on dangers inside the country. A tidy boundary, perhaps, but not one that the nation's enemies paid much attention to. In fact, it was one they were able to exploit in carrying out the September 11 attacks, in which foreign operatives burrowed into American society, only to pop up to stage the biggest assault on American soil since the Japanese attack on Pearl Harbor in December 1941. From President Bush, congressional leaders, and the 9/11 Commission came an inescapable challenge to the agencies: cooperate! "But the organizations' institutional cultures are so different," concluded Gorman, "that real coordination will be very difficult to achieve."[5]

Since its creation in 1947, in the early days of the Cold War, the CIA has focused on building long-term relationships with potential intelligence sources. A field agent may spend long hours in conversation with a subject who is plied with good liquor, swapping tales, and building trust, in the hope that, when things begin to happen, the source may lean toward sharing some important information. Within this clandestine world, where it is always hard to predict what is going to happen where, the CIA—known as "The Company" to insiders—has encouraged a loose, nonhierarchical style of operating. Success here consists in digging out a critical piece of information and passing it along to top policymakers. Field agents often cut corners to make this possible, and then they melt back into the background.

By contrast, the FBI, founded in 1908, has long had an informal motto: "We always get our man." Dogged police work combined with careful training of its agents has always been the hallmark of the FBI. Knowing that their job is to catch and incarcerate criminals, this agency's operatives are scrupulous to avoid crossing legal lines so they won't jeopardize prosecutions. Success means putting bad guys behind bars, one case at a time.

FBI agents take up a case, track it to its completion, file it away, and move on; their work is linear. In contrast, CIA agents circle constantly around problems, pick up on leads until they either solidify or evaporate, and work them like a prospector panning for gold.

These different styles of work lead each agency to recruit a different kind of person. John Vincent, a twenty-seven-year FBI veteran, explains, "The type of people that go into the CIA is completely different from the type of people who go into the FBI." In the FBI, most employees "are pretty normal Joes off the street. The CIA guys—they're a different group of people. Most of the CIA guys I've met are very intelligent but wouldn't know how to put a nut on a bolt."[6] FBI agents, in Gorman's analysis, are from Mars.

Sixteen-year CIA veteran Ronald Marks says that's because, in the CIA, judgment is much more important than rules. "You have a source who will tell you X. Your judgment of that source is based on the time you've spent with them. You're dealing pretty much in a murky world." That, he concludes, is "the world of judgment."[7] As Gorman puts it, CIA agents are from Venus.

These different operating styles have led to very different antiterrorism strategies. The information-based, judgment-driven world of the CIA has focused on rooting out information about possible attacks in advance, even if the information does not come together in sharp focus. The conviction-based, rule-driven world of the FBI has focused on trying to arrest and convict terrorists, often after the fact.

Nevertheless, the stark realities of the post–9/11 world make it essential for the two agencies to cooperate. As the 9/11 Commission warned, "Countering transnational Islamist terrorism will test whether the U.S. government can fashion more flexible models of management needed to deal with the twenty-first-century world."[8] In fact, toward the end of its report the commission quoted the following stark conclusion, drawn from a study of the Pearl Harbor attack:

> Surprise, when it happens to a government, is likely to be a complicated, diffuse, bureaucratic thing. It includes neglect of responsibility, but also responsibility so poorly defined or so ambiguously delegated that action gets lost.[9]

To prevent poorly defined, ambiguously delegated policy in the future—to prevent the government's bureaucratic problems from getting in the way of its war on terror—the commission argued that the nation needed a single, powerful director of national intelligence with the authority to force coordination between the FBI and the CIA, as well as the thirteen other intelligence agencies. That change, the commissioners concluded, was the only way to create a unified homeland security culture from the very different independent organizational cultures that had grown in the vast intelligence community.

But even a new organization, journalist Gorman argued, might not solve the problem. Looking back at Gray's best-seller, Gorman wrote, "Mars and Venus can expect to need couples' counseling for a very long time."

Questions to Consider

1. What are the roots of the different organizational cultures in the FBI and the CIA? How do these cultures affect their work? In both good and bad ways?
2. How likely is it that the two agencies will be able to change their cultures?
3. Do you think that changes in the organizational structure can produce changes in the organizational culture? Is the 9/11 Commission's proposal a good idea? Why—or why not? How else might an organization's culture change, if not by changes to its structure?

Notes

1. John Gray, *Men Are from Mars, Women Are from Venus* (New York: HarperCollins, 1992), 10.
2. Siobhan Gorman, "FBI, CIA Remain Worlds Apart," *GovExec.com,* http://www.govexec .com/dailyfed/0803/080103nj1.htm (accessed August 1, 2003).

3. Chris Strohm, "9/11 Commission Scolds Government over Attacks, Calls for Major Reforms," *GovExec.com,* http://www.govexec.com/dailyfed/0704/072204c1.htm (accessed July 22, 2004). See the Commission's report, *The 9/11 Commission Report* (2004), http://www. 9-11commission.gov/report/911Report.pdf.
4. Gorman, "FBI, CIA Remain Worlds Apart."
5. Ibid.
6. Ibid.
7. Ibid.
8. *9/11 Commission Report,* 406.
9. Thomas Schelling, foreword to Roberta Wohlstetter, *Pearl Harbor: Warning and Decision* (Stanford University Press, 1962), viii.

Key Concepts

agencies **81**

agents **80**

authority **79**

bureaucratic model **84**

charismatic authority **85**

closed-system theorists **86**

feedback loop **87**

formal approach **77**

government-by-proxy approach **77**

hierarchy **77**

human relations movement **92**

humanist approach **77**

inputs **87**

network analysis **101**

open-system theorists **87**

organization culture **97**

organizational structure **77**

outputs **87**

pluralist approach **77**

principal-agent theory **102**

principals **80**

rational-legal authority **85**

scientific management movement **92**

sensitivity training **95**

system boundaries **88**

system purpose **88**

systems theory **86**

throughputs **87**

traditional authority **84**

transaction costs **102**

For Further Reading

Goldsmith, Stephen, and William D. Eggers. *Governing by Network: The New Shape of Government.* Washington, D.C.: Brookings Institution, 2004.

Goldsmith, Stephen, and Donald F. Kettl, eds. *Unlocking the Power of Networks: Keys to High-Performance Government,* edited with Stephen Goldsmith. Washington, D.C.: Brookings Institution Press, 2009.

Gulick, Luther. "Notes on the Theory of Organization." In *Papers on the Science of Administration,* edited by L. Gulick and L. Urwick, 1–45. New York: Institute of Public Administration, 1937.

Katz, Daniel, and Robert L. Kahn. *The Social Psychology of Organizations.* 2nd ed. New York: Wiley, 1978.

Khademian, Anne M. *Working with Culture: The Way the Job Gets Done in Public Programs.* Washington, D.C.: CQ Press, 2002.

McGregor, Douglas. *The Human Side of Enterprise.* New York: McGraw-Hill, 1960.

Moe, Terry M. "The New Economics of Organization." *American Journal of Political Science* 28 (1984): 739–777.

Perrow, Charles. *Complex Organizations.* 3rd ed. New York: Random House, 1986.

Simon, Herbert. *Administrative Behavior.* New York: Macmillan, 1947.

Weber, Max. *From Max Weber: Essays in Sociology.* Translated and edited by H. H. Gerth and C. Wright Mills. New York: Oxford University Press, 1958.

Suggested Websites

For an exploration of academic research about organizational theory, see the website of the Public Management Research Association, **http://www.pmranet.org,** and of the Academy of Management, **www.aomonline.org.** Both provide links to cutting-edge research in the field. In addition, the website prepared by Babson College Assistant Professor Keith Krollag, **http://faculty.babson.edu/krollag/org_site/encyclop/ encyclo.html,** is a useful encyclopedia of the major terms in the organizational theory literature.

5

Strategies and Tactics for Administrative Reform

In the administrative world, nothing has become more constant than change.[1] Indeed, virtually every government—large or small, rich or poor—throughout the world has recently launched a major reform effort. A 2001 report by the Organization of Economic Cooperation and Development, an association of the world's major industrialized nations, concluded,

> As society continues to change rapidly, the solutions of the past are no longer sufficient. Not only is there no "one size fits all" solution across countries, but countries should also learn to use reform to create institutions that can constantly adapt to changes in their own societies and to changing outside forces.[2]

The reforms attempted across the world have been very different and have often had multiple personalities. They have sometimes carried inherent conflicts, usually buried deep under the frenzy of the tough political realities that provoked the reforms in the first place. But beyond the differences is a remarkably universal movement toward reform, reflecting what seems to be an irresistible lure in redesigning the work of government to work better and cost less. These bold promises, however, are extremely difficult to achieve, both because the job itself is tough and because the differing personalities of administrative reform often drive it in conflicting directions.

Reform in America

Three important truths characterize public management reform in the United States. First, from the nation's earliest days, Americans have been devoted to reform. Most presidents, governors, and mayors come into office pledging to make public programs work better (better, in particular, than in their predecessor's administration). American public administration, in fact, revolves around a fundamental paradox: an enduring sense that public bureaucracy is a large, immovable object and that top executives need to produce deep, constant change. Few elected officials champion the cause of public administration per se, but none can ignore the imperative to make public programs work.

Second, in the United States, the most innovative administrative thinking has occurred in the private sector. Public managers anxious to save money and improve service delivery have looked for solutions wherever they could find them, and that search has often led them to corporate strategies and tactics. In part, this is because of the recurring belief, often wrongheaded, that government would be better if it were managed more like the private sector. The match between private solutions and public problems has often not been a good one, but that has scarcely deterred public officials from trying to borrow anything that might prove a good idea.

Finally, many American governmental reforms have tended to bubble up from the experiments of state and local governments, rather than moving from the federal government down; the federal government has often been the last link in the chain. The Government Performance Project, funded by the Pew Charitable Trusts, has produced a series of report cards on the performance of state governments, and the research has uncovered a remarkable array of innovation and ingenuity in the states. In playing catch-up, however, the federal government has often found that its programs, such as food stamps and Social Security, are poor matches for innovative solutions developed for such state and local programs as garbage collection and park maintenance.

from ground up

American public administration's continued commitment to reform springs from a variety of sources. Some of it reflects a fundamental tension in the American political character between great ideals and an underlying pragmatism. Some of it results from the fact that many of the reform ideas are drawn from settings that offer a much different context for the problems they are trying to solve: private-sector strategies applied to government, and state government strategies applied to the federal government. Some of it derives from an ongoing dynamic: government has always tried to do hard things, and reform has always been a coping strategy when results fall short of expectations. And some of it simply demonstrates that Americans have always been tinkerers, and they like tweaking the workings of their institutions.

Conflicting Theories

Despite the peculiar problems that government officials at different levels must tackle, there has been surprising convergence around three basic approaches. Terms such as **downsizing, reengineering,** and **continuous improvement** have quickly entered the administrative vocabulary of managers around the world. The terms themselves are appealing, because they speak to the aspirations of managers and citizens alike. Hardly anyone wants to make the public sector bigger, so reformers resort to downsizing, or shrinking government. When results fail to meet expectations, reformers seek to reengineer organizations. And no one thinks that the incentives in traditional bureaucracy produce the right incentives to help government bureaucrats adapt easily to a quickly changing world, so continuous improvement seems an attractive solution.

Behind these three basic approaches, however, are deceptively complex ideas. The old bureaucratic orthodoxy, founded on traditional authority and hierarchy, promised a clear, straightforward, and universal set of principles: delegation of authority on the basis of expertise, and democratic accountability through hierarchical control. The new ideas driving bureaucratic reform, however, are neither orthodox nor universal. Moreover, at their core are important but often unrecognized contradictions that threaten the success of reform efforts, as recent American experience illustrates.

Downsizing

The concept of downsizing seems quite simple. Arguing that government is too big, conservatives have long battled to shrink its size. In that effort, there is no bigger or more attractive target than the number of government employees; rarely is any more sophisticated goal envisioned by the downsizing movement. Indeed, the theory is nothing more than this: government is too big, so one should do whatever is politically possible to make it smaller—set arbitrary ceilings on taxes or personnel, promise across-the-board cuts, or pledge to trim the middle of the bureaucracy. Angry taxpayers have often proved willing to wield blunt axes in making cuts, even if good programs or key managers are eliminated, if that is what it takes to get their message across.

In the United States, such blunt-edge downsizing originated at the state level, although reducing property taxes imposed by local government has most often been the target of angry state voters. The movement started in the mid-1970s, as inflation fueled real estate prices and spiraling real estate values drove up property taxes. New Jersey legislators began in 1976 by limiting the growth of expenditures to the growth of per capita personal income. California voters fired the loudest shot in 1978 by approving an amendment to the state constitution, Proposition 13, which reduced property taxes to 1 percent of market value and limited future property tax growth to a 2-percent annual increase over the amount calculated from the 1975–1976 base. Massachusetts voters followed with Proposition 2½, which reduced property taxes by 15 percent per year until they reached 2½ percent of full market value, where they had to remain (hence the name applied to the proposition).[3] State legislators passed scores of other tax limitations or special tax breaks in the following decade.[4] Between 1976 and 1982, legislators and voters in nineteen states agreed to limit revenues or expenditures.[5]

The movement continued through the 1990s and the 2000s, led by Colorado's passage in 1992 of a constitutional amendment to limit tax increases—christened the **Taxpayer Bill of Rights,** or TABOR for short—which spread to other states as well. The proposal passed with 54 percent of the vote; a decade later, almost three-fourths of Colorado residents favored its tough approach.[6] The Colorado effort sparked a string of copycats over the next decade. Meanwhile, in 1994 Michigan voters agreed to shift a substantial amount of local property tax revenues for education to state taxes, while Wisconsin legislators voted to replace most local property taxes for schools with state aid, to be financed by state government spending cuts. In both cases, state officials first committed themselves to the broad reform—property tax relief—without deciding how they would produce it, and in both cases, the strategy provoked wild bargaining in the state legislatures to produce the promised aid.

The problem, surveys in the 1990s revealed, was not that citizens were unhappy with the services they were receiving. Instead, they believed that their taxes were too high—that the public sector was fundamentally inefficient and could easily provide the same services for less money.[7] Elected officials discovered that the mantra of cutting the unholy trinity of "waste, fraud, and abuse" resonated well with voters. For better or worse, both elected officials and voters came to believe that public inefficiency was so great that expenditures and revenues could be slashed without hurting the quality of public services; tax and spending limits would force government bureaucrats to wring waste out of the system. E. S. Savas argued that the public, "despairing of the ability or will of its elected government to reduce expenditures, has

In Garland, Maine, Mary Adams campaigned in 2006 for a "Taxpayer Bill of Rights" to cut taxes and bring down government spending. The 68-year-old grandmother helped advance a movement that had spread from coast to coast.

taken the matter directly into its hands and reduced revenue, like a parent rebuking his spendthrift child by cutting its allowance."[8]

The downsizing movement spilled over to the federal government in the mid-1980s, but with far more uneven results. In 1984 the President's **Private Sector Survey on Cost Control** (better known as the Grace Commission, after its chairman, J. Peter Grace) produced 2,478 recommendations that its report said would save $424.4 billion over three years. The commission concluded that the federal government was "suffering from a critical case of inefficient and ineffective management" and that only more businesslike practices and, in particular, huge cuts in government programs could reduce the deficit hemorrhage.[9] Academic critics argued that the report built largely on an ideological, probusiness, antigovernment base; that it contained misrepresentations; and that following its recommendations could actually hurt the work of the federal government.[10] Suspicious Democrats, who controlled Congress, saw it as a partisan maneuver by Republican president Ronald Reagan, and the resulting partisan battles doomed almost all of the report's recommendations.

The Grace Commission report did, however, fuel a downsizing movement at the federal level, helping to promote in 1985 the **Balanced Budget and Emergency Deficit Control Act,** better known as Gramm-Rudman Act, after two of its key sponsors, senators Phil Gramm (R-Tex.) and Warren Rudman (R-N.H.). Among its many important effects, Gramm-Rudman forced both Congress and the president, Democrats and Republicans alike, to begin bringing the burgeoning federal deficit under control; downsizing became an inescapable part of politics at all levels of American government. Even though subsequent efforts nudged Gramm-Rudman aside, it had made downsizing a fundamental part of the strategies used by both political parties. At the state and local levels, the movement bubbled over into the TABOR movement, with an aggressive campaign to cut the rate of state government spending.

Soon after taking office in 1993, President Bill Clinton named Vice President Al Gore to work on **reinventing government,** to make the federal government work better and cost less. The term came from a best-selling 1993 book, *Reinventing Government,* by David Osborne and Ted Gaebler.[11] Gore's campaign, the National Performance Review, promised voters $108 billion in savings by fiscal year 1999. Some of the savings were to come from reforms already under way, while others would derive from proposed policy changes and elimination of field offices of federal agencies. Most of the projected savings, however, were to result from reducing the federal workforce by 12 percent over five years—a total cut of 252,000 positions—to leave the workforce at under 2 million for the first time since 1967. The vice president's report promised that the cuts would consist of pruning away unnecessary layers of the federal bureaucracy:

Most of the personnel reductions will be concentrated in the structures of over-control and micromanagement that now bind the federal government: supervisors, headquarters staffs, personnel specialists, budget analysts, procurement specialists, accountants, and auditors. These central control structures not only stifle the creativity of line managers and workers, they consume billions per year in salary, benefits, and administrative costs. Additional personnel cuts will result as each agency reengineers its basic work processes to achieve higher productivity at lower costs—eliminating unnecessary layers of management and nonessential staff.[12]

The report asserted that the many reforms it proposed—from streamlining the procurement process to giving managers more flexibility to make decisions without endless cross-checking—would improve governmental efficiency, making it possible to eliminate functions and layers of the federal bureaucracy and, therefore, to save billions of dollars. In theory, new efficiencies would produce the savings; in practice, however, the savings were almost totally separate from the administrative reforms. The report promised that strategic planning within the bureaucracy was to determine where the cuts could be made, but when department heads began working to deliver the promised reductions, the cuts had little if anything to do with the plans. In fact, most departments planned to meet their targets by offering employees buyout packages that included financial inducements for taking early retirement.[13] In the end, by 2001, the number of federal civilian employees had declined by 365,000 (17 percent).

The Clinton-Gore effort did indeed reduce the number of government workers to the lowest level since the Kennedy administration. The number of federal employees remained at this lower level until the creation of the Department of Homeland Security in 2003, which added 65,000 airport screeners to the federal workforce. Even with this huge growth of new employees, however, federal employment remained below where it had been forty years earlier. In fact, one of the most striking trends in government service is that, despite the widespread public belief in a rapidly growing bureaucracy, federal employment has been relatively stable since the 1960s (see Figure 5.1). Only in the George W. Bush administration was there a modest increase in the number of federal employees, principally because of the federal government's takeover of the airline security screening function, which had been conducted by private companies before 2001.

This overall trend, however, masks important changes. Driven (not surprisingly) by a huge increase in the number of civilian defense employees, the number of federal workers grew rapidly during World War II. After the war, the number fell back—but to a level twice as high as that of prewar days. Government employment remained larger, in part, because the defense establishment was increased to counter

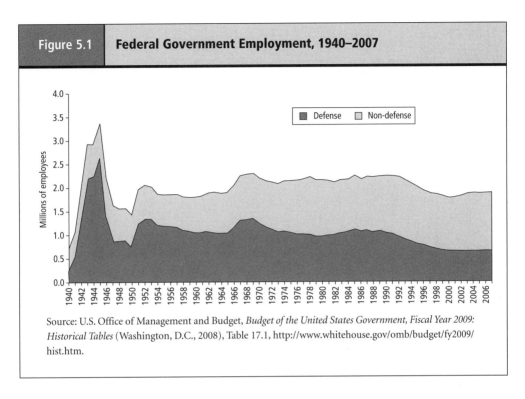

Figure 5.1 | **Federal Government Employment, 1940–2007**

Source: U.S. Office of Management and Budget, *Budget of the United States Government, Fiscal Year 2009: Historical Tables* (Washington, D.C., 2008), Table 17.1, http://www.whitehouse.gov/omb/budget/fy2009/hist.htm.

the growing Cold War threat from the Soviet Union. But this was only part of the story. Defense employment gradually shrank in the late 1960s as the Vietnam War gradually ran toward an unhappy end—but overall government employment did not, because domestic agencies continued to increase in size. That growth trend continued until the Clinton administration's downsizing in the 1990s, and was only partially restored by the hiring of the new Homeland Security employees in the aftermath of September 11.

The real growth in government employment has come at the state and local level, as Figure 5.2 shows. From 1982 to 2005, state and local employment increased by 46 percent. This is not the case of government gone wild. As population has increased, citizens have needed more police officers, fire fighters, garbage collectors, and teachers. Since state and local governments provide most of government's frontline services, the number of employees tends to grow with population.

At the bottom of the recurring battles over the size of the government workforce are important points about the downsizing movement. First, although from time to time it has relied on such wildly different theoretical bases as reinventing government[14] and the idea that bureaucrats seek to maximize their power by maximizing

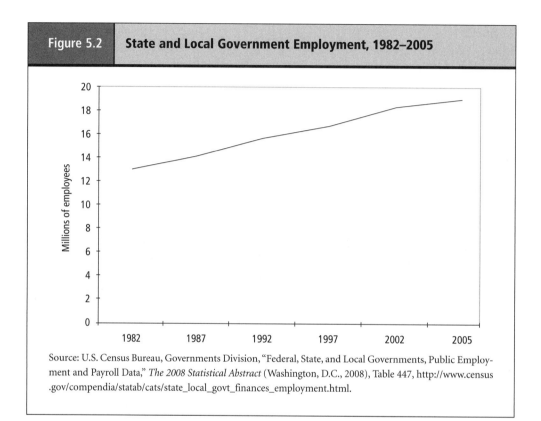

| Figure 5.2 | **State and Local Government Employment, 1982–2005** |

Source: U.S. Census Bureau, Governments Division, "Federal, State, and Local Governments, Public Employment and Payroll Data," *The 2008 Statistical Abstract* (Washington, D.C., 2008), Table 447, http://www.census.gov/compendia/statab/cats/state_local_govt_finances_employment.html.

their numbers,[15] the movement itself has been largely atheoretical. Pragmatic principle has guided it: the only way to force greater governmental efficiency is to hold a loaded gun—in the form of tax and spending limits—to the heads of public managers. Cynics have called it the "starve the beast" strategy: if the beast they see as government cannot be killed in a frontal attack, they suggest, it can instead be shrunk by starving it of tax revenue and, thus, of its employees. Indeed, as President Bill Clinton struggled to resuscitate his presidency in early 1995 by promising a middle-class tax cut, he promised to fund it by cutting government bureaucracy even further.

Second, although there often has been bold talk about cutting away the fat, typically little planning has been done in advance of adopting these measures. Voters and elected officials have imposed limits that have often been set more to hit symbolic targets than to allow for the number of employees needed to do the job. When cuts have come, managers have struggled to find ways of continuing to deliver valued services with fewer employees. Elected officials and managers alike must cope in the

"starve the beast"

short term; long-term planning has become a luxury that the quickly moving political system does not allow. The downsizing movement thus has focused the attention of government officials on coping with immediate pressures instead of charting strategies for lasting performance. As Congress's watchdog agency, the General Accounting Office (GAO; in 2004 it became the Government Accountability Office), concluded in 2002:

> Much of the downsizing was set in motion without sufficient planning for its effects on agencies' performance capacity. Across government, federal employers reduced or froze their hiring efforts for extended periods. . . . This helped reduce their numbers of employees, but it also reduced the influx of new people with new knowledge, new energy, and new ideas—the reservoir of future agency leaders and managers.[16]

Third, while downsizing has in fact limited the growth of government spending and tax revenues in the United States, its effect on the quality of services and the efficiency of administration is anything but clear. American government at all levels, in fact, has tended to invest relatively little in measuring the quality of what it buys.[17] That has been changing with the rise of the performance management movement in the 2000s. At the federal level, the George W. Bush administration introduced an aggressive effort to assess the performance of federal programs and to link that information to budget decisions. State and local governments advanced performance movements (as we will see in chapter 12).

Elected officials, however, have pursued downsizing for primarily symbolic reasons. They have tapped into the anger of taxpayers and have boldly proclaimed government's pathologies, even as some of their remedies risk making those pathologies worse. The downsizing movement has given officeholders a message that resonates with voters without directly attacking the problem of making government work better. Public officials, both elected and appointed, have turned instead to reengineering and culture change for that purpose.

Reengineering

Few management books make it to the best-seller list, but Michael Hammer and James Champy's *Reengineering the Corporation*—a tale of corporations faced not only with new challenges but with threats to their very existence—sat there for months in 1993.[18] To succeed, even to survive, these authors claim, business leaders must move past incremental improvements and instead undertake fundamental reexamination of their operations. Their contention that completely new work processes and organizational structures can produce quantum leaps in performance has proven powerful in the private sector, and its influence has spilled over into government.[19]

Reengineering, Hammer and Champy argue, begins by putting everything on the table. It "means starting all over, starting from scratch," through "discontinuous thinking."[20] Too often, they believe, managers tinker at the edges when they need to start anew. The process begins by having managers consider the "three Cs": customers, competition, and change. The foundation for the new reality builds on customers "who know what they want, what they want to pay for it, and how to get it on the terms that they demand," and the successful companies will be those that build their operations to serve customers' needs. More intense competition means that companies that do not incorporate cutting-edge technology into their operations will not survive. And as change becomes constant, only organizations light on their feet, quick to adapt, will prosper.

Reengineering requires fundamental and radical redesign of work processes. Indeed, *process* is the fundamental building block of reengineering. Effective managers redesign the processes within their organizations to ensure that customers' needs are met. They incorporate the latest technology, especially information technology, to wring extra efficiency out of their operations. Hammer and Champy emphatically argue that reengineering is not the same as downsizing, which is not driven by the need to improve performance; it is not the same as administrative reorganization because reengineers view process as far more important than structure; and it is not the same as **total quality management** (TQM), which seeks to improve quality within existing processes through continuous improvement. Reengineers, by contrast, search for breakthrough strategies instead of incremental improvements—rather than trying to do a job 10 percent better, reengineers look for strategies that can work ten, or a hundred, times better.[21]

As private managers have popularized reengineering, public managers have found the movement irresistible. Massachusetts, for example, reengineered its child-support collection system. Previously, collection efforts had begun with complaints by the caregiving spouse against the nonsupporting spouse; caseworkers, through a labor-intensive system, then tried to track down scofflaws and intervene to try to win support. Under the new system, the state instead began relying on computers to find cases with similar characteristics, to search the database for parents who owed support, and to generate letters insisting on payment. After two years, according to one report, 85 percent of collections had occurred without a caseworker's intervention, the number of cases in which payments were collected had increased 30 percent, and the compliance rate had jumped from 59 percent to 76 percent. In Merced County, California, new software designed for individual workstations replaced mainframe-based programs for processing welfare eligibility claims; in the process, the time from initial application to interview decreased from four weeks to three days or less.[22] Texas, meanwhile, launched several major initiatives to improve the state's tax administration system that supporters believed could produce an additional $51 million in revenues per year.[23] Focus on the program's mission, identify its customers, rethink how best to deliver services, and, the reengineering movement argues, more efficient services will follow. The rise of the performance movement of the 2000s has helped fuel the reengineering movement, as governments at all levels have sought to squeeze extra productivity from their operations.

Not all scholars of public administration agree that a government approach founded on customer service is valid. Many leading figures in public administration have attacked reengineering and reinvention. H. George Frederickson, for example, contends that "governments are not markets" and that "citizens are not the customers. They are the owners."[24] Critics add that the broader movement to make government more entrepreneurial is dangerous; even if entrepreneurial behavior were a good idea, they argue, the concept could never be applied to government because there frequently is little private competition in most public functions.[25] Nevertheless, the reinventers counter that energetic, problem-solving managers would perform far better than more traditional bureaucrats rooted in standard operating procedures and organizational structures.

Moreover, even though citizens quite clearly "own" their government, many reformers argue that citizens could be treated far more responsively—as "customers" of government programs—without violating the fundamental premises of democratic government. Wisconsin's Department of Motor Vehicles, for example, installed new systems to make it much easier to obtain driver's licenses: take-a-number machines that tell citizens how long they can expect to wait; new strategies to minimize those waits; and satellite offices located in shopping malls, open evenings and weekends, that give citizens wider access. The state's Department of Revenue developed a new quick-refund system that got taxpayers their income tax refund checks within two weeks. In Oregon, when the state's driver's license bureau surveyed citizens to determine what problem they most wanted solved, it found that the No. 1 problem was the poor quality of the driver's license photographs that embarrassed citizens had to carry around for years. The state installed a new electronic system that allowed citizens to choose the photos that would grace their licenses, making them much happier with the service. As computer programs like TurboTax and Tax Cut have made it easier for individuals to prepare their tax returns at home, governments have worked hard to make it easier for taxpayers to file their taxes with a touch of a button.

Compared with the private sector, government's **customer service movement** is in its relative infancy. Substantial problems need to be worked out, from the difficult task of identifying customers to developing fresh incentives for government employees to serve citizens better. The very strategies and tactics of government further complicate the problem: as we saw in chapter 3, many government programs operate indirectly, through transfers, grants, and contracts; and most government employees are far from the ultimate customers of their programs. That does not mean that a customer service approach is invalid; it does mean, however, that government's managers must work far more creatively to ensure that managers throughout the system remain focused on the ultimate goals of public programs. The growth of **performance management,** in states such as Virginia and at the federal level, has proven important in reshaping incentives throughout the system.

The reengineers aggressively present their arguments as fresh and novel—all the better, of course, to promote book sales and consultancy contracts. In fact, their focus on customers, radical change, nimble organizations, and information technology represents a creative combination. As we saw in the previous chapter, however, organizational theory has traditionally focused on an organization's purpose and how to maximize its efficiency. Process, in fact, was central to much organizational thinking in the 1930s, especially to the work of Henri Fayol.[26] So, too, was information. As Lyndall Urwick argued, "the underlying principle of any form of administration which aims at scientific precision and integrity must be investigation or research yielding information."[27] Indeed, Luther Gulick's famous paper, "The Theory of Organization," written for the Brownlow Committee, which advised President Franklin Roosevelt on reorganization of his office, explicitly tackled the issue of "organization by major process." Along the way, Gulick noted the critical problem of process-based organization: "while organization by process thus puts great efficiency within our reach, this efficiency cannot be realized unless the compensating structure of coordination is developed."[28]

In the decades that followed World War II, the interest of organizational theorists—especially *public* organizational theorists—in organizational process diminished considerably. Most discussion of process revolved around *due process* and the guarantee of fair treatment for citizens.[29] James Q. Wilson's brilliant book *Bureaucracy,* however, talks about "procedural organizations" as ones where "managers can observe what their subordinates are doing but not the outcome (if any) that results from those efforts."[30] This limited perspective creates a stark tension: in a situation where they cannot determine what results subordinates produce, Wilson warns, government managers often cannot understand, let alone control, the results of their programs. The reengineers, in contrast, contend that controlling process to improve results is essential to better administration. Indeed, organizational process is implicit in the work of most modern public organization theorists, but it is central to almost nothing (except, as noted earlier, to securing fair treatment).[31] Reengineering seeks to reestablish organizational process in the minds of managers, and to elevate it above even the level it enjoyed in the prewar period.

The single-mindedness of the reengineers is both their greatest virtue and their biggest weakness. Hammer and Champy unselfconsciously point to a single book as the predecessor to theirs: Adam Smith's 1776 classic, *The Wealth of Nations.* "We believe that the application of the principles of business reengineering will have effects as significant and dramatic as those created by Smith's principles of industrial organization," they write.[32] Like the authors of most reform-minded books, Hammer and Champy are unabashed in their enthusiasm for their idea and unreserved in touting its promise. They strongly argue, moreover, that halfway measures will always prove inadequate—which, of course, provides the perfect excuse, for any failure can be traced to a failure to reengineer thoroughly enough. Such advice, however, provides scant guidance for coping in an environment full of competing expectations. It offers little counsel about what to do when problems emerge except to try even harder, or about how to sustain the revolutionary spirit over the long haul after the revolution has ended and routine has set in.

Nevertheless, this bold advice has had widespread influence, especially on Vice President Gore's reinventing government task force, whose report indeed promised that the Clinton administration would "reengineer government activities, making full use of computer systems and telecommunications to revolutionize how we deliver services."[33] These reinventers argued the need to eliminate or consolidate obsolete and duplicative organizational structures, replacing governmental units with improved technology to link them together better. The vice president's task force, however, dropped into the usual predicament of reengineers within government: whereas the reengineering movement's theorists argue unequivocally that strategy has to drive tactics, and especially that downsizing has to be a result rather than a goal of administrative reform, the process of framing the Gore report put downsizing as a central goal, and everything else became secondary.

This contradiction became more than theoretical. Reengineers promised sweeping results, but they also argued that the process required great maneuvering room and some time to achieve those results, and they strongly contended that they could not have their hands tied by arbitrary targets. The vice president's task force thus caught itself in a dilemma: by first committing the federal government to arbitrary downsizing targets, the reinventers subverted the reengineering process that was to produce them. The political rationale for the move was inescapable—in the short term, the big headline was the downsizing. The long-run cost of the short-run gain, however, was to undermine the process that was to achieve the bold reforms.

This dilemma scarcely diminished enthusiasm for reengineering in government, however. Reformers everywhere have embraced it, at least at the rhetorical level. But even its most ardent fans admit that process reengineering is a high-risk venture. Some reports suggest that up to 70 percent of private-sector reengineering projects fail. "In the public sector," writes one expert, "there's less motivation to change, and many more structured impediments," so the odds might not be even that good.[34]

These unfavorable odds scarcely deterred the administration of George W. Bush. Soon after taking office, the president announced a new "President's Management Agenda," which proposed two major changes. One was scarcely surprising: as in all new administrations, one of its first steps was to abolish the previous administration's reforms, and the Clinton "reinventing government" office closed shop. However, the other was surprising: the Bush agenda centralized management issues in the Office of Management and Budget, or OMB (whereas the reinventing government initiative had been left as an independent center loosely attached to the vice president's office), coupled them to the budget (to ensure that federal agencies paid attention), and took an aggressive reengineering approach (quite unlike the tension between downsizing and employee empowerment that had dominated the Clinton administration's effort). "To reform government, we must rethink government," the president's management report began.[35]

The Bush administration launched a five-part plan:

1. *Strategic management of human capital.* Charging that, especially because of downsizing, the capacity of the federal workforce had fallen out of sync with the mission to be accomplished, the administration pledged to make the government's personnel system more performance-oriented.

2. *Competitive sourcing.* Convinced that much of the work currently done inside government could be accomplished better and cheaper by private companies, the administration pledged to increase the contracting out of federal goods and services.

3. *Improved financial performance.* Concluding that too many federal programs made erroneous payments that cost the government at least $20 billion per year, the administration pledged tighter financial controls to shrink the problem.

4. *Expanded electronic government.* Believing that greater reliance on the Internet and computer technology could improve government's services to citizens and reduce government's costs, the administration pledged to enhance federal **e-government** initiatives.

5. *Budget and financial integration.* Observing that too many government programs did not work well, while too often poorly performing programs were rewarded with more money, the administration concluded that "scarce federal resources should be allocated to programs and managers that deliver results."[36]

Of all the elements of the Bush management agenda, the promise to increase contracting out and to link spending with results attracted the most attention. (We return to these issues in more detail in chapters 11 and 12.) The overriding message, however, was clear. Quoting from one of Bush's speeches, the OMB report argued:

> Government should be results-oriented, guided not by process but by performance. There comes a time when every program must be judged either a success or a failure. Where we find success, we should repeat it, share it, and make it the standard. And where we find failure, we must call it by its name. Government action that fails in its purpose must be reformed or ended.[37]

The Bush management agenda was a page torn directly from the top-down, manager-centered guidebook of the reengineers. Start from scratch, focus on the mission, reorganize the organization's basic process, change the incentives—it was as blunt an assault on the federal government's management problems as had been seen since the efforts of two reform commissions headed by former president Herbert Hoover in the late 1940s and early 1950s. As always, the federal mountain proved difficult to move, but the Bush administration did prove notably successful at improving the federal government's measurement of its results.

The pressure on government to reduce costs and improve services is so severe that managers, public and private, are often willing to risk the odds of wrestling with the big dilemma of reengineering: overpromising and underdelivering. State governments, including Utah and Virginia, have been aggressively working to improve their management systems for a long time.[38] Although reengineering has barely entered the public administration landscape as more than a slogan, its promise has proved alluring. More important, it has provided a battle flag under which armies of reformers have marched. Most new elected chief executives push aside the reforms of their predecessors, but new executives now have little choice but to introduce new, bold reforms of their own. The imperative of squeezing more services from the tax base and the need to be seen as an effective, cutting-edge leader have combined to make reform an inescapable imperative.

Continuous Improvement

Other administrative reformers have taken a very different tack. In place of the discontinuous, top-down, revolutionary change that the reengineers recommend, they have advocated a more gradual, continuous, bottom-up movement. Since the late 1980s, this movement has been most strongly associated with total quality management (TQM) launched by W. Edwards Deming, but its roots in fact go far deeper.[39] Other theorists have adapted TQM to drive a broader movement toward continuous organizational improvement.

TQM builds on the notion that the quality of the product matters most. Deming contends that costs decline as quality increases. "Better quality leads to lower costs and higher productivity," one admirer explains. "The consequences for an individual company are that increasing quality leads to higher productivity, lower costs, higher profits, higher share price, and greater security for everyone in the company—the managers, the workers, and the owners."[40] Instead of looking backward into an organization to determine how to squeeze out more profit, industry should look forward to improve quality, and profit will take care of itself. Employees dominated by the profit motive tend to be unhappy, while employees pursuing quality take more satisfaction in what they do, feel more secure, and work more productively. Thus, according to the TQM movement, a total commitment to continuous effort to achieve quality in everything the organization does is the key to managerial success.

On one level, this may sound little different from the strategy of the reengineers, who care deeply about quality. The reengineers, however, believe that fundamental organizational processes too often get in the way of achieving quality and that only radical change in those processes can improve results. TQMers, by contrast, argue the need to "think small," to build from the bottom to the top of an organization.[41] In TQM, whether in government or the private sector, workers themselves are the experts who know best how to solve problems, serve customers, and improve the work.[42]

TQM, moreover, views reengineering as only one part of administrative improvement. Changing the process alone is not enough, in the view of the movement's supporters. One of its foremost advocates, in fact, has argued that process is but one of the five pillars supporting management improvement (along with product, organization, leadership, and commitment). The reengineers contend that only large-scale, fundamental change can work; TQMers, in contrast, urge managers to win big by organizing small and improving continuously.[43]

TQM, in part because of its precepts and in part because as an idea it has been around longer than reengineering, has been far more broadly deployed in American government. The Environmental Protection Agency used the technique to improve its management of a program dealing with leaking underground storage tanks, and the Air Force Logistics Command used it to improve the readiness rate of its fighter planes from 40 percent to 76 percent. In the New York City sanitation department, TQM helped to resolve labor union problems. The U.S. Department of Veterans Affairs Philadelphia Regional Office used TQM to improve service to veterans applying for loans.[44] In fact, two students of the process concluded, "quality improvement projects have resulted in significant cost savings, improved services to agency customers and clients, and measurable improvements in employee morale and productivity."[45]

The quality movement has bred a broader range of progeny than has reengineering. Some advocates delete "total" from the label to distance themselves from the zealotry that alienated some managers from TQM. Other writers have suggested modifications to the quality improvement approach based on shaping continuous improvement to help organizations learn and on having individuals assume personal responsibility for organizational results. TQM and its successors focus far more on people than on organizations.[46] They tend to be more holistic than reengineering and its cousins, more driven by a concern for operational-level workers than for top leadership, and more convinced of the ability of workers to improve organizational results as they improve their own work.

Indeed, this approach builds on a long tradition of organizational theory, beginning with Mary Parker Follett[47] and continuing through Abraham H. Maslow[48] to more modern motivation-based theorists. Arguing that personal factors, from motivation to personal satisfaction, matter as much as structure and process in determining organizational results, this tradition has always been influential, but it has never been central to organizational theory. It does not promise quite the same magic in such a short period of time as reengineering. Indeed, its basic precept is that the movement toward quality, once launched, is never finished. No level of quality is ever enough, and only the constant search for quality can keep an organization and its workers sharp.

These ideas, not surprisingly, found deep resonance in American administrative reform, from Vice President Gore's reinventing government task force to state and local government efforts. More than any other set of ideas, the continuous improvement movement drove the Gore report, which promised to "give customers a voice—and a choice" and to "put citizens first," while employees were to be "empowered to get results." Indeed, the footnotes at the end of the report are littered with references to TQM. Similar customer-based, continuous processes have driven reforms at state and local levels as well, from state-based reinvention efforts in Minnesota to sweeping strategic planning in Oregon.[49]

The discussion of continuous improvement, however, proceeds alongside the arguments for downsizing and reengineering. The advocates of continuous improvement argue quite vigorously that managers cannot be expected to take risks when their jobs are on the line. Nor, in their view, can reengineering comprehend the full range of reform needed to make any organization work better. The result, from Gore's task force to other reform efforts around the country, has been an uneasy alliance among competing ideas.

Assessing the Reforms

A side-by-side comparison of the defining ideas of these three major administrative reforms—downsizing, reengineering, and continuous improvement—reveals stark differences. Table 5.1 arrays the reforms according to the goals they seek, the directions

Table 5.1	Administrative Reform Strategies in the United States		
	Downsizing	**Reengineering**	**Continuous improvement**
Goal	Lower expenditures	Efficiency	Responsiveness
Direction	Outside-in	Top-down	Bottom-up
Method	Blunt targets	Competition	Cooperation
Central focus	Size	Process	Interpersonal relations
Action	Discontinuous	Discontinuous	Continuous

in which they are implemented, the methods that characterize them, the central focus of managers following them, and the kinds of action that drive them. In brief, they may be described as follows:

- Downsizing, enforced from the outside in by angry citizens, seeks lower government expenditures. Its methods are blunt targets, driven by the assumption that there is ample waste in government to accommodate the cuts. Downsizers seek to shrink the size of government through strategic intervention, indeed, by firing a weapon of sufficient size to signal their fundamental disdain for existing policymakers and managers.
- Reengineering seeks greater organizational efficiency by pursuing a radical change in organizational process. Top leaders, with the broad strategic sense of where the organization needs to go, attempt to harness competition and the urge to serve customers and thereby to transform their organizations.
- Continuous improvement seeks greater responsiveness to the needs of customers by launching an ongoing process to improve the quality of an organization's products. Advocates of continuous improvement believe that workers know best how to solve an organization's problems, so, unlike reengineering, continuous improvement builds from the bottom up. Cooperation among workers replaces the competition imperative, and stronger relations among employees is more important than organizational structure and process.

The fundamental precepts of each movement directly conflict with the other two. Downsizing begins with the assumption that dramatic action is required to get the attention of public managers and policymakers. Reengineers and continuous improvers, in contrast, believe that greater efficiency and smaller organizations ought

Few areas of public administration attract more attention by citizens than education. Special education teacher Cynthia Phillips prepares her classroom at Capital High School in Charleston, West Virginia.

to be the result, not the cause, of administrative action. Reengineering seeks to transform the behavior of lower-level workers by dramatic policy change at the top; continuous improvement contends that the job of top managers is to promote the conditions that will allow lower-level workers themselves to define the organization's transformation. Downsizers simply seek smaller government. Reengineers focus on process, while continuous improvers concentrate on people. Reengineers promote competition to drive behavior change, while continuous improvers argue that competition can undercut the interpersonal cooperation required to achieve quality.

Assessing the conflicts among the driving ideas of these administrative reform approaches is itself an important problem. We simply do not know which one works best. Finding out is impossible, not only because governments tend to grossly underinvest in program evaluation but also because no organization adopts any reform in its pure form. Elected officials and managers shop around among the reform ideas, selecting the elements that most attract them. As a result, managers often find themselves attempting to cope with externally imposed downsizing targets by reengineering their processes from the top down while encouraging their employees to improve quality from the bottom up. The advocates of each approach often are aghast at such hybrids, because they recognize that ideas for competition and cooperation, for topdown and bottom-up leadership, for process and interpersonal approaches, for discontinuous change and continuous improvement, rarely mesh well. The combination of such antithetical reform plans sends out contradictory signals to workers and creates conflicting expectations about results.

These contradictions, however, have scarcely prevented both public managers and policymakers from embracing the basic ideas. The labels themselves have strong symbolic appeal, and the overall goals of each technique are unassailable. Citizens and elected officials alike find alluring the promise of a smaller government, engineered with better processes and devoted to greater responsiveness to citizens and quality. The contradictions of administrative reform ideas are both fundamentally unresolvable and politically unavoidable.

All the World's a Stage

Around the globe, two undeniable truths about public administration are evident.[50] One is that administrative reform is a fixture of government everywhere—indeed, it may well be the feature that governments share more than any other. Nations that have just broken out of a generation of domination by the Soviet Union are struggling to catch up. They face tasks ranging from inventing a system of public law within which a new private sector can grow to revising a tax system to fund public programs better. Developing nations are rushing to modernize their economies, and reconstructing their governments is a critical part of that strategy.[51] More-developed nations are seeking to reinvent themselves by wringing waste out of the public sector and making government programs more efficient.

The other truth is that, despite the universality of reform, no single set of ideas is driving it. Reform of public administration is as varied as the nations attempting it. The number of basic ideas at the core of the reform movement is small, but they have come together in a remarkable array of combinations.

Downsizing carries a simple goal: shrink the public sector as much as possible, whether by selling off public enterprises, contracting out services that remain publicly provided, or imposing limits to future growth. However, although downsizing is one of the few government reforms that can produce quick cost-savings, it risks pushing government's management capacity out of sync with the job to be done. Downsizing is rarely accompanied by a restructuring of government's workforce, and, as a result, it is very easy to end up with too many of the wrong employees and not enough with the skills government needs most. Nevertheless, virtually every major government around the world has tried it, both to signal its determination to cut costs and to produce real savings.

The reengineering approaches employ both procedural and analytical tactics. Many countries have developed new processes to link operating units together better. For example, New Zealand is training top managers to develop new skills in administering programs that cut across agency boundaries. The French decentralization movement aims, in part, to bring together at the local level all those concerned with similar problems. Spain has introduced information technology to link governmental units, and e-government has spread around the globe. Meanwhile, a world-wide movement to reduce the number of government regulations, launched in the 1980s, is continuing. Countries are relying as well on information and analysis to increase leverage over administrators' actions. Governments also have spent more than a decade developing performance management systems, in which operating managers are given greater discretion in return for accountability for performance measured against agreed-upon indicators. Many nations are linking such performance measurement with reform of financial management systems to promote planning and cost control. Australia, Finland, Iceland, New Zealand, the United Kingdom, and the United States all have moved (some much further and more eagerly than others) from cost toward accrual accounting to improve accountability. Overall, the result is a widely varied collection of strategies that fly loosely under the reengineering banner.

At the same time, many nations are relying on better measurement and training systems as they seek to change the culture of bureaucrats. Performance measurement systems are designed to focus managers on results and outputs instead of budgets and inputs. Countries are working to change expectations about career paths and to enhance managers' leadership ability. Both the Netherlands and the United States have committed themselves to pushing decisions down to the lowest possible level. Many nations are also working to make public services more "customer-centered." In Canada, for example, public officials are working to "co-locate" related services so that citizens needing public services can come to one place instead of having to run from government office to office. Japan has launched a major movement to make its programs more consumer-oriented and transparent to citizens. The United Kingdom has championed "joined-up government" to improve service coordination.

All the world unquestionably has become a stage for administrative reform in the public sector. Indeed, the past decade has seen an unprecedented revolution, in both scale and breadth, in public administration. Not since the immediate post–World War II years have so many governments attempted so dramatic a reshaping of the way they do business. The postwar reforms focused principally on establishing the right structures, organized according to existing administrative orthodoxy to help governments manage their programs most efficiently; those reforms proved remarkably long-lasting. By the 1980s, however, it was clear that they had sowed the seeds of their own undoing. Earlier strategies to create strong bureaucracies for solving postwar problems had evolved into bureaucracies that too often seemed oversized, overbearing, and overcontrolling. Citizens around the world complained that the taxes they paid to governments were far higher than the benefits they received. Meanwhile, governments in less-developed countries and in newly independent countries struggled to catch up. A new, global revolution in public administration sprang up, and as it quickly spread around the world, it often echoed many of the same notes.

Conclusion

One overarching conclusion stands out sharply in this review of administrative reform in industrialized countries. Even though many different ideas have driven administrative reform and even though these ideas have contradictory ideas built into them, reformers have indiscriminately mixed and matched them with little regard for the contradictions. Moreover, because the mixtures tend to come together in very different forms, patterns rarely repeat themselves. That makes it hard to determine whether the administrative reforms work, whether some ideas work better than others, or which work best where. Reformers can and do take credit for any positive change that happens on their watch. Reform theorists do likewise, quickly pointing to inadequate application of their theories to explain any problems.

It would, in fact, be possible to use this explanation to drive a broader, cynical conclusion that administrative reform is nothing but symbolic politics cleverly practiced. Is there, under it all, anything real going on? The cynical challenge has merit, for the symbols have proven to have broad and lasting value, in the United States and around the world. Moreover, the reform movement is about vocabulary and prescription: developing a way to capture the unhappiness that so often surrounds government performance and a strategy for solving government's problems.

It would, however, be far too cynical to stop there, for three reasons. First, the reforms have genuinely produced significant effects. American efforts have had a deep, if uneven, impact.[52] In New Zealand, reforms have profoundly transformed the public sector.[53] Indeed, the reform movement has clearly proven that government *can* change, and many of these changes have made government more efficient and effective. Quite simply, management matters. It provides a symbolic language for understanding government activity and both strategies and tactics for improving results. This may not seem a very bold claim, but it is one that often is underestimated.

An equally important second conclusion is that management matters only to the degree to which it matters politically. It is unrealistic to expect that public administration can live a life independent of politics, or that its most fundamental meaning will be administrative rather than political. The internal theoretical contradictions of most administrative reform efforts matter far less than the fact that the contradictions themselves seem so often to have important political value. It is the politics of the administrative process that matters most.

Third, many of the reforms have created big and sometimes unexpected new problems that demand careful attention. Downsizing has often created imbalances in the workforce. Growing reliance on contracts with the private sector has created problems in supervising those contracts and in ensuring the pursuit of the public interest. More attention to serving the needs of citizens-as-customers has flown directly into the teeth of a basic paradox: most citizens want more public services than they are willing to pay for. If government reforms have solved some problems, they have created new ones. These new issues too often have remained unexplored— and, of course, they thereby plant the seeds of a future round of reforms.

This suggests a pair of important implications. First, public managers themselves must be ready to accommodate conflicting and contradictory demands. Their lives would unquestionably be far simpler if they were allowed to pursue a single administrative approach. For that matter, their lives would be simpler yet if they were free to follow their own ideas independently of the policies established by elected officials or the needs of citizens. But that was not what they were hired to do. In democratic societies, the fundamental mission of public managers is to reconcile such fundamentally irreconcilable demands. As the Office of Management and Budget frankly admitted in 2001:

> Though reform is badly needed, the obstacles are daunting—as previous generations of would-be reformers have repeatedly discovered. The work of reform is continually overwhelmed by the constant multiplication of hopeful new government programs, each of whose authors is certain that this particular idea will avoid the managerial problems to which all previous government programs have succumbed. Congress, the Executive Branch, and the media have all shown far greater interest in the launch of new initiatives than in following up to see if anything useful ever occurred.[54]

The job in the twenty-first century has become harder because expectations have grown even as resources have shrunk. That means that the challenges for public managers have never been higher, nor has the need for good public managers ever been greater.

Second, administrative theorists have perhaps an even more daunting challenge. To a significant degree, the central ideas of *public* administration reform have tended to come from *private* managers. Administrative theory has significantly lagged behind these startling changes. The tasks and environment of public administration are so fundamentally different, however, that no matter how suggestive private-sector reforms may be, they are unlikely to provide very sure guides for the public sector. For example, the "customer service" movement has swept the Western world, but there simply has been little careful thought about who government's customers are, how government activities can be restructured to advance customer service, how to balance the often conflicting expectations of government's multiple customers, and what other important goals might be sacrificed in the process.

Moreover, administrative theorists face an equally imposing job of reconciling the contradictions that political realities impose on neat organizational theories. Too often, like public managers who complain that their jobs would be much easier if elected officials would stop interfering in their work, theorists complain about elected officials whose contradictory messages muddy neat theories. The problem is far more with the theory than with the practice. And the pace of administrative reform around the world demonstrates just how important tackling these issues is.

Case 5

From the Front Lines of Administrative Reform: Punching through on the Bailout

Protesters heckled Lehman Brothers Chief Executive Richard S. Fuld Jr., following his October 6, 2008, testimony on Capitol Hill about his company's collapse. Taxpayers were enraged at the cost of the financial bailout, and many blamed Wall Street executives for the crisis.

On a quiet Sunday, Richard Fuld was working out on a treadmill. Another exerciser, in the corner lifting weights, noticed who was on the treadmill, walked over, and delivered a staggering punch.[1] Fuld was the head of Lehman Brothers, once one of Wall Street's most distinguished investment banking firms. In the previous eight years, he had received about $300 million in pay and bonuses, only to see the firm declare bankruptcy amid the September 2008 financial crisis. The weightlifter did what many Americans were thinking. The deeper the financial markets fell, the more investors wanted to take a shot at those who, they believed, had caused the system to collapse.

Lehman Brothers was one of several companies at the center of the crisis. An investment banking firm, its managers worked hard to raise the money that fueled the economy. When companies needed to borrow money, for everything from building new manufacturing plants to funding big mergers, they went to investment banking firms. The investment bankers took the companies' loans, packaged them, and sold them to investors. They did not have branch offices with tellers and ATMs. Rather, they operated out of big financial centers, especially New York, London, and Tokyo. Employees were the wheelers and dealers who made the deals that made so many of them rich.

The company was born when Henry Lehman, a German immigrant, came to Montgomery, Alabama, in 1844 to open a general store. It proved successful enough that his brothers Emanuel and Mayer joined him six years later. Together, they formed Lehman Brothers, which gradually grew from selling goods to brokering cotton, and they opened an office in New York. By the 1880s, they began making deals with merchants and became a Wall Street player. By its 150th birthday, it had become an international powerhouse, with new buildings in New York and London and high credit ratings to back up its success.

When the markets started going sour toward the end of 2008, however, they took Lehman down with them. Along with many other big banking and investment firms, Lehman had been a major player in the mortgage market. Financiers created new mortgages that allowed individuals to buy homes at below-market interest rates, with little or no money down. In turn, the financiers bought up millions of mortgages, packaged them, and sold them to investors looking for higher-than-normal returns. The flood of cash into the mortgage market helped fuel economic growth for much of the early part of the decade, and the deals made the investment bankers enormous amounts of money.

In 2008, however, the bubble burst. The value of homes dropped and the economy slowed. Homeowners struggled to pay their mortgages. That lowered the value of the mortgage investments that the financiers had sold. To make matters worse, investors had bought complex insurance packages (called "credit default swaps") to back up their investments, but the value of this insurance plummeted. Within just a few weeks, the foundations of distinguished old firms like Lehman and Merrill Lynch crumbled. In just a day, the Bank of America bought Merrill Lynch, and Lehman Brothers declared bankruptcy. Other financial institutions around the world carved up the pieces of Lehman and bought them at bargain-basement prices.

People borrowed money they could not afford, and financial institutions put deals together that no one really understood. In fact, some of the analysts who framed the deals were Ph.D.s in theoretical physics and electrical engineering, who were brilliant mathematical modelers but who knew little about the financial instruments they helped create. In 1999, an editorial in *Physics World* noted the drift of highly trained researchers into investment banks.[2] As an observer blogged nine years later, "What if the rocket scientists make a mess of it?"[3] They did—but they were not alone. Investors lost more than a trillion dollars within hours and the economy staggered.

As the collapse spread, first in the United States and then around the world, federal officials huddled over how best to shore up the economy. On September 6, Treasury Secretary Henry Paulson managed the takeover of the mortgage giants Freddie Mac and Fannie Mae by the Federal Housing Finance Agency. Fannie and Freddie were government corporations, chartered by Congress to help support mortgage lending but whose stock was held by private investors. (Analysts had long called them "quasi-governmental organizations," because of their peculiar place in the nether world between the public and private sectors.) Fannie and Freddie together accounted for about half of the funds in the American mortgage market, and as mortgage investments soured they found themselves in financial trouble. The Treasury concluded it had little choice but to bail them out. Eleven days later, officials from the United States Department of the Treasury and the Federal Reserve System cobbled together a bailout of AIG, an international insurance giant, and helped finance the merger and takeover of several banks. A Pasadena-based bank, IndyMac, had failed in July and had cost the government insurance system $9 billion. More bank failures followed, even after the Treasury and Fed decisions.

Treasury Secretary Paulson concluded that making decisions one financial institution at a time was not working and that the federal government had no choice but to make a giant move to reassure the markets. On September 19, he proposed a $700 billion plan in which the government would borrow money to buy "toxic mortgages," as analysts soon began calling them, from investment houses. By taking the bad loans off their books, Paulson hoped, the government could help stabilize the financial system. Five days later he sent a three-page bill to Congress to give the Treasury enormous power over gigantic sums of money. Political analysts immediately recognized that the idea of using that much government money to purchase loans from Wall Street financiers would be political poison. Rather than becoming known as an economic stabilization program, observers quickly called it a "Wall Street bailout." Members of the House of Representatives balked at the bailout and voted it down by a 12-vote margin on September 29. The stock market plummeted, with the Dow Jones Industrial Average falling 778 points, the biggest one-day point drop to that point in history.

Two-thirds of Republicans and one-third of Democrats voted against the bill because it used an enormous amount of federal debt, backed by taxpayer dollars, to fund the bailout. Throughout American history, rifts between Wall Street and Main Street had often become heated battles. In the late 1700s, Alexander Hamilton had argued for a strong and aggressive national economic policy, and populists rose up against him. Both the First and Second Bank of the United States were closed because of populist opposition. In 1896, presidential candidate William Jennings Bryan mesmerized his audience by arguing, "you shall not press down upon the brow of labor this crown of thorns. You shall not crucify mankind upon a cross of gold," in a powerful argument to help farmers against the power of bankers by increasing the supply of money. The House vote in September 2008 rejecting the bailout joined the monumental moments in American history where business and populist interests collided.

Paulson huddled with Fed Chairman Ben Bernanke to redraft the bill. To counter complaints that the bill was just a bailout and that it did not provide enough accountability over the decisions, the new draft created a Financial Stability Oversight Board to protect the taxpayers. The board comprised the Chairman of the Federal Reserve, the Secretary of the Treasury, the Director of the Federal Home Finance Agency, the Chairman of the Securities and Exchange Commission, and the Secretary of the Department of Housing and Urban Development. It required the Treasury secretary to make regular reports to Congress and to prepare periodic financial statements. In addition, the secretary would be required to recommend changes in the regulatory system. The Comptroller General, who heads Congress's auditing agency, was required to conduct ongoing oversight and to report to Congress every two months on the effort. Congress itself would establish an oversight panel, consisting of five outside experts, and the FBI had power to investigate wrongdoing. The bill gave the secretary the right to set aside standard procurement rules, as set in law, as might be necessary to move quickly to administer the bailout. The Office of Management and Budget and the Congressional Budget Office were each required to issue regular reports on how much money the bailout cost.

With the new provisions—and $150 billion in special tax provisions added to the bill to curry support—the Senate and House both passed the bill within days. It was a tough vote, not only because of the sheer size of the bailout and the complexity of the system. Members of Congress were giving enormous power to the Treasury Department at a time when the only thing certain was that a new president—and, in all likelihood, a new Treasury secretary—would be taking office in just four months. Taxpayers remained furious. The decision by AIG executives to treat seventy top salespersons and executives to a $440,000 retreat at a luxurious

California resort, just days after the Fed bailed out the company, enraged members of Congress. The $23,000 charge for spa treatments proved especially galling. "Shame on you," scolded Rep. Jackie Speier (D-Calif.).[4]

Questions to Consider

1. Once the "Wall Street bailout" label stuck, how did this change the debate over what to do and how to make it work?

2. The original three-page bill would have given the Treasury secretary enormous power with few restrictions and little oversight. What issues do you think this might have raised? Would you have voted for the bill under these circumstances? (Remember that Congress initially failed to approve the $700 billion plan—and the American stock market lost more than $1 trillion in value the same day.)

3. The Federal Reserve is an independent agency, with power to set policy on its own subject to only loose congressional and presidential control. The Treasury Department is an executive branch agency, whose secretary reports directly to the president and which administers policies as enacted by Congress. What implications for policymaking and accountability do you see in combining two such different agency structures in this bailout package?

4. The bailout was placed administratively in the Department of the Treasury. Consider other administrative structures that the government could have used. The job could have been put within the Federal Reserve, into another independent agency, into a new agency which would be closed down as soon as the job was done, or in some other structure. What are the advantages and disadvantage of each? Do you think that Congress made the right decision in the end?

5. Consider the accountability structure created for this effort. Do you feel comfortable that this system will protect taxpayers and ensure that the effort will work well? Are there alternatives you would suggest?

Notes

1. Jon Swaine, "Richard Fuld Punched in Face in Lehman Brothers Gym," *Telegraph.co.uk*, October 7, 2008, http://www.telegraph.co.uk/finance/financetopics/financialcrisis/3150319/Richard-Fuld-punched-in-face-in-Lehman-Brothers-gym.html.

2. Editorial, " 'Rocket Science': The Facts," *Physicsworld.com*, June 3, 1999, http://physicsworld.com/cws/article/print/1081.

3. Hamish Johnston, "Lehman Bros 'Killed by Complexity,' " *Physicsworld.com*, September 16, 2008, http://physicsworld.com/blog/2008/09/killed_by_complexity_1.html.

4. Peter Whoriskey, "AIG Spa Trip Fuels Fury on Hill," *Washington Post*, October 8, 2008, D1.

Key Concepts

Balanced Budget and Emergency Deficit
  Control Act (or, Gramm-Rudman) **117**

continuous improvement **114**

customer service movement **123**

downsizing **114**

e-government **126**

performance management **124**

Private Sector Survey on Cost Control
  (or, Grace Commission) **117**

reengineering **114**

reinventing government **117**

Taxpayer Bill of Rights (TABOR) **116**

total quality management (TQM) **122**

For Further Reading

Kamarck, Elaine C. *The End of Government as We Know It: Making Public Policy Work.* Boulder, Colo.: Lynne Rienner, 2007.

Kettl, Donald F. *The Global Public Management Revolution: A Report on the Transformation of Governance.* Washington, D.C.: Brookings Institution, 2000.

Niskanen, William. *Bureaucracy and Representative Government.* Chicago: Aldine Atherton, 1971.

Osborne, David, and Ted Gaebler. *Reinventing Government: How the Entrepreneurial Spirit Is Transforming the Public Sector, from Schoolhouse to Statehouse, City Hall to the Pentagon.* Reading, Mass.: Addison-Wesley, 1993.

Osborne, David, and Peter Hutchinson. *The Price of Government: Getting the Results We Need in an Age of Permanent Fiscal Crisis.* New York: Basic Books, 2004.

Pollitt, Christopher, and Geert Bouckaert. *Public Management Reform: A Comparative Analysis.* Oxford: Oxford University Press, 2000.

Savas, E. S. *Privatizing the Public Sector: How to Shrink Government.* Chatham, N.J.: Chatham House, 1982.

Wilson, James Q. *Bureaucracy: What Government Agencies Do and Why They Do It.* New York: Basic Books, 1989.

Suggested Websites

The Office of Management and Budget website (**http://www.whitehouse.gov/omb**) contains the administration's most recent management reform initiatives. The congressional Government Accountability Office (**http://www.gao.gov**) conducts independent assessments of the effectiveness of government management. The best source for tracking government reform initiatives around the world is the Organization for Economic Cooperation and Development (**http://www.oecd.org/home**).

6

The Executive Branch

Does organization matter? Some analysts say it doesn't. They dismiss organization with a wave of the hand, saying, "It's people that count. The right people can make any organization work; the wrong people can make any organization fail." Other analysts contend that "all administration is politics—persuasion, advocacy, conflict, negotiation, compromise." In fact, administration is about people, politics, and structure. The personal qualities of individuals and their skill in coping with the complex give-and-take of the political world surely affect public decisions and their results. But it also depends a great deal—far more than many observers often realize—on organizational building blocks. The roles they play are powerfully shaped by the organization's design.

people, politics, & structure

Rufus Miles, a noted Princeton University professor, concocted a "law" to explain this: according to Miles's Law, "where you stand depends on where you sit." [1] It is part of the very nature of bureaucratic politics that the secretary of defense will not advocate a drastic cut in military outlays, that the secretary of agriculture will be more concerned with farmers' income than with consumers' cost of living, and that the secretary of the treasury will be a defender of fiscal prudence and the concerns of the investment community. Governors focus on highways, prisons, the environment, and jobs. Mayors care about crime, education, and housing. The organizational setting both defines the way that government officials see their jobs and creates the capacity for them to do them.

Organizational structure cannot not make things happen. It provides patterns of relations within the executive branch that shape the odds that policies will be well designed and well implemented. [2] Before 1966, federal concern with transportation was fragmented among a number of separate agencies for rail, air, highway, water, and subway. In 1966, Congress created the Department of Transportation. Although that did not ensure coordinated policy, because political cross-pressures for funding different projects continued, at least organizational confusion was not an additional barrier. In the aftermath of the attacks of September 11, 2001, many observers both inside and outside government concluded that the nation's domestic defense system was hopelessly fragmented. That conclusion led to the creation of the Department of Homeland Security in 2003 in an effort to bring better coordination to the fight against terrorism.

In the executive branch, coordination is an important goal in the search for effective public policy. Indeed, as Harold Seidman has pointed out, coordination is the "philosopher's stone" of public administration. In medieval times, alchemists believed that if they found a magical stone, it would help them discover the answers to human problems. Coordination, Seidman argues, has the same appeal for managers and reformers. "If only we can find the right formula for coordination," he wrote, "we can reconcile the irreconcilable, harmonize competing and wholly divergent interests, overcome irrationalities in our government structures, and make hard policy choices to which no one will disagree."[3] Of course, we have never quite found the magic formula for coordination, any more than alchemists ever found their philosopher's stone. But better coordination is still sought as the answer to many of government's problems, while inadequate coordination is the diagnosis of its failures. Organization lies at the root of both.

Organization is a remarkably complex phenomenon. Perhaps all transportation concerns of the government should not be brought under a single department. It can be argued that urban mass transit should be in the department concerned with cities—the Department of Housing and Urban Development—and that regulation of transportation companies' routes, rates, and safety should be left with independent regulatory commissions rather than being placed under a political cabinet member. In fact, as some have argued, intervention by the secretary of transportation in the work of individual industries may be excessive and ill serve the public interest. To focus the air safety agency, the Federal Aviation Administration (FAA), more squarely on protecting travelers, a 1988 commission advocated taking the FAA out of the Department of Transportation. That would dramatically have reduced the size of the department, since the FAA had three-fourths of the department's employees. Despite support from the airlines and the Air Line Pilots Association, however, the proposal died.[4]

In the reorganization that followed the September 11 attacks, however, Congress did decide to move the Transportation Security Administration, which employed the government's security screeners, into the new Department of Homeland Security. Concern about better coordinating domestic security arrangements overrode arguments about keeping transportation-related agencies within the same department. But even that was not enough restructuring, according to the independent commission that examined the attacks, which concluded that the nation's intelligence agencies needed a single head to coordinate their work. The agencies involved—and the congressional committees to whom they reported—quickly pushed back.[5] Then, in 2008, several airlines were virtually shut down for days because maintenance workers had made a half-inch mistake in taping some wires. Some critics condemned the FAA for excessive vigilance. Others said that the FAA had spent years working too closely with industry and that this episode showed the agency had not regulated the airlines closely enough. (See the case study for this chapter for a fuller account of the dispute.)

Debates over the role of government structure spill over to government at all levels. In 2004 the California Performance Review declared, "California's government must reorganize to meet the demands of modern California." The report proposed a massive shift in the responsibilities of state agencies that seeks to align "programs by function, consolidates shared services and abolishes outdated entities." Pointing out that California is the fifth largest economy in the world and that the state has a rich tradition of embracing new ideas, the review nevertheless charged that

> California's state government is antiquated and ineffective. It simply does not mirror the innovative and visionary character of our state. Instead of serving the people, it is focused on process and procedure. It is bureaucracy at its worst—costly, inefficient and in many cases unaccountable.

The performance review recommended a fundamental restructuring of the 11 agencies, 79 departments, and more than 300 boards and commissions responsible for carrying out the state's functions.[6]

"Form follows function," concluded the California Performance Review's report. Indeed, the complexity of government's organizational structure mirrors the complexity of government's many, often conflicting, missions. In this chapter, we begin with an overview of the executive branch; in chapter 7 we focus on critical and persistent organizational problems. While most of our examples focus, for the sake of clarity, on the national government, the same patterns follow in the state and local governments as well.

Many analysts argue that individuals play the central role in organizations. For a variety of reasons, however, reformers contend that only reform of organizational structure can solve big problems. Structure matters—a lot. How structure affects organizations and the way they behave, however, is a deceptively complex puzzle.

Executive Branch Components

Organization by function historically has been at the core of government. Most nations have passed through four basic stages of administrative development as the building blocks of government emerged.

In the first stage, governments focused on four basic functions: (1) revenue collection, expenditures, and debt management (as with a Treasury or Finance Ministry); (2) maintenance of internal law and order (at first through the court system, later with a Justice Department or, in centralized countries, a Ministry of the Interior); (3) defense (or, separately, military and naval defense); and (4) foreign affairs. A postal service and an engineering construction service (for roads, bridges, waterways, and public buildings) also appeared early, though not necessarily with departmental status.

Stages 2, 3, & 4

At a second historical stage, most modern nations built departments around agriculture and commerce (or "trade"). At the same time, they placed other developing functions that did not fit the established pattern into a catchall department (often the Ministry of the Interior). In a third stage, dating from the latter part of the nineteenth century, functions previously placed inside the catchall departments burst out to achieve departmental status in their own right. These generally reflected government's assumption of human welfare responsibilities in such areas as labor conditions, social security, education, public health, and housing. A fourth stage developed to recognize government's responsibilities for science and technology, energy, the environment, and economic planning.

There is little consistent logic behind what makes a department a "department," which typically is the top level of the administrative structure. The federal Department of Veterans Affairs had been an independent agency but was elevated to cabinet status to recognize the contributions of the nation's veterans. ("Elevating to cabinet" status consisted of little more than changing its name, making new signs, and making its head a cabinet secretary. Little else, including the bureau's location and functions, changed.) On the other hand, the Social Security Administration was spun out of the Department of Health and Human Services to insulate its huge spending from the annual budget battles. (We explore this topic further in chapter 11). NASA and the Environmental Protection Agency both have big missions, but as agencies independent of any cabinet department they hold the same legal status as the far smaller National Science Foundation.

What explains these apparent inconsistencies? The organizational pattern of the government is not so much a structure designed as in the private sector to accomplish a mission. Rather, the government's organizational structure tends to follow political motivations: to recognize important constituencies, such as veterans, teachers, and farmers; and to signal the importance of policy problems, such as cities, transportation, energy, and homeland security. Indeed, even though we regularly refer to presidents as "chief executive" and expect them somehow to manage the vast executive establishment, the organizational structure of the executive branch is far more the creature of Congress. It tends to reflect the structure of Congress's committees and subcommittees and the political forces to which members of Congress pay the most attention. This scarcely means that presidents do not themselves pay attention to these political constituencies. President Carter led the campaign to create the Department of Education, and President Reagan championed the Department of Veterans Affairs. President George W. Bush embraced the creation of the Department of Homeland Security. At the state and local level, this combination of recognizing key constituencies and important problems likewise determines which agencies get departmental status and which do not. The decision typically is far more symbolic than managerial.

gov't's structure is built around constituencies + political motivations

Moreover, the structure of the executive branch, at all levels of government, tends to rest on a paradox. We count on the executive (president, governor, or mayor) to serve as chief executive, but the branch atop which they sit is the product of legislative action and reflects legislative interests. At the federal level, for example, creating cabinet departments requires acts of Congress. Managing their missions requires laws that create programs. Spending money requires congressional appropriations. In each case, of course, the president can propose legislation, and the president has the usual power to bargain over its content and to sign or veto the result. However, unlike the private sector, where executives can decide the mission and create the structure for the organizations they run, presidents find themselves overseeing a vast establishment over which they share control and which tends to follow the structure and political interests of the legislative branch. One recent cabinet secretary had a side office housing a treadmill; when exercising, the secretary ran long miles looking out a big window directly at the Capitol dome. That picture captures the basic relationships well. A survey of the federal government's organizational strategy paints the basic picture. State and local structure mirrors the federal strategy.

Cabinet Departments

Discussion about public administration is often confusing because of the wide variety of terms used to describe organizational units. We often speak of "bureaus," "departments," "commissions," "offices," and "agencies." We typically use agencies as the broadest, most generic designation—executive-branch units, after all, operate as *agents* of the government. The other terms refer to more specific units of the executive branch.

The term **cabinet** dates from the sixteenth century, when the English king began meeting with his closest advisers in a cabinet, or small room. (That term, in turn, has its roots in the Old French *cabine*, a gambling room, usually small and private to avoid prying eyes. It was the natural place for the king's advisers to gather.) Over time, the meeting of the king's ministers grew into a more formal structure, and the American government incorporated the concept to describe the relationship between the president and department secretaries. (*Secretary* comes from Old English and refers to a confidential officer; its clerical meaning emerged later.)

Until the 1950s, the American cabinet structure was remarkably stable. Of the fifteen executive departments now operating, three date from 1789 (State, Defense,[7] and Treasury), and a fourth (Justice) was established then as a separate office, though it did not achieve full departmental status until eighty years later. The heads of those four departments are still regarded as the **inner cabinet.** Their heads regularly counsel the president on important policy issues, in part because their missions are among the government's most important and in part because presidents tend to name some of their most trusted advisers to these positions.

In the **outer cabinet,** the Interior and Agriculture departments are over a hundred years old, and the Commerce and Labor departments date from 1903. The seven newer outer departments have appeared since 1950: Health, Education, and Welfare (HEW) in 1953 (split into separate departments for Health and Human Services [HHS] and Education in 1979), Housing and Urban Development (HUD) in 1965, Transportation in 1966, Energy in 1977, Education in 1979, Veterans Affairs in 1989, and Homeland Security in 2002.[8]

Since 2002, with the creation of the Department of Homeland Security, the federal government has had fifteen cabinet departments (see Table 6.1). They range greatly in size, from the Department of Defense, which accounts for a third of all fed-

Table 6.1	**Federal Executive Branch Departments: Estimated Outlays and Employment, FY 2009**

	Outlays (in $ millions)	Employment (in thousands)
Agriculture	94,753	91.1
Commerce	9,246	53.9
Defense-military functions	702,382	677.2
Education	63,500	4.2
Energy	23,325	16.1
Health and Human Services	738,633	60.8
Homeland Security	44,297	166.2
Housing and Urban Development	45,630	9.5
Interior	10,239	68.6
Justice	26,520	115.8
Labor	54,192	16.8
State	22,103	32.2
Transportation	71,104	55.5
Treasury	547,801	109.6
Veterans Affairs	91,815	253.4
Other	561,815	98.7
TOTAL	3,107,355	1,829.6

Source: U.S. Office of Management and Budget, *Budget of the United States Government, Fiscal Year 2009, Historical Tables,* Table 4.1, and *Analytical Perspectives,* Table 24.1

eral civilian employees, to the Department of Education, whose 4,200 employees would make it a small agency within many of the larger cabinet departments. The departments have about 90 percent of the executive branch's civilian employees. (The total does not include the U.S. Postal Service, which is a government corporation separate from regular civilian government employment.) The departments account for 80 percent of all federal spending. But federal outlays are even more concentrated than that number might suggest: 58 percent of total federal expenditures are disbursed through just three departments—Defense, HHS, and the Treasury.

Independent Agencies

Beyond the cabinet departments lie a large number of **independent agencies,** which account for about one-tenth of the federal government's employees and one-fifth of its spending. The Social Security Administration, which was taken out of the HHS in 1995, accounts for much of that spending and most of those employees. But spending and employment figures offer only a rough measure of the size and reach of these independent agencies, which range from the small, such as the American Battle Monuments Commission, to the hugely powerful, such as the Federal Reserve Board. Some are regulatory, such as the Federal Communications Commission, which sets broadcast standards and manages licenses for the nation's broadcasters, while others provide services, such as the Tennessee Valley Authority, which operates flood-control and power-generating dams in the southeastern part of the country.

Congress originally created these agencies as independent bodies to insulate them from presidential control.[9] Many of them are governed by boards that are bipartisan in membership, and board members frequently have overlapping terms that are longer than that of a presidential administration, to prevent the president from immediately changing policy on taking office. The president typically can remove commissioners only for "inefficiency, neglect of duty, or malfeasance in office" (i.e., not on grounds of policy differences with the president).[10]

These agencies have broad discretionary powers over important sectors of the American economy. By various methods (licensing, rate-fixing, cease-and-desist orders, and safety codes, for example), the **regulatory commissions** monitor major features of transportation, communications, power production and distribution, banking, the issuing of corporate securities, commodities and securities exchanges, the prosecution of unfair and deceptive business practices, the safety of consumer products, and labor-management relations. To further complicate the picture, bureaus within many departments—including the Food and Drug Administration (in HHS) and the Occupational Safety and Health Administration (in Labor)—exercise similar regulatory powers. The deregulation movement, lasting from 1975 into the 1980s, stripped some commissions of much regulatory authority over truck and *"independent agencies" not always as independent as they should be*

airline transportation and over telephone communications,[11] but most commissions remain powerful regulators. The chair of the Federal Reserve Board has been rated the second most influential person in the nation, following only the president.[12]

In recent decades, the supposed guarantees of political independence from the president have collapsed.[13] During a president's term, the president can usually appoint a commission's majority, installing members who share similar policy goals and, even more important, designating the chairperson of each commission, who often dominates the commission.[14] The president's Office of Management and Budget reviews commissions' budgets, the Justice Department controls commissions' proposed appeals of cases to the Supreme Court, and the commissions often depend on the president's support in dealing with Congress.

The result is that commissions are responsive to presidential policy concerns.[15] Nearly every president has considered asking Congress to change the structure of the Federal Reserve, whose Board of Governors, with its Open Market Committee, is regarded as probably the most independent of all regulatory commissions. Yet, "when Presidents have known what mix of monetary and fiscal policies they wanted, they usually have gotten it. . . . The history of the Fed is that of an agency rarely far out of step with the President's policies."[16]

What remains of the distinction between dependence and independence surfaces when regulatory commissions make case-by-case decisions. As the process is courtlike, intervention by the president or the president's aides is deemed inappropriate. To be sure, a commission's decisions, even though quasi-judicial in nature, may establish a policy line at odds with that of the president. Even here, though, the president's choice of commissioners and especially the chair is bound to have an impact.

The service-based independent agencies typically arose from special historical conditions. They often represent high-level commitment to particular missions that neither Congress nor the president wanted to submerge within a larger department. The Tennessee Valley Authority (TVA) dates from President Franklin D. Roosevelt's New Deal. Its status flows from Roosevelt's commitment to create "a corporation clothed with the power of government but possessed of the flexibility and initiative of a private enterprise."[17] The TVA soon brought electric power to a region that had long suffered without an adequate supply and dams to areas that had often been overrun by spring floods. Indeed, over the years it has become more like a private electric utility than a government agency. The Peace Corps, established by President John F. Kennedy, has for decades sent workers to improve the lives of people in foreign lands. The National Science Foundation funds research, and NASA runs the nation's space program.

Some of these independent agencies are **government corporations,** mostly engaged in lending, insurance, and other business-type operations.[18] Familiar examples are the Corporation for Public Broadcasting, the Federal Deposit Insurance Corporation, the Legal Services Corporation, the National Railroad Passenger Corporation (Amtrak), the TVA, and the U.S. Postal Service. They vary greatly. Some are wholly government-owned, others are mixed enterprises with both government and private investments, and yet others have only private funding. Some are meant to be profit-making; others are nonprofit organizations. Some support themselves from their revenues; others are wholly or partly dependent on appropriations. Some are integrated into the regular departments; others float freely. And they vary in conformity to standard personnel, budgetary, and auditing practices and controls.

Congress tried to impose some order on this motley collection by passage of the Government Corporation Control Act of 1945, the most important provisions of which included budgetary and auditing controls hitching the corporations to the government that created them. But Congress has often exempted new corporations from various provisions of the act. The debate on the merits turns on a conflict— between the view that every government agency needs to be integrated into the structure of responsibility and accountability of the executive branch and, therefore, needs to be held under tight control and the counterargument that government agencies ought to be managed by business-style standards of efficiency and, therefore, ought to be allowed substantial autonomy and flexibility. The debate remains unresolved.

In sum, in contrast to popular impressions, the president has great leverage over federal spending through just a handful of departments. The regulatory commissions' independence of presidential control has largely evaporated. Only government corporations can claim some degree of independence, but they are such a varied lot that making general conclusions is difficult indeed.

Bureaus

The principal operating organizations of the government are **bureaus.** This general term covers many organizations within the larger departments. Bureaus have a wide variety of titles, such as Bureau of Motor Vehicles, Internal Revenue Service, Geological Survey, Antitrust Division, Federal Highway Administration, Homicide Division, Office of Energy Research, and the famous Federal Bureau of Investigation. These operating units are so important in public administration that they give the field its name: bureaucracy—that is, a government by bureaus.

Bureaus vary dramatically in size and significance. Some of them have long historical roots—longer, often, than those of the departments in which they are currently located. The Public Health Service system traces its origins to 1798, when *bureaus*

Congress authorized marine hospitals to care for merchant seamen. Four years later, Congress established the Army Corps of Engineers and soon charged it with improving the navigability of rivers and harbors for civilian as well as military purposes. The Bureau of the Census in the Commerce Department finds its mission in the Constitution's 1789 provision requiring a decennial population census, though the bureau itself dates only from 1902. (Originally, the census was taken by U.S. marshals under supervision of the State Department; after 1850, the Interior Department did the job.) The Bureau of Land Management succeeded the General Land Office (established in 1812), some of whose records bear the signatures of George Washington and Thomas Jefferson.[19] Many other bureaus are old enough to have developed a distinctive culture—a sense of organic institutional life and a doctrine and tradition to which their staffs are dedicated. As we have seen, bureaus do not easily abandon such culture simply at the command of the temporary officials who fill top executive branch positions.

One of the first things that state and local governments did as they became organized was to set up key bureaus to deal with the safety, public health, and transportation of their citizens. At the local level, many such organizations date from before the birth of the nation. Even as he was tinkering with lightning rods and his famous stove, Benjamin Franklin created a lending library, a fire brigade, a night watchmen unit, a hospital, a militia, and a university. In his stimulating biography of Franklin, Walter Isaacson quotes the sage of Pennsylvania as writing, "The good men may do separately is small compared with what they may do collectively."[20]

@ state & local levels

American state and local governments rely on bureaus as well. Like the federal government, state governments tend to have a collection of cabinet departments and a number of independent agencies. (For example, see the organization chart for California's state government in Figure 6.1.) At the local level, however, the number of bureaus is often dizzying. As Figure 6.2 shows, the City of Miami has a vast array of departments, agencies, and other government offices. That is typical of many cities, and it greatly complicates the administrative tasks of top administrators. As complex as the organizational structure of the federal government is, the structure of many state and local governments is as intricate—or more so, especially given their smaller scale and size.

tons at local level

Field Offices

Most discussions about bureaus and bureaucracy focus on the headquarters organization. That is the source of most news, as cabinet secretaries and bureau heads hold press conferences and produce news releases. It is the center of high-level political conflict, especially when executive-branch agencies battle with legislators over programs and money.

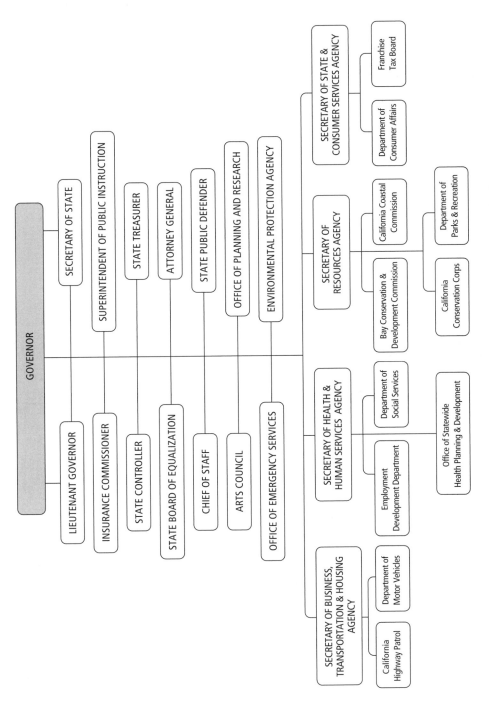

Figure 6.1   Organization Chart of Major California State Bureaus

GOVERNOR

- LIEUTENANT GOVERNOR
- SECRETARY OF STATE
- INSURANCE COMMISSIONER
- SUPERINTENDENT OF PUBLIC INSTRUCTION
- STATE CONTROLLER
- STATE TREASURER
- STATE BOARD OF EQUALIZATION
- ATTORNEY GENERAL
- CHIEF OF STAFF
- STATE PUBLIC DEFENDER
- ARTS COUNCIL
- OFFICE OF PLANNING AND RESEARCH
- OFFICE OF EMERGENCY SERVICES
- ENVIRONMENTAL PROTECTION AGENCY

SECRETARY OF BUSINESS, TRANSPORTATION & HOUSING AGENCY
- California Highway Patrol
- Department of Motor Vehicles

SECRETARY OF HEALTH & HUMAN SERVICES AGENCY
- Employment Development Department
- Department of Social Services
- Office of Statewide Health Planning & Development

SECRETARY OF RESOURCES AGENCY
- Bay Conservation & Development Commission
- California Coastal Commission
- California Conservation Corps
- Department of Parks & Recreation

SECRETARY OF STATE & CONSUMER SERVICES AGENCY
- Department of Consumer Affairs
- Franchise Tax Board

Source: California State Capitol Museum, at http://capitolmuseum.ca.gov/english/citizens/government/executive.html.

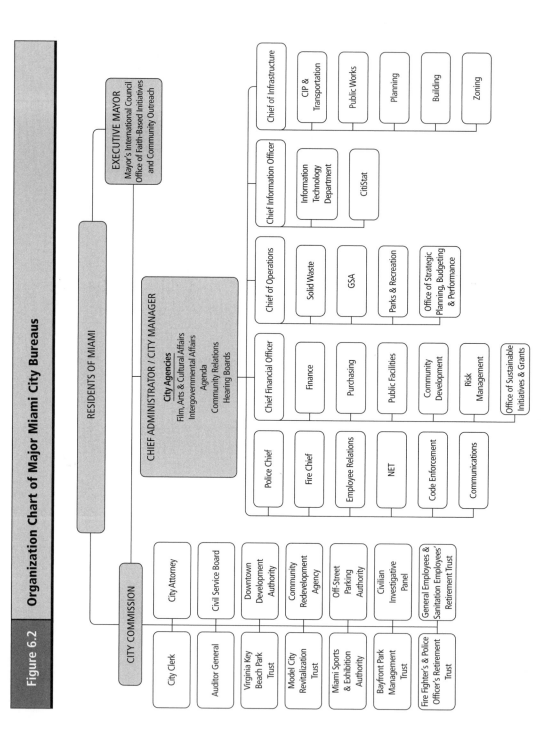

Figure 6.2   Organization Chart of Major Miami City Bureaus

RESIDENTS OF MIAMI

EXECUTIVE MAYOR
Mayor's International Council
Office of Faith-Based Initiatives
and Community Outreach

CITY COMMISSION

City Clerk

City Attorney

Auditor General

Civil Service Board

Virginia Key Beach Park Trust

Downtown Development Authority

Model City Revitalization Trust

Community Redevelopment Agency

Miami Sports & Exhibition Authority

Off-Street Parking Authority

Bayfront Park Management Trust

Civilian Investigative Panel

Fire Fighter's & Police Officer's Retirement Trust

General Employees & Sanitation Employees' Retirement Trust

CHIEF ADMINISTRATOR / CITY MANAGER
City Agencies
Film, Arts & Cultural Affairs
Intergovernmental Affairs
Agenda
Community Relations
Hearing Boards

Police Chief

Fire Chief

Employee Relations

NET

Code Enforcement

Communications

Chief Financial Officer

Finance

Purchasing

Public Facilities

Community Development

Risk Management

Office of Sustainable Initiatives & Grants

Chief of Operations

Solid Waste

GSA

Parks & Recreation

Office of Strategic Planning, Budgeting & Performance

Chief Information Officer

Information Technology Department

CitiStat

Chief of Infrastructure

CIP & Transportation

Public Works

Planning

Building

Zoning

Source: City of Miami Adopted Budget FY 2008, http://www.ci.miami.fl.us/Budget/pages/budget_books/FY08_by_Section/01_IS_Cover_to_052.pdf, p. 17.

The reality, of course, is that most government operations do not happen at headquarters but out in the field. At the federal level, for example, just 12 percent of the federal government's civilian employees are located in the Washington, D.C., metropolitan area. Seven of eight federal employees work in the field, from airport screeners and air traffic controllers to local Social Security Administration representatives and members of the foreign service in embassies around the world. Most police officers patrol neighborhoods and visit headquarters rarely. Firefighters staff their trucks at stations around the city. State natural resources workers manage water and sewer permits and oversee hunters. Highway department employees build roads, patch potholes, and plow snow. The headlines tend to focus on big battles in the capitol or city hall, but most of government's work happens in the field.

Most bureaus establish their own field organization and procedures, including the number of field districts. Most of these field structures, in turn, tend to be organized by **function,** from police precincts and fire stations to drivers license testing facilities and parks. This arrangement contrasts sharply with the **areal** or, as it is often called, **prefectoral system** of field administration that many other nations have adopted. The system dates from the Roman empire, where a member of the army had command of a region. In such a system, the country is divided into administrative regions or districts. Each region has a single national official (in some countries called a "prefect") to oversee all national field agents in the area, regardless of their departmental and bureau affiliations.[21] The French prefectoral system, originated by Napoleon, is the model most widely copied.[22]

The advantage of the area-based prefectoral system is coordination, because all government functions in the area report through a single prefect. The cost of this system is functional specialization, since the prefect is a generalist instead of an experienced specialist. The American system has tended to build instead on functions, which has the advantage of specialization—but that specialization comes at the cost of coordination of field operations.[23] As a result, a major undertaking, the war on drugs, has suffered from lack of cooperation about narcotics smuggling among the Drug Enforcement Administration (in Justice), the Customs Service (in Homeland Security), the Coast Guard (in Homeland Security), and the State Department.[24] In the area of domestic security, which involves coordination not only among multiple federal agencies but among the federal, state, and local governments as well, the problem has proven even more daunting.[25] Administrative analysts have long sought to find a way to combine place-based coordination with high levels of functional specialization, but the inherent conflicts have long proven daunting.

Several students of the problem propose that the president have a presidential representative in each region, whose Washington attachment would be the Office of

Management and Budget or a parallel agency in the executive office.[26] President Johnson's Task Force on Government Organization described the role this way:

> As Presidential representatives, they would have authority to enter interdepartmental and intergovernmental disputes on their own initiative. Through persuasion and mediation they would be expected to resolve program conflicts in the field whenever possible, referring to Washington those issues which require arbitration by the [Executive Office agency] Director or those which have sensitive political implications for the President personally.[27]

This is no prefectoral system, in which the national government has strong power over the field offices—"persuade," "mediate," and "refer" are not the verbs of power. Full-time presidential representatives could improve interdepartmental coordination in the field, but no department wants to cede any of its power to presidential coordination czars. So such plans have never gained traction.

At the state and local level, the focus of bureaus on clearly defined missions sometimes makes this problem a bit easier. Fire and police departments, for example, typically deal with immediate problems whose scale and scope are clear to all on the scene. But that immediacy does not eliminate coordination issues: on the morning of 9/11, New York City police and fire officials did not coordinate their activities well, and long-term tensions between the departments made it hard to devise new coordination plans in the months that followed the attacks. (Refer to chapter 7 for more discussion about the issues of coordination and organizational problems of the New York City police and fire departments.)

To promote responsiveness to the president's policy objectives, the president, the White House aides, and the organizations in the executive office naturally seek to impose some order on the activities of the bureaus, departments, and other major agencies. How well they succeed and what the costs of success may be are the focus of the balance of this chapter. The lessons apply not only to Washington but to state and local governments as well.

Direction of the Executive Branch

Congress creates all executive departments and most of the agencies outside departments. Control of them is exercised by Congress and the courts, as well as by the president—as is amply demonstrated in later parts of this book. Nevertheless, in seeking to understand the organization and structure of the executive branch, we may easily underestimate Congress's importance.

At the same time, however, we can be so impressed by the centrifugal forces drawing agencies away from the president that we underrate the president's comparative advantage in controlling agencies. This advantage eclipses that of many governors and mayors. As we have seen, the executive branch in some state and local governments is less a branch than a heap of twigs. In most state governments, the governor is only one of five or six popularly elected executive officials, and departments' and agencies' executive heads are often chosen by the legislature or by boards and commissions (whose members have overlapping terms) rather than by the governor. On the average, governors appoint less than half their states' administrative officials (whether with or without legislative confirmation). Some mayors in so-called weak-mayor systems have similar handicaps. More strikingly, even those in strong-mayor systems (and city managers, too) find that many functions are vested in other local governments—single-function special districts such as those for schools.

state + local CEOs usually don't have near the same amount of influence over operations as does the president

Against this background, "the executive branch" is a term of considerable substance in the federal government. The president and vice president are the only elected executive officials. The president is vested by the Constitution with "the Executive power," is directed to "take Care that the Laws be faithfully executed," and is authorized to "require the Opinion in writing, of the principal Officer in each of the executive Departments, upon any subject relating to the Duties of their respective Offices." The president is constitutionally empowered to nominate and, by and with the advice and consent of the Senate, to appoint all higher "Officers of the United States" whose appointments are not otherwise constitutionally provided for. Congress can vest appointments of inferior officers only "in the president alone, in the Courts of Law, or in the Heads of Departments." The president can remove executive officers.[28] The president's formal powers, of course, are only the beginning, but they suffice to distinguish the president from most chief executives of American governments, to legitimize the president's resistance to excessive congressional incursions, and to guide courts in their interpretations of the president's powers.

powers of president

In the 2008 presidential campaign, Sen. Barack Obama and Sen. John McCain presented very different ideas on the nation's future, as they sought to make the case on who could best serve as the nation's chief executive.

At the state and local level, the tradition of long ballots—with independent races for many key positions—complicates the problem of coordination. In many states, the attorney general and secretary of state (and sometimes other major positions as well, such as regents for the state university system) are elected independently of the governor. At the federal level, the president at least has appointment power over the key members of the cabinet; at the state level, that is often not the case. In her political biography of George W. Bush, Texas columnist Molly Ivins wrote, only partly in jest, that the Texas governor is the fifth most powerful person in the state, behind the lieutenant governor, attorney general, comptroller, and land commissioner, all of whom are independently elected.[29] In many local governments, positions such as clerk of courts, coroner, county clerk, district attorney, registrar of deeds, sheriff, and treasurer are often independently elected. The fragmentation of administrative organization means that, in many state and local governments, the chief executive may be responsible for the performance of state agencies, but many key officials with whom the executive must work have independent sources of political power.

Problems for Executive Management

Given the scope of executive appointive and removal powers and the general mandate to see to the faithful execution of the laws, the top executive might be expected to assure effective management of the executive branch. As we know, however, this expectation often falls short. Four facts help explain why.

First, top elected executives are not chosen for managerial ability, and they rarely have a lively interest in administrative matters. Presidents quite properly devote much of their energy to making foreign and domestic policy decisions and to resolving crises; they work to influence Congress and to build support with major interest groups and the public. Presidents know that they will not be judged by administrative achievements. Administration captures a president's interest mostly when he perceives its instrumental value for attainment of his policy and power objectives.[30] The same is true for governors, county executives, and mayors—except when major performance problems arise and voters threaten to exact punishment at the polls.

Second, top executives are often disappointed when they count on cabinet members (and heads of noncabinet agencies) to assure a record of administrative effectiveness. Of course, the real work of administration is performed in the departments and agencies. But problems inevitably arise. Presidential appointees, including department heads, their undersecretaries, and their assistant secretaries, often have brief tenures: two years is the median; a third remain in their positions for eighteen months or less, and only a third stay as long as three years.[31] The door is always revolving at the top of the federal executive branch, and the situation is similar in many states and cities.

[handwritten margin note: At state & local levels, power is often diluted due to several elected officials]

Furthermore, department heads rarely have a free hand in assembling their teams of subordinates: because the executive appointment system is centralized in the White House, a department's undersecretary, assistant secretaries, and even lesser officials are appointed independently of the secretary or after intense negotiations. Such negotiations often pit the secretary's need for managerial competence and prior knowledge of the relevant subject matter against the White House's quite different goals, which may include staffing offices with those personally loyal to the president and his ideology, rewarding political service in his presidential campaign, obliging important senators, and consoling defeated candidates for public office. The result is that, despite notable exceptions, secretaries have difficulty in becoming effective executives—and thus in refuting an old charge that they are the weakest links in the chain of authority. The independent base of support enjoyed by many key officials at the state and local level further complicates the problem there. Top-level administrators can rarely assemble their own team. They must find a way to work with the team that political pressures assemble around them.

Third, interdepartmental friction points have multiplied. Because departments are specialized by function, they have often developed deep disputes with other departments over who is in charge of what. What is new is the increase in such cross-cutting issues, which can be traced to the following developments: (1) governmental involvement in economic and social problems has expanded, (2) domestic and foreign policy problems have multiplied their interactions, and (3) the interdependence of factors bearing on solution of each such problem has become more widely recognized. This increasing confluence of interests has two consequences: first, because a department has relatively fewer "whole subjects" to itself, it is more difficult to hold the single department head responsible for results; and, second, what the several departments sharing a subject cannot settle among themselves must be settled, if at all, by coordination at the level of top executives. In New York City's Lower East Side, a September 2005 call for help led to a week-long battle among emergency responders. A woman suffering from Alzheimer's disease was threatening to use a knife to cut herself. A fire department ambulance arrived to help. So did a volunteer Jewish ambulance crew. But an argument erupted between a member of the Jewish ambulance crew and a police officer. The police arrested the ambulance crew member and the battle brewed into a noisy shouting match pitting the police against friends of the arrested crew member. New York State Assembly Speaker Sheldon Silver, who lived in the neighborhood, personally intervened to cool the tempers, but that only enraged the police. Some officers contended that they had been forced to give the ambulance crew member preferential treatment because of political pressure. Supporters of the ambulance crew member contended that their volunteers could have given the woman better care, because they were from the neighborhood and spoke Yiddish.

The dispute simmered for a long time. Should the city pay attention to the special neighborhood/area-based considerations in the case? Or should the functional specialization of the city's ambulance crew rule?[32]

The fourth reason that top executives do not assure effective management is that, given their time constraints and disinterest in administrative problems, the burden of top-level coordination falls on aides and staff agencies. In practice, however, these subordinates tend to undermine department and agency heads; they have little interest in improving administrative management; and responsibilities get dispersed among scores of aides inexperienced in government, infrequently in direct touch with the top executive, and poorly coordinated among themselves.

The various and disputed roles of all three major kinds of participants in overall management of the federal executive branch—the president, the president's aides and staff agencies, and the department and agency heads—become clearer as we examine the growing institutionalization of the presidency.

The Executive Office and the White House

As long ago as 1937, in transmitting to Congress the report of the President's Committee on Administrative Management (the Brownlow Committee), Franklin D. Roosevelt wrote:

> The Committee has not spared me; they say what has been common knowledge for 20 years, that the President cannot adequately handle his responsibilities; that he is overworked; that it is humanly impossible, under the system which we have, for him fully to carry out his constitutional duty as Chief Executive. . . . With my predecessors who have said the same thing over and over again, I plead guilty.
>
> The plain fact is that the present Organization and equipment of the executive branch of the Government defeats the constitutional intent that there be a single responsible Chief Executive to coordinate and manage the departments and activities in accordance with the laws enacted by the Congress.[33]

Immediately after passage of the Reorganization Act of 1939, Roosevelt established the Executive Office of the President, transferred to it the Bureau of the Budget (from the Treasury Department), and set up its other units, among them the White House Office.

From its relatively modest beginnings, with 570 employees in 1939, the Executive Office had expanded by the year 2006 to include about 1,700 employees, of whom 400 work in the White House office.[34] In addition, the White House has long had additional employees detailed to it from executive departments, many of them appointed to department rolls specifically for White House service.[35] "The swelling of the presidency," as Thomas Cronin has called it,[36] was not only quantitative.

Not only has the number of executive office employees increased, but their role has changed as well. In 1937, the Brownlow Committee proposed that six presidential assistants be added to the three White House secretaries (who dealt with Congress, the public, and the media). Contrast the powerful position of recent presidents' aides to the committee's stipulation of the role of the proposed assistants:

> These assistants, probably not exceeding six in number . . . would have no power to make decisions or issue instructions in their own right. They would not be interposed between the President and the heads of his departments. They would not be assistant presidents in any sense. . . . They would remain in the background, issue no orders, make no decisions, emit no public statements. . . . They should be men in whom the President has personal confidence and whose character and attitude is such that they would not attempt to exercise power on their own account. They should be possessed of high competence, great physical vigor, and a passion for anonymity.[37]

Surprisingly, eight former chiefs of staff to presidents from Eisenhower to Carter emphatically endorse this description of the role of presidential assistants.[38]

The White House staff is now so large, multitiered, and specialized that it is itself hard to coordinate.[39] One result of the long-term trend, says a Carter aide, is that "even those at the highest levels—assistants, deputy assistants, special assistants—don't see the President once a week or speak to him in any substantive way once a month."[40] Infighting among staff members to gain the president's ear has plagued every modern president. Even the tightly disciplined staff of George W. Bush has sometimes found itself plagued by books and newspaper stories alleging deep rifts between key advisers.

In recent administrations, order-issuing presidential assistants and their subordinates have weakened the roles of department heads by preempting their decision-making authority and by denigrating them in the eyes of departmental staff and the constituencies served by the departments. Cabinet members have complained of receiving contradictory instructions on the same day from different members of the central staff, each purporting to speak for the president. The president's chief assistants, far from being anonymous, are often more prominent in the news than many cabinet members. Far from providing only "staff assistance" (a role discussed later in this chapter), the president's assistants engage in operational activities. Given their confused roles, their numbers, the White House bureaucracy's complexity, and the priority given to meeting each day's crises, a president needs a chief of staff from the beginning of the president's administration—a lesson learned tardily by some presidents.[41] The chief of staff in turn would benefit if he or she found already in place, at the start, a small, permanent secretariat of career civil servants able to bridge the transition from one administration to another, to

[margin notes: roles have changed, too]

[margin notes: Presidential assistants represent the Pres often, since he's only 1 person]

[margin notes: WH staff too large to coordinate?]

[margin notes: infighting]

[margin notes: Pres assistants have overstepped their purpose & tried to take on presidential powers]

[margin notes: too many cooks in the kitchen]

[margin notes: this structure needs to be on Day 1]

White House Staff

provide an institutional memory, advise . . . on standard operating procedures and administrative processes, and coordinate the flow of papers . . . to and from the Oval Office, . . . insure that materials intended for the President are in the proper format, that they are seen by the appropriate people, that they are presented in a timely manner, and that presidential decisions or actions are effectively transmitted to those who are responsible for their implementation.[42]

It is not clear that these problems could be solved by shrinking the size of the White House staff. A panel of the National Academy of Public Administration urged a reduction,[43] but others have seen the staff's growth as the inevitable result of the president's increasing leadership responsibilities, which are attributed to a weakening of congressional leadership and of political parties, the rise of presidential use of public relations technologies, and other factors. "Instead of trying to wish it away," says Samuel Kernell, "the presence of a large, complex staff must be accepted as a given and its problems addressed forthrightly. . . . The President must give the staff clear direction and vigilantly oversee its performance."[44]

The pattern of White House relations with department heads tends to follow a familiar course. A president comes into office publicly committing to a strong role for cabinet members in direction of their departments. As the administration settles in, however, the president discovers that he must devote most of his time to a handful of key issues, and he depends heavily on his staff to organize information and to follow up on action. Because the president has little time for following the complex issues not on the short list of hot topics, the bureau officials charged with managing them drift away from the inner orbit. In relatively short order, a handful of cabinet officials and the president's own staff soon constitute the president's inner core, and the rest of the cabinet finds itself on the periphery—unless their issues suddenly become hot or unless they publicly stumble into an embarrassing problem.

Apart from the White House Office and the Executive Residence staff, the Executive Office of the President (EOP) includes the following major agencies (numbers of employees indicated in parentheses):

- White House Office (428)
- Office of the Vice President (18)
- Office of Management and Budget (482)
- Office of Administration (223)
- Council of Economic Advisers (24)
- Council on Environmental Quality (18)
- Office of Policy Development (22)
- Executive Residence at the White House (88)

[Margin notes:]

Size of staff needs to shrink, but has grown due to more responsibilities

Pres can become disconnected from issues that aren't crucial or "hot"

WH staff stands in for the Pres out of necessity — more than 1 person can possibly do

part of EOP

EOP (cont.)

- National Security Council (57)
- Office of National Drug Control Policy (105)
- Office of Science and Technology Policy (29)
- Office of the U.S. Trade Representative (223)[45]

Except for the minor Office of Administration and the office tending to the Executive Residence, these are all agencies with primarily policy concerns that cut across the whole government or a major segment of it and that, in most cases, must regularly occupy the president's attention. Their role reflects the concept that the Executive Office agencies should provide institutional support to the president by gathering information for him, advising him, monitoring the execution of his decisions by the operating departments, and facilitating interagency coordination. Most of the Executive Office is devoted to providing policy advice and coordination to support the president.

Of the major EOP agencies, three warrant our special attention: the **Office of Management and Budget,** the **National Security Council,** and the **Office of Policy Development.**

3 major agencies in EOP

The Office of Management and Budget ── not neutral; in the Pres' corner!

The Bureau of the Budget, established in the Treasury Department in 1921, became a part of the new Executive Office of the President in 1939. In 1970 President Nixon renamed it the Office of Management and Budget (OMB). His intent was to emphasize management concerns, but the budget has always been the driving core of OMB's mission and culture. It has long been the largest unit of the Executive Office, accounting now for over a third of the employees.

OMB $

Power is the critical factor in the OMB's (as in the earlier Budget Bureau's) value to the president and in its relations with departments and agencies.[46] At the heart of its power is its annual review of all agencies' spending proposals. OMB analyzes these proposals, makes recommendations to the president for the president's final decision, and compiles all of the requests into the budget that is formally transmitted to Congress. Later we look more closely at the budgetary process, but here we need note only three facts. One, quite obvious, is that because money is the lifeblood of agency programs, agencies care greatly about OMB's treatment of their expenditure proposals. The second, less obvious, is that budgeting is virtually the only comprehensive decision-forcing process in the executive branch; most other decision making is fragmented, episodic, and fluctuating in scope and intensity. The third is that through its review of budgets, the OMB is the only presidential agency commanding a comprehensive body of information about all the nooks and crannies of the executive branch. Together these facts mean that budgeting is a major instrument of policy.

annually reviews all agencies' spending proposals

creates the budget proposal sent to Congress

major

The same close identification with the president characterizes the following nonbudgetary functions of the OMB:

- *Legislative clearance.* Agencies are required to submit to OMB their proposals for new legislation and amendments before transmitting them to Congress. OMB uses this legislative clearance function to ensure that agencies' proposals are "in accord with the president's program."
- *Review of legislation passed by Congress.* OMB is in charge of the time-pressured review of each bill passed by Congress and sent to the president for approval or veto. It rapidly canvasses the views of all concerned agencies about the appropriate action, assures that the president is aware of those views when the president makes decisions, and often recommends what action the president should take.
- *Review of regulations proposed by agencies.* OMB reviews the principal regulations affecting the public that agencies propose to issue, a recent and powerful policy and management tool (which we discuss in chapter 13).
- *Management review.* OMB's efforts to improve administrative organization, management, and coordination in the executive branch are meant to help meet the president's responsibilities as the chief executive.
- *Intelligence about executive branch operations.* Incidental to their other functions, OMB staff members range the corridors of the principal agencies and deal with them daily by telephone and memorandum. OMB can therefore be a rich source of intelligence to the president on what is going on "out there" at all levels of policy generation and program management.

In the course of its half-century of life, the Bureau of the Budget (BOB) developed a tradition of using its resources to serve both the long-term institution of the presidency and the short-term, incumbent president—a difficult combination. Hugh Heclo has come closest to reconciling the bureau's dual mission by stressing "neutral competence" as the essential qualitative factor in its operations.[47] The strategy of staffing most positions with career civil servants and capitalizing on its prestige to attract the ablest of these helps to account for the dominance of this factor in the bureau. Higher positions were mostly filled by promotion, thus ensuring that incumbents were experienced in the bureau's work and had been socialized to the bureau's standard of neutral competence. Often the staff had served under several presidents; their time horizons were such that they could both look back on the road traveled, thus providing an institutional memory otherwise lacking in those around a president,[48] and look down the road ahead with a longer view than the four-year political calendar that otherwise tends to circumscribe the White House staff's vision.

The BOB's and OMB's tradition of service to both the incumbent president and the presidency itself declined in the 1960s and later. As the growth, specialization, and assertiveness of the White House staff in the 1960s lessened presidential dependence on the large and capable career staff of BOB, White House aides had both the time and the inclination to bypass the bureau in dealing with the executive departments. As political factors came to weigh more heavily in presidential decision making, these aides absorbed shares of advisory functions previously lodged with the nonpolitical bureau, leaving the bureau to handle procedural mechanics and to advise on only noncontroversial legislative proposals of agencies and enactments of Congress.

In the 1970s the Nixon OMB adopted a simplistic interpretation of service to the incumbent president and so undid much that had been achieved in the tradition of neutral competence and service to the longer-range institutional interests of the presidency. Nixon's OMB directors and deputy directors were political activists, making political speeches, advocating the president's policies at congressional hearings, and defending massive impoundments of appropriated funds until a number of courts ruled them illegal. A new layer of political appointees was inserted between the director and the career civil servants: in 1974 nearly two-thirds of the heads of OMB's major offices and examining divisions had one year's experience or less in their posts (compared to one-tenth in 1960).[49]

In the 1980s OMB enjoyed a resurgence of power. Reagan's first director of the budget, David Stockman, led the administration's top-priority policy of cutting spending on domestic programs; he centralized decision making in the bureau with little input from the agencies.[50] In other functions as well, some of them enhanced by legislation and executive orders, the bureau has become so fully in tune with the president's political objectives that it has recaptured roles earlier yielded to White House staff members. The dozen or so high-level political appointees in OMB, serving for one to three years, assure that the political orientation will prevail and, as the budget has become even more central to federal policy in the 1990s and 2000s, the bureau's resurgence has continued.

OMB's "M" side—its responsibility for improving administration—has been a victim of OMB's primary interest in budgeting and its growing political orientation. In one view, "Management has become largely ad hoc, short-term responses to immediate political problems. The management 'initiatives' have been geared principally toward those activities which promise a quick political pay-off or have the potential for a salutary impact on budgetary 'spending.' "[51] Despairing of invigorating OMB's management work, a panel of the National Academy of Public Administration urged transfer of that work to a new Office of Federal Management, in the Executive Office.[52] Opponents argued that such an office would lack the power over agencies that inclusion in OMB confers: when budgeting and management improvement are in a single agency, budgeting is sure to predominate, but putting the management function into a new agency could well weaken the top-level focus on administration even further by separating it from the budgetary muscle that never fails to attract the attention of executive agencies and congressional committees. That logic underlay George W. Bush's management agenda to recouple administrative efforts with budgetary clout (see chapter 5). This recurring debate demonstrates the sharp dilemmas in which central budget offices such as OMB always find themselves: the tension between long and short term, between management and budgeting, between inputs and performance.

The National Security Council

NSC

The National Security Council (NSC) was established by statute in 1947, "to advise the President with respect to the integration of domestic, foreign, and military policies relating to the national security."[53] Its statutory members are the president, the vice president, the secretary of state, and the secretary of defense; also attending the meetings as statutory advisers are the chair of the Joint Chiefs of Staff and the director of the Central Intelligence Agency, and the president may ask others to attend as well.[54] An elaborate structure of interagency committees reviews foreign, defense, international economic, and intelligence policy issues and anticipates and manages crisis situations.[55] Recommendations on policy issues are submitted to the NSC, but its role being advisory, the president retains the decision-making responsibility.

gradually gotten more power

Nat'l Security Advisor at odds w/ sec of defense & of state

Over time, the NSC has gradually become the focus of presidential foreign policy making. Indeed, that growing power has regularly rankled secretaries of defense and, especially, state. It is no wonder that some perceive that the United States has two State Departments.[56]

Nat'l Security Adviser's expanding role

The director of the NSC staff—more commonly referred to as the national security adviser—has achieved a dominant role for several reasons. The NSC staff is a unit in the Executive Office, but its director is situated inside the White House as assistant to the president;[57] there, she or he has access, briefing the president every morning and being immediately available for counsel. With staff members serving on all NSC interagency committees and monitoring cable traffic from abroad, the national security adviser has a more comprehensive knowledge of developing issues and impending crises than anyone in the departments and agencies. Interagency conflicts, common between the State and Defense Departments, make the national security adviser the only arbiter short of the president. Free of departmental loyalties, the adviser is well placed to claim primary commitment to the national interest and loyal service to the incumbent president. And, with a staff of short-term, personally selected appointees, the adviser can move with greater dispatch and attentiveness to the president's short-term goals than can the State Department, with its experienced foreign service officers and civil servants and its long-term goals of foreign policy.

In addition, the national security adviser enjoys greater freedom of action than the secretary of state because, unlike the secretary, the NSC's head is appointed by the president without Senate confirmation and is normally not subject to reporting to or questioning by congressional committees. In 2004 President George W. Bush's national security adviser, Condoleezza Rice, broke with this tradition to testify before a special commission investigating the September 11 attacks, but she did so only after long discussions intended to ensure that her testimony would not create a precedent.

If these factors explain the NSC's rise in power, they do not establish its wisdom. In the eight years of the Reagan administration there were only two secretaries of state—the second of whom served over six years—but there were six national security advisers. Such turnover can weaken institutional memory. Indeed, Lt. Col. Oliver North, the major figure in covert operations involving the sale of arms to Iran in exchange for release of hostages (a violation of both a statutory ban on military assistance to Iran and a national policy against dealing with terrorists), found the changing top-level NSC leadership a major advantage in concealing his illegal activities. As North himself became part of the NSC's institutional memory, in the process, he became virtually indispensable.[58]

Proposed remedies for such potential abuse of the NSC's power are interlocking. One is to restrict the national security adviser's role to serving as an "honest broker," charged with inviting and coordinating the policy views of the relevant departments and agencies, summing up the areas of consensus and dissensus, and presenting the president with the pros and cons of the options together with indication of the positions of the departments and agencies; this honest-broker role would reasonably extend to the monitoring of agencies' progress in implementing presidential decisions. This prescription, which excludes direct engagement in operations, conforms to the classic definition of the role of presidential assistants and, more generally, of the role of all staff assistants in the government.

A second remedy, consistent with the first, is to reestablish the secretary of state as the principal foreign policy official of the government. Some would do more, in effect substituting that official for the current national security adviser, with oversight of defense, intelligence, and international economics, as well as political affairs. A third proposal, consistent with both of these suggestions, is to shrink the size of the NSC staff—the consequence of which presumably would be greater reliance on the State Department's regional and functional specialists, whose responsibilities are now duplicated by NSC staff members. Finally, most critics of the current setup support the opinion that operational activities belong outside the White House, in the departments and agencies, accountable to Congress as well as to the president; dissenters are

how do make the Nat'l Security Advisor's role better make advisory

Part of EOP

3) office of Policy Development

likely to include the president and his entourage, who assume that the president's staff aides will move more speedily and loyally than the departments' "cumbersome" bureaucracies. In the end, it is difficult to separate the president from reliance on a close and trusted White House adviser who can always provide a final look at tough issues before the president makes a final policy decision.

The Office of Policy Development

Presidents have experimented with various arrangements for the formulation and coordination of domestic policy. Nixon began the effort to formalize matters by establishing a cabinet-level Domestic Council, "to coordinate policy formulation in the domestic area. This . . . to a considerable degree would be a domestic counterpart to the National Security Council."[59] Its staff was headed by one of the two principal assistants to the president. Since then, presidents have retained a staff for domestic policy, first called the Office of Policy Development and then renamed (in 1993) the Domestic Policy Council, but they have varied the patterns of cabinet-level involvement. Carter relied on the staff, abolishing the council; Ford and Reagan (in his first term) relied heavily on smaller interagency cabinet-level bodies concerned with particular policy domains.[60] In his second term, Reagan did without such bodies, as did George H. W. Bush and Bill Clinton, both depending instead on two cabinet-level councils with exceptionally broad jurisdictions, an Economic Policy Council and a Domestic Policy Council. In the George W. Bush administration, the Domestic Policy Council encompassed (and, indeed, was overshadowed by) several high-profile operations, including the Office of National AIDS Policy, the Office of National Drug Control Policy, and the Office of Faith-Based and Community Initiatives.

The Office of Policy Development has never played a strong role, partly because of a rapid turnover of directors (four in Reagan's eight years), partly because of OMB's overarching policy leverage, and especially because other White House aides compete with the Office of Policy Development's director for influence on domestic policy.[61] The system is not fully disciplined: many initiatives are undertaken by other actors without clearance through the councils or the office.

The domestic policy field differs from the national security field, because its environment is more political, complex, and constraining. Domestic constituencies are more troublesome than those in the foreign affairs and military areas. From time to time, presidents have even complicated the problem further by creating special White House offices to serve as political liaisons to key interest groups. Members of the policy development staff spend much of their time in "firefighting"—meeting day-to-day crises and rapidly responding to requests from the president and the president's aides. The result is neglect of the long- and middle-range planning of gov-

back-and-forth on whether or not this is even used by Presidents

weak reasons

domestic policy field is complicated

ernmental policies that is peculiarly a responsibility of institutionalized staff agencies, for it cannot be performed by individual aides in the White House itself.

E-government

The rise of desktop computers and the Internet in the 1990s led to a radically new approach to some of government's organizational problems. Government officials began recognizing that citizens did not necessarily need to come to government to transact public business. The spread of always-on electronic connections made it possible to build systems to allow citizens to file their taxes, renew their motor vehicle registrations, check on traffic congestion, obtain a police report, pay a traffic ticket, or apply for a job.

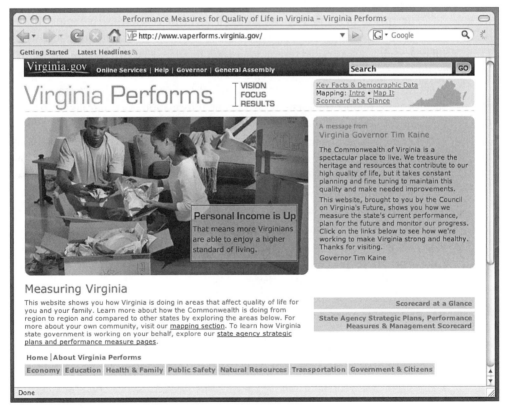

The "Virginia Performs" website, at http://vaperforms.virginia.gov, charts trends in performance of the state's executive-branch agencies.

e-government

The Internal Revenue Service (IRS), for example, increasingly encouraged taxpayers to file their taxes electronically. More than 72 million taxpayers—more than half of those sending in returns—filed online in 2006. The IRS saved money by avoiding the costs of printing, mailing, and then processing millions of paper returns. Electronically filed returns did not have to be hand-keyed into the IRS computer system, and they even proved more accurate than the paper filings, since private-market computer programs such as TurboTax and TaxCut had already double-checked the figures. Taxpayers received their refunds far faster, often in just two weeks. In Phoenix, Arizona, citizens can conduct a wide range of transactions with the government without having to leave their keyboards. They can get permits and pay taxes and fines. They can sign up for classes on irrigation and landscaping, get a parking permit or buy surplus city equipment, view city maps, or watch the city's online television channel, all at http://phoenix.gov/eserv.

The growth of e-government, as the movement is known, has rapidly transformed the operations of many government services.[62] And, although just in its infancy, it already has raised several important implications. First, e-government has tremendous potential for improving government's performance. It allows government to deliver services on citizens' own schedules, allowing them to determine when they want to conduct transactions. Processing information electronically often saves government substantial money as well.

Second, e-government can enhance the ability of citizens to connect more easily with government. Web portals such as the federal government's USA.gov and the Commonwealth of Virginia's Virginia.gov allow citizens to think in terms of the services they want to access, without necessarily having to determine in advance which government agency provides them. For example, it often takes some time to figure out that in order to obtain a passport one needs to obtain a photograph from a private photographer, visit a post office (run by the U.S. Postal Service), and submit a passport application to the U.S. State Department. On USA.gov, one can simply type in "passport" to find these instructions.

Third, the rise of e-government raises questions of access and equity. By 2008, three-fourths of Americans had Internet access, and many local libraries and other public facilities have been expanding free access to break down the digital divide. Inequalities remain, but the technological barriers gradually are falling.

Fourth, the advent of e-government also raises significant organizational questions. Freed from dependence on traditional governmental bureaucracies, e-government can operate in a loose, even invisible network, which offers the chance for creating new virtual strategies for linking government organizations. Such technology is unlikely to solve government's eternal coordination problems, but it does offer new strategies and tactics for doing so. However, in attacking the problem through infor-

implications of e-government

may help with coordination

mation systems instead of through bureaucratic hierarchies, e-government also has the potential for radically altering the existing patterns of bureaucratic behavior, authority, and power. It raises serious questions of security and privacy, to ensure that sensitive information is kept safe. Moreover, as Jane E. Fountain suggested, the e-government movement "may allow bureaucrats less opportunity to use their accumulated experience and judgment, or tacit knowledge, to consider exceptional cases that do not conform to standardized rule-based systems." Indeed, she concluded, "The state is being reconstructed as organizational actors enact new technologies to reshape relationships in the state and the economy."[63] Public officials have sometimes found themselves surprised by issues that bubble up in blogs, and they sometimes have had to scramble to deal with virtual issues that their traditional communication channels had never surfaced.

Given the tremendous changes in information technology over the past half-generation, it is hard to guess where the next generation will take us. Although, as one 2004 study concluded, "E-gov is not yet the 'killer app' among the available tools to contact government,"[64] it is clear that it will continue to develop. These technological changes will present deep and fundamental questions for the operation of government—and for its connections to citizens.

Conclusion

Formal organization is about creating channels for communication and coordination. The goal has long been to ensure continuity between policymaking and administration, but the best path is anything but clear. It is impossible to manage complex work without breaking it down into its component parts and then building strong competence in bureaus to carry it out. But any division of complex jobs into bureaus risks creating overlaps for some problems and gaps through which others may fall. Coordination is essential for administration, and organization is perhaps the most basic tool for achieving it. No matter how hard they try, however, government officials can never fully solve the coordination problem, and their efforts to solve some parts of the problem can sometimes create new and unexpected issues. The search for the philosopher's stone of coordination is never-ending.

This fundamental dilemma of administration points to two other problems. One that afflicts the whole executive branch is the interconnectedness, in the end, of all problems, which means that in order to solve any of them, top officials need to break them down into manageable parts. The other is the distinction between those who carry out government's work—"line" officials—and those who provide advice—"staff" officials. Here, too, the recurring problem of organizing the White House provides a microcosm of a government-wide problem. In the next chapter, we focus on these issues.

Case 6

From the Front Lines of the Executive Branch: Regulating the Airline Industry

On April 9, 2008, passengers waited in line at Chicago's O'Hare International Airport. They struggled to book new seats on rescheduled flights as American Airlines canceled one-third of its fleet while inspectors checked the wiring on its planes.

In April 2008, the frustration of American Airlines passengers was mounting. For three days running, the airline canceled 1,000 flights, delaying some passengers for hours and leaving others stuck in the airport without a connecting flight.

Frustration, in fact, didn't even begin to capture the mounting fury of many passengers. Dean Headly, an expert on airline service, had traveled to Washington, D.C., to announce the findings of a new study. His return back to Wichita, Kansas, where he was a marketing professor at Wichita State University, was a nightmare. His plane from Washington arrived in Dallas, Texas, but the connecting flights had all been grounded. He finally managed to secure a flight out of Dallas to Tulsa, Oklahoma, and had to rent a car to drive three hours to Wichita, arriving at 2:30 a.m. His luggage finally caught up with him two days later.[1]

The reason? Federal inspectors had discovered that American Airlines had not complied with Federal Aviation Administration (FAA) wiring safety requirements. The agency's airworthiness directives specified that groups of wires needed to be tied tightly together at intervals of no more than 1 inch. On the American MD-80 airplanes, the mainstay of the airline's fleet, the ties were one-quarter of an inch farther apart. That tiny error grounded Headly and 100,000 other angry passengers over a three-day span.

Rep. Steve Kagen (D-Wis.) said he had received a complaint from one of his constituents who had been stuck in Columbus, Ohio, for 36 hours.[2] Sara Martinez, a community relations road warrior, repeatedly got stuck in Chicago. While waiting at O'Hare Airport for any transportation back home to San Antonio, Texas, the only seat she could find was on Southwest Airlines. But that plane left hours later, out of Midway Airport, on the other side of the city. She traveled back to the center of the city to visit friends before heading out to Midway, whiling away the extra hours on her BlackBerry.[3]

Sen. John D. Rockefeller (D-W.Va.) sharply criticized the FAA for its decision. "The FAA is an agency that's spiraling downward and approaching the losing of the confidence of the American people," he said during an oversight hearing into the agency's practices.[4] American Airlines employees stood around airline gates handing out orange juice and cereal bars, but that did little to calm the shattered nerves of frustrated fliers.

Was it really worth virtually shutting down the airline, as well as grounding hundreds of flights from other carriers flying the same plane, for just one-quarter of an inch?

Aviation experts said yes. It was not a problem likely to lead to immediate problems, but if wires are not properly secured, they can chafe and fray. That can lead to cracked or broken insulation and sparks near the planes' fuel tanks. And that, in turn, can produce a catastrophic explosion.

This scenario is not hypothetical. In July 1996, TWA Flight 800 had taken off from New York's Kennedy Airport on its way to Paris. Just minutes into its flight, the Boeing 747 exploded over Long Island Sound and all 230 people on board died. Speculation swirled about the cause. Conspiracy theorists suggested that a terrorist or a wayward U.S. Navy missile had brought down the plane. However, investigators from the federal National Transportation Safety Board later concluded that an explosion in the plane's center fuel tank, probably because of a short circuit in the wiring of the plane's fuel gauge, had caused the crash.

Experts pointed to that crash as the reason for their caution about the MD-80s. The planes were old—an average of eighteen years—and FAA inspectors had found that fifteen of nineteen American MD-80s that they checked did not meet the spacing requirements. That led to the FAA's order to ground all of the planes immediately until the problem was fixed.

American Airlines had asked the FAA to allow them to make the repairs over several days while keeping other planes in the air, but the agency refused. Industry representatives quietly pointed to the original wiring regulation, issued in 2006, which allowed the airlines eighteen months to bring their planes up to standards. If the issue was so serious as to require an immediate grounding, why had the FAA permitted airlines a year and a half to fix the problem? Gerald Arpey, American's chief executive, said simply that "I think it would be fair to say the FAA is stepping up surveillance."[5]

The FAA was already under harsh criticism for its oversight of the airlines. Just a month before, the FAA found that several of its own government inspectors had collaborated with employees of Southwest Airlines to hide safety issues. The airline had flown more than thirty-five jets for thirty months past required safety inspection deadlines. FAA officials said that, when its inspectors found the problem, they should have grounded the planes. Instead, inspectors looked the other way, and when supervisors discovered the problem, they accepted the airline's promise it would ground the planes without checking to make sure. The planes continued to fly.

For Southwest, the problem lay in fuselage inspections. Later checks revealed several of the planes had developed cracks, including one that stretched 3.5 inches. Whistleblowers inside the FAA suggested that supervisors had taken a permissive stance toward the airline, especially after the friend of one supervisor joined the airline. "It is obvious that the cozy relationship" between the two friends, one FAA employee wrote, "played a contributing factor."

One member of Congress, Rep. Eddie Bernice Johnson (D-Tex.), charged that the FAA "has been pretty derelict to not follow their guidelines." She concluded, "Anytime that the relationship [between carrier and regulator] is such that it could subject passengers to unsafe conditions, it's time for something to be done about it."[6]

The FAA has long been whipsawed between charges that it was bending safety rules to help airlines protect their business and that it was paying far too much niggling attention to minor rules at the expense of the traveling public. The agency's problems in early 2008 showed that the debate had lost none of its bite.

Questions to Consider

1. Should the FAA have forced American Airlines to ground its entire MD-80 fleet until each plane was checked and fixed—or should it have given the airline a longer time to make the repairs? What issues should overseers consider in making the decision?
2. How should the FAA balance its mission to promote aviation with its mission of ensuring the safety of passengers?

3. How does the FAA's structure affect this question? Would it be better to have different agencies responsible for promoting air travel, ensure effective air traffic control, and upholding the safety of airliners—or to have one agency to oversee all things aviation? How should we balance the need to coordinate the government's relationship with the airlines and the need to ensure functional expertise in the airline industry?

Notes

1. Michelle Higgins, "Flight Chaos Shows Passengers Have Few Rights," *New York Times*, April 16, 2008, http://travel.nytimes.com/2008/04/16/travel/16prac.html?scp=2&sq=michelle%20higgins%20%22dean%20headley%22&st=cse.
2. Lisa Stark and others, "Travel Chaos," *ABCNews.com*, April 9, 2008, http://abcnews.go.com/Business/BusinessTravel/Story?id=4618579&page=1.
3. Jeff Bailey, "American Airlines Cancels 922 More Flights," *New York Times*, April 10, 2008, http://www.nytimes.com/2008/04/10/business/11aircnd.html?_r=1&oref=slogin.
4. Del Quentin Wilber, "More American Flights Canceled over Jets' Wiring," *Washington Post*, April 11, 2008, http://www.washingtonpost.com/wp-dyn/content/article/2008/04/10/AR2008041000991_pf.html.
5. Quoted by Wilber, "More American Flights Canceled over Jets' Wiring."
6. Dave Michaels, "Southwest Airlines, FAA Accused of Falsifying Safety Report," *Dallas Morning News*, March 13, 2008, http://www.dallasnews.com/sharedcontent/dws/bus/stories/DN-southwest_11bus.ART.State.Edition2.46665ec.html.

Key Concepts

areal, or prefectoral, system **155**	inner cabinet **147**
bureaus **151**	National Security Council **163**
cabinet **147**	Office of Management and Budget **163**
function **155**	Office of Policy Development **163**
government corporations **151**	outer cabinet **148**
independent agencies **149**	regulatory commissions **149**

For Further Reading

6, Perri. *E-Governance: Styles of Political Judgment in the Information Age Polity.* New York: Palgrave, 2004.

Arnold, Peri E. *Making the Managerial Presidency: Comprehensive Reorganization Planning, 1905–1980.* Princeton, N.J.: Princeton University Press, 1986.

Campbell, Colin. *Managing the Presidency: Carter, Reagan, and the Search for Executive Harmony.* Pittsburgh: University of Pittsburgh Press, 1986.

Fesler, James W. *Area and Administration.* Tuscaloosa: University of Alabama Press, 2008.

Fountain, Jane E. *Building the Virtual State: Information Technology and Institutional Change.* Washington, D.C.: Brookings Institution, 2001.

Heclo, Hugh. *A Government of Strangers: Executive Politics in Washington.* Washington, D.C.: Brookings Institution, 1977.

Hess, Stephen, and James Pfiffner. *Organizing the Presidency.* Washington, D.C.: Brookings Institution, 2003.

Nathan, Richard P. *The Administrative Presidency.* New York: Wiley, 1983.

Seidman, Harold. *Politics, Position, and Power: The Dynamics of Federal Organization.* 5th ed. New York: Oxford University Press, 1998.

Suggested Websites

The National Academy of Public Administration conducts excellent research on the management of the executive branch and of management problems within individual agencies, making its reports available on its website, **http://www.napawash.org.** In addition, the Government Accountability Office is an invaluable source for analysis of both management and policy issues; see **http://www.gao.gov.**

For information about employment trends in the federal government, see the Office of Personnel Management's "Federal Employment Statistics" web page, **http://www.opm.gov/feddata.**

There is an enormous amount of information about e-government available on the web. An excellent foundation for exploring the federal government's websites is the federal portal, **http://www.firstgov.gov.** Most state and local governments have web pages and portals as well; among the very good ones are those for the Commonwealth of Virginia, **http://www.virginia.gov/cmsportal,** and for the city of Phoenix, **http://phoenix.gov.**

7

Organization Problems

Perhaps the most widely held notion about public administration is that, all too often, it does not perform well. The news media regularly describe problems ranging from overpayment for military equipment to excessive delays in responding to fire calls. In fact, most government programs work well most of the time. Taxpayers, however, do not like paying taxes to begin with, and anything short of exceptional performance tends to disappoint those who do not receive the services they think they are entitled to—and to enrage those who hear the inevitable tales of waste, fraud, and abuse of government programs.

Of course, private-sector organizations are scarcely immune to such problems. The dumpsters behind most restaurants and office buildings are full not only of routine trash but also of major miscalculations about how the businesses located there should be run. Sometimes those miscalculations are so big that a company collapses and goes out of business. In just one week in 2008, three U.S. airlines shut down—Skybus, ATA, and Aloha Airlines. Other miscalculations are simply buried in corporate balance sheets: if the company can recover the costs of its mistakes from profits elsewhere, no one outside the organization is any the wiser. In government, however, policymakers require public administrators to manage programs, and going out of business is not an option. Problems are in public view for all to see—and to criticize. We all share in the benefits of most government programs and in the cost of all of them, so when problems emerge, we tend to take them personally. Moreover, since government tends to do the hard things that the private sector cannot or does not want to take on, problems—and complaints—about its handling of those chores are inevitable.

Indeed, the politics of the administrative process can create barriers to effective performance. As one of President Reagan's speechwriters explained,

> The only thing a government worker really needs to fear is making a mistake
> so big and so public that he becomes that rarest of objects, a government

[handwritten margin notes: "widely believed govt doesn't perform well" and "govts job is harder"]

worker fired for cause. The incentives therefore discourage creative thinking and risk taking.[1]

Beyond the incentives for individual public administrators, Jack Knott and Gary Miller point out that the very choice of organizational structure itself "is inherently political; we must ask 'who gets what?' from any institutional arrangement."[2] Any effort to chart what works in bureaucracy—and what does not—must therefore take account of both the individual and the institutional effects on bureaus: what they do, how they do it, and how they might work better.

These basic puzzles, as Herbert Kaufman recognized in 1956, have long revolved around three basic organizational values: **neutral competence, executive leadership,** and **representativeness.**[3] The quest for neutral competence calls for the creation of a highly skilled bureaucracy insulated from the political interference that can undermine efficiency. This does not mean that bureaucracy is politically unaccountable or unresponsive, but it does mean that organizational designers must take care to minimize political meddling in issues that deal with the technical parts of administration. The quest for executive leadership calls for a strong elected executive—president, governor, mayor—and strong and loyal department heads, all politically chosen. It also calls for a strong hierarchy that assures the responsiveness of organizational units to the elected executive's policy priorities. The quest for representativeness calls for organizational arrangements that respond to legislative interests and to the clienteles most affected by agency decisions.

In American public administration, we have long professed strong allegiance to each of these values; we seek them all, simultaneously and enthusiastically. But because they obviously conflict, we never quite get from bureaucracy what we want because it can never deliver at the same time all the things we ask of it. That dilemma, in turn, sows the seeds for constant discontent and for recurring efforts to restructure the bureaucracy in pursuit of a better balance among these competing values. Sometimes, in fact, we do find a better equilibrium. More often, however, we simply substitute one set of values for another and thereby set the stage for the next round of political complaint and administrative reform.

The Search for Effective Organization

Elected officials, reporters, and citizens alike are often frustrated to discover that fundamental organizational problems recur. For example, in 1988 the New York City police and fire commissioners nearly came to blows in the mayor's presence because of their departments' long rivalry over the handling of emergencies and rescues, most recently evidenced by the police having blocked fire department scuba divers from joining the search for survivors of a helicopter crash in a river. The police were jealously guarding an image as saviors, not just arresters. The city's firefighters, underemployed by a decade's 40 percent decrease in fires and therefore fearing a loss of jobs, were seeking emergency responsibilities comparable to those of other cities' fire departments and, with time on their hands, promising faster response to emergencies than that supplied by the police department. Finally, in 1990, a detailed jurisdictional treaty was negotiated between commissioners appointed by a new mayor.[4]

That treaty scarcely solved the problem. On the morning of September 11, 2001, the NYPD's helicopter hovering above the World Trade Center towers had a better perspective on the buildings' condition than did the rescuers below, but the police helicopter crew had no way of sharing this information with the fire department. Meanwhile, fire commanders in the lobbies of the two buildings discovered that radio and telephone contact with their firefighters in the upper floors often broke down. These communication problems, both technical and bureaucratic, had tragic consequences.[5] In the aftermath of the buildings' collapse, everyone pledged to ensure that such problems would not recur, but years after the terrorist attacks the two departments continued to tussle over who would be in charge of new integrated command centers. Fire officials explained that they could not risk a command structure that put their forces under the control of other officials who did not really understand firefighting; police officials voiced the same argument. These turf battles were understandable, but they only prolonged a problem that had already festered for years. Even new peace treaties failed to resolve the conflict.

Fundamental organizational problems recur with frustrating regularity in most agencies and at a variety of governmental and administrative levels. Most of these problems are old and familiar, so officials already know the best available alternatives and their consequences. When genuinely new problems arise, however, it is not

After an explosion rocked 119th Street in New York's Harlem neighborhood in 2007, police, fire, and other emergency officials worked to coordinate their response.

unusual to discover that the best alternatives developed earlier now only lead to other problems. On one level, this conundrum is immensely frustrating. On another, it helps to explain why problems recur: if there were clear and lasting solutions, they would have been applied long ago and the problems would have ceased being problems. When the government's relief efforts in New Orleans following Hurricane Katrina evaporated into chaos, it surely was not because the administrators had decided to create the biggest administrative failure in American history. Rather, it was because their efforts at collaboration stumbled on the enormous problems the storm created.

Administrators often find it reassuring to learn that the big issues with which they are struggling are not new. They can benefit from knowing that problems recur and that they have no good or easy solutions. Such issues tend to show up most often, as we shall see, in the endless search for better **coordination.** It is often hard to integrate the operations of different agencies—whether police and fire departments or foreign policy and defense departments—without sacrificing the expertise that is their very reason for existence. These recurring dilemmas can tend to make analysts and politicians alike very cynical, for the endless and often irresolvable problems invite criticism—and their very inevitability can invite political interference. Why insist on neutral competence if the approach produces recurring fits of incompetence? Why not at least reap the political benefits of harnessing the bureaucracy's power to partisan ends? American government tends to sort out these issues through four general administrative puzzles: (1) the choice among criteria of good organization, (2) interagency conflict, (3) interagency coordination, and (4) the role of staff in supporting and controlling operating activities.

Organizational Criteria

From the building blocks of organizational theory, it is easy to devise a set of reference points for choosing among alternative structures. A good example is the following checklist developed by an interagency task force:

- *Public acceptance*: the amount of trust the public places in the integrity, fairness, and judiciousness of the information and decisions a system generates
- *Adaptability*: the ability of a system to react quickly and positively to changes in (a) technology, (b) major public policies, (c) international developments, (d) state-federal relationships, and (e) economic conditions
- *Consistency of decisions*: the degree to which a system promotes consistent policy decisions
- *Professional competence*: the degree to which a system makes it easy to recruit high-caliber professionals and makes effective use of their talents

- *Participation, representation, and diversity*: the degree to which a system provides for diverse public inputs to governmental decision making
- *Effective database*: the capacity of the system to generate, verify, and use reliable and complete information
- *Cost and timeliness*: the reasonableness of the expense and time required by a system to yield decisions
- *Promotion of private efficiency*: the extent to which a system avoids unintended pressures on private decision makers in their choices of technology, markets . . . , and other decisions
- *Accountability to the president*: the extent to which a system provides clear lines of executive authority
- *Accountability to Congress*: the extent to which a system provides clear data for congressional review and clear charters of responsibility for carrying out congressional mandates
- *Compatibility with state regulation*: the extent to which a system . . . fosters effective state-federal relationships[6]

Whether we start with this checklist or devise one of our own, one crucial point must be understood. As the task force concluded, "each criterion is important, but all cannot be satisfied at the same time. For example, it is unlikely that a system that yields the fastest decision and also entails the least administrative cost would rank among the best systems with respect to public credibility or public participation. In short, the design of any [organizational] system requires compromises and tradeoffs among desirable attributes."[7]

Because there is no formula to guide these compromises and tradeoffs, we might seem to be adrift on a sea of uncertainty. But this feeling exaggerates the difficulties, and it may invite us to minimize rationality because we cannot maximize it, by resorting to simple hunches or sloppy analogies. The most common of these alternatives is to reach for insight from the private sector, but as we have seen, that experience often does not translate well. The President of the United States is unlike a corporation president, the Congress unlike a corporate board of directors, and the departments and bureaus unlike profit centers that manufacture products and aim for short-run profitability. Sometimes college faculty members make the same mistake in a different way, by assuming that the collegial relations they enjoy in their departments can be transferred to government organizations.[8] Team building can often be an important tool, but it cannot provide enough leverage for directing a large and complex organization. Effective management and organizational design demand a sharper understanding of the underlying issues, especially of the forces shaping conflict among agencies.

Interagency Conflict

The criteria we have quoted from the task force omit any concern for how an organization fits with other organizations at the same level. Yet the very choice of organizational structure often creates the foundations for conflict with other agencies. Spotless windows were a rarity in Queen Victoria's nineteenth-century English palace, because their outside cleaning was under the control of the Woods and Forests department, their inside cleaning was the responsibility of the Lord Chamberlain's department, and the work schedules of the two departments often did not match.[9]

Interagency conflict puts a heavy burden on higher officials, who must attempt to coordinate the agencies under their charge. Such coordination is important to prevent two kinds of errors: duplication, whereby two agencies waste resources trying to do the same thing; and gaps, whereby problems fester because no one is in charge of solving them. One set of conflicts stems from a mismatch of organization bases identified by classical organizational theory: purpose, process, clientele, and place. An organization built on one such base will not fit well with organizations built on other bases; this is especially the case when some are purpose-based and others clientele-based. Another set of conflicts arises when, as is often the case, all relevant organizations have the same base—that of purpose.

Purpose Versus Clientele

The Department of Health and Human Services (HHS) is basically a purpose-based organization, serving the general population through health research and health system financing, welfare programs, and food and drug regulation, among other functions. The Department of Veterans Affairs and the Interior Department's Bureau of Indian Affairs (BIA) are clientele-based. In effect, these single-clientele agencies perform or arrange for many services for their special groups that HHS would otherwise provide for them under its general, national programs. The Department of Veterans Affairs, for example, runs its own hospital system, while BIA has its own health clinics—and each operates independently of other health agencies organized by function at the federal, state, and local levels.

If some agencies are purpose-based and others are clientele-based, certain predictable consequences follow. HHS cannot claim to speak for a unified health or welfare policy, nor can it assert coordinative authority to assure equity and consistency in policy execution. Many of the horror stories of administration—two or three agencies building hospitals in a locality that needs only one, agents of the purpose-based Federal Bureau of Investigation (FBI) being killed while serving warrants on an Indian reservation that is under the jurisdiction of the clientele-based BIA—are results of the crisscrossing of jurisdictions of purpose-based agencies and clientele-based agencies.

A reverse situation occurs when a clientele-based agency embraces inconsistent or even contradictory purposes. Many industry-based agencies seek both to promote and to regulate the industry they are assigned to monitor. For instance, the federal agencies regulating both atomic energy and mines tended to emphasize promotion over control in their respective spheres. Congress feared that the Atomic Energy Commission was neglecting protection of the public health and safety, so it moved that function to a new Nuclear Regulatory Commission and placed nuclear energy promotion in the new Department of Energy. The goal of the Interior Department's Bureau of Mines was "to stimulate private industry to produce a substantial share of the nation's mineral needs in ways that best protect the public interest,"[10] but it also was the agency charged with protection of the health and safety of coal miners through mine inspections and enforcement actions. Mine disasters and the resulting public outcry led Congress to transfer the protective function from the Interior Department to a new Mine Safety and Health Administration in the Department of Labor.

In both the nuclear energy case and the coal mining case, the fostering of an industry and the constraining of it by enforcement of health and safety standards had proven to be incompatible tasks for a single agency. Similarly, state officials have often been criticized for trying both to control and to promote gambling out of a single agency. State environment and parks agencies regularly find themselves caught up in battles between anglers and hunters, who want easy access to the best sporting spots, and environmentalists, who seek to protect scenic parks from snowmobilers and all-wheel-drive vehicles.

Function Versus Area

Other conflicts often grow up within departments. Many departments, from local public works agencies to the federal Forest Service, are organized by both function and area. The State Department, for example, manages the nation's foreign policy, and its traditional internal organization is by region and country. But alongside the place-based offices are functional bureaus focused on politico-military affairs (e.g., arms control), human rights and humanitarian affairs, environmental and scientific affairs, economic and business affairs, refugee programs, and international organizations. No functional issue, whether managing the oceans or aiding refugees, stops at any nation's border. However, it is usually difficult to get action on any functional problem without dealing with individual nations, and that requires the department's traditional country-based structure. One of the secretary of state's most difficult internal management jobs is setting the ongoing balance between these conflicting— and inevitable—approaches.

In chapter 6 we saw that, in contrast to some other countries, the U.S. government has no prefectoral officials to coordinate the field activities of the various departments and agencies within each of the country's regions. Each functional department has field offices, but coordination among the field offices of different departments in the same region occurs irregularly, at best. For decades, presidents have tried different approaches to this coordination problem, from creating uniform regions to establishing super-regions where high-level officials would have the power to pull related agencies together. The individual departments, not surprisingly, have always resisted the more aggressive efforts. Coordination of federal programs, always difficult in Washington, remains a tough problem in the regions.

Conflicts Among Purpose-Based Agencies

Of course, conflicts also occur among purpose-based departments. The names of departments commonly identify a general field of activity; they do not necessarily convey a sharp sense of purpose. The nation's oldest federal departments—State, Treasury, Defense, and Justice—all have fuzzy missions that have evolved radically since these departments were first created. New issues emerge constantly, from the pressures of the Cold War following World War II, the fall of the Soviet Union, pressures on the dollar along with inflation, the rise of the European Union, and the sudden intrusion of terrorism on American soil. These departments, and many others, have worked to adapt their mission and their work, often with little structural change to match the shifting purposes.

Rather than clear and constant purposes, departments focus on core activities that define the issues that they—as well as their leaders and most important constituencies—pay the most attention to. In addition to regarding departments as having assigned fields of activity and concern instead of clear and constant purposes, we can further relax our expectations of harmony by emphasizing that they have core activities instead of firm jurisdictional boundaries.[11] Border warfare among departments occurs along the lines of these core activities, and it happens because borders are not and cannot be precise. Policymakers are eternally tempted to solve these problems by overhauling organizational structure. Such reorganization can remap the terrain, but it can never put an end to border wars. For the agencies involved, jurisdictional boundaries remain crucial.

For example, the commission investigating the September 11 attacks found substantial problems in the sharing of information among the nation's intelligence agencies. Indeed, some observers speculated that the attacks might have been prevented if the government had made better use of the information it had collected before the attacks. (Of course, the attacks were on a scale that most officials had not imagined, and the real meaning of much of that information became clear only after the fact. Indeed, that is why the 9/11 Commission ascribed a large part of the problem to a "failure of imagination.") To reduce the likelihood of future attacks, Congress insisted on creating a new Department of Homeland Security that would answer the constant call to devise a better way of connecting the dots among any pieces of information that might be collected. When the new department emerged from Congress, however, it did not include any of the nation's key intelligence bureaus: the Central Intelligence Agency, the National Security Agency, the Defense Intelligence Agency, or the FBI. Each of them had waged a fierce behind-the-scenes battle to retain its independence—contending that it had critical core activities that would be compromised through a merger—and each one had emerged victorious. So the department that had been prompted by the urgent need to connect the dots ended up leaving most of the dots where they were, with only relatively weak new interagency councils to strengthen information sharing among them.

Interagency Coordination

Conflict among agencies is thus inevitable. Conflict can undermine coordination—yet, as we have seen, coordination is the core of administration. Executives therefore resort to a variety of methods to manage and moderate conflict among agencies.

Coordination is a *horizontal* activity, in that it seeks to draw related agencies together in common purpose. But because no agency willingly surrenders control over its core activities to another, coordination rarely happens naturally or easily. Coordination requires intervention by a coordinator, which is a *vertical* activity.

Horizontal Cooperation

Cooperative approaches depend on the willingness of agencies to come to agreement with one another. Four methods stand out:

1. Thousands of **interagency agreements** ("treaties") have been negotiated between the concerned agencies to establish specific boundaries and, therefore, to clarify which agency will do what without interference from the other.
2. Hundreds of **interagency committees** at the cabinet, subcabinet, and bureau levels exist to promote collaboration in jointly occupied areas.
3. Under the **lead agency formula,** one agency is designated to lead and attempt to coordinate all agencies' activities in a particular area. Ironically, even though the lead agency formula does not work well in the federal government, federal agencies often require state and local governments to create lead agencies as a condition of federal grant programs.
4. A **clearance procedure** links agencies horizontally by requiring that an agency's proposed decisions in a subject-matter area be reviewed, whether for comment or for formal approval or veto, by other interested agencies.[12]

Experience with these devices is not reassuring. Consensus can resolve minor matters, but truly important issues are far harder to solve, and the hard decisions often do not get made.

The Joint Chiefs of Staff (JCS) was, until 1986, simply an interagency committee of the Defense Department, suffering all the disabilities of such committees despite its critical responsibilities. As it was made up of a chair, the army and air force chiefs of staff, the chief of naval operations, and the Marine Corps commandant, the key problem was that the armed services' chiefs were more attentive to their services' interests than to the common defense. Four studies initiated by presidents (Kennedy, Nixon, Carter, and Reagan) roundly assailed the Joint Chiefs as appallingly deficient both as an adviser to the secretary of defense, the National Security Council, and the president[13] and as the supervisor of the regional Unified Commands that execute military operations.[14] In 1978 the study for President Jimmy Carter reported:

> [T]he nature of the organization precludes effective addressal of those issues involving allocation of resources among the Services . . . except to agree that they should be increased without consideration of resource constraints. . . .
>
> Other contentious issues in which important Service interests or prerogatives are at stake tend to be resolved only slowly, if at all. These include basic approaches to strategy, roles and missions of the Services, the organization of Unified Commands, joint doctrine, and JCS decision-making procedures and documents. . . . Changes in these contentious areas are approached reluctantly and deferred to the extent possible.[15]

As long as the members were coequal and unanimity was normally sought (common features of an interagency committee), no solution was possible, despite the high stakes involved. One comic-opera example: because the services had incompatible communications systems at the time of the 1983 invasion of Grenada, American land forces could not call in air support from the navy's nearby ships until an army officer used his AT&T telephone calling card to reach Fort Campbell, Kentucky, on a regular telephone; officials at the base, in turn, called in air support.

Finally, in 1986, Congress reformed the system, following closely the recommendations of the President's Commission on Defense Management.[16] A new member, designated vice-chair, was added to represent the views of the Unified Commands. The chair was named, in place of the Joint Chiefs, as the principal military adviser to the president and the secretary of defense. And the Joint Staff, composed of specially chosen and trained officers, was placed firmly under the chair. New communications systems have eased the coordination problem somewhat; so, too, has the creation of commands in regions around the world to unify operational control of the different armed services. Nevertheless, interservice rivalries remain one of the enduring realities of the armed forces.

Narcotics-control efforts illustrate the common situation when neither horizontal cooperation nor vertical coordination seems a likely solution. With the efforts split among many agencies, the Reagan administration's principal recourse in its "war on drugs" was the creation of multiagency committees.[17] Congress, disenchanted with this weak response, provided in the Anti-Drug Abuse Act of 1988 a "czar" for coordination of narcotics-control efforts, and President George H. W. Bush appointed the first such officer.[18] But if largely voluntary cooperation was no answer, neither, apparently, is a major shift to vertical coordination through a high-level antidrug director. Such directive power as the czar has over bureaus concerned with narcotics conflicts with department heads' authority over the same bureaus. Most such bureaus—including the Customs Service, the Coast Guard, the FBI, the Immigration and Naturalization Service, and the Central Intelligence Agency—have core functions unrelated to narcotics control. Nonetheless, the czar idea is a popular one; it has been advanced, for example, as the cure for the bureaucratic fragmentation that has impeded response to the AIDS crisis.[19] When Congress and President George W. Bush concluded that the White House Office of Homeland Security was not powerful enough to ensure the coordination needed in the area of domestic security, they abandoned the czar approach in favor of a more traditional department, but this arrangement was challenged when the 9/11 Commission countered that a cabinet-level intelligence czar was needed to bring the nation's disparate foreign intelligence together into a coherent picture.

At a tunnel stretching under the Detroit River from Detroit into Ontario, Canada, U.S. Border Patrol agent Mindi Thomas checked a freight train. Government officials had discovered that commercial vehicles were responsible for carrying a substantial amount of contraband across the border.

Vertical Coordination

A principal function of hierarchy is to provide vertical coordination of agencies or of subordinate units having substantial, shared interests. It stands in strong contrast to reliance on the weak reed of horizontal cooperation. The two patterns are quite different: in the vertical coordination model, two warring agencies are brought to book by the organizational superior of both—not a specialized "czar" but a person with the formal authority to impose a decision and to monitor the agencies' compliance with it. Although their willingness to use authority may be limited by many influences, superiors have the strong motivation to ensure that the programs under their responsibility proceed effectively.

The vertical dimension involves much more than arbitrating jurisdictional controversies. Superiors constantly must be on guard to protect themselves—their time, energy, and political capital—against the eagerness of subordinates to push up the ladder tough decisions that they do not wish to make themselves. It can often be tempting for officials to pass along these "hot potato" issues, some of which may involve problems of coordination and some which may hinge on sharp political conflicts. But superiors who allow their subordinates to shirk responsibility in this way can soon find themselves swamped by decisions that they do not need to make. That can make it harder for them to focus on the matters that truly do require their time, and it can make effective coordination more difficult by allowing decisions to rise up above the level at which the issues need to be resolved. If lower-level officials pass the buck instead of working through the problems they encounter, those problems often remain unresolved and the superiors become overwhelmed.

The horizontal and vertical dimensions of the hierarchy interact. If the executive branch had a hundred departments of roughly equal scope, three consequences would be predictable. First, border disputes would multiply beyond the president's (or governor's or mayor's) capacity to arbitrate. Second, individual department and agency heads' access to the president would be curtailed. Third, cabinet and subcabinet committees would be too large for effective discussion and decision (or advice to the president). Hence the tendency of governments everywhere is to hold the number of major departments and agencies to a range of between ten and thirty.[20] (A major exception is the New Zealand government's reforms in the 1980s, which swelled the number of departments to almost forty. However, critics soon began making precisely the point that so many departments hindered the coordination of the government's programs.)

Each department needs to be more than an assemblage of bureaus. If the bureaus in a department do belong together, most jurisdictional battles and policy disputes among them can be kept within the family, with the department head serving as arbitrator. This explains the search for an organizing principle for each department. It is also the rationale most often invoked when policymakers reorganize the executive branch.

However, seeking to limit the number of major departments—to keep the span of control reasonably small—exacts a price. The fewer the number of units at each level of the hierarchy, the greater must be the number of hierarchical levels. The State Department, for example, has a steep pyramid, which contributes to the department's reputation for being highly bureaucratic. The greater the number of hierarchical layers, the more supervisors (instead of employees producing results) the organization must have. Multiplying the levels also increases the distance between the operating levels that do the work and the top-level decision makers. One consequence is that there are more points at which upward-flowing proposals may be blocked and information may get distorted, and at which downward-flowing instructions may be drained of clarity and force. Another consequence is delay, simply because transmission and consideration of messages through a long series of offices take longer than their passage through a short series. Here again, we confront a tradeoff situation for which no general formula provides a solution.

The Role of Staff

So far in this section we have focused mainly on *operating* agencies. That is, we have dealt with people and units responsible for managing programs that directly serve or regulate the public. However, agencies also rely on other kinds of units to promote their functioning. The standard term for these support units is **staff activities,** which are contrasted with **line activities,** or operating activities. Many observers use the word staff to refer to all government employees. More properly, however, employees who manage the core functions of an agency are *line* officials. Those who support their work are *staff* officials.

There are, in fact, three different staff roles: **staff** (sometimes called **pure-staff**), which provides general support to the agency's line activities; **auxiliary staff,** which provides a basic housekeeping function; and **control staff,** which helps top officials secure leverage over the organization. The first two facilitate operations; because persons performing these activities assist in the organization's mission, classical theory prescribes that they should have no power to command the line officials. The third activity is quite different, for control necessarily imposes restraints on the freedom of line officials. This intersection of functions can often create deep conflict, because these staff activities can—and often do—conflict with line activities. We will return to that point shortly.

The Pure-Staff Role

Aides who work in the pure-staff role serve as the top manager's eyes, ears, and auxiliary brain. They assist the manager by originating ideas; gathering, screening, and appraising ideas from others; organizing information for decision making; and keeping track of how quickly relevant agencies execute decisions. In 1975 the Commission on Organization of the Government for the Conduct of Foreign Policy captured well the staff function by listing the appropriate tasks of the president's staff, and then strictly defining their scope:

- Identify issues likely to require presidential attention
- Structure those issues for efficient presidential understanding and decision—ensuring that the relevant facts are available, a full set of alternatives are presented, agency positions are placed in perspective
- Assure due process, permitting each interested department an opportunity to state its case
- Ensure that affected parties are clearly informed of decisions once taken, and that their own responsibilities respecting those decisions are specified
- Monitor the implementation of presidential decisions
- Assess the results of decisions taken, drawing from those assessments implications for future action

The defining characteristic of these tasks is that they embody staff responsibilities rather than line authority. They provide assistance to the president, not direction to department officials other than to convey presidential instructions. There should be only one official with line responsibility in the White House, and that is the president himself.[21]

All top officials need staff assistance. The more complex the organization's mission and structure, the more these officials need help in gathering information, interpreting details, anticipating issues, weighing decisions, and following the process of implementation.

The staff function is so important that it often becomes institutionalized in an organizational unit. For example, in addition to his immediate aides in the White House (the "White House staff"), the president has a number of staff agencies, all charged with informing, assisting, and advising the president. Department heads and bureau chiefs have not only "assistants to" themselves but also organizational units concerned with program analysis, planning, and research. At least at the departmental level, staff units abound, with such assignments as legislative affairs, international affairs, intergovernmental affairs, public affairs (media relations), civil rights and minority affairs, small business, and consumers. In some departments, all or most of the assistant secretaries have primarily staff roles cutting across the bureaus, instead of, as in other departments, being line officials, each supervising a group of bureaus. At the state and local levels, the pattern is precisely the same, on a smaller scale.

Higher officials, of course, receive information and recommendations directly from their subordinate operating officials, as well as from their staff aides and staff units. There are two differences between these patterns of advice. First, the heads of subordinate operating units tend to speak just for their part of the organization, not for the organization as a whole, while the official's staff aides are expected to share the broader perspective of the supervisor and to look to organization-wide issues. Second, subordinate operating officials tend to be immersed in day-to-day operational problems, and, as a result, they tend to have a short time perspective. The official's staff aides, in contrast, are expected to take a long-range view, but given the need for aides to politically protect their superior, short-term crises often drive out long-term perspectives. The staff often finds itself heavily immersed in helping superiors deal with immediate crises and other urgent tasks that the top official views as useful. That can divert the staff's attention from long-range issues—and, as we have seen, if long-range planning does not happen here, it sometimes does not happen at all.

Auxiliary and Control Roles

Organizations rely heavily on auxiliary activities to assist in accomplishing their mission. For example, most governments have central purchasing offices, building management offices, accounting offices, libraries, public affairs offices, and publications units. These jobs tend to be grouped together under the "administrative support" or housekeeping label.

In addition, organizations rely on control activities to monitor performance and enforce compliance with standards and procedures. Federal departments, for example, have inspectors general, who are given broad authority to investigate and report to the secretary and to Congress on suspected fraud, waste, and other mismanagement. In addition, personnel and budget offices enforce civil service laws and regulations as well as appropriations acts and other restrictions on expenditures and programs. Technically, such control activities are not the same as the exercise of line authority. But, technicalities aside, operating officials invariably resent the so-called meddling of controllers, particularly when the controllers divert the operators' energies from what they view as the vigorous implementation of programs to side issues, such as compliance with burdensome red-tape requirements.

Power Building

Despite the formal separations, these staff activities often tend to acquire a kind of power that is difficult to distinguish from command authority. All such persons and units control a scarce resource.[22] A staff assistant often has close and regular access to the chief of the unit; such "face time" is a highly prized resource because it can often bring considerable influence on the chief's decisions. Lower-level line officials, therefore, may cultivate the staff assistant, attempt to learn the assistant's views, and then try to send along proposals that seem likely to get the strongest support. Often, too, a top official facing many tough problems may tell a staff assistant to "just handle it"—staff aides can thus find themselves sliding from a supporting role into the chair of command. Indeed, cabinet officials regularly complain that the president's staff aides often take it on themselves to issue orders and to screen them from the president.

Or take auxiliary units. The volume of work flowing to such a unit is often so great that its head must decide which issues from which operating units should receive priority—this is real power. Operating units assigned low priority may be severely frustrated in trying to meet their own and their superior's deadlines.

The problem of power building is aggravated by a tendency for staff, auxiliary, control, and command functions to be formally combined in the same organizational unit. A department's procurement office may be charged not only with supplying the operating units' needs for a host of supply and equipment items (an auxiliary activity) but also with the authority to question and revise operating officials' specifications of their requirements (a control and command activity). However obvious it may be that line officials cannot be left free to purchase whatever strikes their fancy, the mixing of auxiliary and control functions is a critical organizational problem. Few events annoy operating officials more than finding that their decisions about what kinds of supplies they need have been overruled by purchasing-office employees, who often sit far from the front lines of the agency's activities.

Moreover, these staff, auxiliary, and control activities recur throughout the organization's hierarchy, which multiplies the points of conflict and creates networks of staff officials, thus further enhancing their power. Consider, for example, the network of attorneys inside most federal agencies. Each department has a general counsel, and all lawyers acting as lawyers are appointed by the general counsel and are members of the Legal Division, a staff agency. (Lawyers filling other posts in which they are not acting as lawyers are not included.) Most lawyers are assigned to other bureaus within the department, and they tend to have their offices in these bureaus, but they are part of the Legal Division and so they constitute an interconnected network spread throughout the department. If problems occur—if, for example, one of the bureaus proposes to do something that in its lawyer's view runs against the department's legal policy—the lawyer can report the infraction through the Legal Division's hierarchy. Beyond this legal-control function, however, the Legal Division constitutes a communications network that can keep all its members as well as the general counsel informed about what is happening throughout the department. This information, in turn, makes the general counsel a valued adviser to the department head, who greatly needs information that supplements what comes up through the chain of command from the bureau chiefs.

Staff activities thus differ from line (or operating) activities because their role is one of assistance to, not command of, line officials. However, this seemingly neat line is often breached, for there is a powerful temptation to give orders as well as advice.

The information network can give staff officials a powerful additional source of leverage, and even the apparently modest roles of auxiliary units can be converted to an excuse for the exercise of power. The power of control roles, even though they are based mostly on statutes and regulations, can be magnified at the expense of program managers. The linkages among staff assistants and their units throughout the bureaucracy reinforce this power.

Solutions?

The issues of staff roles discussed above are deep-seated problems that have long resisted easy solutions. The pure-staff activity has one obvious solution: a clear sense of the role of staff by those who serve in these positions. Staff persons need to practice self-restraint: to resist the temptation to go into business for themselves as decision makers and order-givers. Of course, such restraint is often in short supply—it is never easy to fade into the background while others take center stage, and it is hard to push away the temptations of power that the staff role offers. Though the staff-line distinction is not quite as simple as a difference between thinkers and doers, the cultures of most operating organizations tend to put those who "do" into a more valued position than those who "think."

Auxiliary units inevitably exercise specialized control functions, especially because top executives rarely want to invest their scarce time in housekeeping disputes. However, program administrators are often frustrated by the necessity of sharing control over the tools for their jobs with outside auxiliary units that are committed less to program results than to managing the support apparatus, from personnel rules to purchasing standards. As we see in chapter 8, substantial efforts have been made to give operating managers more control over their personnel systems.

For example, prompted by the Clinton administration's reinventing government campaign, many governments have launched purchasing card programs, which allow managers to use the equivalent of credit cards to purchase supplies—from computers to pencils—from private vendors. Government analysts have found that office-supply superstores often offer prices as good as those the government used to be able to negotiate for its bulk purchases, and the purchasing cards produce further savings by allowing government managers to avoid the cost of buying, storing, and shipping the supplies. Although there have been occasional abuses of these cards, they have helped to circumvent some of the old dilemmas that plagued the government purchasing system.

Reorganization

If so many problems are structural, why, some wonder, cannot they be solved by reorganizing the structure? To be sure, executive restructuring efforts have regularly sought to rearrange the organizational building blocks to enhance symmetry, improve the logical grouping of activities, reduce the executive's span of control, and strengthen administrative coordination and efficiency. These efforts fall largely within the neutral competence approach to organization, and they have long been an important part of administrative strategy.[23]

However, a major part of the answer is that government structure is about much more than efficiency—which makes reorganization a political act. The structure determines which issues get priority and which get more priority than others. It also defines which constituencies get prime attention, strengthens government's ability to serve some of these constituencies, and creates powerful symbols about who and what matter most. If a program finds itself in an unsympathetic department, it is less likely that the secretary will fight for adequate financing and staffing; as a result, the program will likely be anemic. If a program is placed far down in the hierarchy, the director's access to the secretary will be impeded; recommendations about resources and policy will have to move through a chain of intermediaries, who may block or change them. And when those in immediate charge of a program feel like orphans in their department, they will look elsewhere for support—for funds, staff, and program autonomy that enables them to ease the burdens of abandonment. All of these issues become folded into the value of representativeness that Herbert Kaufman identified as one of the basic approaches to organization.

For much of the past half-century, the president had statutory authority to propose to Congress reorganization plans creating, renaming, consolidating, and transferring whole agencies (other than cabinet departments and independent regulatory commissions) and any of their component units. By means of an ingenious legislative veto arrangement, the president's plans automatically went into effect in sixty days if neither house adopted a resolution of disapproval. In 1983, however, the Supreme Court ruled unconstitutional the legislative veto provisions appearing in hundreds of statutes, including the Reorganization Act.[24] Now, for a president's reorganization plan to be effective, it must be approved by a joint resolution of the two houses passed within ninety days after receipt and signed by the president (or, if vetoed because of amendments, overridden by Congress).[25] The odds were thus significantly altered: before 1983, the congressional engine's idling in neutral gear was to the president's advantage; now it is to his disadvantage, because he needs the House and Senate gears engaged and propelling action in his favor. Even his proposal for a statute would have a better chance of success, as Congress could pass it any time over a two-year session, whereas it would have to approve a reorganization plan within ninety days. As a result, the presidency lost some of its executive power, marking one more major difference in how the executive function differs between the public and private sectors: private executives can change the structure of their organizations whenever and however they like.

The president therefore has a choice of tactics in seeking to restructure. He can seek comprehensive reorganization of the executive branch through an act of Congress. This option is always tempting, but whatever the potential benefits, it always stirs opposition among the interest groups happy with the existing structure—or at least fearful that change might shrink their power and access. Alternatively, the president can focus his reorganization efforts on a small handful of bureaus. Sometimes the opposition to such limited action can be just as fierce, however, and it always has a less sweeping impact. In fact, some bureaus have proven immovable despite long histories of recommendations for restructuring. Reformers have long sought to move the Forest Service and the civil works functions of the Army Corps of Engineers to the Interior Department, in order to bring natural resource functions together in a single department. But both bureaus—and the interest groups supporting them—have fought off every effort to move them.

Comprehensive Reorganization

Nearly every one of the presidents from Hoover through George W. Bush has supported some kind of sweeping overhaul of the executive branch. (The exceptions were Kennedy and Ford, because of their short tenures in office, and Reagan, who focused his efficiency efforts on privatization.)[26] Even conservatives like George W. Bush could not resist shuffling the organizational boxes. He championed the largest single government restructuring since the end of World War II with the creation of the Department of Homeland Security. Why, given the odds against them, do presidents bother? Some come into office trailing campaign promises to "straighten out the mess in Washington." Some—such as Hoover and Carter, who were engineers—are personally disposed to fix the machinery of government. Some seek popular credit for trying to improve administration—which may count for more politically than would actual achievement, to which they may devote little energy. Some—including the former senators Truman, Nixon, and Johnson, who knew Washington well—may perceive existing executive branch organization as poorly serving the national interest and propose to invest political capital in structural reform.

But political capital is precious. It can quickly evaporate or shift to urgent policy initiatives. Nixon's ambitious plan (described below) failed to win congressional support, and then the Watergate scandal exhausted his political capital. In 1967–1968 Johnson, losing his political capital because of the Vietnam War, neither allowed publication nor advocated adoption of the recommendations of his Task Force on Government Organization. Of Roosevelt's far-reaching proposals, only two were initially approved by Congress.[27] In fact, no president except Truman has obtained much of what he wanted. Two joint congressional-presidential Commissions on Organization of the Executive Branch of the Government, each chaired by former president Herbert Hoover, reported in 1949 and 1955.[28] Over half of the First Hoover Commission's recommendations were adopted, mostly because of Truman's support and a massive public relations campaign. The Second Hoover Commission focused not on major reorganization but on procedural techniques and policy issues—especially how to reduce the government's competition with and regulation of private enterprise. Nevertheless, "not a single major permanent program resulting from the years of depression, recovery, war, and reform was abolished as a result of this prodigious inquiry."[29]

In 1971 President Nixon proposed a drastic reorganization of the executive branch.[30] The plan would have retained unchanged only the four departments whose heads had sat in George Washington's cabinet. Four departments—Commerce, Labor, Transportation, and Agriculture—would be abolished, most of their work being absorbed by a wholly new Department of Economic Affairs. Three newly named and reconstituted departments—Natural Resources, Human Resources, and Community Development—were to supersede the departments of the Interior; Health, Education, and Welfare; and Housing and Urban Development. But Congress refused to act.[31]

President Carter mounted a heavily staffed reorganization study in the Office of Management and Budget, but the results were modest compared with his ambitions; the successes were establishment of the Department of Education (fulfilling a campaign pledge) and the Department of Energy, partition of the Civil Service Commission into two new agencies, and reorganization of the president's Executive Office.[32] President Reagan then futilely sought abolition of the new Education and Energy Departments he had inherited from Carter but proposed no overhaul of executive branch structure.[33] He relied instead on his cabinet councils for harmonizing interagency concerns, on centralized control of agency behavior, on procedural changes, and on political appointments.[34] Congressional Republicans returned to the battle in 1995 and fought—yet failed—to eliminate the Commerce Department. The creation of the Department of Homeland Security in 2002 moved more agencies (twenty-two) and more employees than any restructuring since the creation of the Department of Defense, but critics continued to battle over its effectiveness.

Among state governments, comprehensive reorganizations have come in waves, a recent one centered in the 1965–1978 period when twenty-one states recast their executive branches. Usually the governor initiates the enterprise, and it is achieved through constitutional amendment or statute or both.[35] But the taste for reorganization has scarcely gone away, as shown by the massive 2004 proposal to restructure California's state government.

Obstacles to Reorganization

There never is a shortage of reorganization ideas, both because there always are ways of improving government's efficiency and because past reorganizations create the seeds for new ones. However, relatively few of these ideas are translated into action. Those that are adopted tend to be specifically focused in response to perceived performance failures that are believed to be products of poor organization. And either they promise enough benefits to command political support or they are so unproblematic as to avoid stirring political opposition. Some eventually succeed because they have recurred so often over the years that objections lose credibility.[36]

Indeed, *stability*, not fluidity, characterizes the executive branch's organization.[37] How do we account for this? Most obviously, departments and bureaus resist the loss of functions—they seek to protect their turf. Moreover, although some agencies act imperialistically to expand their realms, protecting what they have tends to be more important.[38] How do agencies attract enough political support to discourage and even defeat reorganization initiatives by presidents and department heads? The answer is that congressional committees and powerful interest groups create powerful counterpressures. Mustering their forces against a reorganization effort is not difficult; often they spring to arms without much invitation.

Congressional committees have their own jurisdictions to protect. One reason that Congress failed to support Nixon's major reorganization effort was dissatisfaction with the impact it would have had on legislative committees: on average, over nine existing committees would have had fragmentary jurisdiction over each of the four new departments. The alternative would have been a reorganization of the committees' jurisdictions to match those of the departments—not a prospect to warm the hearts of the leading members of committees marked for abolition or loss of jurisdiction.

Interest groups that perceive potential harm to their members throw their lobbying strength against proposed reorganizations, allying themselves with the affected departments or bureaus and with sympathetic congressional committees. The result in many a field of government action is an **iron triangle** or "unholy trinity" that resists any reorganization initiative that may threaten its members' shared interest.

Indeed, a major study of government reorganization by Craig W. Thomas teaches several important lessons. First, although we are very long on rhetoric about reorganization, we are very short on evidence. We simply know relatively little about whether changes in government organization do in fact improve efficiency. Second, many efforts to improve the efficiency of government through reorganization have been disappointing: contracting out and creating government corporations can improve efficiency if the changes are well managed, but a common approach—

centralizing authority—often does not improve efficiency. Third, despite the constant rhetoric about trying to reorganize government agencies to improve efficiency, "reorganizations are profoundly and unavoidably political and we should accept them as such."[39] If reformers promote reorganization to produce more efficient and more effective government, they cannot be sure of achieving the results they desire. But they can be sure of provoking deep political battles over the structure and symbols of government programs.

This strong array of forces against restructuring might be overcome more often if theory and experience pointed to one best way to organize the executive branch or to organize a department or bureau. The difficulty is that when those knowledgeable about administration are asked how to organize, they are likely to answer, "It all depends." This does not mean that anything goes. It does mean, as we have seen, that there are persistent organizational problems, several alternative approaches to them, and in any given situation a set of variables that carry different weights from those they carry in another situation. It also means that a reorganization's potential for achieving its objectives is contingent on so many factors that neither theory nor experience can assure that the potential will be fulfilled. Finally, it means that the ultimate choice often depends more on political values than on administrative efficiency.

Conclusion

Responses to organization problems usually seek to promote one or another of the values of neutral competence, executive leadership, or representativeness. All such responses may be infused with politics, concerned for "who gets what?" This is true, we saw, even of responses in the neutral competence mode, because administrators, including careerists, prefer arrangements that protect their units' powers and that assure their control of subordinate units.

Organization problems, we have discovered, are not chance or unique occurrences. Instead, they fall into patterns that not only persist or recur but that, more remarkably, also appear at all levels—presidential, departmental, bureau, and field service. The fact that conflict seems structurally embedded, that things go wrong even when neutral competence is the goal, stems from such causes as organizers' failure to take account of the salient criteria: incompatibilities among the organizational structures; the fuzziness of jurisdictional boundaries; the weakness of voluntary, horizontal cooperation; the limits of vertical, hierarchical coordination; and the frustrations that operating officials suffer because of the controls exercised by staff and auxiliary aides and units.

Although organizational structure seems passive, it should now be clear that it both results from and shapes the dynamics of organizational conflict. Those dynamics are political, reflecting the claims of president and Congress to achieve respectively the values of executive leadership and representativeness, and reflecting as well the clash of interest groups.

As later chapters show, public organizations, however passive they appear in the abstract, come to life when perceived as sets of human beings, both civil servants and political appointees, as wrestlers over policy issues and battlers for scarce budgetary resources, as agents attempting to implement service and regulatory programs that have ambitious and contradictory goals, and as bureaucrats adapting to the control efforts of executive, legislative, and judicial overseers. We turn to those puzzles in the next section.

From the Front Lines of Organization Problems: Sunset, the Golden Retriever

Case 7

For Sunset, a golden retriever, the news from Sacramento wasn't good. Sunset was training to be a guide dog for the blind, and Sunset's instructor, Katryn Webster, was worried about the future of her organization, Guide Dogs of the Desert.[1] The state government agency regulating Sunset's training and Webster's organization, the Board of Guide Dogs for the Blind, was threatened with radical surgery as part of Gov. Arnold Schwarzenegger's new reform agenda, the California Performance Review. Webster wasn't sure whether the performance review's recommendations would permanently change the way her organization worked and how effective it could be.

When he took office in January 2004, Schwarzenegger had launched the performance review program to eliminate waste and inefficiency across state government, in part by reducing perceived duplication in "common functions and responsibilities."[2] The "Gubernator," as he quickly became known to fans of his action-hero movies, faced a huge budget deficit and a public tired of taxes. At his inauguration, he told California's citizens that his performance review could help slash the state government's costs. "I plan a total review of government—its performance, its practices, its cost," he announced.[3]

Luckily for Sunset, when Schwarzenegger's task force made its recommendations in August 2004, it didn't suggest wiping out the guide dog program and the board that supervised it. Rather, it recommended moving the Board of Guide Dogs for the Blind to a new Department of Education and Workforce Preparation—along with similar changes for more than a hundred other boards and agencies that existed independent of the governor's cabinet agencies. But the board's supporters worried the move would weaken their work.

"Guide dogs take you into situations where it's life and death," explained board member Jane Brackman, "and if a dog isn't properly trained or a student isn't properly trained, people die."[4] Sheila Styron, president of Guide Dog Users, Inc., a national support organization, added, "Most people in California are pretty happy with the board." In fact, she said, "We would like it to become stronger."[5]

Eliminating the board, its supporters said, would not even save the state any money—Schwarzenegger's primary goal in launching the performance review—because license fees paid the board's $141,000 annual budget. (Blind persons received the dog and training for free; donations covered the $50,000 per dog training cost, and the three dog training academies that exist in California paid the state a license fee to be allowed to operate.) The board was scarcely a megabureaucracy soaking up taxpayer dollars; its seven members each received $100 (plus expenses) per day for the board's eight meetings per year.

Tough government rules were necessary, said the board's supporters, because some dog owners were taking unfair advantage of the special rules for guide dogs. Dog lovers with perfectly good eyesight, for example, were pretending their pets were guide dogs in order to be able to bring them into restaurants. The board performed important advocacy work as well, such as its effort to get an exemption for guide dogs from Hawaii's rule that dogs moving into the state had to be quarantined (to protect Hawaii from importing rabies). Moving the board into the new department, supporters feared, would make it harder to provide dogs for blind citizens. "You put a small entity like the state board into an overarching entity," explained Mitch Pomerantz, disability law compliance officer for Los Angeles, "and it's going to get lost in the shuffle."[6]

Critics, however, wondered if the California Performance Review had gone far enough. "They did not go to the hard step and say, 'Do we really need to regulate guide dog trainers any more?'" explained Julie D'Angelo Fellmeth, administrative director of the Center for Public Interest Law at the University of San Diego.

"They're not shrinking government. They're just getting rid of multi-member boards and substituting bureaucrats."[7]

The battle over the Board of Guide Dogs for the Blind played itself out hundreds of times over. Schwarzenegger's task force recommended that a third of the state's 339 independent boards and commissions should be moved into executive departments, whose heads would report to the elected governor.

Three months after the California Performance Review issued its report, experts told a public hearing that any kind of reorganization would be difficult to implement. Every board had its own constituency, and every constituency feared its influence over policy would be watered down if the location of its organization was moved lower on the bureaucratic food chain. While searching for billions of dollars of savings, Schwarzenegger and his aides had to decide how far to take a reorganization battle that promised few budgetary savings.

On the other hand, if he were to step back from the reorganization battle, Schwarzenegger risked undermining his credibility. In his 2004 State of the State Address, he had pledged to "blow up boxes" in restructuring the state's bureaucracy—eliminating those boxed entries that are so ubiquitous on organizational charts. Toward the end of his first year in office, however, a *San Francisco Chronicle* editorial said his term so far had mostly been a "victory parade." His performance review offered 1,200 recommendations—ranging from improved electronic government to changing vehicle registration from once a year to once every two years—which would produce $32 billion in predicted savings. "Is he serious about government reform, or is the package for political show?" the newspaper asked.[8]

Schwarzenegger was vastly underrated when he took office. Critics laughed off his campaign as an ego-driven publicity stunt. But they had grossly underestimated the wily Austrian bodybuilder and chess player. In case after case, he proved a far more effective governor than his critics had expected. After a few months, "The only people who are still laughing at Governor Schwarzenegger," explained Jack Pitney, a Claremont McKenna political scientist, "are the people who don't know California."[9]

But his performance review remained a long-running battle. Schwarzenegger had called California's sprawling government bureaucracy "a mastodon frozen in time." He saw the job of restructuring the state bureaucracy—including the Board of Guide Dogs for the Blind—as a symbol to demonstrate his determination to transform the state government. He knew that the reorganization, in itself, would not save billions. But if he could prevail, it would strengthen his hand in controlling the state government apparatus and in enhancing his ability to win on even bigger policy battles later.

The battle had enormous implications, many observers of California politics believed. "To me, the jury's still out on whether he wants real, true structural reform," said Joe Canciamilla, a Democrat from the State Assembly. "If he's not willing to take that step, with the popularity he's had, the independence he's had, the public statements he's made—if this governor isn't willing to go there, it ain't gonna happen for several generations."[10]

The battle hinged on the supervision of Sunset, the golden retriever, and thousands of cases just like it throughout the state and its government.

Questions to Consider

1. Consider the case for moving independent boards and commissions into executive branch departments. What are the advantages and disadvantages of such a restructuring?

2. Government reformers often lose their appetite for the political battle over restructuring the executive branch when they discover that, in itself, it tends to save little money. Are there other reasons to consider such reorganization? Do these reasons make a strong enough case to make it worth the political fight, even if there are not big savings in tax dollars?

3. Consider the symbolic value of an organization's structure. What roles do such symbols play, on both sides of the reorganization battle?

4. Just how much do you believe that the *structure* of government bureaucracies really matters? If you were an adviser to Governor Schwarzenegger, how much of his political capital would you advise him to invest in the battle over eliminating so many quasi-independent boards and commissions?

Notes

1. See the organization's website, http://www.guidedogsofthedesert.org/index2.html.
2. See the report of the California Performance Review (2004), http://cpr.ca.gov.
3. Ed Mendel, "Optimistic Governor Doesn't Pull Punches," *San Diego Union-Tribune*, January 7, 2004, A1.
4. Jordan Rau, "Guide Dog Board Threatened," *Los Angeles Times*, November 29, 2004, B1.
5. Ibid.
6. Ibid.
7. Ibid.
8. "Now, Governor's Second Act," editorial, *San Francisco Chronicle*, November 17, 2004, B10.
9. Alan Greenblatt, "Strong Governor," *Governing*, July 2004, http://www.governing.com/articles/7schwarz.htm.
10. Ibid.

Key Concepts

auxiliary staff **189**

clearance procedure **185**

control staff **189**

coordination **180**

executive leadership **178**

interagency agreements **185**

interagency committees **185**

iron triangle **197**

lead agency formula **185**

line activities (or operating activities) **189**

neutral competence **178**

pure-staff **189**

representativeness **178**

staff **189**

staff activities **189**

For Further Reading

Arnold, Peri E. *Making the Managerial Presidency: Comprehensive Reorganization Planning, 1905–1980.* Princeton, N.J.: Princeton University Press, 1986.

Fesler, James W. *Area and Administration.* Tuscaloosa: University of Alabama Press, 2008.

Kaufman, Herbert. "Emerging Doctrines of Public Administration." *American Political Science Review* 50 (December 1956): 1059–1073.

Knott, Jack H., and Gary J. Miller. *Reforming Bureaucracy: The Politics of Institutional Choice.* Englewood Cliffs, N.J.: Prentice Hall, 1987.

National Commission on Terrorist Attacks upon the United States. *The 9/11 Commission Report.* New York: Norton, 2004.

Thomas, Craig W. "Reorganizing Public Organizations: Alternatives, Objectives, and Evidence." *Journal of Public Administration and Theory* 3 (1993): 457–486.

Suggested Websites

The federal government has moved its extensive guide to its organizational structure, the *U.S. Government Manual,* online to **http://www.gpoaccess.gov/gmanual/index.html.** This is an invaluable resource for understanding the structure and function of governmental agencies.

The California Performance Review (**http://cpr.ca.gov**) has assembled thorough background discussions about the organization of the state's government; it is a useful guide for understanding the structural issues faced by the nation's largest state. Many other state and local governments regularly explore how best to improve their operations, and a web search will uncover the most recent initiatives they are taking.

PART III

People in Government Organizations

The Greek historian Herodotus is credited with the earliest version of the U.S. Postal Service motto, "Neither snow, nor rain, nor heat, nor gloom of night stays these couriers from the swift completion of their appointed rounds." But he could not have foreseen the many demands placed upon the modern postal worker or the postal worker's need to cope with challenges from UPS, FedEx, and other private delivery services. An organization's structure might provide the system's overall framework, but Herodotus would surely agree that people are the core of public organizations no matter what the century.

Doing the public's work—and doing it well—requires finding good people, recruiting and keeping them, ensuring that they work according to the laws and norms of a democratic society, and creating incentives for the highest levels of performance. To pursue all these goals, democratic governments have long relied on a **civil service system** (pursuit of the civil, that is, nonmilitary, functions of government) to minimize political tinkering with the administrative process.

However, finding the right balance between minimizing political abuse and maximizing political responsiveness is an ageless problem. This section examines the foundations of the civil service system, the system of political leadership that guides it, and the efforts to reform it. The quality of the system's people determines the quality of the government's work, regardless of whether the pursuit of that work encounters snow, rain, heat, or gloom of night.

8

The Civil Service

The first man to set foot on the moon was a civil servant, an employee of the National Aeronautics and Space Administration. The day was one of enormous national celebration, and President Johnson designated the day of the moonwalk a holiday for the government's employees. Some employees had jobs that required them to work anyway, but civil servants working on holidays receive premium pay (twice their regular pay). Neil Armstrong's work that day did not qualify, however, because he was at the GS-16 level in the federal civil service system, and Congress forbade provision of premium pay for workers above the GS-15 level. So, despite the enormous risk Armstrong took with that "one small step for mankind," as he put it, providing him premium pay would have been illegal—even though the eight-year moon-landing program had spent $25 billion to put him there.[1]

This unusual case illustrates four basic facts about government civil service systems. First, the government *hires employees by merit.* Armstrong went through a highly competitive process to qualify to be an astronaut. Second, government workers receive *pay according to their position,* not their personal characteristics. Astronauts with Armstrong's level of training qualified for the GS-16 level of salary. Third, once in the civil service system, workers receive many *protections from political interference and dismissal,* in exchange for their agreement to abide by laws and regulations. This safeguard stems from a long-held belief that there is not a Republican or a Democratic way to do most technical government jobs but a best way of doing the government's work—such as flying a moon lander—and the government's workers ought to do what needs to be done in the best way possible. Fourth, in doing their work, government's workers have an *obligation to accountability,* to administer the law to the best of their ability regardless of their personal views. For Armstrong and the nation's other government workers, this meant keeping the public interest paramount. Civil service laws and procedures vary among the federal, state, and local levels, but these basic principles guide the civil service system throughout government.

These principles date from the Pendleton Civil Service Act of 1883, but they capture some enduring tensions. The scale of government's work is so vast, and the potential for political interference so tempting, that standard rules are inescapable. Different people in similar situations need to be treated the same. However, the morale and performance of the workforce depends on reinforcing the motivation of individual workers; being treated as simply one among thousands may quiet a worker's zest for superior performance. Balancing the system's need for a broad set of rules and the individual's need for motivation is a central problem of the civil service.

And why is the civil service so important? As we see in this chapter and the next, the quality of the government's performance depends heavily on the skill of the people working in it. Much of government is labor intensive. Some parts of it build on the work of frontline firefighters, police officers, teachers, and public works employees; other parts of it rely on the ability of employees to leverage the government's vast collection of contracts, regulations, and other tools. As former Comptroller General David M. Walker told Congress in 2001, as he explained the importance of people in the General Accounting Office (now the Government Accountability Office [GAO]), "The more skilled and capable our workforce, the more capable our organization will be to perform its mission."[2] The same is true of every agency in government: the quality of government can only be as good as the quality of the people who work for it.

At the same time, simply trying to understand the civil service system—its laws and traditions—is a daunting job. "For the unanointed," journalist Jonathan Walters explains, "no topic around public administration is considered more baffling—or stultifying—than civil service."[3] Indeed, the system has a terrible reputation in some quarters. As David Osborne and Ted Gaebler argue in *Reinventing Government*, "The only thing more destructive than a line item budget system is a personnel system built around civil service."[4] Some find the topic so dense that they either simply ignore it or relegate it to "inside the system" issues, which top officials do not need to worry about. Others abandon hope of trying to understand it and so surrender to the experts who have devoted careers to building and deciphering the system.

Many students view the topic as boring or arcane (or both). Many analysts of public policy pay it little attention at all and focus instead on the design of public policy and how best to fund it. But the quality of the government is only as good as the quality of the people who work for it—and the quality of the people depends heavily on the civil service system. It is the often hidden, and surprisingly interesting, building block on which the performance of government ultimately depends.

Public Employment

Before exploring the specific features of that system, let us first consider the big picture of public employment in the United States. There is a widespread belief that American bureaucracy is fat and swollen. In reality, however, the proportional size of Amer-ican bureaucracy—when measured by government employment as a share of total employment—falls in the middle range of the world's industrialized nations: smaller than the government bureaucracies of the Scandinavian countries and Canada, a bit larger than those of Mexico, Germany, and Japan. It is about the same size as the gov-ernments of Australia, Portugal, Poland, and the Netherlands (see Figure 8.1).

Moreover, as we saw in chapter 3, government employment at the national level has been relatively flat in the last forty years. Employment at the state and local level has grown, but only by about the pace of overall population growth.

What do most government employees do? More than half of all state and local employees—and almost half of all government employees—work in education and libraries (see Table 8.1). Police officers and firefighters rank next at the state and local

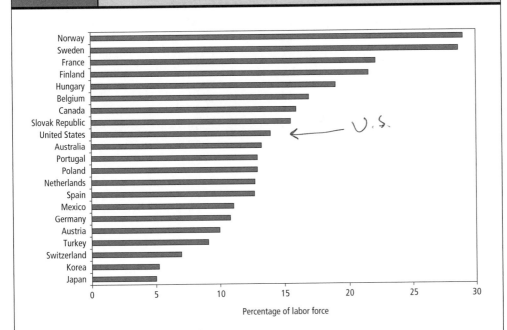

| Figure 8.1 | **Government Employment as a Share of Total Employment** |

Percentage of labor force

Source: Organization for Economic Cooperation and Development, *Employment in Government in the Per-spective of the Production Costs of Goods and Services in the Public Domain*, GOV/PGC/PEM (2008)1 (Paris: OECD, 2008), 20, http://www.olis.oecd.org/olis/2008doc.nsf/LinkTo/NT00000A16/$FILE/JT03239319.PDF. Note: Data are for 2005.

level, followed by hospital employees. At the federal level, workers in national defense and the postal service each account for about one-fourth of employees; other functions that employ sizable numbers of federal workers include natural resources, financial administration, health care, and hospitals. Contrary to yet another popular impression, welfare accounts for less than 3 percent of all government employees.

Fundamental Elements of the Civil Service System

Suppose that an individual wants to work for the government: how does the system work? First, of course, there must be an opening, and vacancies can be scarce when

Table 8.1	**Public Employees by Function**		

| Function | Percentage of total | | |
	Federal	State/local	Total
Air transportation	1.9	0.3	0.5
Corrections	1.3	4.5	4.0
Education and libraries	0.6	53.4	45.7
Financial administration	5.3	2.4	2.9
Health	5.0	2.7	3.1
Highways	0.1	3.5	3.0
Hospitals	5.5	5.9	5.8
Housing and community development	0.6	0.8	0.7
Judicial and legal	2.2	2.6	2.5
National defense	25.3	0.0	3.7
Natural resources	7.1	1.2	2.1
Parks and recreation	1.0	1.7	1.6
Police and fire	4.1	7.5	7.0
Postal service	24.4	0.0	3.6
Public welfare	0.3	3.4	2.9
Social insurance administration	2.5	0.6	0.8
Space research and technology	0.7	0.0	0.1
Water transport and terminals	0.2	0.1	0.1
Other	11.9	9.5	9.8

Source: U.S. Census of Governments, 2002 *Public Employment Data,* http://www.census.gov/govs/www/apes.html.

the economy turns down. Finding government positions, however, has become easier because of the spread of online job services. At the federal level, USAJobs.gov provides a one-stop website for federal vacancies. (The well-known private-sector website, Monster.com, provides the technology that supports USAJobs.gov.) Many state and local governments have produced their own job-hunting websites. The city of Seattle lists its jobs at http://www.seattle.gov/personnel/employment. Job hunters seeking a position in the Utah state government can go to https://statejobs.utah.gov.

But then government job seekers must navigate the three fundamental elements of the civil service system: rules for position classification, staffing, and compensation. The steps involved in filling government jobs constitute a complex chain of issues and actions, both for agencies and for employees, that are outlined in Figure 8.2. Beyond that are policies outlining employee rights and obligations, which make government work so fundamentally different from private-sector jobs.

Position Classification

In civil service systems, as well as in most large corporations, each position is identified in terms of the special knowledge the job requires, its level of difficulty, and the responsibilities (including supervisory duties) that come with it. This process is known as **position classification,** and it is the foundation of the system. Each position is defined according to the occupation (e.g., clerk-typist, civil engineer), and the degrees of difficulty and responsibility are expressed in a grade level. In the federal civil service system, there are fifteen grades in the General Schedule (GS), which governs most employees (though not Neil Armstrong—he and others at the top of the civil service are covered by different rules, which we explore a bit later in this chapter). Civil service systems at the state and local level generally operate in the same way.

Each position opening is thus described by GS level (or its equivalent in other personnel classification systems) and occupation, which, in turn, define the qualifications an applicant must meet to be considered for the position. Once an individual is hired, the position description details the duties and the salary (see Table 8.2 for the grades and the salary ranges, as well as the various roles performed at each level). In the federal GS system, levels 1 through 8 tend to be clerical positions. College graduates often qualify for entry-level professional positions, beginning at the GS-5 level. With a master's degree, an applicant may qualify for placement at the GS-7 or GS-9 levels, while levels 10 and above tend to be managerial levels that require higher levels of experience.

Applicants who want to be considered for a position must demonstrate not only that they have the necessary skills but also that they are better qualified than other applicants. The government therefore has, over time, devised a series of tests to judge an individual's qualifications. Applicants for clerical positions are tested for typing

Figure 8.2	**Personnel Steps for Agencies and Employees**

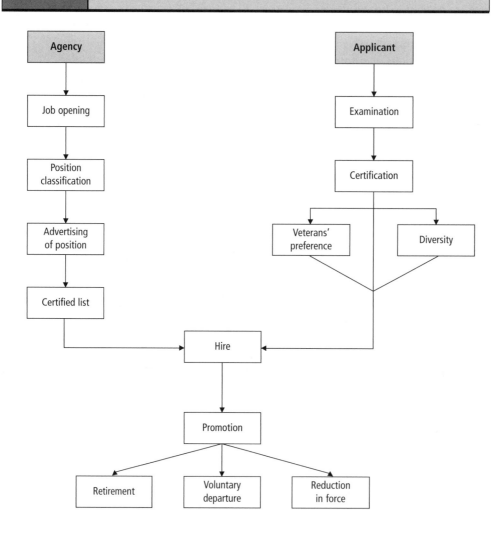

accuracy and speed, while potential firefighters and police officers must pass both written exams and tests of strength and agility. For more professional positions, other systems have been developed to test the applicant's skills; we return to that process later.

This position classification process has endured because governments have not yet devised a better way of screening applicants. The civil service, of course, is devoted to finding the best-qualified employees (to ensure that taxpayers get the most value for their money) and to preventing political interference in the hiring process (to ensure that *what* applicants know, not *who* they know, is what counts). But it is a process that is fraught with problems.

First, no matter how hard government workers in the personnel offices try, the written descriptions rarely match the actual job. Supervisors constantly add to and subtract from the actual duties and responsibilities of their staff members. This mismatch means that the testing process may not produce the best person for the actual job, and it can mean that a system designed to give equal treatment to everyone doing the same job does not in fact work that way.

Second, the system creates strong incentives for **grade creep**: a tendency for agencies to multiply the number of high administrative positions, shift professional specialists to administrative roles, or seek higher classifications for existing positions. The higher the classification, the more supervisors can pay their employees—which

[handwritten margin notes: problems; 1. written position & actual job don't match; 2. grade creep]

Table 8.2	General Schedule (GS) of the Federal Civil Service System		
GS grade	Bottom salary	Top salary	Typical roles
1	17,046	21,324	General entry level and preprofessional
2	19,165	24,115	
3	20,911	27,184	
4	23,475	30,252	
5	26,264	34,139	Senior clerical and entry-level professional and administrative
6	29,276	38,060	
7	32,534	42,290	
8	36,030	46,839	Senior clerical
9	39,795	51,738	Intermediate professional or administrative
10	43,824	56,973	Full professional or administrative
11	48,184	62,593	
12	57,709	75,025	
13	68,625	89,217	
14	81,093	105,420	Executive
15	95,390	124,010	

Source: U.S. Office of Personnel Management, http://www.opm.gov/oca/08tables/pdf/gs.pdf.
Note: Salaries effective January 2008.

problems

makes it easier to hire the workers they want and to keep the good ones they have. Government supervisors worry constantly about losing their best employees to better-paying jobs in the private sector, but within the civil service system, it is impossible simply to give the worker a salary increase, because it is the position, not the worker, that determines the salary level. Therefore, in order to increase the salary, the supervisor seeks to upgrade the position. To guard against such grade creep, government personnel offices employ classification specialists, whose job it is to review every request for reclassification, looking carefully at the technical skills required and the number of persons supervised by the employee in question.

Third, the federal workforce itself has changed, and that makes it difficult to *keeping up* keep the system up to date. The classification system tends to describe well relatively standardized positions, such as clerks and typists, but it often struggles to capture the requirements of professional and policy positions. Moreover, increasing levels of specialization can make individual positions distinctive and unique. The government, for example, might seek not just a mining engineer but one knowledgeable about South African mining. Agencies sometimes define a job so narrowly that only a small handful of persons could possibly qualify, which makes it easier for the competitive hiring system to produce the agency's preferred candidate. Central personnel offices, of course, know all about this strategy, but it is usually difficult for them to distinguish such cases from legitimate efforts to describe a position's qualifications. (At the federal level, the central personnel office is the Office of Personnel Management [OPM]; most state and local governments have similar bureaus.) So, despite the system's basic principles, sometimes the person *can* define the job, instead of having the job define the person.

Staffing

The online job systems have made it much easier to search for job openings. But once an individual finds a job in which he or she is interested, it is usually necessary to qualify for the position through an examination.

The testing process is central to hiring new government employees. The federal government's long-standing regulations require "open, competitive examinations for testing applicants for appointment in the competitive service which are practical in character and as far as possible relate to matters that fairly test the relative capacity and fitness of the applicants for the appointment sought. . . . An individual may be appointed in the competitive service only if he has passed an examination or is specifically excepted from examination."[5] Even for positions for which standardized tests are impractical, the government has long had to devise some alternative to meet both the letter and spirit of the civil service system.

The Hiring Process

In recent years, OPM has given agencies much greater flexibility in devising the best tests for their potential employees. Applicants who meet minimum qualification requirements for white-collar positions are given one of two kinds of examination. An **assembled examination,** a written test administered usually at a number of cities throughout the country, is used mostly for lower positions, but for higher positions—those at GS-9 and up—an **unassembled examination** is more common. In this case, each candidate submits a comprehensive résumé, detailing education, training, and experience. The names of references, such as former employers and teachers, are often required, and hiring officials frequently check these references.

Constant changes in the testing process, along with challenges of writing good tests, have led government agencies to rely far less on traditional exams, a 2008 report by the Merit Systems Protection Board (MSPB) found. In 2005, just 28 percent of new federal employees were hired through competitive exams. Over time, exceptions to the exam process have grown, including special provisions for veterans, internships, and flexibilities for hiring in high-demand positions like airport screeners.[6] MSPB Chairman Neil McPhie said, "There is a role for these exceptions, but their extensive use may have implications for the future." The implications? A dramatic erosion of the long-standing principles that supported the merit system, and a risk that the multiple routes of entry could open the door to favoritism in hiring and a workforce that recruits disproportionately from some groups. With many baby boomers certain to retire in the coming years, these cracks in the tradition worried some observers, who feared that the flexibilities would open the door to favoritism and a return to the patronage that the system was created to abolish.[7]

For the applicants who do attempt entry through the traditional testing process, those who pass the examination are placed on a register of individuals eligible for hire within the class, or group of positions, for which they have qualified. The federal government uses two kinds of registers: a ranked list of all eligibles in the order of their examination grades, used for lower-level positions, and an unranked list, used for most scientific positions and for most positions at GS-9 and above.

Suppose that an agency wishes to fill a vacant position. It may decide to do so by promoting or transferring a civil servant already in the agency or elsewhere in the government. That individual must meet the qualifications for the new position, and the classification of the new position defines the new salary. But if the agency wishes to consider outsiders, the system generally begins with a request to the personnel agency to certify the names of the top three qualified persons from the register of eligibles. On the ranked register, this is a straightforward process of submitting the first three names on the list; on the unranked register, they are persons that the personnel agency has determined are the three best-qualified individuals. The agency can then choose any of the top three candidates. Sometimes, because the personnel system often operates very slowly, the agency's chosen person may already have accepted another position, and so the system typically provides a process for supplying new names. Sometimes, the agency does not find any of the candidates acceptable, and agency officials may then simply keep the position vacant and hope for a better collection of names on the next try.

Because agencies often find this "rule of three" annoying, many personnel reforms, as we see in the next chapter, have sought to change it. Still, it remains one of the fundamental principles of most civil service systems. The examination and certification process reduces the hiring flexibility of agencies and can sometimes prove difficult, even incomprehensible, for applicants. College placement officers sometimes wisely suggest that individuals who want to work for the government find someone who would like to hire them—and then allow that person to figure out from the inside how best to ensure that the applicant's name rises to the top of the list.

Beyond the complexities of the hiring process are two recruitment goals that the government pursues as well: providing favorable treatment for veterans in federal employment and increasing the diversity of the workforce at all levels of government.

Veterans' Preference

In the federal system, veterans earn a five-point bonus; if they are disabled, they get a ten-point bonus. In addition, veterans with service-connected disabilities who receive a passing grade on the examination are placed at the head of the eligibles register (though not for scientific and professional positions at GS-9 and higher). Their names, therefore, must be certified for vacancies before OPM can begin certifying nonveterans with much higher exam ratings.

The system is encumbered with a number of other preferential provisions for veterans. For example, if on the certificate of three names a veteran is listed ahead of a nonveteran, the agency cannot pass over the veteran without stating its reasons and obtaining OPM agreement to the sufficiency of the reasons; both the agency's and OPM's actions are closely monitored by veterans' organizations. The federal government employs 452,757 veterans, one-fourth of all its nonpostal employees; about one-fifth of them are disabled.[8] Some observers think that the nation's obligation to assure employment opportunities for those who have fought its wars could be met by granting veterans' preference in governmental appointments during only the first few years after discharge from military service. But veterans' organizations oppose any modification of lifelong preference, and Congress shares their view.

Diversity

Federal statutes protect federal employees (and applicants for employment) against discrimination on grounds of race, color, religion, sex, national origin, age, or physical or mental impairment; some federal statutes apply as well to state and local governments. In addition, since long before the creation of the United States itself, government jobs have been perceived as good and secure positions. That desirability has enabled government to select and shape its workforce to advance two social goals: to redress past patterns of discrimination and to make the bureaucracy more representative of the overall population.

Pursuing such diversity requires giving preference in appointment to minority, female, and disabled applicants over equally qualified white males, and that practice naturally provokes dispute over whether such preferences contradict the merit principle. There are two issues here: whether merit is the *only* principle on which the government ought to base its employment, and whether the government has such confidence in its system of examination that it should insist on following it to the exclusion of other important objectives. As we discover later, the examination system is imperfect, and that makes it easier to justify balancing merit with other social goals.

At the federal level, these preferences have promoted substantial diversity. Minorities comprise more than 30 percent of the federal workforce (see Figure 8.3), and in many cases the minority groups' share of the federal workforce is greater than

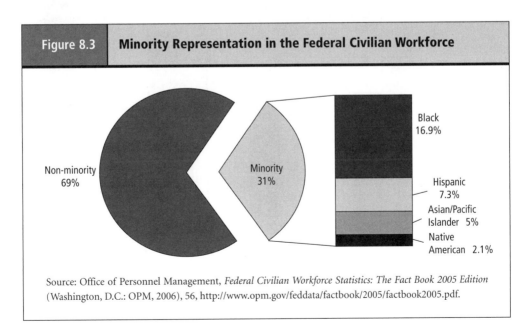

| Figure 8.3 | **Minority Representation in the Federal Civilian Workforce** |

Non-minority 69%

Minority 31%

Black 16.9%

Hispanic 7.3%

Asian/Pacific Islander 5%

Native American 2.1%

Source: Office of Personnel Management, *Federal Civilian Workforce Statistics: The Fact Book 2005 Edition* (Washington, D.C.: OPM, 2006), 56, http://www.opm.gov/feddata/factbook/2005/factbook2005.pdf.

their share of the total workforce. However, the federal workforce is unbalanced by gender: women comprise a far larger percentage of employees at lower levels, while men have a larger share of the jobs at the upper-level managerial positions (see Figure 8.4). As baby boomers working for the federal government (who are predominantly male) retire, and as the federal government seeks to replace them with younger workers (who come from a pool that is disproportionately female, since more women than men are graduating from college), this will become a far sharper and more important issue.

Promotion

Those already holding career positions advance principally by promotion and transfer. Here the operating agencies have great discretion, subject to the promoted or

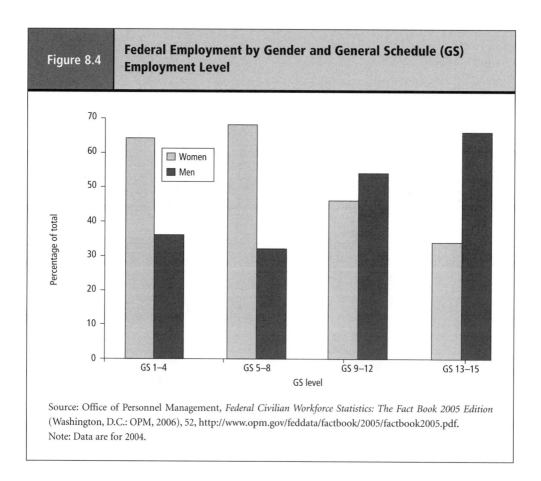

| Figure 8.4 | **Federal Employment by Gender and General Schedule (GS) Employment Level** |

Source: Office of Personnel Management, *Federal Civilian Workforce Statistics: The Fact Book 2005 Edition* (Washington, D.C.: OPM, 2006), 52, http://www.opm.gov/feddata/factbook/2005/factbook2005.pdf.
Note: Data are for 2004.

transferred employee's having at least the minimum educational and experience qualifications for the higher position. The employee need not be put in competition with possibly superior talent outside the government, and the agency does not need to look at all the employees in the government, department, or bureau who might be qualified for the position. Employees can break out of dead-end positions by shopping around to find a unit to which they can be transferred and promoted. The relative ease of transfer, in fact, may encourage individuals to accept a job at a lower level than they might be qualified for, in the hope that in relatively short order they can learn the system to find a better job at a higher salary.

The promotion system rests on the following four premises:

1. *Career service.* The initial recruitment of able candidates for entry to the public service is enhanced by prospects of long, possibly lifetime, careers with advancement by promotion. A mostly closed promotional system, without much lateral entry at higher levels by "outsiders," improves those prospects.
2. *Face-to-face assessment.* Important on-the-job characteristics, such as ability to meet and deal with others, cannot be accurately judged by initial or subsequent formal examinations. They can be accurately judged by an employee's supervisor and an agency promotional board.
3. *Flexibility.* Agency officials need to be accorded much discretion in choosing supervisory personnel and in rewarding demonstrated competence. Effective supervision and high morale depend on finding good matches between people and responsibilities, and the more flexibility managers have to promote from within, the more likely they are to produce high-performing programs.
4. *Chain reaction.* Promotion from within builds staff morale, because each promotion creates a vacancy, which can set off a series of promotions down the line.

Central personnel procedures can still trap managers in cumbersome, time-consuming procedures that do not match the twin goals of choosing the candidate who will do the best job and protecting the system from arbitrary actions tainted by favoritism. Moreover, a closed promotion system, in which most positions are hired from within, can keep new ideas from coming into the system. Some systems, including those for officers of the armed services and in the foreign service, follow a tough up-or-out process: at a certain level, officers either win promotion or must leave the service; at each step up the hierarchy, there are fewer positions at the next level, so the up-or-out process tends to weed out employees along the way. Federal managers sometimes complain that individuals who do not actively seek to get ahead can settle into their positions, produce merely adequate work, be impossible to remove for cause, and lower the overall performance of the organization. Some of the reforms we explore in the next chapter are designed to solve that problem.

Separation

Government employees tend to sustain long careers in civil service: the average length of service of full-time, permanent, nonpostal employees is about seventeen years.[9] It is difficult to compare turnover with that in the private sector, but some studies have suggested that the rate is about the same among white-collar employees.[10] Turnover can have positive or negative effects, depending on whether those who leave are the government's most- or least-skilled employees and how much it costs to recruit and train their replacements. This uncertainty vastly complicates the task of assessing the real cost of layoffs, downsizing, and voluntary departures from government service.

All civil service systems make it possible to remove employees for cause. The larger problem is removal of the mediocre. Supervisors are often reluctant to try to remove employees; it is a long and complex process, and if unsuccessful, they may only find themselves saddled with disgruntled employees who can undermine morale. As a result, a supervisor may instead encourage an inferior employee to transfer elsewhere; indeed, the supervisor may be all too willing to provide a glowing recommendation of such an employee's qualifications—for another job.

Governments sometimes find that tight budgets require them to downsize their workforce. In economic downturns, such as that experienced in the early 2000s, state and local governments have relied on **reductions in force** (RIFs, or "riffing," for short). Governments reduced their personnel ceilings, thus triggering elaborate rules about which employees could be retained and which ones had to be riffed first. In general, lowest-seniority employees are the first to go. A higher-seniority employee whose unit shrinks in size generally can "bump" a lower-seniority employee, even from a job at a lower level than the one he or she originally occupied. That, in turn, can trigger further bumps, until the lowest-seniority employees must leave government service. Needless to say, such RIFs can devastate both an agency's capacity and the morale of its employees.

Starting in the 1990s, the federal government made liberal use of **buyouts** as an alternative mechanism for reducing the number of its employees. In 1993 the Clinton administration first proposed shrinking the federal workforce by 252,000; Congress later increased the total to 272,900. These reductions, which the administration said would come mostly from middle management, were to finance the administration's 1994 crime bill. Rather than relying on RIFs (which administration officials feared would be too disruptive) or attrition (which would not produce large enough reductions), the administration instead offered cash incentives to employees who agreed to leave government employment. The strategy risked encouraging the government's most seasoned employees—not the "checkers of checkers" targeted by the administration—to leave first. GAO, in fact, found that although the workforce reduction had not yet harmed most departments, several agencies complained that it had hurt their ability to accomplish their missions. In one agency, officials said that "the buyout has 'gutted' corporate memory.... The number of key managers who left has resulted in a deleterious domino effect. Depth and coverage in certain offices has been negatively impacted."[11] Nevertheless, the appetite of officials at all levels for further shrinking the size of government led to a host of different strategies to downsize government employment.[12]

Compensation

The government's capacity to attract and keep able people depends heavily on the salaries (and fringe benefits) it offers. Pay, to be sure, is not the only factor that a worker considers in seeking, accepting, or staying in a particular organization.[13] The challenge of the work, the impact one's work can have, the agreeableness of the specific setting (including physical facilities, supervisor's behavior, and stimulus and cooperativeness of one's peers), prospects for promotion, and fringe benefits all weigh on the scales.[14] In the government sector, the sense of working in the public interest is another important motivating force. Still, government must compete in the labor market for competent people, and its employees, current and prospective, naturally weigh their pay in deciding where to work.

The law provides that federal white-collar pay rates shall be comparable with private-enterprise pay rates for the same levels of work. The president therefore annually adjusts the salaries of federal employees to achieve comparability, and the Bureau of Labor Statistics annually surveys private firms to determine how to make the adjustment.

Although the policy is clear, federal pay has tended to lag behind what employees would earn in similar private-sector jobs. In a Congressional Budget Office (CBO) study, analysts found that about three-fourths of federal employees had salaries within 10 percent (plus or minus) of what similar private-sector jobs would pay. In some key professional and administrative occupations, however, 85 percent of federal employees were paid more than 20 percent *less* than they would receive in the private sector. The study, CBO concluded, reinforces

> a long-standing concern about the federal pay system: it allows no variation in pay raises by occupation, with the potential result that employees in professional and administrative occupations may receive smaller pay raises than those needed to match private salaries for similar jobs, and employees in

[handwritten margin notes: "gov't must be competitive"; "lag behind private sector"]

technical and clerical occupations may receive pay raises that are higher than those needed to match salaries in the private sector. Thus, even if the current system was fully implemented as envisioned in [federal legislation], it would fail in its aim to provide federal pay that was comparable to pay for nonfederal jobs.[15]

good benefits

Government, in general, tends to provide relatively generous fringe benefits, including health care and retirement programs. For the jobs where the pay gap is already large, however, a CBO study found that the fringe benefits were not nearly enough to close the gap.[16]

Is comparability a sound goal? A former associate director of the federal Office of Personnel Management, a political appointee during the Reagan administration, argued that it is not: "In fact, the federal government is able to hire the caliber of people it needs at current wage levels and could do so at even lower pay scales. It should be content to hire competent people, not the best and most talented people." The federal government, he wrote, does not "need laboratories full of Nobel laureates, legal offices full of the top graduates of the best schools, administrative offices staffed with MBAs from Wharton, or policy shops full of the brightest whatevers." Indeed, "the brightest and most talented people should work in the private sector."[17]

However, few careful observers would agree that the government's responsibilities for foreign affairs, defense, and economic and social conditions can be well administered by those left over after private employers have taken their pick of the best-qualified job candidates. In fact, a survey of government managers by GAO found that "low federal pay was the factor respondents most frequently cited as a reason for employees to leave the federal government and for applicants to decline a federal job offer."[18] But there remains a doubt that the government is appropriately addressing the comparability issue.

also difficult b/c of differences in cost of living

Because the cost of living varies so significantly among regions of the country, the problem of pay comparability becomes even more complex. The Volcker Commission concluded in 1990 that "the current goal of national pay comparability is unworkable" and recommended "a pay-setting system that recognizes the fact that public employees live and work in localities characterized by widely different living costs and labor market pressures, and adjusts compensation upward accordingly." It also urged "special pay rates for occupations where there are shortages or strong competitive pressure from the private sector."[19] Congress has authorized the government to provide "locality-pay adjustments," and OPM now has special pay scales for the thirty largest metropolitan areas in the country. Employee organizations, however, have bitterly complained that the government has failed to fully fund the program. The American Federation of Government Employees (AFGE) estimates that a GS-9 worker in Atlanta is making more than $5,172 less than would be the case if the system had full comparability, and that in San Francisco, the difference is more than $8,547.[20] AFGE complains, "Pay for performance has a miserable record of failure in the private and public sectors."[21]

Comparable Worth

A core civil service principle is the concept that individuals should receive equal pay for jobs of comparable value. Distinctions in pay should be related to the nature of the job and the level of performance. However, as analysts have pointed out, for many positions traditionally dominated by women (such as secretaries and nurses), the pay in fact has not been equivalent. Moreover, they say, there sometimes are few opportunities for promotion, and sex-based discrimination can block opportunities. These critics have pursued reform based on jobs' **comparable worth.** Many state governments have conducted comparable worth or pay equity studies, most of which have found that sex-based wage differences and sex-based occupational segregation do exist in their bureaucracies, and some state and local governments have taken remedial action.[22]

equal pay for equal work

Defining what is truly comparable, however, is an extremely difficult problem. To what traditionally male-dominated jobs should traditionally female-dominated jobs be compared? Analysts sometimes note that wages for women can be lower because some women leave the workforce for child-rearing duty and then reenter it later. They suggest as well that some traditionally female-dominated jobs require less work experience and, therefore, do not warrant as high a pay level. Some economists ask why, if women believe that they are underpaid in some jobs, they do not simply switch to other positions; other analysts counter that long-term patterns of discrimination can make that difficult or impossible.[23]

As more women enter the workforce, gain more advanced education and training, and advance up the hierarchy, the comparable worth issue is changing dramatically. Moreover, some men are taking on more responsibility for child-rearing, and more women are returning sooner to the workforce after giving birth. These trends are redefining the comparable worth issue, but they are also raising new questions about how best to ensure equity between the sexes in the workplace—and how to accommodate family pressures with career demands. Some governments are adopting more flexible policies for family leave and for telecommuting; others are developing child-care programs. As these social trends continue to reshape the government workforce, such issues will become even more important.

Building a Quality Workforce

The public service can attract the ablest persons only by being competitive, which is partly a product of pay, promotional opportunities, and other conditions of work but is also a product of perceptions held by members of the pool of potential recruits. Recruitment of able candidates (particularly college seniors and recent graduates) has been most successful in periods when the government is perceived as engaged in interesting, innovative, and exciting programs that promise to have high value for society. The New Deal, World War II, the Kennedy administration, and the Johnson administration (with its Great Society programs) were such periods. At other times, particularly in the 1970s and 1980s, however, successful presidential candidates campaigned against Washington and "the bureaucracy," with predictable effects on the morale of civil servants and on potential recruits' choices among their career options. President George H. W. Bush broke with this negative view, expressing in his 1988 campaign "a very high regard for the overall competence of career civil servants and for the vital role they have in our democratic form of government." And, as president, he told an assembly of top careerists that he shared their "belief in public service as the highest and noblest calling."[24] President Clinton likewise did not engage in bureaucrat bashing, although his downsizing initiatives made many employees nervous. President George W. Bush, while a conservative, also embraced the positive role that government plays in American society.

Despite the rising presidential rhetoric in support of the public service, the federal government has struggled to attract the high quality of recruits it needs.[25] The very complexity of the personnel process can create a roadblock. As the National Advisory Council on the Public Service found, "the Federal government now has a confused and incomplete patchwork of recruiting programs. Potential applicants for Federal employment are discouraged by a perplexing and overly complicated process." In addition, "Too often, there is no link between the recruiting initiatives and the hiring process."[26] Indeed, the director of the federal Office of Personnel Management concluded that it was little wonder that potential government employees were confused by a process that is "intellectually confusing, procedurally nightmarish, inaccessible to students, and very difficult to administer."[27] A study conducted by Carolyn Ban and Norma Riccucci for the Winter Commission on the state and local public service likewise found that "probably the most important thing that state and local governments can do to improve the efficiency of their workforce is to improve the quality of the people they hire."[28]

Opportunities for public service continue to be available throughout government, but the Clinton administration's downsizing and the RIFs in many state and local governments have further discouraged many individuals from seeking government careers. At the federal level, moreover, the combination of downsizing and limits on the number of new positions has led to a gradual aging of the workforce. An analysis by the CBO found that the average age of federal employees had grown substantially. In December 2005, one-fourth of the government's salaried employees had

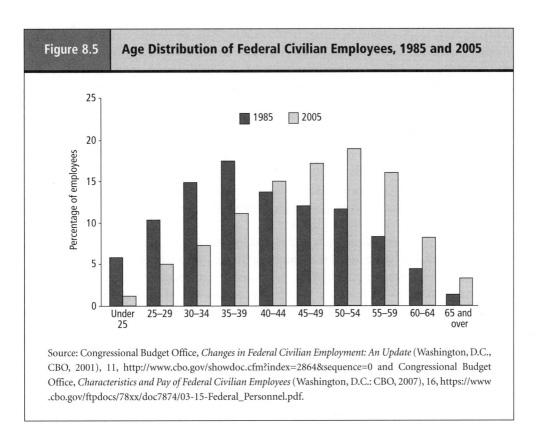

| Figure 8.5 | **Age Distribution of Federal Civilian Employees, 1985 and 2005** |

Source: Congressional Budget Office, *Changes in Federal Civilian Employment: An Update* (Washington, D.C., CBO, 2001), 11, http://www.cbo.gov/showdoc.cfm?index=2864&sequence=0 and Congressional Budget Office, *Characteristics and Pay of Federal Civilian Employees* (Washington, D.C.: CBO, 2007), 16, https://www.cbo.gov/ftpdocs/78xx/doc7874/03-15-Federal_Personnel.pdf.

reached the minimum retirement age of 55. One in ten employees could immediately retire with a full pension. The federal government is gray and getting grayer (see Figure 8.5). Its strategic planners worried increasingly about how best to manage the transition from retiring baby boomers to younger employees.[29]

Employee Rights and Obligations

The norm of equity calls for similar treatment for people in similar situations. It plays a part in each of the key elements of the civil service system: open, competitive examinations; the merit principle; equal pay for equal work within the government; comparability of civil servants' pay with private enterprise's pay rates for the same levels of work; and nondiscrimination by political party, race, national origin, religion, sex, age, or physical disability.

Equity between public and private employees involves issues that extend well beyond pay-rate comparability. Civil service systems have long held that public employees should not be burdened with constraints on their public and private behavior as citizens and human beings beyond those borne by private employees unless such constraints are required by the special nature of government itself. Here our concerns are the right of government employees to organize and bargain collectively through labor unions, their right to privacy, and their right to engage actively in politics.

Unionization and Collective Bargaining

American governments must reckon with a major rise in **unionization** of public employees and an increased use of **collective bargaining** to determine conditions of employment.[30] About 40 percent of all public sector employees are represented by unions, with representation highest at the local level—45.6 percent—and lowest at the federal level—31.5 percent (see Table 8.3).

The issues posed by unionization of public employees run deep. For over fifty years, federal statutes have assured that employees in the private sector can organize, join unions, and bargain collectively through their unions about pay, fringe benefits, promotion, hours of work, and working conditions. Of course, the right to bargain collectively is effective only if unions have the ultimate weapon of the right to strike. The rules are very different in the public sector, however, and they are even more different at the state and local level, where laws and policies on employees' rights to organize, join unions, and strike vary dramatically around the nation. Some states, including Georgia, have moved away from collective bargaining, while Wisconsin allows organized employees to engage in collective bargaining but prohibits them from striking. Many state and local governments, moreover, are engaged

Table 8.3	Union Membership	
	Percent union members	Percent represented by unions
Public sector	35.9	39.8
Federal	26.8	31.5
State	30.4	34.0
Local	41.8	45.6

Source: U.S. Bureau of Labor Statistics, *Union Members Summary* (2008), Table 3, http://www.bls.gov/news.release/union2.nr0.htm.
Note: Data are for 2007.

in substantial reforms, and that process is further transforming the relationship between governments and their employees. Nevertheless, key issues on the right to strike and bargain endure.

The Strike

In considering how governments may be different from the private sector, we notice, first, that governments do not generally concede the right of their employees to strike against the sovereign state. The reason for this reservation has to do with the critical nature of many government services. Citizens would consider it intolerable if they suddenly found themselves without police and fire protection, air-traffic control, schools, and garbage collection. And while Americans might not notice it immediately if the employees of the State, Treasury, or Defense Departments went on strike, the implications could be equally momentous.

But this rationale becomes strained when it is applied to less vital government services, such as cataloguers at the public library or assistants in a federal research lab. Yet no simple rule can sharply distinguish among the occupations of public employees in terms of the tolerability of strikes. A 1977 strike by only 2,500 cleaners and handymen forced New York City's 960 public schools to hold only half-day sessions for their more than 1 million pupils and deprived half a million of them, mostly

In Philadelphia in June 2008, a striking transit police officer distributed flyers to pedestrians shortly after his union declared a strike against SEPTA, the regional transportation authority. The prospect of inadequate security in the city's subway system led to a quick settlement.

from poor families, of free hot lunches.[31] In Philadelphia, transit police officers have the right to strike (and exercised it in 2008), but city police officers do not.

Theory may not matter, however. Public employees do strike, and government officials usually decide that resorting to the courts is not a promising method in getting employees back to work. Firing the strikers, as President Reagan did to the 11,000 air-traffic controllers in 1981, leads to a long process—over many years in the case of the Federal Aviation Administration (FAA)—of recruiting and training a new staff. Meanwhile, the government risks having a public function poorly performed. But even when the government denies employees the right to strike, that prohibition does not prevent employees from resorting to job actions that can tie public administration in knots. A "sick-in" by schoolteachers can shut down the schools even while the teachers receive sick-leave pay. When air-traffic controllers "work to the rule" (strictly adhering to prescribed procedures), they can cripple the flow of landings and takeoffs under the guise of enforcing every safety regulation to the letter. A "slowdown" by postal clerks can build up mountains of unsorted and undelivered mail. Teaching assistants at state universities can grade final exams but refuse to turn the grades over to the registrar, leaving thousands of seniors without the credits they need to graduate.

Who Are the Bargainers?

The second difference is that the civil service system itself, along with budget decisions by elected policymakers, sets the basic conditions of work. As a result, no executive official can bargain over many of the issues about which the union is concerned. Managers cannot agree to pay increases or fundamental changes in working conditions. Since the main decisions are political, often the most that the unions can do is to build their political strength, which turns them into interest group lobbyists—a very different role from that of unions in the private sector. The president of the largest federal union says, "We've got no choice except to try to put pressure on enough congressmen and senators to see things our way. That's our bargaining table."[32]

Faced with this prospect, the executive negotiator may give in too readily to union demands. Union members and their families have substantial voting strength in many legislators' districts and wards; those in local governments may actually be able to determine mayoral elections. The unions' voting strength, lobbying skill, and collective bargaining tactics reinforce one another. In addition, the public is often so angered by the loss of police, trash collection, or school services during a strike or slowdown that it puts pressure on government officials for a speedy settlement of the dispute. Public employee unions, of course, do not get all that they ask for, because government bargainers know that citizens dislike settlements that substantially raise taxes or that pay public employees more than others in the community who are doing comparable work. For the most part, government bargainers try to balance between protecting the merit principle and the civil service system and avoiding bargaining away government's ability to determine public policies and improve administrative performance.

Some governments, at all levels of the federal system, are moving away from traditionally confrontational labor-management relations to partnerships. The Clinton administration, for example, launched the National Partnership Council to bring union leaders into direct negotiations with top officials. In the process, however, the administration did not offer the same arrangement to organizations representing management officials, and many of them felt disenfranchised by the effort. When George W. Bush took office, he ended the partnership council, and that move eroded already difficult relationships with the unions.

The experience taught two important lessons. First, the civil service system and the supervisory arrangements it creates are one thing; labor-management relations often are quite different. At state and local as well as federal levels, the result frequently is a dual personnel system.[33] Second, despite the frequently large gaps between top officials and frontline managers, between management and labor, and between supervisors and subordinates, many managers are coming to recognize the need for fresh alliances. One private-sector executive's conclusion speaks loudly to the public sector as well: "We have lots of team efforts with union involvement. The biggest lesson we have learned is that we are all in the same boat and we need to work together."[34]

The Scope of Issues

Finally, government differs from private enterprise in the scope of issues on which employees and their unions want to, or are able to, bargain. The line between employees' own conditions of work and the government's policies and programs seems a clear one—the former being the stuff of collective bargaining, the latter the responsibility of legislative bodies and political executives. But public employee unions have blurred the line. If a union blocks a mayor's effort to staff police patrol cars with one officer when the past pattern has mandated two, or if it prevents the reduction of the number of firefighters on a fire truck, that may simply reflect the concern that all unions have about workers' safety and the loss of jobs. But what if the mayor wants to shift firefighting companies at nighttime from the depopulated business districts to the most populous and fire-prone areas of the city? Should the size of school classes or the content of school programs be determined by government-union bargaining? Should the size of payments to welfare clients, or the location of welfare centers, be so determined? All these issues have in fact been the subjects of negotiation and strikes.[35]

In the federal government, the scope of negotiable issues is restricted. Bargaining cannot concern matters that are the subject of any law or government-wide rule or regulation, or any agency rule or regulation for which "a compelling need" exists (the Federal Labor Relations Authority [FLRA] settles disputes over compelling need). Further, the Civil Service Reform Act of 1978 (which established the FLRA) preserves the authority of agency management officials "to determine the mission, budget, organization, number of employees, and internal security practices" of their agencies; to hire, assign, lay off, and retain employees; to remove or otherwise discipline employees; and to assign work and determine the personnel by which agency operations shall be conducted. The procedures for exercise of such authority are negotiable, however, as are grievance procedures for adversely affected employees.[36] And, curiously, an agency may choose to bargain about "the numbers, types, and grades of employees or positions assigned to any organizational subdivision, work project, or tour of duty, or on the technology, methods, and means of performing work."

What, given the statutory restrictions, do agencies and unions bargain about? So far, it has been mostly about the assignment and scheduling of work (overtime, workweek definition, temporary assignments, shift hours, work breaks, meal periods), grievance and other procedures, safety, employee counseling, technological displacement, and the color of wall paint. In comparison to the private sector and to state and local governments, the federal bargaining table is a meager one: many highly significant issues relating to pay, job security, promotions, and fringe benefits that are accepted as negotiable in the private sector are precluded from bargaining at the federal level. On many issues, federal statutes accord unions the right to be consulted—but consultation is not bargaining.

In recent years, public employee unions have nervously eyed government officials who have battled the unions. President George W. Bush worked to limit the collective bargaining rights of employees in the new Department of Homeland Security. Many federal managers believe that unions have grown too powerful. FAA managers, for example, have complained that they have great difficulty in scheduling work shifts because union provisions allow air-traffic controllers to come to work early or stay late; this practice allows them to accumulate credit hours, which they can use flexibly at a later time. At the Centers for Medicare and Medicaid Services, negotiations at one point became so tense that a union official said simply, "It's a war."[37]

The Right to Privacy

The rise of drug abuse and the increasing awareness of AIDS in the 1980s provoked new confrontations between government and its employees. In 1986 President Reagan signed an Executive Order requiring federal employees to refrain from the use of illegal drugs and declaring persons who use illegal drugs unsuitable for federal employment.[38] He authorized each agency to test any applicant for illegal drug use and, most important, directed each one to "establish a program to test for the use of illegal drugs by employees in sensitive positions." Such positions include more than the term suggests. Among those affected are employees in positions designated sensitive by their agency, employees with access to classified information, presidential appointees, law enforcement officers, and employees in "other positions that the agency head determines involve law enforcement, national security, the protection of life and property, public health or safety, or other functions requiring a high degree of trust and confidence." In 2004 the federal government extended the testing to include hair, saliva, and sweat samples. However, while many employees are required to submit to these tests, only about one-fourth of federal employees work in jobs covered by these tests.[39] Local governments have also instituted mandatory urinalysis for police, firefighters, schoolteachers, and other employees.

Employee unions oppose mandatory testing of urine for evidence of illegal drug use, if inclusive or random—without, therefore, reasonable grounds for suspicion of the individual employee—as an invasion of privacy and a violation of the Fourth Amendment's protection against unreasonable searches and seizures. In 1989, by a 5-4 vote, however, the Supreme Court, while agreeing on the applicability of the Fourth Amendment, held reasonable the U.S. Customs Service's inclusive drug testing of newly hired and transferred employees whose duties included direct interception of drugs or carrying of firearms.[40] Though granting the government's "compelling interest in protecting truly sensitive information," the Court deferred ruling on the reasonableness of testing those handling classified information, pending a lower court's inquiry into why baggage handlers, messengers, lawyers, and accountants were included.

AIDS testing also invokes the issue of privacy. The standard blood test identifies persons who have AIDS antibodies, but that does not mean that they have AIDS or will get it,[41] and the danger of their infecting others is limited to sexual relations and intermixture of blood (as when drug users inject with needles used by others). The U.S. Foreign Service began in 1987 to test its job applicants, officers, and their dependents for the AIDS virus, rejecting any applicants testing positive for AIDS antibodies and restricting any persons in service abroad—the concerns being both adequacy of medical facilities at some foreign posts and foreign governments' attitudes toward receiving official representatives who have or may develop AIDS.[42]

Political Activity

The right of public employees to engage in political activities intertwines with the right of such employees to join unions, bargain collectively, and strike. The word *right* gives the first clue that a dispute over fundamental values is involved. In both the political and labor spheres, a simple question is put: Why shouldn't citizens who are government employees enjoy the same rights as citizens who are private employees? And in both spheres the claim is made not only that they should enjoy the same rights but that, on constitutional grounds, they must. Otherwise, the argument goes, government employees are denied their First Amendment rights to freedom of speech, press, assembly, and petition. On the other side, too, the argument is consistent in both spheres: government is different, and its operations would be severely compromised by strikes (and perhaps by the collective bargaining style of decision making) and by civil servants' involvement in partisan political activity.

The Hatch Act

To deal with these issues at the federal level, Congress in 1939 adopted "An Act to Prevent Pernicious Political Activities," usually called the **Hatch Act** after its sponsor, Sen. Carl Hatch of New Mexico. The key provision applicable to federal employees reads as follows:

> No officer or employee in the executive branch of the Federal Government, or any agency or department thereof, shall take part in political management or political campaigns. All such persons shall retain the right to vote as they may choose and to express their opinions on all political subjects.[43]

The act's restrictions extend to virtually all employees who are regarded as not in policymaking positions, whether in the merit system or not.[44]

From 1940 to 1974, the Hatch Act's ban on political activity extended to state and local appointive officers and employees engaged primarily in any activity wholly or partly financed by federal loans or grants. In 1974, however, Congress shrank the ban to cover only candidacy for office in a partisan election and use of official authority or influence to affect others' voting or political contributions. The act was further amended in 1993 to allow most employees of the federal government to be more involved in political campaigns. Federal employees therefore have the right to be candidates for office, but only in nonpartisan elections. They can vote and assist in voter registration drives. As Box 8.1 shows, they can make political contributions and express opinions about political issues. (However, some federal employees, including those working for the CIA, the FBI, and the Secret Service, have greater limits on their political activity.) State government and local government employees are allowed a broader range of activities, with fewer restrictions (see Box 8.2). In general, government officials cannot run for office in a partisan election, campaign while on the job, or use their position to influence an election.

Box 8.1	**Hatch Act Rights and Restrictions for Federal Government Employees**

Federal and D.C. employees *may:*

- be candidates for public office in nonpartisan elections
- register and vote as they choose
- assist in voter registration drives
- express opinions about candidates and issues
- contribute money to political organizations
- attend political fundraising functions
- attend and be active at political rallies and meetings
- join and be active members of political parties or clubs
- sign nominating petitions
- campaign for or against referendum questions, constitutional amendments, municipal ordinances
- campaign for or against candidates in partisan elections
- make campaign speeches for candidates in partisan elections
- distribute campaign literature in partisan elections
- hold office in political clubs or parties

Federal and D.C. employees *may not:*

- use official authority or influence to interfere with an election
- solicit or discourage political activity by anyone with business before their agency
- solicit or receive political contributions (may be done in certain limited situations by federal labor or other employee organizations)
- be candidates for public office in partisan elections
- engage in political activity while:
  - on duty
  - in a government office
  - wearing an official uniform
  - using a government vehicle
- wear partisan political buttons on duty

Source: U.S. Office of Special Counsel, http://www.osc.gov/ha_fed.htm.

Box 8.2	**Hatch Act Rights and Restrictions for State and Local Government Employees**

State and local employees *may:*

- run for public office in nonpartisan elections
- campaign for and hold office in political clubs and organizations
- actively campaign for candidates for public office in partisan and nonpartisan elections
- contribute money to political organizations and attend political fundraising functions

Covered state and local employees *may not:*

- be candidates for public office in partisan elections
- use official authority or influence to interfere with or affect the results of an election or nomination
- directly or indirectly coerce contributions from subordinates in support of a political party or candidate

Source: U.S. Office of Special Counsel, http://www.osc.gov/ha_state.htm.

Patronage Restrictions

Three Supreme Court decisions have directly tested the constitutionality of requiring party membership or support for retention of government employment (in two cases) or for appointment, promotion, or transfer (in another case). In *Elrod v. Burns* (1976),[45] Elrod, a Democrat, succeeded the Republican sheriff of Cook County, Illinois (Chicago's county), and proceeded, as was the custom, to dismiss Burns and other non–civil service employees (save those who joined the new sheriff's party or obtained sponsorship from a leader of that party). The Court's plurality opinion condemned such patronage dismissals of non–civil service employees in nonpolicy-making positions as a violation of First Amendment rights of freedom of belief and association (which are protected against both the federal government and, through the Fourteenth Amendment, state and local governments). A concurring opinion answered "no" to the question "whether a non-policymaking, nonconfidential government employee can be discharged from a job that he is satisfactorily performing upon the sole ground of his political beliefs."

In *Branti v. Finkel* (1980),[46] Branti, a Democrat, succeeded a Republican (Finkel) as public defender in Rockland County, New York, and sought to dismiss Finkel and other Republican assistant public defenders. The Court, turning away from the question of a position's policymaking or confidential character, held that the issue was whether party affiliation is an appropriate requirement for the effective performance of the position's duties. It said that in this instance it was not and ruled against the attempted dismissal.[47]

In *Rutan v. Republican Party of Illinois* (1990),[48] the Republican governor of Illinois imposed a hiring freeze in 1980 on the approximately 60,000 positions under his control and permitted exceptions only with his express permission. Rutan and her fellow litigants, "low-level employees" in the Court's words, charged that the governor had used the freeze and exceptions to operate a political patronage system, which, in their cases, denied them appointments, promotions, and transfers because they had not worked for or supported the Republican Party.[49] "Unless these patronage practices are narrowly tailored to further vital government interests," said the Court, "we must conclude that they impermissibly encroach on First Amendment freedoms." Citing the *Elrod* and *Branti* cases, it dismissed claims that the patronage practices furthered the government's interest in securing loyal and effective employees. Indeed, "A government's interest in securing employees who will loyally implement its policies can be adequately served by choosing or dismissing certain high-level employees on the basis of their political views."

These three decisions, covering not just dismissals but also appointments, promotions, and transfers, outlaw the patronage system at all levels of government except for high-level, policymaking positions where party membership or support is deemed an appropriate requirement for effective performance of duties. This dramatic development has mainly affected local governments and some state governments. But political bosses and officials do not lack for ways to pursue their interests even under civil service systems. The most common tactics are choosing loyalists as civil service commissioners and underfinancing the commission so that registers of eligibles are allowed to expire and new examinations are postponed for months or years; "temporary" noncompetitive appointments are then possible, and they tend to go to party supporters.

Revolving-Door Restrictions

Most governments also restrict activities of employees after they leave government service, for two reasons. First, the restrictions seek to prevent government officials from using their positions to set themselves up in lucrative jobs after their government jobs. Many higher-level officials have the power to award contracts, and it would be tempting indeed to use that power to steer contracts to a company and then jump to the other side in a high-paying position to manage it. Second, the restrictions seek to prevent government officials from joining a company and then using their vast network of government contracts to pull business into their new private-sector firms.

For example, in 2004 Boeing was fighting to win a large contract for 767 aircraft, which would be transformed into tankers to replace the Air Force's aging KC-135 models. The company's principal competition was Airbus, a European consortium that was the only other builder capable of producing a long-range tanker. The Air Force's second-highest civilian in charge of procurement, Darleen Druyun, was jailed for a deal she made: she favored Boeing in the competition and negotiated a new job with Boeing after she left the federal government. She received a nine-month prison sentence, plus seven months in-home (or halfway house) detention, a $5,000 fine, and orders to complete 150 hours of community service.

In her plea agreement, Druyun confessed that, as "a parting gift" to her new employer, she had supported a higher price than the deal required and that she had shared data about one of Boeing's competitors with the company. She also had favored Boeing on a $4 billion avionics contract, as well as on a $100 million NATO contract in 2002, and she had pushed for a $412 million settlement with Boeing on a contract dispute between the company and the government in 2000. As a further incentive, Druyun's daughter and son-in-law had been Boeing employees either at the time of or shortly after each of those deals.[50] Congressional heat, including attacks from Senator John McCain (R-Ariz.), led the Air Force to a fresh competition for the contract. In 2008, the Air Force awarded the contract to Airbus, but GAO found that the Air Force had bungled the contract review, and the project went back to the drawing board yet again.

Over the years, GAO carefully examined the issue. In an analysis of 2,435 officials who had previously served in the government, it found

> There are acknowledged benefits to employing former government officials for both DOD [Department of Defense] and defense contractors; for example, former DOD officials bring with them the knowledge and skills in acquisition practices they have developed at DOD which also benefit DOD when communicating with these contractor personnel. However, a major concern with post-government employment has been that senior military and civilian officials and acquisition officials working for defense contractors immediately after leaving DOD could lead to conflicts of interest and affect public confidence in the government.[51]

Rules to prevent such problems vary with the level of government and typically are very complex. In general, however, former officials are permanently barred from joining a company and dealing with their former employer on issues for which they had direct responsibility. Most levels of governments impose "cooling-off periods," ranging form 6 months to several years, during which they may not contact their former employer on government issues. Despite the rules, GAO found that many former military officials had, in fact, worked on contracts related to their former work and some had even worked on the same contracts for which they had responsibility at the Pentagon.[52]

The revolving-door regulations are complicated and can prove difficult for former employees to decipher without hiring an attorney for guidance. In fact, some individuals decide not to seek government employment because of the restrictions they face on leaving public service. No one wants former officials to trade on their former associations for personal wealth. Everyone wants the government to hire the most capable employees for the jobs to be done. The enduring challenge is determining how best to find the balance.

Conclusion

The civil service system is actually a series of interlocking subsystems: one for position classification, one for staffing, and one for compensation. The broad, historically rooted principles of these subsystems help explain the tremendous complexity of the rules shaping the government's workforce. They also outline why so many of government's other problems regularly recur—from an impersonal style that ignores or subordinates individual differences among persons to a preoccupation with red tape. Even noble goals such as equity and merit reinforce these tendencies, and that should give us pause. Indeed, as Patricia W. Ingraham pointed out, the system's "problems highlight the difficulties created by the long-term emphasis on *administering* procedures, rather than *managing* people and programs."[53]

Now, though, we know that several major systems—and values—are in conflict. The civil service system, the collective bargaining system, and the political system start from different premises and embody different values, and they are on a collision course, as governments, unions, and political parties all vie for the loyalty and services of public employees. Reconciliation of these systems, their values, and their claims on citizens serving the public will not occur easily or soon.[54] But careful observers of government agree on one thing: the quality of the government depends critically on the quality of its employees. As a GAO study put it, "Federal employees have often been viewed as costs to be cut rather than as assets to be valued."[55] We turn to the fundamental questions of civil service reform, leadership, and the management of human capital in the next chapter.

Case 8

From the Front Lines of Civil Service: Who Is More Efficient— Government Workers or Private Contractors?

Nothing represents the front lines of public administration more conspicuously than garbage collection. In recent years, however, this most fundamental of government services has been the focus of heated debate over whether the private sector can do a better job at trash removal for less money.

Everyone knows that the private sector is more efficient than the public sector. In fact, a major case for privatizing public work, its proponents say, is that the private sector can do it better, cheaper, and smarter.

But is "everyone" right? Not if they look at the experience of Chesapeake, Virginia. In 1995 the city council told the public works director to get bids from private companies for collecting trash in the city's "Western Branch," the area collected on Mondays. The public works department responded with a "managed competition" model. "The bottom line cost to the citizens was the most important consideration," explained Thomas Westbrook, the department's assistant director.[1]

The city hired a private consultant to manage the competition process. Four bids for the job were received. The winner? As Bill Davis, the city's purchasing director, announced, "the proposal submitted by the city's public works department, solid waste division, was the most responsive and responsible offer and represents the least expensive and most advantageous situation for the city."[2]

In short, the public sector out-competed the private sector. How did this happen? Facing the heat of competition, the city's solid waste division found a way to change its waste-collection process: instead of using two different trucks, staffed by two different crews, to collect overflow garbage and yard waste, it could use a single truck with a single crew and with its capacity split between the two loads. Had it not been for the competition, the department's officials might not have devised this method, which contributed to a 39 percent savings over the previous arrangement. Facing the potential loss of their jobs, however, city workers came up with an innovative approach.

"We felt that we were as cheap as private industry and we wanted to be able to bid on that service as well," Westbrook explained.[3] His employees did so—and he was right.

In this effective bidding process, Chesapeake followed a model established by Phoenix, Arizona, which has been contracting out public services since 1979. In the first twenty years of the process, city officials there estimate that they saved more than $30 million. In six garbage-collection auctions, the city department won three of the competitions, and in those it did not win, it placed second. Between 1979 and 1998, the cost of collecting a ton of garbage in Phoenix fell from $67.88 to $41.96, a 38 percent decrease. Moreover, analysts have determined that Phoenix's costs are less than those of similar cities.[4]

Phoenix established basic ground rules for all the competitors:

1. *Reserve rule.* Wanting to ensure that the city department remained viable in case service problems arose with the private contractors, Phoenix would not allow more than half of its households to be served by private contractors.

2. *Previous experience.* Bidders had to present evidence of garbage collection work in similarly sized areas.

3. *Bond.* Private bidders had to post a bond to guarantee that they would complete the work.

4. *Insurance.* Private contractors had to carry liability insurance in case their vehicles and workers caused property damage or injury.

5. *Medical benefits.* The city required private contractors to provide medical insurance that matched what city workers received.

6. *Displaced city workers.* Private contractors were required to offer employment to any city workers who lost their jobs as a result of the competition.

7. *Fleet restrictions.* Competitors could not use their vehicles for other purposes, and garbage pickup was not allowed on Wednesdays and Saturdays.

When some private competitors chafed under these restrictions, city workers countered that private contractors should have to play by the same rules that they observed. Accepting the ground rules would make it harder for those private companies to low-ball bids, especially by not funding basic benefits to employees and by using equipment for other purposes. Indeed, public employees fought against any competition strategy that would allow private companies to win by providing their employees with fewer fringe benefits, in part because they believed that would be unfair and in part because they feared that it might increase pressure to lower their own benefits. Everyone agreed that competition helped lower costs, but determining how best to create a level playing field proved a deceptively difficult problem.

Analysts concluded that these cases demonstrate that the problem with government efficiency isn't government itself—or the people who work for it. Rather, it is the set of restrictions that limit their flexibility and the lack of incentives to improve their productivity. Create a strong incentive—such as the potential loss of jobs—and city workers can produce remarkable efficiencies. Level the playing field, and they can even win out over the private sector. Private competitors countered that they could provide even cheaper service at lower cost if the city were to change its ground rules.

Beyond the procedural disputes, however, there's a surprising nugget of truth to be found in this mixed experience. What "everyone" knows—that the private sector is more efficient than the public sector—isn't true. Armed with the right incentives, government can out-compete the private sector.

Questions to Consider

1. What factors account for the cost savings in Chesapeake and Phoenix?
2. Are there broader lessons that come from their experiences?
3. Should such competitions be extended to more cities? To more services? To more levels of government?
4. Are there public functions that should *not* be contracted out? Where would you draw the line?
5. Consider *who* does the public's work. How much does it matter if those providing public services are not public employees? Is there a value in having public employees provide public services? And, if so, how can we keep their work accountable, efficient, and effective?

Notes

1. Rob Shapard, "Collection: City's Managed Competition Model Tops Private Sector," *WasteAge,* June 1, 1997, http://wasteage.com/mag/waste_collection_citys_managed.
2. Ibid.
3. Ibid.
4. Robert Franciosi, "Garbage In, Garbage Out: An Examination of Private/Public Competition by the City of Phoenix," Goldwater Institute, Phoenix, Arizona, January 1998, http://goldwaterinstitute.org/article.php?id=102&print=1.

Key Concepts

assembled examination **215**

buyouts **220**

civil service system **205**

collective bargaining **226**

comparable worth **223**

grade creep **213**

Hatch Act **232**

position classification **211**

reductions in force (RIF) **220**

unassembled examination **215**

unionization **226**

For Further Reading

Ingraham, Patricia Wallace. *The Foundation of Merit: Public Service in American Democracy.* Baltimore: Johns Hopkins University Press, 1995.

Johnson, Ronald N., and Gary D. Libecap. *The Federal Civil Service System and the Problem of Bureaucracy.* Chicago: University of Chicago Press, 1994.

Mosher, Frederick C. *Democracy and the Public Service.* 2nd ed. New York: Oxford University Press, 1982.

National Commission on the Public Service (the Volcker Commission). *Urgent Business for America: Revitalizing the Federal Government for the 21st Century,* January 2003. http://www.uscourts.gov/newsroom/VolckerRpt.pdf.

Perry, James L., and Ann Marie Thomson. *Civic Service: What Difference Does It Make?* Armonk, N.Y.: M. E. Sharpe, 2004.

Suggested Websites

The U.S. Census Bureau's "Public Employment and Payroll Data" (**http://www.census .gov/govs/www/apes.html**) is an excellent source of comparative data on public employees at the federal, state, and local levels. At the federal level, the Office of Personnel Management's "Federal Employment Statistics," especially "The Fact Book," is a useful guide; see **http://www.opm.gov/feddata.**

Labor practices vary greatly from state to state—some prohibit collective bargaining, while others allow government employees a limited right to strike. The Legal Information Institute at Cornell University compiles state laws, and its website provides a source for exploring state-by-state variations; see **http://www.law.cornell.edu/ topics/Table_Labor.htm.**

In recent years, more information about working for government, including available positions and (in some cases) applications, has moved online. The federal government's source for job openings is USAJobs, **http://www.usajobs.opm.gov.** Many state and local governments have similar systems. Pennsylvania, for example, has an integrated website that lists private and public sector jobs (at all levels of government), **http://www.pa.gov.**

The National Academy of Public Administration periodically issues reports on the role and function of the civil service; NAPA's studies can be found at **http://www.napawash.org.**

The Government Accountability Office, at **http://www.gao.gov,** consistently produces some of the most thorough analysis of human capital issues.

The Partnership for Public Service examines the policy issues in building a high-performing government workforce. Its studies and analyses can be found at **http:// www.ourpublicservice.org.**

9

Managing Human Capital

If the quality of government depends on the quality of the people who work for it, how good a job is government doing in hiring skilled workers? In the early 2000s, the Government Accountability Office (GAO) explored the issue of **human capital**: the development of a strategy to recruit and retain the workers the government needs and to ensure that they produce strong and effective government programs. Following its review, GAO concluded that "today's federal human capital strategies are not yet appropriately constituted to meet current and emerging challenges or to drive the needed transformation across the government." But, GAO concluded, "federal employees are not the problem." The real problem "is a set of policies that are viewed by many as outdated, overregulated, and not strategic."[1]

Much of government—especially at the federal and state levels, and increasingly at the local level as well—depends not on a straight function of turning inputs into outputs but on leveraging the activity of a vast and complex network of partners, in both the for-profit and nonprofit sectors. Government managers need to know what they need to do, how best to do it, how well they have accomplished results, and how most effectively to build partnerships. In short, they need to *know* perhaps more than they need to *do*.

For society at large, experts have increasingly pointed to the rise of a "knowledge society," as management expert Peter Drucker explains:

> Knowledge workers, even though only a large minority of the work force, already give the emerging knowledge society its character, its leadership, its central challenges and its social profile. They may not be the *ruling* class of the knowledge society, but they already are its *leading* class.[2]

This is even more true for government, whose work increasingly depends on managing information. Indeed, many of the issues we examine in later chapters on implementation and regulation revolve around tracking information and using it to improve performance. In this chapter, we explore the emerging issue of human capital, efforts to transform the civil service system, and strategies for strengthening leadership at the top of the bureaucracy.

The Human Capital Challenge

In January 2001, GAO named human capital management as a high-risk area facing the entire government. The failure to build human capital, GAO worried, courted failure in the government's performance.

Building Human Capital

The challenge of building human capital revolves around four issues in particular.[3]

Leadership

The development of human capital begins at the top, with organizational leaders who focus on continuously improving the organization and building a workforce with the capacity to achieve the organization's goals. In part, this requires top managers to give sustained attention to management. Big policy issues—from scandals to political battles and new legislative proposals to congressional oversight hearings—often drive out a focus on administrative issues. But whenever the urgent (as indeed these policy issues are) drives out the important (especially a long-term focus on organizational performance), government organizations risk spending their time fighting brush fires instead of accomplishing their overall missions.

For example, the Department of Homeland Security (DHS), created in 2002 to bring together more than twenty agencies and over 170,000 federal employees, presents a daunting administrative challenge. The department's secretary and top officials face a bewildering flood of terrorist warnings, intelligence analyses, logistical problems, and bureaucratic battles. Congress insists on regular briefings, and the secretary by necessity must invest a great deal of energy and time in working with the heads of other agencies charged with important pieces of the homeland security function, including the secretaries of defense and state and the heads of the FBI and the CIA. It is very easy for these issues to become all-consuming, but if the big policy questions consume the leadership, there may well be little time and no senior officials left to deal with the critical long-term task of bringing the department's vast bureaucratic empire together into a smoothly functioning operation. The risk is that the department's top officials will busy themselves with policy puzzles but find they do not have the capacity to implement them effectively.

But not only is the job difficult; it is also prolonged. Deep organizational change takes sustained effort over time—five to seven years or more, according to the private sector's experience. Yet high-level political appointees serve, on average, less than three years.[4] That pattern of transience at the top leaves much of the task of long-term transformation in the hands of senior career officials, but, as we see later in this chapter, that part of the government's workforce is aging and many of the most experienced managers are nearing retirement. Leadership, therefore, requires not only sustained attention to management but also careful attention to the problem of building the next generation of leaders.[5]

Strategic Human Capital Planning

While government planning often gets a bad name, it is impossible for government to solve its human capital issues without taking a longer-term view of changing missions and needed capacity. For example, government studies have estimated that the Federal Aviation Administration (FAA) may well lose more than half of its air-traffic controllers by 2012. However, the FAA has not developed a plan for filling in that loss, and that risks leaving the agency—and the nation—short of skilled controllers as the skies get ever busier.[6] Similar problems plague other government agencies, ranging from the Securities and Exchange Commission to the Environmental Protection Agency.

As the government has come to rely more on contracting out, grants, and loan programs (as we saw in chapter 3), the challenge of meshing the government's management capacity with its management strategies has grown. Over time, the government's strategies have gradually shifted and have become more complex and varied, but its personnel system has not. As a result, government agencies risk training employees for jobs that are diminishing while failing to prepare new workers for the new strategies. It is impossible to determine how best to make this transition without developing a strategic sense of where the government is going and how best to get there. Otherwise, personnel policy risks falling out of sync with government's strategies and tactics. As GAO concluded in 2008,

> The importance of a top-notch federal workforce cannot be overstated. The nation is facing new and more complex challenges in the 21st century as various forces are reshaping the United States and its place in the world. These forces include a large and growing long-term fiscal imbalance, evolving national and homeland security threats, increasing global interdependence, and a changing economy. . . . [S]ome federal agencies continue to face persistent performance and accountability problems at a time when taxpayers have come to expect—and need—higher levels of performance and greater responsiveness by public officials and programs.[7]

As government has contracted the production of more goods and services to the private sector, the problem of strategically managing human capital has expanded as well. For example, at the Centers for Disease Control and Prevention (CDC), which is responsible for managing public health issues such as flu and bioterror, the contracting workforce increased 139 percent from 2000 to 2006 while the number of government employees grew just 3.5 percent, but the agency had not planned for how to integrate the contractors' operations into its overall plan.[8] The official responsible for congressional relations in the Department of Health and Human Services, in which CDC is located, replied that contractors were not included in the workforce plan because "the agency does not control their hiring, diversity, compensation, training and other key human capital factors."[9] But because the agency had come to rely so much on contractors, the skills of the contractor workforce increasingly determined the CDC's capacity to do its job. Without looking at that question, CDC inevitably could not be sure it could accomplish the mission.

Acquiring, Developing, and Retaining Talent

Of course, government agencies are not the only organizations seeking to operate effectively in the knowledge society. Private and nonprofit organizations, in the United States and around the world, are competing for the highly skilled workers needed for these tasks. Although there are many advantages to working for the government—from fringe benefits to the rewards that come from serving the public— in many cases government workers can find similar positions in the private sector, and many of these private-sector jobs involve work under the general umbrella of government rules. The government thus needs to compete in hiring top talent—and it needs to work hard to keep its best employees committed to the public service. Indeed, as Kay Coles James, director of the Office of Personnel Management, argued in 2004, "We have no problem attracting people." The crisis, she concluded, "is in the hiring process"—because the restrictive hiring practices many agencies use make it difficult to get interested and skilled employees into the government workforce.[10]

At a 2006 job fair in Oklahoma City, Jenny Chong of the state's personnel management office talked with a student from the University of Oklahoma. Governments at all levels have increased their efforts to recruit "the best and the brightest" university graduates for public service.

The Food and Drug Administration (FDA) has had great difficulty in retaining skilled scientists, even as drug companies have increased their own research and development of complex new drugs. If it is to protect consumers' health and safety, the FDA needs to ensure that its staff members know as much as the scientists developing the new drugs. Otherwise, government will lack the muscle to make an independent judgment of whether new pharmaceuticals are safe and effective. To tackle this problem, the FDA has developed new tactics, including retention bonuses for its most valued employees.

The problem of ensuring an adequate supply of skilled workers is common throughout government. In the Department of Housing and Urban Development (HUD), half of the staff members responsible for monitoring the performance of the contractors managing government housing programs were found to have no training in contract management. Even worse, HUD's procurement officials did not know of the gap.[11]

Results-Oriented Culture

Too often, as we saw in the previous chapter, government personnel processes become ends in themselves: forms to be filed, rules to be followed, regardless of how they contribute to the ability of the bureaucracy to accomplish its mission. Those very processes can, in fact, make it difficult to achieve the mission. In contrast, a focus on the agency's mission—on getting *results*—can make it easier to devise an effective personnel system. In the aftermath of the September 11 attacks, for example, the FBI discovered that the mismatch of rules and missions hindered the bureau's effectiveness. To resolve this problem, top FBI officials reorganized the bureau's structure to match its mission and worked to match the personnel system to the new priorities.

As American governments at all levels develop more aggressive performance management systems, it becomes easier to use those systems to drive the personnel system—and to reshape the personnel system to support the mission. Other nations have been pursuing just such strategies. In Canada, the province of Ontario has redefined its system for measuring employee performance to capture how well its employees contribute to the organization's goals. A similar overhaul has occurred in the Tax Office in Australia. These governments have created a "line of sight" performance management system, designed "to clearly demonstrate how an individual's performance contributes to the overall goals of the organization as well as to broader governmentwide priorities."[12] The idea is simple: measure each employee's performance, and connect that employee's work to the work of the organization. Strengthening the incentives for each employee improves the ability of the organization to accomplish its mission.

Such an approach, of course, is both complex and difficult. Moreover, at least in the United States, it has not moved far beyond the conceptual stage. Nevertheless, some federal agencies—including the Bureau of Land Management, the Internal Revenue Service, and the Federal Highway Administration—have begun launching performance management efforts. There are many barriers to pursuing such systems aggressively, including resistance by all employees, poor training, and a lack of trust. But many analysts have concluded that this approach ought to be the foundation for reform in the United States.[13]

Federal Reform

The federal Office of Personnel Management (OPM), the Office of Management and Budget (OMB), and the GAO have all launched major human capital efforts. OPM has published human capital standards—see Box 9.1, which charts the connections between agency missions, human capital, program performance, and government's accountability (also see the case study at the end of this chapter). When President George W. Bush made human capital a central part of his management agenda, OMB warned that "the managerial revolution that has transformed the culture of almost every other large institution in American life seems to have bypassed the federal workforce." As a result,

> Excellence goes unrewarded; mediocre performance carries few consequences; and it takes months to remove even the poorest performers. Federal pay systems do not reflect current labor market realities: under current law, the entire General Schedule that covers almost every kind of white-collar occupation must be adjusted by a single percentage in each of the 32 localities in the contiguous 48 states. In most agencies, human resources planning is weak.[14]

And former Comptroller General David M. Walker, when he headed GAO, concluded, "Strategic management of human capital should emphasize that people are the key to the success of our government transformation effort. As such, they should be treated more like assets instead of liabilities."[15]

This strong convergence of rhetoric and ideas has begun to have an impact. During the Clinton administration, OPM wiped away two of the most notorious symbols of the troubled personnel system. Accompanied (literally) by a fife and drum corps, OPM director James King dumped the *Federal Personnel Manual* into the trash. This multivolume set of rules contained 10,000 pages of rules—including 900 pages of instructions for filling out just one federal form. As King explained, "It is written in such gobbledygook that it takes a team of Washington's finest attorneys to understand what is required to hire, fire, classify and reward employees."[16] The job of writing rules was instead turned over to federal agencies.

Box 9.1	**Human Capital Standards**

I. Strategic Alignment

Agency human capital strategy is aligned with mission, goals, and organizational objectives and integrated into its strategic plans, performance plans, and budgets.

II. Workforce Planning and Deployment

Agency is citizen-centered, delayered and mission-focused, and leverages e-Government and competitive sourcing.

III. Leadership and Knowledge Management

Agency leaders and managers effectively manage people, ensure continuity of leadership, and sustain a learning environment that drives continuous improvement in performance.

IV. Results-Oriented Performance Culture

Agency has a diverse, results-oriented, high performance workforce, and has a performance management system that effectively differentiates between high and low performance, and links individual/team/unit performance to organizational goals and desired results.

V. Talent

Agency has closed most mission-critical skills, knowledge, and competency gaps/deficiencies, and has made meaningful progress toward closing all.

VI. Accountability

Agency human capital decisions are guided by a data-driven results-oriented planning and accountability system.

Source: U.S. Office of Personnel Management, "Human Capital Standards," http://www.aps.opm.gov/HumanCapital/standards/index.cfm

The Clinton administration followed up that theatrical gesture by eliminating the much-hated SF-171, the federal government's standard résumé form which, when completed, often stretched six feet or more. It was replaced by a computerized system and by acceptance of more-standard résumés. (Some government managers, long used to the layout of the SF-171, kept the form alive with photocopying machines—old traditions proved hard to kill.)

New Flexibility for the Personnel System

In the late 1990s, however, new and more aggressive flexibilities began creeping into the personnel systems at all levels of government. Each was designed to link employee performance with agency missions and to enhance the ability of the government to do its job.

At all levels of government, managers complain that the personnel system has too many layers, with too many subcategories, which makes it difficult to classify employees and even more difficult to manage employees effectively. Because the nature of the job defines the personnel classification and the classification defines who can do the job, managers have a hard time moving employees to where they are most needed or into the jobs in which they might be able to produce the best results.

For example, a 1997 survey of state government personnel managers found that they believed that their states had far too many job titles. The average state reported 1,802 titles that the personnel managers had to track, yet most of these titles covered very few employees—an average of just twenty-four each—which created groupings too small for broad policy. Moreover, the classification and pay systems were very old, averaging twenty-three years since their inception in the mid-1970s.[17] Government's functions and strategies had changed considerably in the meantime, but the personnel system had not.

Broadbanding collapses the typically large number of job categories in most government personnel systems into a far smaller number. The new categories tend to capture broad occupational families, with fewer pay grades and broader ranges within each pay grade. The system has several advantages:

- *Flexibility.* The supervisor has far greater flexibility in assigning workers to tasks; as new tasks emerge, employees can be shifted around the workplace without confronting the traditional barriers that constrain the existing system.
- *Career development.* Employees have more room for moving up the system and more opportunity for shifting horizontally into related jobs.
- *Linking pay to skills.* The system can also make it easier to link employees' pay to their skills and performance, as part of a reengineered human capital system.

However, the system also brings the following risks:

- *Downgrading positions without downgrading the work.* With additional flexibility, managers may be tempted to shift work from higher-skilled to lower-skilled workers. In health care programs, for example, the new flexibility might make it possible to transfer patient care from skilled professional staff to relatively less trained workers. Critics worry that this could lead to "de-skilling" the workforce.
- *Potential for abuse.* The current system limits managers' discretion, which prevents managers from easily shifting employees to different jobs or new assignments. Critics worry that the new flexibility could create the possibility of abuse.
- *Poor performance and stress.* Employees could find themselves facing a broader range of duties, and if their tasks were to change too often or stretch too far into unfamiliar territory, they could become stressed or begin to perform at a low level. Critics worry that this new pressure could leave employees worse off.

- *Failure to reward increased productivity.* Broadbanding often accompanies other performance improvement efforts, including decreases in staff and demands for increases in productivity. If employees do more with less, critics worry, they may not reap the benefits for the efficiencies they gain.[18]

At the federal level, broadbanding has not advanced far past the test stage. A number of federal agencies, including several army facilities, an air force facility, and the Department of Commerce, have experimented with the strategy. The navy's China Lake weapons center, the first of the broadbanding demonstration projects, permanently moved to a flexible broadband system after top officials concluded that performance had improved, supervisors found the system easier to manage, and employee satisfaction with pay and performance management had increased.[19]

Departmental Flexibilities

Many reformers have agreed on the need for an even more fundamental reform of the federal civil service system, but they disagree on how best to pursue it. Some reformers despaired of enacting a broad-based reform that would apply to the entire federal government after the power of public employee unions and a lack of congressional interest in such sweeping change paralyzed the effort. Faced with tough management problems, Congress has allowed some agencies exemptions from portions of the civil service law. But some reformers have worried that a series of ad hoc reforms would produce widespread inconsistency in federal personnel standards. Paul Volcker, the former Federal Reserve Board chairman who headed a series of civil service reform commissions, said that he sensed "something of a thread of incoherence" in the efforts of these agencies.[20] They struggled between doing what could be done—at the risk of undermining more than a century of uniform civil service policies—and seeking a broader reform—at the risk of inviting political conflicts that would make it impossible to do anything.

When the air-traffic controllers went on strike in 1981, President Reagan determined that they had broken the law and he fired them; for years afterward, the FAA struggled to rebuild the system. In 1996, however, Congress approved an agencywide reform granting top managers more flexibility. The law gave the FAA a broadband pay system, requirements for more frequent feedback on employee performance and a linking of performance with pay, better workforce planning, and a competitive hiring practice that bypassed the federal government's central system. The FAA initially clashed with its unions to establish these reforms, and GAO concluded that the FAA had not collected enough data to measure the success of its effort. Employees reported mixed reactions to the new system.[21]

In 1998, following intensive hearings that produced charges of widespread mismanagement, Congress gave similar personnel flexibility to the Internal Revenue Service (IRS). Its new system produced more progress than the one at the FAA, but IRS managers quickly discovered that real reform takes a long time. Of the IRS broadbanding effort, Ron Sanders, the agency's chief human resources officer, explained, "The essence of pay banding is pay for performance. That means you've got to have some way of credibly measuring that performance."[22] That need required both transforming the internal culture and devising new mechanisms for assessing the quality of employees' work. But these IRS personnel reforms did not—and, indeed, could not—solve the problems that had first prompted Congress to act.

The agency had faced an avalanche of embarrassing congressional hearings, reports of abuse of taxpayers, and inadequate customer service. Many of these charges turned out, on later investigation, to be unfounded; others hinged on the basic dilemma of IRS's mission: balancing satisfaction of taxpayers with collection of taxes they do not want to pay—and finding a way to keep IRS employees happy and productive in the process of accomplishing this tradeoff. As IRS worked hard on serving taxpayers better, the inevitable happened: charges soon began to surface that the agency was not collecting all of the taxes owed. Then, as it began shifting more emphasis toward collection, it inevitably devoted less energy to taxpayer satisfaction. The agency's personnel reforms could not resolve this dilemma. But observers did agree that the IRS reforms offered a possible model for the rest of the government.

This debate over agency-based flexibility fell right into the middle of the 2002 debate over creating a new Department of Homeland Security. President Bush opposed the congressional campaign for the department until, faced with strong evidence that information flows throughout the government had been seriously flawed before the September 11 attacks, he announced that he, too, favored creation of the department. The price for his support, however, was a waiver of many of the government's civil service rules. "The new secretary of Homeland Security must have the freedom and the flexibility, to be able to get the right people in the right jobs at the right time so we can hold people accountable," Bush argued in July 2002.[23] He pressed for substantial flexibility in the so-called **Title 5** requirements, which are contained in Title 5 of the U.S. Code: the classic standards for hiring and firing, the preferences for veterans in recruitment, the prohibitions against nepotism, the protections for whistleblowers, and the other requirements that had accumulated over more than a century of legislation and administrative rules. Congressional Democrats, fearful that Bush was using the debate to try to break public employee unions (many of which traditionally supported Democrats), fought the civil service waivers throughout the summer and fall. In the November 2002 midterm elections, however, Republicans won surprising victories over Democratic congressional candidates, and the party took control of both houses of Congress. The Democrats quickly conceded the battle, and Congress approved the new department. (See Box 9.2 for a comparison of the traditional civil service provisions and proposals for change in the new department.)

The creation of this new department framed the broadest civil service changes ever proposed. Indeed, Bush administration officials even proposed that similar flexibility be extended to the entire Department of Defense. However, congressional Democrats stalled that proposal and fought hard against the Department of Homeland Security strategy. In 2008, Congress prohibited DHS from spending any more to implement the new system, and that prohibition effectively killed the plan. But the controversy sharpened the debate about the future of the civil service system, and about whether reforms could—or should—proceed agency by agency or through a comprehensive, government-wide effort. And it focused the most basic question of all: what is the role and meaning of the nineteenth century merit system in the twenty-first century?

Box 9.2	**Proposed Civil Service Rules for the Department of Homeland Security**

Provisions maintained

Merit system principles
Whistle-blower protection
Basic employment rules (e.g., veterans' preference)
Senior Executive Service
Reduction-in-force procedures
Training rules
Incentive awards
Personnel demonstration authority
Payroll administration
Travel rules
Special allowances (e.g., for overseas duty)
Attendance and leave standards
Antidiscrimination
Political activity limits
Gift limits
Drug-use policy
Work life and safety services
Injury compensation
Insurance and retirement benefits

Provisions not maintained

Employee appeal rights
"Rule of three" hiring rule
Performance appraisal system
Position classification
Pay rates and systems
Labor-management relations
Adverse action procedures
Appeal rights

Source: Brian Friel, "Homeland Security Leaders Win Broad Power over Civil Service Rules," *GovExec.com*, November 21, 2002, http://www.govexec.com/dailyfed/1102/112102b1.htm.

Rethinking the Meaning of Merit

Over the past two decades, three states—Texas, Georgia, and Florida—have taken even bigger steps toward escaping the bounds of the current civil service system. They took the advice of Walter Broadnax, former director of the New York State civil service system and long-time analyst of the process, who, in frustration at the system's constraints, said simply, "Blow it up."[24] These three states followed just that course.

The Texas legislature led the way in 1985 by abolishing the Texas Merit Council, a body that did not have control over all the state's employees but did oversee ten agencies' compliance with federal law. Deciding to eliminate the council, the state legislature delegated responsibility for complying with federal civil service standards to the state agencies themselves. The agencies, in turn, were given complete flexibility in setting hiring and firing procedures for their employees. The state government, for example, cannot calculate how long it takes to hire new employees, since the agencies follow their own rules and the state does not keep centralized statistics. Indeed, Texas is the only state without a central personnel office.

Georgia followed in 1996 with an even more radical reform, which Governor Zell Miller made a centerpiece of his effort to transform government management. When the state set up its civil service system in the 1940s, he said, creating "a professional workforce that was free of political cronyism" was important. But, he contended,

> [T]oo often in government, we pass laws to fix particular problems of the moment, and then we allow half a century to roll by without ever following up to see what the long-term consequences have been. Folks, the truth of the matter is that a solution in 1943 is a problem in 1996. The problem is governmental paralysis, because despite its name, our present Merit System is not about merit. It offers no reward to good workers. It only provides cover for bad workers.[25]

Miller won overwhelming support for his plan to abolish the state's merit system. Employees hired after July 1, 1996, would serve **at will,** which meant that they had no civil service protection and could be fired without benefit of the standard civil service procedures. The new employees would receive the same benefits as employees currently in the system, but they would not accrue seniority rights, so, in case of reductions in force, they could not protect their jobs by "bumping" less-senior employees (as described in the previous chapter). They would have no formal rights of appeal of disciplinary actions or performance assessments; managers could promote, demote, transfer, or fire employees as they saw fit. The legislature also abolished the traditional grade-and-step process that set employees' wages.

Despite the worries of many advocates of the traditional civil service, Georgia's new system has been remarkably free of tales of abuse. Investigative reporters found little expansion of patronage; in fact, they determined that patronage in Georgia was little different than in states with tough civil service laws. Different employees doing similar jobs might receive different pay, which would not have occurred in the old system. And managers found that they had lost the ability to blame the system for being unable to respond to requests. As one senior state official put it, the buck stops with managers, who have to shoulder responsibility for their decisions.[26] The 2008 Government Performance Project (GPP) survey of state government management capacity found the state at the cutting edge. "Georgia continues to push the envelope in workforce and human capital planning."[27]

In 2001 Florida made three fundamental changes in its civil service system. First, supervisors became at-will employees—top officials could hire and fire them without having to deal with civil service protections. Second, the state collapsed its existing pay structure into a broadband system. Finally, with a handful of exceptions for police officers, firefighters, and nurses, the state eliminated seniority protections for state employees. As journalist Jonathan Walters explained, "What lawmakers in Florida seemed to have decided was that if it's not possible to eliminate civil service coverage for all state employees outright, then the best thing to do was to drastically reengineer what that coverage amounts to."[28] The state continued to push ahead without a strategic workforce plan, however, and the GPP found the state drifting into growing trouble. Florida outsourced more of its administrative work and made one-fifth of its workforce into at-will employees (that is, they could be fired at the will of their supervisors). Turnover rose, and the state's capacity to get its work done shrank.[29]

What effect did these reforms have? There has been little evidence in any of the three states of widespread abuse, either of hiring substandard workers or of political interference in the hiring process. Few lawsuits alleging discrimination or other violations of the law have arisen. The basic principles for which the civil service system had been created a century before remained intact. Managers simply found it easier to manage: they had more flexibility and could act more quickly, and they had an easier time firing poor performers and, when necessary, shrinking the size of the government workforce.

What would happen if such reforms were to be instituted in other states with stronger traditions of political patronage would be hard to guess. As in the federal system, establishing good performance measurement systems proved difficult, and none of the states systematically assessed the impact of the reforms—with the devolution of responsibility came a hands-off policy on collecting data. But it is clear that, faced with a tension between the restrictions of the current civil service system and the needs of adapting government to fast-changing realities, more state and local governments will be exploring flexible personnel systems.[30]

Virginia's state government, in many ways, has become the national model. The GPP found that

> The commonwealth has a strategic plan for management of human resources (HR) that identifies current and future needs and is linked to the human capital plan. Virginia has readily available comprehensive data about its current and future workforce needs that it uses to make decisions involving human capital management. The commonwealth has evaluated and updated its classification, compensation and management systems and implemented emergency workforce planning.

Virginia developed innovative approaches to recruiting new employees, including a strategy to give state service a special cachet and a contract with a private company to recruit foreign-born nurses to fill high-demand positions. The state has broadband pay ranges and flexible fringe benefits, along with a generous pay-for-performance system. Training and development are high priorities.[31] The state found that making human capital development paid off with higher performance for taxpayers and better jobs for state employees.

Leadership in the Public Service

At the core of all of these reforms is a central concept: high performance in public agencies depends on leadership by top officials. No system for hiring, firing, promoting, and rewarding employees—whether it is a civil service system or not—can work without strong and sustained direction. Building and maintaining human capital begins, as GAO pointed out, with leadership.

Just as the government has grappled with how best to nurture its rank-and-file employees, it has long struggled with how best to recruit and reward its top leaders. In this section, we focus on leadership in the federal government. State and local governments often follow the same general pattern, but they can also present enormous variations.

Every modern government deals with the leadership task by creating a mix of political and administrative officials at the top. The fundamental puzzle is how to set that mix: political officials provide a larger measure of responsiveness, while career administrators bring a larger measure of professional competence. Methods for establishing the mix vary greatly. In Britain, a change of parties brings only about 120 members of Parliament into the executive part of the government, with such titles as minister, junior minister, and parliamentary secretary. In France, the government of the day has only 100 to 150 politicians, mostly ministers, secretaries of state, and their staff aides. In Germany, the strictly political echelon is thin—about 40 members, including ministers and parliamentary secretaries. Denmark has perhaps the thinnest layer of political officials of any major democracy: the minister of each agency is a political official, but all officials below that level are careerists. The American federal government, of course, stands at the opposite extreme.

Political Leadership

In the American executive branch there are over 3,000 political positions, of which about 1,500 are at the higher levels.[32] Of these, approximately 1,000 are leadership positions, including cabinet secretaries, administrators of agencies such as NASA and the Small Business Administration, ambassadors to foreign nations, and regulatory positions in agencies such as the Federal Trade Commission and the Securities and Exchange Commission.[33] By any measure, the United States has a far larger number of political officials at the top of the bureaucracy than other Western democracies. Moreover, the number of executives at the top of the federal bureaucracy has steadily been increasing over the past forty years.

Why does the United States stand out? One explanation is that some presidents—notably Nixon, Carter, and Reagan—have entered office on campaigns vilifying "the bureaucracy" and, believing their own rhetoric, concluded that only a small army of their own selection could assure agencies' responsiveness to presidential policy priorities.[34] Even presidents who have expressed more confidence in government—including Clinton and both presidents Bush—find that political appointments can help build a trusted cadre of officials throughout the government.

More basically, however, the American separation of powers, in contrast to European systems, leaves the president less in command of administrative agencies than are European executives, who have more administrative freedom. In parliamentary systems, leaders can count on legislative support because their party or coalition has the most votes. The U.S. president, in contrast, faces a Congress that engages in active oversight and intervention in administrative agencies' affairs and often confronts a situation in which one or both houses are under the opposite party's control. In addition, as Terry Moe has argued, the mismatch between the public's extravagant expectations of a president's performance and the limited resources available for satisfying those expectations makes the president seize on the tools readily at hand, namely politicization of appointments and centralization in the White House.[35]

No one doubts the need for having a layer of political positions and, immediately below that layer, for mixing political appointees and careerists. It is widely agreed that a president or department head needs people who share the same policy orientation; who will advocate the chosen policies to congressional committees, interest groups, and the public; who can serve as their superiors' loyal agents in bringing the permanent bureaucracy into effective service of those policies; and who have their superiors' confidence. The leader also needs officials who are expendable—who can readily be removed when they lose the president's or department head's confidence, resist policy directives, or become liabilities because they have antagonized relevant congressional committees or interest groups.[36] The question for debate is how deep into the bureaucracy this political appointment process should go.

As Paul Light, a leading scholar of the presidential appointments process, found in an important study of senior officials, the federal government has steadily "thickened" as the number of political appointees has risen. There are, Light discovered, "more layers of leaders" and "more leaders at each layer." The result has been an important transformation in government:

> In the 1950s, the federal bureaucracy looked like a relatively flat bureaucratic pyramid, with few senior executives, a somewhat larger number of middle managers, and a very large number of frontline employees. By the 1970s, it was beginning to look like a circus tent, with a growing corps of senior political and career managers, a sizable bulge of middle managers and professionals, and a shrinking number of frontline employees.
>
> In the 1980s and 1990s, the configuration began to resemble a pentagon, with even more political and career executives at the top, and almost equal numbers of many middle-level and frontline employees.[37]

In his survey, Light found fifty-two potential managerial layers of government from top to bottom in the federal government (see Figure 9.1). Some positions are held by political appointees; others are occupied by careerists. Not all departments have every position: only the Department of Energy, for example, has a principal associate deputy undersecretary. Moreover, the government is getting even thicker: Light also discovered that in 2004 there were sixty-four different categories of supporting positions (chief of staff to the secretary, deputy chief of staff to the secretary, chief of staff to the undersecretary, and so on); that number was up from fifty-one in 1998 and thirty-three in 1992.[38]

Even amid the recent enthusiasm for downsizing the federal government, presidents have shown little inclination to reduce the number of layers or, especially, the number of political appointees who fill them. Every position is an opportunity to reward a valued campaign aide or a generous contributor. But the increase of governmental layers weakens accountability by making it harder to assign clear responsibility for results.

Recruitment

Filling those positions is one of the most daunting problems facing a new president. After the election, a new president has only about ten weeks to assemble the team

Figure 9.1	Layers of Government

SECRETARY
Chief of Staff to the Secretary
Deputy Chief of Staff

DEPUTY SECRETARY
Chief of Staff to the Deputy Secretary
Associate Deputy Secretary

UNDER SECRETARY
Principal Deputy Under Secretary
Deputy Under Secretary
Principal Associate Deputy Under Secretary
Associate Deputy Under Secretary
Assistant Deputy Under Secretary
Associate Under Secretary

ASSISTANT SECRETARY/INSPECTOR GENERAL/GENERAL COUNSEL
Chief of Staff to the Assistant Secretary
Principal Deputy Assistant Secretary
Deputy Assistant Secretary
Associate Deputy Assistant Secretary
Deputy Associate Deputy
Assistant Secretary

ASSISTANT GENERAL COUNSEL/INSPECTOR GENERAL
Deputy Assistant General Counsel/Inspector General

ADMINISTRATOR
Chief of Staff to the Administrator
Principal Deputy Administrator
Deputy Administrator
Associate Deputy Administrator
Assistant Deputy Administrator

ASSOCIATE ADMINISTRATOR
Deputy Associate Administrator
Assistant Administrator
Deputy Assistant Administrator
Associate Assistant Administrator

PRINCIPAL OFFICE DIRECTOR
Office Director
Principal Deputy Office Director
Deputy Office Director
Assistant Deputy Office Director

ASSOCIATE OFFICE DIRECTOR
Deputy Associate Office Director
Assistant Office Director
Deputy Assistant Director

PRINCIPAL DIVISION DIRECTOR/ DIVISION DIRECTOR
Deputy Division Director
Associate Division Director
Assistant Division Director
Deputy Assistant Division Director

SUB-DIVISION DIRECTOR
Deputy Sub-division Director
Associate Sub-division Director
Assistant Sub-division Director

BRANCH CHIEF

Source: Paul C. Light, "How Thick Is Government?" *American Enterprise* 5 (November/December 1994): 60.

that will take over the executive branch on inauguration day. The president must rely heavily on top campaign staff to handle the flood of candidacies self-generated or proposed by political and interest group patrons. Campaign staff members are rarely qualified for the shift of focus from campaigning to governing; the qualifications required for specific positions are poorly understood and often poorly match those of the chosen candidates.[39] After inauguration, the task shifts to the White House personnel office, and haste gives way to delay. By November of his first year, George H. W. Bush had not nominated candidates for 27 percent of departmental and other agency positions requiring Senate confirmation—a higher percentage than in the four preceding major transitions.[40] As Paul Light observed, "It now takes as long, on average, to get an appointee into office as it does to have a child."[41]

The recruitment of political executives is so difficult that one must marvel that it works as well as it does. It succeeds best in the selection of cabinet members, a matter to which the president-elect gives personal attention. Most cabinet members have had federal government experience.[42] They are often generalists with prior service in other cabinet posts, at the subcabinet level, in Congress, or in the White House. Some have served at the state and local level, especially those named to cabinet posts for such departments as Health and Human Services (HHS) and Transportation, which have a heavy state and local government connection. They are likely to be qualified for the processes of advocacy, negotiation, and compromise that dominate governmental policymaking, especially if they are lawyers, though it is less likely to be so with corporate executives and academics, and not at all with ideologues.[43]

The vast number of appointments below the cabinet level poses the real problem, making it virtually impossible for the president-elect (later, the president) to give the selections personal attention. Therefore, the president is dependent at first on the campaign staff and then on the personnel office at the White House. An initial impulse of some incoming presidents is to delegate to cabinet members the selection of their subordinates, but after the inauguration, subcabinet appointments are generally cleared or initiated in the White House personnel office.

Most political executives have solid educational backgrounds, and many have subject-matter knowledge relevant to their particular responsibilities. But there are two important problems. First, many political appointees have suffered from lack of experience in the federal executive branch; former appointees without such prior experience express regret at how poorly prepared they were for the Washington setting of interest groups, congressional committees, and White House staff; the goldfish-bowl exposure to the media; the budget process; and the permanent bureaucracy. A few appointees have even revealed defective appreciation of the Constitution, faithful execution of the laws, and the public service code of ethics. The contrast with Britain is striking. There the political officials are drawn from Parliament. A new cabinet typically consists of individuals who in opposition were members of a "shadow cabinet," each specializing in the affairs of a particular ministry. Often the ministers have had experience in one or more earlier governments when their party was in power.

The second problem is that many political appointees arrive at their positions without extensive management experience.[44] Many come from law firms, university faculties, research institute staffs, interest group organizations, and congressional members' offices and committees; such experience scarcely prepares them well to run a bureau of 5,000 employees, let alone to operate effectively in one of the cabinet departments. Recruits from business are more likely to have experience in large-scale management—although, when Reagan appointed more businesspersons (a fifth of all his appointees) than any president since Eisenhower, his appointees did not exhibit significantly better performance. In 2008, G. Edward DeSeve laid out a set of competencies that political executives need to do their job, but progress remained fleeting.[45]

Turnover

Political appointees serve only briefly in their posts. For decades, the median length of service for presidential appointees has been little more than two years; a third stayed a year and a half or less.[46] This rapid-fire **turnover** creates a host of problems.

First, many presidential appointees leave after they have barely learned their jobs and adapted to the Washington environment; there is wide agreement that appointees need at least a year to become productive performers in their government posts. Some, moreover, are aware that the second year may be their last; to initiate and see results from new projects, they will prefer those that are short range, even though significant achievements in the public interest require emphasis on the long range. Those who do not pay attention to the likelihood they will not be there long may invest energy in substantial undertakings, but the job of carrying them through will be passed on to their successors, who may well push them aside to make way for a new set of priorities. An administration loses sustained focus through such a stop-and-go or go-and-stop process. One career civil servant, who became an assistant secretary of commerce, reported his experience this way:

> I don't know how many assistant secretaries I have helped break in. . . . And there is always a propensity for a new guy to come in and discover the wheel all over again. And then you have the classic case of a political officer who is going to make a name for himself, and therefore he is going to identify one golden chalice he is going after, and he will take the whole goddam energy of an organization to go after that golden chalice. He leaves after

eighteen months, a new guy comes in, and his golden chalice is over here. "Hey guys, everybody, this way."[47]

Turnover at the cabinet level has similar costs. At the Department of Labor, the GAO reported, the then-serving secretary "has demonstrated the strong leadership needed for a well-managed Organization, and his management system established a sound framework for strategic planning and management." Nevertheless, of nearly 200 Labor Department managers polled about this official's efficient system, "about 92 percent believed it should remain despite top-level turnover, whereas only about 35 percent believed it would."[48] Below the cabinet and assistant secretaries, the phenomenon repeats itself: in the decade ending in 1987, the Social Security Administration had seven commissioners or acting commissioners. As the GAO found, "These short tenures, along with commissioners' differing priorities and management approaches, resulted in frequent changes of direction, diminished accountability, and little long-term operational planning."[49]

Second, despite frequent talk of a president's or department head's "team," rapid turnover undermines teamwork. In a department, the set of top executives is constantly changing, as the timing of individual departures is usually set by each official's choice. More broadly, because so many policies and programs involve interdepartmental collaboration, their shaping and constancy depend on interdepartmental networks of political executives sharing concerns with particular policy areas. Such networks, as Hugh Heclo has observed, require "relationships of confidence and trust."[50] But the chemistry of these interpersonal relations develops only over time; the subtraction and addition of new elements can upset the developed formula.

Third, civil servants' incentives to obey political superiors tend to fray when those superiors, here today, are likely to be gone tomorrow. Some high careerists patiently tutor one after another political executive to speed the learning process. But others, if in charge of bureaus and programs, mount defenses to minimize damage by ill-prepared and very temporary political executives.[51] Indeed, hardened top career officials have learned that there are two ways of embarrassing a new political appointee. One, they say, is to do nothing the new boss wants, on the assumption that the appointee will not be around long enough to notice. The other is to do *everything* the new boss wants, on the assumption that the appointee will quickly learn to depend more on the career staff to avoid the inevitable political problems that come from charging ahead too quickly.

Fourth, the high rate of turnover means that staffing the administration never really ends. Departures constantly create vacancies that need filling, which produces both problems and opportunities. A major problem is the many months, sometimes years, required to recruit, nominate, and obtain Senate confirmation of successors to the vacant posts. On the eve of Reagan's second inauguration, HHS lacked three assistant secretaries, a general counsel, and two commissioners. Its Social Security Administration in early 1985 had an acting commissioner (who had served thus for sixteen months) and three acting deputy commissioners (two having served nineteen months).[52] At the beginning of 1986, one-sixth of the 176 cabinet department positions that required presidential nomination and Senate confirmation were either vacant or occupied by persons designated as only "acting" in their positions.[53] During the first years of the George W. Bush administration, the Presidential Appointee Initiative tracked appointments and charted a constant lack of leadership at the top. When a position is vacant or held by a temporary designee, fresh initiatives are rarely taken, on the ground that those should be left for the properly appointed successor. Thus, to the red-and-green traffic light symbols of stop-and-go administration is added an amber light for the long pause in filling vacancies.

In 1998, Congress passed the Vacancies Reform Act, which required agencies to report to Congress and GAO on vacant positions requiring Senate confirmation. The law also limited the service of acting administrators to 210 days. Many agencies, however, proved slow in reporting vacancies and sometimes did not report at all. Many acting administrators served for longer than the 210-day limit.[54]

Finally, during the last year or eighteen months of a presidency there is likely to be a substantial exodus of political appointees, many intent on capitalizing on their government experience by obtaining remunerative employment in the private sector. As a presidency winds down, restaffing can be exceedingly difficult, as few qualified persons will take public office for a predictably brief period. Moreover, no president wants to risk a contentious confirmation battle when launching a reelection campaign. Both problems can lead to weak leadership—or no leadership—in the waning months of an administration.

This constellation of issues posed special problems for the Department of Homeland Security. Turnover in the department in 2005 was 8.4 percent, twice the government-wide average. Among airport screeners, attrition was more than 14 percent. As FEMA, an agency within the department, struggled to respond to Hurricane Katrina, it had 500 vacancies, and eight of its ten regions were headed by acting administrators—including the region overseeing Louisiana. Basic problems of staffing and leading federal agencies continued to pose big problems of performance.

How Many Are Too Many?

There has been an ongoing debate over whether the growing number of political appointees is a good thing for the administrative process. Political appointees are needed, it is argued, to assure that the permanent bureaucracy faithfully serves the chief executive, adapting to a new administration's policy priorities regardless of how much change they may require. But two important questions remain: (1) How many political appointees are needed to achieve the objective? and (2) At what point does the number of such appointees become so large as to frustrate the objective?

There are no precise answers to these questions, but political appointees themselves have proposed some formulations. President Nixon's top political recruiter wrote:

> The solution to problems of rigidity and resistance to change in government is not to increase the number of appointive positions at the top, as so many politicians are wont to do. . . . An optimum balance between the number of career and noncareer appointments . . . should be struck in favor of fewer political appointees, not more. In many cases, the effectiveness of an agency would be improved and political appointments would be reduced by roughly 25 percent if line positions beneath the assistant secretary level were reserved for career officials.[55]

The Volcker Commission, which included fifteen former top political appointees, recommended in 1989 that "the growth in recent years in the number of presidential appointees, whether those subject to Senate confirmation, noncareer senior executives, or personal and confidential assistants, should be curtailed. . . . The Commission is confident that a substantial cut is possible, and believes a cut from the current 3,000 to no more than 2,000 is a reasonable target." On our second question, the commission observed that "excessive numbers of political appointees serving relatively brief periods may undermine the president's ability to govern, insulating the administration from needed dispassionate advice and institutional memory. The mere size of the political turnover almost guarantees management gaps and discontinuities, while the best of the career professionals will leave government if they do not have challenging opportunities at the sub-cabinet level."[56]

If the answers seem so clear, why has it been so hard to translate them into reality? For two reasons: because Congress must act to transform political appointments to career staff, and because presidents claim that they need these positions to steer the administration.

Career Leadership

No matter how strong or problematic the bureaucracy's political leadership, effective performance depends on strong leadership from the bureaucracy's top career officials. Indeed, these executives serve as the critical shock absorber in the administrative system, connecting the expert bureaucracy with elected officials and ensuring that elected officials' policy is transmitted through the bureaucracy.

At the cornerstone of the Civil Service Reform Act of 1978 was the creation of the Senior Executive Service (SES), which was designed to provide this career leadership. The SES absorbed most of the previously GS-16 to GS-18 career and noncareer positions, together with some executive-level positions filled by the president without Senate confirmation. It consists of about 7,700 employees, mostly career officials but including 575 presidential appointees.

They are a well-educated and highly experienced group. Two-thirds have advanced degrees, and 92 percent are college graduates. Most—59 percent—work in administrative and technical occupations; 19 percent are scientists or engineers, and 21 percent work in other professional positions. They are disproportionately men (73 percent) and, compared with the rest of the federal workforce, they disproportionately work in the Washington area (82 percent). Minorities comprised 12 percent of the SES in 2005, and 27 percent of the SES were women.[57]

The 1978 reform act aimed at giving agency heads greater flexibility in assigning members of this cadre among positions and tasks. Under the old system, the position occupied (tenure, grade, and salary) determined a GS-16 to GS-18 career official's status. Under the civil service rules, the agency could dislodge the incumbent (apart from position abolition, firing, or forced resignation) only by promotion, demotion, or transfer to a position at the same grade and matching his or her qualifications. It was often difficult to find a position for which a bureau chief or other high careerist had the requisite qualifications, let alone a position that was vacant or could be made

This swearing-in ceremony for top bureaucratic officials illustrates an important distinction between private- and public-sector management: the job of government executives is not only to manage their agencies but also to serve the public interest and defend the Constitution.

so. Substituting an SES system of rank-in-person (with the salary set by the individual's qualifications) for the old one of rank-in-position (with the salary set by the requirements of the position) promised to remedy this problem.

Operation

In addition to this new flexibility in staffing, reformers believed that the senior levels of the government would be stronger if top officials could assemble their own management teams. Instead of encouraging long-term tunnel vision among executives who rose within their agencies and stayed there, the idea was to create a flexible cadre of skilled managers who could lend their expertise to government management.

Entry

Each agency establishes qualification standards for its SES positions. For the vast majority of positions filled by career officials, a recruitment program in each agency is supposed to reach all qualified individuals both within and outside the civil service. An agency board reviews the qualifications of each candidate and, observing merit principles, makes recommendations to the agency appointing authority. OPM's own qualifications review boards determine whether the agency's candidates have executive qualifications (but not whether they have technical qualifications). In practice, the agency is the key actor, recruiting and choosing both career and noncareer members of the SES.

Reassignment, Performance Appraisal, and Removal

Politically appointed agency executives have in the past been frustrated by the difficulty of moving top careerists from positions in which they were ineffective to positions in which they either would do better or at least would no longer be weak links in the chain of an important program's management. The reform act removed this difficulty, for SES members have no right to particular assignments. A noncareerist can be reassigned to any general position in the agency for which he or she is qualified. So, too, can a career appointee, after a four-month waiting period.

Each agency is required to establish performance appraisal systems and to set performance requirements for each senior executive in consultation with him or her. Appraisal of individual performance is by performance review boards, which, however, have only recommendatory functions. Each executive is to be judged on both individual performance and organization's performance. With the advent of a government-wide performance system through the Government Performance and Results Act (which we explore in chapter 11), executives are assessed as well on their contribution to their agencies' goals.

Issues

Although reformers intended the SES to be the cornerstone of the Civil Service Reform Act, in practice its operations have never been smooth. As a National Academy of Public Administration (NAPA) study found in 2002: "The world has changed dramatically since the SES was established in 1978, but the underlying support structures have not evolved with it. Demands on senior leadership have increased due to changes in international ramifications, and an all-embracing customer orientation." The structure and workings of the SES system create a series of problems, both in managing federal programs and in building strong relationships with political officials.[58]

Rapid Turnover of Political Appointees

The SES is intended as the system's shock absorber, but the short tenure of political appointees—a little more than two years—creates constant shocks for it to absorb. When new political appointees arrive, there often is a settling-in period characterized by mutual distrust between the appointees and SES officials. And, typically, there is no succession plan or other strategy to bridge these recurring gaps between top policymakers and agency administration.

Specialization versus Generalization

The intent of the reform act was to create a cadre of skilled generalists. In fact, the members of the SES have tended to be highly specialized, and there has been relatively little lateral movement among agencies and departments. When they have attempted to exert leadership, it has been "neither visibly valued nor directly sought," NAPA found. The result is a series of stovepipe patterns, with narrow functional thinking that makes it more difficult to create energetic leadership or broad coordination among related problems. It also makes it difficult for SES members to shift to new positions where their skills may best be used.

Proliferation of Top-Level Systems

Another of the reform act's ideas was to create a single cadre of top officials, but since 1978 many new leaderships systems have evolved, especially to help solve the many problems of paying, attracting, and retaining good managers. The proliferation of new systems has made it even harder to manage the SES in integrated fashion.

Compression of Performance Ratings and Pay

The legislation created a pay system designed to recognize and reward top performers. There are two kinds of awards: performance awards, for superior performance in the previous year; and presidential rank awards, for consistent and long-term excellence. However, Congress and a series of presidential administrations have been reluctant to fund the systems—especially bonus systems—adequately. And, in practice, the rewards systems have never worked well.

In performance assessments of top managers, there has been a tendency to rate most managers highly, which has in turn qualified many of them for rewards intended only for the very best performers. An analysis in 2004 found that almost two-thirds of civilian federal employees received bonuses in fiscal year 2002. Within the SES in 2002, 75 percent of the service's members were rated at the very top level of the evaluation system. Although both the Office of the Secretary of Defense (OSD) and the Social Security Administration used three-level rating systems, all but one of the OSD officials and every one of the Social Security managers received top-level ratings.

Such ratings compression is largely the product of complex pressures on each agency's managers. After giving 99 percent of its SES members a top rating in 2001, the Department of Energy resolved to toughen up the system, and its supervisors awarded the top rating to just 18 percent of SES members the next year.[59] But this well-intentioned determination to make distinctions puts the government's personnel managers in a bind: most of the government's SESers probably are superior performers, but if everyone is ranked at the top, the rankings have little meaning. If officials tighten up the system, however, low rankings can discourage SESers, especially if there are no strong incentives connected with the ratings.

Moreover, much of the debate depends on the assumption that bonuses would enhance the performance of government's employees. Evidence from the private sector, however, does not support the enthusiasm that often accompanies the public-sector debate. A survey in 2004 found that 83 percent of companies using some kind of pay-for-performance system concluded that the approach was either somewhat successful or not working at all. In part, that was because top company officials had a difficult time clearly communicating goals to employees and measuring how well employees met those goals; in part, it was because companies do not always set good goals. Pay-for-performance systems sometimes do work, especially when the companies set clear goals and employees feel motivated—but those companies are in a minority.[60]

The result of these problems has been pay compression at the top—sometimes salaries of supervisors are the same as those two and even three levels below—and little support for providing performance-based incentives. Pay is only one incentive for performance, but when pay is compressed, it can discourage managers by signaling that performance does not matter. Interviews with SES members consistently signal that this is a crucial problem.

Lack of Attention to the Human Capital Problem

The government's top officials have paid relatively little attention to the need for excellence in the top levels of the career staff. Leadership from these top careerists is crucial. Indeed, as NAPA found:

> In the United States and abroad, governments and private sector firms have learned that identifying and developing executive talent are some of the most important functions that an organization can undertake. It should not be an afterthought, done once important policy issues are addressed.[61]

Too often, nurturing of top talent is not even an afterthought. The federal government has simply not paid much attention to the problem.

As part of the broader effort in the federal government to develop human capital, OPM, OMB, and GAO are working aggressively on these issues. For example, OPM has developed a more aggressive performance measurement system designed to link employees' performance with the performance of their agencies. On the other side, it has aggressively sought to reduce the tendency for most SES members to receive the highest level of evaluation. (The case study for this chapter explores the issues in more detail.)

At the core, however, the basic problems remain. The large number of political appointees creates continuing friction with the career bureaucracy. The SES has never fully evolved into the "shock absorber" system that its framers intended. In part, this is because SES managers have never become the generalist cadre first envisioned, tending, instead, to remain within the agencies in which they built their careers and displaying little horizontal movement. In part, it is because the performance measurement and incentive systems have never fully developed. These forces tend to reinforce each other—and to frustrate the SES's ability to solve the problems for which it was created.

The human capital quandary runs deep. If we accept departing careerists' views at face value, we then come full circle, back to the issue of how to recruit political appointees who have executive ability and other qualifications for their positions and how to keep them while they learn their jobs and achieve full effectiveness.

Twelve state governments have introduced executive personnel systems of varying comparability to the SES. However, a careful assessment of them concludes that they have neither added to the attractiveness of a career in government nor been consequential in heightening the mobility of executives or their executive development.[62]

The Problem of Top-Level Leadership

Despite recurring attempts to reform the system, the problem of leadership at the very top of the bureaucracy remains one of government's most important and difficult problems. At the core is a dilemma that is hard to break. Elliot Richardson, who has headed four cabinet departments, has summed it up this way:

> The trouble is that all too many [new] political appointees . . . suspect . . . that senior civil servants lie awake at night scheming to sabotage the President's agenda and devising plans to promote their own. Having worked with most of the career services under five administrations, I can attest that this is not true. . . .
>
> Almost any job at the deputy assistant secretary level . . . is more responsible and has wider impact on the national interest than most senior corporate positions. . . .
>
> I have many friends who once held responsible but not necessarily prominent roles in government and who now occupy prestigious and well-paid positions in the private sector—some of them very prestigious and very well-paid. Not one finds his present occupation as rewarding as his government service. . . . Society treats public servants, together with teachers, ministers, and the practitioners of certain other honorable but low-paid callings, as the beneficiaries of a high level of psychic income. But the psychic income of public service is being steadily eroded.[63]

At the end of Ronald Reagan's term, C. William Verity, his secretary of commerce, formerly chief executive officer of a large steel company, added,

> I had always felt that Government people were not motivated, because in industry you have various incentives where you can motivate people, and that perhaps Government people didn't work so hard because they weren't so highly motivated. Well, I was dead wrong.
>
> I find that in this department there are a tremendous cadre of professionals, highly motivated not by financial incentives but to serve their country. It's as simple as that.[64]

A proper balance between financial and psychic incomes in the higher public service varies roughly by rank. Attracting cabinet members is not a serious problem: most are well-off and at an age when family responsibilities are not pressing, and they welcome high public status and the prospect of posthumous life in history books as a suitable culmination of successful careers. None of these conditions apply, however, to most of the potential candidates for noncareer, subcabinet posts—who are, in fact, a diverse group. Consider, first, the individuals accepting presidential appointments. Most suffer salary cuts in accepting a federal appointment. We know that people of high quality decline presidential appointments for financial reasons, forcing the White House to turn to less-preferred candidates.

Consider, second, the SES picture. Both noncareer candidates and career members are younger, their children are likely to be at or approaching college with its high tuition costs, and, for many, the government positions are at a level carrying slight prestige. Yet, such relatively young political appointees, whose primarily private-sector careers are still in the making, are likely to benefit from the government experience (notably in special fields such as taxation and antitrust law), the embellishment of their biographical résumés, and improved eligibility for higher governmental appointments in the future, when their party again wins the presidency. Some political SESers, of course, will in fact earn higher pay in the executive branch than in the think tanks, small advocacy organizations, and congressional staffs from which many come. Nonetheless, as one study concluded, "inadequate salaries are a barrier to recruiting from among one group of especially desirable candidates for government service: those highly trained technicians and midcareer managers whose expertise, energy, and creativity [have] been amply demonstrated in the private sector."[65]

There has been a steady stream of commissions on top-level salaries over the past generation, and every one of them has concluded that top federal officials are critically underpaid. The one reporting in December 1988 found that "the level of salaries of high federal officials are now only about 65–70 percent in constant dollars of what their 1969 salaries were for the same positions."[66] The other commissions produced similar results.

Many citizens express dismay at the salaries paid public officials. Imbued with the egalitarian spirit of democracy, and sensitive to the disparity between their own incomes and those of high officials, they show little patience with arguments that government needs a fair share of the best educated and most skilled managers and professional specialists. They do not easily accept that this fair share must come from an elite pool whose members need incentives for high performance. Yet without some way of solving this problem, citizens will not get the level of performance they expect—and, indeed, deserve—as value for the taxes they pay.

Conclusion

Several matters should be clear by this time. First, the small percentage of federal employees who constitute the higher public service are of crucial importance. These are the managers of major federal programs; the advisers and often the decision makers on large policy questions; the interagency negotiators; the spokespersons to and bargainers with the Executive Office of the President, congressional committees, interest groups, and the general public; and the agents of the current administration who, in trying to induce civil servants to follow the election returns, carry much of the responsibility for assuring democratic control of the bureaucracy.

Second, the number of political appointments at the top of the bureaucracy in the United States is far larger than in other countries.

Third, the top career officials are a highly specialized and high-performing group. However, recruiting and retaining them—and providing incentives for superior performance—is an enduring problem that a series of reforms have not succeeded in solving.

Fourth, the careers of political appointees are short and those of careerists are long. This disparity makes for an uncomfortable relationship, one in which political superiors operate within a brief time frame, initiating enterprises they will not see through to completion, or restricting themselves to short-run ventures for which they can get credit. Careerists, operating within an extended time frame, have a memory of what has worked and not worked in the past, an awareness of the long lead time from genesis of a program to its maturation, and an institutional loyalty and interpersonal network within agency and government that are uncharacteristic of most of the strangers recruited for political posts. Government is like a repertory theater whose regular cast was there before and remains during and after the visit of each celebrity imported to star for a short run.

Fifth, although strong support remains for protecting the civil service system from political interference, frustration is growing with the restrictions that have accumulated in the system over time. Reformers are eager to provide managers with more flexibility, but every reform raises twin problems: fears that the changes will uproot the nation's long and deep commitment to politically neutral administration, and worries that the reforms will not go far enough in ensuring government grows its capacity to meet big, tough problems.

Sixth, these are deep, enduring, and critical issues. In his 2008 book, Paul C. Light tracks the fundamental puzzles back to the debate between Thomas Jefferson and Alexander Hamilton on the nature of the American republic. Light found that although much of government works well, human capital problems cripple its ability to rise to fundamental challenges. He concluded that "the federal service is suffering its greatest crisis since it was founded in the first moments of the republic . . . running out of energy [and] unable to faithfully execute all the laws."[67] Only a fundamental and sweeping reform, Light argues, can help government rise to the challenges it faces. Solving government's most important and fundamental problems depends on resolution of these issues of human capital management—and on linking them to the broader puzzles of government decision making and implementation. Human capital is not an isolated topic in itself but one that is intimately connected to government's capacity to do what must be done. We turn next to the issues raised in that connection.

Case 9

From the Front Lines of Human Capital: A New Take on Old Principles

From the late 1930s into the 1950s, employees of the Social Security Administration ran card-punch machines to maintain Social Security records. The government employed a large number of clerical workers in the days before computers revolutionized office work.

In the annals of modern public administration, few things are more basic than the merit system. It builds on a principle, established by Progressive reformers in the late nineteenth century, that government hiring should be based on what you know, not who you know. Standard tests determined who got government jobs and demonstrated skills determined promotions. Pay went with the job, not with the person.

Critics increasingly condemned the system for being too rigid to meet the needs of modern government. Reformers floated a host of ideas, but they all struggled to get political traction.

In the course of this debate, Dr. Nancy Kingsbury and her team at the Government Accountability Office (GAO) put together a strategy that, they believed, could provide a road map for real reform. What they produced in the summer of 2008 was the following merit system principles matrix.

Modern Management Concepts and Merit Principles = Modern Merit Principles

Purpose: The processes used in administrative systems are often surrogates for the underlying principles those systems are intended to achieve. In the federal personnel system, there is increasing consensus that at least some of the processes used in the system do not work effectively to support and create excellence, flexibility, urgency, and clarity of mission in the current or future environment. To help better understand how those processes might be changed, we have explored the underlying merit system principles and developed illustrative alternative language to highlight how principles may contribute to the existing problems and could be used to inform changes needed. We do not provide these ideas because we think they are the right answers; we do so to stimulate a debate about what the right answers might be, taking into account the organizational needs of federal agencies in the future and the special role and needs of federal employees as public servants. Because changes to the processes are being implemented incrementally, indeed almost chaotically, in various agencies, having a consistent and coherent understanding of the principles underlying federal employment would provide a useful framework for evaluating process change.

Merit system principles	Values embedded in current principles	Updated merit system principles	Values embedded in updated principles	Concepts behind the illustrative language
		1. Organizations should manage their human capital resources based on a clear understanding and communication of their core values, mission(s), and strategic plan, and an organizational alignment and leadership strategy that reflect those mission(s) and values.	Human capital Shared vision Effective communication Strategic alignment Effective leadership	Current MP have no organizational context except the public service writ large. Purpose is to establish a human capital framework within which to consider MP.
1. Recruitment should be from qualified individuals from appropriate sources in an endeavor to achieve a workforce from all segments of society, and selection and advancement should be determined solely on the basis of relative ability, knowledge, and skills, after fair and open competition which assures that all receive equal opportunity.	Competency/fitness Representative workforce Fair and open competition Equal opportunity Selection and advancement according to relative KSAs	2. Recruitment should be from highly qualified individuals to achieve a diverse workforce. Knowledges and skills, and ability to achieve results should determine selection, reward, and advancement within a framework of open competition and equal opportunity.	Competency/fitness Excellence Diversity Fair and open competition Equal opportunity Selection, reward, and advancement according to relative performance and knowledges and skills Achieving results	Setting a higher standard for qualification. Incorporating concepts of performance and results in selection, reward, and advancement. Shift emphasis from "representation" to diversity. Veterans' preference unchanged.

Original Principle	Keywords	Revised Principle	Keywords	Notes
2. All employees and applicants for employment should receive fair and equitable treatment in all aspects of personnel management without regard to political affiliation, race, color, religion, national origin, sex, marital status, age, or handicapped condition, and with proper regard for their privacy and constitutional rights.	Fairness Equity Diversity Protection against discrimination Privacy rights Constitutional rights	[See revised principle 9 for incorporation of fairness and equity concerns.]		[These concepts are important and are the positive side of the "protections" clauses later in the MP. Suggest moving them there to provide directly linked context for the protections.]
3. Equal pay should be provided for work of equal value, with appropriate consideration of both national and local rates paid by employers in the private sector, and appropriate incentives and recognition should be provided for excellence in performance.	Comparable worth Pay parity with the private sector Effective pay parity across localities Incentives and recognition for excellence	3. Equal pay should be provided for work of equal value, with appropriate consideration of national and local rates paid by employers in other appropriate employment sectors for similar skills. [See revised principle 5 for incorporation of issues related to incentives and recognition.]	Comparable worth Pay parity with all appropriate sectors (private, nonprofit, S/L) Effective pay parity across localities	Broaden concept of pay equity to more appropriate sectors. Concept of reward for excellence picked up in broadened MP 5, so dropped here as redundant (and conceptually separate from comparable pay issue).
4. All employees should maintain high standards of integrity, conduct, and concern for the public interest.	Integrity/honesty Conduct above reproach Public interest	4. All employees and applicants should carry out their responsibilities with energy, integrity, and an understanding and commitment to the mission, core values, and goals of their organization, with appropriate recognition of their special responsibilities to protect the collective best interest of the nation and its citizens.	Integrity/honesty Commitment to agency mission, values, and goals Hard work/sense of urgency duty to the collective best interest of the nation	Expand concept of duty to include energy and commitment to agency mission. Expand "public interest" to more specifically incorporate the concept of duty of loyalty to the collective best interest.
5. The federal workforce should be used efficiently and effectively.	Efficiency Effectiveness	5. Incentives and recognition should be provided based on excellence in both individual and team performance based on achievement of organizational results.	Incentives for results and excellence Focus on individual and team performance and organizational outcomes	Expand rather limited concepts of efficiency and effectiveness to incorporate excellence in performance and organizational results.

(continues)

Modern Management Concepts and Merit Principles = Modern Merit Principles (continued)

Merit system principles	Values embedded in current principles	Updated merit system principles	Values embedded in updated principles	Concepts behind the illustrative language
6. Employees should be retained on the basis of adequacy of their performance, inadequate performance should be corrected, and employees should be separated who cannot or will not improve their performance to meet required standards.	Job security for adequate performance Explicit correction of poor performance Removal of consistent poor performers	6. Employees should be retained based on the identified organizational need for their skills and competencies and their demonstrated performance and commitment to public service. Employees should be separated who cannot or will not demonstrate individual performance that contributes to organizational goals.	Assessment of skill and competency needs Job security for performance that contributes to agency goals Public service	Incorporate organizational needs for skills into retention. Shift concept of performance away from "standards" to organizational goals.
7. Employees should be provided effective education and training in cases in which such education and training would result in better organizational and individual performance.	Effective education/training Increase organizational performance Increase individual performance	7. Employers and employees share responsibility to ensure that employees obtain effective education, training, and developmental opportunities to enhance their skills and abilities to contribute to organizational goals and to create human capital growth.	Effective education, training, and development Enhance skills and abilities Contribute to organizational goals Shared responsibility for human capital growth	Validate concept of human capital growth. Broaden training to include developmental experiences. Emphasize shared responsibility.
8A. Employees should be— protected against arbitrary action, personal favoritism, or coercion for partisan political purposes, and 8B. Employees should be— prohibited from using their official authority or influence for the purpose of interfering with or affecting the result of an election or a nomination for election.	Fairness Legal protections Independence Nonpartisan	9. Employees and applicants for employment should receive fair and equitable treatment and respect for their privacy and constitutional rights in all aspects of their employment, and without regard to political affiliation, race, color, religion, national origin, sex, marital status, age, or handicapped condition. To that end, employees should be (a) protected against arbitrary action, personal favoritism, or coercion for	Fairness and diversity Nondiscrimination Legal protections against reprisals [Elimination of prohibiting employees from influencing an election or nomination could	Establish positive rights as rationale for protections. Eliminate details of protections if covered in other statutes. Reduce "weight of words" in favor of protections as opposed to positive principles and organizational interest.

Merit principle	KSA/values		Recommendation
9. Employees should be protected against reprisal for the lawful disclosure of information which the employees reasonably believe evidences—	Legal protections against reprisals	partisan political or ideological reasons, (b) protected against reprisal for legally protected disclosures of information.	be dropped as redundant with existing statutes and inconsistent in logic with the "protections" elements of all of the rest of the principle.]
9A. a violation of any law, rule, or regulation, or	Faithfully uphold the laws		
9B. mismanagement, a gross waste of funds, an absence of authority, or a substantial and specific danger to public health or safety.	Faithfully manage and guard the taxpayers' interest		
10. Managers and employees (and employees' representatives) should work together to balance management responsibilities and employee interests to effectively and efficiently achieve high performance of the organization's mission and goals.		Cooperation Shared vision of achieving agency goals Employee interests Management responsibilities	Rectify current MP silence on labor management relations. Focus on balanced responsibilities (management and labor). Reinforce high performance and organizational mission.

Source: This merit principle matrix comes from Dr. Nancy Kingsbury, managing director for applied research and methods at the Government Accountability Office, who led a team at the GAO to develop this working document.
Note: MP = merit principle; KSA = knowledge, skills, and abilities; S/L = state and local (governments).

Questions to Consider

1. Consider the GAO matrix. Do you think this represents an improvement over existing human resources strategies?
2. What advantages do you think this strategy would have? What disadvantages?
3. Consider the political forces arrayed around the human resources issues, from public employee unions and good government groups to the White House and members of Congress. Which forces do you think would be allied on which sides of this debate?
4. Do you think the federal government ought to adopt this plan? If so, what political strategy would you create to advance it? If not, what would you suggest in its place?

Key Concepts

at-will employment **254**

broadbanding **250**

human capital **243**

Title 5 **252**

turnover **261**

For Further Reading

DeSeve, G. Edward. *The Presidential Appointee's Handbook.* Washington, D.C.: Brookings Institution Press, 2008.

General Accounting Office (now the Government Accountability Office). *High-Risk Series: Strategic Human Capital Management,* GAO-03-120. Washington, D.C.: GAO, 2003.

Heclo, Hugh. *A Government of Strangers: Executive Politics in Washington.* Washington, D.C.: Brookings Institution, 1972.

Ingraham, Patricia W. "Striving for Balance: Reforms in Human Resource Management." In *Handbook of Comparative Administration,* edited by Laurence Lynn Jr. and Christopher Pollitt. Oxford: Oxford University Press, forthcoming.

Light, Paul C. *A Government Ill Executed: The Decline of Federal Service and How to Reverse It.* Cambridge: Harvard University Press, 2008.

Light, Paul C. *Thickening Government: Federal Hierarchy and the Diffusion of Accountability.* Washington, D.C.: Brookings Institution, 1995.

Moe, Terry M. "The Politicized Presidency." In *The New Direction in American Politics,* edited by John E. Chubb and Paul E. Peterson, 235–271. Washington, D.C.: Brookings Institution, 1985.

Nathan, Richard P. *The Administrative Presidency.* New York: Wiley, 1983.

Radin, Beryl A. *The Accountable Juggler: The Art of Leadership in a Federal Agency.* Washington, D.C.: CQ Press, 2002.

Selden, Sally Coleman. *Human Capital: Tools and Strategies for the Public Sector.* Washington, D.C.: CQ Press, 2009.

Suggested Websites

The Government Accountability Office has carefully examined the problem of managing human capital for a long time; see its work at **http://www.gao.gov.** In addition, the Office of Personnel Management (**http://www.opm.gov**) is an important source for both data and analysis of the human capital issue. For independent studies of human capital in government, see the work of the National Academy of Public Administration (**http://www.napawash.org**).

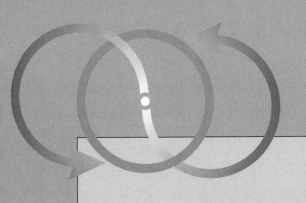

PART IV

Making and Implementing Government Decisions

If structure is the basic building block of administration, decision making is the central administrative act. However, organizational theorists have long disagreed about how best to make administrative decisions. This section probes the competing theories of decision making and applies those theories to the most important of all administrative decisions, the budget. Without money to back them up, most decisions are hollow.

Making good decisions, however, is not enough, because decisions are not self-executing. They require skillful management by effective managers if the bold promises embodied in public policy are not to find disappointment in poor implementation. This section concludes by looking carefully at the link between decision making and implementation.

10

Decision Making

Most early students of public administration concentrated on how to design an organization's structure so that it would function as efficiently as possible. Luther Gulick's classic formulation, discussed in chapter 4, defined basic principles for administrators to use in organizing agencies. In 1945, however, Herbert A. Simon posed a very different approach, contending that "a theory of administration should be concerned with the processes of decision as well as with the processes of action." In fact, Simon argued,

> The task of "deciding" pervades the entire administrative organization quite as much as does the task of "doing"—indeed, it is integrally tied up with the latter. A general theory of organization that will insure correct decision-making must include principles of organization that will include correct decision-making, just as it must include principles that will insure effective action.[1]

Simon thus established decision making as a central element of public administration; indeed, in his view, it was *the* central element.

Decision making occurs through a seamless web, from top to bottom in an organization. The job of administering governmental policy means that, at each step along the way, administrators must determine what the policy is and what their role is in bringing it to life. Decision making thus is the quintessential administrative act: as Simon pointed out, doing is impossible without deciding.

The study of administrative decision making, however, has often been full of conflict. Many different theories of decision making have struggled for acceptance. Moreover, each of these theories has carried with it heavy baggage: descriptive elements—detailing how decision making typically *does* work; and normative elements—prescribing how decision making *should* work. Weighed down with these opposing burdens, no decision-making approach predominates. Each one, however, has helped provide useful techniques for making decisions and has described the fundamental problems that theory must answer. In this chapter, we first examine the

decision-making is key

lots of theories

basic problems with which decision-making theories struggle. Then we probe competing approaches to decision making. We conclude by exploring the enduring problems that plague decision making and those who attempt to develop good descriptions and prescriptions.

Basic Problems

Every approach to administrative decision making must tackle two issues. First, what information can decision makers use in reaching their judgments? Information is the basic raw material of decisions, and decision makers must acquire, weigh, and act on the data they collect. Second, how do political values affect decisions? The sheer complexity of public problems and the overwhelming volume of information force decision makers to simplify the context shaping their decisions. This inevitable simplification is the product of political values. Moreover, for a decision to stick, it must win enough support to prevent others from seeking to overturn it. Building support means finding a common base of values among those who could sustain the decision. Both information and values constantly intermingle as administrators seek to make decisions and as theorists develop arguments about how the process does—and ought to—work.

Information

Decisions, of course, can be made at whim or on the basis of strong opinions. An administrator who believes that overdevelopment harms the environment or that all basic scientific research is useful, regardless of its costs, may be tempted to make decisions accordingly. Common knowledge, instinct, and bias can drive even the most complex of decisions.[2]

Public administrators are hired not for their bias but for their expertise, as Weber long ago pointed out.[3] Indeed, the presumption that specialized administrators will exercise expert judgment provides the basis for legislators' delegation of power. Legislators cannot be expected to anticipate or solve all of the complex problems that typically crop up in the administration of public programs. Furthermore, even when a general policy may be clear, conditions vary so around the country that administrators must often tailor programs to fit local needs. Thus, if decision making is the very life of administrative activity, it is no exaggeration to say that information is the mother's milk of decision making. Expert skills and good information form the core of administrative decisions.

The importance of good information to effective public administration can scarcely be overestimated. That very importance, however, creates a dilemma. On the one hand, it is often deceptively difficult to uncover useful information and channel it to relevant decision makers. On the other hand, knowledge brings power, and it is hard for the inexpert to control expert authority. This is, of course, a reprise of the classic public administration struggle between neutral competence and political accountability, but nowhere in public administration is this struggle sharper.[4]

The problem is that information rarely is an abstract truth but, more typically, is a matter of interpretation. No one ever knows everything, and never does everyone know the same things. Acquiring information is often an expensive activity, and some participants have an advantage over others because they have greater resources. Moreover, participants sometimes have a vested interest in keeping information hidden from others. In short, as Deborah A. Stone points out, "Because politics is driven by how people interpret information, much political activity is an effort to control interpretations."[5] Two aspects of information thus critically affect decision making: who has what information, and how they and others choose to look at the information they have.

Values

"Most important decision puzzles are so complicated that it is impossible to analyze them completely," Robert D. Behn and James W. Vaupel argue. Furthermore, they contend, "Decisions depend upon judgments—judgments about the nature of the dilemma, the probabilities of events, and the desirability of consequences. Decision making is inherently subjective."[6] Any process that includes some questions while leaving others out, estimates the likelihood of different outcomes, and, especially, weighs preferences for different outcomes is a value-laden process. One important question that decision-making theories must face, therefore, is how such value judgments are to be made.

Furthermore, no public policy decision, no matter how expertly reached, can endure if it does not command political support.[7] As Francis E. Rourke points out, political support for administrative decisions can come from higher levels of the executive branch, from Congress, or from the public.[8] Public support typically comes from two sources: an agency's decisions may enjoy a favorable opinion among the general public—what Rourke calls an agency's "mass public"—or they may draw support from its "attentive publics"—groups that have a "salient interest in the agency." These two forms of support are not exclusive, and many agencies actively cultivate both.[9] NASA, for example, works hard to promote the allure of space flight among the general public, while it labors to build support among its contractors for recurring battles on Capitol Hill over financing for its expensive programs.

As important as broad support is, political support from an agency's attentive publics typically is much more crucial. Few private citizens have the resources or the time to follow or comprehend the intricate detail and complex trail that most public policy decisions follow. In most decisions, only those who have the strongest interest are willing to devote the time and money needed to understand and influence the issues. This means, of course, that most difficult administrative decisions are reached within a relatively closed world dominated by those with common and intense interests.[10]

The relatively greater importance of strong support from narrow interests carries with it another dilemma for administrative decision makers: seeking the support of an agency's attentive publics risks sacrificing the broader interests of the public. In contrast, if the decision maker cultivates only mass public support, he or she risks offending powerful interests, which may then use their influence to exact a heavy price. In short, every administrative decision maker needs to win political support for decisions, but how that support is won can raise important problems. Few public decisions are ever stable, because the forces that support them change constantly. Most decisions involve carving out boundaries—what is acceptable and what is not, how much is enough and how much is too much. Such boundary setting is, in Stone's words, an "inherently unstable" process in which "boundaries are border wars waiting to happen."[11]

The complexity of decision making in bureaucracy has led to many different approaches. In this chapter, we explore four of them, noting how each one deals with the fundamental problems of information and values: (1) the rational approach, which seeks to maximize efficiency; (2) the **bargaining approach,** which seeks to maximize political support; (3) the **participative decision-making approach,** which seeks to improve decisions by intimately involving those affected by them; and (4) the **public-choice approach,** which attempts to substitute marketlike forces for other incentives that, its supporters argue, distort decisions.

Rational Decision Making

Rational decision making, which is perhaps the classic approach, builds on the work of microeconomists (who seek to explain the behavior of individuals and firms) and holds efficiency as the highest value. Proponents of this school argue that the goal of any activity, including governmental programs, is to get the biggest return for any investment. Simply put, they seek the most bang for the buck.

The rational method fundamentally rests on the systems theory approach described in chapter 4. The decision maker structures the decision-making problem as a system that processes inputs to produce outputs, and then seeks to produce the most output for a given level of inputs—or, alternatively, to determine the minimum amount of inputs needed to produce a given amount of output. In short, the decision maker seeks to maximize efficiency.

The systems approach is so simple, its logic so overpowering, that it is easy to understand how it has become a classic. After all, we speak of "computer systems," which are hunks and slivers of silicon, wires, and plastic that process inputs (such as letters typed into a keyboard) into outputs (such as letters and reports and books like this one). Computer analysts strive to improve the system: to make computers work more quickly or more cheaply or do things that could not be done before.

Basic Steps

The rational decision-making approach follows five basic steps:

1. *Define goals.* The rational approach starts with a description of a problem to be solved and an output goal to be achieved. For example, a policy analyst might seek to determine the best way to reduce automobile accident deaths by 10 percent or to reduce air pollution below dangerous limits. This is very different from conventional ways of thinking about government programs, which focus on activity measures, such as the number of Social Security checks mailed and the miles of highway built. The systems approach concentrates instead on most effectively producing desired outputs. The goals come to analysts through the legislative process.

2. *Identify alternatives.* Once the decision maker has determined the goal, the analyst tries to identify the different ways the goal can be achieved. In the search, the key is to think innovatively about new options that others might never have tried or even considered.

3. *Calculate the consequences.* The analyst then weighs the alternatives by measuring the costs and benefits of each one. In the strictest form of such analyses, in fact, every cost and benefit is translated into dollar terms. Furthermore, the analyst also considers indirect benefits and costs—often called **externalities** or **spillovers**—that relate to other goals. For example, a highway route that is best in terms of the stated transportation goal may destroy parks and increase downtown traffic congestion.

4. *Decide.* Once the analysis is finished, the decision maker chooses the alternative with the most favorable balance of benefits to costs.

5. *Begin again.* Systems analysis is not a once-and-done process. Instead, analysts see it as an iterative process: a project provides feedback—new information about what works and what does not, as well as consequences (intended and not) of a decision—which then helps the analyst redefine the problem, set new goals, and begin the process again. By continually working to fine-tune the system by learning from past mistakes, systems analysis in theory helps decision makers move ever closer to the best decisions.

Although the rational approach may seem abstract, it has the appeal of common sense: any sensible person will choose the most rational (and efficient) route to his or her goal. Who, after all, wants to be irrational?[12]

Example: The Planning-Programming-Budgeting System

Because of its logic, the rational approach has many followers. As the classic case of the **Planning-Programming-Budgeting System** (PPBS) shows, however, the straight-forward logic of rational decision making has many variations in practice. Further-more, the considerable difficulties of *doing* systems analysis can be its undoing.

In 1961 Secretary of Defense Robert McNamara introduced PPBS in the Penta-gon.[13] The technique involved three phases: (1) planning, in which top-level man-agers developed five-year strategies for defense activities; (2) programming, in which the strategies were transformed into detailed descriptions of the department's needs, including which weapons systems had to be purchased when; and (3) budgeting, in which officials transformed the program into year-by-year budget requests. The basic idea was to link the annual budgetary process with long-range plans instead of making haphazard requests. Furthermore, each branch of the service was to budget by program instead of by organizational unit. The Pentagon, for example, would decide whether the nation's strategic needs required a new jet fighter and, if so, what capabilities it ought to have. Program budgeting, McNamara hoped, would drive down the cost of buying weapons systems by reducing competition among the ser-vices for their own individually tailored weapons systems.

President Johnson was so pleased with the results in the Department of Defense (DOD) that he extended the technique in 1965 to almost all federal civilian depart-ments and agencies. Each agency submitted its budget to the Bureau of the Budget (now the Office of Management and Budget) by program.[14] The program budgets were, in turn, supported by massive memoranda that considered "all relevant out-puts, costs, and financing needs" as well as "the benefits and costs of alternative approaches" to solving problems. Each agency also prepared a five-year projection of its future programs and financial requirements. The plans, however, were often "lengthy wish lists of what the agencies would like to spend on their programs if no fiscal constraints were imposed." The connection between PPBS paperwork and what agencies actually planned to do was often amorphous. Since Congress continued to run its appropriations process the old way, the link between PPBS and congressional decisions was fuzzy indeed.[15]

Instead of integrating and improving presidential and congressional decisions on the budget, PPBS produced its own paperwork domain. PPBS finally collapsed under the burden, and in June 1971 the federal government's PPBS ended, as the

Office of Management and Budget ceased requiring that agencies submit PPBS documents with their conventional budget requests.[16]

In terms of its original objectives, PPBS was a failure. It never was able to transform the base of government planning and link budgets—government's inputs—to its outputs. In foreign governments and nearly all state and local governments that have tried the system, it has produced similar results.[17] Part of PPBS's failure came from budgeters' inability to cope with the system's analytical burdens. More fundamentally, it failed because of a critical design flaw: PPBS's designers left Congress out of the system, and PPBSers "refused to reveal to Congress the studies and information produced by the PPB system . . . [though] without information of this kind, the ability of Congress to even ask the right questions concerning program performance is seriously impaired."[18]

Moreover, although PPBS was solely an instrument of the executive branch, even that limited environment was neglected. PPBS designers were inadequately prepared to neutralize bureaucratic resistance. Any innovation produces such resistance, but PPBSers seemed arrogant to many other government officials. Lower organizational units were upset that PPBS appeared to rob them of authority (centralizing it instead in agency heads and the Bureau of the Budget), that it shifted analytical work from agency staffs knowledgeable about the agency's policy area to PPBS technicians skilled in quantifying but unacquainted with the policy area, and that it required an enormous amount of paperwork without discernible impact on decision making.

Nevertheless, PPBS's results were substantial. It brought into the government a number of able analysts, many of whom remained.[19] It acquainted a large number of top executives and career civil servants with a new style of discourse, one that emphasizes clarification of objectives, generation of alternative ways of serving the objectives, and quantification of benefits and costs where such measurement is appropriate. Multiyear projections of program costs are now transmitted to Congress as a regular part of the budgetary process. The approach has even spilled over into repeated efforts to apply benefit-cost analysis to other government strategies, such as regulation.

The Pentagon, moreover, still actively works on a modified PPBS. Defense officials continue to develop long-range plans, translate those plans into programs, and develop the programs into budgets. The way the process works has varied considerably by administration: Republicans have tended to vest more authority with the individual services, while Democratic administrations have pulled more authority to the defense secretary. Despite the longevity of the process, however, its results continue to be disappointing. Lawrence J. Korb, former assistant secretary of defense, argues that during the Reagan administration, top officials' approach to PPBS "contributed to a near collapse of rational budgeting in DOD and helped undermine the consensus in this country for a buildup. Indeed, when [Defense Secretary Caspar] Weinberger departed the Pentagon in late 1987, the budgeting process was in near chaos." Korb contends that defense planning had "almost no impact on the process," that programming meetings had far too many participants to make meaningful decisions, and that previous decisions never drove final budget decisions.[20]

Appraisal

Because the rational approach to decision making seems so straightforward, it has a large following. Even the most cynical critics of PPBS could scarcely argue against improving the way the federal government formulates its goals and how to achieve them. Still, the rational approach must struggle with several serious problems, dealing with both information and values.

Information

The pure systems approach requires an extraordinary amount of information. Decision makers must consider all alternatives to achieving a policy goal, which, of course, is impossible because no one's wit is equal to a complete search of possibilities. In fact, to some systems-approach critics, the impossibility of comprehensive analysis itself renders the approach useless. As Charles E. Lindblom, perhaps the method's strongest critic, argues: "Men have always wanted to fly. Was the ambition to undertake unaided flight, devoid of any strategy for achieving it, ever a useful norm or ideal? . . . Achieving impossible feats of synopsis [comprehensive analysis] is a bootless, unproductive ideal."[21] Moreover, by trying to do the impossible, Lindblom worries, "they fall into worse patterns of analysis and decision." Even the cost, in time, energy, and money, of a nearly comprehensive search is extremely high, and the decision maker driven by comprehensiveness can never be sure what has been left out. The goal itself is impossible, the gaps are rarely defined, and the result is an uncharted gap in the analysis whose effects are unknown.[22]

In real life, of course, no one ever tries to be completely comprehensive. Decision makers instead simplify the process: (1) they screen out the silly options and restrict themselves to a few major alternatives; and (2) they stop searching when they come upon a satisfactory alternative, even though further search might turn up a better one. James G. March and Herbert A. Simon have called this approach **satisficing.**[23]

Such realism does not carry us very far, for two reasons. First, most of the calculations required for translating benefits and costs into dollars and cents require value judgments: how much worth should be accorded a life, a child's happiness, a scenic view from the highway, or a pleasing architectural design? Economists in fact have developed mechanisms for pricing even such difficult things as the value of a human life.[24] The very attempt to weigh the value of different items, however, often takes us to extremely difficult (and sometimes bizarre) judgments. As Lewis M. Branscomb writes,

> Despite the well-publicized conflict between economic and ecological interests, our appreciation for environmental impact and technology assessment is unique in the world. Where else would (i) a $600-million hydroelectric dam be held up to protect an endangered 3-inch freshwater fish called the snail darter, (ii) a unique butterfly enjoy priority at the end of the main runway of the Los Angeles International Airport, and (iii) the sexual aspirations of a clam threaten the construction of a nuclear power station in New Hampshire?[25]

Second, how do we know when we have found a satisfactory range of alternatives? To study some alternatives and not others is to make a value judgment, yet value-free analysis is the goal of rational decision making. Rational analysts are thus back in the same dilemma between doing their best to guess what alternatives others might have had in mind and imposing their own values on the array of alternatives. Either way, the process for defining standards is vague, and little science remains in the so-called science of rational decision making. That, in turn, raises new questions about values.

Values

The systems approach depends on a clear statement of goals. Without such a statement, in fact, it quite simply cannot work. The classic literature on rational decision making, however, has little to say about *who* sets goals. Instead, the theory presumes that *some* decision maker will define the objective in the precise form needed for rational decision makers at lower levels to proceed with their tasks. Yet we know that Congress's statements of objectives often lack clarity and consistency, that Congress would fight the president if the president attempted to set comprehensive goals, and that executive branch agencies usually get caught between the two. This uncertainty, in turn, leaves the rational decision makers with two choices: to make their own best guess about what Congress, for example, may have intended in passing a law (and risk being told they are wrong when, as is likely, someone disagrees); or to apply subjective values to define the goals (and risk undercutting the very objectivity at the core of systems analysis).

The American political system constantly formulates and reformulates goals as political majorities shift, as the effectiveness of various interest groups waxes and wanes, as population changes, and as new technologies and new information alter the shape of problems and our capacity to deal with them. The art of assembling majority support, among voters and legislators, for each program typically requires fuzzy goals and vague language. The more precisely objectives are defined, the easier it is for competing parties to disagree with them.

The rational, efficiency-minded approach often works very well for small-scale and technical issues, on which agreement over goals is relatively easy. Should a local government buy or lease its police cars? Which paving material will last the longest? How much of which kind of snow-removal equipment should a city buy? On larger questions, however, the constitutional separation of powers, political realities, bureaucratic dynamics, and rapidity of change in world and domestic conditions give little hope of finding a way to define goals clearly. What is the best solution if there is disagreement over what the problem is?

Efficiency is not the only goal we seek. Equality, for example, is often a central objective in public programs. In fact, the economist Arthur M. Okun calls the job of balancing equality and efficiency "the big tradeoff": "We can't have our cake of market efficiency and share it equally."[26] Another economist, Murray Weidenbaum, who served in the Reagan administration as chairman of the Council of Economic Advisers, goes even further, observing that

> it is possible to develop government investment projects which meet the efficiency criterion (that is, the total benefits exceed the total costs) but which fail to meet the simplest standards of equity. . . . Unfortunately, there has been a tendency on the part of some economists to dismiss such "distributional" questions as subjective and political, and hence not within the proper concern of economic analysis.[27]

The rational approach thus has great attraction because it offers an elegant prescription for how the best decisions can be made. In describing the practical policy world, however, it falls short. Its advocates, in fact, often follow rational techniques only as long as those techniques help them achieve their own political ends. Moreover, even in the abstract, rational techniques do not tell decision makers where to draw the line short of the impossible task of comprehensiveness. Nor do these techniques solve the fundamental question of whose values will be used to perform the analysis. Indeed, agreement on goals, as the bargaining approach contends, is the central problem of decision making.

Strategic Planning

The tremendous difficulty of managing a rational decision-making process has scarcely prevented some governments from taking a far more systematic view of their operations and results. As we see in subsequent chapters, government reforms have in many cases centered on defining goals more explicitly and in measuring governments' success in achieving them.

For example, the state of Oregon began in the late 1980s to create a strategic vision for its citizens' quality of life; it defined hundreds of benchmarks and began tracking the state's progress in achieving them, through a series of reports. The Commonwealth of Virginia took an even more systematic approach by creating a Council on Virginia's Future, a body headed by the governor and including legislative and community leaders. The council articulated a statewide long-term vision, including where the state wanted to be in economic growth and educational attainment, and it set up forty measures for assessing progress; finally, it linked these goals to the performance of state agencies as a way of holding them accountable for results. Even some local governments, such as York County in southern Pennsylvania, have devised strategies that identify community goals and the strategies for achieving them.

For all the reasons that had undermined previous comprehensive planning efforts, some critics suggested that such strategic planning exercises were likely to do little more than employ consultants and create meaningless debate. Despite the high obstacles, governments nonetheless seem committed to continuing the effort. They appear to see some value in having the conversation and in elevating the debate beyond the usual day-to-day struggles over budgets to the larger purposes for which the money is being spent. None are likely to be fully successful. However, it is a testimony to the enduring power of the *idea* of comprehensive planning that so many governments continue so vigorously to try to accomplish it.

Bargaining

We have earlier taken note of the pluralistic approach to administrative organization (chapter 4) and of the alliances that sometimes develop among an agency, its related congressional committees, and its clientele interest groups (chapter 7). These issues demonstrate how decision making involves conflict, negotiation, persuasion, and individuals with stakes in particular policies and decisions.

The bargaining approach to decision making builds on these concepts to develop a different view of rationality. The approach's proponents, such as Charles E. Lindblom, argue that it is paradoxically most rational to conduct limited analysis and then to bargain out a decision that can attract political support.

Lindblom offers a simple prescription, **incrementalism,** for the analysis of public decisions.[28] It is best, he says, to limit that analysis to a few alternatives instead of trying to judge them all; to weigh one's values along with the evidence instead of holding them separate as the rational approach would suggest; and to concentrate on the immediate problems to be solved rather than the broader goals to be achieved. The great goals are almost always beyond reach, especially in the short run, and problems presented in smaller chunks are easier to define, diagnose, and solve. It is, furthermore, easier to build support for a series of incremental changes from the current situation and to correct any errors that might creep in. Decision making is thus essentially value laden.[29] Conflicts are the rule and cannot be resolved by rational analysis. Instead, **partisan mutual adjustment**—the pulling and hauling among decision makers with different views—offers the best hope for the best decisions, supporters of the bargaining approach contend.[30]

In fact, regulatory reformers have developed an explicit bargaining strategy to reduce conflict. Many federal regulations are automatically litigated by interest groups that disagree with what the regulators have written. When new rules are promulgated, lawyers flock to the telephones to report to their offices, and their colleagues rush to file appeals. Endless legal delays thus are the rule, not the exception. To produce better rules and to forestall litigation, the Environmental Protection Agency holds **regulatory negotiation sessions** involving the various interests potentially affected by a new rule. In a series of bargaining sessions, they meet to hammer out a mutually acceptable regulation and, in the process, greatly reduce the chances that the rule will be litigated. While this strategy cannot be used for all rulemaking—even when successful it raises some important problems—regulatory negotiation does reduce conflict and promote quicker, cleaner regulation.[31] More often, of course, the bargaining is much less structured, as the classic case of the Cuban missile crisis illustrates.

Example: The Cuban Missile Crisis

In October 1962 the United States came to the brink of nuclear war with the Soviet Union. American intelligence aircraft discovered that the Soviets had built missile bases in Cuba from which they could have launched nuclear strikes against New York, Washington, D.C., and other important East Coast targets. American experts estimated that the resulting war would kill 100 million Americans, more than that number of Russians, and millions more Europeans. President Kennedy's advisers worried about why the Soviets had placed the missiles in Cuba to begin with and how they could convince the Soviets to remove the weapons.

The White House launched a public relations offensive against the Soviets, in which Adlai Stevenson, U.S. ambassador to the United Nations, dramatically revealed reconnaissance photos of the bases, asked for an explanation from the Soviet ambassador, and promised to wait for an answer "until hell froze over." The president's advisers developed several alternatives to deal with the crisis: military officials planned an attack on the missile bases to wipe them out before they could become fully operational; other advisers suggested a naval blockade to turn back further shipments of the missiles and to give the Soviets a chance to dismantle the missiles before hostilities began. Meanwhile, the administration conducted quiet back-channel diplomacy to try to uncover the Soviet Union's motives and to attempt to defuse the crisis.

President Kennedy decided on the blockade, and the nation waited anxiously to see if Soviet freighters bound for Havana would turn around; when they first stopped short of the blockade line and then returned to Soviet ports, tensions eased. Soviet premier Nikita S. Khrushchev agreed to remove the missiles and never again to deploy such weapons in Cuba. Kennedy in return promised not to invade Cuba and to remove the American missiles in Turkey that had worried the Soviets. After thirteen October days of high tension, the crisis ended.[32]

Graham Allison, who studied the crisis, argues that the events could be understood from three different perspectives. First, in what he christened Model I, the Cuban missile crisis could be analyzed from a traditional, rational-actor approach: both the United States and the Soviet Union had unified national positions that guided each side's decisions. Second, he advanced Model II, based on organizational processes: decisions could be understood by analyzing the standard operating procedures of the bureaucracies on both sides. Finally, he proposed Model III, identified as the bureaucratic-politics perspective: decisions could be understood as "a *resultant* of various bargaining games among players in the national government." By examining "the perceptions, motivations, positions, power, and maneuvers of the players," one could understand a decision.[33]

This bargaining model does help to illuminate the missile crisis. Kennedy, for example, was vulnerable because of the failure of the American-supported Bay of Pigs invasion by Cuban exiles trying to overthrow Cuban leader Fidel Castro in April 1961. Americans had come to believe that communist domination of Cuba constituted a serious threat to American security, and the failure of that invasion attempt made Kennedy seem indecisive. As a consequence, when faced with the discovery of missiles in Cuba, his administration had to act forcefully. The options of doing nothing or taking a diplomatic approach therefore lost ground to the prospect of a military response.

Kennedy initially favored what some advisers called a "surgical" air strike, designed to take out the missile launchers without doing more widespread damage. Other participants, however, including Defense Secretary Robert McNamara, worried deeply that even limited shots might immediately escalate beyond either side's control into nuclear war. The president's brother, Robert Kennedy, pointedly asked whether the president, if he launched a surprise attack, would become known as an American Tojo—the Japanese strategist who had planned the raid on Pearl Harbor. In fact, as Allison points out, "after these arguments had been stated so strongly, the president scarcely could have followed his initial preference without seeming to become what RFK had condemned."[34]

Three of the president's closest advisers—Robert Kennedy, McNamara, and presidential counselor Theodore Sorensen—teamed up to press for the blockade. Meanwhile, military advisers, CIA chief John McCone, and Secretary of State Dean Rusk argued in favor of the air strike, but their position weakened when one of the

As tensions with the Soviet Union escalated in 1962, President John F. Kennedy met with his brother, Attorney General Robert F. Kennedy, on the portico outside the Oval Office. The government's decision-making strategies during that month's Cuban missile crisis became a much-studied case of how—and how not—to frame governmental policy.

participants asked how the Soviets would likely respond. The best guess was that the Soviets would strike at American missile bases in Turkey, which would, under the NATO treaty, compel the United States to attack the Soviet Union. No one found that appealing. Finally, military planners began to argue that a surgical air strike was impossible and that, to be effective, any military action against the missile launchers would have to be accompanied by a broad-scale attack against all Cuban military installations and, in all likelihood, an invasion.

The ultimate decision to establish a blockade, along with the other key decisions of the crisis, thus can be viewed as the result of a bargaining process among the key players. Decisions are, in reality, complex arenas in which decision makers must resolve uncertainties and conflicting preferences. As Allison concludes, "What moves the chess pieces is not simply the reasons that support a course of action, or the routines of organizations that enact an alternative, but the power and skill of proponents and opponents of the action in question."[35] Decisions thus are viewed as the product of bargains. In the bargaining game, the perspective of each player is shaped by the player's position: "where you stand depends on where you sit," the saying goes.[36] Who wins depends on who has the strongest hand and who bargains most effectively.[37]

Appraisal

The bargaining approach has drawn withering fire from its critics, especially among proponents of the rational approach.

Information

Critics contend that the bargaining approach is dangerously incomplete and risks depriving decision makers of important information.[38] The political process, they contend, can be counted on to present decision makers with political opinions, but it is far less useful in identifying which alternatives are likely to be the most efficient. The result, they suggest, is that scarce resources can be wasted. When money is tight, bargaining over public programs might produce common ground only by spreading money among the combatants. One economist, Charles Schultze, acknowledges that "it may, indeed, be necessary to guard against the naïveté of the systems analyst who ignores *political* constraints and believes that efficiency alone produces virtue." But in taking aim at the incrementalists, he concludes, "it is equally necessary to guard against the naïveté of the decision maker who ignores *resource* constraints and believes that virtue alone produces efficiency."[39] It is possible, Schultze argues, to take account of political realities while doing systems analysis.

Lindblom replies that systems analysis cannot be done and argues that his decision-making approach is indeed analysis; he merely suggests that limited, successive comparison of alternatives is more successful than attempts at comprehensiveness. The bargaining approach, however, does not really tell the analyst just how comprehensive to be, how much analysis to do. Just how large ought an increment to be? How many alternatives should a decision maker consider? The only answer is a circular one: the increments should be small enough and the alternatives few enough to produce political consensus. A decision maker knows that the approach is right if a consensus forms and wrong if it does not. While this formula may offer a useful description of many decisions, it provides a weak guide for officials trying to design a decision-making process.

Values

The bargaining approach is obviously at its strongest in describing how decisions are made and, in particular, how decision makers build political support for their judgments. Indeed, incrementalism grows directly out of enduring American traditions of participation in politics as well as more recent theories of pluralism. Its rooting in this heritage gives the approach extra appeal.

Nevertheless, the role of interests in decision making varies substantially in the government. In some agencies, such as the Department of Agriculture or the Social Security Administration, relatively broad interests pay careful attention to decisions such as farm price supports or retirement benefits; interest group pressure is intermittent but occasionally intense. In other agencies, such as the Departments of State and Defense, the range of interests is narrower, and public attention is much less intense. For the most part, the partisans at work are those with a direct stake in the decisions, such as military contractors, Defense Department officials, and representatives of other parts of the government. The players and their roles in the bargaining process thus are likely to vary greatly by the type of agency and the nature of its programs. The value of the bargaining approach in resolving decision-making conflicts is likely to vary accordingly.

Furthermore, it is often difficult to bargain out differences. When issues are complicated and the interests narrow, it is easy for broader public interests to be submerged. Intense attentive publics can wield heavy influence over decisions before the general public even knows that a major decision is to be made. Well-financed special interests, furthermore, have a large advantage over an agency's general public: they can play a role in framing the decision to begin with, in producing analyses to influence the decision, and in gaining the ears of decision makers at crucial times. Their intimate familiarity with the issues and the decision makers gives them a strategic advantage that members of the general public can rarely match.

In contrast, especially in foreign policy and national security issues, the range of participants can be very limited, and the possibility of bargaining typically evaporates. Indeed, during the Reagan administration, a small group of White House officials conducted a clandestine policy of selling arms to Iran to win the release of American hostages in the Middle East—a policy developed outside regular State and Defense Department channels and without the benefit of expert advice. In many foreign policy cases, top decision makers often work above the alternatives produced by staff at lower levels.[40]

Bargaining thus provides a useful description of how many, but not all, administrative decisions are made. Just as with the rational approach, however, there are important normative problems with bargaining, particularly because not everyone is represented equally around the table, and some interests may not even be invited. Nevertheless, the approach is important for its assertion of the importance of values in decision making and for its stark contrast with the rational model.

Participative Decision Making

Beyond incrementalism is another approach founded even more directly on political democracy: participative decision making, which calls at the most general level for participation by those who will be affected by the decisions. That generality, however, leaves two ambiguities.

First, what does *participation* mean? It may mean being consulted for advice by someone who has power to make a decision, or it may mean sharing decision-making power, as when those affected vote on a proposed decision and their vote set-

who participates, + what do they get to do?

tles whether the proposal is adopted or rejected. Second, just who should be entitled to participate in decision making? Claims to such status can be made by four groups: (1) the employees of the organization making the decision; (2) the persons whom the organization serves or regulates (the clientele); (3) the taxpayers whose pocketbooks the decision will affect; and (4) the whole public, or at least the voting public, of the country. These participants are potentially in conflict: the course of action that any of these groups may recommend can vary sharply from what any other group might choose.

good

On the surface, the value of such participation seems obvious. Who could object to having the decision-making process enlightened by the views of those who have to live with the decision? The problem, of course, is that each group invokes "democracy" as its battle cry—sometimes to the exclusion of all other claimants. Furthermore, when one group gains leverage on a decision, such influence often comes only at a cost to other groups.

bad

For example, the poor, especially those in inner-city neighborhoods, have for decades sought a greater voice in the programs serving them. Residents of middle-class neighborhoods similarly demand a say about new projects, school closings, and other governmental initiatives that seem boons or threats to their quality of life. Often, in fact, the demand for such participation leads to the **NIMBY phenomenon**: strong pressures to keep potentially objectionable programs "not in my backyard." Federal statutes and administrative regulations require local community or neighborhood participation in decisions about community development, antipoverty programs, community mental health centers, and other programs. Meanwhile, a host of nongovernmental organizations—most of them newly created for the purpose—have been delegated responsibilities for administering government programs. For example, Congress created the Prospective Payment Advisory Commission to advise the Health Care Financing Administration on rates hospitals should be paid for Medicare cases; medical professionals dominate the commission, so physicians have a voice in what the federal government pays them. In a number of large cities, likewise, the board of education has decentralized power to elected neighborhood councils.

New techniques for participation evolved so quickly from the 1960s to the 1980s that many have supposed that clientele participation in decision making is a novel idea. In fact, American public administration has had long and rich experience with consultation and shared decisions, especially at the local level. These arrangements have not always been successful, and fewer frustrations would arise if new ventures toward participatory democracy and grass-roots decentralization took account of the hazards so well marked out by experience.

For decades, the federal government debated where best to build a long-term storage site for the nation's nuclear waste. After scientists recommended that the facility be built in Nevada at Yucca Mountain, 70 miles north of Las Vegas, government officials arrested 34 protesters who opposed the decision.

Example: The Federal Level

Federal agencies have long used advisory committees of private citizens in the decision-making process. Most important among these have been industry advisory committees, which have a painful history of troubles over representativeness, secrecy, conflicts of interest, profiteering on privileged information, temptations to violate antitrust laws, and displacement of responsible government officials as the real decision makers.

The high-water mark of these industry advisory committees came early in the New Deal when the National Recovery Administration relied heavily on trade associations, first, for the drafting of the nearly 500 codes of fair competition controlling the production and prices of as many industries, and second, for selection of members of the code authorities to which enforcement powers were delegated.[41] During World War II, industry advisory committees proliferated—the War Production Board had a thousand of them, and the Office of Price Administration some 650—and at national and regional levels joint industry-labor-government boards were given decisional power in labor disputes.[42] In the 1950s, the Business Advisory Council of the Department of Commerce attracted so much criticism as a privileged big-business channel of influence on administration policy that it was reconstituted as a private organization.[43] Dogging this history of industry advisory committees has been the risk that the government's assembling of representatives of an industry will validate Adam Smith's dictum: "People of the same trade seldom meet together, even for merriment and diversion, but the conversation ends in a conspiracy against the public, or in some contrivance to raise prices."[44]

A second major area of clientele participation through national advisory committees has to do with the allocation of funds for scientific research, including the awarding of research grants and contracts to individual scientists and institutions. The National Science Foundation, the National Institutes of Health, and other research-supporting agencies rely heavily on peer review by committees of scientists in the specialized fields. Here again, issues of representativeness, insiders' advantages, and unconscious bias have been raised about clientele participation.[45] During the Carter administration, the number of federal advisory committees was cut by 30 percent, to 816, but critics continued to complain that secrecy afflicted the committees.[46] In 2001 environmentalists made just that charge about a task force headed by Vice President Dick Cheney, which produced the Bush administration's energy policy.

Example: The Local Level

Over the past fifty years, a variety of national programs have promoted decentralized, grassroots participation by their clients. A few programs, in fact, involve all of their clients, rather than just representative councils and committees. For example, compulsory marketing quotas and marketing orders for several agricultural commodities can be instituted only by a two-thirds favorable vote in a referendum of all growers of the commodity.[47]

More commonly, federal agencies have relied on local committees whose part-time members were intended to be representative of their communities or neighborhoods. In some programs the local committees were appointed by the president or a federal agency after consultation with the governor, local government officials, or the agency's own field agents. This was true of the 5,500 War Price and Rationing Boards established in World War II by the Office of Price Administration (OPA). And it was true of the some 4,000 local Selective Service Boards that administered the draft during the Vietnam War. Though appointive, each board was meant to be "representative of the community as a whole" (OPA) or "composed of friends and neighbors of the registrant it classifies" (Selective Service).[48]

Farmers and Cattle Ranchers

The oldest form of local participation in decision making for federal programs comes in the administration of agricultural programs. In what is literally grassroots participation, farmers since 1933 have been elected to serve on committees in 3,000 counties. Members of the three-member committees are chosen either directly by the county's farmers or indirectly by the members of community committees. A county committee exercises real power: it "is ultimately responsible for program and administrative policies and decisions at the county level."[49] It establishes individual farms' acreage allotments and marketing quotas for some commodities, administers crop-support loans, provides disaster payments, and supervises government-owned commodity storage facilities. Choosing committee members is often difficult—a problem that spills over into other national programs. In one year's election, for example, the turnout nationally was only 23 percent, and in six major farming states the turnout ranged from 5 to 8 percent.[50] In half the communities of one Illinois county, there were more candidates than voters!

The grazing boards in the West, elected by local stockmen who grazed their cattle on prairie lands, are reminders that clientele participation can magnify self-interest at the expense of public interest and, indeed, of other special interests. These boards have effectively made most decisions on the issuance of permits for grazing on public lands, and, as Grant McConnell pointed out, the most influential ranchers have dominated the boards. Participation in district elections has been low, averaging less than 10 percent in Oregon and Idaho, and the committees have been dominated by the same powerful stockmen for a long time. As a result, "the general [public] interest in conservation of the soil has, on occasion at least, suffered from the pattern of power deriving from the autonomous systems of government of these lands."[51]

City Dwellers

Urban America has wrestled with the same problems without any attentiveness to the lessons of the rural experience. A series of federal programs begun in the mid-1960s required communities to establish citizen committees to help determine how the money should be spent. The mandates began with the 1964 Economic Opportunity Act, which required each local community action program in the War on Poverty to be "developed, conducted, and administered with the maximum feasible participation of the areas and members of the groups served." The 1966 Model Cities Act required that any local plan for rebuilding and revitalizing slum or blighted neighborhoods must provide for "widespread citizen participation" from those neighborhoods. In 1974 the Housing and Community Development Act (which superseded the Model Cities Act, among others) required that any local government applying for community development funds offer "satisfactory assurances" that it had provided citizens with "adequate" information, had held public hearings to learn citizens' views, and had provided citizens a chance to shape the application. If you think the quoted congressional phrases are imprecise, you are right: what is maximum or widespread or adequate participation was left an open question, which led to battles over infusing each term with a specific meaning.

Or consider education. There are approximately 16,000 local school boards around the country. As the movement to improve basic education gained steam in the mid-1980s, however, critics began to look seriously at the boards. "The system isn't working, and the reason it isn't working is that the stakes that have become the focus for most of the boards are the jobs involved, not what is happening in the schools and with the kids," said New York City Board of Education president Robert Wagner Jr. In fact, one *New York Times* headline announced, "School Boards Found Failing to Meet Goals," and its reporter concluded that the school district system was little more than a collection of "political clubhouses."[52] Turnout for school board elections in the city was consistently less than 10 percent, while patronage loomed over educational issues.[53] As part of a major 2002 reform the city changed the system to one with thirty-two Community District Education Councils, and each council has an advisory board composed of nine parents, two area residents, and a high school senior (who serves without a vote).[54]

Internet-based methods for encouraging collaboration have broadened the opportunities for participation. So, too, are the spread of neighborhood forums, which bring citizens together with decision makers to explore policies. Nearly everyone finds these processes valuable. The lasting question is what impact they have on decision making—and how they might improve the quality of the decisions made.

Appraisal

Since the mid-1970s, as complaints about decentralization have grown and as budgets have gotten tighter, the trend gradually has been to centralize control and put more decision-making responsibility in the hands of elected officials. This trend underlines the recurring dilemmas of participative decision making.

Information

One of the biggest advantages offered by participative approaches is the wealth of information they provide. Few insights into the management of public programs are better than those of the persons who must administer them, and few observers of any program's effects have keener insights than the citizens most affected by them. The very wealth of this information is a problem, however, because it typically flows to decision makers as a large, undifferentiated mass, with no easy clues about which information is most important. Too much information can sometimes be as bad as too little.

Values

In sorting through the vast amount of information that the participative approach produces, decision makers must also confront important value questions. The approach spawns these recurring dilemmas:

1. *Self-interest versus no interest*: a narrow clientele dedicated to protection of its own self-interest, or a broad, mixed clientele with a less-keen interest in the policy
2. *Too much versus too little representation*: direct participation in decision making by all members of the clientele who wish to participate—at the risk of assembling an impossibly large group to deal with—or direct participation only by those who get appointed or elected to committees, councils, or boards that are officially assumed to represent the clientele—but that may not be very representative
3. *Too much versus too little power*: formal or informal power given to citizens for making government decisions—raising the problem of who looks out for the public interest—or for simply providing advice (and demands) to public administrators who weigh those views with other considerations and make the actual decisions—but who may not take that advice seriously

The choices are hard, but they carry important implications for responsive and effective policymaking. On the one hand, participative decision making has led to new public access to government decisions and to the creation of a new cadre of civic leaders. On the other hand, the system has created some avenues of patronage and new officials seeking to protect their own positions. The record is mixed.[55]

Public Choice

Some microeconomists have developed a different theory to explain how public agencies make decisions, hence the name public choice.[56] Public-choice theory spins off the rational approach described in chapter 4, beginning with the bedrock of all economics—the assumption that human beings are rational and seek to maximize whatever is important to them. The most rational thing, according to the theory, is to promote one's self-interest. Whether choosing where to live or what car to buy, these economists argue, individuals attempt to maximize their utility: the value they derive from their decisions. In the private sector, this makes individuals and corporations competitive and leads to the most efficient distribution of resources.

Public-choice theory argues that public officials, like all other individuals, are self-interested, which leads them to avoid risk and to promote their careers. These objectives, in turn, mean that they seek to enlarge their programs and increase their budgets. As a result, public-choice economists argue, an organization full of self-interested bureaucrats is likely to produce bigger government that is both inefficient and prone to operating against the public's interest.[57] Bureaucrats' pursuit of self-interest, they contend, helps explain the often disappointing performance of American government.

This inference has led proponents of the public-choice school to argue that, wherever possible, governmental functions ought to be turned over to the private sector. From the Japanese government's sale of that nation's largest airline to Mexico's divestiture of 250 government-owned corporations, governments around the world have followed the public-choice prescription in privatizing public services. In fact, Japan has moved even further to a decade-long privatization of its postal system. Where this proves impossible, either for practical or for political reasons, public-choice proponents contend that public functions ought to be contracted out to the private sector. The contracting process, they assert, simulates private-sector competition and dilutes the influence of government bureaucrats.[58] As Stuart Butler, one of the movement's strongest voices, put it, **privatization** is a kind of "political guerrilla warfare" that directs demand away from government provision of services and reduces the demand for budget growth.[59]

The Grace Commission, appointed by President Reagan to study the federal government's management, picked up these themes in the mid-1980s.[60] First, the commission contended, inefficient management gets rewarded with higher appropriations and more staff. Since the current year's budget is usually based on the money spent last year, the incentive is to spend all of the money appropriated whether it is needed or not. There is no incentive to conserve money for return to the Treasury. Second, because government is insulated from competition, it need not respond to changes as, the report alleged, the private sector must. Public agencies can continue on, year after year, administering programs the same way. Finally, powerful constituencies grow up around government programs and protect them from the need to change and adapt. Interest groups often fight change to safeguard their share of government goods and services. As a result, the theory goes, government is not forced to operate efficiently, and nearly everyone involved in the administration of government programs has an interest in keeping it that way.

Example: Banks and Bubbles

The public-choice approach has also led to innovative regulatory strategies. Rather than have government issue rules that require any industry that creates pollution to reduce impurities below a fixed ceiling, regulators can create incentives for industries to reduce pollution more efficiently. The Environmental Protection Agency, for example, set pollution standards allowing companies that reduced their pollution below prescribed levels to "bank" their pollution savings for use in future expansion. Other companies, since 1979, have been allowed to establish a "bubble" around all their facilities in a given area and then find the cheapest way to reduce overall pollution within that area, rather than having to deal with individual rules applying to each polluting facility. In both pollution banking and bubbles, the strategy is to allow each company's assessment of its self-interest to promote the overall goal of reducing pollution.

In 1980, for example, the first bubble plan approved saved an electric utility $27 million when it substituted high-sulfur coal for low-sulfur coal at one plant and switched to natural gas from low-sulfur coal at another. The plan not only saved substantial money but also reduced overall emissions. DuPont engineers, furthermore, estimated that a regional bubble for the company's operations could produce an 85 percent reduction in pollution for $14.6 million in costs, whereas if the company were to reduce each source of pollution by 85 percent, it would have cost more than seven times—$91 million—more.[61] Such bubble plans have significantly reduced emissions for some pollutants and have created a literal market for pollution on the Chicago Board of Trade.[62] In the 2008 presidential election, both John McCain and Barack Obama advanced similar strategies for a national effort to reduce greenhouse gases.

Appraisal

The public-choice approach to decision making attacks governmental programs with a simple diagnosis—that the self-interest of government officials produces inefficient programs—and with a simple prescription—to turn over as many public programs as possible to the private sector and, when that is impossible, to mimic private-sector competition within the government. The approach, however, leaves significant questions of both information and values unanswered.

Information

The attraction of the public-choice approach lies in its embrace of the market. Marketlike competition, whether actually in the market or in market-based mechanisms such as contracts, its proponents believe, maximizes efficiency. Decision makers are driven to seek the right information and make the best decisions; if they do not do so, others will outcompete them, and they will lose their jobs. The power of this logic rests on the basic characterization of the bureaucrat as a rational human being: the administrator will single-mindedly pursue goals of immediate utility to him or her—personal power, security, and income.

It is hard to argue that any individual does not look to enhance his or her position. Nevertheless, Steven Kelman contends, this account of the operation of the political process is a terrible caricature of reality:

> It ignores the ability of ideas to defeat interests, and the role that public spirit
> plays in motivating the behavior of participants in the political process. The

"public choice" argument is far worse than simply descriptively inaccurate. Achieving good public policy, I believe, requires . . . a norm of public spirit-edness in the political action—a view that people should not simply be self-ish in their political behavior. . . . The public choice school is part of the assault on this norm.[63]

It is difficult to accept the notion that in administering government programs, gov-ernment bureaucrats are driven so hard to maximize their own utility that more pub-licly oriented objectives slip out of sight. Thus, the theory's very simplicity may well be its undoing. Are bureaucratic officials really so single-minded of purpose that there is no room for pride in performance, for striving to meet the goals of legisla-tion, for a sense of public service in the public interest?

As we saw in chapter 8, many top administrators could doubtless double or triple their salaries in the private sector, but a sense of devotion to the public good keeps them working in the public sector. An approach to the public service that starts with a cynical view of public servants is dangerously flawed, especially when used as a prescription for managing government programs. Moreover, some economists, as former chairman of the president's Council of Economic Advisers Murray Weiden-baum contends, have a tendency to dismiss difficult questions as "subjective and political" and thus to define them as outside the proper sphere of rational analysis of efficiency.[64]

The public-choice movement's great attraction is its parsimonious explanation of government problems, which dovetails neatly with the antigovernment feeling that has grown up in the aftermath of Watergate, under the conservative philosophy championed by the Reagan administration, and amid the reforms led by the George W. Bush administration. Moreover, it offers a neat solution: replace the decisions of government bureaucrats with the allegedly self-correcting influence of the market. Markets, it is argued, eliminate the need for a conscious search for decision-making information, since the self-interested motivations of the participants ensure that rel-evant data are available. The very parsimony of the explanation, however, greatly oversimplifies the much more interesting problems with which public managers must deal and feeds an unhealthy cynicism about government and the public service. Furthermore, the approach greatly underestimates the tremendous power of public ideas: the concept that some things are good for all of us, and that decision makers seek to achieve those things.[65]

Values

The market analogy, furthermore, suggests that both the goals and the motives of the private sector are identical to those of the public sector. Arguments for privatization, however, sometimes muddle together two very different issues: what government should do and how government should do it. Most fundamentally, privatization is an argument about *how* the government does things, not what it ought to do.

That distinction, in turn, underlines an important question: what functions are, at their core, public—for which government has the basic responsibility? As we said earlier, efficiency is not the only goal of public programs; pursuing other important goals, such as equality, typically means making difficult tradeoffs. The deepest debates are usually about ends—what should or should not be public functions—and the public-choice movement's focus on means thus begs the most crucial point. Some programs are intrinsically public, which means that there is, quite simply, a *public* interest in public administration.[66]

Even if we focus solely on means, the public-choice approach is still unsatisfying. Public-choice proponents typically assume that the self-regulating features of the market will solve any problems plaguing public programs. Instruments are not neutral, however, and the long history of government contracts, as well as more recent horror stories in the newspapers, offer ample proof that this is not so.[67]

One point is very simple yet often overlooked: contracts do not administer themselves. Moreover, relying on contracts often replaces one set of values with another. If directly administered government programs are plagued by self-interested bureaucrats, contracted-out programs must deal with self-interested proxies, each of which is seeking to maximize its own utility, sometimes at the government's expense. And, because contracts must themselves be administered to ensure high accountability and performance, the role of government administrators may be different, but it does not disappear. As Eli Freedman, Connecticut commissioner of administration, persuasively argued, "You can't contract away responsibility to manage."[68] As any defense official facing harsh questions about overpriced weapons could tell, contracting out does not eliminate the government's basic responsibilities; it only changes them. (We discuss this issue more fully in chapter 12.)

The public-choice argument thus leads paradoxically to an important point: there is an irreducible governmental role in shaping government. At the same time, the line between the public and private spheres is not very distinct. The public-choice prescription, therefore, is on the surface an appealing one, but a close examination reveals that it is based on an overly simplistic understanding of government administration. It is, in fact, more useful for the problems it raises than for the answers it provides.

Limits on Decision Making

From this discussion, it is clear that no one approach offers a solution to the problems of making administrative decisions. Each approach has its own special virtues and its own idiosyncratic problems. Every approach, though, shares the fundamental complication that administrative decisions, after all, are made by collections of human beings, each of whom operates in a large organization full of complex pressures, contradictory information, and diverse advice. Even the theories of satisficing and incrementalism do not fully take account of the psychological environment in which government executives must operate. James Webb, who served for eight years as NASA administrator, put the problem well:

> Executives within . . . a large-scale endeavor . . . have to work under unusual circumstances and in unusual ways. . . . The executive trained only in . . . traditional principles, able to operate only in accord with them and uncomfortable in their absence, would be of little use and could expect little satisfaction in a large complex endeavor. So too would the executive who has to be psychologically coddled in the fashion that the participative school of management advocates.
>
> In the large-scale endeavor the man himself must also be unusual; he must be knowledgeable in sound management doctrine and practice, but able to do a job without an exact definition of what it is or how it should be done; a man who can work effectively when lines of command crisscross and move in several directions rather than straight up and down; one who can work effectively in an unstable environment and can live with uncertainty and a high degree of personal insecurity; one willing to work for less of a monetary reward than he could insist on elsewhere; one who can blend public and private interests in organized participation for the benefit of both.[69]

Two social psychologists, Irving Janis and Leon Mann, put the point more poignantly. They see the human being "not as a cold fish but as a warm-blooded mammal," one "beset by conflict, doubts, and worry, struggling with incongruous longings, antipathies, and loyalties, and seeking relief by procrastination, rationalizing, or denying responsibility for his own choices."[70] All approaches to decision making share problems: the enormous uncertainty surrounding complex issues, bureaucratic pathologies that distort and block the flow of important information, and recurrent crises that deny the luxury of lengthy consideration.

Uncertainty

It is easy to underestimate how difficult it is for decision makers to know what results their decisions will produce, or even to get good information about what the current state of the world is. Congress, for example, has charged the Federal Reserve with making monetary policy, but it is deceptively difficult even to decide just what "money" is.[71] The Fed has developed various measures of money—including cash, checking accounts, savings accounts, and long-term certificates of deposit—but these measures have been changed over the years as Americans' banking practices have changed. To make things worse, the supply of money is really only an estimate, subject to constant revision.

Other important economic statistics share the same problems. It often takes months to get good numbers on the growth of the economy or the rate of inflation; what initially seemed to be good months can sometimes become bad months as more data emerge. Furthermore, it is sometimes hard to interpret the numbers: is high economic growth, for instance, a sign of a healthy economy or of an inflationary trend that is starting to take off? There are lots of numbers, but Fed officials constantly struggle to obtain good, reliable, up-to-date information about the true state of the economy. Even worse, there are very few reliable models about what figures from the past may signal for the economy's future. And even if Fed officials could determine the health of the economy and where it is headed, it is even more difficult to determine how—and when—best to use its tools to steer the economy in a different direction. Moreover, before the meltdown of the home mortgage market in 2007 and 2008, analysts had predicted the impending collapse. Determining what to do, who should do it, and when to act, however, proved difficult to determine, until the collapse forced the hands of federal regulators.

The complexity of the scientific world raises similar problems. In early 1976, for example, swine flu (a potentially deadly disease that had caused 20 million deaths in an epidemic in the 1920s) threatened to sweep the country. President Ford's scientific advisers, joined by health specialists within the Department of Health, Education, and Welfare (HEW, which in 1980 was split into the departments of Education and Health and Human Services), urged him to conduct a major nationwide immunization campaign. The president agreed, and 40 million Americans were vaccinated. The epidemic never arrived, but thousands of people were injured and some even killed by Guillain-Barré syndrome, a side effect whose link to the vaccine had previously been unknown. HEW Secretary Joseph A. Califano Jr., during the administration of President Jimmy Carter, pointed out the difficult question posed by the case: "How shall top lay officials, who are not themselves expert, deal with fundamental policy questions that are based, in part, on highly technical and complex expert knowledge—especially when that knowledge is speculative, hotly debated, or when 'the facts' are so uncertain?"[72]

With increasing frequency, in areas ranging from space exploration to homeland security, from new telephone technologies to the risk of new diseases, decision makers must tackle issues on the edge of current knowledge, where experts disagree and the road ahead is uncertain. Indeed, risk is the first cousin to uncertainty, and the costs of being wrong can sometimes be catastrophic (as, for instance, in judging the risk of exposure to known cancer-causing chemicals).[73] Apart from political pressures, this uncertainty makes any one approach to decision making an inadequate guide—and the risk all the more hazardous because many decisions, once made, are irreversible and offer no opportunity for the feedback and correction assumed in both the rational and bargaining approaches.

The threat of swine flu, for example, forced a decision that allowed no halfway steps: in the face of the forecast epidemic, President Ford either had to start a national immunization campaign or not. The case recalls the famous, fateful decision by Julius Caesar at the Rubicon. Roman law forbade him from bringing his army back into Rome, for the Romans knew that armed emperors would be impossible to resist. But as Caesar returned to Rome after a successful military campaign in 49 B.C., he decided to challenge the law and Rome's rulers. Once he crossed the boundary, the Rubicon River, with his army, conflict was inevitable. As Plutarch writes:

> [Caesar] wavered much in his mind . . . often changed his opinion one way and the other . . . discussed the matter with his friends who were about him . . . computing how many calamities his passing that river would bring upon mankind and what relation of it would be transmitted to posterity. At last, in a sort of passion, casting aside calculation, and abandoning himself to what might come, and using the proverb frequently in their mouths who enter upon dangerous and bold attempts, "The die is cast," with these words he took the river.[74]

In an age in which a detection system may incorrectly report an enemy's launching of an atomic attack, the few minutes afforded for decision on whether to launch a counterattack permit little computation and calculation, yet the decision is irreversible. The die will have been cast.

Many decisions less momentous for the world are irreversible, or substantially so: drafting an individual into military service and assignment to a war zone, withholding of a license to practice a profession or operate a business, denial of a loan to prevent bankruptcy of a business or farm, refusal of a pardon to a prisoner scheduled for execution. Decisions often have a stubborn finality for those who suffer loss or risk of life and for those whose livelihoods are impaired. It is often difficult to know what results a decision will produce, and the burden of uncertainty weighs all the heavier on decisions that are irreversible.

Information Pathologies

The very structure of bureaucracy, furthermore, can distort the flow of information as it moves upward through the organization. Not all information collected at the bottom, of course, can be passed along to officials at the top—they would quickly become overwhelmed and uncertain about what is actually happening—and therefore, information must be condensed at each bureaucratic level. The process of condensation, however, often leads to filtering. Public officials, not surprisingly, tend to pass along the good news and suppress the bad. At best, this tendency can distort the information flow; at worst, it can completely block early warnings about emerging problems. Furthermore, the official's own professional training can attune him or her more to some kinds of information than others. An engineer, even one who has assumed a general managerial position, still may attend more carefully to engineering problems than to others that might be more pressing.[75]

Sometimes these information pathologies create continuing, nagging problems. In the Peace Corps, one former official discovered, "Training was usually inadequate in language, culture, and technical skills. Volunteers were selected who were not suited to their assignments." But upper-level officials were usually in the dark about this problem, he explained, because lower-level officials often worked "to prevent information, particularly of an unpleasant character, from rising to the top of the agency, where it may produce results unpleasant to the lower ranks."[76]

Sometimes these pathologies cause disasters. On the night before NASA's launch of the space shuttle *Challenger* in January 1986, for example, engineers for one NASA contractor argued furiously that the cold weather predicted for the launch site the next morning could be dangerous. Mid-level NASA managers rejected the advice and refused to pass it on to top launch officials. The engineers, however, proved tragically good prophets, and the shuttle exploded 73 seconds into the flight. Officials with the responsibility for giving the "go" for the launch did not learn about the worries the engineers had expressed that night until the investigation into the disaster began.[77] When the *Columbia* disintegrated on reentry in 2003, officials later discovered that similar worries expressed by engineers had never made their way to top agency officials.[78]

Decision makers obviously cannot make good decisions without the right information, so they often create devices to avoid the pathologies. They can rely on outside sources, ranging from newspapers to advice from external experts. They can apply a counterbias, using their past knowledge about information sources to judge the reliability of the facts they receive. They can bypass hierarchical levels and go right to the source: some management experts, in fact, advocate "management by walking around," getting the manager out from behind the desk and onto the front lines to avoid the "nobody ever tells me anything" problem.[79] They can develop precoded forms that avoid distortion as they move up through the ranks.[80] Many governmental forms and much red tape, in fact, are designed precisely to prevent uncertainty from creeping into the process ("what information should I pass along?") even if it adds additional headaches to the lives of administrators and citizens.

Nevertheless, attempts to rid the information chain of these pathologies can, paradoxically, create new problems:

- Improvements in incoming information may clog internal channels of information.
- Increasing the amount of information flow to decision makers may simply overload them, as may attempts to eliminate the fragmented features of decision making.
- Greater clarity and detail in the wording of decisions may overwhelm implementing officials.[81]

These paradoxes paint a disturbing but very real picture. Administrators are scarcely defenseless, however, because the problem often is not having too little information but having too much—and then trying to sort through it all to find the right combination of facts on which to make decisions. In fact, top NASA officials had been informed earlier of the problem that caused the *Challenger* disaster, "but always in a way that didn't communicate the seriousness of the problem," a House committee found.[82] Later, the same lack of urgency surfaced again to claim a second shuttle. The key to resolving such problems of information management is redundancy: creating multiple sources of feedback that allow decision makers to blend competing pieces of information together into a more coherent picture—without wasting scarce resources on too much redundant information. Determining how much is just right is one of the hardest tasks that decision makers must face.

Crisis

Crises often precipitate decisions. The deaths of 119 men in a 1951 mine explosion and of 78 men in a 1968 mine explosion led to passage of national coal mine safety acts in 1952 and 1969. Catastrophic floods have time after time broken logjams that had obstructed major changes in national flood-control policy.[83] A 1979 accident in a Pennsylvania nuclear reactor, imperiling the population for miles around, stimulated a fundamental reconsideration of government policy toward the nuclear power industry. The *Challenger* explosion speeded up redesign of the booster rocket and produced plans for a new emergency escape system, while the *Columbia* accident led to new launch procedures and improvements of many parts of the space shuttle.

Crises, of course, are not limited to the federal government. Natural disasters such as fires, floods, snowstorms, and earthquakes, as well as accidents such as train wrecks, can put state and local officials just as much on the firing line. All crises share the common pressure of time—an issue rarely considered in the different approaches to decision making. Accounts of decision making in the Cuban missile crisis indicate that the committee advising President Kennedy would probably have recommended a strong military response had its views been required two or three (instead of five) days after discovery of the missile sites. Throughout the crisis, the pressure of time (and the need for secrecy) precluded the group's dipping lower in the bureaucracy for relevant information and advice.[84]

Crises often reverse the order of normal decision-making procedures. If a federal mine inspector finds an "imminent danger" in a coal mine, the inspector may order the mine closed until improvements are made. If the Food and Drug commissioner concludes that a drug presents an immediate danger to the public safety, the commissioner can order it off the market. In both cases, the niceties of quasi-judicial hearings to weigh the producers' objections are observed *after* the order's issuance and while it remains in effect.

In addition to upsetting the normal sequences of decision making, crises increase the difficulty of many potential strategies: the comprehensive analyses that rational decision making requires, the trial and error of bargaining, the consultation of participative decision making, and the reliance on the private sector of public choice. Crises accentuate the problems of uncertainty, especially in areas of technological complexity. Most important, they underline an issue of decision making in the public sector not well considered in most approaches: in the end, the public official is responsible for ascertaining and ensuring the public interest—a task that always proves difficult.

Crises can be managed. In the private sector, the manufacturers of Tylenol were widely hailed for their aggressive action in dealing with the poisoning of their capsules in 1982. Furthermore, Irving L. Janis argues, "vigilant problem solving" can reduce the risks of crises, as managers aggressively seek to formulate the problem, collect available information, reformulate the situation, and frame the best options.[85] When Governor Richard Thornburgh of Pennsylvania faced the potential of a nuclear disaster during the Three Mile Island nuclear power plant crisis in 1979, he had to follow precisely these steps in finding his way. Nevertheless, the sudden appearance of the unexpected coupled with high risk for wrong decisions poses enormous problems for decision makers.

Conclusion

We have examined several approaches to administrative decision making: rational analysis, bargaining, participative, and public choice. Though in some measure all these approaches have been put into practice, they all are expressions of theories, full of assumptions, which have tended to harden into dogmas. They also offer, as Table 10.1 shows, a wide range of tactics for dealing with the lasting problems of information and values.

The approaches share, in varying degrees, certain basic defects. We have already noted some oversights, especially uncertainty, information pathologies, and crisis, but there are others, such as how a problem or a need for a decision is discovered,

Table 10.1	**Approaches to Decision Making**		
Approach	**Information**		**Values**
Rational	Collect comprehensive information to maximize rationality		Assumed
Bargaining	Limited		Struggled over
Participative	Acquired through those affected by decision		Focus on clients' values
Public choice	Use self-policing forces of the market		Use self-interest of players

formulated, and put on the agenda (most approaches start with a known and stated problem or need). Furthermore, nondecision—the decision not to decide or the avoidance of an issue altogether, whether conscious or unconscious—often has consequences as great as those of decision itself.

More basic are two problematic tendencies. First, each approach tends to focus on a single value, as is evident in economists' eagerness to increase efficiency through systems analysis, incrementalists' dedication to maximizing participation, participative managers' commitment to full public voice in decisions, and public choicers' reverence for the virtues of private-sector competition. These are all important values, however, which means that an approach single-mindedly focused on only one of them is inadequate for the complex reality of the political world.

The second shared tendency is the failure to understand what is required to make an approach succeed. Sometimes, as in systems analysis, the conditions may not exist in the real world, and the theorists do not explain very well how to adapt their approaches to reality. Often, however, the adaptations may need to be so substantial that the approach will be drained of its essential character. For example, attempts to adapt the rational decision-making approach by taking account of the elusiveness of policy goals, the shortage of sufficient quantitative data in many analytic areas, the distortion risked in converting qualitative goals or accomplishments into measurable terms, and the behavior of members of Congress may lead to so truncated a version of the rational approach that it is less useful than, say, the more reality-oriented incremental approach.

It is possible, of course, to identify which approaches work best on which problems.[86] The rational approach, for example, tends to work better for issues with clear objectives, quantitative measures, and minimal political pressures. However, even if we can somehow determine which approaches best fit which problems—itself a very tall order—we are left with the puzzle of how to put these different tactical systems to work as a coherent whole.

Those puzzles come into the sharpest focus in the budgetary process, which we examine in the next chapter. As the government's systemwide decision-making process, budgeting raises the difficult issues of how best to deal with the conflicting pressures toward comprehensive planning and incremental politics that lie at the core of decision making. Theorists and public officials alike have long struggled to manage an elusive marriage between the two so as to capture the value of each while avoiding the flaws of both.

Case 10

From the Front Lines of Decision Making: Steering the Economy

Former U.S. Federal Reserve Board Chairman Alan Greenspan (left) and current Chairman Ben Bernanke appeared together at a 2007 event. Reporters listened for any nuance in their statements as they sought to guess the future of American monetary policy.

No story about former Federal Reserve Board chairman Alan Greenspan, who served from 1987 until 2006, is more famous than the tale of his love of baths. He was said to love nothing more than a good early-morning soak, poring over arcane economic statistics and thinking the big thoughts that would drive his day.

He has a bad back, so the hot bath eased the pain. But Greenspan long cultivated the image of a man whose idea of relaxing is to digest information that would put other people to sleep—and by being in command of the numbers, to run what might well be the most powerful institution in the world.

When the economy began to dip in 2001, the once-invincible Greenspan began taking shots from critics who charged that he had missed the chance to help steer the economy out of its recession. As complaints rose, William Webster, former FBI and CIA director, said simply, "He will shoulder it as he always has, but maybe with 15 more minutes in the bathtub every morning."[1]

Greenspan's power came from his leadership of the Federal Reserve, and the Fed's power comes from its management of the nation's money supply as well as its direct and indirect influence over the world's economies. Decisions Greenspan made about the U.S. domestic economy had ripple effects across the globe.

The Fed is a little-known but highly complex organization that is independent of the executive, legislative, and judicial branches of government. Greenspan was chair of its seven-member Board of Governors, which sits in Washington. Board members are appointed for fourteen-year terms; their long terms, coupled with the fact that they don't face the voters at the polls, give them unusual political independence. (In fact, not counting the lifetime appointment of federal judges, the Fed's board members serve the second-longest terms in the federal government, after the fifteen-year term of the Comptroller General at the Government Accountability Office.)

In addition to that Washington-based board, there are twelve Federal Reserve Banks, scattered around the country, which manage the system's regulations. Five rotating presidents of the Federal Reserve Banks join the seven members of the Federal Reserve Board to comprise the Federal Open Market Committee, which sets the nation's monetary policy.[2]

The Fed doesn't actually set interest rates or directly control the economy. Rather, it uses some highly intricate tools, such as its power to set the rates at which banks borrow from the Federal Reserve and its ability to shape the supply of money and credit, to help manage the economy. Financial reporters often write about the Fed's efforts to guide the nation's economic activity, but its controls are loose. Many other factors also play into economic performance, from the sometimes unpredictable behavior of American consumers to the impossible-to-control behavior of other nations.

As the federal budget has grown increasingly out of control in recent years, spawning large, persistent deficits that suggest that many federal policymakers have given up hope of balancing the budget, the Fed has increasingly seemed to be the only game in town for steering the economy. But how should it operate its steering wheel?

Since the 1930s, Fed officials have tried to guess the direction of the economy and to adjust monetary policy accordingly. When the economy looked like it was slowing down, they would make money "easier" (providing a larger money supply, which tends to reduce interest rates, make it cheaper to borrow, and spur the economy). When the economy started to heat up, they would make money "tighter" to slow down the boom before it overheated into inflation.

For decades, critics such as economist Milton Friedman argued that the Fed often guessed incorrectly the direction and size of the movement. The Fed, they charged, often acted too late and, then, it often overreacted, which only tended to make things worse. It would be better (and more rational), they claimed, to put the Fed on automatic pilot—to adjust the money supply by means of a fixed target and let the economy sort itself out.

Believing that they could do better, Fed officials resisted that argument. And they knew for sure that, if the economy should seem too weak (with too much unemployment) or too blustery (with too much inflation), they would catch political heat for not stepping in. After all, the Fed's history is full of presidents sending signals, sometimes subtle and sometimes not, trying to nudge the Fed to act to make sure the economy won't slow down near an election.

Under Greenspan, the Fed began worrying that it was having an increasingly hard time affecting the economy because the financial markets—and the thousands of financial analysts who worked in those markets—were trying to outguess the Fed. Often, by the time the Fed announced a policy decision, the markets had already anticipated and reacted to the news. Sometimes, when the analysts had guessed wrong, the Fed had not only to steer the economy but to put the financial analysts back on course.

So, in the early 1990s, Greenspan and his colleagues began gearing their efforts toward a concept of "rational expectations": trying to influence economic behavior not only by affecting the money supply but also by seeking to shape *expectations* about the money supply—and what the Fed was going to do about it. Fed officials discovered that they could exert tremendous leverage over the markets by sending subtle signals about what they were likely to do. Like a pebble tossed into a still lake, these signals rippled out with broad effect.

But the Fed also realized that trying to guess too far into the future was dangerous, since both the economy and world events often proved wildly unpredictable. Therefore, rather than jumping suddenly into a new policy, the Fed would signal which way it was leaning toward moving. Then, when it started to move, it would do so in a series of small steps. In response to the weak economy in 2001, for example, the Fed lowered one of its interest rate targets eleven times, moving gradually from 6.5 percent to 1.75 percent.

These incremental moves gave the Fed three advantages. First, it could maintain maneuvering room to adjust its policies along the way. Second, it avoided signaling the markets when it was going to start and when it was going to stop, so it retained flexibility about the total size of its policy change. And, third, by taking small steps, it generated a continuing buzz in the markets about what was going to happen next, and thus encouraged the rational expectations of money managers.

The result, the *Wall Street Journal* concluded, was that Greenspan "has deftly steered the American economy by relying on two strengths: an unparalleled grasp of the most intricate data and a willingness to break with convention when traditional economic rules stop working."[3] There must be something to those hot baths surrounded by statistics.

His successor, Ben Bernanke, was a Princeton economics professor who had no reputation for Greenspan's hot baths or statistical magic. In late 2007 and early 2008, Bernanke had to tackle an enormous financial challenge with a different set of tools. Borrowers had gradually accumulated large amounts of debt for home mortgages, sometimes with little or no money down and with clauses in their mortgages that allowed banks to increase their monthly payments substantially. Many homeowners began having a very difficult time making their payments and the banks foreclosed. Some communities turned into ghost towns. In others, buses took potential investors on tours of foreclosed homes that were available at bargain-basement prices. Bernanke stepped in aggressively to help stabilize the market. Among other things, he led the Fed over a March 2008 weekend in brokering a purchase of a major investment banking firm, Bear Stearns, by the mega-bank JPMorgan Chase. The Fed supplied a $30 billion credit line to help finance the deal. Fed officials also said they would take over the enormous Bear Stearns investment portfolio. With so much of their money invested in the deal, they took over control of many of the investment decisions to reduce the Fed's risk— but at the cost of inserting the Fed ever more deeply into basic financial decisions in the economy.

As the nation's banking problems continued in 2008, the Fed said it might extend its tough oversight powers. Experts acknowledged that Bernanke's emergency intervention into the markets made sense in the middle of the crisis, but extending that role would mean continuing its oversight over financial institutions that the Fed did not regulate, including investment banks (which are institutions that concentrate on raising large sums of money to support big corporate expansions). The announcement, as the *Wall Street Journal* reported, had Bernanke "walking a difficult line." He was signaling he was still worried about the financial system and was trying to keep interest rates low. At the same time, rising energy costs, sinking home values, and tightening credit were all leading the Fed to push interest rates higher, to restrain inflation.[4] He might well have felt he needed one of Greenspan's long soaks.

Questions to Consider

1. Consider Alan Greenspan's decision-making style. How would you characterize it?

2. Its critics have long called for less discretion and more predictability in the Fed's decision making. Apart from the complexities of the economic issues, what are the advantages and disadvantages of discretion in decision making in an institution such as the Fed?

3. How does the concept of "rational expectations" fit in with the theories of decision making we have explored in this chapter?

4. Think about Greenspan's strategy of ratcheting interest rates up and down in small (incremental) steps. What are the advantages and disadvantages of such a strategy of decision making?

5. The institution's relative stability and its status make this perhaps the best place in American government to ask: what constitutes a "good" decision? Can—and should—the Fed try to be "rational"? (And, if so, what does that mean?)

6. Bernanke's idea of "rationality" included leading the short but secret negotiations to help JPMorgan Chase buy out Bear Stearns. Do you think it is good for an organization like the Fed to be helping private organizations make enormous investments? Or is it the price for economic stability in a global marketplace?

Notes

1. Richard W. Stevenson, "Once Unthinkable, Criticism Is Raised against Greenspan," *New York Times,* April 2, 2001, A1.
2. For information on the Fed's structure and role, see its website, http://www.federalreserve.gov/general.htm.
3. Greg Ip, "Fed Chief's Style: Devour the Data, Beware of Dogma," *Wall Street Journal,* November 18, 2004, A1.
4. Damian Paletta and Sudeep Reddy, "Bernanke Moves to Extend Fed's Powers Over Wall Street," *Wall Street Journal,* July 9, 2008, A1.

Key Concepts

bargaining approach **286**

externalities **287**

incrementalism **293**

NIMBY phenomenon **299**

participative decision-making approach **286**

partisan mutual adjustment **293**

Planning-Programming-Budgeting System (PPBS) **288**

privatization **305**

public-choice approach **286**

rational decision making **286**

regulatory negotiation sessions **294**

satisficing **290**

spillovers **287**

For Further Reading

Allison, Graham T. *Essence of Decision: Explaining the Cuban Missile Crisis.* Boston: Little, Brown, 1971.

Cohen, Michael, James March, and Johan Olsen. "A Garbage Can Model of Organizational Choice." *Administrative Science Quarterly* 17 (March 1972): 1–25.

Downs, Anthony. *An Economic Theory of Democracy.* New York: Harper and Row, 1957.

Etzioni, Amitai. "Mixed Scanning: A Third Approach to Decision-Making." *Public Administration Review* 27 (December 1967): 385–392.

Lindblom, Charles E. "The Science of 'Muddling Through.'" *Public Administration Review* 19 (Spring 1959): 79–88.

Simon, Herbert A. *Administrative Behavior: A Study of Decision-Making Processes in Administrative Organization.* 3rd ed. New York: Free Press, 1945, 1976.

Suggested Websites

The study and practice of decision making has produced a vast array of approaches to this important and complex field. Many areas of public policy have developed new methods of decision making, for instance in the environmental arena (see the Global Development Research Center, **http://www.gdrc.org/decision**). In health care, many practitioners have argued for an approach to the field that is based far more on the application of evidence, including work at websites like **http://www.evidencebased .net.** Moreover, the Federal Executive Institute's training programs for the federal government's top managers contains a wide-ranging collection of courses on decision making (see **http://www.leadership.opm.gov**).

The Society for Judgment and Decision Making has prepared a useful website, which contains links to a wide spectrum of work in the field (see **http://www.sjdm.org/ content/related-links**). In addition, the *International Journal of Information Technology and Decision Making,* **http://www.worldscinet.com/ijitdm/ijitdm.shtml,** regularly reviews cutting-edge thinking on the subject.

11

Budgeting

Few fields in public administration have been the subject of more turmoil than budgeting. The debate over raising and spending public money lies at the cross-currents of the major theoretical battles about rationality in administration that we explored in the previous chapter. Its fundamental questions focus sharply the big conflicts of values in the American system. And budgeting regularly is at the center of contention between the branches of government and the political parties. The reason is simple: all budgetary decisions rest on value judgments—which items are the most important for investing public money—so budgeting is perhaps the most essentially political decision in public administration. Most of the big battles in government—and in public administration—sooner or later become budgeting battles.

Budget decisions are important (and political) because they shape government programs, but also because they focus on three central questions that have recurred throughout history.[1]

First, *what* should government do? Budgeting is, at its core, about fundamental decisions about the use of scarce resources. How much should society channel through the government for public purposes, and how much should be left in private hands? And of the resources the government spends, what programs most deserve support: new highways or health programs, weapons or welfare? Budgetary politics is enmeshed in perpetual conflict because it involves the toughest, most central questions that societies must answer.

Second, *who* in government should decide these questions? Throughout the history of the United States, the balance of financial power has shifted between the national and subnational governments, and between the legislature and the executive. The budgetary arena has been the continuing forum for broad policy disputes and pitched battles over not only who should benefit from government programs but also who should decide.

Finally, *how* should citizens and public officials make these decisions? In 1940 political scientist V. O. Key Jr. framed the problem in a classic way: "On what basis shall it be decided to allocate x dollars to activity A instead of activity B?"[2] Throughout history, Americans have struggled with a host of answers to Key's question, but it has yet to be resolved satisfactorily. In part, the question is about process: the way to structure the basic battles. In part, it is about analysis: how much the search for the best answer, which we explored in chapter 10, should shape the debate. And in part, it is about politics: how the struggle among competing interests shapes basic decisions about the public's resources.

In this chapter, we explore these questions in sorting out the functions and processes of budgeting. We begin with an examination of the far-reaching economic and political roles of the budget. We continue by probing the basic parts of the budgetary process: budget making, budget appropriation, and budget execution. Finally, we conclude by reviewing the relationship between budgetary politics and public administration. State and local governments vary tremendously in the way they budget and account for their money, and trying to describe the full range of their practices would fill another book this size. So we will focus heavily on the federal government's budget strategies and tactics to explore the basic issues that stretch across the budgetary issues for all governments.

The Budget's Twin Roles

All budgets are about financial decisions. But at the federal level, the budget takes on extra significance, because economists have long contended that it has a powerful effect in shaping the national economy. And, because these decisions affect the allocation of resources among competing claimants, the budget has important political effects as well.

The Economic Role

The very size of the government's financial activity inevitably makes it a strong player in the national economy.[3] That role is reciprocal: the budget has enormous impact on the economy, and the economy increasingly has a strong role in shaping the budget. These points make it inevitable that, because the budget *can* be used to steer the economy, policymakers have concluded that it *should*.

The Budget's Effect on the Economy

At least since the 1930s, economists and government officials have recognized that government taxation and spending, known as **fiscal policy,** have important effects on the economy.[4] Many of them, furthermore, have argued that the government can, and therefore should, use the budget to steer the economy: to boost employment, to cut inflation, to improve the nation's balance of trade abroad, and to keep the value of the dollar secure. While the British economist John Maynard Keynes is the intellectual father of this movement, pragmatists within Franklin D. Roosevelt's New Deal were preaching the virtues of **compensatory economics** before Keynes's theory was published.[5] The movement has grown into the cornerstone of macroeconomics—the study of the economy's behavior and of the behavior of broad aggregates such as inflation, employment, and economic growth. Belief in the power of fiscal policy to steer the economy reached its zenith with the so-called Kennedy tax cut, a huge decrease in income taxes passed in 1964, after the president's assassination, to spur economic growth.[6]

Cycles of economic growth and recession are inevitable, economists tell us. Keynesian economics preaches that the government can use its taxing and spending powers to moderate those cycles, to offset the dangers of too-rapid growth (inflation) and recession (unemployment). A government **surplus** (more revenues than expenditures in any given budget year—the **fiscal year**) slows economic growth by draining money from the economy, while a government **deficit** (expenditures exceeding revenues within a fiscal year) pumps money into the economy and promotes economic growth. (The deficit accumulated over time constitutes the national **debt.**) In good times, the theory suggests, the government ought to run a surplus to keep the economy from expanding too quickly; in bad times, it should run a deficit to keep the economy from becoming too sluggish.

Such economic policymaking is an exclusive province of the federal budget. Constitutional restrictions and sound fiscal management require that state and local budgets be balanced. The federal budget, however, is not like the family budget or even like state and local budgets, because the federal government has far greater resources to sustain a deficit over time, and it has the authority to create money and regulate its value—giving it a way to finance deficits that neither families nor state and local governments enjoy. The federal budget has an important effect on the economy, and policymakers have often harnessed it to promote high economic growth and low inflation. The availability of such an instrument, even if it does not always work well, tempts decision makers to use it for electoral advantage.[7]

The Keynesian approach to budgetary policy encountered serious problems during the 1970s and 1980s. Regardless of the theory's economic influence, it has always had a political imbalance: politicians have found it far easier to increase spending and run deficits when the economy dipped than to take the more bitter tax-increase/ spending-cut pill when the economy overheated. Especially when a rapid increase in Vietnam War expenditures fueled inflation in the late 1960s, President Johnson and his advisers resisted cutting the president's treasured Great Society social programs and raising taxes to rein in the economy.

Furthermore, economic events in this period undercut the theory's assumption of a relatively simple tradeoff between economic growth and inflation: that more of one tended to mean less of the other. During the 1970s, inflation and unemployment both increased, defying the theory and confounding policymakers. Budget deficits grew, oil shocks battered the economy, and inflation escalated as policymakers struggled to find new tools for economic management. Traditional Keynesian economics suggested that a budget deficit could help reduce unemployment while a surplus could cool inflation, but it could not cope with simultaneous high inflation and high unemployment. The task of economic management thus fell increasingly to the Federal Reserve, which is charged to manage the money supply (and to use an alternative to fiscal policy, **monetary policy**). The Fed struggled to deal with stagnant economic growth and inflation, christened **stagflation.** However, existing theories about monetary policy did not provide a clear guide for dealing with this newfound problem, and that made it difficult for the Fed to chart its strategy for managing the nation's money supply. As deficits immobilized budgetary policymakers through the Ford, Carter, Reagan, and first Bush administrations, the Fed became the only game in town.[8]

The problem reached a crisis during the Carter administration. Under the chairmanship of Paul Volcker, the Federal Reserve Board sharply tightened the money supply to slow inflation. Double-digit inflation fell as interest rates rose to historic levels—more than 20 percent for some short-term investments—and the nation entered the deepest economic decline since the Great Depression of the 1930s.

President Reagan campaigned for office on the platform that the federal budget could be used in a new way to spark economic growth. His "supply-side" economics contended that the government could increase both its revenues and the economy's growth, paradoxically, by cutting taxes: the lower the level of taxes, the more money companies could invest and consumers could spend; the resulting economic growth would increase the amount of tax collected. Reagan pushed through Congress a monumental 25 percent individual income tax cut and a virtual elimination of the corporate income tax.[9] The federal deficit nevertheless continued to grow—to a then-record $220.7 billion in fiscal year 1986.[10] During the Reagan years, in fact, the national debt more than doubled—in those eight years, the nation accumulated more debt than in its entire history. Although supply-siders suggested that the growing deficits were the fault of mismanagement by the Federal Reserve and high spending by congressional Democrats, most experts argued that the huge tax cuts, defense spending increases, and rising outlays for entitlements such as Social Security created the deficit problem. Whatever explanation one believed, the deficit swelled.[11]

The result was unprecedented gridlock. The president's budget came to be taken less seriously and Congress proved unable to pass even routine spending measures. Instead, the participants played budgetary brinkmanship, delaying decisions until the last possible moment in the hope of gaining a tactical advantage over opponents.

As the budgetary stakes grew, the process disintegrated into presidential-congressional struggles. In the meantime, more of the job of trying to steer the economy fell from the budget's fiscal policy to the Federal Reserve's monetary policy. The large deficits often left the Fed's policymakers with limited and unpleasant options, but the budgetary process's immobility left little choice.

Far less clear was the effect of two decades of huge deficits on the economy. In the 1980 Republican primary campaign, George H. W. Bush labeled Ronald Reagan's supply-side proposal "voodoo economics" (a charge Bush never lived down). Economists had warned that Jimmy Carter's $74 billion deficit in fiscal year 1980 was a first step toward financial disaster, but even though that deficit nearly tripled during the Reagan years, the economy performed surprisingly well: inflation came down and economic growth limped ahead. When the economy slowed further during Bush's own administration, Bill Clinton's campaign made "It's the economy, stupid!" its guide. Clinton's promise to boost the economy and cut the deficit took him to the White House.

By the end of his second term, Clinton had pushed through a surprising collection of tax increases and spending cuts, and, for the first time in a generation, the federal government actually balanced its budget. But that balance proved short-lived. Soon after taking office, George W. Bush won big tax cuts and then increased spending for homeland security and wars in both Afghanistan and Iraq. The federal government plunged back into huge deficits—which, as Figure 11.1 shows, have been a central fact of the federal government's economic life over the past forty years.

Most economists agreed that the huge deficits were a dangerous drain on the economy, that money spent financing the deficits left few resources for private investment (and thus for future growth). They argued that deficits made inflation worse than it would otherwise be. They contended that large deficits would tie the federal government's hands in fighting future recessions, since there would be limited room to increase spending and thus stimulate the economy. Finally, they concluded that deficits over the long run would worsen the nation's international trading position by eroding the value of the dollar. Left unchecked, economists warned, large deficits would "fester, creating problems that become harder and harder to solve."[12] Other economists contended instead that the deficits actually contributed to the economy's growth and that bringing them down could induce a recession.[13] Throughout the debate, the deficits added to a growing national debt during the 1980s. The surpluses and economic growth of the 1990s bought down the debt as a share of the economy, but that ratio began heading back up in the early 2000s as the economy slowed and the deficits began rising again (see Figure 11.2).

Budget deficits, especially over the long run, unquestionably are dangerous. The larger the deficit, the more of the federal budget must be devoted simply to paying

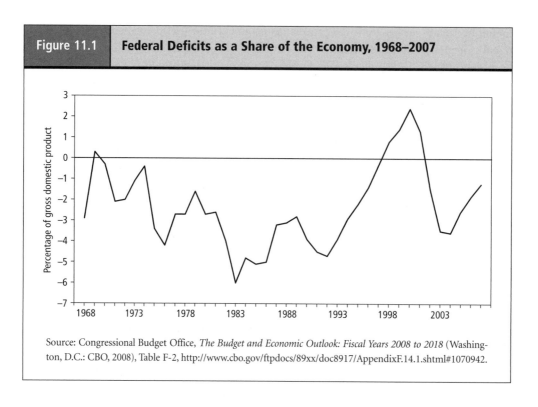

| Figure 11.1 | **Federal Deficits as a Share of the Economy, 1968–2007** |

Source: Congressional Budget Office, *The Budget and Economic Outlook: Fiscal Years 2008 to 2018* (Washington, D.C.: CBO, 2008), Table F-2, http://www.cbo.gov/ftpdocs/89xx/doc8917/AppendixF.14.1.shtml#1070942.

interest. The more money paid in interest, the less money that is available for the things, from new roads to new weapons, that public officials really want to spend money on. Over the years, the share of the budget devoted to interest has dropped, from 14 percent in fiscal year 1994 to 6 percent in 2007, but even the smaller share in 2007 amounted to $237 billion that could not be spent on public programs. Budget deficits also hamstring the political process by giving politicians little maneuvering room. At the federal, state, and local levels, conservatives have sometimes deliberately squeezed government revenues in order to put a brake on government spending. In fact, over the past decade, the strange twists of budgetary politics have turned some liberals into the loudest advocates of balanced budgets and some conservatives into sudden defenders of deficits. The short-lived experience of budget balance made it possible to imagine new government spending; the return of big deficits made that unthinkable.

The Economy's Effect on the Budget

If the budget has become a less useful tool in managing the economy, the economy's performance has become a much more important force in shaping the budget. In

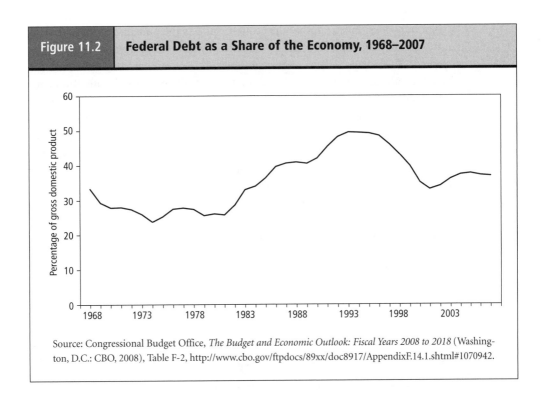

Figure 11.2 | **Federal Debt as a Share of the Economy, 1968–2007**

Source: Congressional Budget Office, *The Budget and Economic Outlook: Fiscal Years 2008 to 2018* (Washington, D.C.: CBO, 2008), Table F-2, http://www.cbo.gov/ftpdocs/89xx/doc8917/AppendixF.14.1.shtml#1070942.

general, a strong economy helps lower the budget deficit. Strong economic growth increases tax revenues and decreases expenditures, especially for such need-based programs as unemployment and welfare. The weaker the economy, the larger the deficit; revenues shrink while spending grows. Similarly, inflation increases spending and usually worsens the deficit; while it swells tax collections, it typically pushes spending up even more rapidly, especially for interest payments on the government's debt and cost-of-living increases in Social Security and other retirement programs. At the state and local levels, these issues have grown as well because, as we saw in chapter 3, retirement and welfare programs coupled with interest payments account for a substantial share of their expenditures.

Budget making, at all levels of government, depends critically on estimating the likely levels of economic growth, unemployment, inflation, and interest rates. Minor errors in the estimates can have huge effects. For example, if the economy were to grow only 0.1 percent per year less than budget makers estimated in 2008, in ten years the cumulative deficit would be $250 billion higher. Just 1 percent higher interest rates would increase the cumulative deficit by $482 billion, and if inflation were 1 percent higher, the cumulative deficit would explode by more than $2.1 trillion.[14]

Not only does this mean that the economy affects the budget, but it also means that budget making depends critically on correctly estimating what the economy is going to do. Even very small errors in economic forecasts can have huge effects on the deficit, the indicator of budgetary health that attracts the most public attention. Figure 11.3 shows the effect of economic uncertainties on the Congressional Budget Office's (CBO) fiscal year 2007 deficit projections. The dark core of the future projections shows CBO's best guess about the size of future deficits. But the lighter outer bands of the trend line show that, with relatively minor errors in forecasting, the deficit could actually be much larger—or much smaller—than the analysts' best estimates. Without making any policy changes at all, policymakers can suddenly discover that they are facing a much bigger—or a much smaller—deficit problem than they expected. Moreover, the farther in the future the projections go, the greater the uncertainty and the bigger the impact of the economic projections.

Preparing the budget therefore depends first on forecasting economic performance. As the political heat rises, the temptation to "adjust" these forecasts for partisan purposes grows. As Rudolph G. Penner, former head of the CBO, and Alan J. Abramson, explain,

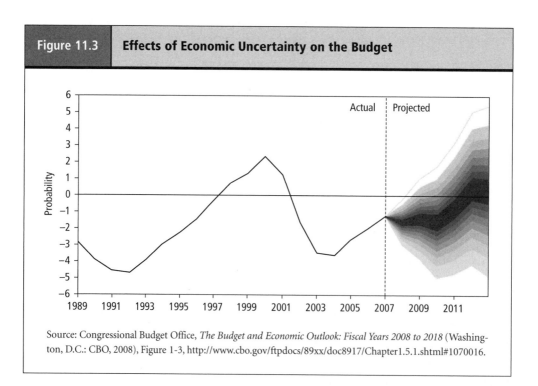

| Figure 11.3 | **Effects of Economic Uncertainty on the Budget** |

Source: Congressional Budget Office, *The Budget and Economic Outlook: Fiscal Years 2008 to 2018* (Washington, D.C.: CBO, 2008), Figure 1-3, http://www.cbo.gov/ftpdocs/89xx/doc8917/Chapter1.5.1.shtml#1070016.

> Changing a deficit estimate by $10 billion by changing an economic forecast is a minor statistical event. Changing policies sufficiently to alter a deficit estimate by $10 billion is a significant political event. This asymmetry creates an enormous temptation to achieve a given target deficit reduction by adopting optimistic economic assumptions rather than by cutting programs or raising taxes. . . . It is little wonder that the economic forecast adopted by Congress for the purposes of formulating the first budget resolution [Congress's initial vote on the budget] was too optimistic on balance every year in FY 1980–87.[15]

Such overly optimistic forecasting recurs almost every year, which helps to explain why, in the long run, policymakers always boldly argue that the deficit can be brought under control. Minor tweaks of the economic projections, all within the range of the reasonable, can make the deficit seem to disappear—when, in reality, it usually has not done so. As former Citicorp president Walter Wriston put it, "A government budget deficit is the intersection of two wild guesses [on expenditures and revenues] a year from now."[16]

These crosscurrents—the effect of the budget on the economy and the effect of the economy on the budget—have taken on greater importance through the years. The federal budget is far more than the sum of the government's expenditures and revenues: it is a statement of the government's relationship with the rest of the economy and of political officials' attempts to influence economic performance. The crosscurrents have, in addition, affected the way the budget is made. The technique and politics of forecasting have taken on a far larger role, and this in turn has opened a new arena in which fundamental budget battles are fought. Finally, the crosscurrents have enhanced the role of the staff members who run the computers that produce the economic estimates.[17]

The Political Development of the Budgetary Process

Budgeting is, of course, much more than an economic decision about how to allocate the nation's wealth among government programs. It embodies fundamental political choices, both about values—which programs get funded and which do not—and institutions, especially the relative sway of the legislative and executive branches of government.

Forecasts of low economic growth, or even a recession, can prove especially difficult for policymakers. A slow economy drives up spending, shrinks tax revenue, and increases the deficit. It is little wonder, therefore, that top officials shy away from forecasts of a slow economy, because they make budgeting even more painful. In the Carter administration, Alfred Kahn, adviser on inflation and later chairman of the Council on Wage and Price Stability, got into trouble with the president's political advisers for talking too much about the risks of a recession. He decided to substitute the word *banana* for recession and, in briefing reporters, said that the nation had to be wary of the risks of a banana. Ignoring the risks of slow economic growth on budget projections never makes them go away, but the economic influences on the budget have a political life all their own.

First Steps

Americans have always distrusted public officials' dealing with their money. Although there was little question in the Republic's first months that the State and War departments would each be headed by a single secretary, Congress considered putting the Treasury under the control of a board (so that no single person could become too powerful) and keeping the board under its own tight control (so that the legislative branch could closely oversee how the executive spent money). Although the Constitution clearly granted the executive branch the power to wage war and make treaties, it gave Congress the power to coin money, levy taxes, and appropriate money. Ever since, budgetary politics has been a forum for sharp competition between the president and Congress.[18] Two different national banks collapsed under populist pressure—and the Internal Revenue Service has long been one of Americans' least favorite agencies.

For America's first century, federal budgeting was mostly a congressional function. The so-called budget submitted to Congress by the executive branch, in fact, was little more than the Treasury Department's collection of agency and departmental requests. Congress was the central force in budgeting.

The Rise of Presidential Power

At the beginning of the twentieth century, the Progressive movement increased citizens' concern about the management of government at all levels. Budgetary reform swept state and local government as part of the broader trend toward strengthened executive powers.[19] By the end of World War I, the congressionally dominated system had proved inadequate for managing the federal government's vastly expanded fiscal functions, and the budget-reform movement launched in the states and cities bubbled up to the federal level.

The culmination of this movement was passage in 1921 of the Budget and Accounting Act, which revolutionized federal budgeting. For the first time, the president was to submit an annual budget to Congress. A Bureau of the Budget was created in the Treasury Department (and later moved to the president's own executive office) to assemble and adjust, if necessary, the department's requests to conform to the president's program.[20] Meanwhile, the Treasury Department's auditing functions were transferred to Congress's new General Accounting Office (GAO, which was renamed the Government Accountability Office in 2004). By gaining the authority to produce their own budget, presidents acquired leverage both over the executive branch departments and agencies—which first had to bargain with the president before having their requests sent to Congress—and over Congress itself, because the document submitted by the president would frame the terms of debate.

The 1921 act thus divided the traditional budget functions into areas of executive and legislative supremacy: budget preparation and execution in the executive branch; budget appropriation and postaudit in the legislative branch; and shared executive-legislative authority over budget control.[21] The division has always been sloppy, but the act nevertheless put the president into a position of preeminence not previously known.

Moreover, the growing pressure of the federal deficit steadily enhanced the power of the president and budget makers, especially within the executive branch. The budgetary process produced strange twists and turns, sometimes with the budget makers' own peculiar vocabulary and complex recordkeeping. As the budgetary process limped along, the short-term bargains that kept it alive required central oversight within the executive branch of each agency's spending patterns, and performing that task in turn enhanced the role of the Office of Management and Budget (OMB), which grew out of the president's Bureau of the Budget.[22]

The Budget and Accounting Act of 1921 proved a significant advance in presidential power—in many ways, it marked the emergence of the modern presidency. It was the beginning of fifty years of steadily growing presidential dominance over Congress in the budgetary process. While Congress has tried, especially since the mid-1970s, to regain its earlier preeminence in the budgetary process, the president has held the upper hand over most of the years since.[23] These struggles between the branches have played themselves out in the arenas of budget making, budget appropriation, and budget execution. (We deal with a related part of the budgetary process, postaudit and performance measurement, in chapter 14.)

Budget Making

At every level of government, the first step in the budgetary process is preparation of the budget: a set of spending and revenue plans combined in a single document.[24] While the details vary by level of government, the process typically includes both top-down and bottom-up features.[25]

Budgeting: Top-Down

A government's budget is not simply a collection of agencies' spending requests. Instead, each government's executive—whether mayor, city manager, county administrator, governor, or president—sets broad targets for overall spending and revenues. These spending targets fix a ceiling under which the agencies are expected to stay in preparing their individual budget requests. The ceiling, in turn, is a product of estimates made by the executive's budget staff: how expected changes in the economy will affect revenues and expenditures (will the economy's growth bring more tax collection, or will its slump put higher demands on welfare?); how demographic changes are likely to affect existing programs (will more school-age children require the school board to hire more teachers?); and how major planned program changes will affect spending (how much money will be required to launch a new defense system?).[26]

At the federal level, preparing the new budget begins almost as soon as the previous one goes to Capitol Hill in late January or early February. During the early spring, the OMB collects information from government agencies about how much money they expect to need for the upcoming fiscal year, both to administer existing programs and to fund new ones. OMB uses these estimates to prepare its spending projections, while the Treasury Department prepares estimates of tax revenues. Then staff members from the OMB, the Treasury, and the president's Council of Economic Advisers gather to assemble economic projections for the coming year. This three-part package of spending, revenue, and economic estimates forms the basis for the president's first policy decisions on the upcoming budget, which are made in June. These decisions focus on the major "policy streams" in the budget: defense spending (including any new programs to be introduced); domestic spending (especially payments to individuals, such as Social Security); and the overall effect of the budget on the economy (especially the size of the deficit). The process at the state and local levels is often similar, with the balance among education, highway, and other programs forming the focus.

OMB uses the president's decisions to define policy directives and spending ceilings for the departments and agencies. During the summer, each agency repeats this process internally, from department secretaries to bureau chiefs, from bureau chiefs to division heads, and so on. The agency's funding request is then assembled, together with supporting documents, and sent to OMB. In the fall and early winter, OMB's budget examiners intensively study the departmental requests and hold budget hearings at which the examiners and others closely question departmental representatives. Then an internal OMB "director's review" of staff recommendations culminates in the OMB director's recommendations to the president. Agencies have one last chance to appeal OMB's recommendations as the president makes final decisions. In some years, in fact, the appeals have stretched into the final days before the budget goes to the printer in early January.[27]

Preparing the federal budget thus begins nearly a full year before the finished document is submitted to Congress, more than a year and a half before the fiscal year begins, and two and a half years before the fiscal year's end. The long time horizon makes the already difficult economic forecasting job even more difficult—and it makes constant tinkering inevitable. At any given time, administrators must deal with three different sets of figures: executing the current fiscal year's budget, defending the next year's requests before Congress, and making budget estimates to submit to OMB for the year after that. Any year's budget battle is thus actually part of interlocking skirmishes reflecting political and economic concerns stretching over many years.[28]

Although the budget game varies by level of government, the federal processes typically are mirrored at state and local levels. Their message, moreover, is that no program or agency ever starts from scratch—every budgetary decision is intimately bound up in past experiences, current battles, and future plans.[29]

Budgeting: Bottom-Up

The top-down picture is the big picture, full of worries about the size of the budget deficit, the budget's role in macroeconomic policy, and large-scale policy changes such as the introduction of new defense systems. From the point of view of lower-level administrators, however, the picture is much different.

The central theory (both descriptively and prescriptively) of bottom-up budgeting is **incrementalism,** originally put forth by Aaron Wildavsky and built on the broader incrementalist theories discussed in the last chapter. How much should an agency official request in the budget preparation process? How should it answer V. O. Key's basic question about how resources are to be allocated? Wildavsky's answer, reflecting the debate we explored in chapter 10, was that officials do, and should, ask for a "fair share" increment over the agency's base. "The base is the general expectation among the participants that programs will be carried on at close to the going level of expenditures," Wildavsky explained. The increments are relatively small increases over the existing base that reflect the agency's share of changes in the budgetary pie.[30]

In budgeting, incrementalism thus has two important implications. First, no one really considers the whole budget. The package is too big for anyone to examine everything, so it is far easier and, Wildavsky argues, more rational to focus on *changes.* Second, the political battles focus on the size of an agency's increment—and of the increment's size compared with those received by other agencies. Budgeting is a battle fought on the margins, with the sharpest struggles focused on changes in the distribution of the government's pie.

Incremental theory, both as a description of how budgeting operates and as a primer on how agency officials should behave, has dominated the budgeting debate since the first publication of Wildavsky's work in 1964.[31] Many theorists have taken sharp issue with his view, for three reasons. First, incremental budgeting begins with the budget base, but the definition of that concept is anything but clear. It can be the current estimate of spending in the previous year, although that estimate constantly changes as Congress acts on the budget and as agencies carry out their programs. It can be the cost of continuing current activities at the same level, which includes increases for inflation and population shifts and decreases for improved productivity. Finally, it can be a spending level set by law, which often can be a different amount from the first two. "OMB actually formulates the base in several ways, which vary substantially over the course of the planning cycle," budget experts explain.[32]

Second, changes from the existing level of spending are not always made in small increments. A study of changes in agency budgets in the U.S. Department of Agriculture from 1946 to 1971, for example, showed that agencies requested budget changes ranging from a decrease (12 percent of the time) to a doubling of their budget (7.3 percent of the time). The average change in budgets from year to year was 11 percent, but some agencies received large cuts, some huge increases. Thus, on the average, budgeting does appear incremental, but the averages hide the rich politics of budgeting: aggressive program managers seeking to build budgets, OMB officials seeking to keep a ceiling on total spending, and presidents and their staffs seeking to pursue new initiatives.[33]

Third, the real focus of budgetary politics is not changes in *agencies'* budgets but changes in their *programs'* budgets. At the agency level, budgets and politics are usually rather stable. "Yet within departmental and agency boundaries (and occasionally between them . . .), there is a constant struggle by program directors, lobbyists, congressmen, state and local politicians, and White House personnel to fund new ideas and to continue the funding of old ones." The competitive success of alternative programs, not changes in the budgets of agencies, occupies budget makers, and in that arena it is the power of the policy entrepreneurs who can build the strongest political case for their ideas that makes the difference.[34]

Attempts to Reform Incrementalism

Especially since the mid-1960s, presidents have experimented with different budget reform techniques to secure greater control over budget preparation. Most notable was Lyndon Johnson's Planning-Programming-Budgeting System (PPBS), which we explored in chapter 10. During the Nixon administration, OMB attempted a different strategy, **management by objectives** (MBO), which was intended to strengthen the ability of managers to manage. Addressed to the efficiency with which programs are implemented rather than to grand objectives and choice among major program alternatives, MBO was both more decentralized and less directly connected to budgeting than PPBS. Agency heads and their principal executives would fix on quantified objectives to be attained in the coming year and then break down each objective into targets for achievement in, say, each quarter year; this process would then be repeated in turn for each subordinate. While MBO was more a management than a budget strategy, it had clear implications for the allocation of money. Once an agency had its goals defined and factored out among its subunits, the money would naturally follow that path. MBO had a mixed record: in some departments and bureaus it made a significant contribution; in others it failed and was quickly abandoned. As with PPBS, there has been "a noticeable disenchantment with MBO as a panacea in the government."[35]

When Jimmy Carter took office in 1977, he brought with him the **zero-base budgeting** (ZBB) approach that he had used as governor of Georgia. ZBB was an assault on incrementalism from a different perspective, but it was not, as the name suggests, budgeting from a zero base. Instead, budgeters began from a certain level of spending (say, 80 percent of current expenditures); they then assembled "decision packages" (consisting of different ways of increasing the level of services) and ranked them. In this way, decision makers could set priorities for spending increases.[36] ZBB seemed attractive at first, but it encouraged agency budget makers to play games with the process (for instance, by ranking very low a project they knew would never be cut, in the hope that they could win funding for other programs at the same time). These tactics, combined with ZBB's paperwork burden, ended the tool's reign at the federal level. At the state and local levels, however, many governments continued to find the process a helpful one for making choices within their smaller budgets.[37]

George H. W. Bush came to the presidency in 1989 with yet another approach. Having campaigned for office promising "no new taxes," he said he could balance the budget instead through a "flexible freeze," in which increases in some programs would be balanced by cuts in others. Almost immediately, however, his flexible freeze encountered deep problems. He announced which programs he wanted to increase but then left it to Congress to decide which programs to cut. Moreover, his plan depended critically on obtaining strong economic growth and low interest rates, but within months of his taking office, the Federal Reserve drove interest rates up in order to stem inflation, and economic growth slowed. And finally, his plan to rescue the savings-and-loan industry promised to cost tens of billions of dollars more than the administration's first estimates. Like other strategies that seem attractive at first blush, President Bush's flexible freeze quickly melted in the political heat of lasting budgetary conflicts. Meanwhile, the National Economic Commission, established in 1987 to develop a nonpartisan approach to resolving the deficit crisis, foundered in 1989 on partisan differences.[38]

The second President Bush took a very different approach to the budgetary process. As part of his management agenda, George W. Bush developed a new

Program Assessment Rating Tool (PART) and sought to integrate measures of agency performance with budgetary decisions. Over a period of several years, the administration required each federal agency—in all, more than 1,000 programs throughout the government—to measure the results of its programs. OMB then assigned a "stoplight score" to each program:

> An agency is "green" if it meets all of the standards for success, "yellow" if it has achieved some but not all of the criteria, and "red" if it has any one of a number of serious flaws. For example, in financial management, an agency is "red" if its books are such a mess that auditors cannot express an opinion on the agency's financial statements, or if an agency has a history of spending more money than has been given to it in law by the Congress.[39]

President Bush and OMB then pledged to use the stoplight score in reviewing the agency's budget, to "focus on results; make decisions based on performance."[40]

Though sweeping in its scope and implications, the PART process struggled with three big issues. First, the job of measuring the performance of all major government programs was a daunting one, because many agencies did not have either clear statements of their goals or information systems that could assess results. While the idea of basing budget decisions on measures of results was certainly a good one, getting good enough information proved a long-term project. Second, if an agency reported low performance, did that mean that more money would only produce more substandard results—or that to move from "red" to "green" required more investment in agency capacity? If an agency was already "green," did that mean that it did not need any more money or that a higher budget would produce even better results? Knowing the level of performance did not explain why the results occurred, or just what budget makers ought to do about it. Third, it was one thing for OMB and the president to include information about performance in their deliberations, but it was quite another for Congress to use performance information in shaping appropriations. Members of Congress have long resisted efforts by the executive branch to impose budget processes or decisions. Bush's OMB officials believed that PART was the right way to do budgeting and that better performance information was in Congress's interest as well. But negotiating past the inherent separation-of-powers tensions proved difficult indeed, and PART barely penetrated Capitol Hill in its early years. In fact, Congress had its own performance measurement process, based in the Government Performance and Results Act of 1993 (see chapter 14), but that process had little more impact.

The Rise of Uncontrollables

None of these reform techniques, however, proved a magic cure because of the larger political and economic issues in which the budgeting system is enmeshed. At the federal level, furthermore, they all encountered the stark reality of the rise of **uncontrollable expenditures.** Indeed, incremental budgeting itself has become less important over the years because much more of the budget has become uncontrollable. As Figure 11.4 shows, the share of the budget that Congress and the president can readily change (control) in any given year fell from 66 percent in 1965 to 38 percent in 2007. The law requires the government to fund entitlement programs and to pay interest on the debt, and that leaves little to spend on discretionary programs. Even here, government officials often have little real discretion: completing existing contracts, operating basic services ranging from federal prisons to the national parks, paying the salaries of the members of the armed forces, and keeping the lights burning in the Capitol and other fundamentals account for almost all remaining federal spending. In any given year, therefore, the president and Congress battle mightily over the tiny share of the federal budget over which they have real control. As controllable spending has shrunk, budgetary politics has become more intense.

State and local governments do not tend to measure uncontrollables as explicitly as the federal government does. But many state governments find that formula-based

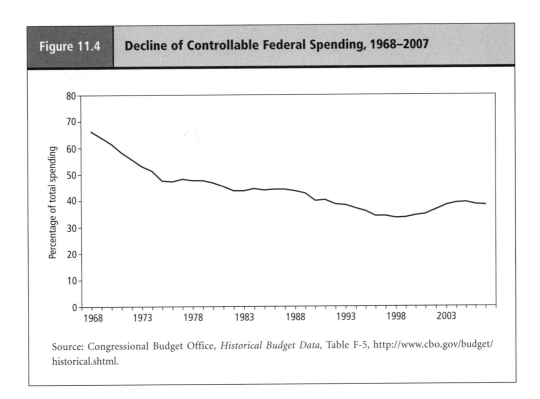

| Figure 11.4 | **Decline of Controllable Federal Spending, 1968–2007** |

Source: Congressional Budget Office, *Historical Budget Data,* Table F-5, http://www.cbo.gov/budget/historical.shtml.

spending for many programs, from aid to local schools to money for highways, takes up a growing share of their budgets. Moreover, years of tight budgets and taxpayer resistance to higher taxes have dramatically reduced the flexibility state and local officials have for reshaping their budget decisions. Although they are not constrained by entitlements in the same way as the federal budget, the political implications for the budget are much the same.

Budget Appropriation

The budget submitted by the president and by the executives at most other levels of government is, in the end, only a set of estimates and recommendations. Congress, like legislatures at other levels, makes the effective decisions, because only it can authorize expenditures and determine how revenues shall be obtained.[41]

Because the president and the agencies know that they propose while the Congress disposes, they tailor their requests in two ways. First, the president and agency officials behave according to the **rule of anticipated reactions**: they adapt their estimates and recommendations to fit their perceptions of how Congress will react to them.[42] A budget maker who expects Congress to cut the agency's spending by 10 percent may submit a request 15 or 20 percent higher. Members of Congress, of course, understand this classic ruse, and they estimate in turn how much padding has been built into the budget.

Second, the executive may play a different game by proposing severe cuts from the previous year's levels—but focusing those cuts in programs that command strong legislative support. Since the executive knows that the legislature will not accept the cuts, the strategy thus transfers to legislators the burden of increasing spending. Members of Congress in 1989, for example, greeted President George H. W. Bush's first budget with enthusiasm until they discovered that he wanted *them* to decide where tough cuts would have to come. At the state level, agencies often use the same strategies. In preparing their budgets, state universities have sometimes argued that if they did not receive more state money, they would be forced to cut enrollment. That, of course, would reduce the number of legislators' constituents who could be enrolled and thus create a tough political dilemma for the legislators. The strategy is so old and well-worn that it even has a name: the **Washington monument ploy**— agencies offer to cut their most popular programs (which, for the National Park Service, would be closing the Washington Monument), in the full knowledge that legislators will never allow such cuts to take effect (see this chapter's case study for the background on the "Washington Monument ploy" and for a recent example of how budgeters use it). The executive may also propose new taxes that the legislature will never pass, so that the proposed budget looks balanced but the legislature will have to take the tough decisions required to bring it into balance.[43]

Congressional Budget Decisions

In dealing with these strategies, Congress has often found itself at a disadvantage. The Constitution gives Congress the power to spend money, but it does not say what process Congress is to use.

By long tradition, Congress had broken the appropriations process into two parts: **authorizations,** which create programs and put limits on how much money they can spend; and **appropriations,** which commit money for spending. Under the old system, authorizations were managed by the subject-area committees, such as the Committee on Armed Services and the Committee on Banking, Housing and Urban Affairs, while appropriations were managed by each house's appropriations committee and its thirteen subcommittees, long known as the "guardians of the Treasury."[44] It is relatively easy to authorize new programs, but members of Congress typically left to their appropriations committees the tough job of deciding how much money actually to spend—and how much of a deficit to risk. That basic functional distinction often led to conflicts between the appropriations and authorizing committees, but the appropriations committees were king: new programs were nothing without new appropriations.

Congress fundamentally changed that process with the Congressional Budget Act of 1974, passed as part of the Watergate-era reforms of government.[45] The act gave Congress more time to work on the budget by pushing the start of the fiscal year (or budget year) forward from July 1 to October 1. The theory was that the extra three months would improve the odds that Congress would finish the budget by the start of the fiscal year; in practice, of course, the change simply postponed the toughest decisions by another three months, and Congress only rarely finishes its work by the start of the fiscal year. The budget act also mandated that the president present a "current services budget" projection: an estimate of the cost of continuing in the new fiscal year all the previous year's programs, at the same level and without policy changes. Members of Congress thus hoped to separate debate over program changes from proposals for continuation of existing programs—that is, to force the president to identify increments, and decrements, in the budget. The act also changed the roles of the appropriations and authorization committees by creating new budget committees in each house and instituting the following three-part legislative process to accompany them:

1. *Setting the totals.* For the first time, Congress obligated itself to prepare a **legislative budget**: an estimate of total expenditures and revenues— and thus of the deficit. To do the job, the 1974 act established a new Committee on the Budget in each house. Early each year, each congressional committee reports to the budget committee of its respective

chamber about the cost of bills it anticipates passing. Each house's budget committee then revises these requests and combines them into a single resolution that sets estimates of revenues and ceilings on expenditures. Each house then considers the committees' recommendations for the budget resolution and passes a concurrent resolution, which sets binding spending ceilings for each of the subject-area committees. The hope was to avoid the "agglomeration of separate actions and decisions" about which the House Rules Committee complained.[46]

The 1974 act also created a new Congressional Budget Office to provide staff support to the budget committees and to give Congress a counterweight to the president's Office of Management and Budget. CBO prepares Congress's own economic forecasts, estimates the costs of proposed legislation, and prepares "scorekeeping" reports that compare adopted and pending bills with the targets set in the concurrent resolution. While CBO has struggled with forecasting problems just as much as OMB has, it has reduced Congress's dependence on the executive branch for forecasts of future trends. Put together, the creation of CBO, the budget committees, and the budget resolutions gave Congress a far stronger hand in dealing with the budget—and a larger responsibility for producing solutions to the budget's difficult problems.

2. *Authorizing programs.* Next, the subject-area committees create authorizations for programs under their purview. These authorizations, approved by both houses of Congress and signed by the president, can be for one year (including much of the government's routine operations); for several years (including many defense programs); or for permanent programs (including Social Security), which remain in effect until the basic law is changed. These authorizations set ceilings on the money that Congress can spend on programs or, in the case of permanent authorizations, define the standards by which benefits are to be paid.

3. *Appropriating money.* While authorizations create the programs, appropriations provide the money to fund them. Congress can authorize a program without providing any appropriations for it, and it often authorizes higher spending than can be covered by the appropriations it is willing to provide. The reverse, of course, does not happen, since appropriations cannot exceed the original authorization. Like authorizations, appropriations can last for varying lengths of time. The appropriations committees in each house decide how much money should actually be spent by recommending **budget authority.**

This three-part process, however, is one step removed from the bottom line: the revenues the government actually collects, the money it actually spends, and the level of the deficit. The level of revenues and expenditures, as we have seen, depends on economic performance and administrative activity. The congressional budget process fixes authorizations and budget authority, while the money expected to be actually spent, known as **outlays,** is only an estimate of the budget authority that will actually be used in any given year. As Figure 11.5 shows, estimating outlays is a complicated process: analysts must determine how much budget authority from past years will be used in a given fiscal year, how much new budget authority will be created and spent, how much previous budget authority will expire at the end of its time limit, and how much budget authority will be carried over into subsequent years. For some uncontrollable spending, such as Medicare, the outlays depend on how many people get sick and what kinds of treatment they require. Outlays can vary according to the rate of unemployment or the progress in building a new fighter at an aircraft plant. Thus, no matter how close a watch Congress keeps on its books, it has only a loose rein on outlays in any given year. Hard-fought congressional deficit battles, which

| Figure 11.5 | **Relationship of Budget Authority to Outlays for 2009** |

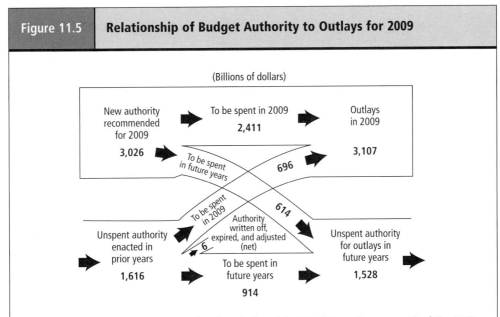

Source: U.S. Office of Management and Budget, *Budget of the United States Government: Fiscal Year 2009, Analytical Perspectives* (Washington, D.C.: OMB, 2008), 402, http://www.whitehouse.gov/omb/budget/fy2009/pdf/apers/concepts.pdf.

revolve around budget authority levels, can be undone when outlay totals do not cooperate—if, for example, economic growth proves sluggish, interest rates rise, or unemployment surges.

Shrinking Power for Authorizers and Appropriators

Both the rise of the budget committees and years of intractable budget deficits have greatly reduced the role of the authorizing committees. Long-term authorizations have limited the subject-area committees' role in annually reviewing programs, and when reviews have occurred, they often have broken down under the pressure of endless debates on amendments to change the programs. Much of what formerly had been the province of the authorizing committees was shifted to amendments to appropriations bills, but the appropriations committees themselves also found their role reduced. Even less of the budget, furthermore, is subject to annual appropriations because Congress has financed more programs through permanent appropriations.

Moreover, the Defense Department pursues a large number of secret projects. The only people in government who know what or how much is in this **black budget** cannot tell, and the size and scale of these secret projects are hidden from all but a handful of members of Congress. Some projects have secret code names, such as "Tractor Rose" or "Retract Larch," while others are funded by vague appropriations that do not describe what the money buys. The black budget hides the size of the Central Intelligence Agency's budget, estimated at $40 billion, and there is no way to tell how much the government spends for its spy satellites, intelligence gathering, and research and development of top-secret weapons programs. One estimate put the Defense Department's black budget at $32 billion in 2008, with billions more hidden in other agencies.[47] The Clinton administration used the black budget to pay for spy satellites, and the second Bush administration expanded it to support its so-called war on terrorism as well as the wars in Afghanistan and Iraq. The entire process, one author wrote, has long been plagued by a "bewildering babble of classified code words and nicknames" that made effective spending control impossible.[48] Officials who work in the programs often sport embroidered patches. One for "Project Zipper" shows a smiling face, with sunglasses and a zipped mouth and the motto, "We make threats not promises." Another has a mushroom on a dark background—mushrooms are grown in the dark—and the motto "*Semper en Obscurus*" ("always in the dark"). A third quotes the first-century Roman emperor Caligula with "*Oderint Dum Metuant,*" which means "let them hate so long as they fear."[49]

Thus, the appropriators' position has shrunk not only because they lost control over spending totals to the budget committees but also because they have control over less of the budget. Nevertheless, the shrinking discretionary budget, especially for domestic programs, has scarcely reduced congressional demands for new spending,

Officials who work on classified black budget programs within the Department of Defense sometimes wear embroidered arm patches, like the one pictured here.

which makes the appropriators' job much less fun. Their role has shifted from guardians of the Treasury to arbiters of the pork barrel: members' requests for individual projects, ranging from new roads to research programs, to take back to their districts.[50] Such pork-barrel spending projects—known on Capitol Hill as **earmarks**—have included a $50,000 tattoo removal program in San Luis Obispo, California; a $500,000 bike trail in North Dakota; and a $270,000 program to combat "goth culture" in Blue Springs, Missouri.[51] The desirability of these earmarks has, paradoxically, increased the appropriators' power: with more competition over less money, their ability to make even small allocations for projects highly valued by members of Congress greatly enhances their position. It has also made them far more visible. In the 2008 presidential campaign, Barack Obama promised a new website to make it easier to find and root out earmarks, and John McCain pledged to shrink the federal deficit by wiping them out.

If the role of the authorizing and appropriations committees has shrunk, the budget committees have often found themselves hamstrung as well. Congress has often been unable to complete its work on time and has often relied instead on all-in-one **continuing resolutions** that circumvent the Congressional Budget Act's procedures. Continuing resolutions combine all the government's spending decisions into one huge package, both those continuing programs at current levels and those incorporating important changes. These stopgap measures often last for short periods of time—sometimes only a matter of hours or days. Congress typically rushes them through to avoid shutting down the government, which cannot operate if Congress

At a news conference held by Citizens Against Government Waste (CAGW) to announce the release of the group's "Pig Book," photographers crowd around Porky the pig. The book exposes the most egregious cases of government pork-barrel spending, as determined by the CAGW.

has not appropriated the money. Continuing resolutions, ironically, have also enhanced the power of some appropriations committee members, since they play the key role in writing them—and can often bury within them small but politically valuable programs such as appropriations for a national weed center, funds to advertise the benefits of eating fish, and higher limits for government honey loans.[52]

Some committee members have also used the resolution-writing process to hide personal attacks on federal programs. One member, for example, planned to travel to Pakistan with his girlfriend, a lobbyist and former Miss U.S.A. World, but the Defense Intelligence Agency (DIA), which was supplying air transport for the junket, refused to allow the girlfriend to accompany the congressman. (DIA rules permit only members of Congress, their staffs, and family members to fly at federal expense.) Two years later, the congressman got even when, in a mad rush toward adjournment, he sneaked into a continuing resolution a provision that took away two aircraft the DIA used to transport ambassadors and their aides. The congressman refused to discuss the ploy, saying, "It just can't help but look like this kind of spoiled congressman with a bloated sense of self-importance trying to get back at someone for not flying his girlfriend around."[53]

Reforming the Budget Process

Growing frustration at what one analyst called a budgetary "ice age"—with the process locked in "a frozen mass of spending priorities that no one has really chosen and that no one really likes"[54]—has prompted a host of proposals to reform the budgetary process. Four of them have received particular attention.

1. *Create a biennial budget.* Since Congress persistently misses its budget deadlines, reformers suggest, it would likely do better if its members took a longer view and made the big decisions less often. Both President Clinton's National Performance Review (NPR) and GAO recommended switching the federal budget to a two-year cycle. As Vice President Gore's NPR report concluded: "Biennial budgeting will not make our budget decisions easier, for they are shaped by competing interests and priorities. But it will eliminate an enormous amount of busy work that keeps us from evaluating programs and meeting customer needs."[55] Former CBO director, and Clinton's budget director, Alice Rivlin agreed: "We spend enormous amounts of time going over the same decisions. . . . In recent years, there hasn't been time for anything else."

    Considering the budget only half as often, however, would increase the pressure for supplemental appropriations bills in the interim and would even further increase the budget's dependence on the long-term economic estimates that have already proven so troublesome. The change, moreover, would weaken the congressional oversight that frequently is conducted through annual budget reviews and would transfer more power to the president for deciding how to put two-year plans into effect.[56] As Allen Schick put it, "Congress would still have the power of the purse, but it would hold the strings more loosely."[57] At the state level, ironically, the trend has been toward annual, not biennial, budgeting. Most states switching their budget systems have moved toward annual budgets because of the pressure to keep on top of rapidly changing programmatic and economic conditions.[58]

2. *Create a capital budget.* At state and local levels, budgets typically differentiate spending for current needs, such as police services or professors' salaries, from spending for capital investment, such as highways and bridges, whose benefits stretch into the future. The basic principle is that the costs of programs should be paid by those who benefit from them. Thus, current taxes should pay for current programs, and borrowing (repaid over time from tax revenues) can pay for capital investments. Most states have separate **capital budgets,** and GAO has argued that a similar approach at the federal level would encourage investment for the future, better capture the cost of federal loan programs, and focus attention on the whole of the government's financial activities.[59] However, a federal capital budget might create a powerful incentive to classify many expenditures, from education to foreign policy, as alleged investment for the future and thus pass their

costs along to future generations. The distinction between capital and current expenditures is not as clear at the federal level as at state and local levels.

3. *Give the president a line-item veto.* Conservatives have long campaigned to provide the president with new veto power over individual line items in the budget. Governors in forty-three states have the power, Republicans since Ronald Reagan have continually insisted, arguing that giving the president the same power would allow the president to make surgical cuts in the budget and save tax dollars.[60] The **line-item veto** solution assumes that the deficit problem stems from congressional spending in excess of the president's requests, but in fact, the two branches tend to differ relatively little. As Allen Schick argues, "variances between the two budgets [presidential and congressional] are often due to differing economic and technical assumptions rather than to policy disagreements."[61] A federal line-item veto thus probably would not produce lower deficits, and it would not attack the entitlement spending that constitutes so much of the budget.

During his long campaign for the line-item veto, critics pressed President Reagan to identify what he would veto if he had the chance. In 1988 he listed $1.5 billion out of a $1 trillion budget. If he had vetoed every one of these programs, many of them pet projects of individual members of Congress, the $150 billion deficit would have been reduced only marginally—and he would have enraged the members of Congress whose projects were killed. Presidents can rarely afford to make enemies, especially since such projects often are crucial to members' votes on other issues important to the president. It is unlikely, therefore, that presidents would often use the line-item veto or that it would significantly change federal spending.

After the recurring budget battles with Richard Nixon, some members of Congress were wary about ceding additional authority to the president.[62] In 1995, however, the Republican majority in Congress took up the line-item veto as a major element in their so-called Contract with America. Even though it risked giving Democrat Bill Clinton extra power, they decided to use their momentum to put the provision on the books, and they passed it into law in 1996.[63] Opponents of the provision immediately challenged it in court, however, and in 1998 the U.S. Supreme Court held that it was unconstitutional. (The Court ruled that an amendment to the Constitution was needed to support the provision.) The idea has continued to resurface since, though generating little of the earlier enthusiasm: its proponents have struggled with the constitutional questions, and many observers have concluded that it is unlikely to produce any substantial savings.

4. *Enact a balanced-budget constitutional amendment.* During the 1990s, Republicans campaigned for a constitutional amendment requiring a balanced budget, but they were unable to collect enough votes to pass it, although the proposal was perhaps the most broadly popular provision in the Contract with America. Every state but Vermont and Wyoming has a requirement to balance its own budget.[64] Experience at the state level, however, shows that defining "balance" is deceptively difficult. The states, moreover, have shown that budget managers can play many games to produce a short-run balance while hiding persistent deficits. As GAO found, "not all states balance every year, even by the relatively flexible state definitions of balance."[65] A budget balance can be created by shifting programs off budget, for example, or expanding guaranteed loans, whose full costs do not show up in the budget.[66] Enforcement of such a constitutional provision would raise even more difficult questions— short of marching the president and Congress off to jail, it is unclear who (but the voters) could seek retribution on whom. And, as Allen Schick reminds us, "the economy often has the last word in determining the fate of presidential and congressional budgets."[67]

All these proposals share a similar theme: *procedural* fixes for the budget's *substantive* problems. "Every reform proposal I have seen so far is really just a way to substitute procedure for substance," argued Sen. Mark O. Hatfield (R-Ore.). "We are not going to work our way out of federal deficit difficulties with procedural gimmicks. There is nothing wrong with our present system if we summon the will to make it work. And if we do not have will, no new procedures will work any better." Carol G. Cox, president of the Committee for a Responsible Federal Budget, agreed: "These are not economic problems. They are not analytical problems. They are political problems."[68]

This is not to say that process does not matter. As Sen. Phil Gramm (R-Tex.) put it, "I submit that procedure produces substance."[69] Neither the president nor Congress establishes a process without considering what substance will result. Negotiations over process often disguise implicit conflicts over substance. In the end, however, no procedure can force elected officials to make political decisions they do not want to make. Budgeting is, at its core, a matter of political judgment.

Back-Door Tactics for Increasing Spending

The peculiar politics of deficit reduction, of course, have promoted new tactics to circumvent the budget-cutting process. "The more rigid are the restraints put on the budgeting process, the more is the motive to be imaginative," explained Roy Ash, OMB director in the Nixon administration. "There is no end to the possibilities."[70] To support new programs, some advocates have argued for trust funds, financed with revenues earmarked for particular programs; that way, they contend, the programs would not add to the deficit.[71] Social Security is the oldest example of such a program, but more recently highway and mass-transit programs have protected their budgets because they were supported by their own trust funds.

Questions about Social Security have especially muddled budgetary politics. In 1985 Congress took the program off budget to protect it from political tinkering and to insulate it from cuts. Since then the program has been running large and growing surpluses, which have been used to reduce the federal government's overall deficit. (The Social Security surplus is, in effect, "invested" for the future by buying Treasury securities, the safest of all investments, which helps finance the national debt.) In fiscal year 2007, for example, the deficit in the budget exclusive of Social Security was $343 billion, but the Social Security trust fund ran a $186 billion surplus, which reduced the overall federal deficit to $162 billion.[72] As the baby boomers begin retiring in the 2010s, however, the Social Security surplus will begin to shrink, while spending for Medicare and other programs will grow. Although analysts on different sides of the debate have disagreed over just how serious the program's long-term problems are, there is no dispute on several basic facts: the growing number of retirees will shrink the Social Security surplus; it will swell spending for programs devoted to older Americans, and the nation will face fundamental choices about how best to fund these programs without imposing crippling tax burdens on future workers. These problems, in fact, may well prove to be the most critical of those shaping budgetary politics in the twenty-first century. Since its inception in 1935, Social Security has always had a special place in American politics, but its deep-seated issues, coupled with deficit politics, have created new budgetary dilemmas.

Furthermore, as the burgeoning deficit has shut off the budget as a source for new programs, Congress has relied more on lending through off-budget entities, such as government corporations and government-sponsored enterprises (which we examined briefly in chapters 3 and 6). Federal loans, both direct and guaranteed loans, have increased rapidly. For example, most housing loans carry the federal government's backing, while nearly half of all college students use the federal government's student loan program—some through direct loans from the federal government and some through bank loans on which the government guarantees repayment if borrowers default.[73] The attractiveness of hiding programs away from usual budgetary politics is obvious, but many federal lending programs carry three significant problems. First, much of the lending does not carry the government's direct guarantee, so those who lend money to the government for these programs demand higher interest rates; costs are therefore greater. Second, congressional oversight typically is weak and irregular, so programs financed through such back-door lending often are not held to the same standard of accountability facing other federal programs.[74] Finally, the potential risk to the government of default by those who have borrowed money is large, but those risks are neither well understood nor well controlled. The expansion of federal programs through lending programs thus carries real danger.

In mid-2008, for example, two public corporations involved in home mortgages, Fannie Mae and Freddie Mac, hit serious financial problems. Together, they helped expand the supply of money available for individuals trying to buy homes. The two corporations did not lend money themselves. Instead, they bought mortgages from individual banks, bundled them together, and sold them to investors. They also borrowed money in the financial markets and purchased mortgages from private lenders. Together, they helped finance half of the nation's mortgages. As more banks and homeowners ran into trouble in 2008, however, the value of the corporations' stock plummeted. The Federal Reserve and Treasury announced plans to step in and prop up the corporations. Both Fannie Mae and Freddie Mac are chartered by Congress to help make it easier to people to buy homes, but private shareholders own their stock. Everyone has always believed, however, that the federal government's credit stands behind them. So when the corporations hit rough waters, the federal government had little choice but to step in—and stand ready in case the government needed to supply billions of dollars to bail them out.

The government has also pursued new programs through the regulatory process. It is tempting to promote new initiatives and transfer their costs to the private sector. The minimum wage, for example, guarantees a floor for workers' pay, and

In 2008, California legislators debated a bill requiring lenders to help state homeowners facing foreclosure on their loans. The mortgage meltdown that swept the country prompted the federal government to devise the largest bailout in American history.

Congress has debated similar regulatory initiatives, from requiring employers to provide all employees with health insurance to guaranteeing husbands (as well as wives) time off to care for newborn babies. Whether the government taxes firms and citizens and then spends the money to provide services or simply requires them to use their resources to do the same thing, the effect is the same—except that in one case the program does not show up in the budget and it does not affect the deficit.

Budget battles between the president and Congress are as old as the Republic, and none of these back-door tactics can resolve that problem. The battles have become fiercer since the mid-1960s, in part because of frequent mixed-party control of the institutions and in part because of the growth of entitlements and interest on the debt along with the steady shrinkage of discretionary spending. The budgetary process embodies these profound struggles: institutional jockeying between the president and Congress over control of the government's business, and substantive debates over the government's relationship to society. No procedural fix will calm the budgetary process unless it embodies a solution to these deep-seated conflicts.

Budget Execution

If the legislature rules the budget appropriations phase of budgeting, the executive is overseer of the execution phase. The authority derives from the president's constitutional role as chief executive and commander in chief, as well as the president's constitutional obligation to "take Care that the Laws are faithfully executed." Allen Schick has noted that "much loss of budget control results from executive actions . . . but executive practices are a 'dark continent' of Federal budgeting."[75] The budget execution process is a delicate balance between ensuring that a program's legislative goals are served and providing adequate flexibility for administrators to do their work.

Controls on Executive Action

The balance comes from congressional tactics to restrain executive discretion, through both legislative controls and limits on executive impoundment.

Legislative Controls on Execution

In 1950 the House Appropriations Committee established the basic rule governing expenditures by the executive branch: congressional appropriations constitute "only a ceiling upon the amount" that can be expended for a given activity. "The administrative officials responsible for administration of an activity for which appropriation is made bear the final burden for rendering all necessary service within the smallest amount possible within the ceiling figure fixed by the Congress."[76] In effect, Congress cannot require that an agency spend all money appropriated, because of two practical considerations. First, conditions may change during the fiscal year so that the funds available for a purpose are not all needed—for example, at the local level, a mild winter may mean that most of the snow-removal budget goes unspent. Second, Congress wants to encourage agencies to achieve a program's objectives at less cost wherever possible.

Legislators nevertheless are frustrated by their inability to propel movement full-speed-ahead by administrators managing their favorite programs. To reduce the possibility of executive nullification of congressional intent, the enabling legislation sometimes commands (rather than simply authorizes) agencies to implement programs. This stipulation, however, neither guarantees that adequate appropriations will be voted nor assures that agencies will spend every dollar appropriated for their programs.

This latter concern is exacerbated by the roles of the president and OMB. Most appropriations are made directly to agencies rather than to the president. In the past, however, an agency sometimes spent its annual appropriation in the first half or three-fourths of the fiscal year and then asked Congress for a supplemental appropriation to avoid closing down the agency.[77] To prevent such shortfalls, Congress has authorized OMB to apportion funds to an agency on a quarterly, monthly, or other time-period basis; and to review and revise each apportionment at least quarterly. Congress has forbidden agencies to exceed such apportioned amounts.

Impoundment

In 1974 Congress enacted the Impoundment Control Act to prevent recurrence of the gross abuse of impoundment authority by the Nixon administration.[78] All presidents from Franklin D. Roosevelt to Lyndon B. Johnson had claimed and exercised authority to **impound**: refusal by the president to spend money appropriated by Congress. The difference between their practice and President Nixon's lay not in failure to claim that presidential power but in their restraint in using it. Earlier presidents' most controversial impoundments withheld funds for particular weapons systems (a category on which a president might claim some authority as commander in chief). Other impoundments partially undid public works legislation, allowing certain projects to proceed while blocking funds for others. A few impoundment actions were justified on deficit-controlling and anti-inflation grounds.

Nixon's impoundments, however, "were unprecedented in their scope and severity," as Louis Fisher, the leading authority on impoundment, put it.[79] Moreover, the long-range consequences of this conflict during the Nixon administration have been unfortunate. One result has been an effort by Congress to draft authorizing statutes and appropriations acts as narrowly as possible, in order to deprive the president and agency heads of discretion in implementing programs. Congress increasingly votes, "The Secretary shall . . . ," instead of the traditional, "The Secretary is author-ized to . . . ."

The Impoundment Control Act distinguishes between **rescissions** and **deferrals** of budget authority; the distinction is roughly between permanent and temporary suspension of outlays. When proposing to rescind budget authority, the president must ask Congress to pass a rescission bill or joint resolution. When the president, the OMB director, or a department or agency head proposes to defer any budget authority for a specific purpose or project—that is, to delay its availability for a period not extending beyond the end of the fiscal year—the president must inform Congress.[80] This provision has helped to restrict the power of the executive to refuse to spend money appropriated by Congress. As the impoundment strategy receded, presidential signing statements arose to replace it, especially in the George W. Bush administration (see chapter 14).

Management Control

In very different fashion, the flow of money throughout the bureaucracy provides a valuable tool for controlling the implementation of government programs.[81] This flow of money provides several important forms of leverage on administrators' activities. First, the money trail demonstrates who is doing what. While a government official can have substantial impact on citizens without spending a large amount of money (through regulatory programs, for instance), it is very difficult to have impact without spending *any* money. While input measures such as money spent do not indicate what output an agency may be producing, they provide a valuable road map to the details of government activity. This tool can be especially important in track-ing the activity of third parties, such as contractors or grantees, who produce many government goods and services.

Second, by controlling the flow of money, the executive can control the direction and pace of governmental activity. Managers sometimes presume that everyone within an organization is working toward the same goal, only to be surprised later by employees' actions that are grossly out of line with the organization's goals. The flow of money is important symbolically because it signals the goals an organization con-siders important. It is important managerially because it helps to secure congruence between the broader goals of the organization and the individual goals of workers.

Finally, the flow of money is important for reporting and evaluating an agency's performance. It can help managers to identify the "hot spots" that need attention, either because a unit is spending too much money too quickly or, paradoxically, because it is spending very little money. More broadly, it provides important raw materials for program evaluation. By measuring what the money goes for, managers can take a first step toward determining a program's, and thus an agency's, efficiency and effectiveness.

"With rare exceptions," Robert N. Anthony and David W. Young explain, "a management control system is built around a financial structure."[82] This structure, in turn, is constructed with the building blocks of accounts—for functions or agencies, for subunits within those functions or agencies, and on to the individual components of an agency. In most governmental accounting systems, every expenditure is tagged with an account number. Account number 3-45983-6803, for example, might identify precisely the source and use of the money: the first "3" might mean that the money comes from a particular funding source, such as an excise tax on gasoline; the "45983" might mean that the money is allocated to the field unit in charge of repairing roads, in the southern part of the state; and the "6803" might mean that the money is going to purchase asphalt patching material. Thus, by means of computers, government managers can monitor the status of all their activities, separated into whatever components they desire.

Weak accounting systems have sometimes cost the government millions of dollars. GAO, for example, discovered that eighteen federal agencies paid 25 percent of their bills late, costing the government millions of dollars in penalties. Another 25 percent of the bills were paid too early, which meant that the government often had to borrow money, costing it $350 million annually in interest. The Department of Defense, meanwhile, could not account for over $600 million that foreign customers had forwarded for the purchase of weapons. Many agency accounting systems are "antiquated," GAO concluded. "As a result, billions of dollars are not being adequately accounted for, managed or financially controlled."[83]

Different governments operate by different systems, but they all rely on management control systems built on accounts.[84] While the intricacies of such fund accounting often seem boring to those worrying over broad legislative-executive conflicts and the politics of deficit reduction, they provide the ultimate control on the government's money. Management control gives executive branch officials important information about the behavior of those who implement government policies, both within and outside government. Through routine auditing functions, it provides the mechanism for discovering problems and correcting them before they become large. Most important, effective management control provides important leverage over the activities of government officials, contractors, and grantees, and thus improves the chances for effective and efficient provision of public services.

One especially intriguing initiative to improve the connection between budgeting and results, inputs and outputs, is the movement in federal, state, and local governments toward performance management. Governments at all levels have increasingly introduced results-oriented management, built around strategic planning, to define more carefully an organization's goals; performance measurement, to develop clear indicators of program outcomes; and the development of new management systems, especially information and human resource systems, to support the broader movement. Such cities as Sunnyvale, California, have moved to focus management more on results—such as the condition of local parks. Oregon launched a long-term effort to define state goals, from success in school to the cleanliness of the environment, and to measure the state's performance against these goals.[85]

In 1993 Congress passed the Government Performance and Results Act, which committed the federal government to a long-term management improvement effort. The act required all federal agencies to prepare annual performance plans and to report annually on the agencies' actual performance. These reforms mirrored even more far-reaching strategies launched in Great Britain, Australia, and New Zealand. We return to this and other performance-based techniques in later chapters.

The reforms have had sweeping implications. They require radically different skills and approaches for government managers, who must focus much more on outputs (such as program outcomes) instead of inputs (such as the budget). The information they produce offers greater potential leverage for such central management agencies as OMB. Indeed, OMB was one of the Government Performance and Results Act's most enthusiastic supporters, and that attainment led to its aggressive effort to launch the PART process during the George W. Bush administration.

The evidence both from the American states and from abroad is that performance management is extremely difficult to develop and use. It imposes daunting measurement and management problems. Moreover, legislators have frequently made limited use at best of the great volumes of information such processes produce, in part because finding consensus on what goals ought to be measured is difficult, and in part because legislators often focus much more on attacking problems by passing laws and appropriating money than on overseeing results (as we examine in chapter 13). Nevertheless, the evidence from both foreign and American experiments is that managers often have found results-oriented management useful in focusing agency staff on high-priority goals and for surviving in the increasingly stringent fiscal environment in which they find themselves. The federal government's effort, however, is the largest such experiment in the world, and observers are looking carefully at whether it will offer real promise or will go the way of such previous reforms as PPBS, MBO, and ZBB.[86]

Budgeting for State and Local Governments

There are as many strategies for state and local government budgeting as there are state and local budgets. But they do share several common features. First, unlike the federal budget, state and local governments must balance their budgets. The federal government can print money and engage in long-term borrowing to cover its operating deficits. State and local governments cannot. If they suffer a temporary shortage, they can slide deficits over into the next fiscal year, dip into rainy day funds, or engage in short-term borrowing, but they cannot engage in the long-term patterns of debt that shape so much of federal budgeting.

Second, state and local governments draw fundamental distinctions between their operating budget (to cover the cost of day-to-day functions) and capital budgets (to cover the cost of long-term expenses for equipment and facilities). Although GAO has long campaigned to create a capital budget for the federal government, state and local governments have long used them. In general, they borrow to fund capital expenditures. The basic principle is that the term of the loan ought to match the life of the equipment or facility. They might issue a twenty-year bond to pay for a sewage treatment plant expected to last two decades or a ten-year bond for a new fire engine. Taxes pay for operating expenses, like the salaries of fire fighters and police officers.

Third, in some governments (like New Jersey), operations shut down if a new budget is not passed by the start of the new fiscal year. Other governments (like Wisconsin) can continue to operate at the same level of spending if the budget is not passed in time. Practice varies widely according to the provisions in the state government's constitution.

Utah has long set the standard by which state and local governments' budgets are judged. It has fully funded its pension system. Many other governments have counted on long-term borrowing or future taxpayers to pay for the pensions of retired government employees. Utah has funded its infrastructure needs and kept its debt under control. As the Government Performance Project found in 2008, Utah has avoided the traps that have so often bedeviled other states.[87]

At the core, however, the basic question of budgeting, as framed by V. O. Key, stretches across all levels of government: "On what basis shall it be decided to allocate x dollars to activity A instead of activity B?"

Conclusion

Our review of the issues arising in the preparation, appropriation, and execution of government budgets underlines the importance of budgetary decisions: the effect of the budget on the economy; the effect of the economy on the budget; and the use of the budgetary arena for fighting out (if not always resolving) battles between the legislative and executive branches. Most of all, budgeting is the arena that most fundamentally shapes public policy decisions. By putting dollars together with often ambitious, and sometimes conflicting, goals, policymakers provide the resources needed to bring programs to life. While the budgetary process varies greatly at all levels of government, the basic issues remain.

The decision-making models we saw in chapter 10 seemed complicated enough. This chapter demonstrates, however, that decisions reached and formalized at one stage of a multistage process may be superseded and reshaped by decisions made at later stages by administrators and control agencies. The decision-making process, then, is considerably more complex than is suggested by theories focused on how one person or one organizational unit makes choices among alternatives at a single point in time. "The decision-making process" is thus a misnomer, for many such processes operate simultaneously in government. The budget process is only one of them, even though the allocation of financial resources is basic to all that the government does.

The next question, of course, is how the administrative process acts on those decisions: how it adapts, refines, and sometimes even reshapes the results of the legislative-executive contests. That is the process we call implementation, to which we turn in the next chapter.

From the Front Lines of Budgeting: Funding SEPTA

Case 11

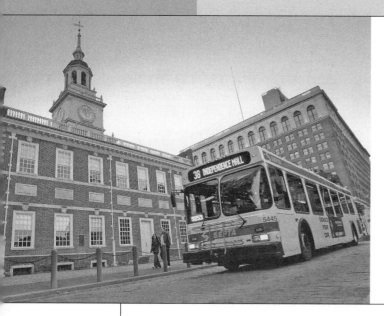

As a Southeastern Pennsylvania Transportation Authority (SEPTA) bus passed Independence Hall in Philadelphia, negotiators haggled over how best to support the mass transit system. SEPTA daily carried half a million people throughout the region.

For years, customers of Philadelphia's mass-transit system could hardly get through their daily commute without bumping into a sign advertising the system's motto: "We're getting there." Disgruntled commuters asked, "When?"

Cynics couldn't help but point out a double meaning: "We're getting there" was meant to suggest progress, but it also implied that the Southeastern Pennsylvania Transportation Authority (SEPTA, for short)[1] had a long, long way to go. Full buses often drove right past impatient commuters waiting at the stops. Long delays left trolley riders fuming. Fares continued to rise, and patrons continued to complain about the service.

By many measures, SEPTA's troubles shouldn't have even existed. Philadelphia has one of the nation's best mass-transit systems, due in large part to its long history and its prime location along the busy New York–Washington corridor. In contrast to cities such as Washington, D.C., that have squeezed their mass-transit lines into already fast-growing suburbs, Philadelphia's suburbs grew up along preexisting mass-transit routes. Despite those advantages, SEPTA has faced chronic budget deficits, and those deficits in turn have created bigger and bigger service problems.

Toward the end of 2004, the system faced a $62 million budget deficit, which SEPTA officials said could lead to a 25 percent fare hike, a 20 percent reduction in service (including the elimination of all weekend service), and a cut of 1,400 jobs. One plan even raised the possibility of boosting the $2 fare to $3, which would have resulted in one of the highest fares in the nation. "This is the worst crisis to face SEPTA in its 36-year history," system chairman Pasquale T. Deon Sr. said. SEPTA's general manager, Faye Moore, added, "The impact of these measures on the lives of our customers, businesses in the region, as well as my fellow SEPTA employees, would be devastating."[2]

In November of that year, the system's budget woes exploded into a statewide issue. SEPTA organized busloads of riders, system managers, and union members for a bus trip to the state capitol in Harrisburg to lobby for state help. These activists pleaded with the governor for aid, and they warned state legislators of the economic crisis that would befall the region if the aid did not arrive in time.

Those who followed Pennsylvania politics recognized that a SEPTA budget crisis was a recurring drama. Every two years, as its budget came up for debate in the state legislature, SEPTA presented a forecast full of red ink. Every two years, it warned riders and employees that, without more state support, the system would face big cutbacks. Every two years, the state provided additional support. And then, by the next year, the whole process began again.

The recurring budget crises made some state officials, both Democrats and Republicans, suspect that the threats of service cuts were SEPTA's version of the "Washington Monument ploy." This was a strategy invented by George B. Hartzog, who directed the National Park Service during the Reagan years. In 1969, the administration cut the service's budget. Hartzog responded by closing all national parks, including the Washington Monument and Grand Canyon, for two days each week. "It was unheard of," he recalled later. "Even my own staff thought I was crazy."[3] He complied with the letter of the policy but created such a political storm that Congress and the administration soon restored the funding. Other leaders copied his lesson and responded to threats of budget cuts by offering up cuts that were politically unacceptable. But it also made policymakers cynical and suspicious, for it became difficult to tell which problems were real and which were just clever budget tricks. In SEPTA's case, a spokesperson for House Majority Leader Samuel H. Smith suggested that "SEPTA creates these budgets to create a crisis."

But the head of the Pennsylvania Public Transit Association, Michael Imbrogno, insisted that the 2004 crisis was real. The implications, he warned, could stretch from Philadelphia to Pittsburgh, which had the state's other large mass-transit system, and from there to "nearly all the systems, including community services that impact senior citizens, the disabled and transit-dependent workers."[4] The system's advocates contended that the spillover effects on the state's economy would be huge, since so many people without cars relied on the system, and that, without a good system, traffic in key transportation corridors would become hopelessly clogged. The chairman of the SEPTA board put it more bluntly, warning that if the agency did not get state help, "The ship is really going down this time."[5]

Whether real or manufactured, SEPTA's critics concluded, the transit system's perpetual crisis was in large part a symptom of deeply rooted management problems. Providing more aid each year gave the system no incentive to fix them. If the state caved in again, they warned, SEPTA would only learn once again just how well its budget strategy worked.

For their part, SEPTA officials claimed that the deepening budget problems were a symptom of the state's failure to provide a firm foundation for the system's financial operations. They never knew how the budget battles would come out, so they could never plan ahead. Because the state provided inadequate support, these officials argued, they had little choice but to divert funds intended to build the system's future to pay for this year's emergency maintenance. As a result, they were forced to delay maintenance that needed to be done and to squeeze riders with higher fares, less service, and more unpredictable trains and buses and trolleys.

SEPTA officials argued that the problem could be fixed once and for all if the state would provide a predictable flow of revenue to the system from a dedicated funding stream (that is, a revenue source whose proceeds would flow automatically to SEPTA). They suggested that a higher gasoline tax would do the trick: it would keep money within the transportation system; it would nudge the cost of gas higher and thus create incentives for riders to switch to more fuel-efficient mass transit; it would get SEPTA out of the battle for other state revenues; and it would allow system officials to make long-term plans for a more reliable system.

Unfortunately, that proposal was not very popular in Harrisburg, where the Republicans who controlled both houses of the legislature were not eager to drive up the price of gasoline for their constituents and then ship the revenues off to Democratic Philadelphia. That city's legislators tried to build a broader coalition with the moderate Republicans who represented the suburbs around the city, but raising taxes was never an easy sell for them. The Philadelphia legislators also hoped for help from Governor Ed Rendell, a Democrat who had previously been mayor of Philadelphia, but he had no love for SEPTA, and other battles he needed to fight with the Republican legislators made him wary about engaging them on this front.

The Republicans, for their part, saw real value in the biennial fight to save SEPTA. It was a must-win issue for their Democratic colleagues from Philadelphia—and every must-win issue created opportunities to extract votes from them on other issues that mattered to legislators elsewhere in the state.

No one really wanted SEPTA to go down the drain—or even to eliminate weekend service—but no one was sure exactly how to fix its chronic problems. Meanwhile, keeping the budget game going worked, sometimes in subtle ways, for many of the players in the state budgetary process.

Questions to Consider

1. How does the "Washington Monument ploy" work? Do you believe it is likely to be an effective strategy? Will players in the process catch on after an agency has tried it once or twice?

2. How does the regular nature of SEPTA's budget battles affect its ability to plan and operate in the long term?

3. What lessons does the biennial budget game teach about the incentives for those who play it?

4. What options might policymakers consider for "fixing" SEPTA? What would you recommend?

Notes

1. See the system's website, http://www.septa.org.
2. "SEPTA Proposes Drastic Actions to Deal with Deficit," press release, September 9, 2004, http://www.septa.org/news/press_releases/090904.html.
3. Matt Schudel, "George B. Hartzog, Jr., 88: Expanded Nation's Park System," *Washington Post,* July 6, 2008, C6.
4. Quoted in "Fund a System in Need," editorial, *Philadelphia Inquirer,* November 11, 2004, A18.
5. Jere Downs, "SEPTA Details Proposed Cuts," *Philadelphia Inquirer,* November 12, 2004, B8.

Key Concepts

appropriations **341**

authorizations **341**

black budget **344**

budget authority **342**

capital budgets **347**

compensatory economics **325**

continuing resolutions **345**

debt **325**

deferrals **354**

deficit **325**

earmarks **345**

fiscal policy **324**

fiscal year **325**

impound **353**

incrementalism **335**

legislative budget **341**

line-item veto **348**

management by objectives (MBO) **336**

monetary policy **326**

outlays **343**

Program Assessment Rating Tool
 (PART) **338**

rescissions **354**

rule of anticipated reactions **340**

stagflation **326**

surplus **325**

uncontrollable expenditures **339**

Washington monument ploy **340**

zero-base budgeting (ZBB) **337**

For Further Reading

Arnold, H. Douglas. *Congress and the Bureaucracy: A Theory of Influence.* New Haven: Yale University Press, 1979.

Key, V. O., Jr. "The Lack of a Budgetary Theory." *American Political Science Review* 34 (December 1940): 1237–1240.

Rubin, Irene S. *The Politics of Public Budgeting.* 4th ed. New York: Chatham House, 2000.

Tufte, Edward R. *Political Control of the Economy.* Princeton, N.J.: Princeton University Press, 1978.

Webber, Carolyn, and Aaron Wildavsky. *A History of Taxation and Expenditures in the Western World.* New York: Simon and Schuster, 1986.

Wildavsky, Aaron, and Naomi Caiden. *The New Politics of the Budgetary Process.* 5th ed. New York: Pearson/Longman, 2004.

Suggested Websites

There is a rich amount of information about the federal budget available on the Internet. An excellent place to start is the Office of Management and Budget (OMB) website, **http://www.whitehouse.gov/omb,** which contains each year's budget as proposed by the president, voluminous supporting information, and historical tables to track the budget's long-term trends. Several databases can be downloaded from this website into spreadsheet programs, which makes analysis and charting easy.

The Congressional Budget Office's website, **http://www.cbo.gov,** contains a wide variety of studies and analyses. In addition, its historical tables provide useful information that often break down government spending and income differently than OMB's data, which often can be useful in considering long-term trends, especially for entitlement, discretionary, and uncontrollable spending.

The president's Council of Economic Advisers publishes analyses at **http://www .whitehouse.gov/cea,** as does the Board of Governors of the Federal Reserve at **http://www.federalreserve.gov.**

12

Implementation
Making Programs Work

Frequent complaints about governmental performance, from overpriced spare parts for the Pentagon to failures in responding to major hurricanes, keep the spotlight on the quality of public administration. But there is nothing new in this debate. More than a hundred years ago, Woodrow Wilson—then a professor, before his days as president—wrote that "it is getting harder to *run* a constitution than to frame one."[1] We can add that it is easier to *write* laws than to *execute* them.

Concerns about the execution of laws gave birth to a new field of study called **implementation.** Traditional public administration focused on government agencies as the basic unit of analysis, seeking to understand the way that bureaus operated. More recent implementation studies, by contrast, concentrate on programs and the results they produce. Implementation analysts use many of the traditional approaches of public administration, but by shifting the focus from the agency to the program, they hope to discover why program performance so often seems disappointing. More important, they seek to determine what can be done to manage programs better.

Every citizen—and taxpayer—is entitled to ask straightforward questions about the administration of government programs. Which programs are successful and should be continued? Which are failures and should be ended? What changes make the most difference in improving the efficiency and responsiveness of government programs? Which of these changes can be made by program administrators themselves, and which require action by elected legislators or executives?

Straightforward answers to these questions are harder to come by. It is hard even to define what success and failure are, let alone to learn how to achieve one while avoiding the other. We explore the rocky terrain of implementation in several ways in this chapter: by considering how to judge a program's success or failure; by studying the special implementation problems of administering government programs through the American intergovernmental system, as well as through private contractors; and, finally, by examining a case study that demonstrates that failure is not inevitable, but that success requires great skill in both politics and administration.

Judging Program Success and Failure

This process we call implementation can be a bit confusing: isn't the entire public administration field about the management of government programs, and thus about implementation? In broad terms, the answer, of course, is yes. As long as people have been engaged in the administration of government, from the earliest days of human civilization, they have been worried about implementation. The book of Exodus in the Bible says that Moses shattered the first version of the Ten Commandments because, as he came down from the mountain, he discovered that his people were already violating the new rules.

However, the study of implementation as a discrete process is more recent. In 1973 Jeffrey L. Pressman and Aaron B. Wildavsky sparked great interest in the process—or, as their subtitle, one of the longest and greatest in literary history, put it: "How Great Expectations in Washington Are Dashed in Oakland; Or, Why It's Amazing that Federal Programs Work at All, This Being a Saga of the Economic Development Administration as Told by Two Sympathetic Observers Who Seek to Build Morals on a Foundation of Ruined Hopes."[2] Their worry: too many programs start with bold objectives that the administrative process fails to realize in practice.

The study of implementation differs from more traditional approaches to public administration because it focuses narrowly on the "*interaction* between the setting of goals and the actions geared to achieving them," as Pressman and Wildavsky noted. In short, implementation analysis concentrates on the *results* of administrative action, not just on its *process.* As their clever subtitle implies, Pressman and Wildavsky turned to the subject because of their observation that a program's performance so often did not match its promise. The reason, they suggest, was that the "seamless web" of programs tends to become very complex—and the greater the complexity, they believe, the greater the chance of failure. Students of implementation see policymaking and policy execution as a web in which each strand depends on all the others.[3]

The studies that followed Pressman and Wildavsky echo their pessimism. One concludes, "Domestic programs virtually never achieve all that is expected of them."[4] Others see the process as "an uphill battle from start to finish."[5] Some scholars of implementation look on themselves as physicians seeking to diagnose the many diseases afflicting government programs.[6] The field is the very embodiment of Murphy's Law: "If anything can go wrong, it will." Indeed, the presumption of failure seems endemic to the study of implementation.[7]

There is a fundamental problem in this approach. While failures of government performance so often seem epidemic, two facts must be kept in mind. First, bad news attracts the most attention. Newspapers never feature banner headlines declaring "Mail Delivered Yet Again Today" or "Thousands of Flights Land Safely Because of Air Traffic Control System." To be sure, the bad news deserves attention, because tax-payers and policymakers alike deserve to know when programs fail. But it would be a mistake to use news coverage and the speeches of public officials as anything more than a rough indicator of how well programs work. Second, the reality is that, from the daily runs of emergency medical technicians to the backwoods work of forest rangers, most government programs work pretty well most of the time. The trick is determining what works well, what does not, and how to transform the latter into the former.

What Are Success and Failure?

To judge whether a program has succeeded or failed, one needs to compare its results with its goals. Implementation analysis thus shares features of the rational decision-making model discussed in chapter 10. This obvious comparison, however, is extremely difficult in practice because legislative objectives typically are unclear, often are many rather than one, and frequently change over time. In the Johnson administration's War on Poverty, for example, the law required local communities to provide "maximum feasible participation" for the poor in making spending deci-sions. This legal standard proved a classic in cognitive fuzziness—according to a clas-sic formulation by Daniel Patrick Moynihan, it only produced "maximum feasible misunderstanding."[8]

Another community development program provided federal grants to local gov-ernments, directing them to spend the money on programs that gave maximum fea-sible priority to programs assisting low- and moderate-income families, or aiding in the prevention of slums and blight, or meeting urgent community development needs.[9] The law, however, did not tell administrators just how strong a priority must be to pass the maximum feasibility test. Nor did it define low- and moderate-income families, so it was hard to tell precisely who was eligible. What constituted an urgent need was anything but clear. So the program found itself engulfed in constant con-troversy over its level of success, precisely because its objectives were so classically vague.

Passing a law in Congress means winning a majority of votes, and the path to coalition building usually is paved with compromises that render its meaning unclear. One frequent tactic in crafting such compromises is to include competing or vague goals in the law; the result, often, is prolonged struggle between those who administer the law and those who are affected by it.[10] Perceptions about a program's success or failure often are a continuation of the political conflict that shaped the program to begin with.

Moreover, goals can change over time. In New Haven, Connecticut, for example, local officials were administering a youth employment program. A slowdown in building construction made it difficult to place program participants in union jobs, as the officials had planned, so they broadened their goals to include nonunion placements. When they found that the sixteen-year-olds in the program were too young to work in some construction jobs, they recruited older participants than first envisioned. And when the officials discovered that most participants lacked the high school degree that many apprenticeship programs required, the director of the program taught an evening General Education Degree class to help participants qualify.[11]

Still, goals and objectives are critical for shaping the success or failure of government programs. Donald Rumsfeld, who had the distinction of serving twice as secretary of defense (for Presidents Ford and George W. Bush) and once as chief of staff (for President Ford), collected a series of axioms outlining the problem—he called them "Rumsfeld's Rules." On one hand: "If you get the objectives right, even a lieutenant can write the strategy," he quotes World War II general George Marshall as saying. On the other, an axiom of his own: "When you're skiing, if you're not falling you're not trying."[12] When objectives are clear, implementation is easy, but government often tackles the very hard problems that the private sector cannot or will not take on. Each painful step in the Iraqi war demonstrated how hard it is to turn Rumsfeld's simple rules into effective government action. Government constantly risks seeming to fall down the slopes because it is trying to contend with some of society's slipperiest challenges.

The Evolution of Goals

Goals evolve through the implementation process because administrative reality is always hard to forecast. Unexpected events continually pop up and require administrators to adjust. As one commentator put it, "One should expect that the expected can be prevented, but the unexpected should have been expected."[13] Goals also change because their definition is inextricably wrapped up in the ongoing political process. The complex system of American government, with its intricate balance of powers and intergovernmental relations, provides many different points of access to the political process. What a policy is can be changed at many points: laws must be interpreted and regulations written by administrators; those interpretations can be challenged in court by those who hold another view; intergovernmental and public-private mechanisms create the possibility of great variation in the way different individuals pursue the same program; and every decision can be challenged somewhere else. (We examine the regulatory issues in chapter 13.) Implementation is a continuing game in which every supposed failure or success sets the stage for the next conflict; those disappointed by the results of one stage of the policy process can always seek better luck around the next turn.[14] Indeed, implementation rarely is a linear start-to-finish process but often is a closed circle in which each event affects the next.

Implementation can thus be understood as the outcome of a continuing, dynamic, often turbulent process in which the many forces of American pluralism struggle to shape administrative action just as they fight over legislative, judicial, and executive decisions.[15] In fact, implementation is a highly interactive, interdependent process. The more the public and private sectors of American society are intertwined, the more all three levels of American federalism become linked. And the more legislative actions are challenged as agencies write regulations and the regulations are challenged in the courts, then the more implementation depends on a loosely coupled structure. The chain of implementation is not a hierarchical set of linkages structured by authority but, rather, a collection of organizations working—often loosely—to collaborate with each other. These continuing interactions shape and reshape policy implementation.[16]

If the goals by which success and failure are to be judged are so mushy, is there no clear standard for measuring how well a program works? The classical approach is to weigh a program's results against its legislative intent, but, as we have seen, legislative language is a poor benchmark—as the result of compromise, goals are typically vague, multiple, and conflicting. Administrators nevertheless have a legal and ethical obligation to pursue these goals as written, and the courts use legislative goals as standards by which to judge administrative action. The very mushiness of goals, however, introduces two different kinds of discretion into the process: that of administrators, in divining what the legislature had in mind; and that of courts, in comparing administrators' interpretations with their own judgments about legislative intent.

Standards for Judging Results

In a legal sense, legislative intent supplies the standards for judging a program's success or failure. It does not provide an objective measure, since, as with Rorschach inkblot tests, everyone reads into the presumed legislative intent just what he or she wishes to see. To deal with this quandary, analysts often employ two additional measures for administrative action.

Economists have always argued that **efficiency** is a premier standard for judging action. Whatever a legislature's goals may have been, we expect public programs to be run efficiently. What outputs are produced for a given level of inputs? Could a different administrative approach produce more outputs for the same level of inputs (or the same level of output for less input)? Invoking the efficiency standard gives one measure by which to judge implementation.

In addition, we expect programs to be responsive: Does implementation reflect the popular will? And who represents that popular will—elected officials or those affected by a program? The problem, of course, is that strategies that emphasize efficiency often sacrifice responsiveness. It is costly, for example, to allow those affected by decisions to have a full chance to make their opinions heard. Efficiency and **accountability** are tradeoffs: more of one usually means less of the other.[17]

The problem of judging implementation is thus the broader problem of American government: although people all hold the performance of governmental institutions to broad standards of efficiency and responsiveness, many have very different ideas about what these standards mean in individual cases. Furthermore, a program's goals are almost always vague. It therefore is often difficult to produce a consistent answer to whether a program succeeds or fails because such judgments vary with the observer. Nevertheless, people naturally prefer successes over failures, want programs that are efficient rather than inefficient, and want programs to achieve their goals. Even if one cannot agree on precisely what these terms mean, they define the overall context in which debate over implementation rages.

Problems of Performance

What factors most make the difference in implementation? If a policymaker desires a particular outcome, what problems may affect his or her chances of getting it? Five specific issues continually resurface: (1) practical uncertainty about how to reach a program's goals; (2) inadequate resources to get the job done; (3) organizational problems that interfere with an agency's handling of its programs; (4) uneven leadership in guiding bureaucracies through difficult issues; and (5) growing dependence on others, whether at other levels of government or in the private sector.

Practical Uncertainty

Difficult problems may have no known solutions. That realization often leads policymakers to embrace the merely plausible, the currently fashionable, or the most powerfully advocated program. The inclination is ageless—as Elliot Richardson, a member of President Nixon's cabinet, wrote:

> Our impatience toward delays in curing social ills reinforces the "don't just stand there, do something" impulse. [This syndrome] encourages . . . the illusion that we know how to cure alcoholism, treat heroin addiction, and rehabilitate criminal offenders. In fact, we do not. The state of the art in these areas is about where the treatment of fevers was in George Washington's day.[18]

In fact, Washington's wife Martha died of fever. Washington himself was bled for a fever he contracted and the treatment contributed to his death.

When policymakers attempt to eliminate poverty, to provide decent housing for every American family, to conquer cancer, to make the country's lakes and rivers fishable and swimmable, to assure everyone's access to adequate health care, and to eliminate discrimination based on race, sex, national origin, age, and physical disability, they are expressing noble hopes that may be dashed because they have not learned how to do these things. As the authors of a study of Medicaid put it, "idealists may frame laws; realists have to administer them."[19]

Even when the uncertainty is technological, formidable challenges often remain. The Soviet nuclear disaster in Chernobyl in 1986 and the tragic disintegration in February 2003 of the space shuttle *Columbia* all too vividly demonstrate the tremendous difficulty of combining complex engineering tasks in never-before-attempted systems. When the problem is social instead of technological, as with welfare programs, the uncertainty about how to deal with complexity is different, though just as troubling. Such uncertainty does not mean, however, that success is impossible in social programs. Indeed, as Lawrence Mead demonstrates in *Government Matters*, Wisconsin's state government vastly reduced the welfare rolls and got many welfare recipients into jobs: "Welfare in its traditional form was virtually abolished." As a result, "This revolution transformed the welfare state and the lives of many former recipients, mostly for good."[20]

The difficulty is imperfect knowledge, particularly when the statute directs an agency to solve a new problem or attack an old problem in a new (but unspecified) way. Moreover, administrators' sophistication is often no match for the imagination of average citizens, let alone the skilled specialist. Programs intended to reduce the oversupply of major agricultural crops have offered subsidies to farmers for taking some of their acreage out of production, but when the farmers choose their poorest-yield acres as the ones to lie fallow and step up the output of their remaining acres, the program's goals for curtailing production are not met. The ingenuity of taxpayers seeking loopholes in the Internal Revenue Service's voluminous regulations is legendary: even when the agency's administrators attempt to anticipate the "unanticipated" consequences of their actions, their judgment can never surpass the inventiveness of thousands, or millions, of clever attorneys, accountants, and other experts who make it their business to find loopholes.

Practical uncertainty thus often handicaps program implementation. Ever more complex technologies, from space shuttles to nuclear reactors, the Internet to electronic commerce, produce problems that are hard to predict. Interactions between people, and between citizens and their government, are even harder to forecast and influence: people often do not know what they want done, not just in government but in many aspects of an intricate society—and, even when they do know, they often do not know how to do it. All these uncertainties hurt the performance of governmental programs.

Inadequate Resources

Resources, both in money and in skilled personnel, are often inadequate for implementing the ambitious programs created by legislatures. Cynics, of course, believe that government is awash in unnecessary bureaucrats, especially at the federal level. Nonetheless, the imbalance between grand objectives and the resources for attaining them is amply documented.

Money

When he was secretary of the Department of Health, Education, and Welfare (later split into the Department of Health and Human Services and the Department of Education), Elliot Richardson discovered that the $100 million Congress had approved for a new elderly nutrition program would reach only 5 percent of those who were eligible, and the Community Health Program only 20 percent of the intended beneficiaries. When he asked his staff to estimate the cost in fiscal year 1972 of having all the department's programs reach every eligible person, he learned that the amount needed was $250 billion—more than the total federal budget at that time. He concluded that "all too often, new legislation merely publicizes a need without creating either the means or the resources for meeting it."[21]

Congress can and often does impose new duties on an agency, expand old ones, or require more elaborate procedures without increasing the agency's appropriations. The president, too, may try to hold back funds or direct an agency to give top priority to a single activity without considering the effects on its full statutory obligations. State and local governments likewise often find that the federal government requires them to meet national guidelines without supplying the money to do so. In mid-1986, for example, officials in St. George, Utah, faced fines up to $25,000 per day for failing to meet federal clean water standards. A new sewage treatment plant they were planning would help the city meet the standards, and city officials had already spent $100,000 trying to qualify for a federal grant that would fund 75 percent of the plant's $13 million cost. At the same time, however, the Reagan administration was attempting to eliminate the grant program entirely. "We've been chasing after EPA [Environmental Protection Agency] dollars for years," said Larry Bulloch, St. George's public works director. "It's like a carrot on a string; we just never catch up with it."[22] The gap between a program's goals and its funding is often substantial—a problem that has grown with the federal deficit.

Staff

As we saw in chapter 8, the number of federal employees has lagged behind the growth of population, federal expenditures, and programs to be administered. Even at state and local levels, government responsibilities have outpaced government employment. A staff too small for its responsibilities will be hard-pressed to interpret the statute, write and amend regulations, answer correspondence, confer with clientele organizations, disburse money to applicants for a program's benefits, and keep accounts on where the money has gone. Moreover, an understaffed organization will not assign enough of its personnel to monitoring a program's performance or detecting program abuse and fraud.

Organizational Problems

The department or agency in which a program is located has much to do with the program's odds of success. Some agencies have an open culture and are extremely friendly toward new programs, whereas others treat new ventures as unwanted children. Often, even when a program does find an inhospitable home, no existing department is likely to be more appropriate, or other factors prevent its being assigned a better location. In such cases, it is useful to know the hazards—and to know that they can be partially countered by protective measures. Three common organizational arrangements illustrate the problem.

First, it is risky to place regulatory responsibilities in an agency whose primary function is service. For instance, many states have regulatory bodies to control industrial activities, which implies an actual (or potential) adversarial relationship between the government agency and the regulated industry. In contrast, promotion of industrial development and employment requires close, sympathetic collaboration between the agency and its clients. No agency could well serve both goals.

Second, it is risky to place a program in an agency whose staff is unsympathetic to the program.[23] In the early years of the Reagan administration, for example, top EPA officials had a negative attitude toward government regulation of business, and many environmental programs suffered. Many critics blamed the move of the Federal Emergency Management Agency (FEMA) from independent status to part of the new Department of Homeland Security for its failure in 2005 to move more swiftly to deal with the disaster that Hurricane Katrina produced. Furthermore, it is easy to assume that any new program needs an imaginative and vigorous administrative staff and that such vigor is not likely to come from an established old-line department, whose civil servants have been there for years. Yet, as we know, the multiplication of government agencies creates new problems: more conflict between agencies, more need for coordination at the chief executive's level (whether president, governor, county administrator, or mayor), and more centralization of authority in the chief executive's staff.

Third, it is risky to assign related programs to different agencies. The program manager's strategy may then depend on the strategies and actions of his or her rivals, and bureaucratic objectives may tend to replace public policy objectives. In the competition for "customers," the manager may overserve or underregulate the clientele shared with other programs. Classic examples include the competition between the Army Corps of Engineers (in the Defense Department) and the Reclamation Service (in the Interior Department) to build dams, and local governments' shopping around among the four federal agencies (the Departments of Agriculture, Commerce, and Housing and Urban Development, as well as the EPA) that can make sewage-treatment construction grants. In the regulatory arena, three federal agencies oversee banks: the Comptroller of the Currency (in the Treasury Department), as well as the Board of Governors of the Federal Reserve System and the Federal Deposit Insurance Corporation (both independent regulatory agencies). The result, said one Federal Reserve chairman, is "a jurisdictional tangle that boggles the mind" and fosters "competition in laxity, sometimes to relax constraints, sometimes to delay corrective measures. Agencies sometimes are played off against one another."[24] That tangle complicated efforts in the late 1980s to solve the savings-and-loan crisis.

Uneven Leadership

A master of epigrams, Ralph Waldo Emerson, set the theme: "an institution is the lengthened shadow of one man."[25] In the bureaucratic world, an exceptional administrator can make the difference in a program's success. For a generation, the Federal Bureau of Investigation was indeed the lengthened shadow of director J. Edgar Hoover. The early success of the Peace Corps owed much to the energetic leadership of Sargent Shriver, and James E. Webb managed NASA's remarkable drive to the moon in the 1960s. Tom Ridge guided the first uncertain steps of the federal government's homeland security operations. Bureaucratic entrepreneurs have radically transformed government agencies with the force of their ideas and energy.[26] Such "fixers" are crucial to smoothing out the inevitable problems that emerge in the implementation process.[27]

As James Q. Wilson has pointed out, however, there are not enough of these leaders: "the supply of able, experienced executives is not increasing nearly as fast as the number of problems being addressed by public policy." And, he continued, "the government—at least publicly—seems to act as if the supply of able political executives were infinitely elastic, though people setting up new agencies will often admit privately that they are so frustrated and appalled by the shortage of talent that the only wonder is why disaster is so long in coming."[28]

Programs whose effectiveness depends on individual leaders tend to falter when their leaders depart. In April 1966, when the Commerce Department's Economic Development Administration (EDA), which had previously had a rural emphasis, moved into urban development with a $23 million public works showcase to relieve unemployment in Oakland, California, the change was led by Eugene P. Foley, characterized as "the enthusiastic, restless and imaginative Assistant Secretary of Commerce who heads EDA." Five months later, however, Foley resigned, and several key staff people soon left. Without his leadership, the program fell back into the normal channels in Washington, where "its priority and singular importance diminished." As Pressman and Wildavsky report, "both Secretary of Commerce Connor and Foley's successor, Ross Davis, felt that the Oakland project was Foley's personal project; they did not share Foley's enthusiasm for a dramatic EDA push in urban areas." The program failed soon afterward.[29]

Dependence on Others

When we think about the implementation of government programs, we tend to think about government officials implementing those programs. It is a fundamental truth of modern public administration, however, that public and private activities are becoming intermingled, "to the point where the dividing line between the federal government's sphere of operations and the rest of the economy has become increasingly blurred, if not eliminated," as economist Murray L. Weidenbaum put it.[30] On the one hand, government has taken an ever-increasing role in setting policy for the entire society, from providing subsistence for the poor to defining the terms of competition for industry. On the other hand, the government has come to rely ever more on third parties—other levels of government, nonprofit organizations, and private organizations—to execute programs. Implementation has thus become a complex business of managing interrelationships between government and the many proxies who carry out its programs.[31]

The reasons are varied. The sheer range of governmental activity makes implementation by any single body impossible, so "farming out" administrative tasks is inevitable. The federal government has decentralized many programs to state and local governments to put them closer to the people and hence make them more responsive. The growing technical complexity of many programs makes it attractive for government to hire contractors to help solve difficult problems. But the rise of contracting out and the other forms of government by proxy we explored in chapter 4 compound the problem of producing results. It is hard enough for a manager at the top of an agency to control the actions of subordinates at the bottom; it is far harder for the manager to control a program when the details of its implementation rest in the hands of persons who are not even part of the agency. The more interrelated the public and private sectors have grown—the more ambiguous the boundaries between public and private activities—the harder it has become to implement programs efficiently and responsively.

The fundamental problem is that different organizations have different purposes, and the people who work for them naturally pursue different goals. Whenever the government relies on a proxy to produce a service, it faces the task of trying to impose its goals on the often very different objectives of the proxy. The least that can result from such a process is conflict; the most, a deflection of the government's goals toward those of its proxy. The two varieties of this implementation strategy raise particular concerns within their separate spheres of operation: relations with different levels of government, and contracts with the private sector.

Intergovernmental Relations

The national government farms out—delegates—implementation of many of its programs to state and local governments. This strategy enjoyed a remarkable growth in the 1960s, in particular, as the federal government sought to advance such values as decentralization, local self-government, and neighborhood power. While federal grants once flowed mostly to the states, the expansion of direct federal-local grants in the 1960s made local governments full and direct administrative partners in federal programs, and that trend has continued since.

But there's the rub. If intergovernmental programs advance state and local values, what becomes of the federal government's policy goals? In such arm's-length administration, the national government's reach may exceed its grasp. The alternative, arm-twisting, is equally unsatisfactory, because autonomous state and local governments may find their own priorities wrenched out of shape as they yield discretion to the federal government. For local governments, sitting at the bottom of the intergovernmental system, the problem is often worse, since they receive intergovernmental aid from both the state and federal governments and therefore must try to accommodate both state and federal goals.

Intergovernmental implementation strategies are of three sorts: (1) grant programs, in which a higher-level government pays lower-level governments to do what it wants done; (2) regulatory programs, sometimes tied to grants and sometimes not, which subtly force changes in governments' behavior; and (3) off-budget programs, such as tax expenditures and loan programs, that provide additional support for governmental goals.

Administration through Grant Programs

As we saw in chapter 3, grants constitute a significant share of government spending. Deficit politics since the late 1970s reduced what had been a very rapid growth in spending for grants, especially at the federal level. Nevertheless, intergovernmental grant programs remain an important tool for government action at all levels, both to advance the funding of government's own goals and to lure recipients into a broad range of regulatory programs. In particular, the federal government has used grants to enlist state governments in managing health care for the poor through the Medicaid program, while state grants finance many local education programs.

Federal grants play an important role in the American system. Although "state and local governments have a vital constitutional role in providing government services," as the Office of Management and Budget (OMB) recognizes, these governments have often lacked the resources—both money and personnel—to do the job. Therefore, as OMB notes, "the Federal Government contributes directly toward that role . . . by providing grants, loans, and tax subsidies to States and localities."[32] The federal government uses state and local governments as its administrative agents; as Martha Derthick has written, "the essence of the grant system is that it entails achievement of federal objectives by proxy."[33] The same can be said of state grants to local governments, which use local governments as administrative agents for state programs.

At the high-water mark of federal aid to state and local governments in 1978, there were about 500 grant programs.[34] The Reagan administration began a major effort in the early 1980s to reduce grant spending and to consolidate programs; by 1986, the number of grant programs had dropped to 340, and 85 percent of federal spending was concentrated in only 25 programs.[35] Since then, federal spending for grants, especially grants to fund projects ranging from job training to urban renewal, has continued to drop, but the number of programs has inched back up to 600.[36] Similar figures for state grants to local governments are notoriously difficult to produce, but most state grants go for aid to local schools.

Grant programs vary in three important ways: by their general function, by their breadth, and by the way in which they are distributed.

Function

About half of all federal grants are, in reality, part of the complex system of government payments to individuals, through such federal programs such as Medicaid and child nutrition, which are run by the state governments. In administering federal grants, state and local governments have always to some degree been deputies for federal policies, but these payment programs put them more squarely in the role of federal field agents. Such federal grants for payments to individuals have grown quickly as a share of all federal grants since the mid-1970s, in part because Congress has increased spending for the programs and in part because other programs have suffered cuts. By 2013, budget officials estimate, 75 percent of federal aid to state and local governments will go to payments for individuals, especially medical assistance, compared with just one-third of payments for such programs in 1960. Indeed, one of the most remarkable shifts in intergovernmental program implementation over the past generation has been the huge shift of federal grants from relatively traditional grant programs, such as urban renewal and social services, to grants for payments to individuals, especially for Medicaid and welfare (see Figure 12.1).

Breadth

Categorized by their functional breadth, federal grants are predominantly of two kinds.[37] **Categorical grants** are for specific, narrowly defined purposes; examples include the federal highway grants that provide funds to states for road construction and the EPA's grants for construction of sewage treatment plants. **Block grants,** in contrast, are for broad purposes and usually are the result of consolidation of related categorical grants.

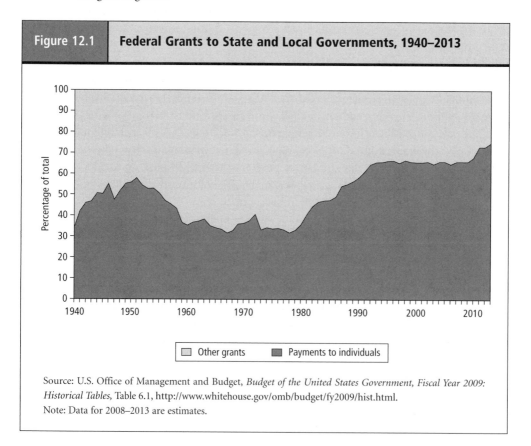

| Figure 12.1 | **Federal Grants to State and Local Governments, 1940–2013** |

Source: U.S. Office of Management and Budget, *Budget of the United States Government, Fiscal Year 2009: Historical Tables,* Table 6.1, http://www.whitehouse.gov/omb/budget/fy2009/hist.html.
Note: Data for 2008–2013 are estimates.

Block grants have long been a favorite of reformers, since they reduce red tape by grouping together related programs and increase the discretion of state and local governments in deciding how to spend the money. The use of block grants grew rapidly during the early 1970s as part of the Nixon administration's reform efforts. A decade later, the Reagan administration used block grants as part of a strategy to reduce federal aid, especially to local governments: it lured state and local governments into accepting less money by promising that they would enjoy more flexibility in spending it. The administration's commitment to reduced federal interference in state and local affairs, however, soon disappeared into the larger issue of deep cuts in some grant programs, and that reversal, in turn, tainted the block-grant strategy. As one intergovernmental analyst pointed out, "What once was regarded by many as a politically neutral technique for simplifying aid management is now likely to be viewed as an instrument of conservative ideology."[38] That turned out to be especially true in the wide-ranging debate over welfare reform and consolidating social service grants into block grants during 1995. Because of these problems, block grants have faded greatly in importance.

Distribution

Federal funds may be distributed either by formula or by project. In **formula-based programs,** statistical procedures determine both who is eligible for money and how much they can receive. The rise of block grants and grants for payments to individuals (mostly Medicaid) has led to a rapid increase in formula-based aid. Distribution of funds by project is strikingly different: each state or local government meeting eligibility requirements may apply for a grant by describing in detail its proposed project, its capabilities for executing it, and the anticipated benefits to the public; the sponsoring federal agency then selects the projects that it will fund (within its budgetary limits). **Project-based programs** thus are competitions that will produce unhappy losers, and they have other problems as well: they impose heavy paperwork burdens on applicants, and they give broad discretion to federal administrators over who actually receives money. A less obvious advantage is that project-based programs permit concentration of limited federal money where it is thought it will do the most good.

The rise of formula-based programs and the relative decline of project grants reflect earlier criticism about **grantsmanship** in the federal aid system, involving complaints that entrepreneurial local and state administrators had exploited the project system for maximum funding.[39] The rapid growth of formula-based grants, however, has changed the site for the fundamental battles over grant distribution from the administrative to the legislative process, where distribution formulas are enacted in law. The decline in grantsmanship, however, has been replaced by new uncertainties in the formulas, which are often incredibly complex. According to OMB, they may involve nearly five hundred different statistical factors, from population to income to numbers of special "in-need" groups, many of which are "of questionable accuracy." The formulas require a "bewildering array of mathematical calculations—addition, multiplication, squaring applied without rationale—which all too frequently produce unsatisfactory results that produce an image of poor public administration." Formula-based programs have proliferated, but the data are often stale or inaccurate. Agencies often cannot predict over time what results the formulas will produce, so long-term planning and budgeting at all levels are hamstrung.[40]

Administration through Regulation

The intergovernmental grant system is more than a device for transferring money. Each grant program brings with it a package of regulations and mandates that further spreads federal influence over state and local government activities. By reserving to the states any powers that are not otherwise given to the federal government, the Tenth Amendment to the Constitution prohibits the federal government from directly ordering states to engage in many activities. In the irresistible lure of grants, however, the federal government has found a way around this impediment: by making the money available, but subject to certain conditions, it can get state and local governments to do what they otherwise might not be inclined to do.[41]

Every program carries its own special rules. Potential Medicaid recipients must meet certain income guidelines, and federal highway funds can be spent only on certain kinds of projects. In addition, the federal government has promulgated a remarkable range of crosscutting rules—fifty-nine by one count—that apply across the board, to all grant programs.[42] Naturally, recipients must properly account for how they spend their money, but they must also survey the environmental effects of any program they plan, they must not discriminate in how the money is spent, and they must make projects accessible to the disabled.

Furthermore, state and local recipients must comply with **crossover sanctions**: failure to meet one program's standard can produce a punishment in another program. For example, during the energy crisis of the 1970s, Congress forbade the secretary of transportation from approving any highway construction project in a state posting a speed limit of more than 55 miles per hour. Since many states, especially in the West, had speed limits of 65 miles per hour on highways, they had the choice of lowering the limits or losing the money; the choice was obvious.[43] From automobile pollution inspection to a minimum drinking age of twenty-one, such crossover sanctions are a favorite instrument for inducing uniform national standards.

The federal government sometimes employs a mixed regulatory strategy, called **partial preemption**.[44] A federal agency sets standards that state and local governments must follow—for example, legislation mandating minimum water quality standards—and if the subnational government does not meet those standards, the federal government steps in to administer the program itself. Thus, in some states, a program will be run by a state or local official; in others, federal field officials will administer it. For example, the Occupational Safety and Health Administration (OSHA) itself conducts inspections and enforces regulations in thirty states while only approving and monitoring programs run by twenty state governments. The financial structure of such a mixed-level program can be equally complicated.

These federally imposed regulations, christened **mandates,** became a hot political issue in 1995.[45] Ending mandates that came without federal funding became a centerpiece of House Republicans' Contract with America, while local officials named unfunded mandates as their top problem—ranked above crime, school violence, and gangs. No one really knows how much such mandates cost: analysts have suggested that they amount to somewhere between 2 and 20 percent of state and local budgets.[46] But if the spending total is unclear, the impact on individual governments has been painful. Mayor Hal Conklin of Santa Barbara, California, complained that the city had to shut down all its parks and spend $400,000 to buy new playground equipment to meet the standards of the Americans with Disabilities Act; the money, he said, was taken out of child-care facilities and after-school programs for disadvantaged youth. "We had to close down a lot of other worthwhile programs in order to meet those particular federal standards which were just passed on without any funding at all," he said.[47] In Rutland, Vermont, the federal Safe Drinking Water Act required local officials to build a $6 million water treatment plant, which, in turn, would increase water bills by 240 percent over three years. "We are facing being mandated to spend millions of dollars to achieve efficiencies which no one has shown will be of any benefit to the public health," Mayor Jeff Wennberg complained.[48]

Attacking the mandates was easy; devising a solution was far tougher. Most reforms would not roll back existing mandates but would only make it harder to impose new ones. Estimating the costs of mandates before they are imposed, however, is an extremely difficult technical problem. Moreover, many interest groups find it far easier to organize in Washington to press for a uniform policy to be applied across the country than to fight fifty separate battles in the state capitals. Many businesses worried about trying to accommodate fifty separate sets of laws and standards may also find uniform standards, enacted in Washington, much more desirable.

Administration through Off-Budget Programs

In addition to grants (and their related regulations), the federal government uses a complex collection of off-budget strategies to advance its goals. For example, individuals are allowed to deduct local property tax payments from their federal taxable income, resulting in a boon both to taxpayers and to local governments. The deductions mean that the federal government shares some of the cost of the local tax and that any tax rate is less painful to taxpayers than it otherwise would be. Exclusions from the federal income tax provide another important form of aid: those who invest in state and local government bonds, for example, do not pay federal income tax on the interest they earn. The governments, therefore, do not have to pay as high an interest rate as they otherwise would, and the result is a substantial savings in interest costs.

The federal government also provides credit to state and local governments, making direct loans for such projects as rural development and college housing, while guaranteeing other loans made to state and local governments, as well as private lending for low-rent public housing and services.[49] Implementation through such programs relies on the creation of incentives for both governments and citizens; whether supporting loans for college dormitories or giving special tax breaks for sports arenas, the federal government supplies the impetus for action and thus powerfully influences the implementation process.

Implementation Problems

Even though policymakers have used intergovernmental strategies during nearly all of American history, implementation problems persist. Four of them merit particular attention: inequity, fragmentation, functionalism, and lax federal control.[50]

Inequity

Where you live determines what you get so long as state and local governments have the option to participate or not in a grant program, to set standards of eligibility for the program, and to fix the level of benefits the program provides. Many state and local governments refused to participate in some federal programs—such as food stamps and Medicaid, which provide food and medical assistance to the poor—during their early years. The grant system thus can exacerbate existing differences in wealth among the states.[51]

Fragmentation

Societal problems rarely respect geographical or programmatic boundaries. Polluted water and dirty air flow across state boundaries. Many metropolitan areas contain over a hundred local governments; the Chicago area has over a thousand. National programs depend for program implementation on state and local governments, each of which has only a piece of a jigsaw puzzle. Furthermore, the multiplicity of federal aid programs—each with its own goals and rules, procedures and forms—creates a maze of great complexity. The rise of block grants has reduced some of this confusion, but less money has at the same time reduced grant recipients' ability to deal with the problems. It is scarcely surprising, therefore, that frustration, impasse, and inconsistency often result.

Functionalism

Delegation, the reliance by the federal government on state and local governments for program implementation, depends heavily on trust—a factor that is made stronger when the delegatee speaks the same language as the delegator. Federal program administrators naturally prefer to deal with state and local officials who work in similar agencies, share their values, have the same kind of training, and are responsive to federal objectives; for example, federal, state, and local health agencies develop a common interest in assuring the autonomy of health agencies at all levels. Cutting through the layers of government, therefore, are vertical functional monoliths, each resisting collaboration with other agencies to integrate delivery of related services to the public, and each resisting direction by elected chief executives and their government-wide coordinating and control agencies.

Lax Federal Control

Federal agencies issue numerous regulations and guidelines, and state and local officials complain about their proliferation. Paradoxically, federal control of state and local implementation is weak, and in block-grant programs, it is intentionally weak because broad discretion is a central federal goal. The federal government may require each state and local government to plan for the use of the grant and to report how the grant was allocated and spent, but it cannot question the money's uses unless the usage clearly violates the law or regulations. In fact, illegal as well as trivial uses of block-grant funds may go undetected and unpunished because of federal reliance on self-reporting by recipient governments, inadequate auditing and enforcement staffs, and the overriding commitment to shift decision making downward in the federal system.

Lax federal control also extends to the categorical-aid programs, so that some categorical programs in practice become block grants. Federal agencies usually impose a large number of *procedural* requirements, but they usually exercise only weak control over the *substance* of state and local decision making and the actual achievement of the program's objectives. The principal sanction for performance problems is withholding a grant—a draconian measure that is rarely invoked—but federal officials otherwise have relatively little leverage. "In our federal system," as Michael Reagan has noted, "no national government can dismiss a state government official."[52]

Even if the federal government were to develop a good reporting system on the use of funds and effective sanctions for poor performance, it still would be difficult to determine what results the grants produced. Because dollars are dollars, one interchangeable with another, a state's or city's money that would have been spent in one program may be replaced with a federal grant, and the freed funds used instead to reduce taxes or increase services in other areas. In effect, the grant extended for one purpose has instead expanded services in another, a problem known as **fungibility.** Thus the uses and effects of federal funding often cannot be fully assessed.

The same issue holds for state governments, which spend a large share of their tax dollars on grants to local governments. In 2006, about 28 percent of all state spending went in aid to local governments, mostly for local schools but also for a variety of other purposes. All of the issues we have explored about federal grants to state and local governments apply to state grants to local governments as well—along with one more: given the enormous variety of patterns in the state-local relationship, state aid takes on remarkably complex forms and is hard to categorize. Over the years, however, local governments have come to depend on these transfers and, as state budgets have gotten tighter, intergovernmental tensions have grown.

A Cornerstone of Implementation

In a system of delegated administration, much depends on the effectiveness with which the delegator and the delegatee both perform their roles. The deficiencies of the federal government in managing the system are numerous,[53] and state and local governments have their own problems. Intergovernmental programs nevertheless have obvious attractions. State and local governments are natural, if sometimes reluctant, administrative partners in federal programs, and by relying on them the federal government promotes the principles of responsive self-government that Americans hold dear.[54] Thus, despite its defects and the strains placed on the intergovernmental system because of budget cuts, the strategy of delegating administration is here to stay.

Contracting

Contracting in American government is older than the government itself. As commander of the Continental army, George Washington constantly struggled with his private suppliers, who schemed to make a quick profit at the expense of his soldiers.[55] Indeed, Julius Caesar wrote of his troubles in dealing with the private merchants on which he relied for supplies.

At the state and local level, the practice of contracting out public services has grown into a major feature. Governments have long relied on for-profit contractors to build roads and on nonprofit contractors to deliver social services, but contracting now extends into nearly every state and local activity, from the administration of prisons to the staffing of libraries. At one point, La Miranda, California, had only sixty employees; in place of a larger municipal bureaucracy, sixty contractors provided everything from fire and police protection to human services and public works.[56] Minneapolis hired a private organization to manage its schools and linked its pay to performance on educational goals. Florida privatized its child welfare program. As tighter budgets have forced state and local officials to be ever more creative, they have relied more on for-profit and nonprofit contractors to deliver services.

The federal government obtains a substantial amount of goods and services for its operations through contracts with private companies, research institutions, and individual consultants. Such procurement accounts for 12 percent of federal outlays and 8.6 million contracts per year. As Figure 12.2 shows, the Department of Defense administers more than two-thirds of all money spent by contract, followed by the Department of Energy, Health and Human Services, NASA, the General Services Administration, Homeland Security, and Veterans Affairs.

Federal contracts cover a remarkable range of activities. Traditionally, contracts have dealt with such needs as the purchase of supplies and equipment and the lease of buildings, but now contractors also provide research and development of everything

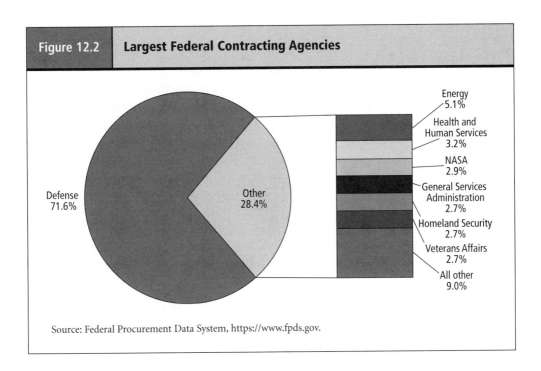

Figure 12.2 Largest Federal Contracting Agencies

Defense 71.6%

Other 28.4%

Energy 5.1%

Health and Human Services 3.2%

NASA 2.9%

General Services Administration 2.7%

Homeland Security 2.7%

Veterans Affairs 2.7%

All other 9.0%

Source: Federal Procurement Data System, https://www.fpds.gov.

from new weapons systems to new treatments for bioterrorism. They do much of the work of the space program; indeed, 90 percent of NASA's budget goes to contracts.

P. W. Singer has documented the rise of a new "privatized military industry," in which hundreds of companies, thousands of employees, and billions of dollars work to support the armed forces.[57] When the United States invaded Iraq in 2003, contractors provided most of the logistical support, from trucking in gasoline to cooking the meals. The contractors trained the Iraqi police force and guarding military convoys. When American administrator Paul Bremer traveled around Iraq, he flew in a helicopter operated by a private security company, which also provided his personal bodyguards. And in 2004, when investigators learned that American soldiers had been caught on camera torturing Iraqi prisoners, they also discovered that the prison personnel included private security officers and interrogators. In the end, there were as many contractor employees as soldiers in Iraq. As Singer concluded,

> the problem is that not all those involved were U.S. soldiers. While the military has established structures to investigate, prosecute and punish soldiers who commit crimes, the legal status of contractors in war zones is murky. Soldiers are accountable to the military code of justice wherever they are located, but contractors are civilians—not part of the chain of command.[58]

Contracting undoubtedly provides invaluable support for a host of government programs. But as the Iraq case illustrates, it can also raise troubling questions.

The federal government has established a general policy "to rely on competitive private enterprise to supply the commercial and industrial products and services it

Security guards working for Blackwater USA, a private company, handled the security for Paul Bremer (left), American administrator for Iraq, and other high-ranking officials. By 2008, there was a contractor employee for every American soldier in Iraq.

needs." However, the government is also committed to perform itself those functions that "are inherently governmental in nature, being . . . intimately related to the public interest."[59] This policy leaves enormous room for dispute over what the government should do for itself and what it should get done outside.

Advantages

Contracting out has several important advantages.

Cost Reduction

To many of its proponents, the greatest advantage of contracting is saving money. During the Reagan administration, a presidential commission concluded that "privatization" of many goods and services would improve them and that it would be better to have government "*provide* services without *producing them*"—that is, by contracting out.[60] In fact, the commission's chairman, J. Peter Grace, concluded that "one of the major inefficiencies in government is that it tries to do everything." By contracting out more services, Grace contended, the government could save $7.4 billion over three years.[61] The actual level of cost savings, however, has been subject to fierce debate: in 1987 the Congressional Budget Office much more conservatively estimated that more contracting out could reduce federal spending by $200 million over five years, a tiny fraction of the Grace Commission's figure.[62] Although figures vary wildly, most analysts agree that contracting can save money.

Special Expertise

Contracts enable the government to obtain the services of outside specialists. An agency may not have workers with the needed skills, or those it has may be fully occupied with their regular duties. For some assignments, the most competent specialists may be found outside government either because the pay is better or because they favor the work environment in universities, research institutes, and private companies.

Avoidance of Red Tape

Contracting also tends to bypass the bureaucratic syndrome that handicaps large government agencies: the very bureaucratic rules designed to promote fairness, competence, and accountability can prevent quick and effective action on problems. An independent organization can assemble an integrated team to study multidimensional problems; within government, such efforts often encounter all the difficulties of interbureau and interdepartmental coordination. Many projects, furthermore, are short term in nature, and a contract (with a built-in termination date) avoids the problem of setting up permanent bureaucratic units for temporary problems.

Additional Flexibility

Contracting is often attractive because contractors' staff members are not counted as government employees and are not subject to regulations governing the civil service. When budget constraints put ceilings on agency size, and when elected officials are leery of appearing to support the unpopular government bureaucracy, policymakers can minimize bureaucratic growth by contracting out. Government's reach thus can be extended without increasing its employment rolls. And because contractors are not subject to many government regulations, especially in the hiring, firing, and pay rates of staff, many government managers welcome the opportunity to contract out.

Problems

Contracting out can also pose problems, some of them the mirror images of the supposed advantages. Most of the problems come down to two questions: How can contractors be selected and their performance controlled so that the government's objectives are achieved? How can contractors preserve their independence in the face of controls that the government attempts to impose? In short, contracting confronts the same issue of control versus autonomy that we found in our consideration of federal grants.

Choice of Contractors

The organizations with which the government contracts for goods and services are a varied lot. Some are operated for profit, while others (such as universities) are nonprofit organizations. Some contractors take on the government's work as only a fraction of their total activity; others are wholly dependent on government contracts; many that have other income, including universities as well as private firms, find government contract income indispensable to their survival. The theory of contracting is that opening government programs up to bid invites competition among contractors that will drive prices down and keep quality up. Nevertheless, many federal contracts, especially smaller ones, are not awarded through competition: one-third of federal contract dollars are awarded noncompetitively.[63]

Large contracts are sometimes so complicated that few potential providers can assemble the expertise needed to do the job. One of the richest contracts in federal government history, a $4.5 billion competition for a new government telephone system, drew sustained interest from only two groups of bidders—and the contract was so complicated that even AT&T did not tackle the project on its own.[64] And even where there is competition, the government often cannot take full advantage of it. For example, because only two American companies are equipped to build submarines, the Pentagon believes that it is in the national interest to keep both companies in the business, so it often splits or alternates contract awards to ensure that both are kept afloat. Boeing found itself enmeshed in a major scandal in 2002 and 2003 because the Pentagon tried to direct a big contract for new air-refueling tankers to the company—and away from its major European competitor, Airbus Industries— although critics, including Sen. John McCain (R-Ariz.), charged that the planes might not be needed, were overpriced, and might not be the best suited to the job.[65]

Though the evidence is mixed, the contracting system appears to reward entrepreneurship more than demonstrated competence.[66] Large firms receive new contracts and extensions of old ones despite expensive past failures, lack of staff qualified for the particular projects, and conflicts of interest. Sometimes a sponsoring agency shows partiality to a firm that is sympathetic to the program, is unlikely to criticize its implementation, enjoys past connections with key agency personnel, or is in a position to facilitate their future careers.

Overspecification

Government contracting, especially for weapons, tends to prescribe "ultra" features to outperform any potential threat or surpass any potential problem. Government naturally wants the best, especially for its fighting men and women, but the procurement bureaucracy has a knack for "goldplating" specifications.[67] In *The Pentagon and the Art of War*, Edward N. Luttwak argued that this problem is the result of over-management caused by an oversupply of senior military officers, which produces "the ultimate case of too many cooks in one kitchen—or rather, of kitchens greatly enlarged to accommodate more cooks around fewer pots."[68] In military weapons, furthermore, contractors must follow a complex collection of MIL-SPECS (military specifications) that prescribe in elaborate detail just how the equipment must perform. The specifications for one military aircraft ranged over 24,000 documents, one of which, for electronic parts, referred to 235 other documents, which in turn referred to 1,374 more, of which half were more than ten years old. To follow the rules precisely meant installing obsolete components into frontline equipment.[69]

Not surprisingly, as problems change over the life of the contract, so too do contracts' goals—which makes the problem of measuring results against objectives ever more complex. Overspecification of the details of a contract can limit the flexibility of government managers and contractors alike, drive up the cost, and lengthen the time needed to produce the goods; it can also enhance "specification creep," whereby more and more requirements get built into the contract. Of course, too few specifications can produce goods that cannot perform in the harsh environments that government goods—especially military hardware—sometimes face. In the absence of a clear financial bottom line, an attitude of "better safe than sorry" often leads to overspecification.

Underperformance

The American Federation of State, County, and Municipal Employees (AFSCME), worried that the growth of contracting would eliminate the jobs of government employees who were union members, compiled an extensive catalog of contract abuses. AFSCME found, for example, that 30 percent of school lunch "meal packs" served by contractors were deficient in basic nutrients: "It would appear that a child eating these meal packs—especially with the usual amount of plate waste—would not be receiving iron and Vitamin A in adequate amounts. Here, it is essentially critical to remember that iron deficiency anemia is the most common of our [nutritional] deficiency diseases." Of thirty-four meals served by one contractor, fourteen were hamburgers, "variously adorned," and eight were hot dogs. Children were served vegetables only six times in a two-month period.[70]

The Government Accountability Office (GAO) surveyed contracts issued by the General Services Administration (GSA) over three years and found that the government had awarded more than $1 billion in contracts to vendors who repeatedly had failed to meet contract specifications and delivery schedules. Despite the problems, "GSA has continued to do business with repeat poor performing vendors." GAO found two reasons for this laxity. First, GSA's managers often had little good information on vendors' past performance; managers could not avoid poor vendors if they did not know who they were. Second, GSA had not always emphasized product quality in making decisions. "Poor performance on GSA supply contracts has been a long-standing problem," GAO concluded.[71]

Overregulation

Contractors face a bewildering array of regulations with which they must comply. It is not unusual for the attachments to a small contract simply listing all these rules to be longer than the stipulations of the contract itself. So in addition to having to deliver goods and services that often are tailor-made to the government's specifications, contractors also must comply with a host of procedural standards, from financial recordkeeping to hiring principles, that can often prove expensive and time consuming.

Sanctions

Government officials supervising private contractors confront the same problem in imposing sanctions as do their colleagues overseeing federal grants: cutting off the contract is often more trouble than it is worth and, in the meantime, deprives government of the good or service it needs. When the space shuttle *Challenger* exploded because of a defect in its solid rocket booster, NASA had no other supplier it could turn to. Punishing the contractor, Morton Thiokol, by canceling the booster contract would have grounded the shuttle for years until a new contractor geared up its operations. Even in the provision of more routine services, such as garbage collection, governments often have relatively few contractors among which to choose.

Corruption

The awarding of valuable contracts has always tempted the unscrupulous to make a quick profit at the government's expense. As the AFSCME study put it, "Government contracting and corruption are old friends."[72] Corruption in state and local contracts has a rich history, as contractors have long paid government officials kickbacks and bribes to win contracts, and contractors have colluded among themselves to fix bids and thus share the government's contract bounty. In New York State, for example, ten road construction companies were indicted for bid rigging: arranging among themselves who would bid how much on which contracts, thus boosting their profits on more than $100 million in contracts over eight years.[73] More recently, the fuzzier lines between the public and private sectors have increased conflict-of-interest problems, in which government employees steer business to firms that have been in the past—or may be in the future—their business connections. Of the enormous growth in what some experts call this "new patronage," one Washington interest group official noted, "The opportunities for misbehavior have increased tremendously as governments have gone to contracting out" as a way to save money.[74] "You make more money rigging bids than robbing banks—more than you could dealing drugs," one federal attorney explained.[75]

Nor are contracting scandals limited to state and local governments. During the Reagan administration, Wedtech, a small Bronx, New York–based tool-and-die manufacturer, used every device at its disposal to acquire more than $200 million in government contracts. The company admitted that it had forged more than $6 million in invoices submitted to the federal government for payment, and, federal prosecutors charged, the company's officials had used their friendship with top administration officials, including presidential counselor and later Attorney General Edwin Meese, to win contracts. The company eventually went out of business, but not before sixteen people connected with the scandal had been indicted, ranging from former White House aide Lyn Nofziger, to a member of Congress, Rep. Mario Biaggi (D-N.Y.), to the New York regional administrator for the Small Business Administration.[76]

It would be tempting to leap to the cynical conclusion that such corruption is epidemic in government contracting, but, of course, it is not. Most contractors are honest and hardworking, and most government officials struggle to get the most for the public's tax dollar. The recurring lessons of corruption in contracting, however, emphasize two broader lessons about implementation through contracting. First, contracting is not an automatic, easy solution to the problems of implementing programs directly through government agencies; instead, it replaces one set of administrative problems with another. Second, to be managed well, contracting requires a sophisticated collection of different administrative tools, which need to be tailored to the special implementation problems of contracting.[77] Also, it requires incorruptible and highly competent government officials to manage the contracts.

The Government's Dilemma

Implementation is, as we have seen, the study of how laws are executed. That definition covers all forms of administration, but students of implementation have concentrated particularly on administrative strategies that rely on proxies—that is, on those strategies, such as grants and contracts, in which the end responsibility for the program's results falls outside the bureaucracy that manages the program. Implementation thus is an untidy domain partly because of the variety of organizations that the government enlists through grants and contracts, partly because of the poor fit between the government's cultures and the complex motivations and internal organizational life of the proxies with which it deals, and partly because of the unresolved conflict between demands for accountability and demands for independence.

The government sacrifices much when it opts for implementation through outsiders. It fails to build its own capabilities for doing the work. Despite the rhetoric of high quality at low price that accompanies proxy federalism and contracting, proxy strategies are sometimes more costly, less effective, and less responsive than work done directly by the government. More critically, by implementing programs through outside agencies instead of through its own bureaucracy, the government has only loose control over grantees and contractors. Often the contracting government agency lacks staff members competent to judge the quality of the contractor's performance.

The fundamental issue is the increasing intermingling of federal-state-local and public-private roles in society. As Bruce L. R. Smith put it, "American politics, if once thought to be frozen in too narrow a range of policy debate, now seems to have an agenda of vast scope. The framework of debate has been not simplified, but vastly complicated, by the value cleavages that cut in strange ways through the political landscape."[78] The boundaries have become ever more blurred, especially since World War II. Fewer activities can now be labeled purely public or private. The government has increasingly relied on private agencies to pursue public purposes, while private institutions have increasingly relied on government support for their very life.

The problems of implementation that emerge thus are not the result of failures in government policy and administration but of the growing ambitions of government programs, the increasing interdependence of government and the private sector, and the greater complexity of society itself. When policymaking and implementation stretch across organizational boundaries—public and private, federal, state, and local—it becomes ever harder to reach agreement on what goals ought to be pursued and to collect information about what results are produced.

What Goals?

Success sometimes can be changed into failure and failure into success. Amtrak's Metroliner, a high-speed train service introduced into the Northeast corridor in the 1960s, was at first a success, but by the late 1970s, the trains were running late because of rough roadbeds (the heritage of privately owned railroads). Reconstruction of the roadbeds in the 1980s helped restore the trains' performance, but not without stirring complaints from conservatives who argued that the government had no place in the railway business to begin with. When Amtrak again encountered financial problems with its high-speed Acela service on the East Coast corridor, the complaints spilled out all over again.

Goals can change over time—as can performance and the standards by which one judges performance. Indeed, two observers can look at the same phenomenon and reach very different conclusions. A new highway may be the answer to a business

Amtrak's high-speed Acela trains quickly proved popular with East Coast travelers. In 2005, however, brake problems caused the railroad to pull all twenty of the trains from service for five months until repairs could be made to disk-brake rotors.

owner's dreams of better access to consumers, while environmentalists decry the danger the highway poses to a local watershed.

Sometimes programs appear to be failures because of "ridiculously high hopes about what might be accomplished with limited funds in a short time," according to former Congressional Budget Office director (and President Clinton's budget director) Alice M. Rivlin.[79] As Rivlin explained elsewhere, "current social problems are difficult because they involve conflicts among objectives that almost everyone holds."[80] Different persons in different organizations are likely to hold different views about the same objectives, which raises some serious problems for reaching agreement on how a program should be implemented. Added to this uncertainty of purpose is the government's ultimate difficulty in ensuring that publicly defined objectives remain paramount. One keystone of the problem of implementation thus is the problem of reconciling goals.

What Information?

It likewise is both important and difficult to collect information about what results a program produces. The presidential commission that investigated the 1986 *Challenger* space shuttle disaster, for example, concluded that it was "an accident rooted in history." Even though managers from NASA and its contractor, Morton Thiokol, knew about the problems with the O-rings (gaskets whose failure caused the shuttle's explosion), senior NASA officials did not understand the problem's seriousness. If they had, the commission concluded, "it seems likely that the launch of 51-L [the *Challenger*'s fatal flight] might not have occurred when it did." The problem was due in part to "a propensity of management at Marshall [the space center charged with managing the solid-fuel rockets] to contain potentially serious problems and to attempt to resolve them internally rather than communicate them forward."[81] The relationship between the contractor and its government supervisors prevented key information from reaching top managers.

The information problem is a critical one. Information distortion is a common enough problem in bureaucracies, but when information must cross bureaucratic boundaries, the problem intensifies. Organizations often hide information from one another, and the temptation to bury reports of poor performance increases when the cost may be loss of a grant or contract. It is hard to manage implementation effectively when managers do not know precisely what results a program produces.

A Program That Works

It would be easy to surrender to feelings of outrage and futility. Yet most programs do work—and work well. Many routine programs are models of remarkable success. Despite all our complaints, the mail does get delivered regularly, and mostly on time.

In Pittsfield, Massachusetts, one postal worker was legendary for never missing his deliveries, despite blizzards and frigid weather.[82] Social Security recipients usually receive their payments on time, and the program's clients rate the quality of service as high.[83] Despite glaring problems, NASA's record of achievement in space is remarkable, as illustrated by pictures of the landscape of other planets and galaxies at the dawn of time.

Less routine programs also often work well. Notable is a housing rehabilitation program funded by the Department of Housing and Urban Development (HUD) and administered through a grant to the city of Baltimore—notable especially for its results when compared with other HUD programs enmeshed in Reagan administration era scandals.[84] The program was an exceptionally ambitious one: local housing officials told HUD that they could renovate 140 public housing units at their Mt. Winans project for 10 percent less than a private contractor would have charged. They planned to do so by hiring participants in a low-income job-training program to fix up their own apartment complex. For months the project had been vacant, and many rooms had been vandalized: walls, floors, kitchens, and bathrooms had to be completely redone.

The combination of unskilled workers, dilapidated public housing, and a job-training program seemed the stuff of which implementation failure stories are written. Yet everyone ended up a winner. HUD saved about $250,000 in the project and received quality work—sometimes even better than what a private contractor would have produced. City officials believed that, since many of the trainees were residents there, the apartment complex was less likely to become run-down in the future, as was the unfortunate case in many public housing neighborhoods, and the city's maintenance costs therefore were likely to be lower.

The trainees won pride in themselves. As the manager of the Mt. Winans project said, the trainees "feel they've contributed to the community. They're very proud of what they've done." Children can point to the work and say, "Look what mama did." In addition, forty of the city's poorest citizens, three-fourths of whom were on welfare, received training in construction skills; just as important, they developed good work habits. "I loved it from the beginning," said one participant who had been on welfare the previous five years. "As soon as they put a ruler in my hand and let me get my knees dirty, I fell in love with it." When the program ended, city officials were hopeful of placing most of the participants in regular jobs and getting them off welfare.

What accounted for this program's unquestioned success? City officials kept the program's reach within their grasp. The program was small—limited to training only forty to fifty people—and flexible. The community already was close: "It's just like a family," explained the head of a local community organization. Furthermore, city officials won the support of neighborhood leaders. "The key point is the leaders in the community have to be involved, have to want it to work," explained one observer. Community leaders helped recruit the workers and became their biggest cheerleaders when the program started. Program managers made it clear that all the trainees would be given was an opportunity; any rewards would have to be earned by the workers—but when they were, they would belong to the workers.

The program began with a training class in basic skills. Any trainee late for class three times was to be dropped from the program—and nobody was expelled. The trainees were excited at what they learned. "We were so hyped," said one participant. "You feel like someone needs you, wants you." Work on the project was often hot and difficult, and the first buildings went way over budget and schedule. Still, by the time the project was finished, HUD had gotten the public housing units rehabilitated more cheaply than would have been the case with private contractors. The city got a larger supply of quality housing, and the workers gained valuable new skills.

There was a darker side to the project. Attrition was high, and one year after the project's start, half the original participants had dropped out, some for attendance or attitude problems, some without giving an excuse, and some to take better-paying private-sector jobs. Wages in the program were low, and some participants lost their welfare and Medicaid benefits. Still, the program was a success, especially when compared with similar training programs that had produced tales of woe. As one participant said, "I didn't think I would graduate. I didn't think I would go that far. I thought it would really be hard. . . . I'm so happy. I'm so happy." The program succeeded because all participants were able to find common ground in the goals they pursued, and because the information that managers needed to correct problems was at hand. The Mt. Winans program thus overcame the twin obstacles that so often doom implementation.

The Importance of Feedback

Effectively steering program implementation depends critically on a manager's obtaining good administrative feedback. The problem, as Herbert Kaufman puts it, is this: "When managers die and go to heaven, they may find themselves in charge of organizations in which subordinates invariably, cheerfully, and fully do as they are bid. Not here on earth."[85] Indeed, noncompliance by subordinates and by an agency's proxies often seems the rule, not the exception. A mismatch between directives and results is frequent—the bulk of the implementation literature is based on this notion, as illustrated by Pressman and Wildavsky's plaintive subtitle, "How Great Expectations in Washington Are Dashed in Oakland."[86]

Furthermore, even though we expect goals and outcomes not to correspond exactly, managers often have a very difficult time discovering the bad news. As we saw in chapter 10, numerous bureaucratic pathologies block and distort the flow of information, especially about problems, from the bottom of an organization (or from outside proxies) to the top. In late 1988, for example, top officials from the Department of Energy and from its predecessor, the Atomic Energy Commission (AEC), denied ever having been told that there were serious safety problems at the department's Savannah River nuclear power plant. The highest officials apparently were unaware that there had been a partial meltdown at the plant in 1970, among thirty other accidents.[87]

Administrative Feedback

Such information blockages pose critical problems for implementers. It is unreasonable to expect any manager to get things right the first time, since difficulties inevitably crop up. Indeed, the crucial problem in implementation is not avoiding problems but detecting and solving them, and solving problems is obviously impossible if managers cannot discover them. Therefore, good implementers must develop strategies for obtaining feedback.

Some feedback comes through routine administrative monitoring. Kaufman, for example, identifies five major sources of information about implementation: (1) the trail of paper that programs generate, which can provide valuable clues about performance; (2) personal inspection, which gets supervisors out from behind their desks to see what is happening in the field; (3) personal contacts outside the agency, which can help administrators bypass internal information problems; (4) investigations, which allow administrators to probe individual problems; and (5) centralization of some services, especially data collection, which can provide early warning about problems.

Unexpected sources of information can also provide valuable feedback. Patterns of complaints by clients can indicate malfunctions at lower bureaucratic levels. Reports by the news media, such as the *New York Times*'s 1988 investigation of the Department of Energy's nuclear power plant problems, can help surface important data. Disaffected employees, often called **whistle-blowers,** can sometimes produce explosive surprises.[88] For example, the federal False Claims Act, passed in 1863 to penalize contractors who were cheating the army, entitles the government to three times the amount of any overcharges or fraudulent claims—and the person who brings the charge to light is entitled to a reward of 15 to 25 percent of the government's takings. The prospect of a multimillion dollar bounty has prompted some employees and former employees of defense contractors to come forward with evidence against their bosses.[89]

Backward Mapping

Understanding what works—and what does not—can provide policymakers with clues about how to design programs better from the beginning.[90] Typically, of course, managers decide what goals they want to accomplish and then define, in increasing detail, the responsibilities of those at each step in the implementation process. Richard F. Elmore calls this **forward mapping,** and he argues that it often causes problems because implementers cannot control all the factors that affect the process. To correct these problems, he contends, managers ought to begin at the end, where "administrative actions intersect private choices." From there, the manager seeks to understand what will affect that relationship and what kind of behavior the manager desires. The manager then works backward, keeping in mind the constraints at each stage, to plan how to make sure that the system is best structured to achieve that behavior.[91]

Backward mapping makes a critical point: no part of the policy process works in isolation; to work best, each phase of the process must be integrated with the others. Evaluation can educate managers about what problems implementers may face; armed with that information, the managers can redesign the implementation process to reduce those risks. More generally, evaluation results can provide valuable feedback for use in reformulating the goals that drive the process. Evaluation is sometimes dismissed as providing information that is too little, too late, but that view misses its true importance. As Giandomenico Majone points out, evaluation is at its best when it promotes adaptation, not when it seeks simple-minded conclusions about success and failure.[92]

Formal Program Evaluation

This feedback, no matter how useful, at best leaves large gaps. Managers therefore often develop formal systems of evaluation to provide regular, high-quality feedback. "With objective information on the outcomes of programs, wise decisions can be made on budget allocations and program planning. Programs that yield good results will be expanded; those that make poor showings will be abandoned or drastically modified," as Carol H. Weiss argues.[93] Faced with the inevitable paradox of too much or too little information, officials seek regular and reliable feedback through formal evaluation strategies.

Formal evaluation has obvious advantages. Managers can design their program evaluations to test precisely what they want and to obtain just the information they need. Moreover, compared with the rest of policy research, the methodology for conducting evaluation research is well accepted and effective.[94] Balancing the potential for such careful experimentation, however, is the risk that, when finished, it will simply collect dust. Careful program evaluation requires controlled experiments and lengthy tests. The political world sometimes cannot tolerate the controls, such as having some groups receive the program while others do not, because most public programs are perceived as benefits, and it is hard to deprive some of the potential advantages for experimental purposes. Furthermore, the long time required to conduct careful research means that results sometimes emerge years after initial interest in new programs—and perhaps years after policy decisions were made. Managers sometimes respond by conducting quick-and-dirty studies that provide useful, if not always fully scientifically valid, feedback. They can also design evaluation strategies that feed more directly into management decisions.[95] But even if evaluations do not directly affect program decisions, they often do affect the intellectual debate over programs by shaping the ideas that structure future decisions. The key, Majone argues, is "to develop methods of assessment that emphasize learning and adaptation rather than expressing summary judgments of pass or fail."[96]

Results-Based Management

Many state and local governments have created quick-response information systems to measure success and failure. Unlike other performance systems, which take long-term perspectives to evaluate the overall performance of government programs, these systems seek to give managers real-time feedback.

Soon after taking office in 1994, New York mayor Rudolph Giuliani committed his administration to reducing crime in the city. His police commissioner, William Bratton, announced that he would seek to reduce crime by 40 percent in three years—a target three times higher than the city's improvement over the previous three years—and he devolved substantial operating decisions to the city's precinct commanders. To help them focus their actions, he then launched a major results-based management system, christened CompStat. A special unit produced weekly reports on crime in each precinct; Bratton and his senior staff made these reports the focus of twice-per-week staff meetings. The centerpiece of these sessions was an array of three eight-by-eight-foot screens, which mapped crime patterns on precinct-based street grids. This geographic information system (GIS) provided an instant snapshot of where crime was occurring, including whether patterns were emerging. If, for example, the GIS showed that a cluster of robberies had occurred in a particular neighborhood over the previous week, the precinct commander could devise a strategy for deploying police officers to break that pattern.

In the past, crime statistics had often appeared months later and had little to do with setting patrol patterns. In contrast, the rapid-response potential of CompStat, coupled with the GIS, gave Bratton and his staff the ability to track which problems were occurring where and to shift police strategy very quickly. It also gave them timely information about the performance of precinct commanders. CompStat thus helped reinforce the crime-control strategy of the department's top officials, and crime statistics fell dramatically—by 12 percent overall, compared with a 1.1 percent decline nationwide.[97] NYPD has continued to use the CompStat system aggressively, and it has led to further dramatic declines in crime. Some critics have suggested that complaints about police misconduct rose at the same time, perhaps because the new police strategy encouraged police officers to be more aggressive. Nevertheless, it was impossible to escape the fact that the results-based management approach had led to a dramatic decline in crime.

Many state and local governments have adopted similar performance systems. Baltimore, for example, developed an aggressive effort to measure the ongoing performance of all city programs and to feed the information into regular meetings between the mayor and top city officials. Called CitiStat, the system shifted analysis from the broad-scale long-term analysis of PPBS (planning-programming-budgeting system) and previous analytical budget systems to a focus on weekly turnaround of information about key indicators. CitiStat transferred these indicators to maps of the city, and the mayor and his top officials used these maps to measure performance, to administer programs, and ultimately to make budgetary decisions. Then-Mayor Martin O'Malley (he was later elected Maryland governor and took the system statewide) outlined four basic tenets of the approach:

- Accurate and timely intelligence
- Effective tactics and strategies
- Rapid deployment of resources
- Relentless follow-up and assessment[98]

For example, city officials tracked the location of fires to identify whether the arson prevention task force was having an effect, the trail of the city's cleanup program, and efforts to rub out rats. Other GIS displays showed the status of solid waste problems, graffiti cleanup, and filled potholes. Like many other cities, Baltimore also created a 311 call center, which allowed citizens to telephone city officials to report nonemergency problems (which go to the 911 number) and to get information about city services. Baltimore created extensive mapping capabilities on its website, http://www.ci.baltimore.md.us/government/citistat/, to allow citizens to track the progress of 311 calls as well as other city services.

CitiStat represents a new strategy for producing better information about the results of government programs and coupling them to budgetary decisions. Baltimore officials have supplemented CitiStat with CitiTrack, a central call system to help solve citizen problems. Citizens can dial "311" and use CitiTrack to connect with the agency that handles the problem. The city not only uses CitiTrack to help streamline citizens' interaction with government but also feeds the complaints back into CitiStat as evidence of what problems are popping up where.[99] New York City created a broad and data-rich City-wide Performance Reporting Tool (CPR, for short), at http://www.nyc.gov/html/ops/cpr/html/home/home.shtml, which revolutionized the way the city collected and managed data on the performance of its programs.

When O'Malley was elected Maryland governor, he took the system with him. Other states, especially in Utah, Virginia, and Washington, have led high-level efforts to strengthen information technology and e-government in improving service delivery. Virginia governor Mark Warner, for example, championed consolidation of the state's vast technology systems into a single new agency that has integrated the state's e-mail systems and funneled more than $1 billion in purchases through the new online procurement system, eVA.[100] Citizens are relying increasingly on e-mail to contact state legislators, and legislators are distributing e-newsletters to their constituents.

These innovative efforts reflect yet again two of the big issues we have examined. First, to make the technology systems work, governments have relied increasingly on private contractors, and that reliance has increased the need to manage these contractors well, because system design problems have sometimes proved costly. Second, the technological issues sometimes pale by comparison to the old and established problems of managing complex organizations. As Texas's chief information officer, Carolyn Purcell, argued, "The complexity is in the relationships, not really in the technology itself."[101]

Conclusion

The perspective on implementation is thus a mixed one, full of hype, hope, and despair. Three considerations may partially shift the balance toward hope.

First, many problems we label implementation actually reflect far larger administrative issues. What we call failure may be the product of goals that policymakers do not agree on and results that they do not like. If true implementation is separated out and defined as "program operations," then many alleged failures turn out not to be breakdowns in the actual process of implementation but the consequence of poor policy choices, impossibly high hopes announced at a program's conception, or misjudgments in legislative prescription of implementation strategies. Sometimes, indeed, the more efficient the implementation of a bad policy, a poor program, or a legislatively mandated faulty strategy, the more conspicuous will be the failure. So-called implementation failures thus often reflect deep and enduring problems in other parts of the policy process.

Second, our principal focus has been on implementation by American governments. But wallowing in government failure stories can make it easy to forget that the private sector's record is scarcely clean. Anyone who has ever worked for a private organization can vouch for substantial waste of materials, inefficient ways of processing paperwork, and problems of bureaucracy that match those of the public sector. Millions of automobiles have been recalled for defects, drugs have been introduced and later found to cause fatal injuries and serious birth defects, computers break down, and other problems in workmanship, services, and materials abound. This catalog of missteps is not meant to compound our misery by suggesting that nothing works anywhere but to emphasize that poor performance is not a purely public-sector problem. In fact, most of the outrageous fraud, waste, and abuse stories about government itself have involved private organizations trying to take advantage of public programs.

Finally, many implementation problems arise out of the increasing complexity of American society rather than from any failing in government itself. The more the boundaries blur—between the public and private sectors, among federal, state, and local governments—the more dependent programs become on the interrelationship of all of these organizations and the more difficult it is to achieve true success.

These mitigating considerations do not mean that implementation by American governments is what it should be. On the contrary, the evidence shows not only that implementation is often unsatisfactory but also that its improvement has been neglected—by Congress, by the president, by operating agencies, and by the research community. The necessary first step toward improved performance is correction of that neglect.[102]

Case 12 From the Front Lines of Implementation: To Tase or Not to Tase?

At a 2007 forum at the University of Florida with Sen. John Kerry (D-Mass.), the Democrats' 2004 presidential nominee, student Andrew Meyer scuffled with university police officers. Meyer tried to press Kerry on several issues. In trying to subdue Meyer, campus police eventually Tasered him, and the episode became a YouTube sensation that drew more than 3 million viewers.

One summer morning in 2004, Sgt. Mark McCallum was forced to make the kind of split-second, life-changing decision that police officers know is part of the job—but that is every officer's nightmare. He and his partner, Deputy John

Watson, spotted a suspect they knew was wanted in three violent armed robberies that had taken place over the previous fourteen hours. They had heard reports that the night before the suspect had put a gun to the back of a liquor store clerk after grabbing her by the back of the neck. A few hours later, he had beaten a min-imart owner with a gun. At a 7-Eleven that morning, he had forced a clerk to open the cash register and then took off with money and cigarettes.

A half hour later, McCallum and Watson spotted the forty-one-year-old sus-pect across from that same 7-Eleven. They ordered him to stop. He refused and began walking away with his hands in the air, but then reached for a gun in his waistband.

McCallum drew his weapon and fired. But instead of a gun, he had pulled out a Taser, a stun gun that shoots a 50,000-volt charge through fishhook-like barbs fastened to a wire. The suspect fell but then struggled back to his feet. McCallum fired the Taser again. He and Watson managed to subdue the man and finally got cuffs and leg shackles on him.

When they searched their captive, the deputies discovered that the weapon in his waistband was a pellet gun, not exactly the sort of lethal weapon they had expected. A spokesman for the Pasco, Florida, sheriff's department proudly told reporters, "This is a case where the Taser saves someone's life because the deputies had every reason and right to shoot him."[1] Local officials had recently added the Taser to the officers' arsenal. "This is just another tool that gives us a step between doing nothing and using deadly force," explained the county's training officer, Sgt. Brian Prescott. "No officer wants to use deadly force."[2] St. Paul, Minnesota, police officials corroborate Prescott's claim, lauding the Taser's effectiveness. There, the Taser helped police avert four "suicide by cop" incidents, in which individuals had threatened force in the expectation that the police would shoot them.

"Taser" is short for the Thomas A. Swift Electric Rifle. Its shock, fired by com-pressed nitrogen and powered by batteries, has a maximum range of twenty-one feet, though it works best at seven to ten feet. The victim loses neuromuscular control, typically for about five seconds, and falls stiffly to the ground. That's long enough for police to subdue and cuff their quarry.

The weapon isn't intended to replace such standard police weapons as pistols and shotguns—its range isn't long enough and, especially in the face of deadly force, its effect isn't sure enough. But officers frequently encounter incidents involving mentally ill suspects or individuals who threaten themselves, as well as cases like the robbery suspect, where a quick electric shock can help the officers gain control of the situation. About 5,400 law-enforcement agencies across the United States have adopted the Taser, and the Federal Aviation Administration has also approved the weapon for use by airline pilots, who were seeking ways of dis-abling attackers without firing bullets inside a pressurized aircraft.

An attorney for the American Civil Liberties Union in northern California, Mark Scholsberg, said, "If police want to use a Taser instead of a gun, that's a welcome development." And Fremont, California, detective Bill Veteran explained its attractiveness to those in the front lines, "I've been in all kinds of wrestling matches, I've been pepper-sprayed, I've been hit by a baton, I've seen people get bit by a police dog." He praised the Taser because, he explained, it's "just a cleaner, safer way to do business."[3]

But some Miami residents aren't so sure. Police there were called to the Kelsey L. Pharr Elementary School following the report of a suspect who had broken a picture frame, picked up a piece of glass, and smeared blood over his face. At the scene, officers tried to calm the suspect, but he grabbed the glass tighter and began cutting his leg with the glass. Miami-Dade officer Maria Abbott fired her Taser, hit the suspect in the torso, and subdued him.

The suspect, who had a history of behavioral problems, was a six-year-old first grader. The boy's mother said, "If there's three officers, it's nothing to tell a 6-year-old holding a glass, if you feel threatened, 'Hey, here's a piece of candy, hey, here's a toy. Let the glass go.'"

A Florida International University psychology professor—and former school principal—was outraged. "I couldn't imagine why a police officer would use that kind of device on a child," Marvin Dunn explained. "I can restrain a 6-year-old with one hand. I don't get it." But police detective Randy Rossman explained, "To further protect the student from injuring himself, the officer felt she needed to deploy the stun gun." The child was taken to a local hospital for psychiatric evaluation.[4]

Miami police found themselves facing similar criticism for their use of the Taser on a twelve-year-old girl. She had skipped school, and police found her drinking and smoking in a swimming pool. When an officer tried to pick her up to take her to school, she began to run. The officer told her to stop and, when she refused, the officer fired the Taser. "I couldn't breathe, and I was, like, nervous, and I was scared at the same time," the girl told a CNN reporter.

Cases of poor or unclear judgment concerning Taser use are not limited to Florida. Critics said that instances of misuse were popping up across the country: Tasering of a nine-year-old Arizona girl already in handcuffs; accidental shocks to children as young as a year old; and a case in which police in Kansas City Tasered a sixty-six-year-old woman, Louise Jones, for improper use of her car horn.[5] Critics also pointed to racial bias in Taser use. An audit overseen by the Houston city controller in 2008 revealed that black people were far more likely than any other suspects to be Tasered by police. Of individuals encountering police, 46 percent were black. However, blacks accounted for 67 percent of the persons Tasered by police. "We need to know why that difference exists," said controller Annise Parker.[6]

These cases, along with those of the two Florida children, have fueled a growing national debate on the use of Tasers by police departments. At stake is not just the occasional use of excessive force by police officers. As critics point out, the device is sometimes lethal. An investigation by the Minneapolis *Star Tribune* found 105 cases throughout the country, between 1983 and 2004, in which a person died after having been shot with an electric stun gun.

A spokesperson for the company that manufactures the Taser admitted that deaths resulting from stun gun use in police custody cases like these may be inevitable, saying, "We know that Tasers are used every day, and we will be involved in tragic deaths that will be very similar to in-custody deaths that have occurred when Tasers have not been used." But, he noted, "We have never been listed as a direct or primary cause of death in our company's existence." The spokesperson concluded, "Taser devices save lives every day."

As is the case with many weapons, the dispute over the Taser quickly spilled over into the marketplace. Individuals can buy the weapon on the manufacturer's website, in a variety of models (though the use is restricted in the District of Columbia, Massachusetts, Rhode Island, New York, New Jersey, Wisconsin, Michigan, Hawaii, and some cities and counties). The Taser C2, for example, sells at $299. A laser sight adds $50. A model in "fashion pink" costs no more, but camouflage or leopard adds an extra $30. The X26C, similar to the model many police departments use, costs $999.

When the nation's largest police department, in New York City, explored whether to issue the Taser to its officers, the debate was fierce. Advocates argued that it could save lives by giving officers an alternative to deadly force for subduing unruly persons, especially mentally ill individuals who sometimes threatened officers but whose basic problems were medical, not criminal. Critics pointed to a previous scandal, when officers used a predecessor of the Taser, the stun gun, during questioning of suspects to loosen their tongues. Critics also worried that the Taser would lessen the officers' inhibition against using weapons of all kinds and make it more likely they would resort to deadly force.

A RAND Corporation study recommended that the department experiment with the Taser but urged the experiment begin with a pilot study.[7] NYPD decided to equip a group of sergeants with Tasers and match them with another group of sergeants who would not receive the weapon. A careful statistical study would then examine how the weapon was used and what impact it had on law enforcement. "This is like turning a battleship around," explained Police Commissioner Raymond W. Kelly. The department wanted to proceed carefully.[8]

As evidence from around the country mounted, the case for the Taser was anything but clear. Studies suggested that police fired their Tasers about 300 times per year, and it usually worked well. However, during a John Kerry rally in the 2004 presidential campaign, a student was Tasered. A video of the event became a YouTube sensation, with 3 million views.[9] In 2008, a civil court jury held Taser International, the manufacturer of the device, partially liable in the death of a California man and awarded his family more than $6 million. A Taser spokesperson countered that the company had won seventy previous civil cases and that the jury found Taser only 15 percent responsible for the Salinas man's death.[10] But the controversy did not end. In July 2008, police in Dayton, Ohio, were criticized for using a Taser on a blind woman. They said she was creating a disturbance. She countered she had no way of being able to tell they really were police.

Questions to Consider

1. Program implementation depends a great deal on the use of discretion by frontline bureaucrats. How does discretion determine the use of the Taser? (Note that rules are one thing; an officer's instantaneous judgment about life-and-death situations can be quite another.)

2. Suppose you were the commissioner of the NYPD. Would you supply all of your officers with the Taser? Why or why not? What rules would you establish for its use?

3. What role, if any, should elected officials play in determining police policy for the purchase and use of such guns?

4. Should Tasers be available for sale to individuals? If so, should they be the same powerful models available to police officers, or should sales be limited to less-powerful models?

Notes

1. "Sheriff's Office Use of Taser Saved a Life," editorial, *St. Petersburg Times,* October 8, 2004, 2.
2. Lisa A. Davis, "Deputies Adding Stunners to Their Crime-Fighting Tools," *Tampa Tribune,* May 29, 2003, 6.
3. Alan Gathright, "Police: Enforcing and Informing," *San Francisco Chronicle,* September 26, 2004, B1.
4. Madeline Baro Diaz, "Use of Taser on 6-Year-Old Prompts Outrage," *St. Louis Post-Dispatch,* November 14, 2004, A2; and "Miami Police Review Policy after Tasers Used on Kids," *CNN.com,* November 14, 2004, http://www.cnn.com/2004/US/11/14/children.tasers/index.html.
5. Matt McKinney, "Stun Guns Pack Uncertain Risk," *Minneapolis Star Tribune,* October 17, 2004, 1A.

6. Roma Khanna, "Audit Says Houston Police More Likely to Taser Blacks," *Houston Chronicle,* September 8, 2008, http://www.chron.com/disp/story.mpl/front/5989712.html.

7. Bernard D. Rostker and others, *Evaluation of the New York City Police Department Firearm Training and Firearm-Discharge Review Process* (Santa Monica, Calif.: RAND Corporation, 2008), http://www.rand.org/pubs/monographs/2008/RAND_MG717.pdf.

8. Al Baker, "Tasers Getting More Prominent Role in Crime Fighting in City," *New York Times,* June 15, 2008, 25.

9. See http://www.youtube.com/watch?v=6bVa6jn4rpE.

10. Baker, "Tasers Getting More Prominent Role in Crime Fighting in City."

Key Concepts

accountability **370**

backward mapping **398**

block grants **378**

categorical grants **378**

contracting **384**

crossover sanctions **380**

delegation **383**

efficiency **369**

formula-based programs **379**

forward mapping **398**

fungibility **384**

grantsmanship **379**

implementation **365**

mandates **381**

partial preemption **380**

project-based programs **379**

whistle-blowers **397**

For Further Reading

Derthick, Martha. *New Towns In-Town.* Washington, D.C.: Urban Institute, 1972.

Hogwood, Brian H., and B. Guy Peters. *The Pathology of Public Policy.* Oxford: Clarendon Press, 1985.

Mead, Lawrence M. *Government Matters: Welfare Reform in Wisconsin.* Princeton: Princeton University Press, 2004.

Pressman, Jeffrey L., and Aaron B. Wildavsky. *Implementation.* Berkeley: University of California Press, 1973.

Wholey, Joseph S., Harry P. Hatry, and Kathryn E. Newcomer, eds. *Handbook of Practical Program Evaluation.* San Francisco: Jossey-Bass, 1994.

Wilson, James Q. *Bureaucracy: What Government Agencies Do and Why They Do It.* New York: Basic Books, 1989.

Suggested Websites

The Internet is full of the new initiatives in the area of program implementation. For New York City's performance management system, see **http://www.nyc.gov/html/ops/cpr/html/home/home.shtml.** Information about Baltimore's CitiStat program can be found at **http://www.ci.baltimore.md.us/news/citistat/index.html.**

For case studies on implementation problems, see the report of the study committee that investigated the *Columbia* space shuttle accident, **http://www.nasa.gov/columbia/home/index.html**; the special report on emergency response in New York on the morning of September 11, 2001, **http://www.nyc.gov/html/fdny/html/mck_report/index.shtml**; and the report of the Arlington County September 11 response at the Pentagon, **http://www.co.arlington.va.us/Departments/Fire/edu/about/FireEduAboutAfterReport.aspx.**

For a fascinating look at one official's views on implementation, see Donald Rumsfeld's "rules" at **http://www.library.villanova.edu/vbl/bweb/rumsfeldsrules.pdf.**

PART V

Administration in a Democracy

Establishing bureaucracy in a democracy creates two sets of issues. As we saw in chapter 1, not only do we want to see programs managed efficiently and effectively, but we also want the process and the result to be responsive and accountable. This section examines the dynamics of bureaucracy's relationship with the larger political and economic system, especially the exercise of administrative power through regulation. We examine as well the methods that legislatures can use in seeking to control the way administrators exercise the power delegated to them.

The core of administrative ethics in the public sector lies in balancing the competing goals of efficiency and accountability. We want administrators to be efficient and accountable, but the crosscutting political forces make it hard to do either, let alone accomplish both. We conclude the book back where we started: with a careful look at how the competing forces shaping administrative behavior affect administration in a democracy.

13

Regulation and the Courts

In July 2008, Yankee Stadium hosted the annual All-Star Game. It was an easy decision, explained Commissioner Bud Selig. "When you think of Yankee Stadium, it is the most famous cathedral in baseball, and, I think, the most famous stadium in the world." The 2008 season was the stadium's last, "So we really believe that this is the way we can honor the cathedral that has meant so much to this sport for so long."[1] It was, at once, a wonderful celebration of the stadium that saw decades of some of baseball's greatest history. Baseball fans everywhere knew it as "the house that Ruth built," an enduring homage to one of the game's most famous sluggers and to legions of other fans who brought championships to the team's home in the Bronx. But it was also a reminder to Yankees' fans of the culture shock coming their way. As a new stadium rose next door, officials were planning the demolition of the old relic and conversion of the land into a park.

During the new stadium's construction, city officials discovered a big problem. New York City investigators found problems with the tests a private company, Testwell Laboratories, had conducted on concrete being poured for the stadium (as well as for the foundation of the Freedom Tower on the former site of the World Trade Center in lower Manhattan and at many other projects). Investigators found that the company sometimes had not properly done preliminary tests on the concrete and then falsely certified later, more thorough tests. The tests were important to ensure that the concrete met the city's standards. To stand the test of years, concrete must be properly mixed and poured. Several city agencies joined in the investigation. When asked why a company might not conduct required tests, an official explained, "I guess it keeps your overhead and costs down if you don't actually do the tests."[2]

It was a case of government by proxy through regulation. The reason for tough city standards for concrete was clear. Having a major facility collapse because of shoddy construction can prove both dangerous and expensive. (A driver was killed in Boston when part of the ceiling in the "Big Dig" tunnel collapsed in July 2006.) City officials contracted with private companies, like Testwell, to conduct tests to

As the New York Yankees finished their 2008 baseball season, a new stadium rose next door. For nostalgic fans, it was a difficult transition. Babe Ruth had christened the old stadium with a home run on its opening day in 1923. The new stadium promised luxury boxes and a martini bar.

ensure that other private contractors were complying with city rules. In the end, the city was neither doing the work nor ensuring that others were doing the work. Its job was to make sure that all these private companies complied with city regulations because, if any problems occurred, everyone knew that citizens and reporters alike would hold the city accountable.

Regulation is a core element of government's work. It frames the way that government officials exercise their discretion. It defines the way that private companies interact with the public, from the safety of foods we eat to the security of bank deposits. Decisions might be the central governmental act, and budgets provide what administrators need to carry out those decisions, but regulations are the central nervous system of government.

Regulation as a Foundation for Government's Work

Government regulation defines the processes by which government administrators do their work. It translates tax laws into the forms that taxpayers love to hate, and it manages the airline standards that keep planes safely in the air. Regulations are everywhere, from the size of reflectors on bicycle wheels to accessibility of public buildings. Rules both empower and limit government employees. They define how far government administrators can push into the lives of ordinary citizens, and thereby restrict their freedom, and how far government administrators can exercise their control, and thereby protect citizens. If public administration revolves around the balance of power and accountability, regulation defines how public administrators balance individual freedom and government control.

Most public programs require rules for their implementation. Indeed, when many people think of government, they think of regulation. Government's rules shape our lives, often in ways we do not much notice. Government regulates the vitamin pills we take and the therapeutic claims that go on our toothpaste tubes. It controls the safety of our prescription drugs and of our cars. It oversees the maintenance of airplanes and buses and sets the standards for highway guardrails and interstate buses. It is literally impossible to get out of bed in the morning without encountering a government regulation, since the government regulates the bedding on which we sleep and, famously, the tags on the pillows on which we rest our heads. (Contrary to popular opinion, it *is* legal to remove the tags on pillows—but only after consumers buy the pillows and take them home.)

Regulation in fact lies at the core of much government policy—and its administration. All governments regulate the behavior of individuals and organizations, with the primary objective of changing that behavior when the unchecked pursuit of self-interest could harm others: consumers, competitors, suppliers, distributors, workers, or members of future generations. Such protective measures become more controversial when aimed at limiting adults' freedom to harm themselves by such means as smoking cigarettes, using narcotics, neglecting to fasten seat belts in cars, or buying excessively risky stocks and bonds. Regulation may be aimed at overseeing the work of manufacturers and distributors (on the "harming others" premise), but sometimes it merely requires full disclosure of the risks, leaving citizens free to make their own choices, even if those choices may endanger their health, safety, or property. At other times, the government decides that some product is not safe enough for consumers to make their own judgments about its use. The Food and Drug Administration (FDA), for example, decided in 2004 not to allow over-the-counter sales of the "morning after" birth control pill. Even though a panel of expert advisers had recommended that the FDA approve such sales, agency officials ruled that there was not enough data to conclude that the drug was safe, so they kept it available by prescription only.

A secondary, but vitally important, objective is to control how government agencies and their employees go about their administrative tasks, particularly those that involve regulation of private behavior.

In the pursuit of both objectives, three features are central. One is the *source of regulatory authority*: the legislation that vests administrative discretion in agencies, specifying the limits of such discretion and the conditions governing how it shall be exercised. A second is the *amount of resources* that Congress and the president make available to the agencies for performance of their regulatory responsibilities. The first and the second features are often not in harmony: Congress may expand an agency's responsibilities without increasing its appropriations, or the president may impose limits on staff size that impair an agency's effectiveness. A third feature is *regulatory procedure*: the interplay between responsibility for regulating private behavior and the rules that Congress, the president, and the courts establish to govern the behavior of regulating agencies and employees. Those rules are intended to keep regulators accountable and responsive and thus to assure a government of laws and not of men, but the rules can prove so complex that regulatory decisions get entangled in red tape, which can delay their issuance for years. These three features—delegation of legislative power, adequacy of resources, and regulatory procedure—occupy much of our attention in this chapter.

The range of regulation of private behavior is very wide. At one extreme are speed limits and stoplights, which govern ordinary behavior in daily life. At the other extreme are restrictions on the ability of individuals to enter a business or profession and the regulation of prices and wages. An individual cannot practice medicine or law without a state license; some states regulate hairdressers and dog groomers as well. In most cities, local governments set the fares that taxicab drivers can charge. In New York State, dentists battled over state rules over who could regulate the state's dentists and what role they can play. This vast array of rules shape a surprising range of economic activity.

The Roots of Regulation

Regulation is old as well as wide. The Constitution in 1789 gave Congress the power "to promote the progress of science and useful arts by securing for limited times to authors and inventors the exclusive right to their respective writings and discoveries."[3] This book is protected against plagiarism by a certificate issued by the U.S. Copyright Office, which administers a statute based on that provision. But this same constitutional grant of power has had far broader impact. In 1988, administering a statute under the same clause, the Patent and Trademark Office awarded the world's first animal-invention patent to Harvard University, whose scientists had transformed a mouse through genetic manipulation.[4]

The scope of government's regulatory power is a major focus of policy disputes (but that question concerns the wisdom of the legislative branch, which we do not explore in this book). Our focus here is on how the executive branch *administers* regulatory laws. Nevertheless, the nonstop political controversy over government regulatory policy deeply affects their administration. A regulatory agency inhabits a relatively serene environment in pursuing its goals when the regulatory policy enjoys wide public support or acquiescence by the regulated interests. But when public support is weak or so diffused that it cannot be mobilized, or when the regulated interests are opposed and well organized, the agency confronts a hostile environment that may threaten its program and perhaps the agency's very existence.[5] Because of the strong support of the industry, an airline regulatory program protected established airlines against the entry of new competitors for decades, even though it kept prices artificially high and deprived many communities of service. In contrast, pollution-control programs that add to the costs of doing business are resisted by many affected companies.

Although the public has mixed feelings about regulation, at a general level, people chafe at government rules and complain about government regulators. Many critics complain that government regulation of business usually does more harm than good. There is widespread belief that there are too many government regulations and that too many rules make too little sense.[6] Yet most people do not favor rolling back government regulations that protect their workplace, safeguard the environment in their neighborhood, ensure the safety of the airplanes on which they fly, or set standards for the security of their bank accounts. Individuals do not like the idea of a big government interfering in their freedom, but they clearly expect government to protect them from danger, even if that means interfering in someone else's freedom. Indeed, the standard reaction to problems ranging from plane crashes to poisoned food is to interview government regulators. Why, reporters ask, did government fail to prevent the problem from happening, even if the problem was the result of mistakes made by private companies?

Some regulations may adversely affect particular regions, communities, or industries, which can increase costs, cause the loss of competitive advantage, and create unemployment. Federal regulations are unquestionably costly, but no one really knows the cost of complying with them. Some members of Congress, in fact, fear that regulators favor "processes over accountability, and paper pushing over content."[7] When legislators get an earful from the affected areas, the regulatory agency may need to back down in order to maintain legislative support; political prudence may take over even if the proposed regulation is in accord with the letter of the law. Thus, not only do regulators need to balance the broad opposition to regulations in general and the strong support for some regulations in particular, but they also need to pay careful attention to *who* pays the costs and receives the benefits.

"The uniqueness of the American approach to regulation," writes David Vogel, "is the one finding on which every cross-national study of regulation is in agreement." In explaining this comment, he anticipates much of what we treat in this chapter:

> The American system of regulation is distinctive in the degree of oversight exercised by the judiciary and the national legislature, in the formality of its rulemaking and enforcement process, in its reliance on prosecution, in the amount of information made available to the public, and in the extent of the opportunities provided for participation by nonindustry constituencies. . . .

The restrictions the United States has placed on corporate conduct affecting public health, safety, and amenity are at least as strict as and in many cases stricter than those adopted by other capitalist nations. As a result, in no other nation have the relations between the regulated and the regulators been so consistently strained.[8]

The Regulatory Job

Regulatory agencies vary in the kinds of regulation they administer.[9] They operate under both vague and highly specific statutory mandates. They are more expert in their particular fields than Congress, the president's office, and the courts, all of which play major roles in regulation. Yet on many matters, they must struggle with the enormous uncertainties of scientific and technological knowledge in framing and implementing regulations.

Kinds of Regulations

Government regulation is of two kinds: economic and social. The expansion of **economic regulation** began in the states, but in the federal government it dates from 1887, when the Interstate Commerce Commission was established to regulate the railroads.[10] It was the dominant form of regulation until the 1960s. Economic regulation has two characteristics. First, it has long sought to assure competition by preventing monopolies and unfair methods of competition (including deception of consumers); these **antitrust laws** embrace all industries where such evils may appear and are administered by the Justice Department and the Federal Trade Commission. Second, in the effort to ensure fair and quality markets, the federal government has regulated the following aspects of economic activity: (1) entry to a business (by issuance or denial of "certificates of convenience and necessity," which are licenses to do business and serve certain routes or areas); (2) prices (by fixing maximum and, in some cases, minimum rates to be charged); (3) safety; and (4) standards of service.

At both the state and the federal levels, government has typically lodged responsibility in independent regulatory commissions. These bodies tend to be headed by boards, and in most cases the law ensures a balance between the political parties (although the party in power can often appoint the chair and secure a majority of commission votes). Each commission regulates a single industry or handful of industries, such as public utilities (gas, water, electric, and telephone companies), taxicabs, and airlines. The single-industry focus gives the regulatory commission special expertise, but it also increases the chance that the commission will fall under the domination of the industry it is supposed to regulate. In the absence of effective consumer organization, this **capture** phenomenon becomes a major concern, with no remedy in sight.[11]

Social regulation, though appearing early in the twentieth century (as with child labor and food and drug regulation), grew enormously in the 1960s and 1970s. It focuses on the quality of life by seeking to safeguard the environment, protect workers' health and safety, assure the safety and quality of consumer products, and prohibit discrimination on grounds of race, color, sex, age, or disability. Responsibility for achieving social regulation is mostly lodged not in independent commissions but in bureaus within departments or, as with the Environmental Protection Agency (EPA), in an independent agency with a single leader. The jurisdictions of these bureaus and agencies are not confined to single industries but cover all industries where threats to health, safety, fair employment, and the environment may occur. Although social regulation is addressed to the quality of life rather than to economic imperfections of the market, it can also have substantial market effects—by reducing a business firm's freedom to act purely in its own self-interest, and more important, by often increasing costs.

Defense of the government's power of intervention rests on the economic concept of **externalities,** sometimes called spillover effects (discussed previously in chapter 10). If a paper mill discharges pollutants into a river, downstream communities must pay the costs of cleaning up the river or purifying their intake to assure safe drinking water for their citizens, while downstream swimmers, fishermen, and boaters pay the price in pleasures forgone. The pollution practice reduces manufacturing costs and so is rational behavior for the company, but the secondary costs—financial, aesthetic, and health-related—exported to people downstream are high. Economists would compare the manufacturer's savings to the downstream costs, and would justify regulatory action to return the costs to the polluter if the benefits accrued downstream were high enough. Thus, government could make an economic case for forcing the paper mill to internalize the externalities.[12]

Analysts apply the concept of externalities broadly. The government has used this approach to justify intervention in the pharmaceutical industry (to ensure that drugs are safe), the food industry (to certify that meat is healthful), and the toy industry (to reduce the chances that children will be injured while at play). It has reached as well into the relationship between employers and employees—to reduce a worker's risk of being injured on the job.

Economic regulation and social regulation are not two sides of a single coin. In the political world, at least, they are two quite distinct coins. Otherwise, it would be hard to explain the federal government's actions in the late 1970s and in the 1980s, when it simultaneously curtailed economic regulation and expanded social regulation. Although retreating from extensive regulation of trucking, airlines, telecommunication, and financial services,[13] the Carter and even the Reagan administrations placed more elaborate protections on the environment, workers' health and safety, and consumers' products. The underlying politics were complex: economists of both liberal and conservative stripes succeeded in convincing both the president and members of Congress that economic deregulation would promote lower prices, better services, and stronger consumer choice. Meanwhile, however, the consumer and environmental movements were growing, building pressure for stronger social regulation.

There are very different political and administrative implications for economic and social regulation. In economic regulation, the regulatory agency often must consider just how much a stronger regulation might hinder market competition at consumers' cost—there is no clear, abstract standard for how high a taxicab fare should be. Regulatory bodies must weigh the interest of taxicab operators and owners in higher profits against the consumers' interest in low fares—and make sure that the balance works out to ensure the community's need for a sufficient supply of taxis to meet the demand.

On the other hand, social regulatory agencies must often act to enforce strong, nonnegotiable standards. For example, the law requires the FDA to act immediately when a food or drug on the market is found to cause death or serious disease—and the procedural niceties must follow, rather than precede, an order to remove the product from store shelves. Sometimes regulatory action simply demands disclosure of information, such as the law requiring the labeling of health hazards on cigarette labels, or the EPA's standards for companies' disclosure of toxic materials they release into the environment. Even such seemingly moderate regulations may meet vigorous opposition from the affected industries, but sometimes the industries actually welcome federal disclosure requirements: in the case of chemicals, the federal ruling replaces a confusing combination of state and local regulations with a uniform national standard; in the case of cigarettes, it transfers responsibility to consumers for choosing to use products that are unsafe (thus shrinking the tobacco companies' corporate liability).[14] Such informational regulations extend even to how frozen pizza boxes must disclose the presence of a cheese substitute—with larger type on the front instead of smaller type in the list of ingredients. The FDA requires such display on all pizzas without meat toppings, while the Department of Agriculture, with jurisdiction over meat-topped pizzas, requires it only if the substitute constitutes more than 90 percent of the cheese topping.[15]

Federal agencies have developed a variety of techniques for measuring a company's compliance with regulations. Some simply set technical standards requiring the use of guards around machines or bicycle reflectors of a certain size. Others set performance standards, which specify, for example, an allowable level of polluting emissions and then let companies choose the method for reaching that goal. The federal government has gone even further by creating a market system for some pollutants. In the effort to reduce acid rain, for example, EPA has implemented a market for sulfur dioxide and nitrous oxide—companies can buy and sell the *right to pollute* on the Chicago Board of Trade (to support the EPA's regulations, yet another case of one private company assisting the government in the regulation of others). This system gives companies economic incentives to reduce their emissions, with the strongest incentives for the companies that can do so most cheaply. As a result, pollution has been dramatically reduced, acid rain levels have declined, and companies have won the flexibility to determine how best to reach the legislative goal.[16]

In addition to market incentives, information provides other pressures on companies' behavior. Crash tests by the federal government's National Highway Traffic Safety Administration and by private groups such as the Insurance Institute for Highway Safety have created strong inducements for automobile manufacturers to build safer cars. Federal research on medical errors has led to consumer scorecards of hospitals. Government inspections of nursing homes and restaurants often lead either to adverse publicity for poor performers or to certificates of approval that high performers can proudly hang on their walls.[17] Other agencies rely on companies' self-reporting of workers' accidents and health impairments, although owners' incentives for accurate reporting in this area are slight.[18]

These examples barely suggest the range of regulation, although they do show that styles of regulatory administration do not fit comfortably into a few broad categories. In general, however, government struggles to accommodate the varieties of its regulatory strategy to the general principles of citizens' rights, fair procedures, health and safety, and control of bureaucratic organization.

State and Local Regulations

Regulation is also a major activity of state and local governments, including New York City's efforts to ensure that concrete for the city's construction is safe. Their regulatory work is of two kinds. One is substantially autonomous, without involvement of the national government. State governments have created public utility commissions to control intrastate rates and services, banking departments to regulate state-chartered banks, and "lemon laws" to impose disclosure and warranties requirements on used-car dealers, as well as minimum-wage and antidiscrimination laws, bottle-deposit and recycling laws, and health and safety laws and regulations that cover a wide range of enterprises—from factory conditions to nursing homes to restaurants and bars to farmers' use of pesticides. The states, not the federal government, regulate insurance companies, despite their nationwide operations. Local governments also regulate broadly, sharing in the assurance of health and safety protections and the honesty of weights and measures (such as grocery scales and gas pumps). They administer land-use zoning, which seeks to control the location, structural features, and uses of buildings.

About 800 occupations are regulated in the United States—20 of them in every state (including attorneys, physicians, pharmacists, barbers, cosmetologists, and real estate agents).[19] Over half the states regulate funeral directors, chauffeurs, milk samplers, plumbers, and hearing-aid dealers, to cite only a few. Typically, licensing laws, which restrict entry to the professions and some other occupations, derive from lobbying by professional associations, which want to keep the number of competitors down and their prices up. They are often administered by substantially autonomous licensing boards whose members are effectively nominated by the associations. Though rationalized as social regulation, necessary to protect the health and safety of consumers of such services, the licensing systems actually tend to produce economic regulation, limiting competition by restricting entry.

The second regulatory role of state and local governments is administration of national regulatory programs.[20] Congress has the power to preempt much state regulatory activity, displacing it with programs executed directly by federal officials. But in many cases it has chosen the alternative of **partial preemption** (see chapter 12).[21] In such fields as environmental protection, occupational safety and health, meat and poultry inspection, and energy regulation, "partial preemption centralizes policy formulation, but it shares policy implementation with the states."[22] Under this arrangement, the national government decides on regulatory standards, and each state government may choose either to administer those prescribed standards or to create and administer its own standards, provided they are at least as stringent as those of the federal government. If a state fits neither situation, the appropriate national agency directly administers its national program within the state. In fact, a state may switch around. In mid-1987, California terminated its occupational safety and health enforcement program, thereby shifting that regulatory function to direct national administration by the Department of Labor's Occupational Safety and Health Administration (OSHA). Two years later, however, California was seeking OSHA's permission to reinstitute its own program, including resumption of enforcement responsibility.

Partial preemption is now a prominent part of the regulatory system, allowing some adaptation to local circumstances and letting individual state governments choose their roles in a regulatory system. It has the advantage of permitting a state to adopt more rigorous standards than those of the national laws and regulations, which would not be possible under full national preemption. It has the disadvantage shared by all farming-out of the implementation of national policies—the weakness of federal sanctions against third-party noncompliance with national directives.[23]

In some cases, moreover, state governments set the standard that other states and even the federal government will eventually follow. California was the first state to require the installation in cars of catalytic converters, which reduce air pollution. No automaker could afford to ignore the huge California market or to build cars just for sale in California, so the catalytic converter soon became a national standard. Even though the George W. Bush administration had backed away from worldwide standards on global warming, California in 2002 passed a bill requiring that all cars sold in the state after 2009 meet tough standards for greenhouse gases, the carbon-based emissions that scientists believe promote global warming. This legislation produced a long battle with the Bush administration, as the case for this chapter illustrates. Yet again, automakers could not ignore the California market, so the state's action helped nudge regulatory policy in a direction toward which the Bush administration did not want to go. In 2008, the Bush administration rejected California's policy, and both sides headed off to the federal courts.

Local governments, of course, issue regulations of their own. Most communities create zoning laws to determine what buildings can be constructed where and to what use their owners can put them. Housing construction is impossible without water and sewage permits, which some communities use to channel their economic development. Some communities have even set their own minimum wages.

Statutory Mandates

Economic regulation and social regulation differ sharply in the content of legislative mandates. At both national and state levels, the economic regulation statutes have vested broad discretion in regulatory agencies: licenses to enter a business field are to be issued to serve "the public interest, convenience, or necessity," and fixed rates are to be "just and reasonable." The Federal Trade Commission is charged to eliminate "unfair methods of competition" and "deceptive practices."

Congress's social regulation statutes often contain broad phrases as well. EPA is empowered to promulgate such regulations for treatment and disposal of "hazardous wastes . . . as may be necessary to protect human health and the environment." The secretary of labor is directed "to the extent feasible" to eliminate worker exposure to toxic substances capable of causing health impairment. The Consumer Products Safety Commission is required "to protect the public against unreasonable risks of injury associated with consumer products." But sometimes the standards are remarkably detailed. The most famous specific provision is the Delaney Clause of the Food, Drug, and Cosmetic Act, which, following general requirements that the FDA approve only substances that are safe, provides that no food additive, color additive, or drug for food animals "shall be deemed to be safe if it is found to induce cancer when ingested by man or animal, or . . . , after tests which are appropriate for the evaluation of the safety of [noningested] additives, to induce cancer in man and animal."[24] The clause's plain meaning is that once an additive has been found to induce cancer in animals, the FDA must ban it despite any finding that humans who ingest or apply the additive face no significant risk—and regardless of costs to manufacturers and merchants. Although the FDA has tried to chip away at the absolute standard—for example, when human risk is rated at one in a million or less—courts have insisted on strict compliance with the statute.[25]

It has always been hard to know just how to deal with the scientific uncertainty and political pressures around such regulatory issues. In 1970 the FDA banned cyclamate, an artificial sweetener, because researchers found that it caused cancer in animals. Saccharin replaced it, but researchers determined that this chemical also caused cancer in animals, although critics complained that the researchers had subjected the animals to enormous doses. Under the law, the FDA had no choice but to remove saccharin from the market, but dieters and diabetics pressured Congress to prevent the ban from taking place, pointing out that they had lost cyclamate and that there were no other good alternatives on the market. The lawmakers stepped in to permit the continued sale of saccharin (in products such as Sweet 'N Low), provided that the packaging carried a warning about the potential risks. Research continued, and in 2000 saccharin was removed from the list of chemicals causing cancer in humans. Congress promptly legislated the removal of the warning notice, although there was no dispute that saccharin caused cancer in animals. The question was how much risk this caused for humans, and whether humans were likely to ingest enough to raise their risks significantly. The scientific debate continued; the legal battle had ended.

The same issues spill over into environmental policy. For example, some statutes name specific air and water pollutants on which EPA must act. The most innovative practice is congressional setting of deadlines for agency accomplishment of statutory objectives. In the 1960s, chemical runoffs into streams often killed fish by the thousands and acid mixed with rain spread pollution even into isolated lakes. A 1969 incident in Cleveland, Ohio, drew national attention—an oil slick on the city's Cuyahoga River caught fire and caused tens of thousands of dollars of damage, especially to bridges overhead. The specter of a burning river drove home the need for fundamental changes to the nation's pollution control policies. The 1972 amendments to the Federal Water Pollution Control Act, more popularly known as the Clean Water Act, directed that navigable waters were to become fishable and swimmable by 1983 and that all discharge of pollutants into navigable waters was to be eliminated by 1985; the "best practicable" control technologies were to be in place by 1977 and the "best available" technologies by 1983—phrases that substantially limited EPA's ability to consider the costs to the regulated interests. In 1984 Congress set over two dozen specific statutory deadlines for EPA regulation of the management and disposal of currently generated hazardous waste.[26] In all, the laws for EPA contain thirty-eight mandatory deadlines for issuance of rules and regulations, and thirty-six deadlines for studies, guidelines, and reports.[27] Though many deadlines have been extended by Congress, their action-forcing is law until amendment occurs, and so they offer a peg on which environmental and other groups can hang a court case against the agency. They also serve as a spur to action, even when achievement falls short of meeting a deadline.

Expertise

Over time, the concentration of regulatory agencies on a limited agenda of concerns builds great experience with what works and what does not. Indeed, it can be difficult to match the level of expertise that the regulators have—which, however, is not all to the good. A specialized agency may develop a myopia that blocks from view the relation of its initiatives to those already taken or being contemplated by other agencies. Over time, the agency's professional focus may harden its commitment to a single way of achieving statutory goals and to one set of procedures for obtaining input from affected interests. Such commitment may be powerfully reinforced by the agency's most influential clientele, whether a regulated interest or public interest group or professional association, which has gotten used to the traditional approach and learned how to benefit from it.

The expertise of regulatory agencies is an important assumption, not least because courts have long cited it as a reason for deferring to the agencies' judgments. It is a valid assumption for most agencies' staffs. The largest regulatory agency, the EPA, has about 18,000 employees, distributed among offices concerned with regulating air pollution, water pollution, solid waste, hazardous waste, toxic substances, radiation, and pesticides, together with others occupied with policy analysis, research, enforcement, and other legal matters. Scientists, engineers, economists, lawyers, and other professional specialists abound. The dynamics of intragency conflict among these specialists tend to counteract the danger of adherence to a time-established orthodoxy of approach.[28] State governments, however, have often contested EPA's rules and, in some cases, have pushed environmental rules much farther than EPA.

When Congress knows what it wants, it wants it sooner rather than later. But in most social regulation, this urgency rarely takes account of the uncertainties of science and technology. What we do not know can hurt us, and in many regulatory programs, experts lack firm knowledge of causes, consequences, and remedies. Part of the problem is time: there are scores, sometimes hundreds, of suspected pollutants in the air and water, and of cancer-causing and other unhealthful and unsafe elements in the workplace; not all can be researched and their threats appraised within a few years. Often the scientific community lacks answers. Similarly, the technologies for eliminating or lessening known threats may be elusive, while newly developed technologies make earlier decisions obsolete.

Cost-benefit analysis has come to play a large role in regulatory programs—an effect that is largely attributable to the increased influence of economists in the government and recent administrations' commitment to reducing regulatory burdens on industry. But it has taken on a strongly ideological flavor as well, with the Reagan and Bush administrations energetically seeking to promote the strategy. Their assumptions have been that government has too many regulations, and that too many of the existing regulations do not produce benefits that exceed their costs. Forcing regulations to meet the cost-benefit standard, they believe, will result in fewer and less-intrusive regulations.

At the core of this effort is an appeal to a basic proposition: that a proposed government regulation should result in greater benefits than costs. On its face, this is a striving for certainty. Some statutes require consideration of costs; others rate some evils so great that they should be eliminated or reduced regardless of cost. The calculations are quantitative, but some costs and especially some benefits are difficult to express in dollar terms. What is the value of an unspoiled national park or forest; of a Grand Canyon view free of noisy, low-flying airplanes; of fishable and swimmable streams; of nondiscriminatory employment?[29]

Translation of these values into dollar figures has what Supreme Court Justice Oliver Wendell Holmes called, in another connection, "delusive exactitude," but it has a powerful impact on public policy. In July 2008, EPA quietly changed the value of a human life. Each of us might well believe we are priceless, but government regulators routinely set a dollar value on human lives. They then use that value to determine whether imposing new regulations is cost-effective, since policymakers have long held that the cost of regulations should not exceed their benefits. EPA had previously used a value of $8.04 million for each human life, but top officials decided to cut that value to $7.22 million. That is still a lot of money, but the lower value makes it that much harder to make an economic case for tougher federal rules: the benefits of a new government regulation would have to be that much greater to make them worthwhile.

For example, the Consumer Product Safety Commission (CPSC) faced a decision on whether to make mattresses less flammable. One proposal would require the industry to pay an extra $343 in manufacturing costs, but CPSC analysts expected the change to save 270 people. The agency used a value of a human life of $5 million, which produced a benefit of $1.3 billion. That big margin for benefits over costs, agency officials concluded, made the new rule economically sensible.[30] Most people get uncomfortable with such calculations, but government has to use *some* standard for deciding which rules make sense and which ones do not. If policymakers do not explicitly set a value on human life, implicit judgments about what regulations are worthwhile will be made anyway. If the value is explicit, citizens and policymakers can debate it. But that does not make the debate any easier—and making the value explicit often draws fierce attack, as was the case with EPA's 2008 decision, because critics believed EPA was using the change to block the flow of new regulations.

Indeed, in a powerful critique of the application of cost-benefit analysis to government regulation, Frank Ackerman and Lisa Heinzerling contend,

> There is no reason to think that the right answers will emerge from the strange process of assigning dollar values to human life, human health, and nature itself, and then crunching the numbers. Indeed, in pursuing this approach, formal cost-benefit analysis often hurts more than it helps: it muddies rather than clarifies fundamental clashes about values. By proceeding as if its assumptions are scientific and by speaking a language all its own, economic analysis too easily conceals the basic human questions that lie at its heart and excludes the voices of people untrained in the field. Again and again, economic theory gives us opaque and technical reasons to do the obviously wrong thing.[31]

Risk assessment has taken its place alongside cost-benefit analysis as a presumably expert approach to regulation. We all are constantly exposed to risks: some risks are more serious than others, and some persons are more exposed than others, yet some risks are a necessary cost of progress, even of progress toward greater safety.[32] Which risks should government try to eliminate or diminish and which to leave unregulated? As with cost-benefit analysis, measurements and tradeoffs are supposed to provide answers. Adequate reporting systems should tell us which industries and occupations have the highest rates of worker injuries and deaths, how many children are strangled by crib toys or hurt by lawn darts. With ingenuity, we can compare risks, suggesting, for example, that (1) traveling the same route by automobile as by a scheduled airline increases the likelihood of death by a factor of seventy; and (2) death is equally probable from one chest X-ray, a thousand-mile scheduled air flight, and living for fifty years within five miles of a nuclear reactor. A nagging problem, though, is that the public's perception of relative degrees of risk often does not fit the risk assessments by agencies' expert staffs. The agendas of both the EPA and the Consumer Product Safety Commission have given priority to citizens' concerns rather than to their staffs' top risk-rated concerns.[33]

Many citizens have distorted perceptions of risk: one airline accident killing 200 people will get far more attention—from journalists and government regulators alike—than 300 traffic accidents across the country that kill twice as many. More people have been killed by traditional power plants than by nuclear plants, but the potentially catastrophic nature of nuclear accidents attracts far more concern. A major issue that surfaced after the devastation that Hurricane Katrina inflicted on New Orleans was that many homeowners had not purchased flood insurance because they believed they did not need it. Risk is in part a matter of statistics, but it is also a matter of perception—and perception shapes the political strategy for dealing with regulatory problems.

Regulatory agencies, regardless of their expertise, find themselves caught between detailed statutory mandates, including often unrealistic deadlines for action, and the uncertainties stemming from inadequate scientific, technological, and economic knowledge. They face heavy pressures to consider benefits, costs, and risks, yet political pressure can force them away from such technical standards. Progress may be possible, but failure to meet expectations is virtually certain. Congress's response tends to be an odd mix of greater specification of mandates and postponement of previously mandated deadlines.

Regulatory Procedure

The Fifth and Fourteenth Amendments to the Constitution prohibit the national government and the states (including their local governments) from depriving any person of life, liberty, or property without due process of law. These amendments, along with an enormous body of case law interpreting them, frame what government regulation can do and the procedures government officials must follow in implementing them. These constitutional prohibitions have long been interpreted to treat corporations as "persons" and to construe deprivation of property as including denial of the opportunity to earn a fair return from prudent management of the property. Historically, the courts have applied these provisions in two ways. One is the obvious approach of requiring fair procedures before taking a depriving action. The other, used against statutes as well as regulatory orders, is not procedural but substantive: a deprivation of property or of a fair return on it must in itself be "reasonable" in the eyes of the courts—a test that has often been failed when conservative judges consider progressive legislation and rate-fixing orders of regulatory commissions. The courts have largely abandoned this directly substantive approach, though sometimes achieving it camouflaged as a procedural question.[34] In the case of regulatory administration, the courts usually avoid reference to the constitutional amendments. Instead, they either accept statutorily prescribed procedures as adequate (fair to citizens and consistent with legal requirements) or add requirements they deem necessary to preserve constitutional guarantees and their own powers.

Congress's prescriptions for rulemaking are found in two sources. One is the Administrative Procedure Act of 1946 (APA), as amended by the Freedom of Information Act and the Government in the Sunshine Act.[35] The other is the organic statute establishing an agency and assigning its functions, together with other statutes on individual programs. The two sources are intertwined, as some APA provisions depend on what agency-specific statutes actually say.[36]

These standards have led to two basic regulatory approaches by administrative agencies. One is **administrative rulemaking,** in which the agency sets forth broad standards that apply to all persons and organizations meeting certain guidelines; for example, the Department of Transportation might spell out the standards for reflectors on bicycles or the lights on eighteen-wheel trucks. The other is **adjudication,** in which administrative law judges within the agencies hear individual cases; over time, these cases cumulate into a body of rules that individuals and organizations must follow. Because administrative rulemaking is far more prevalent and has become far more important in shaping regulatory policy, we concentrate on that approach here.

Administrative Rulemaking

The core of administrative rulemaking lies in Congress's delegation of power to administrators. Such delegation of legislative powers to administrative agencies is an accepted feature of the American political system, but it was not always so. The Constitution says, "All legislative Powers herein granted shall be vested in a Congress of the United States." In 1935 the Supreme Court held two New Deal measures unconstitutional as violative of this provision. Neither before nor since, though, has the Court nullified a statute for this reason.[37] Since then, congressional delegation of power has only increased in importance as government's job has become more broad and complex.

If much administrative power comes from congressional delegation, how should administrators exercise it, especially in the regulatory arena? Most regulatory proceedings are informal, advancing through the following steps: (1) publication of a notice of proposed rulemaking in the *Federal Register,* which is the daily journal containing all rules and notices affecting the public;[38] (2) an interval to give interested parties an opportunity to submit written comments; and (3) after consideration of the relevant material presented, publication of the final rule, together with an explanation of the basis and purpose of the rule. In rulemaking, the APA does not require oral hearings or opportunities for cross-examination of witnesses (which are key elements of adjudicative procedure), unless an agency's particular statutes prescribe them (see Figure 13.1).

Agencies' extensive use of rulemaking is a relatively recent development. In the past, most economic regulatory agencies tended to proceed on a case-by-case basis of adjudication. Critics contended that such regulation failed to build more general policies on which the industry could rely, and that, because of changes in commission membership, policies sometimes proved inconsistent over time. In contrast,

| Figure 13.1 | Federal Regulatory Process |

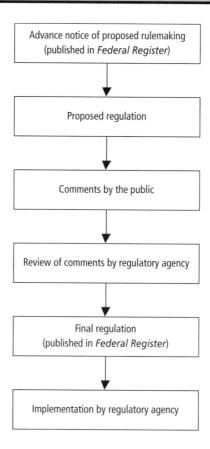

social regulation agencies, facing known evils that needed prompt correction throughout society—such as cancer-causing asbestos in the workplace, schools, and other public places—could not address these problems at the creeping pace of case-by-case actions, so they chose instead to regulate through general rules. It was expected that voluntary compliance would achieve the principal objectives, and the formal case-by-case method could be limited to cases of violation of the rules.

Judicial Review of Rulemaking

Rules written under the APA can be—and often are—challenged in court. The courts are charged with protecting constitutional rights as well as reviewing agencies' actions to determine whether they are "arbitrary, capricious, an abuse of discretion, or otherwise not in accordance with law." These phrases actually restrict the judicial review of rules, because they manifest a concern that bureaucracy should not run amok—a very different standard from inviting the courts to review the evidence and decide whether an agency was factually correct in issuing a regulation. Indeed, judicial review of regulation tends to revolve around whether agencies have followed the proper procedures in issuing their rules, not whether the rules themselves are substantively valid.

Most cases involve a challenge to an agency's action, but parties can also file suit to force an agency to act. The APA empowers a court to "compel agency action unlawfully withheld or unreasonably delayed." This judicial latitude has enabled consumers, environmentalists, and safety-minded citizens and groups to use courts to bring pressure on foot-dragging agencies to meet their rulemaking responsibilities. The opportunity arises especially when Congress has included clear mandates and set calendar deadlines in program-specific statutes.[39]

The courts confront a difficult problem in reviewing informal rules. They need, they say, a record of the agency's rulemaking in order to have something to review—even to test for arbitrariness and the other proscribed abuses. Because oral hearing and cross-examination of witnesses are not required by statute, rulemaking fails to produce the kind of record that courts are familiar with; the rulemaking record instead consists of the mass of written comments received, often a huge collection that includes both significant and trivial contributions. Courts want that record, massive though it is, and they also want to know how the agency reacted to each "significant" objection to the proposed rule. The result is a considerable burden on a regulatory process that is intended to be informal; it goes well beyond the agency's obligation to provide a concise general statement of the basis and purpose of a rule. Once they have the record of evidence, the courts are tempted to regard agency failure to deal satisfactorily with one or another significant objection as a sign of arbitrariness. Their range of tolerance is then likely to vary, depending on whether a court does or does not choose to emphasize, and defer to, the expertise of the regulatory agency.

Courts' Regulation of the Regulators

Courts regulate the regulatory system in many ways. Often, as we have indicated, they arbitrate appeals from agency rules and specific decisions. At other times, they deal with suits filed against agencies to require the issuance of rules mandated or implied in statutes. Sometimes, an agency sues a company, seeking to punish noncompliance with a rule or order by obtaining a court order requiring compliance. Apart from these agency-involvement suits are suits between private parties in which a corporation as defendant is charged with violation of a statute or rule.

Consider a set of simultaneous cases—all within the metropolitan area of New York City—involving the regulation of asbestos (a harmful air pollutant that can cause cancer and lung disease, though the effects may not appear for many years). In November 1987 about two hundred employees sued the Consolidated Edison Company, seeking millions of dollars in damages because of asbestos exposure. In January 1988 the EPA filed a civil suit against Consolidated Edison, seeking civil penalties of over $1 million and a court order requiring the company's full compliance with the Clean Air Act; the violations charged were failure to follow prescribed asbestos-removal procedures and failure to inform EPA fully and promptly of the removal operations. A few days earlier, the government had filed a criminal suit against officials of twenty-three companies removing asbestos materials; they were charged with bribing a federal inspector to overlook violations of federal regulations.[40] Here are three suits—a civil suit for damages brought by private citizens, a civil suit brought by the government, and a criminal suit brought by the government. None is an appeal from an agency, though all relate to EPA and its regulations.

Amid the legal questions about regulation, one is paramount: who has **standing to sue** under what circumstances? That legal question, in turn, suggests a practical question: who can afford the costs of litigation?

Access to the Courts

Doctrines governing the right to sue have changed over time. Many laws governing particular programs provide an opportunity for judicial review of agency actions. In addition, the Administrative Procedure Act of 1946 offers a blanket authorization: "A person suffering legal wrong because of agency action, or adversely affected or aggrieved by agency action within the meaning of a relevant statute, is entitled to judicial review thereof." This apparently wide-open invitation is qualified, however, for it does not apply if "(1) statutes preclude judicial review; or (2) agency action is committed to agency discretion by law." Nor does it apply to persons who, though unhappy about an agency decision, are held not to have suffered a "legal wrong." Until 1989, Congress made the Veterans Administration's denial of claims under the Veterans' Benefit Act unreviewable by the federal courts. In sum, despite generous judicial interpretations of the main provision of the APA, access for aggrieved persons is not so broad as it seems at first reading.

Class-Action Suits

Recourse to a class-action suit has proved important in cases involving a number of citizens most of whom have suffered so small a monetary loss that it is not worthwhile for each to hire a lawyer for representation in legal proceedings, though the damage to the whole class of affected individuals (and the profit to a corporation) may amount to millions of dollars. A **class action** is a private lawsuit for money damages, usually brought against a private person or corporation. Though the active plaintiff is typically only one or a few of the persons damaged—who are presumably sufficiently indignant and well-off to afford the lawyer—the suit is brought on behalf of all the affected individuals. Class-action suits are relevant here because the plaintiffs often claim damages on the ground that the defendant has violated statutes or rules. A class-action suit, therefore, may complement government agencies' efforts to enforce the law or, indeed, substitute for such efforts when agencies neglect their responsibilities. As in other kinds of damage suits (automobile injury cases, for example), the defendant often prefers to settle out of court rather than risk the court's (especially a jury's) making of a generous award. Defendant corporations are inclined to regard class-action suits as "legalized blackmail," but they and others in the same business are also likely to mend their ways so as to conform to statutes and avoid future class-action suits.

In the early 1970s, class-action suits were gaining popularity as a way for otherwise helpless citizens to deter corporate damage to their interests and indirectly to spur agency enforcement of statutes protective of those interests. In 1974, however, a Supreme Court decision held that the plaintiff could not seek damages for himself and the other 6 million persons in his "class" unless he first notified all the more than 2 million persons whose names were known.[41] Giving this notice would have cost him $225,000, though his own damage claim was for only $70. Faced with such a notification requirement, few will venture a class-action suit, even though its claims may rest on violations of antitrust and security statutes (as in this case) or of other laws protective of the public. In 1988 an appeals court required the National Wildlife Federation, in challenging the Interior Department's strip-mining regulations, to spend tens of thousands of dollars obtaining 1,300 pages of affidavits from its members in order to establish standing.[42]

In this area, as in some others, the courts' decisions are inconsistent. The most dramatic class-action suit was brought against seven corporations on behalf of over 15,000 named persons who had severe illnesses or whose children suffered birth defects that they claimed had resulted from exposure to a herbicide, Agent Orange, that had been used by the army during the Vietnam War. In 1985 the case ended with what, to that date, was the largest tort-case settlement in history, $180 million plus interest.[43]

In 1998, however, an even bigger settlement was reached. Years earlier, the Mississippi attorney general had begun a long legal campaign against the tobacco companies, seeking to recover damages to the state and its taxpayers that, he said, had been caused by smoking. This legal action snowballed into an action eventually involving all the states, promising to pay them an estimated $246 billion over twenty-five years and imposing new restrictions on the advertising of tobacco products. By cleverly claiming standing to sue the tobacco companies on the ground of their need to recover Medicaid costs incurred in the treatment of smokers, the states won an enormous settlement and forced a major change in tobacco companies' business practices. Martha Derthick, however, raises serious questions about whether this entrepreneurial litigation circumvented constitutional practice by inserting executive-branch officials in a province of policymaking that should have been left to the legislature.[44]

Private Attorneys General

Individuals and organizations may cast themselves in the role of **private attorneys general,** filing suit not for money damages but to compel a government agency or a corporation to do or cease doing something that affects a major public interest or group—the environment, consumers, and the like. This issue has become more important because the courts have become more liberal in granting standing to sue.

To have standing to sue, the traditional rule is that the plaintiff must show that a so-called legal wrong is involved—that is, he or she must plausibly claim to have individually suffered a wrong protected against by the Constitution, legal statutes, or the common law. The APA, which acknowledges this traditional rule, extends standing to any person "adversely affected or aggrieved within the meaning of a relevant statute." Interpretation of this provision was liberalized in the 1960s and early 1970s, to recognize that the adverse effect or grievance might be recreational, environmental, or aesthetic, rather than only economic or physical.[45] Agency-specific legislation, beginning in the 1970s, has often specified that any person may sue administrators for taking unauthorized action or for failing to perform nondiscretionary duties (such as those mandated by law). And in the liberalization period, the courts often found an implied, even if not statutory, right to redress.

Tort Liability of Governments and Officials

A **tort action** is a civil suit seeking monetary damages for harm allegedly done to the plaintiff by the defendant. The majority of tort actions in America arise out of automobile accidents, but they also are used extensively against manufacturers of products claimed to be dangerous or detrimental to users' health and against employers of workers exposed to hazardous conditions. From 1976 to 1986, asbestos suits accounted for 60 percent of the growth in product-liability tort cases in federal courts.[46] Suits relating to product liability and working condition supplement or substitute for governments' direct regulation.

The tort liability of governments and their officials has evolved through a tangled history and will continue to evolve.[47] Summarized simplistically, the federal and state governments cannot be sued for torts without their consent; this principle derives from English law, which long held that "the king can do no wrong" and could not be sued without his consent. However, government employees can be sued: schoolteachers, policemen, and FBI and narcotics agents are frequent targets of tort suits.

Governments can waive their sovereign immunity by consenting to be sued. The Federal Torts Claims Act of 1946 provided a partial waiver, permitting a damage suit against the government for personal injury, death, or property damage caused by the "negligent or wrongful act or omission" of any federal employee acting within the scope of his or her employment.[48] However, the statutory qualifications and exceptions severely narrow this apparent waiver. Most notably, the government is not liable for an act or omission when the government employee is "exercising due care, in the execution of a statute or regulation, whether or not such statute or regulation be valid," or when he or she is performing or failing to perform "a discretionary function or duty on the part of a federal agency or an employee . . . whether or not the discretion involved be abused." Other significant limitations are (1) that the government is liable only to the extent that a private individual would be liable under the relevant state's law (though some government actions have no private counterpart), and (2) that the government is not liable for interest prior to judgment or for punitive damages (as distinguished from merely compensatory damages), for both of which a private defendant might be liable.

In the 1960s, courts accorded federal officials absolute immunity from tort actions when performing duties committed by law to their control or supervision.[49] In the 1970s, the Supreme Court made a sharp turn, holding officials liable for violation of constitutional rights if they knew or reasonably should have known that they were violating them.[50] It is presumed that an official should know the rights protected by the Constitution, although the presumption has been criticized on grounds that every such right has been and continues to be interpreted through court decisions, which an official cannot be expected to have mastered. In 1988 the Supreme Court held that federal employees could be held personally liable for damages caused by negligent performance or omission of nondiscretionary conduct (such as, in this case, negligence in handling and storing hazardous material). Congress responded by passing a statute that makes the government, rather than the employee, the defendant in such suits.[51]

State governments, under the Eleventh Amendment, are immune from damage suits in federal courts, but local governments are not immune. State and local officials are liable under an 1871 act that provides: "Every person who, under color of any statute [or] regulation . . . of any State, subjects . . . any citizen . . . to the deprivation of any rights, privileges, or immunities secured by the Constitution and laws, shall be liable to the party injured in an action at law."[52] This provision is known as Section 1983 (from its location in the *U.S. Code of Federal Regulations*). Beginning in

1961, the federal courts experienced a great increase in Section 1983 tort actions, consistent with the Supreme Court's narrowing of officials' defenses. The principal defense is now lack of knowledge or presumptive knowledge of relevant provisions of the Constitution and laws.

Tort law's evolution cannot be understood without considering the dilemma expressed in many court opinions. On the one hand are citizens' rights to receive monetary compensation for damages done them by overzealous, negligent, or malicious government officials and employees—plus the promise of deterrence that such court victories will exert on other bureaucrats. On the other hand is the need for prompt and effective administrative action in executing laws and regulations—a need that entails considerable scope for discretionary judgment. The deterrent effect can be considered a virtue, but it also invites officials to avoid risks and even disobey superiors' orders (for such orders are no shield against personal liability); the result could be a serious weakening of the administrative system and of its responsibility for achieving legislative objectives.

The solution to the courts' dilemma, it appears, is abandonment of the immunity of governments from torts and the substantial freeing of officials and employees from personal liability. That solution, however, implies that agencies will have administrative systems strong enough to control the behavior of subordinate officials and employees. Readers of this book may have doubts about how easy it might be to create such a rigorous environment, given the great hierarchical distance between agency heads and "street-level bureaucrats,"[53] as well as the huge expansion in delegation of discretionary powers.[54]

Systems and Values

The question of access to the courts leads to a more fundamental issue: how interventionist should courts be in reviewing regulatory agencies' policymaking and enforcement activities? How aggressively should the courts themselves work to open the doors for judicial redress of grievances? The question raises two issues: (1) the difference between the judicial system and the administrative system in which regulatory agencies operate, and (2) the array of public values that everyone—citizens and policymakers alike—want to see in the regulation of private affairs. How one balances these considerations has much to do with the balance between the regulatory agencies and the courts.

The Judicial and Administrative Systems

In regulatory administration, courts and agencies make strange partners. The two institutions have different traditions and are staffed with very different kinds of people.[55] Courts are *passive*—they depend on parties to bring cases before them. Because of that passivity and because their jurisdiction is broad, they hear cases in sequence, with no discernable connection; most of these cases are unrelated to governmental regulation. With few exceptions (the federal district and appeals courts in the District of Columbia), the judges have expertise neither in regulation generally nor in particular regulatory programs, and they lack expert supporting staffs, so must rely instead on evidence and analysis offered by lawyers for the two sides.

The most significant characteristic of judicial involvement in the regulatory field is a court's focus on the single case before it. Long-standing judicial practice holds that courts must decide only on the basis of the case before it and the court's interpretation of how the law affects that case. Courts cannot, on their own, reach beyond the case to make broader law. For regulation, this means that the issue is the reasonableness of a single agency's decision, made at a single point in time and affecting a single individual, corporation, or group. The court's judgment fits in a setting of legal doctrine and precedents, but it largely ignores how the particular agency's decision fits with the agency's full responsibility for achieving program objectives with limited funds and staff. Instead, a court may require the agency to respond to the particular case before it, without considering how this requirement may subtract from the resources supporting the agency's other programs.

By contrast, most agencies are *active*—each one develops an agenda of priorities that balances its resources against relative opportunities for a significant impact. An agency makes decisions through time, linking each one with others in an effort to assure coherence both in technical foundations and in program effectiveness. Within that agenda and continuity of focus, its staff gathers facts, analyzes problems, and consults with interested persons and organizations, all as a basis for framing regulatory rules and orders. In sharp contrast to the courts, agencies specialize in their assigned subjects, and they have career staffs expert in economics, science, and engineering, as well as in law. Except for agency lawyers, the judges and agency staff members march to different drummers.[56] It would be a wonder if the two sides kept in step—and they rarely do.

Two strategies have emerged to accommodate these differences.[57] First, the courts have pressed the agencies to widen the participation of interested citizens and groups in the formulation of rules, and, though less clearly, they have widened access to the courts for such interested parties.[58] Second, the courts have tended to "make law," attributing intentions to Congress that are not apparent in the language of statutes.[59] The agencies tend to regard both of these strategies as helpful: increased participation has favored environmental and other public interest groups whose efforts support the agencies' missions; and in giving statutory weight to program activities not clearly specified in statutes, the courts have expanded the jurisdictions of the agencies. Shep Melnick reports, "While complaining about some decisions,

EPA officials generally credit the courts with improving the agency's competence and programs."[60] Reconciliation of the two systems has also advanced because of what Jerry Mashaw characterizes as the Supreme Court's "significant retrenchment from its procedurally interventionist posture in the early 1970s."[61]

Values: Conflict or Harmony?

Regulatory administration revolves around three basic values: procedural fairness, substantive correctness of decisions, and achievement of public policy goals. Everyone agrees that the process leading up to agency issuance (or nonissuance) of a rule or individual order should be fair. But it is tempting for courts to say, "Why can't administrative agencies be more like us?" The question applies principally to agencies' adjudicative procedures, though courts have often wished that administrators would behave more like the courts in their regulatory functions as well. In fact, the APA and many agency-specific statutes, as we have seen, support the courts' view, requiring notice, oral hearings, and cross-examination of witnesses. To be sure, these procedures are less rigorous in the rulemaking setting than in ordinary court cases, but they are, nonetheless, enough alike that lawyers play the leading roles, paperwork mounts, and tactics of delay are practiced by companies facing regulatory action. Despite these similarities, however, the trend in regulation is away from formal toward informal rulemaking—away from the procedures that are more judicial and toward those that the courts find troublesome.

The second value is not procedural, but substantive: the correctness of the decision reached. Theoretically, what the system should assure is a correct decision, and if the agency does not make one, the court should. But neither agency nor court can assure that its decision is correct, because scientific and technological uncertainties plague policy issues, and even when there is relative clarity on the technical issues, different political judgments can muddy any sense about which decision is the right one. Both the agency subsystem and the court system provide opportunities for appeal to higher levels, but even in the judicial branch there is no certainty that the highest court's decision will be correct. The possibility of appeal can often simply create new arenas for political interests to continue—and to try to change—policy debates. At best, the courts can hope to limit error to a low, but not zero, tolerance level. Judges' self-restraint, reinforced by deference to agency expertise, permits agency discretion to operate in accord with this objective.

Of course, many issues turn out to be such a mixture of fact and law that a court cannot decide the legal question without also deciding a factual question. Appellate courts have historically often capitalized on this mixed focus to substitute their judgment for that of lower courts, by treating as a question of law whether the evidence was sufficient to support the lower court's decision. Their doctrines have varied on whether they were merely looking to determine if there was "substantial" evidence on the winning side to warrant the decision, or whether they were completely second-guessing the lower court by weighing the evidence on both sides; in the latter case, disagreement about the preponderance of evidence can lead to overturning the lower court's decision. In reviewing agency decisions, the courts have applied the substantial-evidence test, but they take "a hard look."

The third value is achievement of public policy objectives. Here lurks a danger that two very different institutions—judicial and administrative—will find their traditional modes of operation at loggerheads. Excessive formalization of procedure can tie administrative regulation in knots—causing delay, absorbing budgetary and staff resources, increasing red tape, and inviting passivity in agency pursuit of policy goals. Some agencies react to the risk of judicial reversal by adopting even more cumbersome procedures than courts are likely to demand; others seek to demonstrate the evidence behind a decision with massive accumulations of documents. Even in rule-making, the courts' insistence that an agency respond to every significant objection filed by individuals, groups, and companies imposes a burden that is likely to be exaggerated by agencies' uncertainty as to which objections the courts may deem significant. Meantime, the agency is charged by Congress with implementing programs fully and expeditiously—an assignment whose shortfalls may expose the agency to congressional retribution.

The administrative tasks of some agencies are enormous, and their huge burden makes courtlike procedures inappropriate. In the new Department of Homeland Security, which is charged with reviewing applications for immigration and naturalization, the backlog of cases in 2004 was more than 6 million and growing. As T. Alexander Aleinikoff concluded, "If the process is not improved, millions of people will continue to wait many years for naturalization and immigration benefits to which they are entitled as a matter of law."[62] A hidden side effect of this backlog was that homeland security officials were lagging behind the effort to determine whether any of those on the list might be members of terrorist sleeper cells, quietly preparing for a new attack.

The three values of regulatory administration—fair procedures, sound decisions, and policy achievement—are interlinked and in conflict. Each is important in its own right, but to elevate one over the others is to invite trouble. Fairness in regulatory procedure may be enough to reassure everyone, including the courts, about the correctness of the decision reached. Relaxation of the expectation that regulatory procedures mimic that of courts may promote effective implementation of policy objectives. In the end, the courts have tended to reconcile these issues through the doctrine of judicial deferral to agencies' expertise, but this is not an ideal formula, as courts will differ on how much deferral is appropriate, how expert agencies really are, and whether in a particular decision the claim of expertise covers other issues on which the courts might weigh in. It is little wonder, then, that the courts' relationship with regulators continues to evolve.

Presidential Regulation of the Regulators

Presidents seek to control regulatory agencies, insisting that the agencies are part of the executive branch and thus must be accountable to the president. Otherwise, goes the argument, their policymaking, via rules and regulations under broad delegations from Congress, would flout the American democratic system of government. This argument rests on three concepts (all familiar from earlier chapters of this book): (1) the need for coordination, lest agencies contradict or duplicate one another; (2) the need for consistency with the president's policy agenda, lest one executive function conflict with another; and (3) the need for economy and efficiency, lest the president's budgetary and policy agenda be undermined by the cost of federal regulations.

Especially since the Reagan administration, presidents have been working hard to exert greater control over government regulation. Republican presidents—Reagan and both Presidents Bush—have tried to use cost-benefit regulation and the Office of Management and Budget (OMB) review of draft regulations to rein in the number and cost of federal regulations. The Reagan administration was the first to require that agencies prepare and submit to OMB for review a cost-benefit analysis of each proposed major rule and that, to the extent permitted by law, they not act unless benefits exceed costs to society, net benefits are at a maximum, and among alternative approaches the one with the least net cost to society is chosen. No agency may publish a notice of proposed rulemaking until OMB review is completed, nor may it publish a final rule until the OMB director has communicated any views and the agency has responded. Moreover, each agency is required annually to prepare and submit to OMB a regulatory program detailing every significant agency regulatory action (later defined as a "rule") "planned or underway," explaining, among other things, how they are consistent "with the Administration's policies and priorities." Any proposed regulatory action not included in the earlier regulatory program or materially different from an action described in that program must be submitted to the OMB for review and, except for cases of statutory or judicial deadlines and emergency situations, must be deferred until completion of that review. In the case of both the regulatory program and proposed actions later contemplated, the OMB director may return agency submissions for reconsideration.[63]

The George W. Bush administration in 2003 expanded this review through OMB Circular A-4, which requires stringent economic review of regulations before they can take effect. OMB's circular makes the case in two ways: "The motivation is to

(1) learn if the benefits of an action are likely to justify the costs or (2) discover which of various possible alternatives would be the most cost-effective."[64] But even the Clinton administration worked hard through OMB to manage better the flow of federal regulations. In general, recent presidents have wanted to integrate regulatory policy more tightly into the overall thrust of their management efforts. And some presidents have tried to use these techniques to restrict regulations for ideological reasons. In both cases, it is a sign of pushing government regulation from a quasi-judicial arena to policy control more like that presidents seek in other parts of the executive branch.

The regulatory management process has thus provoked much friction.[65] The OMB has gained review authority not only over the final stages of rulemaking but also over such early stages as initiation of research studies meant to contribute to agency consideration of whether or not to start rulemaking proceedings.[66] Delays of months and years have characterized some reviews. The small review staff, in the OMB's Office of Information and Regulatory Affairs, consists of persons trained in economics, business administration, and law, often young and with scant prior knowledge of the agency programs they oversee; understandably, agencies' expert staffs have chafed at the sometimes nitpicking objections and the revisions imposed. OMB has consulted industry representatives (a practice sharply reduced by the George H. W. Bush administration) and communicated with agency officials, often by telephone, without such contacts or their substance being reflected in the rule-making record. These criticisms escalated during the George W. Bush administration, in which several high-ranking officials resigned because of their disagreement with the administration's regulatory policies. For example, Eric V. Schaeffer, director of EPA's Office of Regulatory Enforcement, complained in his letter of resignation that "we seem about to snatch defeat from the jaws of victory. We are in the 9th month of a '90 day review' to reexamine the law, and fighting a White House that seems determined to weaken the rules we are trying to enforce."[67]

The focus is on rulemaking. For better or worse, many people view the actions of regulatory agencies as part of the president's executive function, and they expect the president to manage the flow of federal regulations. For presidents seeking to demonstrate their control over the bureaucracy, efforts to rein in the regulators have been irresistible. In principle, no one wants regulations whose costs vastly exceed their benefits. But it is much easier to measure—and display—costs than it is to assess benefits. Moreover, many benefits of government regulations come in the form of saving lives and improving the health and safety of individuals. It is economically possible to make estimates about such values. Indeed, in the aftermath of the September 11 attacks, one official found himself charged with setting the level of payment to each of the families who had lost a loved one in the attacks—and calculating those payments according to the economic value of each life lost. But what is economically possible often becomes politically difficult. Explicit discussions about the values of health and safety bring many citizens and policymakers into genuinely uncomfortable territory.

That discomfort factor brings an implicit bias to such analysis: a focus on the things easier to measure—the costs—and a tendency to slide past the more difficult puzzles—especially the benefits. Such bias, in turn, makes it easier to make the case against regulations, which fits the interest of conservative Republicans in slowing the flood of regulations. Their opponents, however, have pointed to the inherently imprecise nature of the analysis as one of the reasons why government regulates, "to demand and produce legal protections for health and the environment," as Ackerman and Heinzerling argue. Indeed, they conclude, "we must give up the idea, reassuring to many, that there is, somewhere, a precise mathematical formula waiting to solve our problems for us."[68] The debate between precision and measurement, more and less regulation, is at its core about values: about government's role and how best to pursue it.

Conclusion

Regulation of the behavior of private individuals and corporations to protect others from harm is a central responsibility of government. The scope and methods of such regulation are disputed issues of public policy. However those issues are resolved, there is no doubt that some discretion must be vested in regulatory agencies and that discretion is subject to abuse. Legislatures, courts, and chief executives all seek to reduce opportunities for such abuse, but, in using this control authority, they often seek to advance their own policy preferences or to impose regulatory procedures that, intentionally or not, impede regulatory effectiveness.

The balance between effective and ineffective regulation shifts from time to time, largely reflecting public opinion, elections, and appointments and attitudes of administrators and judges. As we move deeper into the twenty-first century, signs of a shift toward effective regulation are visible, most clearly in the field of environmental protection and workers' health and safety. Yet signs of success have hardly protected regulatory agencies from political attack.

Administrative discretion is tolerable only when not misused, and therein lies a major problem. One distinguished scholar of the legal aspects of public administration, Phillip Cooper, puts it this way: "Just how we ensure that the public interest is served and that administrative power is not abused is the problem of administrative responsibility. . . . [While] the formal legal constraints have received the most attention . . . there is a risk that excessive concern with avoiding suits will cause us to ignore many aspects of the responsibility question of equal or greater significance."[69] We address those ignored aspects in the next chapter.

From the Front Lines of Regulation: Who Should Set Environmental Policy—California or the Federal Government?

Case 13

California Gov. Arnold Schwarzenegger championed an effort to reduce greenhouse gas emissions in the state by 30 percent. Auto congestion, like this backup at the intersection of the 405 Freeway with the 10 West Freeway, contributed significantly to the dirty air.

Is the Environmental Protection Agency (EPA) irrelevant? In late December 2007, it blocked California's cutting-edge plan to reduce greenhouse gases, but that decision is looking increasingly like the last gasp of a losing battle. The new fight is how the nation will fight the campaign against global warming and who—EPA or the states—will call the shots.

At the center of the struggle is California's tough air pollution law, which requires auto manufacturers to reduce greenhouse gas emissions by 30 percent by 2016. EPA Administrator Stephen L. Johnson, standing alone against even his own agency's policy and legal experts, rejected California's request for a waiver to pursue its standards. He could not allow the states to set their own course, Johnson said, because a "patchwork of state rules" would cause chaos. But Johnson's plan, critics charged, would take far too long to bring any meaningful improvement in air quality.

California Governor Arnold Schwarzenegger countered that "Anything less than aggressive action on the greatest environmental threat of all time is inexcusable." Republican Jim Douglas, Vermont's governor, called Johnson "out of touch with the reality of climate change." Democrat Jon Corzine of New Jersey labeled the decision "horrendous." In all, sixteen states sued to challenge Johnson's decision.

Fueling the political battle were back-channel conversations Vice President Cheney and other top White House officials had with automakers. They were fighting hard to block California's tough standards and the costly investments they would require. In the short run, they won. Even if EPA loses in the federal courts or a new administration switches course, the automakers will have delayed those investments for at least a couple of years.

The long run is another matter, for the lawsuit is a twentieth-century-style tussle over one of the biggest twenty-first-century issues. We've moved away from the question of whether we should try to reduce global warming to how: what strategies will work best? The Bush administration is not only fighting a losing battle but also fighting the wrong battle. Some kind of greenhouse gas strategy will come. The questions are what will work best and who will shape it.

The smart money is that the next round of clean air standards will be market-driven, especially through "cap and trade" plans. Both the Obama and McCain campaigns proposed just such a strategy as the cornerstone of their environmental program. In "cap and trade," the government would set overall pollution-reduction targets. Companies could then buy, sell, and trade pollution credits. Companies that find it cheapest to reduce their emissions can sell credits to companies where pollution reduction requires larger investments. The 1989 Clean Air Act reduced acid rain by creating such a market on the Chicago Board of Trade for sulfur dioxide credits, and the success of the strategy surprised even its critics.

A market-driven plan for greenhouse gases would be much tougher to create, however. Europe has struggled to find the right caps for its carbon trading market because the greenhouse gas problem is far more complex than acid rain. Tweaking the system along the way could undermine the predictability that companies find attractive about it.

But two things are certain: EPA's decision only benefits those playing for time, and it doesn't resolve the question of who will run a market-driven strategy. It's impossible to build markets completely from the states, because the scale would be too small, even in California. And it's impossible to develop market-based strategies from Washington without bringing in the states, because they do much of the front-line work on air quality. There is no escaping the need to act on climate change, but there's also no avoiding the fact that an effective climate change strategy is going to require a new environmental partnership between Washington and the states.

On this and other fronts, the Bush administration left behind a fractious legacy on federalism. The states lost their battles on lowering greenhouse gases and increasing health coverage through the State Children's Health Insurance Program. They struggled over the renewal of No Child Left Behind and the creation of Real ID driver's licenses. But it's hard to escape the sense that they have the feds on the run. The Bush administration's decisions were holding actions. Pressures are building for everyone to dance more to the states' tune, but they can't dance alone.

That shapes the environmental challenge for the next administration. The next steps will require a move from stonewalling to stronger incentives for collaboration, because neither the states nor the federal government will be able to take the inescapable next steps alone. EPA will need to find a strategy that makes it relevant in one of the policy issues sure to define this century.

Questions to Consider

1. Is it wise national policy to allow individual states to set the most aggressive standards for pollution control? Or does waiting for Washington mean that policy will float to the least common denominator, with standards that are acceptable to everyone and, therefore, slow to emerge and lower than would be the case with far-reaching, fast-moving states?

2. What ethical standards do you think that a government regulator ought to follow? Was Johnson right to issue a decision that was consistent with the Bush administration's policy, even though that meant overruling his own technical staff?

3. Is a private cap and trade system, which relies on private markets for setting the cost of meeting government standards, a good strategy? Or should the government set clear standards that all companies must meet, regardless of cost?

4. What regulatory strategy should government—federal, state, and local—pursue in the effort to manage climate change?

Note

Portions of this case originally appeared in *Governing* magazine in February 2008. See http://www.governing.com/articles/0802poto.htm.

Key Concepts

adjudication **427**

administrative rulemaking **427**

antitrust laws **416**

capture **416**

class action **431**

cost-benefit analysis **424**

economic regulation **416**

externalities **417**

partial preemption **420**

private attorneys general **432**

risk assessment **425**

social regulation **417**

standing to sue **430**

tort action **432**

For Further Reading

Ackerman, Frank, and Lisa Heinzerling. *Priceless: On Knowing the Price of Everything and the Value of Nothing.* New York: New Press, 2004.

Bardach, Eugene, and Robert A. Kagan. *Going by the Book: The Problem of Regulatory Unreasonableness.* A Twentieth Century Fund Report. Philadelphia: Temple University Press, 1982.

Cooper, Phillip J. *Governing by Contract: Challenges and Opportunities for Public Managers.* Washington, D.C.: CQ Press, 2002.

Derthick, Martha A. *Up in Smoke: From Legislation to Litigation in Tobacco Politics.* 2nd ed. Washington, D.C.: CQ Press, 2005.

Howard, Phillip. *The Death of Common Sense.* New York: Random House, 1994.

Skowronek, Stephen. *Building a New American State: The Expansion of National Administrative Capacities, 1877–1920.* New York: Cambridge University Press, 1982.

Wilson, James Q., ed. *The Politics of Regulation.* New York: Basic Books, 1980.

Suggested Websites

The issues of government regulation provide rich puzzles for Internet-based research. Many complex public policy questions have played out through studies and analyses, which can easily be found through web search engines.

The federal government's catalog of regulations can be found at the website for the *Code of Federal Regulations,* **http://www.gpoaccess.gov/cfr/index.html.** Daily changes to federal regulations are published in the *Federal Register;* see **http://www.gpoaccess .gov/fr/index.html.**

The National Academy of Public Administration has conducted an exhaustive study of federal clean air regulations. See *A Breath of Fresh Air: Reviving the New Source*

Review Program (Washington, D.C.: NAPA, 2003), **http://www.napawash.org/Pubs/Fresh%20Air%20Summary.pdf.** In addition, the Government Accountability Office (**http://www.gao.gov**) regularly reviews regulatory issues through its studies.

Moreover, many government regulatory agencies have their own websites, which are invaluable for tracking policy issues. See, for example, the website for the National Highway Traffic Safety Administration (**http://www.nhtsa.com**) for information about the safety of cars and trucks; the Food and Drug Administration (**http://www.fda.gov**) for the safety of prescription and over-the-counter drugs; and the Environmental Protection Agency (**http://www.epa.gov**) for clean air and water regulations.

Executive Power and Political Accountability

As reports swirled about of the abuse of suspected terrorists at Abu Ghraib prison in Iraq, a national debate erupted. Was the use of torture ever justified? If the military had custody of a prisoner who might have knowledge of a pending terrorist attack—for example, if one of the September 11 hijackers had been captured before that fateful morning—would interrogators be justified in using any means at their disposal, no matter how distasteful, to extract information that could save hundreds or thousands of lives? Or was the use of torture morally wrong and practically limited?

It was as sharp a question about the role of executive power as the nation has ever seen. The president and the president's administration would make such a decision, on behalf of all Americans. What standards should they follow? If the executive decided to use torture, what limits could—and should—Congress set? And how could Congress enforce these limits? The debate quickly sharpened not only into one of moral justice and military effectiveness but also into the separation of powers. It was a central puzzle in the role of executive power and how it should be held politically accountable.

In 2006, the debate came to a head. Congress passed a bill that made torture illegal. President George W. Bush signed it, and the prohibition against torture became law. As he signed the law, however, the president also issued a **signing statement** that contained the administration's interpretation of the law and how it would be enforced. The signing statement read, in part, that "The executive branch shall construe [the law] in a manner consistent with the constitutional authority of the President . . . as Commander in Chief." The approach, Bush contended, "will assist in achieving the shared objective of the Congress and the President . . . of protecting the American people from further terrorist attacks."

But what did this mean? A Bush administration official reassured observers that "We are not going to allow this law" and "We consider ourselves bound by the prohibition on cruel, unusual, and degrading treatment." The official added a reservation, however. "Of course the president has the obligation to follow this law, [but] he also has the obligation to defend and protect the country as commander in chief, and he will have to square those two responsibilities in each case." If the responsibilities came into conflict, the official left no doubt that President Bush was willing to use torture if he believed it necessary for national defense. A New York University law professor who specialized in executive power, David Golove, was more blunt. "The signing statement is saying 'I will only comply with this law when I want to, and if something arises in the war on terrorism where I think it's important to engage in cruel, inhuman, and degrading conduct, I have the authority to do so and nothing in the law is going to stop me,' " Golove explained.[1]

The phenomenon of signing statements was largely unknown until a series of articles by the *Boston Globe*'s Charlie Savage, a sharp reporter with a keen eye for important issues. In April 2006, he wrote a long story that pointed to more than 750 signing statements that the Bush administration had signed. In these cases, ranging from affirmative action to immigration, the administration asserted its executive power to push aside laws if the president concluded it was essential for pursuing the executive function.[2] Savage's reporting rocked the political debate and won him the 2007 Pulitzer Prize. Just what effect did these signing statements actually have on executive branch behavior? The Government Accountability Office (GAO) found that federal officials did not execute the law as written in at least nine cases.[3] Savage found that an adviser to Vice President Dick Cheney routinely scanned legislation for provisions that might challenge executive power and on which the president might issue a signing statement.[4] The debate spilled over into the 2008 presidential campaign, where reporters pressed both John McCain and Barack Obama on whether they would follow a similar course. Both candidates, who both were legislators, pledged to avoid using signing statements to reverse congressional action.

The Separation of Powers

In the classical view of the policy process, the legislature makes policy and the executive branch implements it. But, of course, the legislative and executive roles are far more complex and intertwined than that. In much of the American system, the Constitution creates elaborate checks and balances, not just a separation of powers—which means that political responsibility is shared, and so, too, is policy guidance. Furthermore, as one scholar of congressional oversight has pointed out, "oversight is in many respects a continuation of preenactment politics."[5] That is, the policy pressures that shape legislative politics often continue on through the administrative process. Political forces that lose in the legislature often try to regain the advantage as administrators take over, and the forces that win the early battle must continue to struggle to make sure they retain their edge. The rules instituting checks and balances in the American states tend to mirror the federal setup, but in the wide variety of American local governments, the system of accountability is often even muddier.

The Constitution gives Congress a powerful claim to control of administration: the president may be responsible for faithfully executing the laws, but Congress makes those laws, and the bureaucracy is thus a creature of them both. Congress creates the organizational structure within which administrators work, authorizes their positions and the programs they administer, appropriates funds to pay for them, and retains the right to investigate how they spend the money and run the programs.[6] Congress delegates power to the bureaucracy to administer the law. The president is vested with the faithful execution of the law, but in serving as chief executive, the president shares prerogatives with Congress.[7] The same pattern holds true at the state and local levels. Thus, while hierarchy tends to govern the most basic administrative relationships, it does not shape all the relationships at the top of the bureaucracy. Skillful bureaucratic leaders know they must look as much—if not more—to the legislature as they do to the chief executive.

The relationship between legislature and executive branch agency is very much a reciprocal one, but it is complicated by the function of oversight.

The Paradox of Oversight

At the core of legislative oversight is a profound paradox: although much of what Congress does is oversight, in one form or another, the activity tends to rank low among congressional priorities. Nevertheless, oversight is essential to effective administration because, as we saw in chapter 12, policy has little meaning except in its implementation.

As one panel of experts has pointed out, "oversight permeates the activities of Congress."[8] Many congressional actions involve some form of supervision of administrative actions, from the enactment of laws and budgets to committee hearings to program reviews by congressional staff agencies, such as the GAO and the Congressional Budget Office. Variations in the level of oversight can be quite remarkable, from investigation of a program's overall performance to probes of the most detailed of program activities. In 1987 the Senate attached eighty-six amendments to a bill authorizing the State Department's budget; policy questions addressed in the amendments ranged from the Chinese government's treatment of Tibetan monks to traffic tie-ups caused by long, honking motorcades for foreign dignitaries in Washington.[9] Nothing the federal government does lies beyond the reach of congressional oversight.

In fact, critics have blamed congressional micromanagement for problems in many defense systems. In 1985, for example, the Pentagon submitted 24,000 pages of documentation to Congress in order to comply with 458 different reporting requirements established in previous legislation. The number of these reports, Defense officials estimated, had increased 1,000 percent since 1970.[10] Such a penchant for particulars, moreover, imposes a heavy burden on top administrative officials. Former secretaries of state Henry Kissinger and Cyrus Vance, for example, have complained: "Surely there are better ways for the executive and legislative branches to consult than having the secretaries of state and defense spend more than a quarter of their time on repetitive congressional testimony."[11] As the federal government tried to strengthen its homeland security system in the aftermath of September 11, investigators found that many of the worst problems originated in the Immigration and Naturalization Service, which, they discovered, was allowing too many security breaches and struggling to cope with a rising paperwork backlog. One critic felt that congressional micromanagement had caused many of the agency's problems; what Congress most needed to do, he concluded, was to make up its mind and then get out of the way.[12]

Yet there is substantial evidence that control of administration has traditionally ranked low among the priorities of members of Congress. The reelection imperative is all-important, and much routine oversight does little to enhance a member's reputation back in his or her district. Instead, passing legislation, taking stands on issues, and tending to constituents' needs through casework dominate members' attention.[13] Also, there rarely are regular procedures for conducting oversight.[14] Members are typically more interested in shaping the immediate future than in investigating what has gone wrong in the past, unless past events prove so scandalous that an investigation will win wide publicity and be embarrassing to the opposition party.

Much oversight involves difficult issues, such as devising measures to improve administrative organization, procedures, and staffing, and this kind of detailed work is unlikely to engage legislators' interest. This is not because members of Congress prefer the general to the particular; nothing could be more detailed than the casework that dominates so much of the time of the members' staffs. Constituents often want help in getting Social Security and disability benefits, Medicare reimbursements, admission to a veterans' hospital, and emergency home leave from military service, or a flag that flew over the Capitol. Members of Congress know that constituents care a lot about such requests, and they devote great energy to meeting them. Moreover, even though it is not a direct form of congressional oversight, casework—especially if it reveals patterns of problems—often provides legislators with information on which direct oversight can be conducted. Legislators also pay a great deal of attention to earmarking appropriations bills for projects in their districts—roads, dams, and economic development and social service projects that depend on federal grants and loans.

This disparity of focus frames the paradox of oversight: while nearly all congressional activities can be considered a form of oversight, such devoted attention to local and individual needs yields little useful information about persistent problems of administrative mismanagement or systematic solutions that could make programs work better. Suspicion about major failures in implementation, especially if investigation of the failures promises newspaper headlines and time on the evening news, often sparks members' interest. Especially when these problems offer members of Congress a chance to embarrass a president of the opposite party, the taste for oversight often grows.[15] Nevertheless, when oversight occurs, it is likely to be unsystematic, sporadic, episodic, erratic, haphazard, ad hoc, and initiated on the basis of a crisis.[16] Long-term improvement of implementation requires systematic, sustained attention. Congressional incentives thus run at cross-purposes to the needs of administrative improvement.

Mathew D. McCubbins and Thomas Schwartz have christened this approach the "fire alarm" style of oversight, in which members of Congress respond to complaints as they arise—as opposed to "police patrol" oversight, in which they conduct routine patrols at their own initiative. These analysts argue, in fact, that fire-alarm oversight "serves congressmen's interests at little cost" and that it produces oversight that is much more effective: through periodic interventions sparked by apparent problems, members of Congress can more clearly define the goals they have in mind. Moreover, they contend, responding to problems as they arise is much more likely to detect troubles than is maintaining a regular police-patrol style.[17] This argument is the subject of much debate, but it demonstrates at the least that congressional oversight of administration is a much more subtle process than the formal checks-and-balances system might suggest.

The Purposes of Oversight

Even if it is intermittent and ad hoc, oversight nevertheless serves a number of important purposes for legislators.[18]

- *Assurance that administrators follow the intent of Congress.* Members of Congress naturally wish to ensure that administrators' actions are consistent with what Congress intended in passing legislation. That intent is sometimes hard to determine, of course, because acts of Congress are notorious for their imprecision; often, in fact, Congress does not know what it wants until it sees what it gets. In these cases, oversight provides an opportunity for communicating more clearly, if often informally, to administrators just what results Congress expects.

- *Investigation of instances of fraud, waste, and abuse.* This unholy trinity is a frequent target of congressional investigations. From stories of overpriced hammers purchased by the Pentagon to suggestions of irregularities by contractors serving Native American reservations, allegations of inefficiencies and illegalities frequently fuel the kind of press attention that draws members of Congress, which often sparks oversight.
- *Collection of information.* Since many programs must be reauthorized, congressional oversight gives members of Congress and their staffs the opportunity to obtain basic data that will help them determine how laws ought to be changed and which new laws ought to be enacted.
- *Evaluation of program effectiveness.* Oversight can also provide Congress with information about how well a program is performing. This information can help Congress determine how best to improve an agency's effectiveness.
- *Protection of congressional prerogatives.* Members of Congress also sometimes use oversight to protect what they view as their constitutional rights and privileges from encroachment by the executive branch. The checks-and-balances system often breeds boundary-line disputes, and oversight gives members of Congress an opportunity to defend their points of view.
- *Personal advocacy.* Oversight frequently gives members of Congress their own "bully pulpits" from which to advance programs of interest to them and to attract publicity. Some members of Congress have built their reputations by championing particular causes, while others have used televised hearings to promote their careers.
- *Reversal of unpopular actions.* Finally, oversight provides members with leverage to force agencies to reverse unpopular decisions. Through veiled threats and direct confrontation, Congress can signal administrators about what activities are unacceptable and what can be done to address members' concerns.

Congressional oversight occurs through several channels, which we investigate in this chapter: (1) the work of congressional committees and their staffs; (2) program reviews conducted by the GAO; and (3) performance-based information. All three channels revolve around the flow of information.

Committee Oversight of Administration

Even more than is the case with its legislative work, Congress depends heavily on its committees for monitoring administrative agencies and their implementation of programs. Indeed, the connection between congressional committees and administrative agencies is one of the most important in government.[19] The old saying, "Congress at work is Congress in committee," applies especially to the executive-legislative relationship. Committee members write the legislation and fund the programs that bureaucrats must implement; the bureaucrats' decisions affect the members' abilities to claim credit for governmental action. It is an exchange relationship: "The ability of each to attain his goals is at least partially dependent on the actions of the other," R. Douglas Arnold writes.[20]

Legislators have powerful sanctions in their arsenal, but their use of these tools varies. Some committees engage more frequently in oversight, especially those watching over agencies that must receive annual appropriations; some committees are far tougher in approving budgets than others. Furthermore, some committees tend to be largely populated by members whose goal is constituency service, and, in providing that service, bureaucrats can gain powerful allies. When a committee has a broad national agenda, such as education or labor, instead of a narrow constituency focus, however, oversight may be harsher.[21] Nevertheless, "committees in both houses tend to give more attention to investigations of broad policy questions than to inquiries into agency implementation of programs."[22]

Varieties of Committee Review

Three sets of standing committees have responsibility for **legislative review** (the official term for legislative oversight): the regular legislative committees (usually known as **authorizing committees,** because they prepare the laws that authorize programs); the **appropriations committees**; and committees on government operations.

Authorizing committees can initiate, review, and report out bills and resolutions in particular subject-matter areas (such as labor, commerce, education, foreign affairs). Each has the oversight responsibility to review the administration of laws within its jurisdiction. While some legislative committees have conducted extensive oversight, the overall tendency is for these subject-area committees to concentrate more on the passage of new laws than on reviewing the execution of existing ones. Further decreasing the frequency of oversight here is the growth in the number of programs receiving permanent authorizations (as we saw in chapter 11); when program managers do not need to appear regularly to request continuation of their programs, the likelihood of oversight diminishes. Some committees are also moving toward longer reauthorizations to help reduce their workload, which has further reduced the opportunities for oversight.[23] Furthermore, some legislative committees (and subcommittees) are so favorably disposed toward the agencies and programs under their purview that they are not eager to initiate penetrating inquiries into possible administrative mismanagement or program ineffectiveness.

Appropriations committees have the most impressive credentials for control of administration: prestige, broad scope, power, and competence. Committee members, and especially their staffs, typically command a knowledge of agencies and programs rivaling that of career administrators and surpassing that of political executives. Yet Congress cannot rely mainly on the appropriations committees for the oversight function, because the members of these committees are already heavily burdened by their primary responsibility: they operate under the time pressure of the annual appropriations process, and their focus is on dollar figures and incremental changes from the previous year. The House Appropriations Committee's oversight, a staff member has said, is wide but not deep, whereas legislative committees' oversight is deep but not wide.[24] Moreover, with the rise of the omnibus acts and reconciliation measures discussed in chapter 11, the influence of the appropriations committees, on both budgeting and congressional oversight, has decreased. The committees have responded by adding more riders and earmarks—detailed requirements about how money appropriated for individual programs can be used—but, in general, the effectiveness of oversight by the appropriations committees remains mixed.

The Senate Committee on Homeland Security and Government Affairs and the House Committee on Oversight and Government Reform have the broadest responsibility and strongest powers for overseeing administrative activities. (After September 11, Congress rolled the new homeland security mission into governmental affairs to create a more unified look at governmental operations.) Since the early 1800s, Congress has used such committees to go beyond the usual grasp of legislative and appropriations committees. They are *the* oversight committees of Congress, and their jurisdiction is not constrained by the usual departmental or committee boundaries.[25]

While their potential for effective oversight is great, their performance has often fallen short. Both committees have traditionally ranked relatively low in prestige.[26] One consequence is that the committees' members focus their primary interest elsewhere: members serve on multiple committees, and their other committee assignments often offer more of what they need for reelection. The oversight committees rarely have adopted any strategy to guide their work in monitoring administrative agencies, and the subject-area committees have jealously guarded their jurisdictions from review. When investigations promise big headlines, other committees are quick to seize the agenda. Both houses' oversight committees have been highly selective and episodic in the choice of the administrative activities to be reviewed, generally reflecting their own specific areas of legislative jurisdiction (e.g., executive reorganization and intergovernmental relations), reacting to public scandals, or registering the special concerns of leading committee members. They rarely have been able to pursue sustained investigations, however, because they have received only modest funding.[27] When major issues surface, such as the conduct of the second Bush administration's war in Iraq or decisions about licensing a new drug, the authorizing committees tend to take center stage.

Oversight and Redundancy

The problem of legislative control, at all levels of government, is clearly not a shortage of committees with oversight responsibilities and opportunities. Indeed, the multiplicity of committees and the overlaps among their jurisdictions provide many different avenues for legislative influence on administrative activities. In Congress, the increasingly decentralized system has expanded the points of access and the number of hearings, but "it has at the same time weakened the ability of Congress to conduct serious oversight and administrative control." The growing complexity of administrative activities, the difficulty of developing good information about program performance, and the counterbalancing power of interest groups all combine to lessen Congress's direct leverage over the executive branch.[28] As experts debated the creation of the new Department of Homeland Security in 2002, congressional scholar Norman J. Ornstein counted thirteen House and Senate committees with at least some jurisdiction over the issue, and there were more than sixty subcommittees sharing jurisdiction—for a total of eighty-eight committees and subcommittees in all.[29] Similar phenomena have occurred at the state and local levels.

Redundancy, in fact, has magnified, not solved, Congress's oversight problem. Changes in the budget process have duplicated the number of reviews to which agencies are subjected and have blurred the responsibilities of each committee. As one Georgetown University study on defense oversight argued, "redundancy in the congressional review process seriously aggravates the oversight problem." The redundant steps mean that "Congress rarely takes conclusive action on any issue," as a Senate Armed Services Committee staff report concluded.[30] One estimate is that assistant secretaries must spend as much as 40 percent of their time preparing for congressional testimony and responding to inquiries by members of Congress.[31] Thus, congressional committee structures and operating rules serve to hinder rather than help in the oversight of administration. The multiplicity of committees overseeing the Department of Homeland Security led to constant complaints by senior officials, who said they needed to spend so much time tending their congressional relationships that they had little time left for their work. In 2008, Stephen R. Heifetz, the department's deputy assistant secretary for policy development, argued that "Congress should step back, streamline the number of committees with responsibility for homeland security—and give us room to do our job."[32] Congressional committees might reply that there was nothing more important in doing the job than ensuring accountability to Congress.

Congress's ability to monitor administrative activities effectively depends on its access to information, most of it generated in the executive branch. On the one hand, there are significant barriers to obtaining information about what is happening in the executive branch; on the other hand, legislators typically are awash in data. Effective oversight requires separating the truly useful information from the huge volumes of paper that flood Washington—as well as state capitals and city halls. Distilling the key issues from the mass of detailed data evokes the classic problem of trying "to distinguish the forest from the trees."

Barriers to Information Flow

Since Congress depends heavily on outside forces for the information needed to drive oversight, barriers in the way of the flow of information have a huge impact on the quality of oversight. Several kinds of barriers, both institutional and political, can effectively impede this information flow.

Secrecy

Secrecy, particularly in the conduct of foreign affairs, the planning of military strategy and tactics, and the pursuit of intelligence activities, is the most formidable barrier.[33] Few would argue that these matters should be carried on in full view of the public or, for that matter, of the 535 members of Congress. The problem is that under the guise of national security, it is possible for administrators to classify any documents they choose as "top secret," "secret," or "confidential." Classification, once done, is difficult to undo, however trivial or improper the reasons for its having been done. During World War II, for example, documents often received security classifications simply because that sped their delivery to government offices. In the Defense Department, newspaper clippings have been stamped "secret," and a memorandum urging less use of the top secret classification was itself classified top secret.[34]

Forty years after the war's end, the Tower Commission, investigating the Reagan administration's elaborate plan to sell arms to Iran to secure the release of Americans held hostage there, and then to divert the arms-sales profits to aid the *Contras* in Nicaragua, concluded that "concern for preserving the secrecy of the initiative provided an excuse for abandoning sound process."[35] Congressional investigators, furthermore, found that secrecy concerns enormously complicated their probe. When administrative officials argued the need for flexibility in conducting foreign relations and said they had planned to notify Congress after the hostages were released, Sen. William S. Cohen (R-Maine) acknowledged that the president needs flexibility but warned, "flexibility is too often taken as license, and then after the fact it's rationalized as a constitutional power that cannot be diluted or diminished by congressional action." He concluded, "comity is important, but it has to run in two directions on Pennsylvania Avenue."[36]

Almost fifteen years later, members of Congress continued to complain that they had not received timely information from the Pentagon about problems with the war in Iraq, especially about abusive treatment of Iraqi prisoners by American soldiers. Sen. Carl Levin (D-Mich.) sternly admonished Defense Secretary Donald Rumsfeld in 2004 that consultation with Congress "is not supposed to be an option but a long-standing and fundamental responsibility" of administration officials.[37]

The problem of excessive security classification has two dimensions. One is the denial to Congress of information that in fact has no valid claim to secrecy or confidentiality. The other is the withholding from Congress of information that, though secret or confidential, is essential to congressional decision making and oversight with respect to the nation's foreign relations, military posture, and intelligence gathering. The typical solution proposed for this problem has been furnishing classified information to only a selected few committees (usually the House and Senate Intelligence Committees) in executive session, to only the chairpersons and ranking minority members of such committees, or to only their pro-Pentagon members. However, the disclosure that high Reagan administration officials had been secretly using the proceeds from their arms sales to Iran to fund the White House's Central American program revealed how inadequate such a solution often is. So, too, does the growing share of the Pentagon budget that is devoted to the so-called black—that is, secret—programs that are hidden from all but select members of Congress, as we saw in chapter 11.

Executive Privilege

A second barrier to the flow of information is **executive privilege**—a prerogative never mentioned in the Constitution but now asserted to be inherent in the president's powers. Presidents have claimed that this immunity from compulsion to disclose information is akin to the legal doctrine of "privileged communications," such as those between husband and wife, doctor and patient, attorney and client, and priest and parishioner. In the government, the doctrine has most powerfully been invoked to protect the confidentiality of oral and written communication between the president and White House aides, especially during the Nixon administration's Watergate affair. It has continued to resurface ever since, however, constricting the ability of courts and Congress to elicit information in incidents ranging from Bill Clinton's appearance before a grand jury investigating his personal conduct in office to George W. Bush's testimony before a commission investigating the September 11 attacks. Executive privilege is the core of George W. Bush's case for the use of signing statements. Senior Bush aide Karl Rove claimed executive privilege as a defense against testifying before Congress on the leak of the identity of the name of one of the CIA spies to the media.

In 2007, the House Committee on Oversight and Government Reform held a hearing to investigate how Valerie Plame Wilson's identity as a CIA agent had been leaked to the press. President Bush later acknowledged that the leak came from the White House. Administration critics charged that the leak was an effort to embarrass her husband, former Ambassador Joseph Wilson, who had argued that the Bush administration had exaggerated the threat posed by Iraq to justify going to war.

Administrative Confidentiality

A third, but lower, barrier to legislative access to information is **administrative confidentiality,** which covers two distinct practices. One is the protection of private information: individuals' tax returns, completed census forms, possibly derogatory personal details collected in investigative agencies' files, and businesses concerns' trade secrets and financial data. Such information is normally collected by government agencies under pledges of confidentiality, and the administrators often resist committee demands for such records. They argue, with considerable force, that abuse of confidentiality could impair the government's ability to obtain full and accurate information.

The other claim to administrative confidentiality relates to drafts, memoranda, and other internal records bearing on policies and decisions that may or may not be under serious consideration. Agencies' concern is that premature disclosure of such internal records may lead to distorted publicity and public misunderstanding—many memoranda by subordinate staff members make suggestions that will in fact be rejected at higher levels, but newspaper headlines drawn from them could give the impression that the agency is about to adopt the suggestion. Equally important (and paralleling the argument for executive privilege at the presidential level), the possibility that they will have to defend their memoranda before congressional committees may inhibit those on whom a department head relies for imaginative ideas and frank advice. Congressional committees and their staffs are nevertheless often eager to share in the shaping of agency policies, partly because once announced, such policies are difficult to reverse.[38]

Balancing Issues

Secrecy, executive privilege, and administrative confidentiality are all embroiled in disputes that essentially pit the separation of powers against the checks-and-balances system. There remain moral, prudential, and practical considerations that need to be balanced against these institutional concerns, weighing in favor of restoration of a freer flow of information. On one side are citizens' stake in the confidentiality of personal information in government files, the president's and department heads' need for candid advice from their immediate assistants, the effects of disclosure of preliminary proposals, and the special need for secrecy in matters affecting defense and the conduct of foreign affairs. On the other side are the often deplorable results of official activities cloaked in secrecy; the people's right to know so that they can participate in democratic government; Congress's oversight responsibilities as creator, empowerer, and financier of agencies and their programs; and its role as investigator and exposer of corrupt, illegal, and unethical behavior in the executive branch. With so many constitutional, moral, prudential, and pragmatic considerations in conflict, no formula, however complex, can provide a solution to this dilemma of administrative accountability.

Staffing to Stem the Tide

Congress is buried in paradox: it struggles to obtain some important but sensitive information, but it is also overwhelmed with information from administrative agencies. A large amount comes in the form of regular reports—annual, quarterly, monthly—that their authorizing statutes require. This tidal wave of information, in fact, is mainly of Congress's own making. The Pentagon reports cited earlier are only one sign of Congress's increasing insistence that administrative agencies provide regular reports on their activities as well as answer detailed intermittent inquiries. The Environmental Protection Agency, for example, must respond to more than 4,000 letters per year from Congress requesting information.[39] In addition, "elaborate public relations programs in some agencies blanket congressional committees with more—and often irrelevant—'information' than they can possibly handle, befogging issues and distorting facts in the process."[40] Congress's informational problem stems, in part, from a deliberate agency strategy of communications overkill, but, more commonly, it reflects the lack of fit between congressional interests and the way that information is organized and summarized in administrative agencies. The increasingly scientific and technological character of many fields of governmental activity has further complicated the problem.[41]

For years, Congress dealt with the problem of information overload by vastly increasing the size of its own staff. In a move mirrored in state legislatures around the country, it attempted to close its expertise gap with the executive branch by taking three steps: increasing the personal staffs of members, hiring more staff for committees, and strengthening the three staff agencies that serve Congress (the Congressional Research Service, the Congressional Budget Office, and the GAO, to which we turn shortly).[42] "Committee staffs grew when it became apparent that even specialized committee members needed help if Congress was to get the information required for making informed decisions," Michael J. Malbin argues. "Without its staff, Congress would quickly become the prisoner of its outside sources of information in the executive branch and interest groups."[43]

In fact, from 1965 to 2009, these various congressional staffs doubled in size, while executive-branch employment rose only slightly (see Figure 14.1). As part of their takeover of Congress in 1995, the Republicans significantly cut the congressional staff as a symbol of their commitment to shrinking government, but the staffing levels quickly recovered. By global standards, Congress's staff is large indeed; the second most heavily staffed legislature in the world, Canada's parliament, had a staff just one-tenth as large.[44]

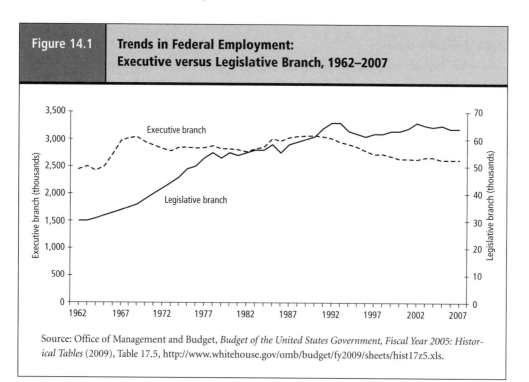

| Figure 14.1 | **Trends in Federal Employment: Executive versus Legislative Branch, 1962–2007** |

Source: Office of Management and Budget, *Budget of the United States Government, Fiscal Year 2005: Historical Tables* (2009), Table 17.5, http://www.whitehouse.gov/omb/budget/fy2009/sheets/hist17z5.xls.

These staffs have helped members of Congress devote more time to casework for constituents. When a constituent writes to complain about a slow Social Security check, malfeasance by local grant recipients, or even allegedly abusive treatment by a relative's commanding officer in the military, the letter is assigned to a worker in a member's office. Congressional mail receives special treatment in government offices; special, brightly colored "buck slips" are usually stapled to the top. Most agencies require quick turnaround times for responses, and they maintain congressional liaison units that monitor responses, to ensure that quick and accurate replies are sent.

Members of Congress and administrators take such letters very seriously, because no one wants to seem indifferent to constituents. There is evidence, however, that such referrals often are not very effective at solving the problems, "since they are usually handled at the same level of the agency (often by the same official) where the complaint arose in the first place." Furthermore, because the complaints are random and extremely detailed, they rarely provide good evidence for broad administrative oversight issues. Occasionally, patterns of complaints or particularly unusual issues may surface, but evidence of wrongdoing does not often emerge through such casework.[45]

No one seriously supposes that a committee can or should match the expertise of the administrative agencies under its jurisdiction. Even a moderate expansion of committee staffs could mean multiplication of little congressional bureaucracies, each requiring direction and coordination by the committee or its chair—responsibilities for which members of Congress have little time and, often, little talent. In the absence of such control, staff members have been known to go off on their own, harassing agency officials and, in effect, participating in agency decision making. Such staff members purport to be representing their committees but in fact may be representing only themselves.

The alternative to the building up of committee staffs is increased reliance on congressional support agencies, including the Congressional Budget Office and the Congressional Research Service. But these two agencies mostly focus their informational and analytical studies on pending legislative proposals and future policy options, rather than on investigation of administrative operations. Such potential as they have for aiding Congress's oversight activities has not been fully realized, and each receives mixed reviews on its sense of priorities, quality of products, and internal administration. However, a third support agency, the Government Accountability Office (GAO, previously called the General Accounting Office), has become "Congress's most valuable oversight support agency" in the opinion of the Senate Committee on Governmental Affairs. Ernest S. Griffith, the former director of what is now the Congressional Research Service, goes further, declaring that "the General Accounting Office is the finest instrument in any nation in the world to serve as watchdog over a bureaucracy and enable its parliament or legislature to keep it under control—if GAO wills to do so."[46] We examine it in the next section.

The Government Accountability Office

In 1921 Congress transferred the government's auditing functions from the Treasury Department, where they had been based since 1789, to a new General Accounting Office.[47] GAO originally was an agency wholly devoted to accounting: its staff reviewed all of the federal government's spending, and employees wearing green eye-shades processed piles of paper. That role has changed radically over the years; GAO now is Congress's chief arm for examining the performance of government programs—and that evolution was recognized with the change in the agency's name.

The comptroller general of the United States, who heads GAO, is appointed by the president with the advice and consent of the Senate. Because Congress wanted to ensure that GAO was protected from interference by the executive branch, the comptroller general holds a fifteen-year term (the longest in the government, except for the lifetime appointment of federal judges) and can be removed only by a joint resolution of Congress or by impeachment.

GAO performs functions with both executive and legislative roots: its legislative branch duties include auditing the expenditures of executive branch agencies; its executive branch duties involve approving agencies' payments and settling their accounts. This ambiguous position has been a source of continuing controversy. When the Competition in Contracting Act of 1984 gave GAO the power to halt a contract under dispute, President Reagan objected to this power, and Attorney General William French Smith instructed executive branch agencies not to comply with the provision. A federal district judge ruled Smith's action illegal, and Congress backed up the decision by withholding all funds from the attorney general's office until he agreed to go along with the law; Smith's successor, Edwin Meese III, eventually backed down. Meanwhile, a federal appeals court agreed with Congress, holding that GAO was a "hybrid agency" that could exercise such executive functions as reviewing contracts before their execution.

In 1986, however, the Supreme Court held, in *Bowsher v. Synar,* that the comptroller general was an agent of Congress and so could not constitutionally exercise executive budget-cutting powers.[48] Thus, GAO is a hybrid whose constitutional position is a vague one. Much of its work revolves around the detailed examination of individual programs, although during the first George W. Bush administration GAO sued Vice President Cheney in an attempt to force him to reveal the names of those with whom his special energy task force had consulted. GAO lost that suit, but its work sparked objections from others in Washington and fueled a continuing controversy over corporate influence on the Bush administration's policies.

An Era of Detailed Control

Two major provisions in the 1921 Budget and Accounting Act's definition of GAO's powers created the basis for much of this friction.[49] One reads: "The Comptroller General shall prescribe the forms, systems, and procedure for . . . accounting in the several departments and establishments, and for the administrative examination of fiscal officers' accounts and claims against the United States." This meant that the government's accounting systems could be designed primarily with GAO's preferences in mind and without attention to the accounting needs of the operating departments, the Treasury Department, and the budget bureau. GAO's external-control needs could be met at the expense of the executive branch's internal-control needs.

The 1921 act's second major provision reads as follows: "All claims and demands whatever by the Government of the United States or against it, and all accounts whatever in which the Government of the United States is concerned, either as debtor or creditor, shall be settled and adjusted in the General Accounting Office." This appeared to mean (and was so interpreted by the first comptroller general, John R. McCarl) that no financial transaction of the government could legally be completed until specifically approved by GAO. Agency officials continued to spend money for goods and services, but the vouchers for all transactions were transported from all over the world to Washington for review by the GAO; if it disapproved any expenditure, the public official who had approved the expenditure would, by law, be personally responsible for the difference.[50] The risk of such personal liability was so threatening that spending officers often asked GAO for advance opinions, and GAO increasingly preaudited expenditures before they were made. As a result, GAO not only delayed actions but became less an after-the-fact auditor than an active participant in the very transactions it was supposed to audit later.

For the first fifteen years, Comptroller General McCarl cherished his role as "watchdog of the Treasury"—he usually interpreted grants of spending power narrowly and statutory restrictions broadly. *Interpreted* is the key word here, and one that is often overlooked in discussions of external control. Statutory provisions, as we observed earlier, are often open to varying interpretations, and their meaning depends on who has the last word.[51] Lawyers from an agency and the Treasury might interpret a provision one way and, in case of doubt, obtain an official opinion from the attorney general. The comptroller general, however, did not accept the attorney general's rulings as binding. If GAO disallowed an expenditure as "contrary to law," the ruling would stand unless the executive branch carried the dispute to court. Thus, giving the last word to an external-control official can—and, in this case, did—open opportunities for hamstringing of programs with which that official—here, the comptroller general—is unsympathetic.[52]

Reorientation

Remarkable changes have taken place in recent decades. Although GAO still has power to, and does, audit some individual transactions, it has come to emphasize the strengthening of agencies' internal audit and control systems, whose effectiveness in turn relieves GAO of the need to audit every transaction. Instead, it can concentrate on programs that are important in financial terms and those that have provoked criticism or congressional interest. GAO, in short, has moved from cost accounting to program auditing, from examining the money trail to measuring program performance. Its reports on cost overruns in weapons procurement have often created sensations, but in more routine audits of agencies, GAO uses statistical sampling and other strategies to test the effectiveness of internal control systems, thus again removing itself from the burden of second-guessing every transaction. GAO has also begun identifying and tracking "high-risk programs," federal activities that have an unusually high threat for waste, fraud, and abuse.

Most audits are done "on site"—that is, in the agencies and their field offices—so freight-car loads of vouchers need no longer be shipped to GAO in Washington. These and other changes have reduced GAO staff numbers from 15,000 in 1946 to 3,200 today.

GAO has moved far toward becoming an all-purpose, external-control agent. Former comptroller general Elmer B. Staats observed that governmental auditing "no longer is a function concerned primarily with financial operations. Instead, governmental auditing now is also concerned with whether governmental organizations are achieving the purpose for which programs are authorized and funds are made available, are doing so economically and efficiently, and are complying with applicable laws and regulations."[53] Legislation enacted during the 1970s emphasized that GAO "shall review and evaluate the *results* of Government programs and activities."[54] GAO's reviews are remarkable for both their detail and their variety, as a sample of report titles shows:

- "Women in the Military: Impact of Proposed Legislation to Open More Combat Support Positions and Units to Women"
- "File Sharing Program: Users of Peer-to-Peer Networks Can Readily Access Child Pornography"
- "Highways: How State Agencies Adopt New Pavement Technologies"
- "Seafood Safety: Seriousness of Problems and Efforts to Protect Customers"
- "Contract Management: DOD Needs Measures for Small Business Subcontracting Program and Better Data on Foreign Subcontracts"
- "AIDS Education: Reaching Populations at Higher Risk"

- "Reserve Forces: Observations on Recent National Guard Use in Overseas and Homeland Missions and Future Challenges"

After the past several presidential elections, moreover, GAO has released a transition series, providing advice to members of Congress and newly elected presidents on topics ranging from the budget deficit and the public service to NASA and national defense.

As a direct congressional agent exercising delegated control authority over administrative agencies, GAO occupies a powerful position. In addition, it has a substantial, skilled investigative and analytical staff that aids congressional committees in their oversight of agency performance and sometimes conducts reviews on its own initiative.

GAO has two handicaps that make it hard for the agency to focus public attention on its work.[55] The first is its "green eyeshade" image, partly recalling its past and partly reflecting the preponderance of accountants on its staff, particularly at executive levels. But the staff pattern has been shifting toward recruitment of business and public administration specialists, economists and other social scientists, engineers, and computer and information specialists. The lingering image problem led Comptroller General David M. Walker to win approval of the agency's name change in 2004.

The second handicap is the time required to investigate and audit programs. This stems largely from GAO's commitment to accuracy, thoroughness, and objectivity, but the result is that its reports often lack timeliness for Congress's agenda. Nevertheless, GAO's reports—and their handy "highlights" pages that summarize key findings—are staples at congressional hearings and in news reports of government activities. In the 1980s, GAO's computer experts provided much of the data used to track down the secret financial transfers used by Reagan aide Oliver North to channel arms-sale profits to Central American guerrillas. GAO's influence, moreover, has spilled over into the states, where many legislatures have established their own "mini-GAOs" to conduct evaluations of state programs.

State and Local Legislative Control

Although GAO is the unquestioned master of legislative staff agencies, many state governments have similar bodies. They often have arcane titles, such as the Virginia Joint Legislative Audit and Review Commission, California's State Joint Legislative Audit Committee, and Wisconsin's Joint Committee on Audit, but their work is just as important and far-reaching. State legislators share the same information mismatch with their federal legislative colleagues, since administrators have far more expertise at their disposal. In the states where legislative service is part time, the problem is even worse. These state-level versions of GAO are typically small but highly professional, and their work often makes headlines.

In local governments, legislators (members of city councils and county boards) rarely have a separate GAO-style staff. They tend to rely on their own staffs. In small communities, such support is often meager, but in larger communities, legislators often have personal staffs that rival those of members of Congress.

Performance-Based Information

A final form of congressional control of administration is performance-based information. In 1993 Congress passed the **Government Performance and Results Act** (GPRA), which required all federal agencies to produce strategic plans and to measure their success in achieving those goals. GPRA was exceptionally ambitious: it committed the government to measuring its outcomes within a very short time—just seven years. In short, Congress required the federal government to go farther and faster than other governments around the world, such as that of New Zealand, which had ventured down the performance management road.[56]

For example, the Social Security Administration (SSA) laid out its goals and indicators to assess how well it was achieving those goals (see Box 14.1). SSA ranked among the most effective government agencies in meeting the challenges of the new GPRA system, but all federal agencies worked hard to produce the reports required by the legislation, evolving five different measures:

- *Outputs:* the goods and services provided
- *Efficiency:* the price for the goods and services
- *Customer service:* citizen satisfaction with the goods and services
- *Quality:* the value of the goods and services
- *Outcome:* the social impact of the goods and services

GAO found that managers increasingly developed performance measures in each of these areas. "Ten years after enactment, GPRA's requirements have laid a solid foundation of results-oriented agency planning, measurement, and reporting," GAO concluded. Moreover, "Performance planning and measurement have slowly yet increasingly been part of agencies' culture."[57]

But as has long been the case with new strategies that put heavy reliance on planning and measurement, GPRA has faced major challenges. The advance of GPRA's techniques has depended heavily on the commitment of top managers: where there has been strong leadership, GPRA has advanced; progress has been halting where top leaders have not used it as a tool. Moreover, in many agencies, the information has been collected but not used. This point, of course, connects to the last: if top leaders are not committed to the process and see little value in it, they are unlikely to use the information, even if Congress requires them to collect it.

Box 14.1	**Social Security Administration: Performance Results**

Strategic Goal A: To deliver high-quality, citizen-centered service.
  Objective 1: Make the right decision in the disability process as early as possible.
  Objective 2: Increase employment for people with disabilities by expanding opportunities.
  Objective 3: Improve service with technology, focusing on accuracy, security, and efficiency.

Strategic Goal B: To protect the integrity of Social Security programs through superior stewardship.
  Objective 4: Detect and prevent fraudulent and improper payments and improve debt management.
  Objective 5: Strengthen the integrity of the Social Security Number issuance process to help prevent
        misuse and fraud of the Social Security Number and card.
  Objective 6: Ensure the accuracy of earnings records so that eligible individuals can receive the proper
        benefits due them.
  Objective 7: Manage Agency finances and assets to link resources effectively to performance outcomes.

**Strategic Goal C: To achieve sustainable solvency and ensure Social Security programs meet the
needs of current and future generations.**
  Objective 8: Through education and research efforts, support reforms to ensure sustainable solvency and
        more responsive retirement and disability programs.

Strategic Goal D: To strategically manage and align staff to support the mission of the Agency.
  Objective 9: Recruit, develop, and retain a high-performing workforce.

Program results: link to Program Assessment Rating Tool Measures

↑   Average processing time for initial disability claims
        • Goal: 88 days   Actual: 83 days

↑   Average processing time for SSA hearings
        • Goal: 524 days   Actual: 512 days

↑   Disability Determination Services net accuracy rate
        • Goal: 97%   Actual: 97%

N/A   Supplemental Security Income overpayment and underpayment accuracy rate.
        • Goal: 95.7% (overpayment)   Actual: Not available.
        • Goal: 98.8% (underpayment)   Actual: Not available

Selected performance measures shown. For an analysis of the Program Assessment Rating Tool (PART) process,
see chapter 11.

Source: Social Security Administration, "GPRA Performance Results," *FY 2007 Performance and Accountability Report* (2003), http://www.ssa.gov/finance/2007/Performance_Section.pdf.

Most of all, GPRA's progress has depended on Congress itself. Top federal managers have been concerned about "the reluctance of Congress to use performance
information when making decisions, especially appropriations decisions," according

to a GAO survey. The evidence is that Congress is making far more use of this information than in the program's early days—and to a significantly greater extent than cynics would have predicted. However, one unsurprising conclusion has emerged: "the information presented and its presentation must meet the needs of the user," Congress. GAO found that the more Congress has been involved as a partner in defining agency goals and in shaping the presentation of the data, the more members of Congress and their staffs tend to use the data.[58]

GPRA has significantly changed the fabric of congressional oversight. By requiring agencies to prepare performance reports, Congress has increased the amount and quality of information. It has forced agency managers to pay far more attention to the goals they are trying to achieve and to demonstrate that they are producing results. It has heightened Congress's own attention to agency management and to oversight. And, in ways that are perhaps surprising, it has promoted a conversation between agency managers, members of Congress, and congressional committee staffs about what goals the programs are seeking. Given the ambiguity that often surrounds the creation of federal programs, this is no mean feat. The problem, however, is that neither Congress nor the agencies *use* the information very often to improve the results of federal programs.

The ultimate goal of linking presidential budgeting, congressional oversight, and agency management remains a distant goal, however. One skilled observer of the process concluded:

> As a result of the PART [Program Assessment Rating Tool, George W. Bush's performance reform], GPRA and the residual effects of the previous acronyms, federal managers are paying more attention to the results of their programs. But the idea of "performance budgeting," in which program effectiveness is directly linked to spending decisions, is one grail that will likely remain far out of reach.[59]

Moreover, the long history of analytical techniques to improve government management suggest several lessons. One is that many acronym-based changes—from PPB (planning-programming-budgeting) through MBO (management by objectives) and ZBB (zero-base budgeting) to PART—rarely last long after the president who created them leaves office. Another is that Congress, always eager to protect its own prerogatives, has rarely bought into these presidential agendas. But GPRA is different in at least this one important respect: Congress itself established its steps and requires agencies to submit annual reports. Because it is based in law instead of on the Office of Management and Budget's (OMB) instructions, GPRA has the potential for becoming hardwired into the federal government. And by trying to provide better answers to the questions that Congress regularly asks, it has the potential for becoming an important tool of federal oversight.

An Assessment of Legislative Control

Legislative control of administration is based on the sound proposition that legislators, not just executives, have a legitimate concern with seeing to it "that the laws be faithfully executed." Legislators can by law fix the objectives and methods of implementing the programs they authorize, determine the funding of each program, and organize and reorganize agencies. They can limit the life span of program authorizations and appropriations. Through committees and accountability offices, such as GAO, they can make their own investigations of agency performance. The circle is completed by legislative alteration of enabling statutes, appropriations, and organizations so as to make agencies' future performance conform more closely to congressional intent.

As Christopher H. Foreman Jr. has observed, following a study of congressional oversight of regulatory policies:

> Oversight emerges as a sometimes painful, inevitably self-interested process of consultation and second-guessing that reasonably well keeps administration sensitive to the concerns of persons and groups affected by or attentive to regulatory policy. As a system for monitoring agency decision making and adherence to approved procedure—that is, as a set of mechanisms for enforcing accountability regarding agency behavior and policy choice—oversight succeeds.

While the process is often confusing, with muddled jurisdictional boundaries and uncertain leverage, the whole entourage comprises "an intricate and impressive system of screens or 'fire alarms.' "[60] It is a system that defies easy description or rational organization, but the intricate relationships nevertheless provide an impressive range of information and leverage, both formal and informal, for legislative influence on administrative activities. It is also a system in which members of Congress can transmit signals—sometimes blunt, sometimes subtle—about their expectations of administrators' actions.

We have discovered two major problems. One is that Congress—as well as legislatures at other levels—has often proven to have limited interest and modest capacity for oversight.[61] Its oversight efforts are at best intermittent, and sustained congressional attention to major administrative issues is rare. New information-based reforms, such as GPRA, provide grounds for hope, but the basic problems are deeply rooted.

The other problem is the danger that legislators (especially in committees and subcommittees) will intrude excessively into the executive function, sometimes to promote their own self-interest.[62] Legislators should not—for reasons of both constitutional comity and administrative efficiency—so confuse their roles as to become, in effect, coadministrators of agencies and programs. A long-time chairman of the

House Naval Affairs Committee, for example, was dubbed "the Secretary of the Navy." The involvement of judges in administration raises similar issues, as we saw in the previous chapter.

How Does Accountability Work?

The central problem of public administration, as we saw in chapter 1, is how to give administrators enough power to accomplish the work that policymakers want done, without having them exercise that power in a way that threatens democracy and liberty. Accountability, at its core, is *who is responsible to whom for what, through what means.* It is a relationship more than a process. It is dynamic rather than static. And it is the most important question of public administration.

Systems for holding public administrators accountable have at least four elements: voluntary compliance, standard setting, monitoring, and sanctions.

The foundation of accountability is *voluntary compliance.* Even though people are not saints, most people most of the time voluntarily comply with most of the significant constraints on their behavior. They do so for a variety of reasons, ranging from moral standards to indifferent acquiescence to self-interest. As Max Weber stressed, they often do so because they believe in the legitimacy of the system of authority. Were it unrealistic to rely on substantial voluntary compliance, the scope and intensity of control systems would be unbearable.

The second element, *standard setting*—the crafting of rules to guide administrative discretion—accomplishes several things. It tells administrators what they are supposed to do (and what behavior they will be punished for). Some standards are obvious: few people need to be told that stealing is wrong, although petty theft—from pilfering government office supplies to using government photocopy machines to duplicate favorite recipes—is common. At the other extreme, some standards are so complicated that no one can know all of the rules that apply to their actions: the question of how—and how much—to pay government's contractors fills thick manuals. Frontline administrators rarely understand all the rules, and they rely on agency lawyers, procurement specialists, and masters of accounting regulations to raise a red flag about potential problems. Observing the standards, however, can become mechanical and trivial; nearly everyone has had experience in dealing with administrators so obsessed with rules and forms that the basic mission of public service becomes lost. The key to effective administration lies in ensuring that attention to the details does not undermine effective pursuit of the broader policy.

Third, an effective accountability system must *monitor* whether the standards are met. Sometimes that happens in advance—an administrator may need to get an action approved in advance. Some state governments, for example, require advance approval of all administrative rules before they become effective. Sometimes, before it becomes final, an action must "incubate"—lie in a congressional committee—for, say, sixty days, during which time committee members may (or may not) seek to persuade the agency to abort the action. Other forms of monitoring call for reviewing actions already completed. For example, monitors often conduct postaudits of financial transactions and review the error rate in payments to welfare clients; the auditors can criticize any improprieties they find and demand that the administrative agency mend its ways in the future. The newer forms of performance monitoring—including OMB's Program Assessment Rating Tool, the Government Performance and Results Act, and Baltimore's CitiStat (discussed in chaps. 11 and 12)—provide government officials with quick feedback about policy impacts.

Should policymakers use monitoring to identify, prevent, or correct all possible errors?[63] It is tempting to answer yes, but, in fact, that can make programs more expensive and less effective. An effort by the Internal Revenue Service to wring out every last nickel of taxes owed by every citizen would cost far more (in the time of revenue agents) than it would collect, and in the process, the heavy-handed approach would infuriate taxpayers. So, instead, overseers selectively review administrators' actions, often in response to complaints by citizens, members of the press, congressional committees, or employees.[64] They may use sampling—by examining, say, every fifth case or by reviewing all of an agency's units' cases in one out of five years; the sampling process shifts the focus from correcting individual errors to identifying those agencies or units that have so poor a pattern of actions that they need fundamental change. Or they may concentrate on areas—such as the awarding of government contracts or the operation of lottery programs—that might be especially prone to problems, or on programs in which government officials—such as inspectors, social workers, police officers, and other "street-level bureaucrats"—frequently must make quick decisions or exercise broad discretion, which present special problems of accountability.

Finally, to be credible, an accountability system needs the ability to impose *sanctions*; if overseers find problems, there must be consequences. The delicate task here is to devise sanctions strong enough to be taken seriously by administrators but not so strong as to disrupt an agency's mission. They cannot be so punitive as to be impossible to enforce or so repressive as to require an impossible burden of proof. Sanctions can sometimes be too tough, as when a federal agency offends Congress and Congress responds with a sharp budget cut, forcing the curtailment of important public services. Sometimes sanctions may be too mild or too poorly directed to serve as adequate punishment or deterrent, as when a congressional investigation produces only a critical report—but no change in law or budget—so the agency may simply ignore the proceeding.

Accountability is thus a matter of balancing internal norms with external processes. The external processes can be within the agency or from oversight bodies in both the executive and legislative branches. If the nation's founders created a separation-of-powers system to restrain government's power, American public administration has over time evolved a complex and layered system for holding administrators accountable.

The process relies on two principles to make this layered accountability system work. One is *independence*: making each control agency autonomous and insulated from those individuals and forces that might corrupt or restrain it. Independence helps assure integrity by insulating it from the cross-pressures that often engulf elected institutions. For example, Congress's principal control agency, GAO, is designed to be independent of the executive departments and is separate from Congress's own day-to-day work. The other answer is *redundancy*: multiplying the control agencies and overlapping their functions.[65] If one control agency misses a problem, having other control agencies with overlapping jurisdictions can increase the chances of catching it. Furthermore, competition among control agencies may stimulate energy in all of them. Inspectors general are likely to be more vigilant because they know that GAO, OMB, and congressional watchdog committees may catch anything they miss—and possibly embarrass them for having missed it.

Redundancy, of course, can itself be a problem. On the one hand, multiple control agencies can make conflicting demands. For example, until the 1950s, GAO, the Treasury Department, and the Bureau of the Budget separately prescribed the kinds of information that agencies' accounting systems had to produce. On the other hand, when several control agencies have jurisdiction over an especially troublesome case, each may await another's move—and in the end, nothing may happen. Finally, redundancy has one very obvious drawback: duplication of oversight is expensive, and at some point the costs may overwhelm the advantages produced. The trick lies in getting the watchdogs to bark loudly enough to alert policymakers to problems but not so obsessively that they become a distracting nuisance.

Consider the case of Gina Gray, appointed by the Pentagon as public affairs director of Arlington National Cemetery in early 2008. She discovered that top Department of Defense officials were imposing limits on media coverage of the burial of soldiers killed in Iraq. After poking through the regulations, she found no regulation against media coverage. If families approved the coverage, she allowed it. But just ten days into the job, she found that a senior cemetery official moved the media fifty yards from the service, which made it impossible for reporters to hear or photograph the service. Her supervisors took away her BlackBerry, demoted her, and ultimately fired her. "Had I not put my foot down, had I just gone along with it and not said regulations were being violated, I'm sure I'd still be there," Gray told a *Washington Post* reporter. "It's about doing the right thing."[66]

The "right thing," of course, was precisely what the issue was about. Who should make policy? What obligations do government officials have in following it? What should they do if they believe that the decisions of their supervisors violate policy or ethical standards? In a close call, should the decisions of supervisors or an official's internal norms rule? Gray decided that the rules did not forbid media coverage of the funerals and she was fired for her stand. In her termination letter, her supervisor said she had "been disrespectful to me as your supervisor and failed to act in an inappropriate manner." It was an unusual typo—a double negative that created profound irony. The *Washington Post* reporter concluded, "Only at Arlington National Cemetery could it be considered a firing offense to act appropriately."[67]

Conclusion: Ethics and the Public Service

No matter how many layers of accountability policymakers build, the responsiveness and effectiveness of public administration depend ultimately on the ethics of individual public administrators. One implication of Michael Lipsky's theory of street-level bureaucrats, which we explored in the previous chapter, is that many administrators operate far from the view of elected officials and top policymakers. They have broad discretion on how they do their jobs, they have a big impact on the lives of citizens, and there are few watchdogs on hand to catch misdeeds. Roving television news helicopters might occasionally catch an unusual event, and investigative reporters are always on the prowl for a good story. The inescapable fact, however, is that the quality—as well as accountability—of the administrative system depends critically on the decisions that individual administrators make and the values they hold in making them.

Debates flourish over whether ethics can be taught. Researchers into child development constantly remind us that the values of most children are formed by the age of three. Moreover, debates constantly swirl over whether ethics can be reliably enforced. No amount of oversight can fully control the uncountable numbers of individual decisions that administrators make every day to make public administration work.

The surest course to an ethical public administration is a careful balance. It requires a balance between the individual values of public administrators and the professional training they bring to the job. It requires a balance between the cultures of their agencies and the oversight of external forces. Most of all, it requires a strong relationship between public administrators and the citizens to whom they ultimately are responsible, for the effective use of public power and for the responsible protection of individual freedom.

Case 14

From the Front Lines of Government Responsibility: How Should Government Communicate with Citizens?

In June 2008, comedian George Carlin died. For decades, he had been an acerbic observer of American society, but he was perhaps best known for his routine about "seven words you can never say on television." Milwaukee police arrested him in 1972 for performing the sketch, and the case went all the way to the U.S. Supreme Court, which ruled the dirty words in fact could not be said on television.

A week before Carlin's death, the Local Government Association (LGA) in the United Kingdom took its own stand about words that bureaucrats shouldn't use. It released a list of 100 words (see facing page) that bureaucrats should not use, along with a suggested substitute for most of them. The LGA suggested banning popular buzzwords like *citizen empowerment, coterminosity, empowerment,* and *stakeholder.* It also took aim at words it thought sloppy, like *facilitate* and *incentivising.*

The Top 100 Banned Words[1]

Ambassador—leader

Agencies—

Beacon—leading light

Best Practice—best way

Bottom-Up—listening to people

CAAs—Why use at all?

Can do culture—get the job done

Capacity—

Capacity building—enough room in
the system

Cascading—Why use at all?

Cautiously welcome—devil in
the detail

Champion—best

Citizen empowerment—people
power

Community engagement—getting
people involved

Conditionality—Why use at all?

Consensual—everyone agrees

Contestability—Why use at all?

Core Message—main point

Core Value—belief

Coterminosity—all singing from the
same hymn sheet

Coterminous—all singing from the
same hymn sheet

Cross-cutting—everyone
working together

Customer—people/person

Democratic mandate/legitimacy—
elected to put people first

Distorts spending priorities—ignores
people's needs

Early Win—success

Empowerment—people power

Engagement—working with people

Engaging users—getting
people involved

Enhance—improve

Evidence Base—research shows

External challenge—outside pressures

Facilitate—help

Fast-Track—speed up

Flexibilities and Freedoms—more
power to do the right thing

Framework—guide

Fulcrum—pivot

Good Practice—best way

Governance—Why use at all?

Guidelines—guide

Holistic—taken in the round

Holistic governance—Why use at all?

Improvement levers—using the tools
to get the job done

Incentivising—incentive

Income/funding streams—
money/cash

Initiative—idea

Joined up—working together

Joint working—working together

LAAs—Why use at all?

Level Playing Field—

Localities—places/town/city/village

Meaningful consultation/dialogue—
talking to people

MAAs—Why use at all?

Menu of Options—choices

Multi-agency—many groups

Multidisciplinary—many

(continued)

The Top 100 Banned Words[1] (continued)

Outcomes—results

Output—results

Participatory—joining in

Partnerships—working together

Pathfinder—Why use at all?

Peer challenge—Why use at all?

Performance Network—Why use at all?

Place shaping—creating places where people can thrive

Predictors of Beaconicity—No idea

Preventative services—protecting the most vulnerable

Priority—most important

Process driven—shouldn't everything be people driven?

Quick Hit—success

Quick Win—success

Resource allocation—money going to the right place

Revenue Streams—money

Risk based—safest way

Scaled-back—cut/reduce

Scoping—work out

Seedbed—idea

Service users—people

Shared priority—all working together

Signpost—point in the direction of

Single Point of Contact—everything under one roof

Slippage—delay

Social contracts—deal

Stakeholder—other organisations

Step Change—improve

Strategic/overarching—planned

Streamlined—efficient

Subsidiarity—federal (still not great though)

Sustainable—long term

Sustainable communities—environmentally friendly

Symposium—meeting

Synergies—what use at all?

Tested for Soundness—what works

Third sector—charities and voluntary organisations

Top-Down—ignores people

Transformational—change

Transparency—clear

Value-added—extra

Vision—ideal/dream/belief

Visionary—as above

Welcome—necessary and needed/step in the right direction

The LGA list was a shot literally heard around the world. CNN picked up the story, as did many British newspapers. For the LGA, it was part of an ongoing campaign, and previous versions attracted fierce attacks. One blogger asked, "Who in the world thought this up? I would suggest that he/she be re-assessed and transferred to Mars." The blogger thought that the LGA was suggesting citizens might not be up to sophisticated conversation. As another asked, "Are we really going to dumb down the English language to such a point that we speak to every adult as though they were a child?" Yet another: "[S]top thinking we are a bunch of illiterate buffoons unaware of what Councils [British local governments] are saying or unable to question to our satisfaction. Has there ever been a more patronising missive from LGA? Excuse me whilst I doff my cap, m'lud! I'd call it claptrap but that's probably a word 'we wouldn't understand.' "

But one blogger came to LGA's defense, writing "Some of these are mild," compared to other jargon that ruled government reports. An Australian commenter put it sharply in terms of administrative responsiveness: "I agree that the majority of the words should be avoided as many are overused" and lack any idea about how to "reinforce accountability." A third: "When acronyms, poor grammar, and words that have inappropriate meaning are cobbled together reports become unintelligible."[2]

The BBC had fun with the story by posting a photo on its website of a woman getting a holistic body massage and suggesting it was "apparently unrelated" to holistic government. Many of the words had roots in British governmental policy. One official denounced "holistic" as "gobbledegook," but pointed to past government efforts that sought to improve the coordination among government programs and thereby make government more "holistic."[3]

To American ears, British language battles can sometimes be both amusing and hard to penetrate. What can we make of a country that has car parks instead of parking lots, lifts instead of elevators, nappies instead of diapers, bangers instead of sausage, and take away for food carried out from a restaurant to be eaten elsewhere. (Some language mavens have observed that British English often makes more sense than American English—after all, elevators lift more than they elevate.) Is this a *Masterpiece Theater, Monty Python and the Holy Grail* kind of battle that is most amusing because it is quaint to Americans?

The LGA officials responsible for the list argue otherwise. One plaintively said that it really came down to communication with citizens and how accountability works—how government connects with citizens, and how clearly the connections happen. "My big point has always been that the private sector is good at this and the public sector isn't." Look at the Nintendo Wii, he said. "It has lots of high-tech gizmos in it that are truly cutting edge but when they talk to people about it . . . in marketing, etc., they don't mention the 87 wigabite memory or the Atheon Rayon xd36sdjd processor—they just say it's great fun." [Don't try to look up this configuration—his tongue was firmly in cheek.] Otherwise, he said, they wouldn't sell their machines and they would go broke. The public sector, by contrast, doesn't really connect with people in terms they want or appreciate. His conclusion: too often, government officials just don't get it, and accountability is weaker for the failure.[4]

Questions to Consider

1. Do you think words matter in how government officials communicate with the public? What suggestions would you have for the list of 100 words? Are there any you would propose taking off the list? (Remember that commentators often hail the Declaration of Independence and the Gettysburg Address as great pieces of literature, though language scholars have battled for centuries over Jefferson's use of "inalienable" rights in the Declaration.)

2. Do you think that the choice of words affects the accountability of government? If so, how? Do mystical words or expressions full of jargon enhance government's power or weaken its connection with citizens? Or both?

3. Think about your role as citizen. How would you like government to communicate with you? About what?

4. How would you view the issue if you were a government official? How do you think you ought to communicate with citizens?

Notes

1. Local Government Association (London: LGA, 2008), http://www.lga.gov.uk/lga/core/page.do?pageId=41517.
2. http://www.idea.gov.uk/idk/core/page.do?PAGEID=77-1430.
3. http://news.bbc.co.uk/1/hi/magazine/7470076.stm.
4. Email to the author, June 26, 2008.

Key Concepts

administrative confidentiality **458**

appropriations committees **453**

authorizing committees **453**

executive privilege **457**

Government Performance and Results Act (GPRA) **466**

legislative review **453**

signing statement **447**

For Further Reading

Aberbach, Joel D. *Keeping a Watchful Eye: The Politics of Congressional Oversight.* Washington, D.C.: Brookings Institution Press, 1990.

Arnold, R. Douglas. *Congress and the Bureaucracy: A Theory of Influence.* New Haven: Yale University Press, 1979.

Dodd, Lawrence C., and Richard L. Schott. *Congress and the Administrative State.* New York: Wiley, 1979.

Foreman, Christopher H., Jr. *Signals from the Hill: Congressional Oversight and the Challenge of Social Regulation.* New Haven: Yale University Press, 1988.

Heclo, Hugh. "Issue Networks and the Executive Establishment." In *The New Political System,* ed. Anthony King. Washington, D.C.: American Enterprise Institute, 1978, 87–124.

Mayhew, David R. *Congress: The Electoral Connection.* New Haven: Yale University Press, 1974.

Mosher, Frederick C. *The GAO: The Quest for Accountability in American Government.* Boulder, Colo.: Westview Press, 1979.

Scher, Seymour. "Conditions for Legislative Control." *Journal of Politics* 25 (August 1963): 526–551.

Suggested Websites

Each federal agency annually publishes the reports required by the Government Performance and Results Act; the reports are available on the agencies' websites. For example, the reports for the Department of Defense can be found at **http://www .defenselink.mil/comptroller/par.** For the Food and Drug Administration, the report can be found here: http://www.fda.gov/ope/gpra/gpraext.htm.

The Government Accountability Office website, **http://www.gao.gov,** is a treasure trove of reports on the performance of government agencies.

Finally, the Office of Management and Budget website (**http://www.whitehouse .gov/omb**) contains a great deal of useful information on the performance of government agencies, including the reports OMB requires in support of the annual budgetary process.

1. Politics and Administration

1. H. Josef Hebert, "EPA Scientists Complain about Political Pressure," Associated Press, http://ap.google.com/article/ALeqM5jiG8PT3cEiOqXFkMJuutD97RCoeQD907NRL00 (accessed April 23, 2008).

2. Letter from EPA Administrator Stephen L. Johnson to California Governor Arnold Schwarzenegger, December 19, 2007, http://www.epa.gov/otaq/climate/20071219-slj.pdf.

3. Janet Wilson, "EPA Chief Is Said to Have Ignored Staff," *Los Angeles Times,* December 21, 2007, http://www.latimes.com/news/printedition/california/la-me-epa21dec21,0, 7077099,full.story?coll=la-headlines-pe-california.

4. Margaret Kriz, "EPA Is Missing in Action on Major Environmental Issues, Observers Charge," GovExec.com, April 14, 2008, http://www.govexec.com/story_page_pf.cfm? articleid=39772.

5. Woodrow Wilson, "The Study of Administration," *Political Science Quarterly* 2 (June 1887): 220.

6. *Responses of the Presidents to Charges of Misconduct,* ed. C. Vann Woodward (New York: Dell, 1974), 9.

7. John P. Burke, *Bureaucratic Responsibility* (Baltimore: Johns Hopkins University Press, 1986), 10. He claims, too boldly it appears, that "one of the essential claims of formal legalism is that bureaucrats should have no discretion in either making or implementing policy" (11). A close analogy to the formal-legal concept is the legal doctrine of principal-agent relations, which allows for the agent to use discretion on behalf of his or her principal's interests.

8. See Douglas Yates, *Bureaucratic Democracy: The Search for Democracy and Efficiency in American Government* (Cambridge, Mass.: Harvard University Press, 1982), esp. 8–61; and Arthur M. Okun, *Equality and Efficiency: The Big Tradeoff* (Washington, D.C.: Brookings Institution Press, 1975).

9. Judith E. Gruber, *Controlling Bureaucracies: Dilemmas in Democratic Governance* (Berkeley: University of California Press, 1987), esp. 202–214.

10. This effect is not guaranteed. As noted in chapter 12, the Office of Management and Budget's (OMB) requirement that regulatory agencies submit proposed studies and regulations for its review resulted, during the Reagan administration, in OMB rejection of some important regulatory initiatives closely attuned to statutory mandates.

11. Peter Self, *Administrative Theories and Politics* (London: Allen and Unwin, 1972), 277–278. (Emphasis in original.)

12. Juvenal, *Satires,* line 347. Our free translation communicates more immediately and less ambiguously than the standard translations, such as "Who will be guarding the guards?" "Who is to keep guard over the guards?" and "Who will watch the Warders"—particularly as Juvenal's point is distrust of the eunuchs guarding a man's mistresses.

13. "The need for operative ideas on how to make accountability a reality under modern conditions is urgent, but it must be admitted that there is a remarkable dearth of such ideas despite great dissatisfaction with the present state of affairs and with the older . . . notions of accountability." *The Dilemma of Accountability in Modern Government,* ed. Bruce L. R. Smith and D. C. Hague (New York: St. Martin's, 1971), 28.

14. Smith and Hague, *Dilemma of Accountability,* 29.

15. We should not be interpreted as going so far as one scholar: "Bureaucrats ought not determine which of several competing demands they should follow, nor should they themselves 'scale down' impossibly high expectations. They should, however, refuse to be 'passed the buck,' and they should encourage higher authorities to make proper decisions." And "Bureaucrats incur responsibilities to make sure that policy makers provide the resources necessary to their policy tasks." Burke, *Bureaucratic Responsibility,* 51, 82.

16. Albert O. Hirschman, *Exit, Voice, and Loyalty: Responses to Decline in Firms, Organizations, and States* (Cambridge, Mass.: Harvard University Press, 1970).

17. See Carl J. Friedrich, "Public Policy and the Nature of Administrative Responsibility," in *Public Policy,* ed. Carl J. Friedrich and E. S. Mason (Cambridge, Mass.: Harvard University Press, 1940), 3–24; and Herman Finer, "Administrative Responsibility in Democratic Government," *Public Administration Review* 1 (Summer 1941): 335–350.

18. Ethical breakdowns in the 1980s partly account for growth of the literature about governmental ethics. See John A. Rohr, *Ethics for Bureaucrats: An Essay on Law and Values,* 2nd ed. (New York: Marcel Dekker, 1989); James S. Bowman and Frederick A. Elliston, eds., *Ethics, Government, and Public Policy: A Reference Guide* (Westport, Conn.: Greenwood Press, 1988); and Robert N. Roberts, *White House Ethics: The History of the Politics of Conflict of Interest Regulation* (Westport, Conn.: Greenwood Press, 1988).

19. G. Calvin Mackenzie, " 'If You Want to Play, You've Got to Pay': Ethics Regulation and the Presidential Appointments System, 1964–1984," in *The In-and-Outers: Presidential Appointees and Transient Government in Washington,* ed. G. Calvin Mackenzie (Baltimore: Johns Hopkins University Press, 1987), 77.

20. Michael A. Nutter, Inaugural Address, January 7, 2008, http://media.philly.com/documents/NutterInauguralSpeechFinal.pdf.

21. Preamble to the Constitution of the United States.

22. "Remarks to the Members of the Senior Executive Service," January 26, 1989, *Weekly Compilation of Presidential Documents* 25, 117–119.

2. Administrative Responsibility

1. Dwight Waldo, *The Administrative State: A Study of the Political Theory of American Public Administration* (New York: Ronald Press, 1948).

2. See, for example, *A Centennial History of the American Administrative State,* ed. Ralph Clark Chandler (New York: Free Press, 1987); John A. Rohr, *To Run a Constitution: The Legitimacy of the Administrative State* (Lawrence: University Press of Kansas, 1986); Lawrence C. Dodd and Richard L. Schott, *Congress and the Administrative State* (New York: Wiley, 1979); Emmette S. Redford, *Democracy and the Administrative State* (New York: Oxford University Press, 1969); David H. Rosenbloom, *Building a Legislative-Centered Public Administration: Congress and the Administrative State, 1946–1999* (Tuscaloosa: University of Alabama Press, 2000).

3. Honorè de Balzac, *Les Employès*. English translations carry various titles (e.g., *The Civil Service, Bureaucracy,* and *The Government Clerks*).

4. These and other meanings are fully analyzed in Martin Albrow, *Bureaucracy* (New York: Holt, Rinehart, and Winston, 1971).

5. Nikolai I. Ryzhkov, speaking to the seventeenth Communist Party Congress, quoted in Philip Taubman, "Soviet Premier, in Congress Talk, Criticizes Economy," *New York Times,* March 4, 1986; Zhao Ziyang (later named general secretary of China's Communist Party), quoted in Edward A. Gargan, "More Change Due in China's Economy," *New York Times,* October 26, 1987.

6. For example, see Donald F. Kettl, *The Global Public Management Revolution: A Report on the Transformation of Governance* (Washington, D.C.: Brookings Institution, 2000).

7. For a well-documented and well-argued case explaining and defending bureaucracy, see Charles T. Goodsell, *The Case for Bureaucracy: A Public Administration Polemic,* 4th ed. (Washington, D.C.: CQ Press, 2004).

8. For a thorough exploration of the definitional problem, see A. Dunsire, *Administration: The Word and the Science* (New York: Wiley, 1973).

9. Dwight Waldo, *The Study of Public Administration* (Garden City, N.Y.: Doubleday, 1955), 5–6; and Herbert A. Simon, *Administrative Behavior* (New York: Macmillan, 1947; 3rd ed., New York: Free Press, 1976), 72–73. How one ascertains what the goals are and relates rational action to them is a difficult problem, recognized by both Waldo and Simon, as is the nonrational dimension of human behavior.

10. For a review of these arguments, see Harold F. Gortner, Julianne Mahler, and Jeanne Bell Nicholson, *Organization Theory: A Public Perspective* (Chicago: Dorsey Press, 1987), 16; and Gary L. Wamsley and Mayer N. Zald, *The Political Economy of Public Organizations: A Critique and Approach to the Study of Public Administration* (Bloomington: Indiana University Press, 1973), 4.

11. Douglas Yates Jr., *The Politics of Management* (San Francisco: Jossey-Bass, 1985), 7.

12. Barry Bozeman, *All Organizations Are Public: Bridging Public and Private Organization Theories* (San Francisco: Jossey-Bass, 1987), 83–85.

13. William A. Robson, "The Managing of Organizations," *Public Administration* (London) 44 (Autumn 1966): 276.

14. Dwight Waldo, *The Enterprise of Public Administration: A Summary View* (Novato, Calif.: Chandler and Sharp, 1980), 164. Compare Bozeman, *All Organizations Are Public,* 5; and Hal G. Rainey, Robert W. Backoff, and Charles H. Levine, "Comparing Public and Private Organizations," *Public Administration Review* 36 (March–April 1976): 234.

15. See Graham T. Allison Jr., "Public and Private Management: Are They Fundamentally Alike in All Unimportant Respects?" in *Current Issues in Public Administration,* 3rd ed., ed. Frederick S. Lane (New York: St. Martin's, 1986), 184–200.

16. Some theorists, for example, argue that the distinction is based on who benefits; public agencies are those whose prime beneficiary is the public. See Peter M. Blau and W. Richard Scott, *Formal Organizations: A Comparative Approach* (San Francisco: Chandler, 1962), 42–43. Others have argued that they are distinctive because of who owns and funds them; public agencies are those "owned" by the state. See Wamsley and Zald, *Political Economy of Public Organization,* 8.

17. Gortner, Mahler, and Nicholson, *Organization Theory,* 26.

18. U.S. Code 31, § 1341.

19. There are, of course, requirements for private officials and their organizations to comply with governmental standards. But, in general, the point applies: in the private sector, officials and their organizations are free to follow their own judgment except as the law applies.

20. Steven Kelman, presentation to Seventeenth Intergovernmental Audit Forum (Philadelphia: May 22, 2008).

21. These distinctions are based on comparisons developed by John T. Dunlop and summarized in Allison, "Public and Private Management," 17–18. See also Ralph Clark Chandler, "Epilogue," in Chandler, *Centennial History*, 580–586; and Rainey, Backoff, and Levine, "Comparing Public and Private Organizations."

22. Anthony Downs, *Inside Bureaucracy* (Boston: Little, Brown, 1967), 30.

23. Arthur Okun, *Equality and Efficiency: The Big Tradeoff* (Washington, D.C.: Brookings Institution, 1975).

24. See Marver H. Bernstein, *The Job of the Federal Government Executive* (Washington, D.C.: Brookings Institution, 1958), 26–28; James W. Fesler et al., *Industrial Mobilization for War* (Washington, D.C.: Government Printing Office, 1947), 971–972. The "goldfish-bowl" phenomenon applies specifically to the United States, rather than to public administration everywhere. See Harold L. Wilensky, *Organizational Intelligence* (New York: Basic Books, 1967), 116–118.

25. Wallace Sayre, "The Unhappy Bureaucrats: Views Ironic, Helpful, Indignant," *Public Administration Review* 10 (Summer 1958): 245.

26. See *Revitalizing Federal Management: Managers and Their Overburdened Systems: A Panel Report* (Washington, D.C.: National Academy of Public Administration, 1983); and National Commission on the Public Service, *Urgent Business for America: Revitalizing the Federal Government for the 21st Century* (Washington, D.C.: January 2003), http://www.brook.edu/dybdocroot/gs/cps/volcker/reportfinal.pdf.

27. For example, see Anne M. Khademian, *Working with Culture: How the Job Gets Done in Public Programs* (Washington, D.C.: CQ Press, 2002).

28. For the variety of approaches, see *Public Administration: The State of the Discipline*, ed. Naomi B. Lynn and Aaron Wildavsky (Chatham, N.J.: Chatham House, 1990); and Chandler, *Centennial History*.

29. Dwight Waldo, "Politics and Administration: On Thinking about a Complex Relationship," in Chandler, *Centennial History*, 89–112, at 96–104.

30. See Frank J. Goodnow, *Politics and Administration* (New York: Macmillan, 1900). Wilson is discussed later in this chapter.

31. Nicholas Henry, "The Emergence of Public Administration as a Field of Study," in Chandler, *Centennial History*, 37–85. See also *American Public Administration: Past, Present, and Future*, ed. Frederick C. Mosher (Tuscaloosa: University of Alabama Press, 1975).

32. Luther Gulick, "Time and Public Administration," *Public Administration Review* 47 (January–February 1987): 115–119.

33. Carl J. Friedrich, *Man and His Government* (New York: McGraw-Hill, 1963), 464–483. The remarkable and lasting innovations in British and French administrative institutions and methods in the twelfth to fourteenth centuries are treated in James W. Fesler, "The Presence of the Administrative Past," in *American Public Administration: Patterns of the Past*, ed. James W. Fesler (Washington, D.C.: American Society for Public Administration, 1982), 1–27, at 3–16. A comprehensive administrative history, much broader

than its title, is Carolyn Webber and Aaron Wildavsky, *A History of Taxation and Expenditure in the Western World* (New York: Simon and Schuster, 1986).

34. Alexis de Tocqueville, *Democracy in America* (New York: Knopf, 1945), 1:211–212; paperback ed. (New York: Vintage Books, 1954), 1:219–220.

35. All quotations of Woodrow Wilson are from his "The Study of Administration," *Political Science Quarterly* 2 (June 1887), as reprinted in *Political Quarterly* 56 (December 1941): 481–506. As the first scholarly article urging attention to public administration, it is often described as "seminal"; however, the article was not widely read until its reprinting in 1941. For a full canvass of Wilson's significance, see *Politics and Administration: Woodrow Wilson and American Public Administration,* ed. Jack Rabin and James S. Bowman (New York: Marcel Dekker, 1984); and Daniel W. Martin, "The Fading Legacy of Woodrow Wilson," *Public Administration Review* 48 (March–April 1988): 631–636.

36. Fesler, *American Public Administration.* An excellent starting point is Stephen Skowronek, *Building a New American State: The Expansion of National Administrative Capacities, 1877–1920* (New York: Cambridge University Press, 1982).

37. Christopher Pollitt, *Time, Policy, Management: Governing with the Past* (Oxford: Oxford University Press, 2008), 2.

38. The list is not exhaustive. See James G. March, "How We Talk and How We Act: Administrative Theory and Administrative Life," in *Leadership and Organization Culture: New Perspectives on Administrative Theory and Practice,* ed. Thomas J. Sergiovanni and John E. Corbally (Urbana: University of Illinois Press, 1984, 1986), 18–35, esp. 21.

39. For a broad critique, see Charles Perrow, *Complex Organizations,* 3rd ed. (New York: Random House, 1986).

40. The concept of overlays is presented in John M. Pfiffner and Frank R. Sherwood, *Administrative Organization* (Englewood Cliffs, N.J.: Prentice Hall, 1960), 16–32. They propose a basic sheet portraying the formal structure of authority, with five overlays: sociometric ("contacts people have with each other because of personal attraction"); functional (arising out of "the relationships created by technical experts" and the authority they exercise "because of their superior Knowledge and skills"); decisional; power; and communication.

3. What Government Does—And How It Does It

1. Seymour Martin Lipset and William Schneider, *The Confidence Gap: Business, Labor and Government in the Public Mind,* rev. ed. (Baltimore: Johns Hopkins University Press, 1987), 378, 380.

2. Ibid., 380.

3. John 7:24, quoted by Frederick C. Mosher and Orville F. Poland, *The Costs of American Governments: Facts, Trends, Myths* (New York: Dodd, Mead, 1964), 1.

4. Press Office Fact Sheet, "Social Security Basic Facts," http://www.ssa.gov/pressoffice/basicfact.htm.

5. *Wall Street Journal,* March 17, 1989, A1.

6. Philip Shenon, "Chilean Fruit Pulled from Shelves as U.S. Widens Inquiry on Poison," *New York Times,* March 15, 1989, http://query.nytimes.com/gst/fullpage.htm?res=950DE4DC1430F936A2570C0A96F948260&sec=&spon=&pagewanted=all.

7. National Air Traffic Controllers Association, "Air Traffic Control: By the Numbers," http://www.natca.org/mediacenter/bythenumbers.msp.

8. New York City, Citywide Performance Reporting (2008), http://www.nyc.gov/ html/ops/cpr/html/themes/all_frame.shtml?http://a858-anltw.nyc.gov/analytics/ saw.dll?Dashboard&PortalPath=/shared/NYC311%20OTW/_Portal/CPR%20OTW&P age=Agency%20Performance&Options=f&Action=Navigate&P0=1&P1=eq&P2=Agen cy.AgencyName&P3=1+Fire%20Department%20of%20New%20York&NQUser=aye4 85xAWZp&NQPassword=ksTT3caK2a2z&Syndicate=Siebel.

9. Port of Los Angeles, http://www.portoflosangeles.org/newsroom/about.asp.

10. For the classic exposition of the "marble cake" argument, see Morton Grodzins, *The American System: A New View of Government in the United States,* ed. Daniel J. Elazar (Chicago: Rand McNally, 1966).

11. Robin Toner, "Pollsters See a Silent Storm that Swept Away Democrats," *New York Times,* November 16, 1994, A13. Budget figures from Congressional Budget Office, *The Economic and Budget Outlook: Fiscal Years 1995–1999* (Washington, D.C.: Government Printing Office, 1994).

12. Program on International Policy Attitudes, "Americans on Foreign Aid and World Hunger: A Study of U.S. Public Attitudes" (2001), http://www.pipa.org/OnlineReports/ BFW/finding2.html.

13. Calculated from Office of Management and Budget, *Budget of the United States Government, Fiscal Year 2005: Historical Tables and Analytical Perspectives.*

14. Christopher C. Hood, *The Tools of Government* (Chatham, N.J.: Chatham House, 1983), 2. For other examples of the "tools" approach to public administration, see Donald F. Kettl, *Government by Proxy: (Mis?) Managing Federal Programs* (Washington, D.C.: CQ Press, 1988); and Lester M. Salamon, ed., *Beyond Privatization: The Tools of Government Action* (Washington, D.C.: Urban Institute, 1989).

15. See Lester M. Salamon, "The New Governance and the Tools of Public Action: An Introduction," in *The Tools of Government: A Guide to the New Governance,* ed. Salamon (New York: Oxford University Press, 2002), 1.

16. Salamon, "The New Governance and the Tools of Public Action," in Salamon, *The Tools of Government,* 5.

17. Donald Haider, "Grants as a Tool of Public Policy," in Salamon, *Beyond Privatization,* 93.

18. Office of Management and Budget, *Budget of the United States Government, Fiscal Year 2009: Analytical Perspectives* (Washington, D.C.: Government Printing Office, 2008), 289.

19. For a review of tax expenditures, see Stanley S. Surrey and Paul R. McDaniel, *Tax Expenditures* (Cambridge, Mass.: Harvard University Press, 1985); John F. Witte, *The Politics and Development of the Federal Income Tax* (Madison: University of Wisconsin Press, 1985); and Paul R. McDaniel, "Tax Expenditures as Tools of Government Action," in Salamon, *Beyond Privatization,* 167–196.

20. Lester M. Salamon, "Rethinking Public Management: Third-Party Government and the Changing Forms of Government Action," *Public Policy* 29 (Summer 1981): 260.

21. Ted Kolderie, "The Two Different Concepts of Privatization," *Public Administration Review* 46 (July–August 1986): 285–291.

4. Foundations of Organizational Theory

1. For an exceptionally thoughtful review of organizational theory, see H. George Frederickson and Kevin B. Smith, *Public Administration Theory Primer* (Boulder, Colo.: Westview Press, 2003).

2. Daniel Katz and Robert L. Kahn, *The Social Psychology of Organizations,* 2nd ed. (New York: Wiley, 1978), 188, 196. Note, however, the caveat: "Role expectations are by no means restricted to the job description as it might be given by the head of the organization or prepared by some specialist in personnel, although these individuals are likely to be influential members of the role set of many persons in the organization" (p. 190).

3. Here we are merely laying the ground for the structural approach to governmental administration. For more substantial analysis of the complex issue of authority, see, for example, Carl J. Friedrich, *Man and His Government* (New York: McGraw-Hill, 1963); and Charles E. Lindblom, *Politics and Markets* (New York: Basic Books, 1977), 17–32.

4. Luther Gulick, "Notes on the Theory of Organization," in *Papers on the Science of Administration,* ed. L. Gulick and L. Urwick (New York: Institute of Public Administration, 1937), 1–45. For an attack on that essay, see Herbert Simon, *Administrative Behavior* (New York: Macmillan, 1947, and later editions), 20–44. For reviews of the controversy, see Alan A. Altshuler, "The Study of Administration," in *The Politics of the Federal Bureaucracy,* 2nd ed., ed. Alan A. Altshuler and Norman C. Thomas (New York: Harper and Row, 1977), 2–17; Vincent Ostrom, *The Intellectual Crisis in Public Administration* (Tuscaloosa: University of Alabama Press, 1973), 36–47; Brian R. Fry, *Mastering Public Administration: From Max Weber to Dwight Waldo* (Chatham, N.J.: Chatham House, 1989), 73–97; and Thomas H. Hammond, "In Defense of Luther Gulick's 'Notes on the Theory of Organization,' " *Public Administration* (London) 58 (Summer 1990).

5. Gulick, "Theory of Organization," 31.

6. Weber's views became accessible to American readers through two translations of portions of his works, which appeared in 1946 and 1947 and were reprinted in the following paperback editions: *From Max Weber: Essays in Sociology,* trans. and ed. H. H. Gerth and C. Wright Mills (New York: Oxford University Press, 1958), and *The Theory of Social and Economic Organization,* trans. A. M. Henderson and Talcott Parsons (New York: Free Press, 1964).

7. Weber, *Theory of Social and Economic Organization,* 328.

8. Weber, *From Max Weber,* 209.

9. Weber, *Theory of Social and Economic Organization,* 330.

10. Ibid., 337.

11. Weber, *From Max Weber,* 196–197.

12. Ibid., 228.

13. See Talcott Parsons's introduction to Weber, *Theory of Social and Economic Organization,* 56, 58–60n.

14. Systems theory and its organizational derivatives are more fully treated in Katz and Kahn, *Social Psychology of Organizations,* 17–34; and Chadwick J. Haberstroh, "Organization Design and Systems Analysis," in *Handbook of Organizations,* ed. James G. March (Chicago: Rand McNally, 1965), 1171–1211.

15. For a trenchant argument that an organization's survival is the lucky result of natural selection processes rather than of efforts to achieve that objective, see Herbert Kaufman, *Time, Chance, and Organizations: Natural Selection in a Perilous Environment* (Chatham, N.J.: Chatham House, 1985).

16. Sir Eric (later Lord) Ashby, *Technology and the Academics* (New York: Macmillan, 1958), 67–68.

17. President-elect Nixon, announcing his choice of cabinet members, quoted in *Congressional Quarterly Weekly Report* 26 (December 13, 1968): 3263.

18. President Nixon's Message to Congress, March 25, 1971, in Office of Management and Budget, Executive Office of the President, *Papers Relating to the President's Departmental Reorganization Program* (Washington, D.C.: Government Printing Office, March 1971), 7.

19. *United States Government Manual 1973/74* (Washington, D.C.: Government Printing Office, 1973), 94.

20. *USDA Performance and Accountability Report for FY2003,* http://www.usda.gov/ocfo/usdarpt/pdf/par04.pdf.

21. Systems theories vary in attentiveness to authority. For a work that does incorporate authority and its hierarchical structuring in a systems framework, see Katz and Kahn, *Social Psychology of Organizations,* esp. 199–222.

22. Frederick Winslow Taylor, *The Principles of Scientific Management* (New York: Harper and Brothers, 1911; Mineola, N.Y.: Dover, 1998). See Fry, *Mastering Public Administration,* 47–72.

23. Taylor, *Principles of Scientific Management,* 28.

24. An early canvass of this literature is in James G. March and Herbert Simon, *Organizations* (New York: Wiley, 1957), although it is puzzling that the findings were not brought to bear on the book's later concerns with organizational structure and processes.

25. For reports of the research and reappraisals of the findings, see George C. Homans, *The Human Group* (New York: Harcourt Brace Jovanovich, 1950); and H. M. Persons, "What Happened at Hawthorne?" *Science* 183 (March 8, 1974): 922–932.

26. "Group members tend to feel better satisfied under moderate degrees of structure than under overly structured or totally unstructured situations. But they prefer too much structure over none at all. Groups tend to be more productive and more cohesive in structured rather than unstructured situations. Formal structure does not necessarily block satisfaction of needs for autonomy and self-actualization. Some degree of structure is necessary for the satisfaction of follower needs." Bernard M. Bass, *Stogdill's Handbook of Leadership: A Survey of Theory and Research,* rev. and exp. ed. (New York: Free Press, 1981), 588–589.

27. Edwin A. Locke, "The Nature and Causes of Job Satisfaction," in *Handbook of Industrial and Organizational Psychology,* ed. Marvin D. Dunnette (Chicago: Rand McNally, 1976), 1297–1349, at 1332. As Locke points out, the human relationists' causal arrow may point the wrong way; that is, high productivity may be a cause of high satisfaction.

28. Chris Argyris, "Being Human and Being Organized," *Transaction* 2 (July 1964): 5. See also his "Some Limits of Rational Man Organization Theory," *Public Administration Review* 33 (May–June 1973): 253–267, esp. 253–254, 263–265.

29. For a full description and critique of the human relations model, see Charles Perrow, *Complex Organizations,* 3rd ed. (New York: Random House, 1986), 79–118. See also H. Roy Kaplan and Curt Tausky, "Humanism in Organizations: A Critical Appraisal," *Public Administration Review* 37 (March–April 1977): 171–180.

30. Douglas McGregor, *The Human Side of Enterprise* (New York: McGraw-Hill, 1960), 33–57.

31. Lawrence B. Mohr, *Explaining Organizational Behavior: The Limits and Possibilities of Theory and Research* (San Francisco: Jossey-Bass, 1982), 125–153; and Bass, *Stogdill's Handbook of Leadership,* passim.

32. Abraham H. Maslow, "The Superior Person," *Transaction* 1 (May 1964): 12–13. For a major test of "the participation hypothesis" in public administration, see *Government*

Reorganizations: Cases and Commentary, ed. Frederick C. Mosher (Indianapolis: Bobbs-Merrill, 1967).

33. Bass, *Stogdill's Handbook of Leadership,* 560–565.

34. Among the many writings illustrative of the pluralistic approach to public administration, three classics are David B. Truman, *The Governmental Process,* 2nd ed. (New York: Knopf, 1971), esp. 395–478; J. Leiper Freeman, *The Political Process: Executive Bureau–Legislative Committee Relations,* rev. ed. (New York: Random House, 1965); and Francis E. Rourke, *Bureaucracy, Politics, and Public Policy,* 3rd ed. (Boston: Little, Brown, 1984).

35. Rourke, *Bureaucracy, Politics, and Public Policy.* See also Carl E. Van Horn, William T. Gormley Jr., and Donald C. Baumer, *Politics and Public Policy,* 3rd ed. (Washington, D.C.: CQ Press, 2001).

36. A good introduction is J. Steven Ott, *The Organizational Culture Perspective* (Chicago: Dorsey Press, 1989). See also Edgar H. Schein, *Organizational Culture and Leadership* (San Francisco: Jossey-Bass, 1987); Michel Crozier, *The Bureaucratic Phenomenon* (Chicago: University of Chicago Press, 1964); and Anne Khademian, *Working with Culture: The Way the Job Gets Done in Public Programs* (Washington, D.C.: CQ Press, 2002).

37. Spatial relations are rarely treated in the literature. For a valuable exception, see Frederick C. Mosher, *A Tale of Two Agencies: A Comparative Analysis of the General Accounting Office and the Office of Management and Budget* (Baton Rouge: Louisiana State University Press, 1984), 87–98. The whole book usefully contrasts the organizational cultures of the two agencies.

38. Harold Seidman and Robert Gilmour, *Politics, Position, and Power: From the Positive to the Regulatory State,* 4th ed. (New York: Oxford University Press, 1986), 167. See pp. 166–194, on "The Executive Establishment, Culture and Personality."

39. Donald F. Kettl, *Leadership at the Fed* (New Haven: Yale University Press, 1986). The dominance issue is treated at pp. 30–32 and 85–88.

40. Herbert Kaufman, *The Forest Ranger: A Study in Administrative Behavior* (Baltimore: Johns Hopkins University Press, 1960).

41. National Aeronautics and Space Administration, *Assessment and Plan for Organizational Culture Change at NASA* (Washington, D.C.: NASA, 2004), 4.

42. Warren E. Leary, "Better Communication Is NASA's Next Frontier," *New York Times,* April 14, 2004, A22.

43. Frederick C. Mosher, "The Changing Responsibilities and Tactics of the Federal Government," in *American Public Administration: Patterns of the Past,* ed. James W. Fesler (Washington, D.C.: American Society for Public Administration, 1982), 198–212; quoted passage at 201. See also Lester H. Salamon, "Rethinking Public Management: Third-Party Government and the Changing Forms of Government Action," *Public Policy* 29 (Summer 1981): 259–278; and Lester H. Salamon, ed., *The Tools of Government: A Guide to the New Governance* (New York: Oxford University Press, 2002).

44. See, for example, Howard Aldrich and David A. Whettan, "Organization-Sets, Action-Sets, and Networks: Making the Most of Simplicity," in *Handbook of Organizational Design,* vol. 1, *Adapting Organizations to Their Environments,* ed. Paul C. Nystrom and William H. Starbuck (New York: Oxford University Press, 1981), 385–408; W. W. Powell, "Neither Market nor Hierarchy: Network Forms of Organization," in *Research in Organizational Behavior,* ed. B. Staw and L. L. Cummings (Greenwich, Conn.: JAI Press, 1990), 295–336; Robert Agranoff, "Human Services Integration: Past and Present Challenges in Public

Administration," *Public Administration Review* 51 (1991): 533–542; H. Brinton Milward and Keith G. Provan, "Services Integration and Outcome Effectiveness: An Empirical Test of an Implicit Theory," paper presented at the 1993 annual conference of the Association for Public Policy Analysis and Management; Fritz W. Scharpf, "Coordination in Hierarchies and Networks," in *Games in Hierarchies and Networks: Analytical and Empirical Approaches to the Study of Governance and Institutions,* ed. Fritz W. Scharpf (Boulder, Colo.: Westview Press, 1993), 125–165; and Eugene Bardach, "Generic Models in the Study of Public Management," paper presented at the 1993 conference of the Association for Public Policy Analysis and Management.

45. Eugene Bardach, "But Can Networks Produce?" paper prepared for the conference on "Network Analysis and Innovations in Public Programs," La Follette Institute of Public Affairs, University of Wisconsin–Madison, 1994, 2.

46. Rosemary O'Leary, Lisa Blomgren Bingham, and Catherine Gerard, guest eds., Special Issue on Collaborative Public Management, *Public Administration Review* 66 (2007).

47. The section that follows is adapted from Donald F. Kettl, *The Transformation of Governance: Public Administration for the 21st Century* (Baltimore: Johns Hopkins University Press, 2002), 88–90.

48. See Harrison C. White, "Agency as Control," in *Principals and Agents: The Structure of Business,* ed. John W. Pratt and Richard J. Zeckhauser (Boston: Harvard Business School Press, 1985), 187–212.

49. See Ronald H. Coase, "The Nature of the Firm," *Economica* 4 (1937): 386–405; and Oliver E. Williamson, *Markets and Hierarchies: Analysis and Antitrust Implications* (New York: Free Press, 1975).

50. See B. Dan Wood and Richard W. Waterman, "The Dynamics of Political Control of the Bureaucracy," *American Political Science Review* 85 (1991): 801–828.

51. Charles Perrow, "Economic Theories of Organization," *Theory and Society* 15 (1986): 41.

52. Terry M. Moe, "The New Economics of Organization," *American Journal of Political Science* 28 (1984): 739–777; and "An Assessment of the Positive Theory of 'Congressional Dominance,'" *Legislative Studies Quarterly* 12 (1987): 475–520.

53. For a comprehensive review of theories we have discussed—and many more (reinforcing the impression of disparity)—see Jeffrey Pfeffer, "Organizations and Organization Theory," in *Handbook of Social Psychology,* vol. 1, ed. Gardner Lindzey and Elliot Aronson (New York: Random House, 1985), 379–435.

5. Strategies and Tactics for Administrative Reform

1. Portions of this chapter were originally presented at a conference in Brisbane, Australia, sponsored by the Australian Fulbright Symposium on Public Sector Reform. The conference, "New Ideas, Better Government," was held on June 23–24, 1994, and was organized by the Griffith University Centre for Australian Public Sector Management. We are grateful to the conference organizers, Glyn Davis and Patrick Weller, for their support of the research and for their permission to use the material developed for the conference in this chapter.

2. Organization for Economic Cooperation and Development, *Government of the Future* (Paris: OECD, 2001), 15.

3. Roy Bahl, *Financing State and Local Governments in the 1980s* (New York: Oxford University Press, 1984), 184–185.

4. Irene Rubin, *The Politics of Public Budgeting: Getting and Spending, Borrowing and Balancing,* 2nd ed. (Chatham, N.J.: Chatham House, 1993), 51–52.

5. J. Richard Aronson and John Hilley, *Financing State and Local Governments,* 4th ed. (Washington, D.C.: Brookings Institution, 1986), 223–224.

6. Ciruli Associates, "Coloradans Support TABOR Amendment Limits on Taxes and Government Spending," February 19, 2003, http://www.ciruli.com/polls/tabor03.htm.

7. See Bahl, *Financing State and Local Government.*

8. E. S. Savas, *Privatizing the Public Sector: How to Shrink Government* (Chatham, N.J.: Chatham House, 1982), 16–17.

9. President's Private Sector Survey on Cost Control (Grace Commission), *A Report to the President* (Washington, D.C.: Government Printing Office, 1984), II-1.

10. Charles Goodsell, "The Grace Commission: Seeking Efficiency for the Whole People," *Public Administration Review* 44 (May–June 1984): 196–204.

11. David Osborne and Ted Gaebler, *Reinventing Government: How the Entrepreneurial Spirit Is Transforming the Public Sector, from Schoolhouse to State-house, City Hall to the Pentagon* (Reading, Mass.: Addison-Wesley, 1993).

12. Al Gore, *From Red Tape to Results: Creating a Government That Works Better and Costs Less* (Washington, D.C.: Government Printing Office, 1993), iii–iv.

13. General Accounting Office, *Federal Employment: The Results to Date of the Fiscal Year 1994 Buyouts at Non-Defense Agencies,* GGD-94-214, September 1994.

14. Osborne and Gaebler, *Reinventing Government.*

15. William Niskanen, *Bureaucracy and Representative Government* (Chicago: Aldine Atherton, 1971); Savas, *Privatizing the Public Sector;* and Andrè Blais and Stèphane Dion, *The Budget-Maximizing Bureaucrat: Appraisals and Evidence* (Pittsburgh: University of Pittsburgh Press, 1991).

16. General Accounting Office, *High Risk Series: An Update,* GAO-01-263, January 2002, 73.

17. Donald F. Kettl, *Sharing Power: Public Governance and Private Markets* (Washington, D.C.: Brookings Institution, 1993).

18. Michael Hammer and James Champy, *Reengineering the Corporation: A Manifesto for Business Revolution* (New York: HarperBusiness, 1993).

19. Jerry Mechling, "Reengineering Part of Your Game Plan? A Guide for Public Managers," *Governing* 7 (February 1994): 41–52; Russell M. Linden, *Seamless Government: A Practical Guide to Re-Engineering in the Public Sector* (San Francisco: Jossey-Bass, 1994); and Sharon L. Caudle, *Reengineering for Results* (Washington, D.C.: National Academy of Public Administration, 1994).

20. Hammer and Champy, *Reengineering the Corporation,* 2, 3.

21. Ibid., 47–49.

22. Mechling, "Reengineering Part of Your Game Plan?"

23. General Accounting Office, *Management Reforms: Examples of Public and Private Innovations to Improve Service Delivery,* AIMD/GGD-94-9, 1994, 37–38.

24. H. George Frederickson, "Painting Bull's Eyes around Bullet Holes," *Governing* 5 (October 1992): 13.

25. Ronald C. Moe, Edward Davis, Frederick Pauls, and Harold Relyca, "Analysis of the Budget and Management Proposals in the Report of the National Performance Review" (Washington, D.C.: Congressional Research Service, September 1993, photocopied), 4.

26. Henri Fayol, *General and Industrial Management* (London: Pitman and Sons, 1925).

27. L. Urwick, "The Function of Administration," in *Papers on the Science of Administration,* ed. Luther Gulick and L. Urwick (New York: Institute of Public Administration, 1937), 124.

28. Luther Gulick, "The Theory of Organization," in ibid., 25.

29. Michael M. Harmon and Richard T. Mayer, *Organization Theory for Public Administration* (Boston: Little, Brown, 1986), 42–47.

30. James Q. Wilson, *Bureaucracy: What Government Agencies Do and Why They Do It* (New York: Basic Books, 1989), 163.

31. For an excellent survey, see James L. Perry, ed., *Handbook of Public Administration* (San Francisco: Jossey-Bass, 1989).

32. Hammer and Champy, *Reengineering the Corporation,* 6.

33. Gore, *From Red Tape to Results,* 94.

34. Mechling, "Reengineering Part of Your Game Plan?," 50.

35. Office of Management and Budget, *The President's Management Agenda: Fiscal Year 2002* (Washington, D.C.: Government Printing Office, 2001), 3.

36. Ibid., 27.

37. Ibid.

38. See the findings of the Government Performance Project. For example, consider the findings of the 2001 GPP survey of state performance, offered in *Governing* (February 2001), http://governing.com/gpp/2001/gp1intro.htm.

39. See W. Edwards Deming, *Out of Crisis* (Cambridge, Mass.: Massachusetts Institute of Technology Center for Advanced Engineering Study, 1986); and Rafael Aguayo, *Dr. Deming: The American Who Taught the Japanese about Quality* (New York: Simon and Schuster, 1990).

40. Aguayo, *Dr. Deming,* 19.

41. Bill Creech, *The Five Pillars of TQM: How to Make Total Quality Management Work for You* (New York: Dutton, 1994), 27, 54.

42. Steven Cohen and Ronald Brand, *Total Quality Management in Government: A Practical Guide for the Real World* (San Francisco: Jossey-Bass, 1993).

43. Creech, *Five Pillars,* 78.

44. Cohen and Brand, *Total Quality Management in Government,* 175–197.

45. Ibid., 197.

46. Peter M. Senge, *The Fifth Discipline: The Art and Practice of the Learning Organization* (New York: Doubleday, 1990); and Donald F. Kettl, "Learning Organizations and Managing the Unknown," in *New Paradigms for Government: Issues for the Changing Public Service,* ed. Patricia W. Ingraham and Barbara S. Romzek (San Francisco: Jossey-Bass, 1994), 19–40.

47. H. Metcalf and L. Urwick, *Dynamic Administration: The Collected Papers of Mary Parker Follett* (New York: Harper & Brothers, 1942).

48. Abraham Maslow, "A Theory of Human Motivation," *Psychological Review* 50 (July 1943): 370–396.

49. See, for example, Michael Barzelay with Babak J. Armajani, *Breaking Through Bureaucracy: A New Vision for Managing in Government* (Berkeley: University of California Press, 1992); and Harry P. Hatry and John J. Kirlin, "An Assessment of the Oregon Benchmarks: A Report to the Oregon Progress Board," June 1994 (mimeo).

50. For two excellent surveys of administrative issues around the world, see Randall Baker, ed., *Comparative Public Management: Putting U.S. Public Policy and Implementation in*

Context (New York: Praeger, 1994); and B. Guy Peters, *The Future of Governing: Four Emerging Models,* 2nd ed., rev. (Lawrence: University of Kansas Press, 2001). The Organization of Economic Cooperation and Development also publishes regular updates on reforms in public administration; see the OECD website, http://www.oecd.org/topic/0,2686,en_2649_37405_1_1_1_1_37405,00.html.

51. An important commentary on reform in the developing world is Allen Schick, "Why Most Developing Countries Should Not Try New Zealand Reforms," *World Bank Research Observer,* 13 (February 1998): 123–131.

52. See Donald F. Kettl and John J. DiIulio Jr., eds., *Inside the Reinvention Machine: Appraising the National Performance Review* (Washington, D.C.: Brookings Institution, 1995).

53. Allen Schick, *The Spirit of Reform: Managing the New Zealand State Sector in a Time of Change* (Wellington, N.Z.: State Services Commission, 1996).

54. OMB, *President's Management Agenda,* 3.

6. The Executive Branch

1. Rufus E. Miles, "The Origin and Meaning of Miles' Law," *Public Administration Review* 38 (September–October 1978): 399–403.

2. This proposition is persuasively demonstrated in Thomas H. Hammond, "Agenda Control, Organizational Structure, and Bureaucratic Politics," *American Political Science Review* 30 (May 1986): 379–420.

3. Harold Seidman, *Politics, Position, and Power: The Dynamics of Federal Organization* (New York: Oxford University Press, 1998), 142.

4. See Laura Parker and Martha M. Hamilton, "Air Safety Regulatory Overhaul Urged," *Washington Post,* April 19, 1988, A1.

5. See National Commission on Terrorist Attacks upon the United States, *The 9/11 Commission Report* (New York: Norton, 2004).

6. California Performance Review, *Form Follows Function,* 2004, chap. 1, http://www.report.cpr.ca.gov/cprrpt/frmfunc/index.htm.

7. The War Department is here treated as the antecedent of the Department of Defense, established in 1949; the War Department included naval concerns until establishment of the Navy Department in 1798.

8. Three of these six were substantially conversions to departmental status of the previously established Federal Security Agency (1939), Housing and Home Finance Agency (1947), and Veterans Administration (1930). For the latest two departmental creations, see Beryl A. Radin and Willis D. Hawley, *The Politics of Federal Reorganization: Creating the U.S. Department of Education* (New York: Pergamon Press, 1988); Terrel H. Bell (first secretary of education), *The Thirteenth Man: A Reagan Cabinet Memoir* (New York: Free Press/Macmillan, 1987); and *Evaluation of Proposals to Establish a Department of Veterans Affairs* (Washington, D.C.: National Academy of Public Administration, 1988).

9. See "The Independent Status of the Regulatory Commissions," in U.S. Senate Committee on Governmental Affairs, *Study on Federal Regulation,* vol. 5, *Regulatory Organization* (Washington, D.C.: Government Printing Office, 1977), 25–81.

10. The restriction on the president's removal power was upheld in *Humphrey's Executor v. United States,* 295 U.S. 602 (1935). The Supreme Court characterized the Federal Trade Commission as "wholly disconnected from the executive department" and, rather, "an agency of the legislative and judicial departments," one that Congress intended to be

"independent of executive authority, except in its selection, and free to exercise its judgment without the leave or hindrance of any other official or any department of Government."

11. For an insightful account of how deregulation came about, see Martha Derthick and Paul J. Quirk, *The Politics of Deregulation* (Washington, D.C.: Brookings Institution, 1985).

12. Donald F. Kettl, *Leadership at the Fed* (New Haven: Yale University Press, 1986), 1.

13. William E. Brigman, "The Executive Branch and the Independent Regulatory Agencies," *Presidential Studies Quarterly* 11 (Spring 1981): 244–261; and David M. Welborn, *Governance of Federal Regulatory Agencies* (Knoxville: University of Tennessee Press, 1977).

14. The chairman appoints and supervises the staff, distributes the workload, and allocates funds. Often several fellow commissioners are patronage appointees, content to follow the chairman's lead. For a disheartening assessment of the quality of appointments from 1949 to 1974 (especially to the Federal Communications Commission and the Federal Trade Commission), see U.S. Senate Committee on Commerce, *Appointments to the Regulatory Agencies* (Washington, D.C.: Government Printing Office, 1976).

15. It was not always thus. In 1937 the Brownlow Committee characterized the regulatory commissions as "a headless 'fourth branch' of the Government, a haphazard deposit of irresponsible agencies and uncoordinated powers." President's Committee on Administrative Management, *Report with Special Studies* (Washington, D.C.: Government Printing Office, 1937), 40.

16. Kettl, *Leadership at the Fed*, 205–206.

17. Tennessee Valley Authority, "A Short History of the TVA," http://www.tva.gov/abouttva/history.htm.

18. Because no accepted definition of government corporations exists, counts differ. The figures cited are respectively from Ronald C. Moe, *Administering Public Functions at the Margin of Government: The Case of Federal Corporations*, Report No. 83-236 GOV, processed (Washington, D.C.: Congressional Research Service, 1 December 1983); and General Accounting Office, *Congress Should Consider Revising Basic Corporate Control Laws* (Washington, D.C.: Government Printing Office, 1983). Both reports are valuable reviews of the status and problems of government corporations.

19. For organizational history to 1922, see Lloyd M. Short, *The Development of National Administrative Organization in the United States* (Baltimore: Johns Hopkins University Press, 1923).

20. See Walter Isaacson, *Benjamin Franklin: An American Life* (New York: Simon and Schuster, 2003).

21. Problems of the functional and areal systems are explored in James W. Fesler, "The Basic Theoretical Question: How to Relate Area and Function," in *The Administration of the New Federalism*, ed. Leigh E. Grosenick (Washington, D.C.: American Society for Public Administration, 1973), 4–14.

22. In France, as elsewhere, functional pressures by central departments force departures from the model, followed periodically by efforts to reestablish its purity.

23. The general problem is reviewed in James W. Fesler, *Area and Administration* (University: University of Alabama Press, 1949, 1964).

24. For a vivid account, see "Turf Wars in the Federal Bureaucracy," *Newsweek,* April 10, 1989, 24–26. For much of the 1980s, coordination of the war on drugs was under the

National Drug Enforcement Policy Board, but it was ineffective in dealing with interagency disputes. A drug "czar" was appointed in 1989.

25. See Donald F. Kettl, *System under Stress: Homeland Security and American Politics* (Washington, D.C.: CQ Press, 2004); and The Century Foundation, *The Department of Homeland Security's First-Year Report Card* (New York: Century Foundation, 2004).

26. Advisory Commission on Intergovernmental Relations, *Improving Federal Grants Management* (Washington, D.C.: Government Printing Office, 1977), 181–199; and James L. Sundquist, *Making Federalism Work* (Washington, D.C.: Brookings Institution, 1969), 272–275.

27. President's Task Force on Government Organization, "The Organization and Management of Great Society Programs," June 15, 1967, 8, processed. Available at the Lyndon B. Johnson Presidential Library, University of Texas, Austin.

28. U.S. Constitution, Art. 2; *Myers v. United States*, 272 U.S. 52 (1926), as modified for quasi-judicial officers by *Humphrey's Executor* (1935) and by *Weiner v. United States*, 357 U.S. 349 (1958).

29. Molly Ivins, *Shrub: The Short but Happy Political Life of George W. Bush* (New York: Vintage Books, 2000).

30. See Peri E. Arnold, *Making the Managerial Presidency: Comprehensive Reorganization Planning, 1905–1980* (Princeton, N.J.: Princeton University Press, 1986), 361–364; and, more generally, Richard P. Nathan, *The Administrative Presidency* (New York: Wiley, 1983); and Colin Campbell, *Managing the Presidency: Carter, Reagan, and the Search for Executive Harmony* (Pittsburgh: University of Pittsburgh Press, 1986).

31. *Leadership in Jeopardy: The Fraying of the Presidential Appointments System* (Washington, D.C.: National Academy of Public Administration, 1985), 4–5.

32. Kareem Fahim and Colin Moynihan, "An Emergency Call Brings So Much Help a Scuffle Breaks Out," *New York Times*, September 3, 2005, p. B1.

33. President's Committee on Administrative Management, *Report with Special Studies*, 40.

34. Herbert Emmerich, *Federal Organization and Administrative Management* (University: University of Alabama Press, 1971), 199; and U.S. Bureau of the Census, *Statistical Abstract of the United States: 1994* (Washington, D.C.: Government Printing Office, 1994), 346. Here and later in this section, official data are presented; however, their accuracy has often been questioned. For the varying counts, see John Hart, *The Presidential Branch*, 2nd ed. (Chatham, N.J.: Chatham House, 1995), 42–46, 112–125; Gary King and Lyn Ragsdale, *The Elusive Executive* (Washington, D.C.: CQ Press, 1990), Tables 4.1 and 4.2; Office of Personnel Management, *Employment and Trends*; and Office of Administration, Executive Office of the President, "Aggregate Report on Personnel Pursuant to Title 3," *U.S. Code of Federal Regulations*, sec. 113 (annual), processed.

35. General Accounting Office, *Personnel Practices: Detailing of Federal Employees to the White House* (Washington, D.C.: Government Printing Office, July 1987), and *Personnel Practices: Federal Employees Detailed from DOD to the White House* (Washington, D.C.: Government Printing Office, March 1988).

36. Thomas E. Cronin, "The Swelling of the Presidency: Can Anyone Reverse the Tide?" in *American Government: Readings and Cases*, 9th ed., ed. Peter Woll (Boston: Little, Brown, 1984), 345–360.

37. President's Committee on Administrative Management, *Report with Special Studies*, 5.

38. Samuel Kernell, "The Creed and Reality of Modern White House Management," in *Chief of Staff: Twenty-Five Years of Managing the Presidency,* ed. Samuel Kernell and Samuel L. Popkin (Berkeley: University of California Press, 1986), 193–222.

39. For a full and admiring description of the White House staff, see Bradley H. Patterson Jr., *The Ring of Power: The White House Staff and Its Expanding Role in Government* (New York: Basic Books, 1988).

40. Greg Schneiders, "My Turn: Goodbye to All That," *Newsweek,* September 24, 1979, 23. Cf. "Even when working a seventy-hour week the President does not see most of his White House Office staff, or most of his Cabinet." Carter devoted a third of his time to seeing senior staff members and a sixth to seeing cabinet and other officials. Richard Rose, *The Postmodern President: The White House Meets the World* (Chatham, N.J.: Chatham House, 1988), 151–152.

41. Kernell and Popkin, *Chief of Staff,* 229–231.

42. *The Executive Presidency: Federal Management for the 1990s* (Washington, D.C.: National Academy of Public Administration, 1988), 7. Both Stuart Eizenstat, former president Carter's domestic policy chief, and former president Ford have also proposed a permanent secretariat.

43. Ibid., 6. See also Stephen Hess, *Organizing the Presidency,* 2nd ed. (Washington, D.C.: Brookings Institution, 1988), 172–174.

44. Samuel Kernell, "The Evolution of the White House Staff," in *Can the Government Govern?* ed. John E. Chubb and Paul E. Peterson (Washington, D.C.: Brookings Institution Press, 1989), 235.

45. U.S. Office of Personnel Management, "Federal Civilian Employment and Payroll," September 2007, Table 9, http://www.opm.gov/feddata/html/2007/september/table9.asp.

46. The best comprehensive review of the OMB is U.S. Senate Committee on Governmental Affairs, *Office of Management and Budget: Evolving Roles and Future Issues,* 99th Cong., 2d. sess., February 1986, S. Rpt. 99–134 (Washington, D.C.: Government Printing Office, 1986). For OMB's and the Budget Bureau's history, see also Larry Berman, *The Office of Management and Budget and the Presidency, 1921–1979* (Princeton, N.J.: Princeton University Press, 1979); and Frederick C. Mosher, *A Tale of Two Agencies: A Comparative Analysis of the General Accounting Office and the Office of Management and Budget* (Baton Rouge: Louisiana State University Press, 1984).

47. Hugh Heclo, "OMB and the Presidency—The Problem of 'Neutral Competence,' " *Public Interest* 38 (Winter 1975): 80–98.

48. This will seem unimportant only to those who have not observed the frequency with which "new" ideas are enthusiastically advanced and acted on by newly recruited high officials who are unaware that the same idea, or a near-analog, was earlier introduced and failed.

49. Hugh Heclo, *A Government of Strangers: Executive Politics in Washington* (Washington, D.C.: Brookings Institution, 1977), 80–81.

50. See David A. Stockman, *The Triumph of Politics: The Inside Story of the Reagan Revolution* (New York: Harper and Row, 1986; paperback ed., New York: Avon Books, 1987).

51. Ronald C. Moe, "Assessment of Organizational Policy and Planning Function in OMB," in U.S. Senate Committee on Governmental Affairs, *Office of Management and Budget,* 147–167, at 163. See also General Accounting Office, *Managing the Government: Revised*

Approach Could Improve OMB's Effectiveness (Washington, D.C.: Government Printing Office, 1989).

52. *Revitalizing Federal Management: Managers and Their Overburdened Systems* (Washington, D.C.: National Academy of Public Administration, 1983), 10–13.

53. 50 *U.S. Code* 401. Reorganization Plan No. 4 of 1949 placed the NSC in the Executive Office of the President.

54. Attendance was expanded by President Reagan to include the attorney general, the secretary of the treasury, the director of OMB, and the chief delegate to the United Nations.

55. For details on the interagency committee structure and national security advisers' conceptions of their role before and after the Iran-Contra scandal of 1985–1986, see Robert C. McFarlane, Richard Saunders, and Thomas C. Shull, "The National Security Council: Organization for Policy Making," in *The Presidency and National Security Policy,* ed. G. Gordon Hoxie et al. (New York: Center for the Study of the Presidency, 1984), 261–273; and Colin L. Powell, "The NSC System in the Last Two Years of the Reagan Administration," in *The Presidency in Transition,* ed. James P. Pfiffner, R. Gordon Hoxie, et al. (New York: Center for the Study of the Presidency, 1989), 204–218. (McFarlane and Powell were national security advisers.) The first Bush administration simplified the interagency committee structure; see Bernard Weinraub, "Bush Backs Plan to Enhance Role of Security Staff," *New York Times,* February 2, 1989.

56. Bert Rockman, "America's Departments of State: Irregular and Regular Syndromes of Policy Making," *American Political Science Review* 75 (December 1981): 911–927.

57. The NSC staff's organizational status is ambiguous. Fifteen staff members are special assistants to the president, thus bringing them within the White House Office. Nine of these assistants head staff units (e.g., Asian Affairs, African Affairs, Defense Policy, Intelligence Programs). *The Capital Source,* Spring 1996, 11–12.

58. Keith Schneider, "North's Record: A Wide Role in a Host of Sensitive Projects," *New York Times,* January 3, 1987.

59. Reorganization Plan No. 2, and Message of the President, in 5 *U.S. Code of Federal Regulations,* 1982, Appendix 1129–1132.

60. The experience of President Ford's most active council is related by its executive secretary, Roger B. Porter, *Presidential Decision Making: The Economic Policy Board* (New York: Cambridge University Press, 1980). Few of the other cabinet councils were more than marginally active. James P. Pfiffner, "White House Staff versus the Cabinet: Centripetal and Centrifugal Roles," *Presidential Studies Quarterly* 16 (Fall 1986): 666–690, at 682–683. Reagan had seven cabinet councils in his first term, which collectively held nearly 500 meetings. Ralph C. Bledsoe, "Policy Management in the Reagan Administration," in Pfiffner and Hoxie, *Presidency in Transition,* 54–61, at 59.

61. See, on Reagan's and earlier domestic policy offices and councils, Margaret Jane Wyszomirski, "The Role of a Presidential Office for Domestic Policy: Three Models and Four Cases," in *The Presidency and Public Policy Making,* ed. George C. Edwards et al. (Pittsburgh: University of Pittsburgh Press, 1985), 130–150.

62. See, for example, Perri 6, *E-Governance: Styles of Political Judgment in the Information Age Polity* (New York: Palgrave, 2004); Jane E. Fountain, *Building the Virtual State: Information Technology and Institutional Change* (Washington, D.C.: Brookings Institution,

2001); and Organization for Economic Cooperation and Development, *The E-Government Imperative* (Paris: OECD, 2003).

63. Fountain, *Building the Virtual State*, 205–206.

64. John B. Horrigan, *How Americans Get in Touch with Government* (Washington, D.C.: Pew Internet and American Life Project, 2004), http://www.pewinternet.org/PPF/r/128/report_display.asp.

7. Organization Problems

1. Peter Robinson, quoted by John Tierney, "Every Administration Has Its Naysayers," *New York Times,* April 25, 2004, sec. 4, p. 3.

2. Jack H. Knott and Gary J. Miller, *Reforming Bureaucracy: The Politics of Institutional Choice* (Englewood Cliffs, N.J.: Prentice Hall, 1987), 274.

3. Herbert Kaufman, "Emerging Doctrines of Public Administration," *American Political Science Review* 50 (December 1956): 1059–1073. He assigns their relative dominance historically in this sequence: representativeness, neutral competence, and executive leadership.

4. Todd S. Purdom, "Scuba Feud Pits Idled Bravest against Prideful Finest," *New York Times,* May 5, 1988; and Ari L. Goldman, "New Rules Set for Handling Emergencies, *New York Times,* July 5, 1990.

5. For an analysis, see National Commission on Terrorist Attacks upon the United States, *The 9/11 Commission Report* (New York: Norton, 2004), chap. 9.

6. Federal Regulation Study Team, *Federal Energy Regulation: An Organizational Study* (Washington, D.C.: Government Printing Office, April 1974), appendix D, D1–D2.

7. Ibid., D2.

8. The bias appears most clearly in members of the human relations school of thought (reviewed in chapter 4), but when leaders of that school acquire experience as heads of organizations, their views change. See Douglas McGregor, "On Leadership," in *Leadership and Motivation: Essays of Douglas McGregor,* ed. Warren G. Bennis and Edgar N. Schein (Cambridge, Mass.: MIT Press, 1966), 66–70; and Warren G. Bennis, *The Leaning Ivory Tower* (San Francisco: Jossey-Bass, 1973). McGregor was president of Antioch College from 1948 to 1954; Bennis was provost and vice president of the University of Buffalo from 1967 to 1971 and president of the University of Cincinnati from 1971 to 1977.

9. E. S. Turner, *The Court of St. James's* (London: Michael Joseph, 1959), 305–306.

10. *United States Government Organization Manual, 1977–1978,* 312.

11. The concept of core activities is akin to the concept of "organizational essence" in Morton H. Halperin, *Bureaucratic Politics and Foreign Policy* (Washington, D.C.: Brookings Institution, 1974), 28–40. Halperin soundly argues that an organization must vigorously protect its organizational core or essence.

12. See Allen Schick, "The Coordination Option," in *Federal Reorganization: What Have We Learned?,* ed. Peter Szanton (Chatham, N.J.: Chatham House, 1981), 85–113, esp. 95–99.

13. William J. Lynn, "The Wars Within: The Joint Military Structure and Its Critics," in *Reorganizing America's Defense: Leadership in War and Peace,* ed. Robert J. Art, Vincent Davis, and Samuel P. Huntington (Washington, D.C.: Pergamon-Brassey's, 1985), 168–204, esp. 174–183.

14. Both deficiencies are well documented and analyzed in Senate Committee on Armed Services, *Defense Organization: The Need for Change: Staff Report,* 99th Cong., 1st sess., October 16, 1985, S. Rpt. 99-86 (Washington, D.C.: Government Printing Office), 157–179 (re Joint Chiefs), and 302–324 (re Unified Commands). Note that the Unified Command problem (the individual armed services vs. the regional commanders) is an example of the function versus area conflict we have earlier examined.

15. *The National Military Command Structure: Report,* prepared by Richard C. Steadman, July 1978 (Washington, D.C.: Department of Defense, 1978), 52, 55.

16. President's Commission on Defense Management (chaired by David Packard), *A Quest for Excellence: Final Report to the President,* June 1986 (Washington, D.C.: Government Printing Office, 1986), 35–37; and *Department of Defense Reorganization Act of 1986,* 100 *U.S. Statutes* 1005.

17. For details on interagency strife in narcotics control, see W. John Moore, "No Quick Fix," *National Journal* 20 (November 21, 1987): 2954–2959; and "Turf Wars in the Federal Bureaucracy," *Newsweek,* April 20, 1989, 4–6.

18. 102 *U.S. Statutes* 4181. The czar is formally the director of National Drug Control Policy.

19. Sandra Panem, *The AIDS Bureaucracy* (Cambridge, Mass.: Harvard University Press, 1988).

20. See Jean Blondel, *The Organization of Governments: A Comparative Analysis of Government Structures* (Beverly Hills, Calif.: Sage, 1982).

21. Commission on the Organization of the Government for the Conduct of Foreign Policy, *Report* (Washington, D.C.: Government Printing Office, 1975), 32–33. (Emphasis in original.)

22. Robert T. Golembiewski, *Organizing Men and Power: Patterns of Behavior and Line-Staff Models* (Chicago: Rand McNally, 1967), 62. Pages 60–89 provide the definitive analysis of the tensions between line and staff-auxiliary-control activities.

23. For major critiques of the neutral competence approach, see Knott and Miller, *Reforming Bureaucracy* and *Organizing Governance and Governing Organizations,* ed. Colin Campbell and B. Guy Peters (Pittsburgh: University of Pittsburgh Press, 1988). See also Harold Seidman and Robert Gilmour, *Politics, Position, and Power: From the Positive to the Regulatory State,* 4th ed. (New York: Oxford University Press, 1986); James G. March and Johan P. Olsen, "Organizing Political Life: What Administrative Reorganization Tells Us about Government," *American Political Science Review* 77 (June 1983): 281–296; and Terry M. Moe, "The Politics of Bureaucratic Structure," in *Can the Government Govern?,* ed. John E. Chubb and Paul E. Peterson (Washington, D.C.: Brookings Institution, 1989), 267–329.

24. *Immigration and Naturalization Service v. Chadha,* 462 U.S. 919 (1983). See Barbara Hinkson Craig, *Chadha: The Story of an Epic Constitutional Struggle* (New York: Oxford University Press, 1988; paperback ed., Berkeley: University of California Press, 1990).

25. 98 *U.S. Statutes* 3192 (November 8, 1984). The president cannot use this method to propose creating a new agency outside a department or existing agency.

26. See Peri E. Arnold, *Making the Managerial Presidency: Comprehensive Reorganization Planning, 1905–1980* (Princeton, N.J.: Princeton University Press, 1986).

27. Others, however, led to later reforms. See James W. Fesler, "The Brownlow Committee Fifty Years Later," *Public Administration Review* 47 (July–August 1987): 291–296.

28. See Ronald C. Moe, *The Hoover Commissions Revisited* (Boulder, Colo.: Westview, 1982).

29. Herbert Emmerich, *Federal Organization and Administrative Management* (Tuscaloosa: University of Alabama Press, 1971), 127.

30. Office of Management and Budget, *Papers Relating to the President's Departmental Reorganization Program,* March 1971 (Washington, D.C.: Government Printing Office, 1971). See also the revised edition of February 1972.

31. Frustrated by Congress's failure to act, Nixon set out in 1973 to do by fiat what Congress would not let him do by law: four cabinet members were additionally given White House posts as counselors to the president, each with powers over the existing departments in the fields of the proposed departments. In May 1973, with Watergate unraveling, Nixon abandoned this scheme of "supersecretaries."

32. The major success claimed was reform of the civil service, but this was mostly nonorganizational.

33. Reagan supported creation of the Department of Veterans Affairs, but its success in Congress was already assured.

34. The success of Reagan's strategy is assessed in *The Reagan Legacy: Promise and Performance,* ed. Charles O. Jones (Chatham, N.J.: Chatham House, 1988), esp. chaps. 1 and 4.

35. James K. Conant, "In the Shadow of Wilson and Brownlow: Executive Branch Reorganization in the States, 1965 to 1987," *Public Administration Review* 48 (September–October 1988): 892–902. One state, Iowa, reorganized in 1985–1986.

36. March and Olsen, "Organizing Political Life," 288, 292.

37. See Herbert Kaufman, *The Limits of Organizational Change* (Montgomery: University of Alabama Press, 1971) and *Are Government Organizations Immortal?* (Washington, D.C.: Brookings Institution, 1976).

38. For a classic analysis of the expansive tendencies, see Matthew Holden Jr., " 'Imperialism' in Bureaucracy," *American Political Science Review* 60 (December 1966): 943–951.

39. Craig W. Thomas, "Reorganizing Public Organizations: Alternatives, Objectives, and Evidence," *Journal of Public Administration and Theory* 3 (1993): 457–486.

8. The Civil Service

1. Associated Press dispatch, *New Haven Register,* July 18, 1969; and 5 *U.S. Code of Federal Regulations,* 5546, 5547.

2. Statement of David M. Walker, *Human Capital: Taking Steps to Meet Current and Emerging Human Capital Challenges,* GAO-01-965T (July 17, 2001), 1.

3. Jonathan Walters, *Life after Civil Service Reform: The Texas, Georgia, and Florida Experiences* (Washington, D.C.: IBM Endowment for the Business of Government, 2002), 7.

4. David Osborne and Ted Gaebler, *Reinventing Government* (Reading, Mass.: Addison-Wesley, 1992).

5. 5 *U.S. Code of Federal Regulations* 3304(a). The substance and much of the language date from the Pendleton Civil Service Act of 1883.

6. U.S. Merit Systems Protection Board, *Federal Appointment Authorities: Cutting through the Confusion* (Washington, D.C.: MSPB, 2008), http://www.mspb.gov/netsearch/viewdocs. aspx?docnumber=350930&version=351511&application=ACROBAT.

7. Brittany R. Ballenstedt, "MSPB: Competitive Hiring on the Decline," *GovExec.com,* July 29, 2008, http://www.govexec.com/story_page.cfm?articleid=40577&dcn=e_gvet.

8. Office of Personnel Management, *Federal Workforce Statistics: The Fact Book 2005 Edition* (Washington, D.C.: OPM, 2005), 32, http://www.opm.gov/feddata/factbook/2005/factbook2005.pdf.

9. Ibid., 10.

10. Congressional Budget Office, *Employee Turnover in the Federal Government* (Washington, D.C.: Government Printing Office, 1986). The "technical adjustments" take into account, among other things, different federal and private workforces' blue- and white-collar proportions and age distributions.

11. General Accounting Office, *Federal Employment: The Results to Date of the FY 1994 Buyouts at Non-Defense Agencies*, T-GGD-94-214 (September 22, 1994), 4–5.

12. For an analysis of the economics of workforce reduction, see Congressional Budget Office, *Reducing the Size of the Federal Civilian Work Force* (Washington, D.C.: Government Printing Office, 1993).

13. One study found that clerk-typists and secretaries, with small pay gaps compared to private salaries, had high quit rates, while chemists, accountants, and engineers, with large pay gaps, had low quit rates. General Accounting Office, *Federal Workforce: Pay, Recruitment, and Retention of Federal Employees* (Washington, D.C.: Government Printing Office, 1987), 2–3. For more comprehensive occupational analysis of voluntary separations, see Congressional Budget Office, *Employee Turnover*, 6–8.

14. For a comparison of government and private-sector employees' evaluation of a number of such job features, see Michael P. Smith and Steven L. Nock, "Social Class and the Quality of Work Life in Public and Private Organizations," *Journal of Social Issues* 30 (1980): 59–75; and Barry Bozeman, *All Organizations Are Public: Bridging Public and Private Organizational Theories* (San Francisco: Jossey-Bass, 1987), 15–23. Federal workers' appraisals are surveyed in Merit Systems Protection Board, *Federal Personnel Policies and Practices: Perspectives from the Workplace* (Washington, D.C.: Government Printing Office, 1987).

15. Congressional Budget Office, "Measuring Differences between Federal and Private Pay," November 2002, http://www.cbo.gov/showdoc.cfm?index=3992&sequence=0&from=1.

16. Congressional Budget Office, "Comparing Federal Employee Benefits with Those in the Private Sector," 1998, http://www.cbo.gov/showdoc.cfm?index=821&sequence=0.

17. Terry W. Culler, "Most Federal Workers Need Only Be Competent," *Wall Street Journal*, May 21, 1986.

18. General Accounting Office, *Recruitment and Retention: Inadequate Federal Pay Cited as Primary Problem by Agency Officials*, GGD-9117 (September 1990), 3.

19. *Leadership for America: Rebuilding the Public Service*, Report of the National (Volcker) Commission on the Public Service and Task Force Reports (Lexington, Mass.: Lexington Books, 1990), 38. About 40,000 GS employees are already covered by special rates for particular occupations. See also the Commission's Task Force Reports, 231–233, 236.

20. The estimates come from a web-based calculator on the AFGE website, http://www.afge.org/Index.cfm?Page=FEPCACalculator.

21. American Federation of Government Employees, "Federal Pay," 22, http://www.afge.org/Documents/2004_IP_03_Fed_Pay.pdf.

22. The leading case, that of Washington State, is assessed in Peter T. Kilborn, "Wage Gap between Sexes Is Cut in Test, but at a Price," *New York Times*, May 31, 1990. For Minnesota and Oregon, see Sara M. Evans and Barbara J. Nelson, *Comparable Worth and the*

Paradox of Technocratic Reform (Chicago: University of Chicago Press, 1989). See also Joan Acker, *Doing Comparable Worth: Gender, Class, and Pay Equity* (Philadelphia: Temple University Press, 1989); Steven R. Rhoads, *Incomparable Worth: Pay Equity Meets the Market* (New York: Cambridge University Press, 1993); Elaine Sorensen, *Comparable Worth: Is It a Worthy Policy?* (Princeton: Princeton University Press, 1994); and Michael W. McCann, *Rights at Work: Pay Equity Reform and the Politics of Legal Mobilization* (Chicago: University of Chicago Press, 1994).

23. June Ellenoff O'Neill, "Comparable Worth," in *The Concise Encyclopedia of Economics*, http://www.econlib.org/library/Enc/ComparableWorth.html.

24. George H. W. Bush, statement issued October 5, 1988; and "Remarks of the President to the Career Members of the Senior Executive Service," January 26, 1989. Reprinted in *Bureaucrat* 18 (Spring 1989): 3.

25. See Merit Systems Protection Board, *Attracting College Graduates to the Federal Government: A View of College Recruiting* (Washington, D.C.: Government Printing Office, 1988); and *Leadership for America Report*, 3–4, 24, and Task Force Reports, 84–88.

26. National Advisory Council on the Public Service, *Ensuring the Highest Quality National Public Service* (Washington, D.C.: National Advisory Council on the Public Service, 1993), 20.

27. Constance Horner, OPM director, as quoted in Judith Havemann, "U.S. Plans New System for Hiring," *Washington Post*, June 23, 1988. Ms. Horner announced a new student-recruitment program, but its realization depended on its appeal to her successor under the Bush administration. See Office of Personnel Management, "New Program to Fill GS-5 and GS-7 Entry-Level Jobs," June 23, 1988, processed.

28. Carolyn Ban and Norma Riccucci, "Personnel Systems and Labor Relations: Steps toward a Quiet Revitalization," in *Revitalizing State and Local Public Service: Strengthening Performance, Accountability, and Citizen Confidence*, ed. Frank J. Thompson (San Francisco: Jossey-Bass, 1993), 83.

29. Congressional Budget Office, *Characteristics and Pay of Federal Civilian Employees* (Washington, D.C.: CBO, March 2007), 8, https://www.cbo.gov/ftpdocs/78xx/doc7874/03-15-Federal_Personnel.pdf.

30. For a thorough coverage of the issues, see Richard B. Freeman and Casey Ichniowski, eds., *When Public Sector Workers Organize* (Chicago: University of Chicago Press, 1988).

31. Leonard Buder, "Walkout Is Hobbling Schools in New York," *New York Times*, February 24, 1977.

32. Quoted in Frank Swoboda, "AFGE's Optimistic Organizer," *Washington Post*, January 21, 1988.

33. Joel M. Douglas, "State Civil Service and Collective Bargaining Systems," *Public Administration Review* 52 (January–February 1992): 162–171.

34. Quoted in National Academy of Public Administration, *Leading People in Change: Empowerment, Commitment, Accountability* (Washington, D.C.: NAPA, 1993), 10.

35. Ibid., 89–111; and Steven M. Goldschmidt and Leland E. Stuart, "The Extent and Impact of Educational Policy Bargaining," *Industrial and Labor Relations Review* 39 (April 1986): 350–360.

36. For the Federal Labor Relations Authority's interpretations of "compelling need" and "procedures," see Sar Levitan and Alexandra Noden, *Working for the Sovereign: Employee*

Relations in the Federal Government (Baltimore: Johns Hopkins University Press, 1983), 36–40; and annual reports of the FLRA.

37. Brian Friel, "Labor Pains," *GovExec.com,* October 1, 2002, http://www.govexec.com/features/1002/1002s1.htm.

38. Executive Order 12564, September 15, 1986. For its implementation, see General Accounting Office, *Drug Testing: Federal Agency Plans for Testing Employees* (Washington, D.C.: Government Printing Office, 1989); and *Drug Testing: Action by Certain Agencies When Employees Test Positive for Illegal Drugs* (Washington, D.C.: Government Printing Office, 1990).

39. Amelia Gruber, "New Policy Would Broaden Drug-Testing Methods," *GovExec.com,* April 6, 2004, http://www.govexec.com/dailyfed/0404/040604a1.htm.

40. *National Treasury Employees v. Von Raab,* 109 S. Ct. 1384 (1989).

41. The relation is a matter of dispute. For technical discussion, see "The Cause of AIDS," *Science* 242 (November 18, 1988): 997–998.

42. Richard L. Berke, "State Department to Begin AIDS Testing," *New York Times,* November 29, 1986.

43. 5 *U.S. Code of Federal Regulations* 7324–7327. For specifically permissible activities and prohibited activities, see 5 *U.S. Code of Federal Regulations* 733.111 to 733.122. Exceptions to the ban exist (1) for nonpartisan elections and with regard to questions (such as constitutional amendments and referenda) not specifically identified with a national or state political party; and (2) in certain local communities near Washington, D.C., and elsewhere (designated by OPM) where federal employees are a majority of voters. OPM restricts activity in such communities' partisan elections to candidacy as, or advocacy or opposition to, an independent candidate.

44. Those free of the restrictions are the president and vice president, aides paid from appropriations for the president's office, heads and assistant heads of executive departments, and officers who are appointed by the president, by and with the advice and consent of the Senate, and who determine policies to be pursued by the United States.

45. 427 U.S. 347 (1976).

46. 445 U.S. 507 (1980).

47. For a criticism of the two cases, see Kenneth J. Meier, "Ode to Patronage: A Critical Analysis of Two Recent Supreme Court Decisions," *Public Administration Review* 41 (September–October 1981): 558–563.

48. 497 U.S. 62 (1990); and Linda Greenhouse, "Court Widens Curb on Patronage in Jobs for Most Public Workers," *New York Times,* June 22, 1990.

49. In contrast, the City of Chicago's Democratic administration substantially ended its patronage hiring system when it settled federal court suits by signing a consent decree. For an excellent review, see Anne Freedman, "Doing Battle with the Patronage Army: Politics, Courts, and Personnel Administration in Chicago," *Public Administration Review* 48 (September–October 1988): 847–859.

50. George Cahlink, "Ex-Procurement Chief Gets Jail Time," *GovExec.com,* October 1, 2004, http://www.govexec.com/dailyfed/1004/100104g1.htm. The plea agreement can be found at this link.

51. Government Accountability Office, *Defense Contracting: Post-Government Employment of Former DOD Officials Needs Greater Transparency,* Report GAO-08-485 (2008), 6.

52. Ibid.

53. Patricia Wallace Ingraham, *The Foundation of Merit: Public Service in American Democracy* (Baltimore: Johns Hopkins University Press, 1995), 74. Emphasis in original.

54. Ronald N. Johnson and Gary D. Libecap, *The Federal Civil Service System and the Problem of Bureaucracy* (Chicago: University of Chicago Press, 1994).

55. Government Accountability Office, *High-Risk Series: Strategic Human Capital Management,* GAO-03-120 (2003), 7.

9. Managing Human Capital

1. General Accounting Office, *High-Risk Series: Strategic Human Capital Management,* GAO-03-120 (Washington, D.C.: 2003), 3–4. For a broad examination of the issues, see Jonathan D. Breul and Nicole Willenz Gardner, eds., *Human Capital 2004* (Lanham, Md.: Rowman and Littlefield, 2004).

2. Peter Drucker, "Knowledge Work and Knowledge Society: The Social Transformations of This Century," 1994 Godkin Lecture (Cambridge, Mass.: John F. Kennedy School of Government, Harvard University, 1994).

3. GAO, *High-Risk Series,* 8–21.

4. Ibid., 10.

5. For a discussion of these issues, see Donna D. Beecher, "The Next Wave of Civil Service Reform," *Public Personnel Management* 32 (Winter 2003): 457–474.

6. See Statement of Robert N. Goldenkoff, U.S. Government Accountability Office, *Human Capital: Transforming Federal Recruiting and Hiring Efforts,* GAO-08-762T (May 2008), 2, http://www.gao.gov/new.items/d08762t.pdf.

7. Goldenkoff, *Human Capital,* 1.

8. Government Accountability Office, *Centers for Disease Control and Prevention: Human Capital Planning Has Improved, but Strategic View of Contractor Workforce Is Needed,* Report GAO-08-582 (May 2008).

9. Alyssa Rosenberg, "CDC's Human Capital Plan Overlooks Contractors, GAO Says," *GovExec.com,* July 3, 2008, http://www.govexec.com/dailyfed/0708/070308ar1.htm.

10. David McGlinchey, "Unwieldy Hiring Process Can Be Fixed, Top Personnel Official Says," *GovExec.com,* June 8, 2004, http://www.govexec.com/dailyfed/0604/060804d1.htm. See also General Accounting Office, *Human Capital: Status of Efforts to Improve Federal Hiring,* Report, GAO-04-796T (Washington, D.C.: June 7, 2004).

11. General Accounting Office, *HUD Management: Actions Needed to Improve Acquisitions Management,* GAO-03-157 (Washington, D.C.: November 15, 2002).

12. General Accounting Office, *Results-Oriented Cultures: Insights for U.S. Agencies from Other Countries' Performance Management Initiatives,* GAO-02-862 (Washington, D.C.: August 2, 2002), 4.

13. For an excellent analysis of human resource reform, see Patricia W. Ingraham, "Striving for Balance: Reforms in Human Resource Management," in *Handbook of Comparative Administration,* ed. Laurence Lynn Jr. and Christopher Pollitt (Oxford: Oxford University Press, forthcoming).

14. Office of Management and Budget, *The President's Management Agenda: Fiscal Year 2002* (Washington, D.C.: 2001), 11–12.

15. Keynote address by David M. Walker, Comptroller General of the United States, Joint Financial Management Improvement Program, 32nd Annual Financial Management Conference (March 11, 2003), http://www.gao.gov/cghome/jfmip32.pdf.

16. Stephen Barr, "OPM Turns over 10,000 New Leaves," *Washington Post*, January 28, 1994, A21.

17. American Federation of State, County, and Municipal Employees, "Broadbanding" (Spring 1997), http://www.afscme.org/wrkplace/cbr297_1.htm.

18. Ibid.

19. Office of Personnel Management, "Demonstration Project Factsheets," http://www.opm. gov/demos/demofact.asp.

20. Quoted in Stephen Barr, "Is Road to Chaos Paved with 'Ad Hoc' Reform?" *Washington Post*, February 22, 2004, C2.

21. General Accounting Office, *FAA's Reform Effort Requires a More Strategic Approach*, GAO-03-156 (Washington, D.C.: February 2003).

22. Eric Yoder, "The IRS Hopes to Hit Paydirt," *GovExec.com*, April 1, 2001, http://www. govexec.com/features/0401/0401s1s3.htm.

23. Keith Koffler and Mark Wegner, "Bush Urges Waiver of Civil Service Rules in Homeland Department," *GovExec.com*, July 22, 2002, http://www.govexec.com/dailyfed/0702/ 072202cd1.htm.

24. Quoted in Jonathan Walters, *Life after Civil Service Reform: The Texas, Georgia, and Florida Experiences* (Washington, D.C.: IBM Endowment for the Business of Government, 2002), 7. The discussion that follows draws heavily on Walters's analysis of the civil service reforms in these three states.

25. Quoted in ibid., 22.

26. Ibid., 28.

27. See http://www.pewcenteronthestates.org/uploadedFiles/PEW_WebGuides_GA.pdf.

28. Ibid., 30.

29. See http://www.pewcenteronthestates.org/uploadedFiles/PEW_WebGuides_FL.pdf.

30. For a broad assessment, see Jerrell D. Coggburn, "Personnel Deregulation: Exploring Differences in the American States," *Journal of Public Administration Research and Theory* 11 (2000): 223–244; Sally Coleman Selden, Patricia Wallace Ingraham, and Willow Jacobson, "Human Resource Practices in State Government: Findings from a National Survey," *Public Administration Review* 61 (September–October 2002), 598–607; and J. Edward Kellough and Sally Coleman Selden, "The Reinvention of Public Personnel Administration: An Analysis of the Diffusion of Personnel Management Reforms in the States," *Public Administration Review* 63 (March–April 2003): 165–176.

31. See http://www.pewcenteronthestates.org/uploadedFiles/PEW_WebGuides_VA.pdf.

32. We have interpreted "higher levels" strictly (i.e., at Executive Schedule levels, in the Senior Executive Service, at GS-16 to GS-18, or serving in the White House, or serving as ambassadors and ministers). About 1,650 persons are political appointees under Schedule C ("positions of a confidential or policy-determining character") at GS-15 and below; as noted earlier, about 1,000 of them are at GS-13 to 15.

33. The Presidential Appointee Initiative, *A Survivor's Guide for Presidential Nominees* (Washington, D.C.: Brookings Institution, 2000), http://www.appointee.brookings.edu/ sg/intro.htm.

34. On Nixon and Reagan, see Richard P. Nathan, *The Administrative Presidency* (New York: Wiley, 1983).

35. Terry M. Moe, "The Politicized Presidency," in *The New Direction in American Politics,* ed. John E. Chubb and Paul E. Peterson (Washington, D.C.: Brookings Institution, 1985), 235–271.

36. Expendability is impaired when, as often, a political appointee is the darling of a congressional committee or interest group or both.

37. Paul C. Light, "How Thick Is Government?" *American Enterprise* 5 (November–December 1994): 60–61. See also the book based on his study, *Thickening Government: Federal Hierarchy and the Diffusion of Accountability* (Washington, D.C.: Brookings Institution Press, 1995).

38. Paul C. Light, "Fact Sheet on the Continued Thickening of Government," July 23, 2003, http://www.brookings.edu/views/papers/light/20040723.htm.

39. For qualifications needed to perform well in one set of political posts, see John H. Trattner, *The Prune Book: The 100 Toughest Management and Policy-Making Jobs in Washington* (Lanham, Md.: Madison Books, 1988).

40. G. Calvin Mackenzie, "Appointing Mr. (or Ms.) Right," *Government Executive* 22 (April 1990): 30–35; the transitions exclude Johnson's and Ford's rises from the vice-presidency. Cf. Burt Solomon, "Bush's Laggard Appointment Pace . . . May Not Matter All That Much," *National Journal* 21 (December 2, 1989): 2952–2953. Through 1989 and often beyond, the Consumer Products Safety Commission lacked a quorum; only four of eighteen top Energy Department officials were in place, as was true of six of eleven assistant secretaries of Labor; the Census Bureau's director had not been appointed, although the 1990 census was soon to start; and in HHS the headships of the National Institutes of Health, Food and Drug Administration, and the Health Care Financing Administration were unfilled.

41. Quoted in Christopher Lee, "Bush Slow to Fill Top Federal Posts," *Washington Post,* October 18, 2002, A35.

42. From 1953 to 1976, 55 percent of the initial appointees and 85 percent of replacement appointees had had such experience. James J. Best, "Presidential Cabinet Appointments: 1953–1976," *Presidential Studies Quarterly* 11 (Winter 1981): 62–66.

43. This and later paragraphs draw on James W. Fesler, "Politics, Policy, and Bureaucracy at the Top," *Annals of the American Academy of Political and Social Science* 466 (March 1983): 23–41, and sources cited there.

44. For informative analyses of political officials who had such capability, see Jameson W. Doig and Erwin C. Hargrove, eds., *Leadership and Innovation: A Biographical Perspective on Entrepreneurs in Government* (Baltimore: Johns Hopkins University Press, 1987).

45. G. Edward DeSeve, *The Presidential Appointee's Handbook* (Washington, D.C.: Brookings Institution Press, 2008).

46. *Leadership in Jeopardy: The Fraying of the Presidential Appointments System,* November 1985 (Washington, D.C.: National Academy of Public Administration, 1985), 4–5. Regulatory commissioners, who have fixed terms and are removable only "for cause," are excluded from the figures we use. The figures measure tenure in specific positions; appointees' median service within the same agency was 3 years, and within the government 4.3 years.

47. For details, see Linda L. Fisher, "Fifty Years of Presidential Appointments," in *The In-and-Outers: Presidential Appointees and Transient Government in Washington,* ed. G. Calvin Mackenzie (Baltimore: Johns Hopkins University Press, 1987), 21–26; Carl Brauer, "Tenure, Turnover, and Postgovernment Employment Trends of Presidential Appointees," in Mackenzie, *In-and-Outers,* 174–194; and Trattner, *Prune Book.* See also General Accounting Office, *Political Appointees: Turnover Rates in Executive Schedule Positions Requiring Senate Confirmation* GGD-94-115 FS (Washington, D.C.: April 1994).

48. Robert Thalon Hall, quoted in Brauer, "Tenure, Turnover, and Post-government Employment," 178–179.

49. General Accounting Office, *Department of Labor: Assessment of Management Improvement Efforts* (Washington, D.C.: Government Printing Office, 1986).

50. General Accounting Office, *Social Security Administration: Stable Leadership and Better Management Needed to Improve Effectiveness* (Washington, D.C.: Government Printing Office, 1987), 3.

51. Hugh Heclo, *A Government of Strangers: Executive Politics in Washington* (Washington, D.C.: Brookings Institution, 1972), 158 and passim.

52. For an entertaining fictional account of the comparable interplay between a British minister and his ministry's permanent secretary, see *The Complete Yes Minister: The Diaries of a Cabinet Minister by the Right Hon. James Hacker MP,* ed. Jonathan Lynn and Anton Jay (Topsfield, Mass.: Salem House, 1987).

53. HHS (including SSA) data from Robert Pear, "Many Policy Jobs Vacant on Eve of Second Term," *New York Times,* January 14, 1985. In 1987, when five Central American countries proposed a regional peace plan, the United States had ambassadors in only two of those countries; lesser-ranked diplomats represented the United States in the other three. Neil A. Lewis, "U.S. Envoys Told to Convey Doubt over Latin Plan," *New York Times,* August 18, 1987. The president's special envoy for Central America had also resigned.

54. U.S. General Accountability Office, Federal Vacancies Reform Act: Key Elements for Agency Procedures for Complying with the Act, GAO-03-806 (July 2003), http://www.gao.gov/new.items/d03806.pdf.

55. General Accounting Office, *Temporary Appointments: Extended Temporary Appointments to Positions Requiring Senate Confirmation* (Washington, D.C.: Government Printing Office, 1986), appendix 1.

56. Frederick V. Malek, *Washington's Hidden Tragedy* (New York: Macmillan, 1978), 102–103.

57. Office of Personnel Management, *Federal Civilian Workforce Statistics: The Fact Book—2005 Edition* (February 2006), 73, https://www.opm.gov/feddata/factbook/2005/factbook2005.pdf. See also *Leadership for America: Rebuilding the Public Service,* Report of the National [Volcker] Commission on the Public Service and Task Force Reports (Lexington, Mass.: Lexington Books, 1990), Task Force Report, 7.

58. National Academy of Public Administration, *Strengthening Senior Leadership in the U.S. Government* (Washington, D.C.: December 2002), 1–2.

59. See ibid., esp. 3–4.

60. David McGlinchey, "OPM Seeks 'Rigorous and Realistic' Executive Ratings," *GovExec.com,* February 19, 2004, http://www.govexec.com/story_page.cfm?articleid=27701&printerfriendlyVers=1& on the issue.

61. Kathy Chu, "Employers See Lackluster Results Linking Salary to Performance," *Wall Street Journal,* June 15, 2004, D2. For analysis of the broader issues, see National Academy of Public Administration, *Recommending Performance-Based Federal Pay* (Washington, D.C.: National Academy of Public Administration, 2004).

62. Ibid., 4.

63. Frank P. Sherwood and Lee J. Breyer, "Executive Personnel Systems in the States," *Public Administration Review* 47 (September–October 1987): 410–416.

64. Elliot L. Richardson, "Civil Servants: Why Not the Best?" *Wall Street Journal,* November 20, 1987. In the Nixon period he was undersecretary of state and then headed the Health, Education, and Welfare, Defense, and Justice Departments; under Ford he was ambassador to the Court of St. James's and secretary of commerce; under Carter, he was ambassador-at-large.

65. John W. Macy, Bruce Adams, and J. Jackson Walters, *America's Unelected Government: Appointing the President's Team* (Cambridge, Mass.: Ballinger, 1983), 82.

66. *Fairness for Our Public Servants,* Report of the 1989 Commission on Executive, Legislative and Judicial Salaries, December 15, 1988 (Washington, D.C.: Government Printing Office, 1988), 1; see chart 2.

67. Paul C. Light, *A Government Ill-Executed: The Decline of the Federal Service and How to Reverse It* (Cambridge: Harvard University Press, 2008), 4.

10. Decision Making

1. Herbert A. Simon, *Administrative Behavior: A Study of Decision-Making Processes in Administrative Organization,* 3rd ed. (New York: Free Press, 1945, 1976). A few years earlier, Chester I. Barnard had also argued the importance of decision making; see *The Functions of the Executive* (Cambridge, Mass.: Harvard University Press, 1938). Simon's work, however, has proved more influential.

2. See, for example, Charles E. Lindblom and David K. Cohen, *Usable Knowledge: Social Science and Social Problem Solving* (New Haven: Yale University Press, 1979).

3. Max Weber, "Bureaucracy," in *From Max Weber: Essays in Sociology,* trans. and ed. H. H. Gerth and C. Wright Mills (New York: Oxford University Press, 1946), 196–244. Francis E. Rourke discusses this point more generally in *Bureaucracy, Politics, and Public Policy,* 3rd ed. (Boston: Little, Brown, 1984).

4. See, for example, Don K. Price, "The Scientific Establishment," *Proceedings of the American Philosophical Society* 106 (June 1962): 235–245; and idem, *The Scientific Estate* (Cambridge, Mass.: Harvard University Press, 1965). The Congressional Research Service has assembled a useful collection of readings on the role of science in decision making. See House Committee on Science and Technology, *Expertise and Democratic Decisionmaking: A Reader,* Science Policy Study, Background Rpt. No. 7, prepared by the Congressional Research Service, 99th Cong., 2d sess., 1986.

5. Deborah A. Stone, *Policy Paradox and Political Reason* (Glenview, Ill.: Scott, Foresman, 1988), 21.

6. Robert D. Behn and James W. Vaupel, *Quick Analysis for Busy Decision Makers* (New York: Basic Books, 1982), 19, 20.

7. See Charles O. Jones, *An Introduction to the Study of Public Policy,* 3rd ed. (Monterey, Calif.: Brooks/Cole, 1984), esp. chap. 6.

8. Rourke, *Bureaucracy, Politics, and Public Policy,* 49.

9. Ibid., 50.

10. This follows Hugh Heclo's argument in "Issue Networks and the Executive Establishment," in *The New American Political System,* ed. Anthony King (Washington, D.C.: American Enterprise Institute, 1978), 87–124.

11. Stone, *Policy Paradox and Political Reason,* 309.

12. Donald W. Taylor, "Decision Making and Problem Solving," in *Handbook of Organizations,* ed. James G. March (Chicago: Rand McNally, 1965), 70.

13. For sympathetic accounts of PPBS in the Department of Defense, written by those in charge of its application, see Charles J. Hitch, *Decision Making for Defense* (Berkeley: University of California Press, 1965); and Alain C. Enthoven and K. Wayne Smith, *How Much Is Enough? Shaping the Defense Program, 1961–1969* (New York: Harper and Row, 1971). Compare James R. Schlesinger, "Uses and Abuses of Analysis," in Senate Committee on Government Operations, *Planning, Programming, Budgeting: Inquiry,* 91st Cong., 2d sess., 1970, 125–136; and Blue Ribbon Defense Panel (Gilbert W. Fitzhugh, chair), *Report to the President and the Secretary of Defense on the Department of Defense* (Washington, D.C.: Government Printing Office, 1970), 112–118, which reports, "the PPBS does not contribute significantly to the decision-making process for consideration of programs which center on major weapons systems" (114).

14. Bureau of the Budget, *Bulletin No. 68–69,* April 12, 1968. All descriptive, but no evaluative quotations are from this text.

15. Jack W. Carlson (assistant director for program evaluation, Bureau of the Budget), "The Status and Next Steps for Planning, Programming, and Budgeting," in U.S. Congress, Joint Economic Committee, *The Analysis and Evaluation of Public Expenditures: The PPB System,* 91st Cong., 1st sess., 1969, 2: 613–634; and his testimony in U.S. Congress, Joint Economic Committee, *Economic Analysis and the Efficiency of Government,* Hearings, 91st Cong., 2d sess., 1970, Pt. 3, 694–706.

16. For the leading analysis of why PPBS failed, see Allen Schick, "A Death in the Bureaucracy: The Demise of Federal PPB," *Public Administration Review* 33 (March–April 1973): 146–156.

17. Allen Schick, *Budget Innovation in the States* (Washington, D.C.: Brookings Institution, 1971); Aaron Wildavsky, *Budgeting: A Comparative Theory of Budgetary Processes* (Boston: Little, Brown, 1975), 335–352; Jack Rabin, "State and Local PPBS," in *Public Budgeting and Finance,* 2nd ed., ed. Robert T. Golembiewski and Jack Rabin (Itasca, Ill.: Peacock, 1975), 427–447. The most searching critiques of PPBS's inherent defects are in Aaron Wildavsky, *The New Politics of the Budgetary Process* (Glenview, Ill.: Scott, Foresman, 1987), 416–420; idem, *The Revolt against the Masses* (New York: Basic Books, 1971); and Leonard Merewitz and Stephen H. Sosnick, *The Budget's New Clothes: A Critique of Planning-Programming-Budgeting and Benefit-Cost Analysis* (Chicago: Markham, 1971). See also Ida R. Hoos, *Systems Analysis in Public Policy: A Critique* (Berkeley: University of California Press, 1972).

18. U.S. Congress, Joint Economic Committee, *Economic Analysis and the Efficiency of Government,* Report, 91st Cong., 2d sess., 9 February 1970, 9.

19. For an illuminating study of these and other analysts (mostly oriented to economics), see Arnold J. Meltsner, *Policy Analysts in the Bureaucracy* (Berkeley: University of California Press, 1976).

20. Lawrence J. Korb, "Ordeal of PPBS in the Pentagon," *Bureaucrat* 17 (Fall 1988): 19–21.

21. Charles E. Lindblom, "Still Muddling, Not Yet Through," *Public Administration Review* 39 (November–December 1979): 518. As we see shortly, Lindblom himself has been subjected to vigorous counterattack.

22. To make matters worse, "rational decision makers" never use all the information they get, yet continue to seek even more. See Martha S. Feldman and James G. March, "Information in Organizations and Signal and Symbol," *Administrative Science Quarterly* 26 (1981): 171–186.

23. James G. March and Herbert A. Simon, *Organizations* (New York: Wiley, 1958), 140–141.

24. See Steven E. Rhoads, ed., *Valuing Life: Public Policy Dilemmas* (Boulder: Westview, 1980).

25. Lewis M. Branscomb, "Science in the White House: A New Start," *Science* 196 (May 20, 1977): 848–852. To protect the snail darters, a court injunction enforcing the Endangered Species Act held up an almost completed $120 million Tennessee Valley Authority (TVA) water project. *Tennessee Valley Authority v. Hill*, 437 U.S. 153 (1978). Congress then established a review commission to grant exemptions from the act, but the commission refused to exempt the TVA project. In 1979, Congress itself voted the exemption.

26. Arthur M. Okun, *Equality and Efficiency: The Big Tradeoff* (Washington, D.C.: Brookings Institution, 1975), 2.

27. Murray Weidenbaum, *The Modern Public Sector* (New York: Basic Books, 1969), 178.

28. The most persuasive and comprehensive descriptions and defenses of the incremental decision-making model are by Charles E. Lindblom. A good, brief statement is his "The Science of 'Muddling Through,'" *Public Administration Review* 19 (Spring 1959): 79–88. The model is further elaborated in *The Intelligence of Democracy: Decision Making through Mutual Adjustment* (New York: Free Press, 1965); *Politics and Markets: The World's Political-Economic Systems* (New York: Basic Books, 1977), 314–324; and *The Policy-Making Process,* 2nd ed. (Englewood Cliffs, N.J.: Prentice Hall, 1980). He responds to criticisms of the model in "Still Muddling, Not Yet Through."

29. The incremental approach, moreover, has not been limited to politics. For applications to business decision making, see James Brian Quinn, "Strategic Change: 'Logical Incrementalism,'" *Sloan Management Review* (Fall 1978): 7–21; "Strategic Goals: Process and Politics," *Sloan Management Review* (Fall 1977): 21–37; and "Managing Strategic Change," *Sloan Management Review* (Summer 1980): 3–20, in which he promotes Lindblom's "muddling-through" approach.

30. The bargaining model has also spun off several related procedures, most notably the "garbage can" approach, in which participants dump problems and solutions into a garbage can; decisions are not made but rather "occur," in response to many ambiguous values and objectives. See Michael Cohen, James March, and Johan Olsen, "A Garbage Can Model of Organizational Choice," *Administrative Science Quarterly* 17 (March 1972): 1–25.

31. See *National Journal,* November 15, 1986, 2767; Philip J. Harter, "Negotiating Regulations: A Cure for Malaise," *Georgetown Law Journal* 71 (October 1982): 1–118; Henry J. Perritt Jr., "Negotiated Rulemaking in Practice," *Journal of Policy Analysis and Management* 5 (Spring 1986): 482–495; and Daniel J. Fiorino and Chris Kirtz, "Breaking Down Walls: Negotiated Rulemaking at EPA," *Temple Environmental Law and Technical Journal* 4 (1985): 40.

32. Robert Kennedy's dramatic first-person memoir of the crisis, *Thirteen Days* (New York: Norton, 1969), provides a detailed description of the events. For an analytical version, see Graham T. Allison, *Essence of Decision: Explaining the Cuban Missile Crisis* (Boston: Little, Brown, 1971), from which the discussion that follows is drawn. In particular, see chap. 6.

33. Allison, *Essence of Decision*, 6.

34. Ibid., 203.

35. Ibid., 145.

36. The aphorism, first discussed in chapter 6, is credited to Rufus Miles and is often known as "Miles's Law." See Rufus E. Miles, "The Origin and Meaning of Miles' Law," *Public Administration Review* 38 (September–October 1978): 399–403. See also Allison, *Essence of Decision*, 176.

37. For another case study of bargaining in decision making, see the study by two *Wall Street Journal* reporters of the passage of the tax reform act of 1986: Jeffrey H. Birnbaum and Alan S. Murray, *Showdown at Gucci Gulch: Lawmaking, Lobbyists, and the Unlikely Triumph of Tax Reform* (New York: Random House, 1987).

38. See Charles L. Schultze, *The Politics and Economics of Public Spending* (Washington, D.C.: Brookings Institution, 1968).

39. Ibid., 76. (Emphasis in original.)

40. For a thoughtful treatment of this and related matters, see Alexander L. George, "The Case for Multiple Advocacy in Making Foreign Policy," *American Political Science Review* 66 (September 1972): 751–785; and his *Decisionmaking in Foreign Policy: The Effective Use of Information and Advice* (Boulder: Westview, 1980).

41. Leonard S. Lyon and others, *The National Recovery Administration* (Washington, D.C.: Brookings Institution, 1935).

42. Edythe W. First, *Industry and Labor Advisory Committees in the National Defense Advisory Commission and the Office of Production Management, May 1940 to January 1942* (Washington, D.C.: Civilian Production Administration, 1946); selected portions appear in *Public Administration: Readings and Documents*, ed. Felix A. Nigro (New York: Holt, 1951), 406–426. See also Harvey C. Mansfield, *A Short History of OPA* (Washington, D.C.: Government Printing Office, 1948), 311; and Allan R. Richards, *War Labor Boards in the Field* (Chapel Hill: University of North Carolina Press, 1953).

43. Grant McConnell, *Private Power and American Democracy* (New York: Knopf, 1966), 276–279. For a more recent look at the role of interest groups in decision making, see Jeffrey M. Berry, *The Interest Group Society* (Boston: Little, Brown, 1984).

44. Adam Smith, *The Wealth of Nations*, Everyman's ed. (London: Dent, 1910), 1:117.

45. See National Academy of Sciences (Committee on the Utilization of Young Scientists and Engineers in Advisory Services to Government, National Research Council), The Science Committee, *Report* and (separately) *Appendixes* (Washington, D.C.: National Academy of Sciences, 1972); and Thane Gustafson, "The Controversy over Peer Review," *Science* 190 (December 12, 1975): 1060–1066.

46. "The President's War on Advisory Committees," *National Journal*, May 12, 1979, 800; U.S. Comptroller General, *Better Evaluations Needed to Weed Out Useless Federal Advisory Committees* (Washington, D.C.: General Accounting Office, 1977); Kit Gage and Samuel S. Epstein, "The Federal Advisory Committee System: An Assessment," *Environmental Law*

Reporter 7 (February 1977): 50, 101–112; and Henry Steck, "Private Influence on Environmental Policy: The Case of the National Industrial Pollution Control Council," *Environmental Law Reporter* 5 (Winter 1975): 241–248.

47. An illuminating case study is Don F. Hadwiger and Ross B. Talbot, *Pressures and Protests: The Kennedy Farm Program and the Wheat Referendum of 1963* (San Francisco: Chandler, 1965).

48. Imogene H. Putnam, *Volunteers in OPA,* issued by Office of Price Administration, U.S. Office of Temporary Controls (Washington, D.C.: Government Printing Office, 1947); and James W. Davis and Kenneth M. Dolbeare, *Little Groups of Neighbors: The Selective Service System* (Chicago: Markham, 1968). Membership of OPA's local boards totaled 125,000; Selective Service Boards, 17,000.

49. Agricultural Stabilization and Conservation Service, U.S. Department of Agriculture, Programs and Services (Washington, D.C.: Information Division, Agricultural Stabilization and Conservation Service, 1977), 17. See also the service's "Farmer Committee Administration of Agricultural Programs" (Washington, D.C.: Agricultural Stabilization and Conservation Service, 1975).

50. U.S. Department of Agriculture, *Review of the Farmer Committee System: Report of the Study Committee* (Washington, D.C.: Agricultural Stabilization and Conservation Service, U.S. Department of Agriculture, 1962), Pt. 4, 132.

51. McConnell, *Private Power and American Democracy,* 207, 210–211.

52. *New York Times,* December 5, 1988, B1.

53. *New York Times,* December 16, 1986, B8.

54. See http://www.lwvnyc.org/TRY_school.html.

55. The most comprehensive survey, covering 269 case studies of decentralization in urban areas, is Robert K. Yin and Douglas Yates, *Street-Level Governments* (Lexington, Mass.: Lexington Books, 1975). For private interest groups' participation in national and state administration, McConnell, *Private Power and American Democracy* is the classic source.

56. "Microeconomists" deal with decision making by individuals and organizations; "macroeconomists," in contrast, study the broad economy of society, including governmental finance.

57. For the roots of the theory, see Anthony Downs, *An Economic Theory of Democracy* (New York: Harper and Row, 1957); James M. Buchanan and Gordon Tullock, *The Calculus of Consent* (Ann Arbor: University of Michigan Press, 1962); Gordon Tullock, *The Politics of Bureaucracy* (Washington, D.C.: Public Affairs Press, 1965); Anthony Downs, *Inside Bureaucracy* (Boston: Little, Brown, 1967); and William A. Niskanen, *Bureaucracy and Representative Government* (Chicago: Aldine-Atherton, 1971).

58. For a discussion, see the "Symposium on Privatization," *International Review of Administrative Sciences* 54 (December 1988): 501–583.

59. Stuart Butler, *Privatizing Federal Spending* (New York: Universe Books, 1985), 58, 166.

60. President's Private Sector Survey on Cost Control (Grace Commission), *Report on Privatization* (Washington, D.C.: Government Printing Office, 1983), vii. See also Butler, *Privatizing Federal Spending;* and E. S. Savas, *Privatization: The Key to Better Government* (Chatham, N.J.: Chatham House, 1987).

61. This discussion draws on Steven E. Rhoads, *The Economist's View of the World: Government, Markets, and Public Policy* (Cambridge: Cambridge University Press, 1985),

44–50; and Joseph E. Stiglitz, *Economics of the Public Sector* (New York: Norton, 1986), chap. 8.

62. For a review of market approaches in air pollution programs, see National Academy of Public Administration, *A Breath of Fresh Air: Reviving the New Source Review Program* (Washington, D.C.: NAPA, 2003).

63. Steven Kelman, " 'Public Choice' and Public Spirit," *Public Interest* 87 (Spring 1987): 81.

64. Weidenbaum, *Modern Public Sector,* 178. More broadly, compare Rhoads, *Economist's View of the World.*

65. See Robert B. Reich, ed., *The Power of Public Ideas* (Cambridge, Mass.: Ballinger, 1988).

66. See Ted Kolderie, "The Two Different Concepts of Privatization," *Public Administration Review* 46 (July–August 1986): 285–291; Ronald C. Moe, "Exploring the Limits of Privatization," *Public Administration Review* 47 (November–December 1987): 453–460; and James W. Fesler, "The State and Its Study: The Whole and Its Parts," *PS* 21 (Fall 1988): 891–901.

67. The American Federation of State, County, and Municipal Employees, for example, compiled a lengthy collection of stories illustrating that privatization-as-contracting often breeds its own problems. American Federation of State, County, and Municipal Employees, *Passing the Bucks* (Washington, D.C.: AFSCME, 1983); and *When Public Services Go Private: Not Always Better, Not Always Honest, There May Be a Better Way* (Washington, D.C.: AFSCME, 1987).

68. Speech to Spring Meeting, National Academy of Public Administration, Washington, D.C., June 6, 1986.

69. James E. Webb, *Space Age Management: The Large-Scale Approach* (New York: McGraw-Hill, 1969), 136–137.

70. Irving L. Janis and Leon Mann, *Decision Making: A Psychological Analysis of Conflict, Choice, and Commitment* (New York: Free Press, 1977), 15.

71. See Donald F. Kettl, *Leadership at the Fed* (New Haven: Yale University Press, 1986), 7–8.

72. Richard E. Neustadt and Harvey V. Fineberg, *The Swine Flu Affair: Decision-Making on a Slippery Disease* (Washington, D.C.: Government Printing Office, 1978), iv.

73. *Science,* 236 (April 17, 1987): 267–300, contains a useful symposium on the problems of risk and uncertainty in public policy; see R. Wilson and E. A. C. Crouch, "Risk Assessment and Comparisons: An Introduction"; B. N. Ames, R. Magaw, and L. S. Gold, "Ranking Possible Carcinogenic Hazards"; P. Slovic, "Perception of Risk"; M. Russell and M. Gruber, "Risk Assessment in Environmental Policy Making"; L. B. Lave, "Health and Safety Risk Analyses: Information for Better Decisions"; and D. Okrent, "The Safety Goals of the U.S. Nuclear Regulatory Commission."

74. Plutarch, *The Lives of the Noble Grecians and Romans* (New York: Modern Library, n.d.), 874.

75. See Peter M. Blau and W. Richard Scott, *Formal Organizations* (San Francisco: Chandler, 1962); Tullock, *Politics of Bureaucracy,* 137–141; Downs, *Inside Bureaucracy,* chap. 10; Harold L. Wilensky, *Organizational Intelligence* (New York: Basic Books, 1967), chap. 3; and Brian W. Hogwood and B. Guy Peters, *The Pathology of Public Policy* (Oxford: Oxford University Press, 1985), chap. 4.

76. Charles Peters, "From Ouagadougou to Cape Canaveral: Why the Bad News Doesn't Travel Up," *Washington Monthly,* April 1986, 27.

77. See Presidential Commission on the Space Shuttle *Challenger* Accident [Rogers Commission], *Report to the President* (Washington, D.C.: Government Printing Office, 1986).

78. See *Columbia* Accident Investigation Board, *Final Report* (2003), http://www.caib.us.

79. Thomas J. Peters and Robert H. Waterman Jr., *In Search of Excellence* (New York: Warner Books, 1982).

80. See Downs, *Inside Bureaucracy,* 118–127, for a discussion of antidistortion factors.

81. Hogwood and Peters, *Pathology of Public Policy,* 85.

82. House Committee on Science and Technology, *Investigation of the* Challenger *Accident,* Report, 99th Cong., 2d sess., 1986, 172.

83. Senate Report No. 91-411, *Federal Coal Mine Health and Safety Act of 1969,* 91st Cong., 1st sess., September 17, 1969, 5–6; Henry C. Hart, "Crisis, Community, and Consent in Water Politics," *Law and Contemporary Problems* 22 (Summer 1957): 510–537.

84. All rational (in the broad sense) models assume that crisis decisions made under severe time pressures are usually worse than those affording more time for data assemblage, specialists' advice, and deliberation. For the view that "a 'hasty' decision made under pressure may on average be better than a less urgent one," see Wilensky, *Organizational Intelligence,* 75–77. A full treatment of decision-making behavior under stress of crisis and shortness of time is provided by Janis and Mann, *Decision Making,* 45–67.

85. Irving L. Janis, *Crucial Decisions: Leadership in Policymaking and Crisis Management* (New York: Free Press, 1989).

86. See Amitai Etzioni, "Mixed Scanning: A Third Approach to Decision-Making," *Public Administration Review* 27 (December 1967): 385–392.

11. Budgeting

1. For a broad look at the history of budgeting, see Carolyn Webber and Aaron Wildavsky, *A History of Taxation and Expenditures in the Western World* (New York: Simon and Schuster, 1986). On what questions a theory of budgeting must answer, see V. O. Key Jr., "The Lack of a Budgetary Theory," *American Political Science Review* 34 (December 1940): 1237–1240; and Verne Lewis, "Toward a Theory of Budgeting," *Public Administration Review* 12 (Winter 1952): 42–54.

2. Key, "Lack of a Budgetary Theory," 1237.

3. See, for example, Herbert Stein, *Governing the $5 Trillion Economy* (New York: Basic Books, 1989).

4. The word *fiscal* is Old French in origin and appears to have roots in the Latin word for "treasury" or "basket," which, put together, sum up the topic well.

5. Keynes is best known for *The General Theory of Employment, Interest, and Money* (1936; repr. New York: Harcourt Brace Jovanovich, 1964). On compensatory economics in the Roosevelt administration, see Donald F. Kettl, "Marriner Eccles and Leadership in the Federal Reserve System," in *Leadership and Innovation: A Biographical Perspective on Entrepreneurs in Government,* ed. Jameson W. Doig and Erwin C. Hargrove (Baltimore: Johns Hopkins University Press, 1987), 318–342.

6. See Herbert Stein, *The Fiscal Revolution in America* (Chicago: University of Chicago Press, 1969); and James E. Alt and K. Alec Chrystal, *Political Economics* (Berkeley: University of California Press, 1983), 54–77.

7. See Edward R. Tufte, *Political Control of the Economy* (Princeton, N.J.: Princeton University Press, 1978).

8. The Federal Reserve operates through three principal policy tools: fixing reserve requirements that banks must hold against deposits (the higher the reserves required, the less money banks can lend out, and thus the higher interest rates become and the more economic growth is slowed); setting the discount rate (the rate at which the Fed lends to banks, which then affects interest rates across the nation); and managing open-market operations (in which the Fed purchases government securities to increase the money supply—thus lowering interest rates and fueling economic growth—and buys securities to decrease the money supply—thus raising interest rates and slowing economic growth).

   The classic treatment of the history of monetary policy is Milton Friedman and Anna Jacobson Schwartz, *A Monetary History of the United States, 1867–1960* (Princeton, N.J.: Princeton University Press, 1963). For a favorable account of the Volcker era, see Donald F. Kettl, *Leadership at the Fed* (New Haven: Yale University Press, 1986), chap. 7. William Greider, in *Secrets of the Temple: How the Federal Reserve Runs the Country* (New York: Simon and Schuster, 1987), takes a far more critical view.

9. Congress increased corporate taxes once again while cutting individual taxes in the 1986 tax reform act. See Jeffrey H. Birnbaum and Alan S. Murray, *Showdown at Gucci Gulch: Lawmakers, Lobbyists, and the Unlikely Triumph of Tax Reform* (New York: Random House, 1987).

10. The federal fiscal year begins on October 1 and runs through the following September 30. Fiscal years are numbered according to the year in which they end; the fiscal year ending September 30, 1992, for example, is known as FY 1992.

11. For a sympathetic look at supply-side economics, see Paul Craig Roberts, *The Supply-Side Revolution: An Insider's Account of Policymaking in Washington* (Cambridge, Mass.: Harvard University Press, 1984). David Stockman gives an unsympathetic insider's account in *The Triumph of Politics* (New York: Harper and Row, 1986). For an analysis of the debate, see Herbert Stein, *Presidential Economics: The Making of Economic Policy from Roosevelt to Reagan and Beyond* (New York: Simon and Schuster, 1984).

12. Lester Thurow, "Budget Deficits," in Daniel Bell and Lester Thurow, *The Deficits: How Big? How Long? How Dangerous?* (New York: New York University Press, 1985), 140. See also Benjamin M. Friedman, *Day of Reckoning: The Consequences of American Economic Policy* (New York: Vintage Books, 1989).

13. Robert Eisner, "The Federal Deficit: How Does It Matter?" *Science* 237 (September 25, 1987): 1577–1582. See also his *How Real Is the Federal Deficit?* (New York: Free Press, 1986).

14. Congressional Budget Office, *The Budget and Economic Outlook: Fiscal Years 2008 to 2018* (Washington, D.C.: CBO, 2008), Table C-1.

15. Rudolph G. Penner and Alan J. Abramson, *Broken Purse Strings: Congressional Budgeting, 1974–88* (Washington, D.C.: Urban Institute Press, 1989), 99.

16. *Wall Street Journal*, August 21, 1986, 22.

17. An excellent survey of the federal budget process is Allen Schick, *The Federal Budget: Politics, Policy, Process* (Washington, D.C.: Brookings Institution, 1995).

18. For a history of these issues, see Leonard D. White, *The Federalists* (New York: Macmillan, 1956), 116–127; Frederick C. Mosher, *A Tale of Two Agencies: A Comparative Analysis of the General Accounting Office and the Office of Management and Budget* (Baton Rouge: Louisiana State University Press, 1984), 13–34; and Jerry L. McCaffery, "The Development of Public Budgeting in the United States," in *A Centennial History of the*

American Administrative State, ed. Ralph Clark Chandler (New York: Free Press, 1987), 345–377.

19. See William F. Willoughby, *The Movement for Budgetary Reform in the States* (New York: Appleton, 1918).

20. In the wake of the Brownlow Committee's report (1937), the Bureau of the Budget was transferred from the Treasury Department to the newly established Executive Office of the President.

21. Mosher, *Tale of Two Agencies,* 32.

22. See David G. Mathiasen, "The Evolution of OMB," *Public Budgeting and Finance* 8 (Autumn 1988): 3–14; and Peter M. Benda and Charles H. Levine, "Reagan and the Bureaucracy: The Bequest, the Promise, and the Legacy," in *The Reagan Legacy: Promise and Performance,* ed. Charles O. Jones (Chatham, N.J.: Chatham House, 1988), 102–142.

23. See Howard E. Shuman, *Politics and the Budget: The Struggle between the President and the Congress* (Englewood Cliffs, N.J.: Prentice Hall, 1984).

24. The federal budget is a two-inch-thick volume, the size of a large city's telephone directory, printed on very thin paper with tiny type. The task of publishing such a huge volume of information, in the quantities needed by members of Congress, the press, and interested members of the general public, preoccupies the Government Printing Office for more than a month each year. Copies of the budget are available at nearly all college and university libraries, usually in the government documents section.

25. See Lance T. LeLoup, "From Microbudgeting to Macrobudgeting: Evolution in Theory and Practice," in *New Directions in Budget Theory,* ed. Irene S. Rubin (Albany: State University of New York Press, 1988), 19–42.

26. On forecasting, see, for example, Larry D. Schroeder, "Forecasting Revenues and Expenditures," in *Management Policies in Local Government Finance,* ed. J. Richard Aronson and Eli Schwartz (Washington, D.C.: International City Management Association, 1981), 66–90. On the problems of forecasting the federal budget, see "Uncertainty and Bias in Budget Projections," in Congressional Budget Office, *The Economic and Budget Outlook: An Update* (Washington, D.C.: Government Printing Office, 1987), 63–86.

27. See David C. Mowery, Mark S. Kamlet, and John P. Crecine, "Presidential Management of Budgetary and Fiscal Policymaking," *Political Science Quarterly* 95 (Fall 1980): 395–425. For a broader examination of budgeting that includes state and local issues, see Irene S. Rubin, *The Politics of Public Budgeting,* 4th ed. (New York: Chatham House, 2000).

28. R. Douglas Arnold argues, for example, that congressional decisions may be used "partly as rewards for past support, partly as payments for support during the current year, and partly to create a favorable climate for future years." Arnold, *Congress and the Bureaucracy: A Theory of Influence* (New Haven: Yale University Press, 1979), 56.

29. For a look at the problems posed by the annual budget process, see Naomi Caiden, "The Myth of the Annual Budget," *Public Administration Review* 42 (November–December 1982): 516–523.

30. Aaron Wildavsky, *The New Politics of the Budgetary Process* (Glenview, Ill: Scott, Foresman, 1988), 83.

31. Wildavsky's work received support at the federal level by Otto A. Davis, M. A. H. Dempster, and Aaron Wildavsky, "A Theory of the Budgetary Process," *American Political Science Review* 60 (September 1966): 529–547; and at the state level by Ira Sharkansky, "Agency

Requests, Gubernatorial Support and Budget Success in State Legislatures," *American Political Science Review* 62 (December 1968): 1220–1231. In his later work, Wildavsky moved away from incrementalism. For a discussion, see Irene Rubin, "Aaron Wildavsky and the Demise of Incrementalism," *Public Administration Review* 49 (January–February 1989): 78–81.

32. Mark S. Kamlet and David C. Mowery, "The Budgetary Base in Federal Resource Allocation," *American Journal of Political Science* 24 (November 1980): 804 and, more generally, 808–810. For another criticism of incrementalism, see Allen Schick, "Incremental Budgeting in a Decremental Age," *Policy Sciences* 16 (1983): 1–25.

33. Lance T. LeLoup and William B. Moreland, "Agency Strategies and Executive Review: The Hidden Politics of Budgeting," *Public Administration Review* 38 (May–June 1978): 232–239; see also Peter B. Natchez and Irwin C. Bupp, "Policy and Priority in the Budgetary Process," *American Political Science Review* 67 (September 1973): 951–963.

34. Natchez and Bupp, "Policy and Priority in the Budgetary Process," 956, and, more generally, 951–963. On the role of entrepreneurs in building support for their programs, see *Leadership and Innovation: A Biographical Perspective on Entrepreneurs in Government*, ed. Jameson W. Doig and Erwin Hargrove (Baltimore: Johns Hopkins University Press, 1987).

35. Frank B. Sherwood and William J. Page Jr., "MBO and Public Management," *Public Administration Review* 36 (January–February 1976): 11. The Office of Management and Budget agrees; see Clifford W. Graves and Stefan A. Halper, "Federal Program Evaluation: The Perspective from OMB," in Senate Committee on Government Operations, *Legislative Oversight and Program Evaluation*, committee print, 94th Cong., 2d sess., 1976, 266–267. The MBO experience is perceptively analyzed in James A. Swiss, "Implementing Federal Programs: Administrative Systems and Organization Effectiveness" (PhD diss., Yale University, 1976). See also Richard Rose, *Managing Presidential Objectives* (New York: Free Press, 1976).

36. Peter A. Pyrrh introduced the system at Texas Instruments and helped Carter install it in Georgia. See his *Zero-Base Budgeting: A Practical Tool for Evaluating Expenses* (New York: Wiley, 1973). More broadly, see "Forum: ZBB Revisited," *Bureaucrat* 7 (Spring 1978): 3–70; Thomas P. Lauth, "Zero-Base Budgeting in Georgia State Government: Myth and Reality," *Public Administration Review* 38 (September–October 1978): 420–430; and George Samuel Minmier, *An Evaluation of the Zero-Base Budgeting System in Governmental Institutions* (Atlanta: School of Business Administration, Georgia State University, 1975), excerpted in Senate Committee on Government Operations, Subcommittee on Intergovernmental Relations, *Compendium of Materials on Zero-base Budgeting*, committee print, 95th Cong., 1st sess., 1977.

37. Stanley B. Botner discusses the spread of PPBS, MBO, and ZBB, among other tools, in "The Use of Budgeting/Management Tools by State Governments," *Public Administration Review* 45 (September–October 1985): 616–620.

38. See *Report of the National Economic Commission* (Washington, D.C.: Government Printing Office, 1989). Both Republican and Democratic members of the commission did concur on the need to protect the Social Security trust fund for future retirees, but they could not agree on a plan for doing so.

39. "The President's Management Agenda," http://www.results.gov/agenda/scorecard.html.

40. "Budget and Performance Integration," http://www.results.gov/agenda/budgetperformance11-03.html.

41. For an analysis of how congressional and presidential policies have differed, see Mark S. Kamlet and David C. Mowery, "Influences on Executive and Congressional Budgetary Priorities, 1955–1981," *American Political Science Review* 81 (March 1987): 155–178.

42. Carl J. Friedrich, *Man and His Government* (New York: McGraw-Hill, 1963), 199–215.

43. For a catalog of the many strategies used in the budget game, see Wildavsky, *Politics of the Budgetary Process,* 21–62.

44. See Richard E. Fenno Jr., *The Power of the Purse: Appropriations Politics in Congress* (Boston: Little, Brown, 1966).

45. *Congressional Budget and Impoundment Control Act of 1974,* Public Law 93-344, 88 Stat. 337. For an analysis of the act's effects on Congress, see Dennis S. Ippolito, *Congressional Spending* (Ithaca, N.Y.: Cornell University Press, 1981); and Allen Schick, *Congress and Money: Budgeting, Spending, and Taxes* (Washington, D.C.: Urban Institute Press, 1980).

46. House Committee on Rules, *Budget and Impoundment Control Act of 1973: Report,* House Rpt. No. 93-658, 93d Cong., 1st sess., 1973, 21–22.

47. William J. Broad, "Inside the Black Budget," *New York Times,* April 1, 2008, http://www.nytimes.com/2008/04/01/science/01patc.html?pagewanted=all.

48. David C. Morrison, "Truth Elusive in 'Black' Maze," *National Journal,* October 10, 1987, 2552.

49. Broad, "Inside the Black Budget."

50. See Schick, *Congress and Money,* 415–481.

51. Ronald D. Utt, PhD, and Christopher B. Summers, "Can Congress Be Embarrassed into Ending Wasteful Pork-Barrel Spending?" (Washington, D.C.: Heritage Foundation, March 15, 2002), http://www.heritage.org/Research/Budget/BG1527.cfm#pgfId=1011528.

52. The "gimmicks" include purposely underfunding entitlements and then tacking on new programs to the inevitable supplemental appropriations bill, and squeezing some spending into different fiscal years to reduce the deficit temporarily. Ibid., 2025, 2028. See also Gary Klott, "Your Taxes at Work: A National Weed Center, an Ad Drive on Fish," *New York Times,* May 26, 1987, B4.

53. Steven Engelberg, "A Congressman, a Plane Ride and the Budget," *New York Times,* January 4, 1988, sec. I, 1.

54. Jonathan Rauch, "The Fiscal Ice Age," *National Journal,* January 10, 1987, 58. For an appraisal of the process, see Donald F. Kettl, *Deficit Politics: The Search for Balance in American Politics,* 2nd ed. (New York: Longman, 2003); Wildavsky, *Politics of the Budgetary Process*; Schick, *Congress and Money*; Allen Schick, ed., *Making Economic Policy in Congress* (Washington, D.C.: American Enterprise Institute, 1983); and Allen Schick, *The Capacity to Budget* (Washington, D.C.: Urban Institute Press, 1990).

55. Al Gore, *From Red Tape to Results: Creating a Government That Works Better and Costs Less* (Washington, D.C.: Government Printing Office, 1993), 17. See also the statement of Susan J. Irving, General Accounting Office, before U.S. House of Representatives, Committee on Rules, *Budget Process: Some Reforms Offer Promise,* T-AIMD-94-86, March 2, 1994.

56. Congress experimented with a two-year budget in December 1987 when it negotiated with the White House a continuing resolution that set a two-year plan for meeting the Gramm-Rudman spending ceilings.

57. Schick, *Federal Budget,* 201.

58. Jonathan Rauch, "Biennial Budgeting Taking Root," *National Journal,* September 27, 1986, 2318–2319; and General Accounting Office, *Budget Issues: Current Status and*

Recent Trends of State Biennial and Annual Budgeting (Washington, D.C.: Government Printing Office, 1987), 2.

59. Statement of Frederick D. Wolf, General Accounting Office, "Capital Budgeting for the Federal Government," Before the Subcommittee on Public Works and Transportation, Committee on Public Works and Transportation, House of Representatives (Washington, D.C.: GAO, 1987).

60. The debate over line-item vetoes predates the Constitution. See, for example, Forrest McDonald, "Line-Item Veto: Older than Constitution," *Wall Street Journal,* March 7, 1988, 16. The Constitution of the Confederate States of America, moreover, provided President Jefferson Davis with a line-item veto as well as a six-year term.

61. Allen Schick, "The Evolution of Congressional Budgeting," in *Crisis in the Budget Process: Exercising Political Choice,* ed. Allen Schick (Washington, D.C.: American Enterprise Institute, 1986), 19.

62. Ronald C. Moe argues that experiences in the states have limited applicability to the federal government and that "practices found useful at one level may produce just the opposite effect if employed at the other level." The line-item veto might, moreover, cause more damage in the relations among the principal branches of government than any financial advantages it might produce. See *Prospects for the Item Veto at the Federal Level: Lessons from the States* (Washington, D.C.: National Academy of Public Administration, 1988). See also U.S. House of Representatives, Committee on the Budget, *The Line-Item Veto: An Appraisal,* committee print, 98th Cong., 2d sess., 1984.

63. For an analysis of the line-item veto, see Louis Fisher and Virginia A. McMurtry, "The Line Item Veto Act" (Washington, D.C.: Congressional Research Service, 1996), http://www.ncseonline.org/NLE/CRSreports/government/gov-4.cfm?&CFID= 16504730&CFTOKEN=5170619.

64. Ibid. See also National Association of State Budget Officers, "State Balanced Budget Requirements: Provisions and Practice," Washington, D.C., June 24, 1992. Photocopied.

65. Ibid., 2.

66. For two different arguments for a constitutional amendment, see Aaron Wildavsky, *How to Limit Government Spending* (Berkeley: University of California Press, 1980); and Milton and Rose Friedman, "Constitutional Amendment to Limit the Growth of Spending," in *Control of Federal Spending: Proceedings of the Academy of Political Science,* ed. C. Lowell Harriss (New York: Academy of Political Science, 1985), 132–136.

    At the state level, it is far more difficult to define what a government's fiscal status is, and balanced-budget requirements often induce governments to discover imaginative devices for shifting unpleasant news to future fiscal years. See Robert B. Albritton and Ellen M. Dran, "Balanced Budgets and State Surpluses," *Public Administration Review* 47 (March–April 1987): 143–152.

    State and local spending limitations have sometimes produced unexpected, and unsatisfactory, results. See Terry Schwardon, ed., *California and the American Tax Revolt: Proposition 13 Five Years Later* (Berkeley: University of California Press, 1984); and Elaine B. Sharp and David Elkins, "The Impact of Fiscal Limitation: A Tale of Seven Cities," *Public Administration Review* 47 (September–October 1987): 385–392.

67. Schick, *Federal Budget,* 198.

68. Lawrence J. Haas, "If All Else Fails, Reform," *National Journal,* July 4, 1987, 1713.

69. Lawrence J. Haas, "An Open Window for Budget Reforms," *National Journal*, May 23, 1987, 1362.

70. Quoted in Jeffrey H. Birnbaum, "As Lawmakers Devise Ways to Trim Deficit, Backdoor Projects Rise," *Wall Street Journal*, November 19, 1987, I, 7.

71. Many taxes hide under the umbrella of "user charges." See Jonathan Rauch, "Swing toward Spending," *National Journal*, April 18, 1987, 926. For an exploration of the basic issues, see E. S. Savas, *Privatization: The Key to Better Government* (Chatham, N.J.: Chatham House, 1987).

72. Congressional Budget Office, "Historical Budget Data," Table 1, http://www.cbo.gov/budget/historical.shtml.

73. June Kronholz, "Student Loans Take Political Stage," *Wall Street Journal*, May 3, 2004, A4.

74. For a look at federal guaranteed loan programs for student aid, see Donald F. Kettl, *Government by Proxy: (Mis?)Managing Federal Programs* (Washington, D.C.: CQ Press, 1988), chap. 5. See also Herman B. Leonard, *Checks Unbalanced: The Quiet Side of Federal Spending* (New York: Basic Books, 1986); Eric A. Hanushek, "Formula Budgeting: The Economics and Analytics of Fiscal Policy Under Rules," *Journal of Policy Analysis and Management* 6 (Fall 1986): 15; and Ronald C. Moe and Thomas H. Stanton, "Government-Sponsored Enterprises as Federal Instrumentalities: Reconciling Private Management with Public Accountability," *Public Administration Review* 49 (July–August 1989): 321–329.

75. House Committee on the Budget, *Congressional Control of Expenditures*, Report prepared by Allen Schick, committee print, 95th Cong., 1st sess., 1977, 126.

76. House Committee on Appropriations, *General Appropriations Bill, 1951*, Report, 74th Cong., 1st sess., 1950, 9.

77. Members of Congress were outraged one year when the Post Office, having spent about $400 million in each of the first three quarters of the fiscal year, had only $9 million left for the final quarter and sought a supplemental appropriation from Congress. See Louis Fisher, *Presidential Spending Power* (Princeton, N.J.: Princeton University Press, 1975), 155.

78. The Impoundment Control Act is Title X of the *Congressional Budget and Impoundment Control Act of 1974* (see note 45 above).

79. Fisher, *Presidential Spending Power*, 176. See 147–201 for a detailed analysis of presidential impoundment. We have drawn heavily on this account for this discussion.

80. If the budget authority was provided for only one fiscal year, however, withholding of funds is regarded as a rescission, not a referral.

81. This discussion draws on Robert N. Anthony and David W. Young, *Management Control in Nonprofit Organizations*, 4th ed. (Homewood, Ill.: Irwin, 1988), esp. 3–49.

82. Ibid., 21. Emphasis in the original omitted.

83. U.S. Comptroller General, *Financial Integrity Act: Continuing Efforts Needed to Improve Internal Control and Accounting Systems* (Washington, D.C.: General Accounting Office, 1987). See also these other GAO reports: *Financial Management: Examples of Weaknesses* (Washington, D.C.: GAO, 1988); and *Managing the Cost of Government: Building an Effective Financial Management Structure* (Washington, D.C.: GAO, 1985).

84. For an examination of these issues, see Leo Herbert, Larry N. Killough, and Alan Walter Steiss, *Governmental Accounting and Control* (Monterey, Calif.: Brooks/Cole, 1984); and Leon E. Hay, *Accounting for Governmental and Nonprofit Entities*, 8th ed. (Homewood, Ill.: Irwin, 1989).

85. For example, see Oregon Progress Board, *Oregon Benchmarks: Standards for Measuring Statewide Progress and Institutional Performance* (Salem: Oregon Progress Board, 1994).

86. See, for example, General Accounting Office, *Managing for Results: State Experiences Provide Insights for Federal Management Reforms,* GGD-95-22, December 1994; and John J. DiIulio et al., *Performance Measures for the Criminal Justice System* (Washington, D.C.: Bureau of Justice Statistics, 1993).

87. See http://www.pewcenteronthestates.org/uploadedFiles/PEW_WebGuides_UT.pdf.

12. Implementation: Making Programs Work

1. Woodrow Wilson, "The Study of Administration," *Political Science Quarterly,* 2 (June 1887): 212.

2. Jeffrey L. Pressman and Aaron B. Wildavsky, *Implementation* (Berkeley: University of California Press, 1973). They cite their debt to an earlier work on implementation by Martha Derthick, *New Towns In-Town* (Washington, D.C.: Urban Institute, 1972).

3. Pressman and Wildavsky, *Implementation,* xv.

4. Randall B. Ripley and Grace A. Franklin, *Policy Implementation and Bureaucracy,* 2nd ed. (Chicago: Dorsey Press, 1986), 2.

5. Daniel A. Mazmanian and Paul A. Sabatier, *Implementation and Public Policy* (Glenview, Ill.: Scott, Foresman, 1983), 277. See also Eugene Bardach, *The Implementation Game: What Happens after a Bill Becomes a Law* (Cambridge, Mass.: MIT Press, 1977).

6. Brian W. Hogwood and B. Guy Peters, *The Pathology of Public Policy* (Oxford: Clarendon Press, 1985).

7. For a spirited rebuttal to the literature of failure, see Sar A. Levitan and Robert Taggart, *The Promise of Greatness* (Cambridge, Mass.: Harvard University Press, 1976). See also Henry J. Aaron, *Politics and the Professors: The Great Society in Perspective* (Washington, D.C.: Brookings Institution, 1978); Robert H. Haveman, ed., *A Decade of Federal Antipoverty Programs: Achievements, Failures, and Lessons* (New York: Academic Press, 1977); and Malcolm L. Goggin, Ann O'M. Bowman, James P. Lester, and Laurence J. O'Toole, *Implementation Theory and Practice: Toward a Third Generation* (Glenview, Ill.: Scott, Foresman/Little, Brown, 1990).

8. See Daniel P. Moynihan, *Maximum Feasible Misunderstanding: Community Action in the War on Poverty* (New York: Free Press, 1970).

9. *Housing and Community Development Act of 1974,* 88 U.S. Statutes 633.

10. Ripley and Franklin, *Policy Implementation and Bureaucracy,* 22–23.

11. Martin A. Levin and Barbara Ferman, *The Political Hand: Policy Implementation and Youth Employment Programs* (New York: Pergamon Press, 1985), 72–73.

12. Donald Rumsfeld, *Rumsfeld's Rules* (typescript, 1974), available at http://www.library.villanova.edu/vbl/bweb/rumsfeldsrules.pdf. For an examination of these rules, see Jeffrey A. Krames, *The Rumsfeld Way: The Leadership Wisdom of a Battle-Hardened Maverick* (New York: McGraw-Hill, 2002).

13. Norman R. Augustine, *Augustine's Laws* (New York: Viking, 1986), 313.

14. Stephen Percy, *Disability, Civil Rights, and Public Policy: The Politics of Implementation* (Tuscaloosa: University of Alabama Press, 1990).

15. See Giandomenico Majone and Aaron Wildavsky, "Implementation as Evolution," in Jeffrey L. Pressman and Aaron Wildavsky, *Implementation,* 3rd ed. (Berkeley: University of California Press, 1984), 163–180.

16. Paul Berman, "The Study of Macro- and Micro-Implementation," *Public Policy* 26 (Spring 1978): 165.

17. See Arthur M. Okun, *Equality and Efficiency: The Big Tradeoff* (Washington, D.C.: Brookings Institution, 1975).

18. Elliot Richardson, *The Creative Balance* (New York: Holt, Rinehart and Winston, 1976), 128.

19. Robert Stevens and Rosemary Stevens, *Welfare Medicine in America: A Study of Medicaid* (New York: Free Press, 1974), 73.

20. Lawrence M. Mead, *Government Matters: Welfare Reform in Wisconsin* (Princeton: Princeton University Press, 2004), 1.

21. Richardson, *Creative Balance,* 130, 132–134.

22. W. John Moore, "Mandates without Money," *National Journal,* October 4, 1986, 2366.

23. See Mazmanian and Sabatier, *Implementation and Public Policy,* 24.

24. Quoted in Louis M. Kohlmeier, "Banking Reform Chances Grow Dimmer," *National Journal,* September 20, 1975, 1341.

25. Ralph Waldo Emerson, "Self-Reliance," in Emerson, *Essays* (Boston: Houghton Mifflin, 1865, 1876, 1883), 62.

26. See Jameson W. Doig and Erwin C. Hargrove, eds., *Leadership and Innovation* (Baltimore: Johns Hopkins University Press, 1987); and John Kingdon, *Agendas, Alternatives, and Public Policies* (Boston: Little, Brown, 1984), 129–130.

27. Bardach, *Implementation Game,* 274–275. See also Levin and Ferman, *Political Hand,* 5.

28. James Q. Wilson, "The Bureaucracy Problem," *Public Interest* 6 (Spring 1967): 7. See also his *Bureaucracy: What Government Agencies Do and Why They Do It* (New York: Basic Books, 1989).

29. Pressman and Wildavsky, *Implementation,* 1, 31, 48, 100. All quotations come from this source.

30. Murray L. Weidenbaum, *The Modern Public Sector: New Ways of Doing the Government's Business* (New York: Basic Books, 1969), 4. See also Bruce L. R. Smith, "Changing Public-Private Sector Relations: A Look at the United States," *Annals of the American Academy of Political and Social Sciences* 466 (March 1983): 149–164.

31. See Lester M. Salamon, "Rethinking Public Management: Third-Party Government and the Changing Forms of Government Action," *Public Policy* 29 (1981): 255–275; and Donald F. Kettl, *Government by Proxy: (Mis?)Managing Federal Programs* (Washington, D.C.: CQ Press, 1988).

32. Office of Management and Budget (OMB), *Budget of the United States Government, Fiscal Year 1988: Special Analyses* (Washington, D.C.: Government Printing Office, 1987), H-1.

33. Martha Derthick, *The Influence of Federal Grants: Public Assistance in Massachusetts* (Cambridge, Mass.: Harvard University Press, 1970), 197.

34. Advisory Commission on Intergovernmental Relations, *A Catalog of Federal Grant-in-Aid Programs to State and Local Governments: Grants Funded FY 1978* (Washington, D.C.: Government Printing Office, 1979).

35. OMB, *Budget, Fiscal Year 1988: Special Analyses,* H-25.

36. General Accounting Office, *Federal Assistance: Grant System Continues to Be Highly Fragmented,* Report GAO-03-718T, April 29, 2003.

37. A third variety, general-purpose grants, virtually ended in 1986 when Congress failed to reauthorize General Revenue Sharing, which provided nearly strings-free aid to all state and general-purpose local governments. A few general-purpose grants remain, such as

federal payments to the District of Columbia, but general-purpose aid is now a relatively insignificant part of the intergovernmental landscape.

38. David R. Beam, "New Federalism, Old Realities: The Reagan Administration and Intergovernmental Reform," in *The Reagan Presidency and the Governing of America,* ed. Lester M. Salamon and Michael S. Lund (Washington, D.C.: Urban Institute, 1985), 427.

39. See General Accounting Office, *Fundamental Changes Are Needed in Federal Assistance to State and Local Governments* (Washington, D.C.: Government Printing Office, 1975), 12.

40. GAO, *Grant Formulas: A Catalog of Federal Aid to States and Localities* (Washington, D.C.: Government Printing Office, 1987), 13.

41. See, for example, Donald F. Kettl, *The Regulation of American Federalism* (Baltimore: Johns Hopkins University Press, 1987); Advisory Commission on Intergovernmental Relations, *Regulatory Federalism: Policy, Process, Impact and Reform* (Washington, D.C.: Government Printing Office, 1984); and Edward I. Koch, "The Mandate Millstone," *Public Interest* 61 (Fall 1980): 42–57.

42. OMB, *Managing Federal Assistance in the 1980's* (Washington, D.C.: Government Printing Office, 1980), 20–26.

43. Congress reversed itself in 1996 and allowed states to increase the speed limit back to 65 miles per hour.

44. For an examination, see Joseph F. Zimmerman, *Federal Preemption: The Silent Revolution* (Ames: Iowa State University Press, 1991).

45. John M. Goshko, "Unfunded Mandates Top Cities' List of Problems," *Washington Post,* January 19, 1995, A13.

46. Bruce D. McDowell, "Federally Induced Costs: Mandate Relief Comes of Age," *Intergovernmental Perspective* (Summer–Fall) 1994: 21.

47. Rochelle L. Stanfield, "Thanks a Lot for Nothing, Washington," *National Journal,* March 26, 1994, 726–727.

48. Margaret Kriz, "Cleaner Than Clean?" *National Journal,* April 23, 1994, 947.

49. OMB, *Budget, Fiscal Year 1990: Special Analyses,* H-41–42.

50. For a full review of administrative problems of the grant system, see Advisory Commission on Intergovernmental Relations (ACIR), *Improving Federal Grants Management* (Washington, D.C.: Government Printing Office, 1977).

51. See Martha Derthick, *Uncontrollable Spending for Social Services Grants* (Washington, D.C.: Brookings Institution, 1975).

52. Michael D. Reagan, "Accountability and Independence in Federal Grants-in-Aid," in *The New Political Economy: The Public Use of the Private Sector,* ed. Bruce L. R. Smith (New York: Wiley, 1975), 206.

53. See National Governors' Conference, *Federal Roadblocks to Efficient State Government,* 2 vols. (Washington, D.C.: Government Printing Office, 1976, 1977); and ACIR, *Improving Federal Grants Management.*

54. Robert P. Stoker, *Reluctant Partners: Implementing Federal Policy* (Pittsburgh: University of Pittsburgh Press, 1991).

55. See John D. Hanrahan, *Government by Contract* (New York: Norton, 1983), esp. chap. 3.

56. *National Journal,* March 1, 1986, 504. See also Harry P. Hatry, *A Review of Private Approaches for Delivery of Public Services* (Washington, D.C.: Urban Institute Press, 1983); and Philip E. Fixler Jr., Robert W. Poole Jr., and Lynn Scarlett, *Privatization 1987: Second Annual Report on Privatization* (Santa Monica, Calif.: Reason Foundation, 1988).

57. P. W. Singer, *Corporate Warriors: The Rise of the Privatized Military Industry* (Ithaca, N.Y.: Cornell University Press, 2003).

58. Peter W. Singer, "Beyond the Law" [London], *Guardian*, May 3, 2004, http://www.guardian.co.uk/comment/story/0,3604,1208237,00.html.

59. OMB, Circular No. A-76 revised, March 29, 1979.

60. President's Private Sector Survey on Cost Control, *Report on Privatization* (Washington, D.C.: Government Printing Office, 1983), 1. Compare President's Commission on Privatization, *Privatization: Toward More Effective Government* (Washington, D.C.: Government Printing Office, 1988).

61. J. Peter Grace, *Burning Money: The Waste of Your Tax Dollars* (New York: Macmillan, 1984), 175.

62. Congressional Budget Office, *Contracting Out: Potential for Reducing Federal Costs* (Washington, D.C.: Government Printing Office, 1987), vii–ix.

63. General Services Administration, Federal Procurement Data Center, *Federal Procurement Data System: Fiscal Year 1993* (Washington, D.C.: Government Printing Office, 1994), 13.

64. Steve Coll and Judith Havemann, "Dispute Threatens U.S. Phone Contract," *Washington Post*, July 31, 1987, B1. See also Donald F. Kettl, *Sharing Power: Public Governance and Private Markets* (Washington, D.C.: Brookings Institution, 1993), chap. 4.

65. Amy Svitak, "Boeing Lobbying on Tankers Faces Critical Review on the Hill," *GovExec.com*, September 2, 2003, http://www.govexec.com/dailyfed/0903/090203cd1.htm.

66. For scathing critiques, see Garry Brewer, *Politicians, Bureaucrats, and the Consultant* (New York: Basic Books, 1973); Daniel Guttman and Barry Wilner, *The Shadow Government: The Government's Multi-Billion-Dollar Giveaway of Its Decision-Making Powers to Private Management Consultants, "Experts," and Think Tanks* (New York: Pantheon, 1976); and Hanrahan, *Government by Contract*. For a broad look at the evidence, see John D. Donahue, *The Privatization Decision: Public Ends, Private Means* (New York: Basic Books, 1989).

67. Senate Armed Services Committee, *Defense Organization: The Need for Change,* staff report, 99th Cong., 1st sess., 1985, 558. For one example, see Nick Kotz, *Wild Blue Yonder: Money, Politics, and the B-1 Bomber* (New York: Pantheon, 1988).

68. Edward R. Luttwak, *The Pentagon and the Art of the War* (New York: Simon and Schuster, 1984), 184.

69. *New York Times,* June 15, 1986, sec. 3, 4.

70. American Federation of State, County, and Municipal Employees, *Passing the Bucks* (Washington, D.C.: AFSCME, 1983), 38.

71. General Accounting Office, *General Services Administration: Actions Needed to Stop Buying Supplies from Poor-Performing Vendors,* GGD-93-34, January 1993, 2, 4.

72. AFSCME, *Passing the Bucks,* 69.

73. Selwyn Raab, "U.S. Indicts Ten Road Contractors on Bids," *New York Times,* June 26, 1987, B1.

74. W. John Moore, "Grass-Roots Graft," *National Journal,* August 1, 1987, pp. 1963, 1966.

75. AFSCME, *Passing the Bucks,* 69–70.

76. Josh Barbanel, "Wedtech: Rise and Fall of a Well-Connected Bronx Company," *New York Times,* January 19, 1987, B1; George Lardner Jr., "Wedtech Going Out of Business," *Washington Post,* July 25, 1987, A5.

77. Effective contracting requires careful management. For a discussion of this problem, see John A. Rehfuss, *Contracting Out in Government: A Guide to Working with Outside Contractors to Supply Public Services* (San Francisco: Jossey-Bass, 1989).

78. Smith, "Changing Public-Private Sector Relations," 152.

79. Alice M. Rivlin, "Social Policy: Alternate Strategies for the Federal Government," Woytinsky Lecture, Department of Economics and Public Policy, University of Michigan, Ann Arbor, 1973, 10–11. For a vigorous, well-documented argument that the Great Society programs "had a massive, overwhelmingly beneficial impact," see Levitan and Taggart, *Promise of Greatness.* Most writers do not share this view.

80. Alice M. Rivlin, "Why Can't We Get Things Done," *Brookings Bulletin* 9 (Spring 1972): 6.

81. Presidential Commission on the Space Shuttle *Challenger* Accident, *Report to the President* (Washington, D.C.: Government Printing Office, 1986), 103.

82. "Never Missed a Day or a Delivery," *Washington Post,* December 28, 1987, A5.

83. U.S. Comptroller General, *Social Security: Clients Still Rate Quality of Service High* (Washington, D.C.: General Accounting Office, 1987).

84. This discussion, including questions, is drawn from Kitty Krause, "Hammers and Nails in Mt. Winans," *Washington Monthly* 18 (April 1986): 21–26.

85. Herbert Kaufman, *Administrative Feedback: Monitoring Subordinates' Behavior* (Washington, D.C.: Brookings Institution, 1973), 2.

86. Pressman and Wildavsky, *Implementation.*

87. Keith Schneider, "Ex-Nuclear Aides Deny Being Told of Plant Mishaps," *New York Times,* October 5, 1988, A26.

88. Kaufman, *Administrative Feedback,* chap. 3. See also Myron Peretz Glazer and Penina Migdal Glazer, *The Whistleblowers: Exposing Corruption in Government and Industry* (New York: Basic Books, 1989).

89. James Hirsch, "Singer Case Whistle-Blower Says Decision Was Difficult," *New York Times,* March 16, 1989, D1.

90. See, for example, Stephen H. Linder and B. Guy Peters, "From Social Theory to Policy Design," *Journal of Public Policy* 4 (1984): 237–259.

91. Richard F. Elmore, "Backward Mapping: Implementation Research and Policy Decisions," in Walter Williams and others, *Studying Implementation: Methodological and Administrative Issues* (Chatham, N.J.: Chatham House, 1982), 261, and, more generally, 18–35.

92. Giandomenico Majone, "Policy Analysis and Public Deliberation," in *The Power of Public Ideas,* ed. Robert B. Reich (Cambridge, Mass.: Ballinger, 1988), 173.

93. Carol H. Weiss, *Evaluation Research: Methods of Assessing Program Effectiveness* (Englewood Cliffs, N.J.: Prentice Hall, 1972), 2.

94. See, for example, ibid.; Donald T. Campbell and Julian C. Stanley, *Experimental and Quasi-Experimental Designs for Research* (Chicago: Rand McNally, 1966); and Joseph S. Wholey, Harry P. Hatry, and Kathryn E. Newcomer, eds., *Handbook of Practical Program Evaluation* (San Francisco: Jossey-Bass, 1994).

95. See Harry Hatry, Richard E. Winnie, and Donald M. Fisk, *Practical Program Evaluation for State and Local Governments,* 2nd ed. (Washington, D.C.: Urban Institute Press, 1981); and Joseph S. Wholey, Kathryn E. Newcomer, and Associates, *Improving Government Performance: Evaluation Strategies for Strengthening Public Agencies and Programs* (San Francisco: Jossey-Bass, 1989).

96. See Majone, "Policy Analysis and Public Deliberation," 173.

97. An excellent summary of CompStat is "Assertive Policing, Plummeting Crime: The NYPD Takes on Crime," C16-99-1530.0 (Cambridge, Mass.: Kennedy School of Government Case Program, Harvard University, 1999).

98. Baltimore CitiStat, http://www.ci.baltimore.md.us/news/citistat/index.html.

99. Melissa Conradi, "Leadership, Process, and People," *Governing.com,* July 10, 2003, http://www.governing.com/conf/mtech3cr.htm.

100. See http://www.eva.state.va.us.

101. Quoted in Conradi, "Leadership, Process, and People."

102. For one effort, see James D. Carroll, "Public Administration in the Third Century of the Constitution: Supply-Side Management, Privatization, or Public Investment?" *Public Administration Review* 47 (January–February 1987): 106–114.

13. Regulation and the Courts

1. Jack Curry, "Yankee Stadium Gets One Last All-Star Game," *New York Times,* February 1, 2007, http://query.nytimes.com/gst/fullpage.html?res=9905E3DA153FF932A35751C0A9619C8B63&scp=1&sq=all-star+game+2008&st=nyt.

2. William K. Rashbaum, "Company Hired to Test Concrete Faces Scrutiny," *New York Times,* June 21, 2008, http://www.nytimes.com/2008/06/21/nyregion/21concrete.html?scp=2&sq=concrete&st=nyt.

3. U.S. Constitution, Art. 1, § 8, cl. 8. The current statute permits "fair use" of copyrighted material; the term's reach is judicially determined in individual cases.

4. Keith Schneider, "Biotechnology Advances Make Life Hard for Patent Office," *New York Times,* April 17, 1988.

5. For a more developed analysis, see *The Politics of Regulation,* ed. James Q. Wilson (New York: Basic Books, 1980), 364–372.

6. See Philip K. Howard, *The Death of Common Sense* (New York: Random House, 1994).

7. House Committee on Commerce, *The Cost of Regulations,* http://www.house.gov/commerce/fedregs/survey.htm.

8. David Vogel, *National Styles of Regulation: Environmental Policy in Great Britain and the United States* (Ithaca, N.Y.: Cornell University Press, 1986), 267.

9. The best guide to each regulatory agency's activities, including problems encountered, is the *Federal Regulatory Directory,* 11th ed. (Washington, D.C.: CQ Press, 2003). In particular, see the section on the regulatory process.

10. For the development of Interstate Commerce Commission railroad regulation to 1920, see Stephen Skowronek, *Building a New American State: The Expansion of National Administrative Capacities, 1877–1920* (New York: Cambridge University Press, 1982), 248–284.

11. The classic work on the capture phenomenon is Marver H. Bernstein, *Regulating Business by Independent Commission* (Princeton, N.J.: Princeton University Press, 1955).

12. Our treatment draws on Michael D. Reagan, *Regulation: The Politics of Policy* (Boston: Little, Brown, 1987), 38–40.

13. For an insightful account and analysis of the deregulation movement, see Martha Derthick and Paul Quirk, *The Politics of Deregulation* (Washington, D.C.: Brookings Institution, 1985).

14. See A. Lee Fritschler, *Smoking and Politics,* 4th ed. (Englewood Cliffs, N.J.: Prentice Hall, 1989). On worker and community "right-to-know" laws, see Margaret E. Kriz, "Fuming over Fumes," *National Journal,* November 26, 1988, 3006–3009.

15. General Accounting Office, *Food Marketing: Frozen Pizza Cheese—Representative of Broader Food Labeling Issues* (Washington, D.C.: Government Printing Office, 1988).

16. See National Academy of Public Administration, *A Breath of Fresh Air: Reviving the New Source Review Program* (Washington, D.C.: NAPA, 2003).

17. Regulatory inspectors' roles and performance are a major subject of Eugene Bardach and Robert A. Kagan, *Going by the Book: The Problem of Regulatory Unreasonableness,* a Twentieth Century Fund report (Philadelphia: Temple University Press, 1982).

18. See General Accounting Office, *Occupational Safety & Health: Assuring Accuracy in Employer Injury and Illness Records* (Washington, D.C.: Government Printing Office, 1988).

19. See Reagan, *Regulation,* 203–204; and Kenneth J. Meier, *Regulation: Politics, Bureaucracy, and Economics* (New York: St. Martin's Press, 1985), esp. 175–201, on occupational licensing.

20. See, especially, Reagan, *Regulation,* 178–202; Donald F. Kettl, *The Regulation of American Federalism* (Baton Rouge: Louisiana State University Press, 1983); and Advisory Commission on Intergovernmental Relations (ACIR), *Regulatory Federalism: Policy, Process, Impact and Reform* (Washington, D.C.: Government Printing Office, 1984).

21. ACIR, *Regulatory Federalism,* 9–10, 82–88.

22. Ibid., 82.

23. However, individuals claiming entitlement to benefits under federal statutes that a state fails to provide may sue to obtain the benefits for themselves and others with like entitlements. *Maine v. Thiboutot,* 448 U.S. 1 (1979).

24. 21 *U.S. Code of Federal Regulations* 348, 360b, 576.

25. *Public Citizen v. Young,* 831 F.2d [Federal Circuit Court for the District of Columbia, 1987], 1108. The FDA's revisionary efforts and the court's decision are fully treated in Richard A. Merrill, "FDA's Implementation of the Delaney Clause: Repudiation of Congressional Choice or Reasoned Adaptation to Scientific Progress?" *Yale Journal on Regulation* 5 (Winter 1988): 1–88.

26. Reagan, *Regulation,* 96–97.

27. Lee M. Thomas, EPA administrator, address to the National Academy of Public Administration, June 6, 1986. Compare, on EPA's and other agencies' deadlines, *Congressional Oversight of Regulatory Agencies: The Need to Strike a Balance and Focus on Performance* (Washington, D.C.: National Academy of Public Administration, 1988), 20.

28. See R. Shep Melnick, *Regulation and the Courts: The Case of the Clean Air Act* (Washington, D.C.: Brookings Institution, 1983), 38–43, 258–261; and William F. West, "The Growth of Internal Conflict in Administrative Regulation," *Public Administration Review* 48 (July–August 1988): 773–782.

29. For a detailed critique, see Reagan, *Regulation,* 123–131.

30. David A. Fahrenthold, "Cosmic Markdown: EPA Says Life Is Worth Less," *New York Times* July 19, 2008, A1.

31. Frank Ackerman and Lisa Heinzerling, *Priceless: On Knowing the Price of Everything and the Value of Nothing* (New York: New Press, 2004), 9.

32. One of many provocative points made by Aaron Wildavsky, *Searching for Safety* (New Brunswick, N.J.: Transaction, 1988). The risk-assessment literature is large. Entry to it and

the issues may be pursued through ibid.; Charles Perrow, *Normal Accidents: Living with High-Risk Technologies* (New York: Basic Books, 1984); and Leroy C. Gould et al., *Perceptions of Technological Risks and Benefits* (New York: Russell Sage Foundation, 1988).

33. Peter Passell, "Life's Risks: Balancing Fear against Reality of Statistics," *New York Times,* May 8, 1989, and "Making a Risky Life Bearable: Better Data, Clearer Choices," *New York Times,* May 8 and 9, 1989; Adam Clymer, "Polls Show Contrasts in How Public and EPA View Environment," *New York Times,* May 22, 1989; and Cathy Marie Johnson, "New Agencies: What They Do and Why They Do It—The Case of the Consumer Product Safety Commission," paper prepared for the 84th annual meeting of the American Political Science Association, September 1–4, 1988.

34. For an argument that courts have moved to substantive review of regulatory agencies' actions, see Martin Shapiro, "The Supreme Court's 'Return' to Economic Regulation," in *Studies in American Political Development* (New Haven: Yale University Press, 1986), 1:91–141; and idem, *Who Guards the Guardians? Judicial Control of Administration* (Athens: University of Georgia Press, 1988).

35. 5 *U.S. Code of Federal Regulations,* 551–559; and 702–706 (judicial review).

36. For example, the APA's adjudicative requirements apply only if the agency's statutes require that its cases must "be determined on the record after opportunity for an agency hearing."

37. For a review of the delegation issue's development, see Louis Fisher, *Conflicts between Congress and the President* (Princeton, N.J.: Princeton University Press, 1985), 99–139; and Theodore J. Lowi, *The End of Liberalism: The Second Republic of the United States,* 2nd ed. (New York: Norton, 1979)—the latter a spirited critique of "the end of the rule of law." We should note that courts tend to interpret narrowly a statute that otherwise would be vulnerable to the constitutional attack.

38. See Office of the Federal Register, National Archives and Records Administration, *The Federal Register: What It Is and How to Use It,* rev. ed. (Washington, D.C.: Government Printing Office, 1985).

39. For the problems associated with the "statutory duty" concept, see Shapiro, *Who Guards the Guardians?* 115–124.

40. Leonard Buder, "U.S. Is Suing Con Edison over Asbestos," *New York Times,* January 8, 1988.

41. *Fisen v. Carlyle & Jacquelin,* 417 U.S. 156 (1974).

42. Rochelle L. Stanfield, "Out-Standing in Court," *National Journal* 20, February 13, 1988, 388–391. The case, *National Wildlife Federation v. Hodel* (earlier titled *In Re: Permanent Surface Mining Regulation Litigation*), was pending in the Federal Court of Appeals for the District of Columbia. The case had been in the courts since 1979(!).

43. See Peter H. Schuck, *Agent Orange on Trial: Mass Toxic Disasters in the Courts* (Cambridge, Mass.: Harvard University Press, 1986). In 1989 the Department of Veterans Affairs abided by, instead of appealing, a federal court decision that could result in government payments to up to 35,000 veterans who claimed disabilities from Agent Orange. Charles Mohr, "U.S. Not Appealing Agent Orange Case," *New York Times,* May 12, 1989.

44. For an analysis of this story, see Martha A. Derthick, *Up in Smoke: From Legislation to Litigation in Tobacco Politics,* 2nd ed. (Washington, D.C.: CQ Press, 2005).

45. *Data Processing Service Organizations v. Camp,* 397 U.S. 150 (1970). This decision propounded the "zone of interests" doctrine: even if a plaintiff cannot tie his claimed injury

directly to a particular statutory or constitutional provision, the suit may proceed if the plaintiff's interest is "arguably within the zone of interests to be protected or regulated by the statute or constitutional guarantee in question." Ibid., 151–152.

46. General Accounting Office, *Product Liability: Extent of "Litigation Explosion" in Federal Courts Questioned* (Washington, D.C.: Government Printing Office, 1988).

47. For the history, see Phillip J. Cooper, *Public Law and Public Administration,* 2nd ed. (Englewood Cliffs, N.J.: Prentice Hall, 1988), 363–389. An admirable review, with proposals for increasing governments' liability, is Peter H. Schuck, *Suing Government: Citizen Remedies for Official Wrongs* (New Haven: Yale University Press, 1983). Our treatment draws extensively on this work and on Jerry L. Mashaw and Richard A. Merrill, *Administrative Law* (St. Paul, Minn.: West, 1992), 783–843. See also Jeremy Rabkin, "Where the Lines Have Held: Tort Claims against the Federal Government," in *New Directions in Liability Law: Proceedings of the Academy of Political Science* 37, no. 1, ed. Walter Olson (New York: Academy of Political Science, 1988), 112–125.

48. 28 *U.S. Code* 1346, 2674, 2680. A 1974 amendment specified tort liability for assault, battery, false imprisonment, false arrest, abuse of process, and malicious prosecution by federal "investigative or law enforcement officials." Ibid., sec. 2680 (h).

49. The leading case is *Barr v. Matteo,* 360 U.S. 564 (1959).

50. *Bivens v. Six Unknown Named Agents of the Federal Bureau of Narcotics,* 403 U.S. 388 (1971), and *Wood v. Strickland,* 420 U.S. 308 (1975). Curiously, absolute immunity continues to protect judges, administrative law judges, and prosecutors from tort actions (though not from criminal prosecution). The Supreme Court's reasoning, seemingly serving the self-interest of its branch's members and associates, has been criticized as indistinguishable from the reasoning that would ensure executive officials' risk-free exercise of discretionary judgment.

51. *Westfall v. Erwin,* 108 *Supreme Court Reporter* 580 (1988). Federal Employee Liability and Tort Compensation Act, 102 *U.S. Statutes* 4563. The key question becomes whether the employee was acting "within the scope" of his or her official duties, not whether the duties were discretionary or nondiscretionary.

52. 42 *U.S. Code* 1983.

53. See Michael Lipsky, *Street-Level Bureaucracy: The Dilemmas of the Individual in Public Services* (New York: Russell Sage Foundation, 1980).

54. For an exploration of the issues of administrative law, see Phillip J. Cooper, *Governing by Contract: Challenges and Opportunities for Public Managers* (Washington, D.C.: CQ Press, 2002).

55. For further development of the contrasts, see Donald L. Horowitz, *The Courts and Social Policy* (Washington, D.C.: Brookings Institution, 1977).

56. So do agency lawyers and those in the Department of Justice, which claims (not always successfully) a monopoly of litigating authority. For the conflicting attitudes, see Donald L. Horowitz, *The Jurocracy: Government Lawyers, Agency Programs, and Judicial Decisions* (Lexington, Mass.: Lexington Books, 1977). For agency lawyers' attributes and incentives, see Eve Spangler, *Lawyers for Hire* (New Haven: Yale University Press, 1986), 107–143.

57. See Phillip J. Cooper, "Conflict or Constructive Tension: The Changing Relationship of Judges and Administrators," *Public Administration Review* 45 (Special Issue, November 1985): 643–652.

58. The classic analysis of the courts' emphasis on wide participation in agency proceedings is Richard B. Stewart, "The Reformation of American Administrative Law," *Harvard Law Review* 88 (June 1975): 1667–1813.

59. The courts derive such intentions from the legislative history of a statute. For an argument that this has unhappily magnified the role of congressional subcommittees and their staffs, which compile the legislative history (reports, floor statements, and hearings), see R. Shep Melnick, "The Politics of Partnership," *Public Administration Review* 45 (Special Issue, November 1985): 651–660.

60. Melnick, *Regulation and the Courts,* 379. Melnick's book is an admirable review of the throes of developing policies in a court-monitored setting.

61. Jerry Mashaw, *Due Process in the Administrative State* (New Haven: Yale University Press, 1985), 160–161. The shifting attitudes are well traced and appraised in this work. For greater detail, see Mashaw and Merrill, *Administrative Law.*

62. T. Alexander Aleinikoff, "Immigration," in *The Department of Homeland Security's First Year: A Report Card,* ed. Donald F. Kettl (Washington, D.C.: Brookings Institution, 2004), 94.

63. Executive Orders 12,291, 3 *U.S. Code* (1981 compilation), and 12,498, ibid. (1985 compilation).

64. Office of Management and Budget Circular A-4, September 13, 2003, http://www.whitehouse.gov/omb/circulars/a004/a-4.pdf.

65. Major assessments are Morton Rosenberg, "Regulatory Management, in U.S. Senate Committee on Governmental Affairs," *Office of Management and Budget: Evolving Roles and Future Issues,* 98th Cong., 2d sess., Senate print 99–134 (February 1986), 185–233; *Presidential Management of Rulemaking in Regulatory Agencies: A Report by a Panel of the National Academy of Public Administration* (Washington, D.C.: National Academy of Public Administration, January 1987); and William J. Pielsticker, "Presidential Control of Administrative Rule Making: Its Potential and Its Limits," paper delivered at the 1988 annual meeting of the American Political Science Association, Washington, D.C., September 1–4, 1988. See also General Accounting Office, *Regulatory Review: Information on OMB's Review Process* (Washington, D.C.: Government Printing Office, 1989).

66. This is reinforced by OMB's power, under the Paperwork Act of 1980, to review and disapprove agencies' proposals to collect information. But the Supreme Court overturned OMB's use of the act to block agencies' regulations that require private parties such as employers to disclose information (e.g., exposure to hazardous substances) to other private parties such as employees. *Dole v. U.S. Steelworkers of America,* 110 *Supreme Court Reporter* 929 (1990).

67. Letter of resignation to EPA Administrator Christie Todd Whitman, February 27, 2002, available on the Environmental Working Group web page, http://www.ewg.org/reports/epa/schaefferltr.html.

68. Ackerman and Heinzerling, *Priceless,* 234.

69. Cooper, *Public Law and Public Administration,* 398–399.

14. Executive Power and Political Accountability

1. Charlie Savage, "Bush Could Bypass New Torture Ban," *Boston Globe,* January 4, 2006.

2. Charlie Savage, "Bush Challenges Hundreds of Laws," *Boston Globe,* April 30, 2006.

3. Statement of Gary L. Kepplinger, *Presidential Signing Statements: Agency Implementation of Selected Provisions of Law,* GAO-08-553T (March 11, 2008).

4. Charlie Savage, "Cheney Aide Is Screening Legislation," *Boston Globe,* May 28, 2006.

5. Christopher H. Foreman Jr., *Signals from the Hill: Congressional Oversight and the Challenge of Social Regulation* (New Haven: Yale University Press, 1988), 12. For a thorough and careful look at oversight, see Joel D. Aberbach, *Keeping a Watchful Eye: The Politics of Congressional Oversight* (Washington, D.C.: Brookings Institution Press, 1990).

6. See Richard E. Neustadt, "Politicians and Bureaucrats," in *The Congress and America's Future,* 2nd ed., ed. David B. Truman (Englewood Cliffs, N.J.: Prentice Hall, 1973), 119.

7. For a history of congressional-administrative relations, see James L. Sundquist, "Congress as Public Administrator," in *A Centennial History of American Public Administration,* ed. Ralph Clark Chandler (New York: Free Press, 1987), 261–289.

8. National Academy of Public Administration, *Congressional Oversight of Regulatory Agencies: The Need to Strike a Balance and Focus on Performance* (Washington, D.C.: NAPA, 1988), 1.

9. Nathaniel C. Nash, "Telling State Dept. How to Run Foreign Policy . . . ," *New York Times,* October 12, 1987.

10. J. Ronald Fox with James L. Field, *The Defense Management Challenge: Weapons Acquisition* (Boston: Harvard Business School Press, 1988), 76. See also David C. Hendrickson, *Reforming Defense: The State of American Civil-Military Relations* (Baltimore: Johns Hopkins University Press, 1988), 30–34. More broadly, see Louis Fisher, "Micromanagement by Congress: Reality and Mythology," in *The Fettered Presidency: Legal Constraints on the Executive Branch,* ed. L. Gordon Crovitz and Jeremy A. Rabkin (Washington, D.C.: American Enterprise Institute, 1989), 139–157.

11. Henry Kissinger and Cyrus Vance, "Bipartisan Objectives for American Foreign Policy," *Foreign Affairs* 66 (Summer 1988): 901.

12. Siobhan Gorman, "Experts Say INS Restructuring Won't Solve Management Problems," *GovExec.com,* May 3, 2002, http://www.govexec.com/dailyfed/0502/050302nj4.htm.

13. See David R. Mayhew, *Congress: The Electoral Connection* (New Haven: Yale University Press, 1974).

14. See Seymour Scher, "Conditions for Legislative Control," *Journal of Politics* 25 (August 1963): 526–551.

15. Ibid., 527.

16. These and similar terms are scattered throughout Senate Committee on Government Operations, *Study on Federal Regulation,* vol. 2, *Congressional Oversight of Regulatory Agencies,* committee print, 95th Cong., 1st sess., 1977. Despite the restrictive title, this volume is one of the best reviews of performance and problems of oversight of both regulatory and nonregulatory agencies by both the House and the Senate. See also NAPA, *Congressional Oversight of Regulatory Agencies,* which reached similar conclusions.

17. Mathew D. McCubbins and Thomas Schwartz, "Congressional Oversight Overlooked: Police Patrols versus Fire Alarms," *American Journal of Political Science* 28 (Fall 1984): 169, 172.

18. This list comes from NAPA, *Congressional Oversight of Regulatory Agencies,* 7–9.

19. See Hugh Heclo, "Issue Networks and the Executive Establishment," in *The New Political System,* ed. Anthony King (Washington, D.C.: American Enterprise Institute, 1978), 87–124.

20. R. Douglas Arnold, *Congress and the Bureaucracy: A Theory of Influence* (New Haven: Yale University Press, 1979), 35.

21. Ibid., 67–68.

22. Lawrence C. Dodd and Richard L. Schott, *Congress and the Administrative State* (New York: Wiley, 1979), 170. More generally, see Morris S. Ogul, *Congress Oversees the Bureaucracy: Studies in Legislative Supervision* (Pittsburgh: University of Pittsburgh Press, 1976).

23. NAPA, *Congressional Oversight of Regulatory Agencies,* 9.

24. See Foreman, *Signals from the Hill,* chap. 4.

25. Dodd and Schott, *Congress and the Administrative State,* 166.

26. On the basis of members' shifts to and from other committees prior to 1973, the House Government Operations Committee ranked eighteenth in prestige among the twenty standing committees, and its Senate counterpart ranked thirteenth among the sixteen standing committees. See Leroy N. Rieselbach, *Congressional Politics* (New York: McGraw-Hill, 1973), 60–61n.

27. Dodd and Schott, *Congress and the Administrative State,* 168.

28. Ibid., 173–184.

29. Norman J. Ornstein, "Perspectives on House Reform of Homeland Security," testimony before the Subcommittee on Rules, Select Committee on Homeland Security, U.S. House of Representatives, May 19, 2003, http://www.aei.org/news/newsID.17514/news_detail.asp.

30. Senate Committee on Armed Services, Staff Report, *Defense Organization: The Need for Change,* committee print, 99th Cong., 1st sess., 1985, 581–582. The Georgetown University study is quoted in this report.

31. Thomas P. Murphy, "Political Executive Roles, Policymaking, and Interface with the Career Bureaucracy," *Bureaucrat* 6 (Summer 1977): 107.

32. Stephen R. Heifetz, "The Risk of Too Much Oversight," *New York Times,* July 21, 2008, http://www.nytimes.com/2008/07/21/opinion/21heifetz.html.

33. For one interest group's discussion of these issues, see Stephen L. Katz, *Government: Decisions without Democracy* (Washington, D.C.: People for the American Way, 1987).

34. Improper classification and other issues are reviewed in House Committee on Government Operations, *Executive Classification of Information . . . Third Report,* House Rpt. 93–221, 1973.

35. Summary of the board's findings by Edmund S. Muskie, in John Tower, Edmund Muskie, and Brent Scowcroft, *The Tower Commission Report* (New York: Bantam Books, 1987), xvii.

36. Christopher Madison, "Flexibility v. Congress's Right to Know," *National Journal,* July 4, 1987, 1727.

37. Pauline Jelinek, "Rumsfeld Apologizes for Iraq Prison Abuse," *Miami Herald.com,* May 7, 2004, http://www.miami.com/mld/miamiherald/news/breaking_news/8607028.htm?1c.

38. In 1972 both the Justice Department and the White House refused to furnish the draft of Executive Order 11753 (on classification of documents!) to the House Committee on Government Operations, arguing that it was only a working draft; this occurred after a newspaper's disclosure of details of the draft. See House Committee on Government Operations, *Executive Classification of Information . . . Third Report,* 53.

39. NAPA, *Congressional Oversight of Regulatory Agencies,* 24.

40. Frederick C. Mosher and others, *Watergate: Its Implications for Responsible Government* (New York: Basic Books, 1974), 115.

41. Excellent treatments of earlier congressional efforts to cope with scientific and technological issues are Thomas P. Jahnige, "The Congressional Committee System and the Oversight Process: Congress and NASA," *Western Political Quarterly* 21 (June 1968): 227–239; and House Committee on Science and Aeronautics, Subcommittee on Science, Research, and Development, *Technological Information for Congress*, 92d Cong., 1st sess., 1971.

42. Francis E. Rourke, "Bureaucracy in the American Constitutional Order," *Political Science Quarterly* 102 (Summer 1978): 217–232.

43. Michael J. Malbin, *Unelected Representatives: Congressional Staff and the Future of Representative Government* (New York: Basic Books, 1979), 5. On the role of staffs in helping with congressional casework, see Morris P. Fiorina, *Congress: Keystone of the Washington Establishment* (New Haven: Yale University Press, 1977). See also Harrison W. Fox and Susan Webb Hammond, *Congressional Staffs: The Invisible Force in American Lawmaking* (New York: Free Press, 1977).

44. Malbin, *Unelected Representatives,* 10.

45. Dodd and Schott, *Congress and the Administrative State,* 270–271.

46. Senate Committee on Government Operations, *Study on Federal Regulation,* 2:71; and Ernest S. Griffith, in Senate Commission on the Operation of the Senate, *Congressional Support Agencies,* committee print, 94th Cong., 2d sess., 1976, 126.

47. For a study of the history, development, and role of the General Accounting Office, see Frederick C. Mosher, *The GAO: The Quest for Accountability in American Government* (Boulder, Colo.: Westview, 1979).

48. See Louis Fisher, *The Politics of Shared Power: Congress and the Executive,* 2nd ed. (Washington, D.C.: CQ Press, 1987), 125–129; and *Bowsher v. Synar,* 106 S. Ct. 3181 (1986).

49. *Budget and Accounting Act of 1921,* Secs. 309, 305 (31 *U.S. Code* 49, 71).

50. These officials could then attempt to collect disallowed payments from the recipients; failing that, they might seek passage of congressional acts reimbursing them. In the 1940s, about a million federal employees paid almost $2 million annually to insurance companies to cover any liabilities for disallowed payments of public funds. Finally, in 1955, Congress authorized agencies themselves to purchase blanket surety bonds for their employees. See Senate Committee on Government Operations, *Financial Management in the Federal Government,* 92d Cong., 1st sess., 1971, 2:233–238.

51. Nicely illustrative of the point, as well as of auditors' petty tendency to question commonsense judgments of ambassadors and other officials, are the case studies in Gerald C. Schulsinger, *The General Accounting Office: Two Glimpses,* Inter-University Case No. 35 (Syracuse, N.Y.: Inter-University Case Program, 1956). For a full set of case studies illustrating past and current practice, see *Cases in Accountability: The Work of the GAO,* ed. Erasmus H. Kloman (Boulder, Colo.: Westview, 1979).

52. See the classic study, Harvey C. Mansfield, *The Comptroller General* (New Haven: Yale University Press, 1939).

53. General Accounting Office, *Standards for Audit of Governmental Organizations, Programs, Activities and Functions* (Washington, D.C.: Government Printing Office, 1973), 1.

54. *Congressional Budget Act of 1974,* 88. Stat. 326; 31 *U.S. Code of Federal Regulations* 1154. (Emphasis added.)

55. These and other problems are treated by Joseph Pois and Ernest S. Griffith in Senate Commission on the Operation of the Senate, *Congressional Support Agencies*, 31–54, 126–133; Joseph Pois, "Trends in General Accounting Office Audits," and Ira Sharkansky, "The Politics of Auditing," in *The New Political Economy: The Public Use of the Private Sector*, ed. Bruce L. R. Smith (New York: Wiley, 1975), 245–318; and John T. Rourke, "The GAO: An Evolving Role," *Public Administration Review* 38 (September–October 1978): 453–457. A full history and analysis is Mosher, *The GAO*.

56. For an exploration of other approaches to performance management, see Robert L. Cardy, *Performance Management: Concepts, Skills, and Exercises* (Armonk, N.Y.: M. E. Sharpe, 2004); and Paul R. Niven, *Balanced Scorecard: Step-by-Step for Government and Nonprofit Agencies* (New York: Wiley, 2003).

57. Statement of Patricia A. Dalton, General Accounting Office, *Results-Oriented Government: GPRA Has Established a Solid Foundation for Achieving Greater Results*, GAO-04-594T (March 31, 2004), 3.

58. Ibid., 15.

59. Tom Shoop, "The Missing Link," *GovExec.com*, April 7, 2004, http://www.govexec.com/features/0404-1/0404-1outlook.htm.

60. Foreman, *Signals from the Hill*, 6, 7. See also McCubbins and Schwartz, "Congressional Oversight Overlooked."

61. Complicating Congress's role is the era of divided government, with different parties in control of Congress and the presidency, for nearly all of the post-Vietnam period. See James L. Sundquist, "Needed: A Political Theory for the New Era of Coalition Government in the United States," *Political Science Quarterly* 103 (Winter 1988–1989): 613–635.

62. Judith E. Gruber, *Controlling Bureaucracies: Dilemmas in Democratic Governance* (Berkeley: University of California Press, 1987), 57.

63. See chapter 12's discussion of "The Importance of Feedback."

64. For the prevalence and the inadequacy of this approach to internal control, see U.S. Comptroller General, *Federal Agencies Can and Should Do More to Combat Fraud in Government Programs* (Washington, D.C.: Government Printing Office, 1978); and Jerome B. McKinney and Michael Johnston, eds., *Fraud, Waste, and Abuse in Government: Causes, Consequences, and Cures* (Philadelphia: Institute for the Study of Human Issues, 1986).

65. The classic argument for redundancy in administrative organization and process is Martin Landau, "Redundancy, Rationality, and the Problem of Duplication and Overlap," *Public Administration Review* 29 (July–August 1969): 346–358.

66. Dana Milbank, "Putting Her Foot Down and Getting the Boot," *Washington Post*, July 10, 2008, A3.

67. Ibid.

A

accountability: the process of holding administrators responsible for their actions, especially their compliance with the law and their effectiveness in managing programs.

adjudication: one of two basic regulatory approaches used by administrative agencies wherein administrative law judges within agencies hear individual cases and develop a body of rules.

administrative confidentiality: privacy protections afforded by government to individuals and organizations; and restrictions of access to internal records collected by government organizations.

administrative responsibility: the process of holding specific individuals responsible, within the bureaucracy, for specific actions.

administrative rulemaking: one of two basic regulatory approaches used by administrative agencies wherein public managers write regulations that apply to all persons and organizations meeting certain guidelines.

administrative state: Dwight Waldo's term to describe the rising importance and power of bureaucracy in American democracy.

agencies: the generic term for public bureaucracies, which carry out public programs on behalf of policymakers.

agents: those who carry out policies on behalf of superiors (known as principals).

Antideficiency Act: the federal law that forbids government officials from spending money not specifically appropriated for a purpose. The act limits the discretion of administrators.

antitrust laws: legislation intended to promote free competition by eliminating the power of monopolies.

appropriations: legislation that commits money to be spent (compare authorizations).

appropriations committees: standing committees that manage the annual appropriations process.

areal (or prefectoral) system: an approach to government that structures its organizations by a particular geographic region.

assembled examination: a written test used principally to qualify individuals for lower levels of the civil service.

at-will employment: an employment system in which employees can be fired at the discretion of managers.

authority: the basic skeleton of bureaucracy, through which a government, an agency, or an individual is vested with the rightful power to make decisions within constitutionally defined limits with the expectation of widespread compliance.

authorizations: legislation that creates programs and puts a limit on the money to be spent managing them (compare appropriations).

authorizing committees: standing committees that can initiate, review, and report out bills and resolutions in particular subject-matter areas.

auxiliary staff: the staff of an agency that provides basic housekeeping functions, including management of the personnel and budgetary processes.

B

backward mapping: a strategy of improving implementation that begins with the objectives to be achieved and then charting the steps required to reach those objectives.

Balanced Budget and Emergency Deficit Control Act: an act sponsored by Sens. Phil Gramm, Warren Rudman, and Ernest Hollings, and passed in 1985, which set automatic spending cuts if Congress and the president could not agree on budget reductions. Its goal was to eliminate the federal deficit by 1990. Also known as the Gramm-Rudman Act.

bargaining approach: a method of making decisions in which parties negotiate their differences. This approach seeks to maximize political support.

black budget: the spending authorized for secret government activities.

block grants: a strategy of intergovernmental assistance that gives the recipient broad discretion in how the money may be used (compare categorical grants).

broadbanding: a civil service reform that replaces multiple levels of job categories ("bands") of the civil service system with fewer, wider categories that encompass more employees and more skills.

budget authority: legislative approval of programs and the ability to spend money, which must be supported by an appropriation.

bureaucratic model: the traditional approach to bureaucracy, based on hierarchy and authority.

bureaus: the basic building blocks of government organizations.

buyouts: offers of lump-sum payments to government employees in exchange for their agreement to retire from government service.

C

cabinet: the collection of administrative departments, as well as those additional offices that the chief executive (such as the president) raises to that rank.

capital budgets: the portion of the budget for items with long useful lives, like roads and fire trucks.

capture: the use of political influence by interest groups to shape the decisions of administrators.

categorical grants: a strategy of intergovernmental assistance that gives the recipient relatively narrow discretion in how the money may be used (compare block grants).

charismatic authority: an approach to authority that relies on the personal magnetism of the leader.

civil service system: the collection of rules and procedures that govern the employees who work in career positions in government.

class action: legal action taken by a small group of individuals on behalf of a far larger group of people who share the same complaint.

clearance procedure: a method of cooperation among agencies that entails that an agency's proposed decisions in a subject-matter area be reviewed, whether for comment or for formal approval or veto, by other interested agencies.

closed-system theorists: an approach to systems theory that focuses on the internal workings of the system.

collective bargaining: negotiation by members of a union over employee rights and compensation.

comparable worth: the principle that individuals ought to receive equivalent pay for equivalent responsibilities.

compensatory economics: use of the budget to steer the economy.

continuing resolutions: Congressional actions that continue the level of spending after the fiscal year at its current level while Congress and the president negotiate the details of a new budget.

continuous improvement: a management strategy devoted to developing ongoing feedback about an organization's results to enhance its success.

contracting: legal arrangements in which a seller agrees to provide a good or service to a buyer for a mutually agreeable price. Government at all levels has increasingly relied on contracts with private sector experts and outside organizations for the delivery of public services.

contracts: legal agreement in which a seller agrees to provide a good or service to a buyer for a mutually agreeable price. Government has increasingly relied on contracts with private-sector experts and outside organizations for the delivery of public services.

control staff: the staff of an agency that helps top officials maintain a check on the behavior of other agency employees.

coordination: the process of orienting the activities of individuals and organizations so they are mutually supportive.

cost-benefit analysis: a comparison of the expenditures required for a program with the gains it produces. An example is risk assessment.

crossover sanctions: punishments incurred in a program that were caused by failures to meet another program's standards.

customer service movement: a management strategy devoted to focusing an organization's efforts on improving the satisfaction of its "customers"—those who benefit from its goods and services.

D

debt: the net deficit that accumulates over time.

deferrals: the decision by executive-branch officials to postpone spending for a program (compare impoundment).

deficit: the excess of expenditures over revenues in any given fiscal year (compare surplus).

delegation: legislative assignment of power to administrators to implement public programs; and reliance on one level of government to accomplish the goals of another.

direct delivery of services: the provision of public goods and services by government agencies themselves (compared with contracts and other tools of indirect government).

direct tools: instruments of government action through which government agencies themselves provide government goods and services.

downsizing: a focus on reducing the size and cost of government operations, especially through reductions in the workforce.

E

earmarks: decisions made by legislators and put into appropriations bills to fund narrow, particular projects (usually as "pork-barrel" spending).

economic regulation: the portion of public sector rulemaking that affects the behavior of private markets (compare social regulation).

efficiency: a measure of the level of inputs required to produce a given level of outputs.

e-government: a strategy of using information technology, especially the Internet and the World Wide Web, to make it easier for citizens to interact with government.

entitlements: government programs through which an individual is automatically guaranteed services—typically, a payment—because the individual meets requirements set in law.

executive leadership: strategic direction provided by the top officials of an organization.

executive privilege: the claim by presidents that communication with aides is protected from outside scrutiny, including investigation by Congress.

exit: the decision by members of an organization to leave, especially because they disagree with policies and programs.

externalities: an economic term referring to indirect benefits and costs beyond the direct costs and benefits of a project. Also called spillovers.

F

federal grants: transfer of money from the federal government to state and local governments in pursuit of national objectives.

feedback loop: an element of systems theory that connects the outputs an organization produces to its inputs.

fiscal accountability: a method of accountability that focuses on the flow of money through an organization.

fiscal policy: decisions about government spending and taxing, and their effect on the economy's performance (compare monetary policy).

fiscal year: the government's budget year (starting October 1 for the federal government, July 1 for many state and local governments).

formal approach: a theory of bureaucracy that relies on a rigorous model of the relationships between actors, especially between principals and agents.

formula-based programs: intergovernmental grant programs in which the amount of the grant is determined by criteria defined by law.

forward mapping: the opposite of backward mapping. In this mode of implementation, managers decide on goals and then define the responsibilities of those at each step in the implementation process, with the result that implementers cannot control important factors that affect the process.

function: the specific role or duty performed by a part of an organization.

fungibility: the ability of grant recipients to transfer the proceeds from a grant to cover the expenses of another activity.

G

government by proxy: the rise of government's use of indirect tools of public action (including contracts, grants, regulations, and special tax provisions) to pursue public goals.

government-by-proxy approach: an approach to organizations that notes that government delegates authority to other governments, to private organizations, and to mixed public-private enterprises as well as within its own organizational structure.

government corporations: organizations that perform public functions but that are organized—and operate—like private companies, with a profit-and-loss bottom line (including Amtrak and the Federal Deposit Insurance Corporation).

Government Performance and Results Act (GPRA): legislation passed by Congress in 1993 that requires executive branch agencies to define their goals and measure their performance in achieving them.

grade creep: the tendency for agencies to increase over time the number of top administrative positions and to seek higher classifications for existing positions.

grantsmanship: the aggressive search for money from other sources of funds, especially the search by governments for aid from higher levels of government.

H

Hatch Act: federal legislation passed in 1939 restricting political activity by government employees. Also called An Act to Prevent Pernicious Political Activities.

hierarchy: the relationship between levels of a bureaucracy.

human capital: an approach to management that focuses on identifying the skills employees need to accomplish an organization's work and in developing those skills to ensure that they produce strong and effective government programs.

human relations movement: an approach to organizations that holds that the relationships among individuals, especially in motivating employees, is the most important element of organization theory. Also called the humanist approach.

I

implementation: the process of transforming policy goals into results.

impoundment: refusal by the president to spend money appropriated by Congress (compare deferrals).

incrementalism: a theory that decisions typically are—and should be—made in small steps, with the opportunity to make adjustments in between. This approach is the basis for bottom-up budgeting.

independent agencies: government organizations that exist separately from the cabinet departments.

indirect tools: the provision of public goods and services by nongovernmental partners (and partners outside the level of government creating a program), through instruments like grants, contracts, regulations, and special tax provisions.

inner cabinet: the Departments of State, Defense, Justice, and Treasury, which constitute the federal government's oldest functions and manage its most important missions.

inputs: the resources, especially money and employees, that organizations use in producing outputs.

interagency agreements: mutual understandings reached by several organizations, which detail the contributions each organization will make to a common goal.

interagency committees: committees that exist to promote collaboration between jointly occupied areas at the cabinet, subcabinet, and bureau levels.

iron triangle: a theory that suggests agency managers, congressional committees and subcommittees, and interest groups work closely to shape policy, and that their shared work is more important than other forces on the process.

L

layer cake federalism: a theory of intergovernmental relations that holds that the responsibilities of federal, state, and local governments can be cleanly separated, like the layers of a cake.

lead agency formula: a method of cooperation wherein one agency is designated to lead and attempt to coordinate all agencies' activities in a particular area.

legislative budget: fiscal policy decisions framed by the actions of the legislature, compared with budget recommendations made by the executive branch.

legislative review: the official term for legislative oversight.

line activities: those actions that contribute directly to the mission of an organization (compare staff activities). Also called operating activities.

line-item veto: authority granted to executives (principally governors) to strike individual items from legislation. Presidents have long asked for the same line-item veto power that governors enjoy.

loan programs: an indirect tool of government that seeks to fund public goals by making credit available to individuals and organizations, either by the government's making a direct loan or by the government guaranteeing the repayment of a loan made by a private organization.

M

management by objectives (MBO): a strategy in which managers chart quantitative objectives for a program to accomplish in the coming year, which in turn determines the budget required for the program.

mandates: requirements that must be met as a condition of aid.

marble cake federalism: the theory of intergovernmental relations that holds that the responsibilities of federal, state, and local governments cannot be cleanly separated and that, instead, they tend to mix and swirl like the colors of a marble cake.

monetary policy: decisions by the Federal Reserve on interest rates and the money supply, and their effect on the economy's performance (compare fiscal policy).

N

National Security Council: an organization within the Executive Office of the President, established in 1947, to advise the president on matters of foreign and military policy.

network analysis: an approach to organizational theory that focuses on the relationships among organizations in sharing responsibility for programs.

neutral competence: the public administration principle that administrators ought to perform their jobs to the highest possible level, without political favoritism.

neutrality doctrine: the principle that public administrators ought to manage programs without political favoritism.

NIMBY phenomenon: the aversion of citizens for projects they perceive will have a direct negative effect on them and their local area (short for "not in my backyard").

nongovernmental organizations: nonprofit organizations, typically devoted to the social purposes of its members, which play an increasingly important role as front-line providers of governmentally funded services.

O

Office of Management and Budget: an organization within the Executive Office of the President, to advise the president on budgetary and management policies. Initially established in 1921 in the Treasury Department, it came under the purview of the Executive Office in 1939.

Office of Policy Development: an organization within the Executive Office of the President, to advise the president on domestic policies.

open-system theorists: those who advocate an approach to systems theory that focuses on the relationship of the system with the environment.

organization culture: the ethos and philosophy that shape the behavior of individuals within an organization.

organizational structure: the arrangement of elements within an organization.

organizational theory: the collection of concepts that seeks to describe and predict the way that organizations—and the people within them—act.

outer cabinet: the remaining cabinet-level departments outside the inner cabinet.

outlays: expenditures that occur within any given fiscal year.

outputs: the goods and services that an organization produces.

oversight: review of the behavior of individuals within organizations, and organizations themselves, by those with authority over them. In public administration, the term is used most commonly to refer to the review of administrative acts by legislatures.

P

partial preemption: the decision by a higher level of government that, if a lower government does not meet predetermined standards, the higher level of government will step in and administer the program itself.

participative decision-making approach: a strategy of decision making that attempts to build support for decisions by including those affected in the decision-making process.

partisan mutual adjustment: a strategy of bargaining in which those involved in a decision (partisans) bargain out their differences (mutual adjustment).

performance management: a strategy to improve the results of government programs by focusing on evaluation of results.

performance measures: assessments of success, of organizations and individuals, in achieving the goals set for them.

Planning-Programming-Budgeting System (PPBS): a budgeting system first introduced in the federal government in the early 1960s, which seeks rational decisions through the identification of goals, developing those goals into programs, and translating the programs into a long-term budget plan.

pluralist approach: an approach to organizations that focuses on the interaction of political forces in shaping organizational behavior.

policy-administration dichotomy: the separation of political decision making from administrative policy implementation.

policymaking: the process of defining the goals that public organizations are charged with seeking. Also referred to as policy formation.

position classification: the identification of the specific knowledge a job requires, the job's level of difficulty, and the job's responsibilities.

principal-agent theory: a formal approach to organizations that focuses on the relationship between principals and agents.

principals: the superiors who shape the behavior of agents.

private attorneys general: role played by individuals or organizations in which a suit is filed not for money damages but to compel a government agency or a corporation to do or cease doing something that affects a major public interest or group.

Private Sector Survey on Cost Control: a commission appointed by President Ronald Reagan and chaired by industrialist J. Peter Grace, which focused on efforts to reduce the costs of government, especially by eliminating federal government programs and relying more on contracting out. Also called the Grace Commission.

privatization: a strategy for turning over public responsibilities to the private sector, either by selling public assets or transferring responsibility to the private sector, or by relying on private companies to supply a good or service through contracts.

process accountability: a method of accountability that focuses on how an organization pursues its objectives.

program accountability: a method of accountability that focuses on an organization's achievement of its policy objectives.

Program Assessment Rating Tool (PART): a budgeting system, developed during the George W. Bush administration, in which agency managers define their goals and measure their performance in meeting them.

Progressives: reformers who campaigned for stronger government regulation to protect citizens from private power and more public programs to improve the lives of ordinary Americans.

project-based programs: intergovernmental grant programs in which the amount of the grant is determined by the details of an approved project.

public administration: the process of translating public policies into results.

public bureaucracy: the organizations charged with public administration.

public-choice approach: a method of decision making that assumes individuals pursue their self-interest and derives propositions about their behavior—and the behavior of organizations—from this assumption. According to this approach, individuals are best motivated by market forces.

R

rational decision making: a method of decision making that seeks the most efficient solution for problems.

rational-legal authority: an element of traditional organizational theory that focuses on hierarchy and authority to accomplish an organization's goals.

reductions in force (RIFs): involuntary layoff or termination of government employees.

reengineering: a strategy for improving an organization's results by transforming the organization's basic processes.

regulations: rules set by government to govern the behavior of individuals and organizations.

regulatory commissions: government organizations, typically independent agencies, whose function is to write and enforce rules governing private-sector behavior and whose policies are set by a multimember board.

regulatory negotiation sessions: a strategy of bargaining in which all parties work out a mutually acceptable regulation and, in the process, greatly reduce the chances that the rule will be litigated.

reinventing government: the Clinton administration's strategy for producing "a government that works better and costs less."

representativeness: the degree to which the employees of a government agency, or of the government overall, reflect the demographic makeup of society at large.

rescissions: joint action by the president and Congress to take back budget authority.

risk assessment: a type of cost-benefit analysis that evaluates whether to regulate risks based on the tradeoffs between expenditures and gains.

rule of anticipated reactions: a strategy by executives to frame their budgetary requests according to how they believe legislators will react to them.

S

satisficing: a strategy of decision making that seeks a satisfactory (not necessarily the best or most efficient) alternative.

scientific management movement: an approach to bureaucracy that seeks to improve performance by improving efficiency, especially in transforming inputs into outputs.

sensitivity training: an element of the human relations movement that seeks to make members of an organization more cognizant of the needs and incentives of their fellow organization members.

signing statement: statement signed by the president that contains the administration's interpretation of a law and how it will be enforced.

social regulation: the portion of public sector rulemaking that affects the health, safety, and well-being of citizens (compare economic regulation).

staff: the common term used to refer to the employees of an organization, not to be confused with staff activities. Sometimes also called pure-staff to distinguish from auxiliary and control staff.

staff activities: those actions (like personnel and budgeting) that support the mission of an organization (compare line activities).

stagflation: a simultaneous increase in inflation and decrease in economic growth, which stymied policymakers in the 1970s.

standing to sue: the legal right of an individual or organization to file a legal action.

surplus: an excess of revenues over expenditures in any given fiscal year (compare deficit).

system boundaries: the border between a system and the rest of the environment.

system purpose: the function for which a system exists.

systems theory: an approach to organizations that focuses on how they translate inputs into outputs.

T

tax expenditures: special advantages in the tax code to create incentive for behavior the government wants to encourage. Tax expenditures include deductions (in which individuals can reduce their income by the amount of an expendi-

ture, such as a home mortgage) and credits (in which individuals can reduce the tax due by the amount of an expenditure, such as payments for child care).

Taxpayer Bill of Rights (TABOR): Colorado's effort to reduce the growth of state government. The strategy has since been debated in other states as well.

throughputs: in systems theory, the process of transforming inputs into outputs.

Title 5: the classic standards for hiring and firing in the civil service.

tort action: a wrongful action, which causes damage or injury, for which individuals or organizations can file a civil suit.

total quality management (TQM): a strategy for improving an organization's results by focusing all of its processes and employees on the goal of increasing the value of the organization's work.

traditional authority: an orientation toward authority that relies on a belief in the sacredness of longstanding customs and that relies on the loyalty of individuals to someone who has become a leader in a long-established way.

transaction costs: the expenses, in time and money, incurred in how an organization conducts its operations.

turnover: the rate at which employees leave an organization.

U

unassembled examination: a comprehensive résumé, detailing an applicant's education, training, and experience, which a personnel office uses to assess the applicant's qualifications for a position.

uncontrollable expenditures: outlays required by law, typically for formula-based payments to individuals such as social security. The expenditures are not strictly speaking uncontrollable; they can be changed by law, but such changes are difficult and frequently take a long time.

unionization: the effort by organized unions to increase their membership and bargaining power in government.

V

voice: the decision by members of an organization to remain within an organization and protest policies and programs with which they disagree.

W

Washington monument ploy: a tactic used by administrators to shield themselves from budget cuts by threatening to eliminate their most popular programs (like tours of the Washington Monument) if legislators reduce appropriations.

whistle-blowers: individuals who divulge details about the behavior of other members of their organization who might be in violation of the law.

Z

zero-base budgeting (ZBB): a budget strategy that rejects incrementalism and asks administrators to analyze the implications of different packages of spending, from substantial reductions in current spending (the base) through significant increases.

Donald F. Kettl is the Robert A. Fox Leadership Professor and professor of political science at the University of Pennsylvania. He is also a nonresident senior fellow at the Brookings Institution in Washington, D.C. Kettl is the author of numerous books, including *The Next Government of the United States: Why Our Institutions Fail Us and How to Fix Them, The Global Public Management Revolution,* and *Leadership at the Fed.* Kettl has twice won the Louis Brownlow Award for the best book in public administration, for *The Transformation of Governance: Public Administration for Twenty-first Century America* in 2003 and *System under Stress: Homeland Security and American Politics* in 2005. In 2008 he received the John Gaus Award of the American Political Science Association for lifetime contributions to the scholarship in the joint tradition of political science and public administration. Kettl has consulted broadly for government organizations and is a regular columnist for *Governing* magazine.

James W. Fesler, who died in 2005, was the Alfred Cowles Professor Emeritus of Government at Yale University. He received the Dwight Waldo Award of the American Society for Public Administration "for distinguished contributions to the professional literature of public administration" and the John Gaus Award in 1988. His books include *Area and Administration, The Independence of State Regulatory Agencies,* and a special new edition of *Area and Administration,* which appeared posthumously in 2008.

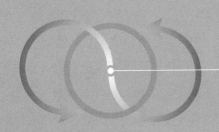

Image Credits

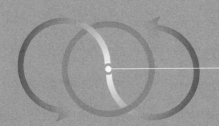

Index

Note: Page references with *t, f, b, p,* or *n/nn* refer to tables, figures, boxes, photos, or note(s), respectively.

Aaron, Henry J., 521*n*7
Aberbach, Joel D., 531*n*5
Abramson, Alan J., 330–331, 515*n*15
Abu Ghraib prisoner abuse, 447
Accountability. *See also* Public power
   administrative reform and, 115
   bureaucratic language clarity and, 474–478
   bureaucratic responsibility and, 7
   CIA torture policies and, 15–17
   civil service obligation to, 207
   definition of and control in, 9–11,
     481*n*10, 482*n*13
   democratic, Wilson on techniques of, 6
   efficient government operations and, 12–13
   elements in, 11–12, 482*n*13
   level of government and its partners and, 68
   mechanisms of, 470–473
   and performance management in foreign
     nations, 133
   political decisions and, 19
   principal-agent theory on, 102
   public service and, 14–15
   as standard for judging results, 370
   theories about, 7–9
   in Weber's bureaucratic organization model, 85
Acker, Joan, 502*n*22
Ackerman, Frank, 425, 440, 527*n*31, 530*n*68
Adams, Bruce, 508*n*65
Adams, John, 5
Adjudication, 427, 428–429
Administrative authority, 80. *See also* Regulatory
  authority
Administrative confidentiality, Congressional
  oversight and, 458, 532*n*38
Administrative feedback, 397
Administrative Procedure Act (APA, 1946)
   court challenges to rules written under,
     428–429
   on judicial review, 430, 528*n*36
   rulemaking and adjudication under, 426–427
Administrative process. *See also* Public
  administration; Public power
   accountability systems, 9–13
   ethics and politics in, 2–3

   historical roots of tensions in, 4–5
   theories about accountability in, 7–9
   Wilson on science of, 39–42
Administrative reform
   assessing each type of, 129–132, 130*t*
   conflicting theories for, 114–132
   continuous improvement, 127–129
   downsizing, 115–121
   effects of, 134
   financial bailout, 136–140
   in foreign nations, 132–134
   in industrialized countries, 134
   problems due to, 134–135
   reengineering, 121–127
   in the United States, 113–114
   worldwide, 113
Administrative responsibility. *See also* Public
  administration
   American expectations for, 22, 409
   internalized controls on, 37
   Kettl's Philadelphia to DC trip and, 21
Administrative rulemaking, 427–429, 430, 435,
  439–440
Administrative state. *See also* Public
  administration
   contradictory images of, 25–26
   misperception about size of, 23–24, 23*f*
   reliance on, 24
   rise of, 22–23
   size of private companies' operations vs.,
     26–28, 27*t*
Agencies. *See also* Regulation(s); Regulatory
  commissions
   administrative rulemaking by, 427–428
   budgetary politics of, 336
   cabinet status of departments vs., 146
   as executive branch units, 147
   independent, 149–151, 152
   judicial systems and, 434–436
   jurisdictions of, 88–89
   organizational problems and performance of,
     373–374
   pluralist model of organizational structure
     and, 97